PUBLICATIONS OF THE
PERRY FOUNDATION FOR BIBLICAL RESEARCH
IN THE HEBREW UNIVERSITY OF JERUSALEM

A COMMENTARY ON THE BOOK OF EXODUS

by

U. CASSUTO

Late Professor of Bible at the Hebrew University of Jerusalem

Translated from the Hebrew by

ISRAEL ABRAHAMS

Professor of Hebrew, University of Cape Town

JERUSALEM
THE MAGNES PRESS, THE HEBREW UNIVERSITY

מ. ד. קאסוטו: פירוש על ספר שמות

*First published in Hebrew, Jerusalem 1951
and reprinted in 1953, 1959 and 1961*

First English edition, Jerusalem 1967
and reprinted in 1974

*Distributed in Great Britain, the British Commonwealth
and Europe by the Oxford University Press*

©
Printed at Central Press, Jerusalem

Photographed at Keren Or

TRANSLATOR'S FOREWORD

The late Professor Umberto Cassuto ז״ל — Magnes Professor of Bible at the Hebrew University — had originally planned to write in Hebrew a monumental commentary on the Bible that would comprise a series of detailed expositions of the Book of Genesis, and less elaborate commentaries, consisting of one volume to each book, devoted to the remaining four books of the Pentateuch. It was also his intention to compose a compendious Introduction to the Torah as a whole, and a comprehensive commentary on the Book of Psalms. Unhappily the author died after completing only three of his commentaries (two on Genesis and one on Exodus), preceded by a smaller work dealing, in the form of lectures, with the Documentary Hypothesis as a whole, in which he summarized his larger Italian book *La Questione della Genesi*. The present volume, *A Commentary on The Book of Exodus*, is the last of the commentaries to be rendered into English.

The untimely demise of Cassuto was undoubtedly a major tragedy in the field of Biblical scholarship. The few commentaries, however, that the great savant was able to bequeath to the world constitute a veritable storehouse of Scriptural learning and lore, whose value for both the student and lay reader of Holy Writ cannot be overestimated. It would be invidious, and in truth pointless, to compare the respective merits of the exegetical works that Cassuto has left us. Each book serves its assigned purpose with profound erudition and consummate expositional skill. Yet the Commentary on Exodus is unquestionably outstanding in a number of respects deserving of our special attention.

The contents of the second book of the Pentateuch, apart from all other considerations, endow this volume with exceptional importance. In the words of our author: 'we must realise that is the book whose significance is so great in the history of Israel and all mankind.' It is in Exodus that we find the initial description of the Revelation on Mount Sinai and the first version of the Decalogue. The spiritual concepts inherent in the Ten Commandments are fundamental to the entire structure of Biblical religious and ethical teaching, constituting, as it

TRANSLATOR'S FOREWORD

were, the base of a pyramid whose apex is love of God expressed in loving-kindness towards man.

The form of this commentary also differentiates it from the two exegetical volumes on Genesis. It is larger and at the same time briefer than the books entitled *From Adam To Noah* and *From Noah To Abraham*. It is more voluminous since it covers the entire *ḥumash* of that name, whereas the other two commentaries deal with one pericope each. However, the annotations on Exodus are much more condensed, taking the form of a running commentary. But this brevity must not be misunderstood; it is not symptomatic of an unscientific treatment of the text. Cassuto himself makes this pellucidly clear in his Preface: 'I endeavoured to make my commentary as succinct as possible. At times I compressed into a single line, and even into a single word, the results of research or meditation that could fill pages, trusting that the thoughtful reader would infer the unstated from the stated.' These words find corroboration in almost every line of this commentary.

At the same time it should be noted that Cassuto's comments have a vivid quality seldom found in the exegetical writings of other Biblical expositors, who all too often prefer a jejune and lifeless approach to their subject. Our author succeeds in injecting a sense of dramatic excitement into his interpretations. Without neglecting the scientific data provided by archaeological and philological research, he makes us conscious of the literary attributes of the Bible. By his insights into the refinements of Biblical style and grammar, he enables us to view the Scriptural writings as immortal classics whose Divine inspiration in no way diminished the beauty of their expression. Cassuto was an exegete with the soul of a poet.

While not overlooking the question of the sources, which are not in his opinion those recognized by the Documentary Hypothesis, Cassuto seeks primarily to explain the existing text to the reader. His encyclopedic learning is evident on every page, and his penetrating analytical comments, which are marked by a brilliant and resourceful originality, lend a colourful significance to the Biblical narrative not often paralleled in other commentaries. Above all he endeavours with compelling scholarly arguments, many of them of a completely unprecedented character, to demonstrate the underlying unity of the Book of Exodus. But he remains throughout wholly objective, following the truth irrespective of the conclusions to which his investigations may lead him. He resists with equal determination the 'vivisection' of the Higher Critics and the 'plastic surgery' of the apologists. He thus

TRANSLATOR'S FOREWORD

blazes a new expository path, which I am convinced future scholars will tread in increasing numbers and with growing conviction.

Unlike the volumes dealing with the first two pericopes of Genesis, the present work does not separate the annotations from the Biblical text, but forms a continuous, unified commentary in which the Scriptural citations are interlinked with the exposition. This type of commentation requires a special technique, and caused the author, wherever possible, to fit his 'comments into the words of Scripture, so that the nexus between the annotations and the text should be close and direct, and the reader would have no need constantly to refer to the Pentateuchal wording.' The effect of this exegetical method has been to make the entire book a mosaic of Scriptural verse and comment. The elements are so closely and artistically interwoven as to form a new literary entity — not a text with notes, but a homogeneous expository work, which must rank among the finest modern contributions to the treasury of Biblical learning.

In the translation of this volume I have followed the principles that I adumbrated in my Foreword to the English version of *From Adam to Noah*. But the external form of the present commentary, its 'mosaic' character as a running commentary, has necessitated certain changes in my translation methods. In so far as the Scriptural passages are concerned, I have, where possible, continued to give preference to modern English usage. Thus I write 'eighty' instead of 'fourscore', 'listen' rather than 'hearken', 'to' and not 'unto'; but 'Thou' has been retained for the Deity. At times the expository nature of the work has compelled me to resort to very literal rendering of the Biblical texts in order to make the annotations fully comprehensible. I have in consequence not confined myself to any particular English version, but I have laid under tribute various translations (such as *The Holy Bible*, *Revised Standard Version*; *The Holy Scriptures* [Jewish Publication Society of America]; *The Torah* [JPS]; and *A New Translation of The Bible*, by James Moffatt), and on occasion I have given my own rendition, my invariable guide-line being the requirements of the context.

To distinguish the Biblical text from the commentary, the former is printed in italics; but where a Scriptural passage is quoted from a part of the Bible outside the Book of Exodus, or even from a section of Exodus that is not the immediate subject of commentation, the quotation appears in roman type and between inverted commas. For technical reasons, however, I found it advisable to omit the inverted commas in the case of Scriptural *oratio recta*, following in this respect the example of the Authorized Version.

TRANSLATOR'S FOREWORD

In regard to the annotations, I have adopted a dual method: comments that are of a supplemental character simply follow the Biblical citation as a continuous part of the sentence; but expositions that are purely explanatory are placed between dashes. I have also interpolated in this volume, as in my translation of the Genesis Commentaries, a number of glosses in square brackets to elucidate for the English reader what the translation alone might have left obscure. On the other hand, I have in certain instances omitted an explanation that was necessary in the Hebrew but was rendered redundant in the English version, since the translation implicitly incorporated the interpretation. Occasionally, for the sake of smoothness, I have added 'in the words of Scripture', or a similar phrase, before a quotation, although the Hebrew text was content with a colon only. To make reference easier, the verse numbers are placed opposite the initial quotation from each verse, and not, as in the original, at the head of the relevant paragraph. Hebrew words retained in the text are given in Hebrew characters and in English transcript; they are also fully vocalized except in the case of stems, which are left unvocalized wherever the vowels are omitted in *BDB*.

Having now completed, after many years of intensive labour, my translation of Cassuto's Biblical commentaries, I wish once again to express my abiding gratitude to Mr. Silas S. Perry for having made it possible for me to execute this work under the auspices of the Foundation that bears his name. Without his unfailing encouragement and support my onerous undertaking could not have been begun or completed. The Book of Exodus has, I am aware, a special significance and attraction for him in as much as it enshrines the Decalogue, which, in a sense, stands at the heart of Judaism and is the ultimate foundation on which alone the structure of world civilization can endure. I earnestly and confidently trust that Mr. Perry's high hopes for the wide circulation and far-ranging spiritual influence of this great commentary in its English garb will be fulfilled in fullest measure.

My appreciative thanks go out to Professor S.E. Loewenstamm and to Professor Ch. Rabin for the scholarly advice they have given me in the course of my work; it has served to enhance the scientific value of my rendition.

I am also grateful to Professor D. Ayalon and Professor J. Blau for their learned guidance on Arabic words and stems appearing in this volume, and to Dr. M. Spitzer for his counsel on various typographical questions.

I am particularly indebted to Dr. Milka Cassuto-Salzmann for the

TRANSLATOR'S FOREWORD

painstaking care with which she revised the proofs of this book and prepared the Indexes, for the many valuable suggestions that she made, and for the outstanding devotion she displayed in seeing the volume through the press in all its stages.

It is likewise my pleasurable duty to thank Mr. Ch. Toren, of the Magnes Press, for the interest he took in the publication of this commentary and for his ever-ready assistance in overcoming the inevitable problems and 'gremlins' that beset the printing of a major work of this nature. But for his help publication would undoubtedly have been considerably delayed.

The task of the Printer has also in many respects not been an easy one. I take this opportunity of thanking all the members of the staff of the Central Printing Press who participated in the production of this volume for their patience, courtesy and cooperation.

Last, but by no means least, my grateful thanks are due to the Hebrew University for leading its distinguished name to the publication in English of the Cassuto Biblical Commentaries. I voice the conviction that in thus honouring the scholarship of the illustrious author of these exegetical works the University of Jerusalem will have made a notable contribution to the advancement of Biblical knowledge and to the spread of Scriptural ideas and ideals throughout the English-speaking world.

ISRAEL ABRAHAMS

Cape Town.
April, 1967.
Nisan, 5727.

KEY TO THE TRANSLITERATION

Hebrew

(a) Consonants

א	= ʾ	ל	= l
בּ	= b	מ ,ם	= m
ב	= bh	נ ,ן	= n
גּ	= g	ס	= s
ג	= gh	ע	= ʿ
דּ	= d	פּ	= p
ד	= dh	פ ,ף	= ph
ה	= h	צ ,ץ	= ṣ
ו	= w	ק	= q
ז	= z	ר	= r
ח	= ḥ	שׂ	= ś
ט	= ṭ	שׁ	= š
י	= y	תּ	= t
כּ ,ך	= k	ת	= th
כ ,ך	= kh		

Note: (1) Unsounded ה at the end of a word is not represented in the transcription;
(2) the customary English spelling is retained for Biblical names and rabbinic works and authorities.

(b) Vowels

Long		Short	
ָ *(Qāmeṣ gādhōl)* = ā		־ = a
י ִ ,ִ *(Ḥireq gādhōl)* = ī		ֶ = e
ֵ ,י ֵ = ē		ִ *(Ḥireq qāṭān)* = i
וֹ ,ֹ = ō		ָ *(Qāmeṣ qāṭān)* = o
וּ = ū		ֻ = u
ְ *(Šewāʾ)* = ᵉ		
ֲ = ă		
ֳ = ŏ		
ֱ = ĕ		

Note: Capital *E* represents ֵ, ֶ and ֱ; thus אֱלֹהִים is transliterated ʾElōhīm, and אֵל is transcribed ʾEl.

Arabic and other languages

The method commonly used in scientific works was followed in the transliteration of Arabic, Akkadian, Egyptian and Ugaritic words.

CONTENTS

Translator's Foreword V
Key to transliteration X
Preface 1

Part I: THE BONDAGE AND LIBERATION (I–XVII)

SECTION ONE: The bondage (i 1–22) 7

First Paragraph: The children of Israel become a people (i 1–7) . . 7
Second Paragraph: The first two stages of bondage (i 8–14) . . 9
Third Paragraph: Pharaoh's command to the midwives (i 15–21) . . 12
Conclusion of the Section (i 22) 16

SECTION TWO: The birth of the saviour and his upbringing
(ii 1–22) 17

First Paragraph: The birth and rescue of Moses (ii 1–10) . . . 17
Second Paragraph: Moses and his brethren (ii 11–15) . . . 21
Third Paragraph: Moses in Midian (ii 16–22) 24

SECTION THREE: Moses' mission (ii 23–iv 31) 28

The Exordium: 'God's in His Heaven' (ii 23–25) 28
First Paragraph: The theophany on Mount Horeb (iii 1–15) . . 30
Second Paragraph: The instructions (iii 16–22) 40
Third Paragraph: Moses' doubts and how they were resolved (iv 1–17) . 45
Fourth Paragraph: Moses' journey (iv 18–23) 52
Fifth Paragraph: The encounter at the lodging place (iv 24–26) . . 58
Sixth Paragraph: Moses and Aaron before the children of Israel
(iv 27–31) 62

CONTENTS

SECTION FOUR: The first attempt and its failure (v 1–vi 1) . 65

    First Paragraph: Moses and Aaron before Pharaoh (v 1–5) . . . 65
    Second Paragraph: Edict upon edict (v 6–9) 67
    Third Paragraph: The new burden imposed on the people (v 10–14) . 69
    Fourth Paragraph: The complaint of the foremen (v 15–19) . . 70
    Fifth Paragraph: The encounter with Moses and Aaron (v 20–21) . 72
    Sixth Paragraph: Moses' remonstrance and the Lord's reply (v 22 – vi 1) 73

SECTION FIVE: Prelude to successful action (vi 2–vii 7) . . 76

    First Paragraph: The Lord's declaration (vi 2–9) 76
    Second Paragraph: Moses and Aaron are commanded to go to Pharaoh (vi 10–13) 82
    Third Paragraph: The genealogy of Moses and Aaron (vi 14–27) . 84
    Fourth Paragraph: The narrative is resumed (vi 28–30) . . . 88
    Fifth Paragraph: Detailed instructions to Moses and Aaron (vii 1–5) . 89
    Conclusion of the Section (vii 6–7) 90

SECTION SIX: The plagues (vii 8–xi 10) 92

    Prologue: The presentation of credentials (vii 8–13) . . . 94
    First Paragraph: Blood (vii 14–25) 96
    Second Paragraph: Frogs (viii 1–15 [Hebrew, vii 26–viii 11]) . . 100
    Third Paragraph: Gnats (viii 16–19 [Hebrew, vv. 12–15]) . . 104
    Fourth Paragraph: Swarms of flies (viii 20–32 [Hebrew, vv. 16–28]) . 107
    Fifth Paragraph: Pest (ix 1–7) 110
    Sixth Paragraph: Boils (ix 8–12) 112
    Seventh Paragraph: Hail (ix 13–35) 115
    Eighth Paragraph: Locusts (x 1–20) 122
    Ninth Paragraph: Darkness (x 21–29) 129
    Tenth Paragraph: The warning regarding the plague of the first-born (xi 1–8) 131
    Epilogue (xi 9–10) 134

SECTION SEVEN: The exodus from Egypt (xii 1–42) . . . 136

    First Paragraph: Instructions on the observance of Passover in Egypt (xii 1–13) 136
    Second Paragraph: Directives for the observance of Passover in the future (xii 14–20) 140
    Third Paragraph: The instructions are conveyed to the people and Passover is celebrated in Egypt (xii 21–28) 142
    Fourth Paragraph: Plague of the first-born (xii 29–32) . . . 144
    Fifth Paragraph: Preparations for the exodus (xii 33–36) . . . 146
    Sixth Paragraph: The exodus (xii 37–42) 147
    Appendixes to the Section (xii 43 – xiii 16) 149
        First Appendix: The ordinance of Passover (xii 43–50) . . 149
        Second Appendix: The laws of the first-born and a memorial to the exodus (xii 51 – xiii 16) 151

CONTENTS

SECTION EIGHT: The division of the Sea of Reeds
(xiii 17–xv 21) 155

First Paragraph: The journey in the wilderness (xiii 17–22) . . . 155
Second Paragraph: The encampment by the Sea of Reeds (xiv 1–4) . . 159
Third Paragraph: The pursuit by the Egyptians (xiv 5–8) . . . 161
Fourth Paragraph: The meeting of the two hosts (xiv 9–14) . . . 162
Fifth Paragraph: The way of salvation (xiv 15–18) 165
Sixth Paragraph: The Israelites pass through the midst of the sea
(xiv 19–22) 166
Seventh Paragraph: The discomfiture of the Egyptians (xiv 23–25) . . 169
Eighth Paragraph: The punishment of the pursuers (xiv 26–29) . . 170
Ninth Paragraph: The deliverance (xiv 30–31) 172
Tenth Paragraph: The song of the sea (xv 1–21) 173

SECTION NINE: The travails of the journey (xv 22–xvii 16) . 183

First Paragraph: The waters of Mara (xv 22–27) 183
Second Paragraph: The manna and the quails (xvi 1–36) . . . 186
Third Paragraph: The waters of Meribah (xvii 1–7) . . . 200
Fourth Paragraph: War with the Amalekites (xvii 8–16) . . . 204

Part II: THE TORAH AND ITS PRECEPTS (XVIII–XXIV)

SECTION ONE: Israel is welcomed as one of the nations of the
world (xviii 1–27) 211

First Paragraph: Jethro's visit (xviii 1–12) 213
Second Paragraph: The advice to appoint judges and its acceptance
(xviii 13–26) 217
Conclusion of the Section (xviii 27) 221

SECTION TWO: The revelation at Mount Sinai (xix 1–xx 21) . 223

First Paragraph: The preparations (xix 1–15) 223
Second Paragraph: The elements of nature in commotion (xix 16–19) . 231
Third Paragraph: The final instructions (xix 20–25) . . . 233
Fourth Paragraph: The Decalogue (xx 1–17) 235
Conclusion of the Section (xx 18–21) 252

SECTION THREE: Statutes and ordinances (xx 22–xxiii 33) . 254

The Exordium: Introductory observations (xx 22b–26) . . . 254
The legal paragraphs: (xxi 1 ff.) 257
First Paragraph: The laws of the Hebrew slave (xxi 2–6) . . 265
Second Paragraph: The laws of the bondwoman (xxi 7–11) . . 267
Third Paragraph: Capital offences (xxi 12–17) 269

CONTENTS

Fourth Paragraph: Laws appertaining to bodily injuries (xxi 18–27) . 272
Fifth Paragraph: The ox and the pit (xxi 28–36) 278
Sixth Paragraph: Laws of theft (xxii 1–4 [Hebrew, xxi 37–xxii 3]) . . 281
Seventh Paragraph: Damage by grazing and burning (xxii 5–6 [Hebrew, vv. 4–5]) 284
Eighth Paragraph: Four classes of bailees (xxii 7–15 [Hebrew, vv. 6–14]) 285
Ninth Paragraph: The law of the seducer (xxii 16–17 [Hebrew, vv. 15–16]) 288
Tenth Paragraph: Statutes against idolatrous customs (xxii 18–20 [Hebrew, vv. 17–19]) 289
Eleventh Paragraph: Love and fellowship towards the poor and the needy (xxii 21–27 [Hebrew, vv. 20–26]) 291
Twelfth Paragraph: Reverence towards God and the leaders of the community (xxii 28–31 [Hebrew, vv. 27–30]) 293
Thirteenth Paragraph: Justice towards all men (xxiii 1–9) . . . 296
Fourteenth Paragraph: The Sacred Seasons (xxiii 10–19) . . . 300
Epilogue of the Section (xxiii 20–33) 305

SECTION FOUR: The making of the Covenant (xxiv 1–18) . 310

First Paragraph: The instructions given to Moses (xxiv 1–2) . . . 310
Second Paragraph: Details of the agreement relative to the making of the Covenant (xxiv 3–8) 311
Third Paragraph: In audience with God (xxiv 9–11) . . . 313
Fourth Paragraph: Moses' ascent (xxiv 12–18) 315

Part III: THE TABERNACLE AND ITS SERVICE (XXV–XL)

SECTION ONE: Directions for the construction of the Tabernacle (xxv 1–xxxi 18) 319

First Paragraph: The contribution to the Tabernacle (xxv 1–9) .. 324
Second Paragraph: The ark and the *kappōreth* (xxv 10–22) . . . 328
Third Paragraph: The Table (xxv 23–30) 336
Fourth Paragraph: The lampstand (xxv 31–40) 340
Fifth Paragraph: The Tabernacle and the Tent (xxvi 1–14) . . 345
Sixth Paragraph: The boards (xxvi 15–30) 354
Seventh Paragraph: The veil and the screen (xxvi 31–37) . . 359
Eighth Paragraph: The altar (xxvii 1–8) 362
Ninth Paragraph: The court of the Tabernacle (xxvii 9–19) . . 365
Tenth Paragraph: First directions for the Priesthood (xxvii 20 – xxviii 5) 369
Eleventh Paragraph: The priestly garments (xxviii 6–43) . . 372
Twelfth Paragraph: The induction (xxix 1–46) 387
Thirteenth Paragraph: The altar of incense (xxx 1–10) . . . 389
Fourteenth Paragraph: The half shekel (xxx 11–16) . . . 392
Fifteenth Paragraph: The laver and its base (xxx 17–21) . . 395

CONTENTS

Sixteenth Paragraph: The oil of anointment (xxx 22–33) . . . 396
Seventeenth Paragraph: Incense of spices (xxx 34–38) . . . 399
Eighteenth Paragraph: Appointment of artisans (xxxi 1–11) . . . 401
Nineteenth Paragraph: Abstention from work in the Sabbath day (xxxi 12–17) 403
Twentieth Paragraph: The handing over of the tables of the Covenant (xxxi 18) 405

SECTION TWO: The making of the calf (xxxii 1–xxxiv 35) . 407

First Paragraph: At the foot of the mountain (xxxii 1–6) . . . 411
Second Paragraph: On Mount Sinai (xxxii 7–14) 414
Third Paragraph: Moses' action (xxxii 15–29) 417
Fourth Paragraph: Moses is assured that Israel will possess the Land (xxxii 30–35) 422
Fifth Paragraph: The directives for the construction of the Tabernacle are annulled (xxxiii 1–4) 425
Sixth Paragraph: A parallel passage to the previous theme (xxxiii 5–6) . 427
Seventh Paragraph: The Tent of Meeting (xxxiii 7–11) . . . 429
Eighth Paragraph: A dialogue between Moses and the Lord (xxxiii 12–23) 432
Ninth Paragraph: Preparation for the renewal of the Covenant and the Revelation of the Lord to Moses (xxxiv 1–10) 437
Tenth Paragraph: Instructions for the observance of the Covenant (xxxiv 11–26) 442
Eleventh Paragraph: The writing of the Covenant documents (xxxiv 27–28) 447
Twelfth Paragraph: The skin of Moses' face becomes radiant (xxxiv 29–35) 448

SECTION THREE: The execution of the work of the Tabernacle and its erection (xxxv 1–xl 38) 452

First Paragraph: Cessation of work on the Sabbath (xxxv 1–3) . . 454
Second Paragraph: The contribution to the Tabernacle (xxxv 4–20) . 455
Third Paragraph: The bringing of the contribution (xxxv 21–29) . . 456
Fourth Paragraph: The appointment of the craftsmen and the commencement of the work (xxxv 30 – xxxvi 7) 459
Fifth Paragraph: The Tabernacle and the Tent (xxxvi 8–19) . . . 461
Sixth Paragraph: The boards (xxxvi 20–34) 463
Seventh Paragraph: The veil and the screen (xxxvi 35–38) . . . 463
Eighth Paragraph: The ark and the *kappōreth* (xxxvii 1–9) . . . 464
Ninth Paragraph: The Table (xxxvii 10–16) 464
Tenth Paragraph: The lampstand (xxxvii 17–24) 465
Eleventh Paragraph: The altar of incense (xxxvii 25–29) . . . 465
Twelfth Paragraph: The altar of burnt offering (xxxviii 1–7) . . . 466
Thirteenth Paragraph: The laver and its base (xxxviii 8) . . . 466
Fourteenth Paragraph: The court of the Tabernacle (xxxviii 9–20) . . 467

CONTENTS

Fifteenth Paragraph: An inventory of materials used for the Tabernacle (xxxviii 21 – xxxix 1) 468
Sixteenth Paragraph: The priestly garments (xxxix 2 – 31) . . . 473
Seventeenth Paragraph: Completion of the work (xxxix 32) . . . 476
Eighteenth Paragraph: The work is brought to Moses (xxxix 33–43) . 476
Nineteenth Paragraph: The command to erect the Tabernacle (xl 1–16) . 478
Twentieth Paragraph: The erection of the Tabernacle (xl 17–33) . . 481
Conclusion of the Section and the Book (xl 34–38) 483

Abbreviations 486

Bibliographical Notes and Addenda 487

INDEXES 493

    I.   Biblical References 493
   II. Other Literary References 505
  III. Notabilia 507

PREFACE

THIS commentary on the Book of Exodus is entirely new, being based on new exegetical principles.

Its aim is to expound the Book of Exodus scientifically, with the help of all the resources that modern scholarship puts at our disposal today. To achieve this purpose, its approach differs considerably from that of the majority of contemporary scientific commentaries. The primary differences between the present commentary and others are, in the main, three, to wit:

(a) The commentaries written in our generation on any book of the Pentateuch are, in most instances, chiefly devoted to investigating the sources and to determining the process by which they have been fitted together. They annotate the documentary fragments that they discern in the book rather than the book itself. The great importance attached by exegetes to the question of the sources diverts their attention from the study of the work that has grown out of these documents. In their opinion, the study of the sources takes precedence over that of the book as we have it. To my mind, the reverse view is the more reasonable. A scientific exposition of any literary work should aim at elucidating and evaluating the work itself; whereas the dissection of its sources is only a means to this end. Admittedly it is an important means, and I, too, have accorded it no small place in my commentary, but at no time have I lost sight of the fact that my main task was to explain the book before us. Ultimately we must realize that this is the book whose significance is so great in the history of Israel and of all mankind, and that it alone has factual existence, not the imaginary work that rests on mere conjecture. Consequently my commentary can be of interest to every type of reader, irrespective of his views on the history of the Book of Exodus. Those who accept the documentary hypothesis will find here an interpretation of the work of the last editor, the final R; for those who hold other opinions regarding the origin of Exodus, my annotations will likewise provide an exposition of its latest recension; whilst those who

PREFACE

are concerned solely with the received form of the text will find here a straightforward answer to their requirements.

(b) The sources of the Book of Exodus are not in my view those recognized by the current hypothesis, namely, P (Priestly Code), E (Elohist), J (Jahwist) and their different strata. One of the principal sources — possibly *the* principal source — was, if I am not mistaken, an ancient heroic poem, an epos dating back to earliest times, that told at length the story of the Egyptian bondage, of the liberation and of the wandering of the children of Israel in the wilderness. In the course of my commentary I frequently indicate, in detail, the use made of this poem, and I point out the traces of the epic still perceptible in the Scriptural text.

(c) Owing to the fact that the origins of the scientific study of the Pentateuch go back to a period anterior to the new discoveries relating to the culture of the ancient East, and that the methods of investigation which crystallized in that epoch continue to exert a fundamental influence on the work of scholars to this day, modern Biblical commentaries do not make adequate use of our current knowledge of the literature and culture of the neighbouring nations of Israel. In this commentary, on the other hand, I have paid constant attention to the literary works of these peoples, as well as to all that archaeological research has taught us regarding their cultural achievements, for it is impossible to gain a correct understanding of Scripture without continual reference to the environment in which the Israelites lived and worked, and in which the books of the Bible were composed.

My commentary is concerned with the plain meaning of the text. I have aimed to explain the natural sense of Scripture according to its original import, eschewing interpretations based on דְּרָשׁ *d^eraš*.* This type of exegesis also has intrinsic importance, particularly for halachic purposes; but the Talmudic sages already taught that 'a Biblical verse never loses its primary sense.' Our task is obviously to search out, to the utmost of our capacity, the true meaning of the Scriptural text. Noteworthy in this respect are the observations of Rashbam [R. Samuel b. Meir] in his introduction to pericope מִשְׁפָּטִים *Mišpāṭīm* [Exod. xxi–xxiv].

To enable us to comprehend the words of Scripture fully, I have invariably given consideration to their aesthetic qualities as well.

---

* This term, which means literally 'exposition', is used broadly for any kind of exegesis that is not in accord with the simple or actual sense of the Biblical text. More specifically, it is the method that characterizes the interpretations of the Midrashim (both halachic and haggadic) and the Talmudim. *Tr.*

PREFACE

The Book of Exodus is not only a sublime religious document; it is also a literary masterpiece, and our understanding of any literary work depends on our understanding of the artistic criteria which governed its composition, and on our appreciation of the beauty with which it is imbued.

For this purpose I sought, in the first place, to determine the inherent divisions of the Book down to its smallest subdivisions. I discerned in it three major parts, each of which is separable into sections, and each section into a number of paragraphs. In this very analysis, and in the titles that I have given the parts, sections and paragraphs, there is to be found, as it were, a general commentary and an elucidation of the architectonic structure of the work. In annotating the details of the passages, I have endeavoured to clarify the way in which the literary techniques of the ancient Orient have been applied, explaining the Eastern concept of 'order', which is unlike the Greek and modern concepts, the principles underlying the sequence of the sections, the repetitions (of words, phrases, paragraphs or complete sections), the numerical symmetry, the symbolism of the numbers according to the sexagesimal and heptadic systems, and so forth.

With the general question relating to the origin of the Book of Exodus, the date of its composition, its history and all the other problems that are usually discussed in an 'introduction', I shall deal in detail in the Introduction to the Pentateuch that I intend publishing at the end of my series of commentaries.* But even in the present volume I took the opportunity, on a number of occasions, of alluding incidentally to many matters of this nature.

I also paid attention to the various recensions, which, even after the final form of the books of the Torah has been fixed in its essential aspects, still differed in textual particulars, as we clearly see from the Samaritan Pentateuch and the ancient versions, as well as from citations in Talmudic literature and in MSS discovered in modern times, like the Nash Papyrus. Apparently the position with regard to the Torah was similar to that which obtained in the case of the Book of Isaiah, according to what we have learnt from the Dead Sea Scrolls, which comprise two divergent recensions of Isaiah, which existed side by side. There were also, it seems, different versions of the Pentateuch, namely, a recension intended for the sages and scholars, on which the Masoretic text is mainly based, and along with it, like

---

* It is to be regretted that the untimely demise of the author prevented him from carrying out his intention. *Tr,*

PREFACE

the Isaiah MS I, a number of popular editions (one of which was preserved by the Samaritans) the traces of which are discernible in the ancient translations.

Seeing that this book is designed primarily as a textual *commentary*, I did not deal — or I dealt only incidentally — with historical problems, such as the date to be assigned to the Exodus from Egypt, and the like; and in general I did not touch upon the question of the historical evaluation of the Scriptural records. Historical discussion of this kind is the function of the historian not of the commentator; the duty of the exegete is only to furnish the historian with material for his study by the proper elucidation of the text.

I endeavoured to make my commentary as succinct as possible. At times I compressed into a single line, and even into a single word, the results of research or meditation that could fill pages, trusting that the thoughtful reader would infer the unstated from the stated. Likewise I have nearly always refrained from controverting, or even citing, the views of other expositors, unless there was a special reason for doing so.

And now a few words about the external form of the commentary. Wherever possible I fitted my comments into the words of Scripture, so that the nexus between the annotation and the text should be close and direct, and the reader would have no need constantly to refer to the Pentateuchal wording; italics are used to mark the Biblical citations. On occasion, when I deemed it necessary, I added prefatory notes at the beginning of the sections or paragraphs, or concluding remarks at the end.

After seeing this volume through the press, I propose, *Deo Volente*, to start work immediately on the publication of the third volume of my commentary on Genesis, in accordance with the scheme that I outlined in the preface to the second volume, entitled *From Noah to Abraham*.*

JERUSALEM, ELUL, 5711 (1951)

U.C.

---

* Unhappily the author's sudden death prevented him from realizing his intention. He succeeded in completing only a small part — perhaps a fifth — of the third volume. This fragment has been added, in reprints of the Hebrew edition and also in the English version, as a supplement to the second volume, *From Noah to Abraham. Tr.*

PART ONE
THE BONDAGE AND LIBERATION
A Commentary on Exodus I—XVII

SECTION ONE

THE BONDAGE

CHAPTER I, 1–22

FIRST PARAGRAPH

THE CHILDREN OF ISRAEL BECOME A PEOPLE

(I 1–7)

Chapter I

This paragraph, which forms the exordium of the section and of the Book, describes briefly how the family of the Patriarchs became a numerous and mighty people. It marks the transition from the Book of Genesis to the Book of Exodus, and serves, as it were, to link the two books together. *And these* [וְאֵלֶּה *wᵉʾēlle*] *are the names of the sons of Israel who came* [הַבָּאִים *habbāʾīm*] *to Egypt with Jacob.* The sense is: Now (this is the force of the *Wāw* copulative at the beginning of the word וְאֵלֶּה *wᵉʾēlle*) these are the names of the sons of Israel, who, as was already narrated in Genesis, went down to Egypt with their father Jacob. It was fitting to record their names here, in the preface to the account of the great events to be chronicled later, in the same way as, prior to describing any massive collective action, such as war, revolution, migration, and the like, it is appropriate to mention the names of the heads of the armies, or parties, or groups who took part in the action referred to.

The sons of Jacob — 'the tribes', as they are termed in Jewish tradition, that is, the ancestors of the tribes of Israel — are twelve, the number customarily comprised in the organization of the Amphictyonies or associations of tribes. We know of the twelve chieftains of Ishmael and the twelve sons of Nahor, and it would seem that also the league of the Edomite chiefs was at first organized on the basis of this number. This numerical system is reflected likewise in the list of genealogies ['histories'] of Noah's descendants given in Gen. X. In the West, too, we find examples of it. It will suffice to mention the Greek Amphictyonic Council of Delphi, which was also originally composed of twelve tribes. But the sons of Jacob did not go down to Egypt alone; the verse repeats the verb בּוֹא *bō'* ['to come'], found in the word הַבָּאִים *habbā'īm* ['who came'], when it continues: *every man and his household came* [בָּאוּ *bā'ū*], that is, each one came with the members of his family. This prepares the way for the mention in *v.* 5 of the total number of those who went down to Egypt. The names of the tribes are arranged symmetrically, in three series, which are marked off by the use of the copulative *Wāw* ['and']. To begin with the first 2 four sons of Leah are listed: *Reuben, Simeon, Levi and Judah*. Thereafter, in the second series, are mentioned the last two sons to whom Leah gave birth after she had temporarily ceased bearing, and also the second son of Rachel (the first son, Joseph, was 3 already in Egypt): *Issachar, Zebulun and Benjamin*. Finally, in the third group, come the two pairs of the handmaids' sons: *Dan* 4 *and Naphtali, Gad and Asher.*

After the names of the tribes who emigrated to Egypt with Jacob, we are given the sum total of all the persons comprising 5 the House of Jacob: *And all the souls that came out of the loins of Jacob were seventy souls*, counting all those who went down to Egypt as well as *Joseph*, the elder son of Rachel, *who was in Egypt* already. This number — seventy — commonly indicates the perfection of a family blessed with offspring, both in the pre-Israelitic and in the Israelitic traditions. The Canaanites, as we know from the Ugaritic texts, used to speak of the seventy sons of the gods; whilst the tradition of the Israelites refers to the seventy descendants of Noah, and subsequently to the seventy sons of Jerubbaal-Gideon, and the seventy sons of Ahab. Similarly Jacob's family was perfect in the number of its children. Just as the nations of the entire world number seventy, according to Genesis X, so the children of Israel total seventy; they form a small world that parallels the great world, a microcosm corresponding to the macrocosm.

Another point. In the same way as the sons of Noah proceeded to multiply in great abundance, and seventy souls became millions, so, too, the children of Israel continued to increase exceedingly. 6 Although all who migrated to Egypt gradually died out — *Then Joseph died, and all his brothers, and all that generation* — yet the life of the family did not cease but expanded. In the course of time, in the tranquil period of which the Bible does not speak in detail, behind the enveloping mist that conceals the history of the passing generations, the family, by Divine grace, grew larger and spread abroad. The ancient blessing bestowed upon the macrocosm, 'Be fruitful and multiply, and fill the earth,' which God had uttered to Adam and Noah (Gen. i 28; ix 1), and which was confirmed in particular to Abraham, the father of the microcosm (*ibid*. xvii 2–6), was completely fulfilled, in overflowing measure, in the descendants of Israel in Egypt, as it is written: *And the children of Israel were* not merely *fruitful*, but they *teemed*; they not only *multiplied*, but *grew mighty*; *exceedingly* [בִּמְאֹד מְאֹד *bimeʾōdh meʾōdh*, literally, 'with strength, strongly'], in keeping with the promise given to Abraham; *so that the land was filled with them*, in accordance with the assurance given to Adam and Noah. We are now enabled to understand how the children of Israel could, for the first time, be called a people in *v*. 9.

Seven expressions for increase are used in this verse, a number indicative of perfection: (1) *were fruitful*; (2) *and teemed*; (3) *and multiplied*; (4) *and grew mighty*; (5) *with strength* [בִּמְאֹד *bimeʾōdh*]; (6) *strongly* [מְאֹד *meʾōdh*]; (7) *so that the land was filled with them*. Harmonious perfection is implied here, with the object of teaching us that all that happened was brought about by the will of God in conformity with His predetermined plan.

SECOND PARAGRAPH

THE FIRST TWO STAGES OF BONDAGE

(I 8–14)

This prosperity and fecundity, however, aroused envy, hatred and suspicion, particularly after a change had taken place in the monarchy. *Now there arose a new king over Egypt*, possibly a member of a different dynasty from that which reigned at the time when the family of Jacob went down to Egypt, a king *who did not know Joseph*, and consequently was not bound to the Israelites by any ties of gratitude for what Joseph had done for Egypt. The Torah was not concerned to inform us who this king was. Its purpose was not to write history but a poetic saga, intended not for scholars but for the people as a whole; and pedantry in respect of historical details was not appropriate to a poem addressed to the nation's heart. Only, from what we are subsequently told about the store cities we can infer, indirectly, to which monarch the text alludes.

As we shall see from various indications later, it may be assumed that the Torah had before it an epic poem describing the enslavement of the Israelites in Egypt and their liberation from there. Many of the characteristics of this ancient epic can be traced in the narrative of the Book of Exodus.

9 Also the following verses, *And he said to his people*, etc., are poetically styled and accord with popular conceptions. The complex process of political change in the life of the nation is portrayed here in the form of a simple dialogue between the king and his people. The king begins by stating a fact: *Behold the people of the children of Israel*, who live in our midst and increase in number year by year, *are* already *too many and too mighty for us*. The statement is, of course, an exaggeration, but it is one understandably prompted by hostility and fear. The Torah tells a similar story concerning another enemy of Israel, namely, Balak king of Moab (Num. xxii 6: 'since they are too mighty for me'). From the literary viewpoint, the words *many and... mighty* serve to link the beginning of this paragraph with the end of the one preceding, in which it is stated, *they multiplied and grew... mighty*.

After the statement of fact, the king proceeds to draw a deduction therefrom. 10 *Come, let us deal shrewdly with them*: we must therefore act shrewdly against them, devise an astute plan, *lest they multiply* even beyond their present numbers, and bring calamity upon us; *and it come to pass, that, when* — meaning, 'if' — *war break out* (תִּקְרֶאנָה *tiqre'nā*; the stem קָרָא *qārā'* here is equivalent to קָרָה *qārā* 'happen', 'befall', and the termination נָה- *-nā* serves to emphasize the verbal idea, as in Arabic and Ugaritic), this numerous and mighty people become an ally of the foe, *and they also join our enemies, and fight against us and go up from the land*, that is (see Naḥmanides), they will go up from Egypt without our being able to avenge ourselves on them as we should wish.

11 On account of this fear, the Egyptians arose *and set over them* — over the people of Israel — *captains of labour-gangs*, that means, they appointed over them overseers or taskmasters who would compel them to do forced service, *in order to afflict them with their heavy burdens*, that is, to undermine their strength by means of the burden of toil, so that they should cease multiplying. The Israelites carried out the work imposed upon them, *and they built for Pharaoh store cities* [עָרֵי מִסְכְּנוֹת *'ārē miskᵉnōth*]. That the expression *'ārē miskᵉnōth* signifies 'store cities' [literally, 'cities of

EXODUS I 14

storage (-places)'] is evident from ii Chron. xxxii 28: 'Storehouses [מִסְכְּנוֹת *misk^{e}nōth*] also for the yield of grain, wine, and oil' (the term *misk^{e}nōth* is a loan-word from Akkadian). The text mentions these cities by name: *Pithom*, in Egyptian *Pr 'tm*, in Herodotus Πάτουμος, that is, 'the house of (the god) Atum [or Etom]', today, Tell er Retabeh in the Delta; *and Raamses*, in Egyptian *Pr R^{c}mss*, 'the house of Rameses', which is Zoan [Tanis] of Egypt. Archaeological exploration at the site of the two cities has revealed that they were built (or, more exactly, were rebuilt) in the time of Rameses II, in the thirteenth century B.C.E. It was after this king that the city of Raamses, which became his capital, was then named, and apparently he is the monarch to whom the text refers.

This is how the Torah describes the beginning of the bondage, the first phase of the travail with which the Egyptians afflicted the Israelites. But it immediately adds that they failed of their purpose. The more they sought to persecute the Israelites and to weaken them, the more the latter continued to multiply in increasing measure, as Scripture narrates: *But* [*Wāw* adversative] *the*
12 *more they were oppressed, the more they multiplied* [כֵּן יִרְבֶּה *kēn yirbe*] *and the more they spread abroad.* The king of Egypt said, 'lest they multiply', [פֶּן־יִרְבֶּה *pen-yirbe*]; but the King of the universe said, 'the more they shall multiply' [כֵּן יִרְבֶּה *kēn yirbe*; in the translation of the verse the imperfect, as a frequentative, is rendered by the past tense]; this antithesis is the actual sense, not just the homiletical interpretation, of the verse. Now the anxiety of the Egyptians also increased in like measure: *And they were in dread of the children of Israel.* Here, too, we have an expression similar to that used of Moab: 'and Moab was overcome with dread of the people of Israel' (Num. xxii 3). Apparently the parallelism between the two narratives is intended by Scripture.

Seeing that their effort was unsuccessful, and the work did not reduce the strength of the Israelites, the Egyptians made the yoke heavier, and embarked on the second stage of the servitude. In the first phase the labour was of an ordinary nature; now it became
13 rigorous: *So the Egyptians made the children of Israel work with rigour* [בְּפָרֶךְ *b^{e}phārekh*], that means, with toil that breaks [מְפָרֶכֶת *m^{e}phārekheth*; the stem פרך *prk* signifies 'to crush small'] the body and embitters one's life. The use here of the words, *and*
14 *made their lives bitter*, serves to prepare us for the subsequent statement in connection with the ceremony of the feast of liberation (xii 8): 'with bitter herbs they shall eat it.' The Egyptians

11

embittered the lives of the Israelites *with hard service, in mortar and brick* (the prepositional *Bēth* at the beginning of the word בַּעֲבֹדָה *baʿăbhōdhā* ['with service'] is connected with the verb וַיְמָרְרוּ *wayᵉmārᵉrū* ['and they made bitter'], hence it is rendered 'with'; but the *Bēth* prefixed to the words בְּחֹמֶר וּבִלְבֵנִים *bᵉḥōmer ūbhilᵉbhēnīm* is related to preceding substantive עֲבֹדָה *ʿăbhōdhā* ['service'], hence it is translated 'in'), *and in all* kinds of *work, in the field; with* [the preposition אֵת *'ēth*] *all their work, wherein they made them serve with rigour*, that is, together with the other kinds of work that they forced them to do with rigour.

The words derived from the stem עבד *ʿbd* ['serve, service, work'] follow one another in these verses like hammer blows; and the word *rigour*, which also occurs twice, reverberates like an echo that strengthens and deepens the impression: 'So the Egyptians made the children of Israel *work* with *rigour* and made their lives bitter with hard *service*, in mortar and brick, and in all kinds of *work* in the field, in addition to all their (other) *work*, wherein they made them *serve* with *rigour*.' These recurring words number seven; here, as well as in the preceding paragraph, the key words of the paragraph occur *seven* times.

THIRD PARAGRAPH

PHARAOH'S COMMAND TO THE MIDWIVES

(I 15–21)

The second phase of the oppression also proved abortive; still the Israelites continued to multiply. The king of Egypt then proceeded to the third stage. Since he saw that it was not possible to weaken the Israelites by indirect methods, he decided to put an end to their power by direct action. But he did not as yet dare to issue a decree to this effect openly, and endeavoured to achieve his object covertly. He ordered the midwives to slay the male children of the Israelites. They were to kill them, of course, secretly, in such a way that the parents and relatives would be unaware of the crime, and would think that the infant had died of natural causes either before or during birth.

The entire episode of the midwives is likewise presented poetically, in a manner beloved of ordinary folk. Conversations of this nature between the great king, who was revered by the Egyptians as a deity, and the Hebrew midwives (*Then the king of Egypt said to the Hebrew midwives*, etc.) would not be conducted literally in the form described. Yet it is precisely to its poetic character and the simplicity of its presentation that the narrative owes the impression it leaves on the mind of the reader or listener.

The attributive *Hebrew* applied here to the midwives represents the first use in Exodus of this term, which is due to recur a number of times in the continuation of the Book. This is not the place to deal with the complicated question of the relationship between this designation [עברי '*bry*] and the similar appellations found in other Eastern tongues (*Ḫabiru* or *Ḫapiru* in Akkadian, *'pr* in Ugaritic and Egyptian,) which denote people belonging to a certain social class. It will suffice for the proper understanding of the passage to pay attention to the following points:

(a) The Akkadian documents of the city of Nuzu make it clear that the word in question signifies in general people who were aliens in their environment, and were mostly employed as servants or slaves.

(b) In Egyptian texts, the aforementioned Egyptian term refers to enslaved people, who were compelled to do forced labour in the service of Pharaoh. In the Bible the children of Israel, or their ancestors, are called *Hebrews* particularly when the writer has in mind their relationship to the foreign environment in which they find themselves (for example, Gen. xiv 13: *Abram the Hebrew*; Jonah i 9: *I am a Hebrew*, etc.), and more especially when they are in the position of slaves (for instance, in Gen. xxxix 14, 17, Joseph, when in Potiphar's house, is described as a *Hebrew man* or *Hebrew servant* (slave); so, too, ibid. xli 12: *A young Hebrew, a servant of the captain of the guard*). Here, in Exodus, whilst the children of Israel are still free men, they are called by their honoured designation, *children of Israel*, even when Pharaoh speaks of them (*v.* 9). But after the commencement of their servitude, they are usually referred to as *Hebrews*. We shall deal with the legal term *Hebrew slave* later, in our commentary to chapter xxi.

The Bible mentions here two midwives, *one of whom was named Shiphra and the other Puah*. The smallness of the number, which would not appear to be consonant with the needs of an entire people, as well as their names, in which there is possibly implied etymologies of the type found in rabbinic expositions (it will suffice to note that the stem שפר *špr* means 'beautiful', whilst the stem

EXODUS I 15

פעה *pʿh* is used in connection with child-birth in Isa. xlii 14), is to be explained, in the same way as we elucidated various points in the preceding passages, by the poetic character of the narrative.

16 Pharaoh, therefore, spoke to the midwives, *and he said* (the word 'said' is repeated because the narration was interrupted by the mention of the midwives' names): *When you serve as midwife to the Hebrew women, you shall look upon the birthstool* [אָבְנָיִם *'obhnāyim*; a dual form, meaning literally, 'two stones'], etc. The word *'obhnāyim* in Jer. xviii 3 denotes the double circular table on which the potter does his work [the potter's wheel]. Here, apparently, it signifies the seat on which the woman about to give birth was customarily placed. Possibly the two meanings of the word are interconnected. The Egyptians used to attribute the creation of human beings to the god Khnum, and in their portrayal of this divinity they depict him as a rule sitting like a potter beside the wheel to fashion thereon human figures out of clay. Due to this notion, the word came to mean the birthstool, on which human beings actually came into existence out of their mother's womb.

And Pharaoh continued: *if it is a son, you shall kill him; but if it is a daughter, she shall live.* Abram, when he went down to Egypt with his wife Sarai, was afraid of a similar eventuality (Gen. xii, 12): 'then they will kill me, but they will let you live.' The parallelism is apparently intended by Scripture in accordance with its principle that the experiences of the fathers foreshadow those of the descendants.

17 However, Pharaoh's new plan also failed: *But* [*Wāw* adversative] *the midwives feared* [וַתִּירֶאןָ *wattīre'nā*] *God, and did not do as the king of Egypt commanded them.* They feared the King of the universe, not the human monarch, *and let the male children live* [וַתְּחַיֶּין אֶת הַיְלָדִים *wattᵉḥayyenā 'eth hayᵉlādhīm*]. A word-play may be intended in regard to *wattīre'nā*; Pharaoh said to them: 'you shall look [וּרְאִיתֶן *ūrᵉ'īthen*, which is an anagram of וַתִּירֶאןָ *wattīre'nā*] upon the birthstool', but they did not do so; they feared and did not look.

18 Then Pharaoh summoned them to him to rebuke them: *So the king of Egypt called the midwives, and said to them, Why have you done this* (in truth they did not do anything, on the contrary they refrained from taking action; but this is the way the wicked despot puts it: he who refuses to obey him acts, as it were, against him), *and let the male children live* [*wattᵉḥayyenā 'eth hayᵉlādhīm*]? It should be noted that the words *wattᵉḥayyenā 'eth hayᵉlādhīm* are

14

repeated (concluding this verse as well as the one preceding) like an echo. This is possible in Hebrew because the forms of the second and third person feminine plural [in the imperfect] are identical.

The answer of the midwives is also cast in a form consonant with the poetic character of the narrative, which speaks to the heart of the people words that they love to hear, words redounding to the credit of their sons and daughters. We are not guilty, the 19 midwives say to the king, *Because the Hebrew women are not like the Egyptian women; for they are vigorous*, full of vitality, and consequently *before ever the midwife comes to them, they are* already (so quick are they) *delivered*; and once the infant son is born, and his father and mother and relatives have seen him, it is impossible to kill him secretly.

20 God rewarded the midwives in accordance with their upright conduct. The sequence of the clauses, which, at first sight, may appear in disorder on account of the incongruity between the division of the verses and the ideas, should be understood as follows: *So God dealt well with the midwives*, that means, He blessed them and their work. On the one hand, He blessed their work in that the children of Israel continued to be fruitful and to multiply — *and the people multiplied and grew very mighty*; and on the other hand, 21 *it came to pass, because the midwives feared God* (compare v. 17), that He blessed them in particular. Since they had helped to make the *houses* of the Israelites great and numerous (we must remember v. 1: 'every man and his household came'), He requited them according to their work — measure for measure — *and made them* [לָהֶם *lāhem*] *houses* [בָּתִּים *bāttīm*] (לָהֶם *lāhem* [masc. form] is used instead of לָהֶן *lāhen* [fem. form] on account of the letter *Bēth* [*Mēm* and *Bēth* being both labials] at the beginning of the word בָּתִּים *bāttīm*; on the concept of 'making houses' compare i Kings ii 24). Towards the close of the section, the opening words are recalled.

Also, at the conclusion of this, the third paragraph, there is a parallelism between the words, *and the people multiplied and grew very mighty*, and the end of the first paragraph (v. 7) as well as that of the second (v. 12). At the termination of each paragraph the main thought is reiterated, namely, that despite all the efforts of Israel's enemies, the blessing bestowed upon them by the Almighty receives corroborative fulfilment in them, and causes them to grow increasingly in numbers and in strength.

In this paragraph, too, the key-word *midwife* occurs, in the singular and in the plural, seven times.

CONCLUSION OF THE SECTION
(I 22)

After the three paragraphs, each of which is divided by the Masoretes into seven verses, comes a single, concluding verse. Pharaoh was compelled to recognize that all his attempts at suppression had been in vain. What he had *said* to his people had failed, and what he had *said* to the midwives had likewise proved abortive; neither ordinary work nor hard service had enfeebled the Israelites, and his plot to kill the Israelite male infants secretly with the help of the midwives had also not been crowned with success. Hence he realized the necessity not merely to *say* but to *command*, and

22 no longer clandestinely but openly: *Then Pharaoh commanded all his people, saying, Every son that is born* to the Israelites *you shall cast into the river* (*Nile*), *and* only *every daughter you shall let live.* This time he issued an open decree, similar to the scheme that he had previously envisaged, and resembling also, as we have explained, what the father of the nation had feared that the Egyptians of his day might do (Gen. xii 12): 'then they will slay me, but they will let you live.' He, however, that saved Abram and Sarai delivered their descendants, too, and it was owing to this very decree that the redeemer came and salvation sprang forth.

In this section, as in the concluding sections of Genesis (except for the poetic verse xlix 18) and in the continuation of Exodus up to the story of the Lord's revelation to Moses, the name '*Elōhīm* and not the Tetragrammaton is used. Apparently the Torah intended to intimate thereby that since they were in a foreign land, the children of Israel were unable to preserve their spiritual attachment to *YHWH* [rendered: 'Lord'], the God of their fathers, or their knowledge of Him, to which their ancestors had attained in the land of Canaan. Although there remained with them the knowledge of God, that is, the general belief in the Godhead, which is shared also by enlightened people among the Gentiles, yet it was not the concept of the Deity that belongs specifically to Israel and finds expression in the name *YHWH*. Moses was the first to succeed in rising again to the plane of the knowledge of the Lord, and he it was who once more raised his people to these heights of spiritual understanding.

SECTION TWO

THE BIRTH OF THE SAVIOUR AND
HIS UPBRINGING

CHAPTER II, 1–22

Chapter II
The inner nexus between this section and the one preceding is possibly hinted at in the outward connection provided by the repeated use of the word *daughter*. This word, which occurs at the end of chapter i, recurs here in the first verse and another five times in the continuation of the first paragraph — in all, seven times consecutively.

FIRST PARAGRAPH

THE BIRTH AND RESCUE OF MOSES

(II 1–10)

This paragraph describes the birth of the saviour and his rescue from the waters of the Nile. His father and mother are mentioned,
1 but not by name. *Now a man from the house of Levi went and took to wife the daughter of Levi*; there is no reference here, at the beginning of the narrative, to any other children of theirs. Nevertheless, it does not follow from this that a different tradition is reflected in our passage from that underlying the continuation of the Scriptural story, which gives the name of his mother and speaks of a brother and sister who were born before him. With fine artistic understanding, the Bible refrains from introducing here details of secondary import, which might deflect our attention from the main theme. The narrative records events of the highest significance, and has no place for genealogical particulars; these will receive due mention subsequently, when the tension will have subsided. At this point Scripture's aim is to inform us that from an ordinary man, a member of the house of Levi, and from an ordinary woman, the daughter of Levi (that is, the only daughter of Levi the son of Jacob), whose names there was no need to mention, God raised up a redeemer unto his people.

2   The sentence, *The woman conceived and bore a son*, does not mean that she conceived and gave birth for the first time, but merely that, at the very time when Pharaoh issued his decree, it happened that this woman became pregnant and gave birth to a male child.

The clause, *and she saw that he was a goodly* [literally, 'good'] *child*, like many others beginning with such expressions as 'and he saw', 'and she saw', and so forth, is to be understood as giving the reason for the statement that follows (compare Gen. 1 15, which describes what happened after Jacob had died, and the forty days of embalming and the seventy days of weeping for him had passed, and his sons had gone up to the land of Canaan to bury him and had returned to Egypt: 'And Joseph's brothers saw that their father was dead, they said, It may be that Joseph will hate us,' etc., that means, since their father was no longer alive, they thought possibly Joseph would hate them and requite them according to their deed). In modern phraseology we should say: Since she perceived that he was good, that is, beautiful and healthy, she did so-and-so. Even if the child had been weak and sickly, his death would have caused his mother much grief; but seeing that he was comely and well, her suffering was all the greater. Hence the mother's concern for his safety was so much more intense, and *she hid him three months*. But at the end of this time, the child's voice had become stronger, and

3   could be heard even outside the walls of the house, *and she could hide him no longer*. Thereupon she decided to entrust him to God's care, *and she took* [וַתִּקַּח *wattiqqaḥ*] *unto him*, that is, for him, for his deliverance (an allusion to the profound anxiety in the mother's heart), *an ark of bulrushes* — a kind of chest made of interwoven papyrus stems — *and daubed it with bitumen and pitch*, so that not a drop of water should seep into it (another token of the mother's anxious precautions), *and she placed the child in it, and placed* the ark *among the reeds at the river's brink*. The repetition of the word *placed* appears to imply that the mother put the ark down very gently, with the same tender care with which she had put the child into the ark.

The word *ark* [תֵּבָה *tēbhā*] occurs in only two sections of the Bible: here and in the section of the Flood. This is certainly not a mere coincidence. By this verbal parallelism Scripture apparently intends to draw attention to the thematic analogy. In both instances one worthy of being saved and destined to bring salvation to others is to be rescued from death by drowning. In the earlier section the salvation of humanity is involved, here it is the salvation of the chosen people; in the former passage, Scripture tells of the deliverance of the macrocosm, in the latter it speaks of the deliverance of the microcosm.

Loth to rely on a miracle, but yet hoping that one would happen, the mother wanted someone to watch over the fate of the ark and the child: *So his sister took her stand at a distance, to know what would be done to him.* Now an incident occurred that brought about the miracle and the salvation: for the time being the rescue of the child, subsequently the deliverance of the enslaved people.

5 *And the daughter of Pharaoh came down to bathe at the river, and her maidens walked beside the river.* The princess's name, like that of her father, is not stated. The name is not important to the theme proper; only the fact that she is Pharaoh's daughter is of significance. The princess *saw the ark among the reeds, and sent her maid* ('her' expresses general definition — i.e. the particular maid that she happened to send) *to fetch it* [וַתִּקָּחֶהָ *wattiqqāḥehā*, literally, 'and she took it'].

6 *When she opened* the ark, out of curiosity, *she saw it* [וַתִּרְאֵהוּ *wattir'ēhū*], *the child.* This construction, in which the noun ['child'] is specifically mentioned after the pronominal suffix [הוּ- *-hū*, 'it'] referring to it, is not to be regarded as pleonastic or a later addition. In Phoenician, too, we find examples of this usage for the purpose of giving emphasis to a noun. So, for example, in the inscription of king Azitawadda (i 17–18): *lšbtnm Dnnym*, which means literally, 'for their dwelling, the *Dnnym*.' After narrating objectively that Pharaoh's daughter saw the child — with the definite article, that is, the child already known to us — Scripture proceeds to tell us her subjective impression: *and lo, she sees inside the ark a weeping boy* — without the definite article, because to her it was not the known child but just a boy. The thing that immediately attracted her attention was his weeping. He is crying, therefore he is not dead, but is suffering and arouses compassion. *So she took pity on him and said* (that is, she thought to herself), *This is one of the Hebrews' children.* Here, in the verses referring to the one who is to become the foster-mother of the child, there occur the expressions 'she saw', 'she saw it' and 'she took it', which resemble those used earlier of the real mother. Such parallels are beloved of the writers of Israel and of the neighbouring peoples.

The young sister of the infant, who saw from where she was

EXODUS II 7

standing what had happened, and perceived signs of compassion in the princess, did not hesitate; she approached her at once and
7 made, as though enquiring, a clever suggestion: *Shall I go and call you a nurse from the Hebrew women to suckle the child for you?* For there were many Hebrew women who had borne children and were bereft of them, and they could suckle another child. In the girl's question the word לָךְ *lākh* ['for you,' 'you'] is used twice, as though to give the impression that she is making her suggestion only for the sake of the princess.

8 The princess, who is deeply moved, can answer only with a brief word of assent: '*Go.*' *So the girl went* — at once — *and called the child's mother*. The word *went*, coming in the Hebrew immediately after *Go*, indicates the celerity with which the order was carried out. Compare Gen. xii 1–4: 'Go you... So Abram went', etc.

9 The mother ran to the place forthwith. *And Pharaoh's daughter said to her, Take this child away, and suckle him for me* — on my behalf, for the child is mine, for I found him and he is entirely mine — *and I* (אֲנִי *'ănī*; the pronoun is emphatic) *will give you your wages. So the woman took* [וַתִּקַּח *wattiqqaḥ*] *the child and suckled him*. Again we find *wattiqqaḥ* ['and she took'], which had already been used initially when the mother took the ark in the first instance [*v.* 3], and subsequently *wattiqqāḥehā*, when the maid of Pharaoh's daughter took the ark [*v.* 5]. This third occurrence marks the denouement, which is crowned with success. Now the happy mother is able *to take* her son without anxiety for his life.

10 The days passed. *And the child grew* and was weaned, *and she* (his mother) *brought him unto Pharaoh's daughter, and he became her son* — that is, she adopted him — *and she called his name Moses* [מֹשֶׁה *Mōše*], *for she said, Because I drew him out* [מְשִׁיתִהוּ *mᵉšīthīhū*] *of the water*. The explanation does not fit the name accurately, because the form of the word is active not passive. Nevertheless, it seems incorrect to regard the interpretation, with most contemporary exegetes, as a popular etymology. The author of the verse undoubtedly had a fine feeling for the Hebrew language, and he knew quite well the difference between מֹשֶׁה *mōše* ['one who draws out'] and מָשׁוּי *māšūy* ['one who is drawn out']. It is also difficult to suppose that Scripture attributed to the Egyptian princess a knowledge of Hebrew and the choice of a Hebrew name. The naming is to be explained in a different way. First, it is stated that 'he became her son; and she called his name מֹשֶׁה *Mōše*', that

is, *son* in Egyptian (an Egyptian word that was actually pronounced thus — *Mōse* — at that period and in that locality). Thereafter it is stated, in the manner of homiletical name-etymologies, that the sound of this Egyptian name recalled the Hebrew verb מָשָׁה *māšā* ['draw out'], and it appeared as though the princess had this in mind ('for she said' = 'for she thought'): 'Because I drew him out of the water.' This apart, the Bible possibly intends to indicate, by inference if not expressly, that this child was destined to be 'the deliverer [מֹשֶׁה *mōše*] of his people' (Isa. lxiii 11) from the sea of servitude.

The key-word in this paragraph is *child*, which occurs seven times. Also emphasized in the paragraph, by being used three times, are the words *took, called, went* and *suckled*.

SECOND PARAGRAPH

MOSES AND HIS BRETHREN

(II 11–15)

Between what is narrated at the end of the previous paragraph and what is here recorded there was undoubtedly an interval of many years, and the expression, *And it came to pass in those days*, refers not to the period described above but to the time when the events to be related immediately afterwards took place. The wording resembles that of i Sam. iii 2: 'And it came to pass in that day, when Eli was lying down in his place.' No specific day is mentioned in the preceding narrative; the meaning, therefore, is: And it came to pass on a certain day, the day on which the events that we are about to recount happened. Similarly it is stated in Gen. xxxix 11: 'And it came to pass on a certain day, when he went into the house to do his work,' etc.

The words, *when Moses had grown up* [וַיִּגְדַּל *wayyighdal*], at the beginning of the narrative, form a link with the end of the preceding paragraph (v. 10: 'and the child grew' [וַיִּגְדַּל *wayyighdal*]). The identical word *wayyighdal* occurs in both passages, although in a different connotation. In v. 10 the signification is relative, the subject being still *the child*; in the present verse the meaning is absolute: Moses grew up and matured and became a young man.

The youth, although brought up as the son of Pharaoh's daughter in her palace, did not forget his brethren in bondage; *he went out from the royal palace so that he might draw near to his brethren, and he looked* [וַיַּרְא *wayyar'*] *on their burdens*. The word *wayyar'* ['and he saw, looked'] occurs thrice in this paragraph and is thereby emphasized; it thus parallels the word וַתֵּרֶא *wattēre'* ['and she saw'], which is used three times in the previous paragraph. Such parallels are not fortuitous in Biblical style. It implies that just as his mother and Pharaoh's daughter took pity on him, even so he took pity on his brethren; he felt compassion for them and was grieved at their burdens. Likewise the word בְּסִבְלֹתָם *b^esibhlōthām* ['on their burdens'] exactly duplicates the term used in the section of the Bondage (i 11) [where it is rendered: 'with their heavy burdens'], and suffices to remind us of that whole melancholy chapter.

On one of the visits that Moses paid to his brethren, an incident occurred: *and he saw an Egyptian* — one of the taskmasters, a captain of the labour-gangs (i 11) — *smiting a Hebrew*; not any Hebrew slave (see above, on i 15), but actually *one of his brethren*, 12 an Israelite. *He looked this way and that, and seeing no one* that might testify (this is mentioned here in order to explain why Moses was surprised when he discovered that the incident was known, *v.* 14), or, no one that could come to the Hebrew's aid (compare Isa. lxiii 5: 'I looked but there was no one to help; I was appalled, but there was no one to uphold; so my own arm brought me victory, and my wrath upheld me'). So Moses arose and *he smote the Egyptian and hid him in the sand*. The Egyptian smote, therefore justice demanded that he, too, should be smitten. However, the verb *smite* is repeated with a somewhat different nuance: when first used it means 'to beat', the second time it signifies 'to kill'. Nevertheless, the repetition points to the principle of measure for measure.

By this act Moses showed the qualities of his spirit, the spirit of a man who pursues justice and is quick to save the oppressed from the hand of the oppressor, the spirit of love of freedom and of courage to rise up against tyrants. A man possessed of these attributes was worthy to become God's messenger to deliver Israel from the bondage of Egypt and to *smite* their oppressors with ten *plagues* [literally, 'smitings'].

13 *He went out* again to his brethren the *second day* — the following day — and he saw, *lo, two Hebrews were striving together, and one of them was striking his fellow*. This time, too, Moses

EXODUS II 15

intervened in order to save the victim from the hand of the smiter. *And he said to the guilty person* (not guilty in the legal sense, that is, one who is wrong juridically, for Moses had not asked them to state their arguments, but guilty morally in that he was committing an assault): *Why* [לָמָּה *lāmmā*] *do you smite your fellow*? The word לָמָּה *lāmmā* is used here as an expression of rebuke, like מַדּוּעַ *maddūa‘* ['Why'] in Pharaoh's reproof to the midwives (i 18). But the aggressor reacts to the rebuke insolently, countering with two

14 questions. The first is: *Who made you a prince and a judge over us?* The reference is not to actual judgement; 'judge' is a synonym here for 'prince', and both words express a single idea — a kind of hendiadys — sometimes forming a parallelism with each other, both in the Bible (cf. Prov. viii 16: 'By me princes rule, and nobles, even all the judges of the earth') and in Ugaritic (*zbl — tpṭ* ['prince — judge']). The second question is even more impudent: *Do you mean to kill me as you killed the Egyptian?* The accused turns accuser. *Then Moses was afraid, and said* (= thought): *Surely, the thing is known.* Apparently, the man whom Moses protected the day before had told what had happened.

The very ring of the man's words convey the deep anger in his heart. It will suffice to note the recurrence (alliteration) of the sibilants *Šīn Šīn* in his first question (מִי שָׂמְךָ לְאִישׁ שַׂר וְשֹׁפֵט *mī śāmekhā le’īš śar wešōphēṭ*), and of *Rēš* in his second question (הַלְהָרְגֵנִי אַתָּה אֹמֵר כַּאֲשֶׁר הָרַגְתָּ אֶת־הַמִּצְרִי *halehorghēnī ’attā ’ōmēr ka’ăšer hāraghtā ’eth hammiṣrī*).

Scripture's intention is to indicate that everything occurred by Divine design in order to warn Moses of the peril to his life. The

15 news spread abroad. *When Pharaoh heard of it* — of the killing of the Egyptian — *he sought to kill Moses* in accordance with the law of murder (the repetition of the verb 'kill' is not accidental). But Moses, who had already been warned, forestalled him: *Moses fled from Pharaoh, and stayed* [וַיֵּשֶׁב *wayyēšebh*] *in the land of Midian, and he sat down* [וַיֵּשֶׁב *wayyēšebh*] *by a well* [הַבְּאֵר *habbe’ēr*]. Here, too, one word is used in two senses: the first וַיֵּשֶׁב *wayyēšebh* signifies 'he settled', and the second that he actually 'sat'. Moses stayed in Midian, and one day he was sitting by one of the wells in the land (the definite article of *habbe’ēr* denotes general definition [i.e. the particular well at which he happened to sit — a well]). At the end of the third paragraph this verb is used again, in yet a third connotation. The Septuagint translators did not grasp the word-play and altered the text to make it simpler.

23

EXODUS II 15

What happened at that well will be narrated in the next paragraph.

This paragraph contains no key-word; yet here, too, there are verbal repetitions that are not coincidental, but are employed for emphasis. At the beginning of the passage, וַיַּרְא *wayyar'* ['and he saw'] occurs three times, thus providing a link, as we have explained, with the preceding paragraphs. Thereafter the term *smite* is used thrice, and this is followed by the threefold occurrence of the verb *to kill*.

THIRD PARAGRAPH

MOSES IN MIDIAN

(II 16–22)

16 The paragraph commences with the sentence, *Now the priest of Midian had seven daughters*; this preliminary information is intended to help us understand the subsequent narrative. The name Midian serves to establish a close nexus with the previous paragraph.

After this prefatory statement it is related: *and the daughters of the priest came* [וַתָּבֹאנָה *wattābhō'nā*] *to the well by which Moses was sitting, and drew water from the well, and filled the troughs* [הָרְהָטִים *hārᵉhāṭīm*] — the conduits through which the water runs (in Aramaic רְהַט *rᵉhaṭ* means 'run') — *to water their father's flock.*

17 *But* (the *Wāw* at the beginning of v. 17 is adversative) they were unable to water the flock: *the shepherds came* [וַיָּבֹאוּ *wayyābhō'ū*] — aggressive, tyrannical fellows — *and drove them away* [וַיְגָרְשׁוּם *wayᵉghārᵉšūm*], by force, in order to use the water that they had drawn (the word *wayᵉghārᵉšūm* ends with a *Mēm* [pronominal suffix, third person *mas.* pl. = 'them'] instead of *Nūn* [pronominal suffix, third person *fem.* pl.], so as to make it clear that the ending is the pronoun and not the simple form [with *Nūn paragogicum*] of the verb without the object). However, Moses was there, and he showed courage, and promptness of action in helping to deliver the weak from the hand of the strong. *But* (again an antithetic *Wāw*) *Moses stood up and helped them, and watered their flock* [צֹאנָם *ṣō'nām*] (here at the end of the second half of the verse, final *Mēm* [pronominal suffix, third person *mas.* pl. = 'their'] is again used for *Nūn* [the corresponding *fem.* form] for the sake of parallelism with וַיְגָרְשׁוּם *wayᵉghārᵉšūm* at the end of the first half of the verse).

18 After Moses had watered the sheep, the girls returned home: *And when they came* [וַתָּבֹאנָה *wattābhō'nā*] *to their father Reuel.* Three consecutive sentences begin with the same or similar words: וַתָּבֹאנָה *wattābhō'nā* [*v.* 16]—וַיָּבֹאוּ *wayyābhō'ū* [*v.* 17]—וַתָּבֹאנָה *wattābhō'nā* [*v.* 18], the purpose, this time, being not to express a given idea, but to produce a stylistic effect. The name Reuel we shall discuss later on, at the beginning of chapter iii.

Their father *said to them: How is it that you have come so soon today?* He is surprised that they came sooner than the tyranny 19 of the shepherds normally permitted them to do. *And they said, An Egyptian* (they thought him to be an Egyptian on account of his dress and speech) *delivered us out of the hand of the shepherds, and even drew water for us and watered the flock.* The statement that the Egyptian had drawn water for them presents no difficulty, even though it is related in *v.* 17 that he had only watered the flock, because the act of watering includes also the drawing of water; this is also the case in Gen. xxix 10. The necessity for drawing water again is easily understood: possibly the shepherds had used up some of the water that Reuel's daughters had drawn for themselves, or the water was partly spilled during the altercation, or the whole incident occurred before the girls had finished drawing their water.

20 The father enquires at once, *And where is he?* The *Wāw* copulative links his question to the story of his daughters, the sense being: If this be so, then, after all that he has done for you, why is he not here with you? *Why have you left the man? Call him, that he may eat bread.* Go, invite him on my behalf to come to our house and to partake of our meal ('bread' here signifies food in general).

It is self-understood, though the Bible does not state this expressly, that his daughters returned to the well and invited Moses, in their father's name, to come to their home. Similarly in epic poetry, although the normal practice is to describe the execution of each command in detail and in the same words as were used in the injunction, there are occasional exceptions where the implementation is not narrated but is taken for granted. This abridgement is even more usual in narrative prose, as in our case. Another inference is also to be drawn from the context, although not ex-
21 plicitly recorded: since it is written, *And Moses agreed* [וַיּוֹאֶל *wayyō'el*, *Hiph'īl* of יָאַל *yā'al*] *to dwell* [לָשֶׁבֶת *lāšebheth* from the stem יָשַׁב *yāšabh*] *with the man,* it follows that Reuel suggested to

25

Moses that he should dwell with him. The verb הוֹאִיל *hō'īl*, which occurs in the Bible in various senses [be willing, be pleased, determine, undertake], is used here in the sense of 'agree', as we learn from another verse similar to this. Thus we read in Judges xvii 11: 'And the Levite agreed [וַיּוֹאֶל *wayyō'el*] to dwell with the man', after it had been stated earlier (*v.* 10): 'And Micah said to him, Dwell with me.' This passage in Judges likewise shows that the verb יָשַׁב *yāšabh* ['dwell'] is not to be related, as some have conjectured, to the marriage of the Midianite priest's daughter; it means only 'to dwell'.

It is after this that the marriage is mentioned: *and* Reuel *gave Moses his daughter Zippora*; and immediately thereafter we are told of the birth of the first-born: *She bore a son and called his name Gershom.* In this instance, too, an explanation of the name is given: *for he said, I have been a sojourner* [גֵּר *gēr*] *in a foreign land*, and here likewise we must not regard it as a popular etymology. The writer of this sentence undoubtedly knew full well that the name Gershom [גֵּרְשֹׁם *Gēreš̌ōm*] was derived from the verb גָּרַשׁ *gāraš* [in the Pi'el, 'drive away', 'banish'] and not from גּוּר *gūr* ['sojourn'], and he certainly did not intend to convey that Moses was the first to invent this name. His intention was merely to inform us that of the fund of names in use, Moses had chosen this one because its sound recalled the fact that he was a sojourner in a foreign land. It was precisely in Moses' family that the name was already to be found: Gershon or Gershom (this form occurs in i Chron. vi 1, etc.) was the first son of Levi. Furthermore, the name גֵּרְשֹׁם *Gēreš̌ōm* may possibly echo and form a parallelism with the word וַיְגָרְשׁוּם *wayeghāreš̌ūm* ['and drove them away'], from the stem גָּרַשׁ *gāraš*, at the beginning of the passage [*v.* 17].

The story of this paragraph is very similar to two narratives in the Book of Genesis:

(a) The story of Abraham's servant, the oldest of his house (Gen. xxiv). He journeyed to Mesopotamia to take from thence a wife for Isaac, and he sat by a well, and there he met Rebekah, who came and filled her jar and gave him and his camels to drink, etc.

(b) The story of Jacob (Gen. xxix). He also travelled to the same country to take a wife from there, and by the well he met Rachel the daughter of Laban, who was coming with her father's sheep, and he forestalled the shepherds and watered her sheep; thereafter he agreed to stay with Laban and tend his flock (for Moses, compare iii 1), and he married his two daughters, etc.

The parallelism between the three narratives is intended by the Torah, apparently, to inculcate its familiar lesson that the experiences of the fathers prefigure those of their descendants.

In this passage, too, we note the triple occurrence, for emphasis, of the expressions, *flock, water, draw water*.

The section is characterized by its harmonious and consummate structure. It begins and ends with a marriage and the birth of a son. At the conclusion of the first paragraph a son is named and the name is explained; this also happens at the end of the third paragraph. The first paragraph speaks of the daughter of Levi and the daughter of Pharaoh, and the third tells of the seven daughters of Reuel and, in particular, of his daughter Zipporah; and to the number of the daughters, which is expressly stated in the text to be seven, corresponds the number of times that the word *daughter* in the singular occurs throughout the section. With the interconnecting links between the three paragraphs, as well as with the threefold iterations in each of them, for the sake of emphasis, we have already dealt.

The three episodes narrated in this section serve as an introduction to Moses' mission to redeem Israel. They prove that his qualities of character and his courage fitted him worthily for this mission. It is not without significance, therefore, that the account of the third episode employs specifically expressions of *salvation* and *deliverance*.

SECTION THREE

MOSES' MISSION

CHAPTER II, VERSE 23 — CHAPTER IV, VERSE 31

THE EXORDIUM

'GOD'S IN HIS HEAVEN'

(II 23–25)

The cry of the children of Israel, who are enslaved and afflicted, rises before the throne of God, and He decides to deliver them. How and by whom the work of salvation will be wrought will be told in the continuation of the narrative.

Here the people are again called by their honoured title 'the children of Israel'. Although in the eyes of the Egyptians they were just Hebrews — nameless, foreign slaves — yet in God's sight they were the children of Israel, the descendants of Israel the Patriarch.

23 The opening words, *And it came to pass in the course of those many days*, are similar and parallel to those at the beginning of the second paragraph of the previous section (*v.* 11), and have the same meaning; only here the adjective *many* has been added, indicating that the period referred to was a long one, and that a considerable time had elapsed since the day that Moses fled from Egypt until the day that he undertook his mission. This indication of the passage of time is intended to resolve chronological difficulties, as will be explained later.

In order to find a connection between the clause, *the king of Egypt died* and the following clause, *And the children of Israel groaned from* [E.V. 'under', 'by reason of'] *their bondage, and cried out* [וַיִּזְעָקוּ *wayyizʻāqū* from the stem זָעַק *zāʻaq*], various unscientific interpretations and far-fetched suggestions have been put forward. But according to the simple sense of the passage, it appears that the two sentences are not connected but deal with two separate matters The death of the king of Egypt is mentioned only to provide us with preliminary information such as we found above, in *v.* 16: 'the priest of Midian had seven daughters.' Now that the king who sought to *slay* Moses was dead, there was nothing to prevent Moses returning to Egypt (compare iv 19: 'for all the men who were *seeking* your life are dead').

'From their bondage' — that is, from the place of their bondage and because of the burden thereof — the children of Israel were groaning brokenheartedly and crying unto God, *and their cry for help* [שַׁוְעָתָם *šawʿāthām* from the stem שָׁוַע *šāwaʿ*] *from the bondage came up to God. And God heard their groaning* [נַאֲקָתָם *naʾăqāthām* from the stem נָאַק *nāʾaq*], etc. The three synonymous stems, זָעַק *zāʿaq* — שָׁוַע *šāwaʿ* — נָאַק *nāʾaq*, which follow one another, emphasize the gravity of the position. Poetically the text describes three stages in the course of the Israelites' supplications :(a) the children of Israel *cry* out from their place of bondage; (b) their cry for help *rises* from their place of servitude heavenward; (c) this cry — the cry of those who *groan* under their burden — is *heard* by God.

And God remembered His covenant with Abraham, with Isaac and with Jacob. The cry of the Israelites recalls before God the covenant that He made and the promises that He gave to their ancestors. *And God saw the children of Israel* — He looked upon them with paternal love — *and God knew*, that is, He took cognizance of the matter, in the sense of the verb *ydʿ–wdʿ* in ancient Arabic idioms and in Aramaic.

The four consecutive clauses that begin with a verb followed by the subject *'Elōhīm* ['God'] ('and God heard', 'and God remembered', 'and God saw', 'and God knew'), form a harmonious parallelism with each other, and describe, stage by stage, the Divine response to the groaning of the children of Israel: first He hears the groaning, then He remembers the covenant, thereafter He considers the position of the Israelites, and finally He decides to intervene in the matter. The verbs *remember, see, hear* have already occurred a number of times in the narratives of the Book of Genesis to indicate the paternal relationship of God to his suffering, pain-racked creatures. Thus He remembered Noah and the beasts, etc. (viii 1); He remembered Abraham for the benefit of Lot (xix 29); He remembered Rachel who was barren (xxx 22); He saw the affliction of Leah (xxix 31), and the suffering of Jacob in Laban's house (xxxi 12, 42); He heard the affliction of Hagar (xvi 11), the voice of Ishmael (xxi 17), the voice of Leah who was disliked (xxix 33), the voice of childless Rachel (xxx 6), and, again, the prayers of Leah and Rachel (xxx 17, 22). Similarly, these characteristic verbs recur in regard to the Israelites, in bondage in Egypt (Exod. iii 7, 9; iv 31; vi 5). In this case, too, the experiences of the fathers foreshadowed the history of their descendants, whilst their merit stood by their children.

FIRST PARAGRAPH

THE THEOPHANY ON MOUNT HOREB

(III 1–15)

Chapter III

In the opening verses Scripture directed our glance upward, towards the throne of God, and momentarily distracted our mind from Moses. Now the Torah returns to Moses, in order to relate how Moses was chosen to implement what the Heavenly Court had decided. Hence the Bible puts the subject before the predicate, and does not say, ...וַיְהִי מֹשֶׁה רֹעֶה *wayᵉhī Mōše rōʿe*... [literally,
1 'And was Moses keeping (the flock)'], but וּמֹשֶׁה הָיָה רֹעֶה *ū-Mōše hāyā rōʿe*... ['And Moses was keeping (the flock)'], as though to say: Now as for Moses, he was keeping the flock, etc.

Like Jacob in his day, Moses was tending the flock of his father-in-law: *the flock of his father-in-law, Jethro, the priest of Midian*. This work also helped to prepare Moses for the task to which he was to devote himself, the task of shepherding the flock of the Lord (Isa. lxiii 11). His father-in-law is called here Jethro, and seemingly this presents a difficulty, for earlier the Bible referred to him as Reuel. The difficulty is not to be explained by the usual premise that the redactor excerpted mechanically texts from different sources, for it is inconceivable that the editor should not have noticed the discrepancy between the sources, and should unwittingly have put the two conflicting names within a few lines of each other. It seems more probable to suppose that there existed among the Israelites variant traditions concerning the man's name, which were well known to the people, and that the Torah deliberately chose the name Reuel when alluding to him only as the priest of Midian, but preferred to use here, when speaking of him as Moses' father-in-law, the name Jethro [יִתְרוֹ *Yithrō*, from a stem meaning 'abundance', 'superiority'], the more honoured designation, which points to his pre-eminent status. His importance rose in our estimation when he became Moses' father-in-law.

EXODUS III 2

Now one day an incident occurred: Moses *led his flock after grassland*, that is, he was seeking after good pasture (מִדְבָּר *midhbār* [which is usually rendered 'desert'] signifies here 'pasture', and so Onkelos translates: שְׁפַר רַעְיָא *šᵉphar raʿyā* ['choice pasture']; and אַחַר *'aḥar* indicates the object of his search, as in Job xxxix 8: 'He ranges the mountains as his pasture, and he searches *after* [אַחַר *'aḥar*] every green thing'), *and he came*, as he wandered to and fro for this purpose, *to Horeb the mountain of God*. Possibly, in the view of Scripture, this mountain had already been hallowed by theophanies, and consequently was called 'the mountain of God', but Moses was not aware of this. More probably, however, the mountain is so called proleptically: the mountain that was destined to become God's mountain. The name Horeb and the problem of its identification we shall discuss later, in the section on the Revelation at Mount Sinai.

On this mountain Moses was vouchsafed a vision of God. In the sentence, *And the angel of the Lord* [YHWH] *appeared to him*, the expression, *the angel of the Lord*, means a manifestation of the Lord. The Biblical text here and in the continuation of the narrative is meticulously careful to avoid referring to any likeness whatsoever, except the burning bush. The angel, or the theophany, appeared to Moses *in a flame of* [לַבַּת *labbath*] *fire* rising *out of the midst of a bush*, that is, in the form of a flame of fire of a unique kind — the bush was alight with it, producing the fire out of itself, and yet it remained whole: *and lo, the bush was burning with fire, yet it was not consumed*. At any rate, what presented itself to Moses' vision was a miracle. Although the bush (i.e. blackberry, *Rubus discolor*) is commonly found in steppe country, and it is no unusual phenomenon for a bush dried by the summer's heat to catch fire, yet the bush that Moses saw was not consumed in the flame (לַבַּת *labbath* stands for לְהָבַת *lahăbhath*, as in Psa. xxix 7: 'flames of [לְהָבוֹת *lahăbhōth*] fire', and thus, in fact, in its fuller and more usual form, the word is found in the Samaritan Pentateuch).

Numerous attempts of various kinds have been made to explain the bush symbolically, but it is highly doubtful if this represents the actual intention of the text. It is likewise dubious if there is any connection between the name of the bush [סְנֶה *sᵉne*] and that of Sinai [סִינַי *Sīnay*]. Just in this verse, it will be noted, the mountain is not called Sinai but Horeb.

The word הַסְּנֶה *hassᵉne* (even at its first occurrence it has the

31

definite article as an expression of general definition) is used three times in one verse, for emphasis, and twice more in the two succeeding verses. Also expressions of 'seeing' keep recurring, like hammer strokes: וַיֵּרָא *wayyērā'* ['and was seen', 'and appeared'], וַיַּרְא *wayyar'* ['and saw'], וְאֶרְאֶה *weʾerʾe* ['and I shall see'], הַמַּרְאֶה *hammarʾe* ['sight'], וַיַּרְא *wayyar'* ['and saw'], לִרְאוֹת *lirʾōth* ['to see']. This should cause no surprise, since it is 'seeing' and 'appearing' that form the primary theme of this paragraph. Following upon these six words from the stem רָאָה *rāʾā* ['see'], there occurs a seventh time, and with special emphasis, a final twofold echo thereof in the utterance of God: 'I have surely seen' [רָאֹה רָאִיתִי *rāʾō rāʾīthī*, literally, 'seen I have seen'] (v. 7).

3 The strange phenomenon arouses the attention of Moses. *And Moses said* to himself, *I will turn aside* to the place and *see this great* (i.e. wonderful and strange) *sight* at close quarters and fathom its mystery, *why the bush is not burnt*. There is no discrepancy to be discerned between this and the earlier statement that *the bush was burning with fire*; this constitutes the wonder, that the bush burns and is not burnt.

4 *When the Lord* [*YHWH*] *saw that he turned aside to see, God* [*'Elōhīm*] *called to him out of the bush*. The sudden change of Divine name — *YHWH* in the first clause and *'Elōhīm* in the second — which is difficult to explain by the mechanical division of the text between different sources, is easily explicable in the light of what we have stated above, at the end of our commentary to chapter i. The children of Israel, including hitherto even Moses, forgot in the land of their exile the direct knowledge of *YHWH*, the God of their ancestors, and retained only a general and vague understanding of the concept ''*Elōhīm*'. Now Moses is vouchsafed a special revelation that elevates him to that knowledge of *YHWH* to which the patriarchs of the nation had attained. Consequently the Divine names change in these verses, which precede the revelation of the Tetragrammaton to Moses, in accordance with the following principles: whenever the Lord is spoken of objectively, the name *YHWH* occurs; but when the reference is to what Moses saw or heard or felt subjectively, the name *'Elōhīm* is used. Here in v. 4 the text has, *When YHWH saw*, because an objective statement concerning what the Lord saw is intended; but Scripture says, *'Elōhīm called to him*, because the call heard by Moses appeared to him at the moment as the voice of *'Elōhīm*. He learns only subsequently that it is the voice of *YHWH*.

This Voice called unto Moses out of the bush, *and said, Moses, Moses!*, repeating the name in order to warn him of the urgency and the importance of the call. *And* Moses *said, Here am I* — I am prepared to hear and obey. Moses only hears, but sees no image; nevertheless, he understands that something exalted and sublime confronts him. The Voice continued to speak, *and said, Do not come near* — stand reverently at a distance, for the vision you have seen is holy. *Put off your sandals from your feet* — do not tread on this ground with your travel-soiled sandals — *for the place on which you are standing is holy ground.* Moses obeys the command and waits in silence. Again he hears the Voice, which tells him who it is that is speaking. *And He said, I am the God of your father, the God of Abraham, the God of Isaac, and the God of Jacob.* The names of the Patriarchs recall the opening paragraph, which declares that God remembered, for the sake of the enslaved Israelites, the covenant He had made with Abraham, Isaac and Jacob, and we begin to understand the purpose of this revelation.

As soon as Moses hears that it is the God of the Patriarchs who is addressing him, he quickly hides his face: *And Moses hid his face, for he was afraid* out of reverence *to look at God.* Although the Bible is careful not to mention any corporeal form apart from the fire in the midst of the bush, it emphasizes that Moses did not dare to look even at this vision, when he knew that it was a vision of God. But even though he refrains from looking, he listens attentively to what God is pleased to tell him. Once more the Voice is heard, and it announces great tidings. Here it is written, *And YHWH said*, and not 'And *'Elōhīm* said', since it is not explicitly stated that He said *to Moses* or *to him*, as in *v.* 4 and in *vv.* 14–15. To the objective narrator the speaker is none other than *YHWH*, even though to Moses He is still only God in a general sense. Particularly when conveying these tidings, the Torah wished to make the announcement in the name of *YHWH*: He who uttered these words was *YHWH* Himself!

The announcement begins with solemn words: *I have surely seen the affliction of My people who are in Egypt.* Alongside the verb 'see', there occur in this initial verse the other verbs that have already been used together with it in the opening paragraph (ii 24–25); thus we find here, too: *see* — *hear* — *know.* What happened in the Divine Court on high is now made known to those who dwell upon the earth below. From My holy habitation in heaven I have seen the affliction of My people (the expression 'My' indicates a special relationship of love) who are there in Egypt, in the land which you were compelled to leave, *and I have heard their cry because of their taskmasters; for I know their sufferings.* Consequently, I decided to save them, *and I have come down to deliver them out of the hand of the Egyptians.* It seems strange that the Bible should use the expression *I have come down*, which apparently presupposes that the Godhead needs to descend to earth in order to act thereon, after employing the verbs *see — hear — know*, which imply that God hears and sees and knows everything from His throne of glory. But the difficulty can be explained in the light of the history of the Hebrew language. The term 'come down' is, in such a context, merely the normal idiom for describing Divine intervention in human affairs, and was inherited by the Hebrew tongue from the Canaanite literary tradition, which, when using this or similar phrases, understood them in their literal signification (see the example I cited from the Ugaritic writings in my annotations to Genesis xi 7). In Hebrew this expression, like many other Canaanite phrases, continued to be used despite the fact that the concepts that the Israelites expressed by such idiomatic phrases were far different from the original Canaanite notions.

8 The promise of deliverance from the hand of the Egyptians is only the first part of the annunciation; the second and principal part thereof is the assurance concerning the acquisition of the land: *and to bring them out of that land* — from the land of Egypt, whose afflictions they would ultimately forget and which consequently deserved no more than this cursory reference — to a land that merited considerable praise. This eulogy is expressed in three consecutive phrases. The first is, *to a good and broad land*, that is, good in its products and broad in extent, and was capable, therefore, of providing the Israelites with abundant sustenance and ample room for settlement. The second expression comes to elaborate the meaning of the adjective 'good': *to a land flowing with milk and honey*. This formula was at first coined by the nomadic shepherds to denote a land blessed with pastures for cattle producing milk and with trees whose boughs afforded man, without the necessity for hard toil, food as nourishing and as sweet as bees' honey. In the course of time the signification of the phrase was extended to include also land that yielded rich harvests as a result of human labour. The spies whom Moses sent

EXODUS III 11

to explore the land of Canaan brought samples of the fruit of the land — grapes, pomegranates and figs — and said of the land that 'it flows with milk and honey and this is its fruit' (Num. xiii 27). The third phrase, which serves to clarify the meaning of the attributive 'broad' and to specify the land alluded to, is: *to the place of the Canaanites, the Hittites, the Amorites, the Perizzites, the Hivites and the Jebusites*. This land is now the 'dwelling-place' of six peoples; the Israelites could therefore settle there in their thousands and myriads. The list of nations comprises here and in other passages six names, a round number based on the sexagesimal system that obtained in the ancient East. But there are also verses that list five or seven or ten names; this is solely due to the fondness for diversification, which is a common feature of Biblical style. On the various names, see my commentary on the Book of Genesis.

After the announcement of the tidings comes the conclusion, to wit, the commissioning of Moses. The conclusion begins, as
9 is customary in ancient Hebrew, with the expression *And now* [וְעַתָּה *we'attā*]; but it is immediately followed by a recapitulation of the essential points of the preceding statement so as to recall and emphasize it: *behold, the cry of the people of Israel has come to Me, and I have seen the oppression with which the Egyptians oppress them*. Hence it is necessary to repeat the expression *And now* at the beginning of v. 10, in order to indicate the main con-
10 clusion: *And now, Moses, hear what I require of you. Come, and I will send you* (as in Gen. xxxvii 13, when Jacob sent Joseph on his mission) *to Pharaoh that you may bring forth My people, the children of Israel, out of Egypt*. You must go as My agent to the king of Egypt, and carry out, on My behalf, the task of bringing forth the children of Israel from the house of bondage. The announcement included not only the exodus from Egypt but also the entry into the land of Canaan; nevertheless, when Moses is charged with the mission only the exodus from Egypt is mentioned, because Moses was not to lead the people into the land.

So ends the Divine utterance. In its last words we encounter again the expression 'My people' used at the beginning, the designation 'children of Israel', which occurs in the middle, and the name 'Egypt', which is found at the beginning and also in the middle of the communication. The conclusion comes to sum up and confirm, as it were, what had previously been stated in detail.
11 *But Moses said to God* [אֱלֹהִים *'Elōhīm*] (Moses had not yet

attained to the knowledge of the name *YHWH*): *Who am I that I should go to Pharaoh, and bring the children of Israel out of Egypt?* This is not, as most commentators explain, a refusal to accept the mission or an expression of doubt as to his ability to implement it. The doubts will be mentioned in chapter iv, after reference has been made to the details of the undertaking. At this stage, when Moses is confronted with the plan as a whole, and realizes at the outset the terrible difficulties of his commission, his initial response is to voice his sense of humility and to stress his unworthiness relative to the magnitude of the enterprise. This is the meaning of such phrases as 'Who am I?' or 'Who is your servant?' and the like, whether they occur in the Bible, in the Lachish Letters, or generally in the idiom of the ancient East. In like vein Moses speaks here: Who am I, a simple shepherd, that I should be able to fulfil the exalted mission wherewith Thou art minded to honour me, a twofold mission (he reiterates the two matters spoken of in *v.* 10): to come before the king after I have long ago left his palace and have become a shepherd, and to become the head and leader of an entire people in order to bring it forth from Egypt?

12 The answer to his question came forthwith: *And He [God] said*: *But I will be with you.* You need not rely upon your own powers only; I shall be with you, and help you, and give you strength to succeed in your commission; and in order that you may be sure that what you have seen and heard emanates from none other than Me, and that it is I who have charged you with this task, I shall give you a sign: *And this shall be the sign for you, that I have sent you*: I apprise you now that *when you have brought forth the people out of Egypt, you shall serve God upon this mountain.* The very fact that I inform you today of what will happen after you have brought forth the people from Egypt — and the matter is a cause for wonder, for Mount Horeb is not situated on the direct road from Egypt to Canaan — will serve as a sign to you that the deliverance of the children of Israel from the hand of the Egyptians was decreed by Me, and the implementation of the decree is beyond all doubt. It is not just after the fulfilment of what I tell you today that you will be certain that you are sent by Me, but even prior to that, whenever you contemplate and await the Convocation at this mountain, which I appoint unto you now, you will have this assurance.

At this stage Moses asks the name of the God who is speaking to him. According to the conception prevailing in the ancient

East, the designation of any entity was to be equated, as it were, with its existence: whatever is without an appellation does not exist, but whatever has a denomination has existence. The meaning of an object's name indicates its nature and determines its characteristics; in Talmudic parlance (B. Berakhoth 7b): 'the name is a formative factor.' Thus two things were clear to Moses: (a) that the God of the Patriarchs has a specific name, although his people had forgotten it after leaving the place where He had revealed Himself to their ancestors; (b) that this name expresses the attributes of the God of the Patriarchs. He realized that the knowledge of this designation was necessary to him in the propagation of his mission amongst his brethren. He himself was prepared to obey and to devote his capacities, to their full extent, to fulfilling the charge of his ancestral God, but he anticipated that, when he appeared before his kinsmen as the messenger of the God of the Patriarchs, they would ask him the name of Him who had sent him, and, especially, the meaning of the designation. He deemed it essential, if they were to believe in him and in the One who sent him, to know how to answer these questions. Conse-

13 quently Moses enquired: *Then Moses said to God* [אֱלֹהִים *'Elōhīm*] (Moses still uses the term *'Elōhīm*, because the Specific Name was not yet known to him): *If I come to the children of Israel and say to them, The God of your fathers has sent me to you, and they ask me, What is His name? what shall I say to them?* God gives a twofold reply to this question: one answer (not two) in v. 14, and another in v. 15. The former provides a prefatory explanation of the meaning of the name, that is, it describes the attribute of God that is expressed by His specific designation; the latter discloses this name and proclaims it in exalted terms.

The first answer given by God to Moses (here, too, of course,
14 the text has *'Elōhīm*: *Then God* [*'Elōhīm*] *said to Moses*) is this: *I am who I am*. We should certainly not seek to find in these words a philosophic or theological doctrine in accordance with the concepts of later epochs; they contain a very simple idea only, connected with the word אֶהְיֶה *'eh*ᵉ*ye* [rendered here: 'I am'], which had already been used in the Divine utterance to Moses in v. 12: *But I will be* [אֶהְיֶה *'eh*ᵉ*ye*] *with you*. We are given here an explanation of the name *YHWH* that connects it with the stem *haya* הָיָה ['to be']. Irrespective of the actual etymology of the name (the reader will find the various theories dealing with the etymology of this designation in my article 'The Names of God' in the *Encyclopaedia*

Biblica [Hebrew], s.v. אֱלֹהִים 'Elōhīm), the Torah regards it as a derivation of the stems הָיָה — הָוָה hāyā–hāwā. The meaning assigned to it in our passage corresponds to the *present*. The form of the verb that is called in Hebrew today 'future' [i.e. the imperfect] could signify in Biblical language any tense — past, present or future — and approximated in some instances to the use of the 'present' in Modern Hebrew. The name *YHWH*, by which the God of Israel is designated, is the 'future' tense, third person, and it is interpreted in our text in the sense of יִהְיֶה *yihᵉye* [literally, 'He will be', understood as 'He is']. Hence, when the explanation is given by *YHWH* Himself, the verb appears in the first person (see Rashbam [Rabbi Samuel ben Meir] *ad locum*): אֶהְיֶה *'ehᵉye* ['I am']. The sense is: It is I who am with My creatures (compare B. Berakhoth 9b) in their hour of trouble and need — as I have already declared to you: 'But I will be (אֶהְיֶה *'ehᵉye*) with you' (v. 12) — to help them and save them. And I am who I am, always, and just as I am with you, so am I with all the children of Israel who are enslaved, and with everyone who is in need of My help, both now and in the future. There is also implicit in this interpretation the thought of implementing the promises: I am who I am always, ever alike, and consequently I am true to My word and fulfil it (compare Mekhilta of Rabbi Simeon ben Yoḥai on Exod. vi 2). When the Israelites realized, after their exodus from Egypt and their deliverance from Pharaoh's host, which pursued after them, that in truth the Lord was with them and kept His promises to them, they proclaimed in the Song of the Sea (xv 3): '*YHWH* is His name', that is, He and His name are worthy of each other, His deeds being in accord with His designation.

The answer given to Moses comprises only these words: 'I am who I am', no more. The second part of *v.* 14, which begins with the reiteration of the words *And He said*, is to be understood in the way that I have often explained the duplication *and he said... and he said* in the Book of Genesis, to wit, the first occurrence of the clause *and he said* is followed by the quotation of the words spoken, whereas the second use of this expression serves to introduce the elucidation of the inner meaning of these words. To Moses' question: What shall I say to them if they ask me for the name of Him that sent me, the reply is given 'I am who I am', the meaning of which is: *Say this to the children of Israel*, I AM (who I am) *has sent me to you*, that is, He who sent me to you is the God who says of Himself, *I am*.

EXODUS III 15

15 The second answer, which is introduced by the sentence, *God also said to Moses* (the word *also* indicates that there is an additional utterance here) is worded in an elevated style, in part poetic. It is headed by the solemn formula, *Say this unto the children of Israel*, which has a broader rhythm than the corresponding clause in the previous verse (אֶל *'el* instead of לְ־ *l^e*-[both prepositions mean 'to', 'unto']) and is identical with that which prefaces the poetic verses of Exod. xx 22 ff. Thereafter follow the words that Moses is bidden to tell the Israelites: first, the Specific Name, *YHWH*, which stands, as it were, alone, before the series of designations separating it from the predicate *has sent me*. Juxtaposed to it are the following appellations: to begin with, the general title, *the God of your fathers*, which is succeeded by three terms that particularize and confirm it, emphasizing the idea of unbroken continuity, namely, *the God of Abraham, the God of Isaac, and the God of Jacob*. After the solemn proclamation of the Name and its by-names, the fact of the mission is to be mentioned, *has sent me to you*. He Himself sent me to you; although we forgat His name, He did not forget us. He remembered His covenant with our ancestors, and has sent me to you to fulfil His covenant. Finally, there is a noble concluding sentence, constructed in true poetic form, according to the style of Eastern poetry of antiquity; *this is My name for ever, and this is My remembrance* [i.e. title] *throughout all generations*. The parallelism between שֵׁם *šēm* ['name'] and זֵכֶר *zēkher* ['remembrance'] recurs in Prov. x 7, Job xviii 17 (cf. also Isa. xxvi 8); and the parallelism between עֹלָם *'ōlām* ['ever'] and דֹּר(וָ)דֹר *dōr (wā)dhōr* ['all generations'] is one that was already common in ancient Canaanite poetry, as is evidenced by the Ugaritic texts, where it occurs frequently, and from the Canaanite usage it passed over to Hebrew literature, the Bible employing it not less than twenty-eight times. The extent to which the recollection of this verse survived among the Israelites throughout the generations we can infer from the passages that were patterned after it. Already in Hosea xii 5 [Hebrew, *v.* 6] we find: 'the Lord [*YHWH*] the God of hosts, the Lord is His name [literally, 'remembrance']'; in Psa. cii 12 [Hebrew, *v.* 13]: 'But Thou, O Lord, art enthroned for ever; Thy name [literally, 'remembrance'] endures to all generations'; *ibid.* cxxxv 13: 'Thy name, O Lord, endures for ever, Thy renown [literally, 'remembrance'], O Lord, throughout all ages'. This poetic line forms a fitting conclusion to the subject and an appropriate ending to the paragraph.

Our interpretation of this paragraph, which explains all the aspects of the theme simply and clearly, shows the incorrectness of the view prevailing among contemporary scholars, who hold, on the basis of a mechanical and superficial study of the verses, without any attempt to delve into their inner meaning, that we have here before us a fragment taken from a given source that states that the name *YHWH* was unknown to the Patriarchs and was first revealed to Moses. This is not the place to controvert this view in detail (the reader will find a full discussion of the subject in my Italian work, *La Questione della Genesi*, pp. 82–92); it will suffice to indicate one point only. It is precisely in these verses, which are regarded as incontrovertible proof of the existence of an Elohistic source, according to which the Tetragrammaton was not known to the Patriarchs, that it is specifically written (v. 15): '*YHWH* [E.V. *Lord*], the God of your fathers, the God of Abraham, the God of Isaac, and the God of Jacob', and thereafter (v. 16): '*YHWH* the God of your fathers.' In order to nullify this decisive testimony, the proponents of the aforementioned theory usually assert that these verses have been amended by later redactors or interpolators — an answer of despair, which generates new difficulties and is based on the arbitrary expunction of all contrary evidence, a method that permits a scholar to advance whatever hypothesis occurs to him, even if the witness of Scripture is clearly opposed to it.

SECOND PARAGRAPH

THE INSTRUCTIONS

(III 16–22)

Having been apprised of the essential nature of his mission, Moses is given detailed instructions concerning the manner of its execution: *Go and gather the elders of Israel together, and say to them,* etc.

First, he must go to Egypt and convoke the elders of Israel, the heads of the people and their representatives (obviously he could not speak to the whole people at once), in order to tell them of the theophany that the God of their ancestors had vouchsafed him, and to bring them the good tidings of the approaching redemption. In the wording of the announcement that Moses has to make to them, there are repeated, in conformity with the usual style of Biblical narrative, expressions that have already occurred in the preceding narration with a few changes in keeping with the altered situation. In this instance, too, the communication begins with the proclamation of the name *YHWH* as in *v.* 15, and the by-names that accompanied it there also occur here. But this time the words describing the action (*has appeared to me*) do not come after the substitute designations as in the previous passage, for it was proper that at the commencement of his first address to the people Moses should state at once what had happened, and should not preface this information with a long list of appellations like that in verse 15, whose main purport was actually to make known the Divine Name and its surrogates. Immediately following the Tetragrammaton and the general epithet — *YHWH, the God of your fathers* — the announcement concerning the theophany is made — *has appeared to me* (compare *v.* 2: 'And the angel of the Lord appeared to him') and only thereafter comes the particularization, *the God of Abraham, of Isaac, and of Jacob* (the omission of the word *God* before each patriarch's name is merely a variation in the external form). The fact of the theophany itself is the first thing that Moses must tell the Israelites, and the second is the substance of the promise: *I have surely remembered you,* etc. According to the sequence of the Pentateuchal narratives, this expression was well known to the children of Israel, for before his death Joseph had said to his brothers as follows (Gen. *l* 24): 'But God will surely remember you, and bring you up out of this land to the land which He swore to Abraham, to Isaac and to Jacob.' He then took this oath of them (*ibid. v.* 25): 'God will surely remember you, and you shall carry up my bones from here', and the recollection of this adjuration was handed down among the Israelites in Egypt, generation after generation, until they fulfilled it (Exod. xiii 19). The underlying intention of the phrasing in our passage is to awaken in the hearts of the enslaved people in Egypt the consciousness that the time of redemption has arrived. The succeeding words, *and what has been done to you in Egypt*, revert to what had been said previously in *v.* 7, and to the assurance given in the 'Covenant between the Pieces' (Gen. xv 14); whilst the continuation of the address in *v.* 17, *And I have said,*

17 *I will bring you up out of the affliction of Egypt to the land of the Canaanites,* etc., refers back to the statement in *v.* 8 (the word

EXODUS III 17

affliction occurs in *v*. 7). Here the nations of Canaan are mentioned before the phrase, *a land flowing with milk and honey*, in order to conclude on a happy note.

18 After the elders of the people will have hearkened to Moses' voice (although the text reads, *And they will hearken to your voice*, the form being that of a coordinate principal clause, as required by ancient Hebrew style, yet the sense is that expressed in modern diction by a subordinate clause), and will be ready to cooperate with him, they must appear together with Moses before Pharaoh in order to commence the negotiations (*And you shall come, you*, etc.). The words spoken by Moses and the elders to Pharaoh are formulated in a manner suited to the latter's understanding; hence the name *YHWH* ('The Lord') is followed by the designation *the God of the Hebrews*. The name itself is not known to Pharaoh (v 2: 'And Pharaoh said... I know not the Lord'), and a title like 'the God of Abraham, Isaac and Jacob' would have been equally obscure. But the appellation *the God of the Hebrews* he was able to understand. It was generally recognized that every people had its own god or gods; the same applied to the Hebrews — a group of foreign slaves whom Pharaoh knew well and whom he himself called by the name of Hebrews (on this name see my commentary on i 15). 'The Gods of the Hebrews' or the 'Hebrew gods' (in Akkadian *ilâni ḥapiri*) was actually the expression current in the ancient East.

Another point: Moses and the elders were to tell Pharaoh that God *lighted* [נִקְרָה *niqrā*] upon them (to be exact: upon one of them on behalf of all of them), that means, that He revealed Himself to them by chance; whereas in the narrative above (*v*. 2) the verb *appeared* [וַיֵּרָא *wayyērā'*] occurs; so, too, when Moses speaks to the elders (*v*. 16) he uses the term *has appeared* [נִרְאָה *nir'ā*]. Also in this distinction between 'appeared' and 'lighted' there is discernible the intention to adapt the language to the Gentiles' way of thinking. For in the Canaanite tongue the verb נִקְרָה *niqrā* signified a theophany (thus, for example, in the Ugaritic epic of Aqhat, II, vi, ll. 43–44, the goddess Anath says to Aqhat the son of Daniel: 'If I light upon you [*l'aqryk*] in the path of transgression', etc.). Consequently, the Bible also uses this verb in accounts of theophanies to non-Israelites, like Balaam the son of Beor, or in conversations with them, as in the present instance.

The words *and now* introduce, as usual, the conclusion: since our God lighted upon us, we request your permission to go forth

42

EXODUS III 21

from your land in order to draw near unto Him in the wilderness, in the place where He manifested Himself to one of us, and to offer sacrifices to Him as a thanksgiving for His having vouchsafed us this theophany; in the words of Scripture: *let us go, we pray you, three days' journey into the wilderness, that we may sacrifice to the Lord our God*. This first request is not yet a demand that a general exodus of all the Israelites be authorized, but only that the men, who would take part in the offering of the oblations, should be allowed to go; the women and the children and their possessions were to remain in Egypt. We must not, therefore, discern here, as several commentators have thought, the intention to achieve the possibility of leaving the country for good. At this stage Moses and the elders make a modest and limited request as the starting-point of their diplomatic negotiations with Pharaoh, the purpose being to uncover his real feelings and thoughts. God, it is true, perceives the secret intentions of his heart, and knows *a priori* that he will refuse (regarding this fore-
19 knowledge, see my annotation to iv 21): *But I know that the king of Egypt will not give you leave to go, not even* [literally, 'and not'] *by a mighty hand*, that is, even if you make your demands militantly (Naḥmanides). But to enable the world to learn the moral of these events, it is essential that the heart and mind of the king should be laid bare for all to see. His refusal would clearly prove that he persists in his stubbornness and that he is absolutely determined to keep the heavy yoke of bondage on the necks of the Israelites permanently and incessantly. Thereby shall God's judgement be
20 vindicated: *And I will put forth My hand, and smite Egypt with all My wonders which I will do in the midst thereof*, namely, the ten plagues, *and after that* — after the execution of this judgement — *he*, the king of Egypt, *will let you go*, that is, he will liberate the entire people.

These verses contain a word-play on the use of the noun יָד *yādh* ['hand'] and the verb שָׁלַח *šālaḥ* [which means both 'to put forth' and 'to let go']: your *strong hand* will not induce Pharaoh to let you go even on a three days' journey; but when *I put forth* [אֶשְׁלַח *'ešlaḥ*] *My hand, my strong hand* (compare vi 1), then *he will let you go* completely.

On that day, when you go forth, you will not leave like foes who have been thrust out of the country in enmity, but you will
21 depart like people taking leave of their friends in peace: *And I will give this people favour in the sight of the Egyptians*, and there

43

shall be fulfilled in you the promise that was given to Abraham at the 'Covenant between the Pieces' (Gen. xv 14): 'and afterward shall they come out with great substance', *and it shall come to pass, that, when you go, you shall not go empty, but every woman shall ask of her neighbour, and of her that sojourns in her house,* etc. Many different interpretations have been put forward regarding this incident, to wit, the request for *jewels of silver*, and *jewels of gold, and raiment*; but both the derogatory and apologetic explanations are superficial and do not fathom the real significance of the passage. The true and objective explanation emerges, as I suggested many years ago (in 1923), when we compare this verse with what is stated in Deut. xv 13–14 concerning the manumission of the *Hebrew slave* at the conclusion of his period of service. Here it is written: 'and it shall come to pass, that, when you go, you shall not go empty'; and there we are told: 'And when you let him go free from you, you shall not let him go empty; you shall furnish him liberally out of your flock, and out of your threshing floor, and out of your winepress', etc. This law of the Book of Deuteronomy is undoubtedly of ancient origin, and our passage alludes to its substance and phraseology, using similar language. *The Hebrew slaves* who went forth from Egypt had already served their masters the number of years that Providence had predetermined (Gen. xv 13; Exod. xii 40–41), and consequently they were entitled to liberation, and upon liberation the bounty was also due to them. This was required by law — that is, absolute justice demanded it — and although no earthly court could compel the king of Egypt and his servants to fulfil their obligation, the Heavenly Court saw to it that the requirements of law and justice were carried out, and directed the course of events to this end.

With the jewels that the Egyptians will give you when you leave, you will be able to adorn not only the women but also your boys and girls — *and you shall put them upon your sons, and upon your daughters* — and it will seem to you as though *you had spoiled the Egyptians*. These last words appear to us highly exaggerated if we only consider the enormous wealth of the Egyptians and the modest value of the jewels that the Israelites were able to receive from the Egyptians. But it is all relative; in the eyes of the poverty-stricken slaves it seemed as if these ornaments constituted great riches (Gen. xv 14), and that, by taking these possessions, they spoiled, as it were, the Egyptians.

THIRD PARAGRAPH

MOSES' DOUBTS AND HOW THEY WERE RESOLVED

(IV 1–17)

Chapter IV

1 The words, *And Moses answered and said*, mark the beginning of a new theme. This formula, 'so-and-so answered and said', which was inherited by Israelitic literature from Canaanite literature, as we learn from the Ugaritic texts, often does not signify just a simple reply, but serves to indicate the enunciation of a new thought or plan on the part of the speaker. This is its meaning at the beginning of the speeches in the Book of Job, and this is also its signification in our verse. The new point here is the doubts expressed by Moses. Till now Moses was confronted by his task in its general aspect, and his reaction was confined to voicing his feelings of humility at the importance and exalted nature of his commission, and in asking for instructions concerning what he was to tell the children of Israel. The possibility of his refusing never entered his mind. Only after he had been given detailed directions and had begun to cogitate them, did doubts begin to assail his spirit: he doubted his powers and capabilities. His uncertainties were three, and in respect of each of them he received an unanswerable reply from the Lord.

The first doubt was, *But, behold, they will not believe me, nor hearken unto my voice; for they will say, The Lord has not appeared unto you*. In this instance, too, there is no refusal, as many exegetes have supposed. On the contrary, Moses pictures to himself what may happen when he stands before the Israelites at the commencement of his mission. The allegation, 'nor hearken unto my voice', is not to be regarded as a contradiction of the earlier statement by God (iii 18): 'And they will hearken to your voice'; in truth, the two verses are interdependent. It is the very words of the Divine utterance, 'And they will hearken to your voice' (the meaning of which is, as we have explained: And after they will have hearkened to your voice, etc.), that arouse uncertainty in his mind: How shall I succeed in persuading my brethren, the children of Israel, to hearken to my voice? *Behold* (הֵן *hēn* = הִנֵּה) there is reason to fear that *they will not believe me*, when I tell them that the Lord appeared unto me, and will consider me a liar; and if they will not believe me, *they will not hearken to my voice*, and will not associate themselves with my undertaking.

The difference between שָׁמַע לְקוֹל *šāmaʿ lᵉqōl* and שָׁמַע בְּקוֹל *šāmaʿ bᵉqōl* [both expressions signify 'to hearken to the voice', although literally לְ *lᵉ* means 'to' and בְּ *bᵉ* 'in'] is one of form only, such as we find even in epic poetry, though the style of the latter is not marked by variations of this kind to the same extent as that of narrative prose.

The Lord's answer is suited to Moses' doubt; I shall enable you to perform signs before them, wonders that an ordinary person cannot do. Thus they will believe that you have divine power, and when you tell them that the Lord appeared to you, they will realize that you are not lying.

These signs (the noun אוֹת *'ōth* ['sign'] is masculine here) are three in number. The first is the transformation of the rod into a
2 serpent and its subsequent restoration to the form of a rod. *And the Lord said unto him, What is that in your hand? And he said, A rod*. The purpose of the question was to draw Moses' attention to the fact that the object in his hand was only an ordinary stick, and thereby to make his amazement at the sign that would be wrought before his eyes all the greater. The expression מַזֶּה *mazze*, written as one word [normally it is spelt thus: מַה־זֶּה *ma(h)z-ze*], is intended to emphasize the word-play מַזֶּה־מַטֶּה *mazze—matte*.
3 *And he said, Cast it on the ground. And he cast it on the ground, and it became a serpent*. The rod turned into a serpent, and Moses
4 was astonished and frightened: *and Moses fled from before it. And the Lord said unto Moses, Put forth your hand, and take it by the tail*. So Moses overcame his terror and did what he was commanded: *and he put forth his hand, and laid hold of it, and it became a rod in his hand*. If Moses will re-enact this sign before the Israelites, he will prove to them a number of things:

(a) that he is not only not inferior to the Egyptian enchanters, who know how to charm snakes and to make them as completely motionless as a rod, and afterwards to change them back to their normal vitality, but that he is also able to perform the opposite processes, which are even more amazing;

(b) that he has the power to achieve marvels comparable to those attributed by the Egyptians to their greatest magicians, as in the Egyptian story that relates of a famous sorcerer who made a sea-monster of wax and cast it into the water, where it became alive, until the magician took hold of it with his hand and it became a waxen model again (see further on this in my annotations to vii 8–12);

(c) that, with the help of his God, he is able to put forth his hand and take hold of the *tail* of the serpent without fear (as a rule, snakes are held by their necks to prevent them from biting), and thus he would show how great is his trust in his God, and he would make his brethren as courageous as himself.

5   The words *that they may believe that the Lord, the God of their fathers*, etc., in *v.* 5, are a continuation of the Lord's utterance in *v.* 4 (the intervening text, *and he put forth his hand*, etc., is a parenthetic statement, describing what Moses did whilst the Lord was still speaking), and iterate, almost word for word, the doubt expressed by Moses in *v.* 1, with the addition of the designations, *the God of Abraham, the God of Isaac and the God of Jacob*, repeated from chapter iii, in order to stress that the children of Israel would have perfect faith in all that he would tell them.

The second sign is that of leprosy. At once, without permitting Moses to speak again and to express any misgiving in regard to
6   the first sign, the Lord continues to speak to him: *And the Lord said furthermore unto him, Put now your hand into your bosom. And he put his hand into his bosom; and when he took it out, behold, his hand was leprous, as white as snow.* And again the reverse:
7   *And he said, Put your hand into your bosom again. And he put his hand into his bosom again; and when he took it out of his bosom, behold, it turned again as his other flesh.* This sign, too, is in keeping with the Egyptian environment, for leprosy was widespread in Egypt. Since it was accounted an incurable disease, its removal from Moses' hand was a miraculous feat calculated to leave a deep impression on the minds of all who witnessed it. At the same time, Moses' willingness to subject himself to so grievous a malady, would demonstrate his courage and his readiness to endure whatever was necessary for the fulfilment of his mission.

8   In this case, too, the statement in *v.* 8, *And it shall come to pass, if they will not believe you, neither hearken to the voice of the first sign, that they will believe the voice of the latter sign*, is only the continuation of the Lord's utterance in the preceding verse, and the words in between, from *And he put* to *as his other flesh*, are in brackets. There is likewise here a kind of recapitulation of Moses' words, when he expressed his apprehension that they might not believe him nor hearken to his voice. It is precisely on account of this reiteration that 'voice' is applied also to the signs.

EXODUS IV 9

9 A further repetition of Moses' observations occurs in *v.* 9, as a prelude to the delivery of the third sign. God speaks gently, with paternal love, as it were, and complete understanding of Moses' state of mind: You are afraid, My son, that your brethren will not believe you nor hearken to your voice, and I have already given you two signs designed to prove to them the truth of your statements; but if you are still concerned lest *they will not believe even these two signs*, and that even after seeing them, *they will not hearken unto your voice*, know that I am delivering to you a third sign, which will assuredly prove decisive. This sign, which cannot be performed here, but only in Egypt, is as follows: *you shall take of the water of the Nile, and pour it upon the dry land; and the water which you take out of the Nile shall become blood upon the dry land.* The Nile, the source of life and fertility in the land of Egypt, is regarded by the Egyptians as a deity, and if you show your brethren that He who sent you rules even over the Nile, they will see therein clear proof that He is able to overcome all the forces that exist for the benefit of Egypt, not excluding those that are held to be divine powers, and they will no longer doubt your mission. This sign, moreover, also contains an allusion to the first plague, which was to be the initial punishment inflicted on the Egyptians, if they were unwilling to let Israel go.

After he had received the signs, Moses' first misgiving is completely removed. He can no longer fear that the Israelites will not believe him, when he comes and tells them that the Lord, the God of their fathers, manifested Himself to him. He does not, therefore, revert to the subject.

But another objection occurs to Moses. The mighty enterprise with which the Lord intends to entrust him — to make propaganda among the Israelites and to enter into diplomatic negotiations with Pharaoh — requires high gifts of eloquence and oratory. Moses, however, observes no such capabilities in himself. Hence

10 he beseeches: *Oh* (בִּי *bī*, an expression of entreaty) *Lord* (the Name customarily used, as a vocative, when addressing God), please remember *that I am not eloquent* [literally, 'a man of words'], that is, I am not an orator whose words flow easily. I never possessed this quality in the past — *neither heretofore* — and I do not discern it in myself even today — *nor since you have spoken to your servant* (compare the expression in the Lachish Letters: 'Since you have sent to your servant'). *For*, on the contrary, *I am heavy of mouth and heavy of tongue.* The words do not signify,

as many have supposed, that Moses was actually a stammerer; the meaning is only that he did not feel within himself the distinguished talents of an orator, and, in his humility, he expressed the thought with some exaggeration.

However, in regard to this objection, too, Moses received a
11 reply that could not be gainsaid. *And the Lord said unto Him, who has made man's mouth?* who is it that gives a man the power of speech? — *or who makes a man dumb, or deaf?* — that is, who withholds this power from his? — *or seeing, or blind?* — that is, who is it in general who determines the abilities or disabilities of people? — *is it not I the Lord* who has sent you? Seeing that I have sent you, you may rest assured that I shall give you all the
12 powers requisite to the execution of My mission. *Now therefore* (a formula indicating the commencement of the conclusion following upon the premises) *go*, without further hesitation, *and I*, just as I have already told you (iii 12) that 'I will be with you', even so *I will be with your mouth*, and help you with your speech, *and teach you what you shall speak*.

This reply provides an answer to Moses' second objection in the same way as the previous reply set at nought his first apprehension. However, his mind is not yet at ease. Possibly the magnitude and difficulty of the task frighten him; possibly, in his humility, he does not deem himself worthy of the Divine help promised him; or it may be that he himself does not clearly understand why he continues to hesitate; yet he is still unable to say: 'Here am I; send me.' He now puts forward only a humble
13 entreaty: *O Lord, send, I pray thee, by the hand of him whom Thou wilt send* — that is, by the hand of whomever Thou dost wish to send, except me. This restriction, 'except me', he does not dare to utter explicitly, and his words are so phrased as to be construed even as an expression of assent: by the hand of whom Thou wishest, and if it is Thy wish to send by my hand, I shall obey. But the Lord, looking on his heart, understands that he is still hesitant and full of misgivings and that if he will agree, he will do so without enthusiasm. Moses ought not to have reacted thus to so exalted and important a task as he was given; nor should he have evinced so much doubt and hesitation, and so persistently, towards the Divine mission. Hence the reply he receives now is unlike the gentle answers that he was given in regard to his earlier
14 objections, but is uttered in wrath: *And the anger of the Lord was kindled against Moses*. This reply thus contains an element

of retribution. The punishment resembles that of the Israelites who hesitated to receive the precious gift of the Promised Land, and were punished by being denied the privilege of seeing the Land in that generation; only their children took possession of it. In a similar way, Moses, who did not willingly accept the commission with which God wishes to honour him, was punished in that the glory of fulfilling the task did not belong to him alone, but was shared in part by his brother Aaron.

To the latter God now gives part of the assignment: *Is there not Aaron your brother the Levite?*, etc. On the mention of Aaron, who appears here for the first time, no reference having been made to him in the story of Moses' birth, see my remarks above, in my commentary to that narrative, and my annotations on vi 14–27. Regarding the designation *the Levite*, applied here to Aaron, many forced and fanciful explanations have been advanced. The correct interpretation, in accordance with the simple meaning of the text, is that the Torah intended here a word-play. Aaron belongs to the tribe of Levi, and in keeping with his name [which means, 'joined to'], he is worthy of accompanying Moses on his mission; compare Num. xviii 2: 'And your brethren also, the tribe of Levi, the tribe of your father, bring near with you, that they may be joined to you, and minister to you.'

Aaron certainly will not be able to plead that he lacks eloquence: *I know that he can speak well*. The pronoun *he* comes [in the Hebrew] at the end of the clause as though to emphasize the thought: he is not like you. Furthermore, Moses, know that I shall awaken in his heart the desire to go forth to meet you: *And also, behold, he comes forth to meet you; and when he sees you he will be glad in his heart*. He will not doubt or hesitate as you did, but will rejoice greatly at seeing you and will collaborate with you in the accomplishment of My mission.

15 Now this will be the procedure in your joint work: first of all, *you shall speak to him* — this you will be able to do without difficulty, since no one has to be a great orator in order to talk to his brother — *and put the words in his mouth*, and from his mouth they will issue with ease. *And I will be with your mouth, and with his mouth* (again the expression, 'I will be with') *and will teach you what you shall do*; here the Lord repeats and completes the assurance He gave in v. 12: I shall teach you not only what you
16 have to say, but also what you have to do. *And he shall speak for you* [literally, 'to you'] — on your behalf, in your stead, in

your name — *unto the people, and it shall be* as follows: that *he shall be to you a mouth*, that is, a spokesman mediating between you and the people, after the manner of the high Egyptian official who was designated 'the mouth of the king', and acted as an intermediary between Pharaoh and the officials below him. *And you shall be to him as God*, and you will teach him what he must say to the people, just as God instructs his prophet and inspires him, and as the king of Egypt, who is regarded as a divinity by his people, makes his will known through the medium of the officer who bears the honoured title of his 'mouth'.

In the Lord's present announcement to Moses there is not a single word reverting to His command, such as Go and do so-and-so. This silence creates a deeper impression than any confirmatory injunction: there is no need to say that you are duty-bound to go, and that you will go and carry out your commission. Moses is only told how, and by what means, he should execute his task.

17 At the end of the paragraph, the signs mentioned at the beginning are referred to again: *And you shall take in your hand this rod, wherewith you shall do the signs.* Here, too, it is not stated: You must perform the signs that I have delivered to you. This is self-understood; and the detail of the rod is mentioned only as an indirect reminder to Moses that he must obey, and not forget anything that he has been told. Moses feels, as did other prophets, particularly Jeremiah, that the hand of the Lord overpowers him and masters him, and that perforce he must obey and carry out his commission. It is precisely in this that the greatness of the prophet manifests itself, namely, that ineluctably he does all that the will of God imposes upon him.

The rod was mentioned above (*vv.* 2–4) as an object that changed its form in the performance of the first sign, but here it is spoken of as an instrument and means for achieving all the signs; it is similarly referred to a number of times later on, even in the story of the dividing of the Sea of Reeds. In *v.* 20, the Bible calls it 'the rod of God' (so, too, xvii 9, and elsewhere). Apparently, there existed in Israel an ancient tradition, which was incorporated in the epic poem dealing with the Bondage and Liberation, concerning a Divine rod that was given to Moses in order that he might perform the signs therewith. This tradition was preserved in the memory of the people through the generations, and found expression in the rabbinic legends that relate the history of the rod (how it was handed down from Adam, generation by genera-

EXODUS IV 17

tion, until it came into the possession of Moses), and tell of the Specific Name [Tetragrammaton], which was inscribed thereon, of the mnemonics of the Ten Plagues, which were also engraved on it, and of other details of this nature. At times the Talmudic sages even use a concept redolent of mythology, and refer to the rod of God as the sceptre of the Holy One blessed be He, which He gave to Moses (Exod. Rabba viii 2). The Rabbis certainly did not invent these legends, but found their authority in a very early tradition which even predated the Torah. But the latter, following its customary practice, sought to minimize as far as possible, all mythological and cognate elements, and to this end it presents the rod to its readers, at the outset, as an ordinary shepherd's staff. However, there still remain traces of the ancient epic tradition in the expression 'the rod of God', and in the use of the rod as a wonder-working instrument.

The stem דבר *dbr*, which is characteristic of the verses pertaining to Moses' third doubt and to God's answer thereto (*vv.* 10–17), occurs seven times in this passage. The compound expression דַּבֵּר יְדַבֵּר *dabbēr yᵉdhabbēr* ['he can speak well'] in *v.* 14 is counted, as usual, as a single unit. The word *mouth*, which is also a feature of Moses' third objection, is likewise found in these verses seven times.

FOURTH PARAGRAPH

MOSES' JOURNEY

(IV 18–23)

Moses now ceases to hesitate; from now on he devotes his whole
18 life and all his capacities to the execution of his mission. *And Moses went* from Mount Horeb, *and returned to Jether* [יֶתֶר *Yether*] *his father-in-law* to receive his permission to go to Egypt. The father-in-law is here called יֶתֶר *Yether*; this name differs from the name יִתְרוֹ *Yithrō* [Jethro] only in its grammatical form. In the name *Yithrō* there is preserved a relic of the ancient ending of the nominative case (although the original significance of the case has not been retained), whilst the form יֶתֶר *Yether* has no suffix.

Moses does not disclose to his father-in-law explicitly the object of his journey; diplomatic negotiations cannot be done openly. He merely says, in general terms: *Let me go, I pray, and return to my brethren who are in Egypt, and see whether they are still alive.* The words *my brethren* and *see* remind us of what was stated earlier (ii 11): that 'he went out to his brethren, and looked on their burdens', and thus establish an inner connection between the two episodes. The clause *whether they are still alive* does not express apprehension that the brethren may have died, but only concern to know how they are. It will suffice to compare Joseph's enquiry (Genesis, xlv 3): 'is my father still alive?' after he had already heard from his brothers that their father was alive and awaiting their return.

Jethro (here the text reverts to the full and normal spelling of the name) consents to Moses' departure and blesses him: *And Jethro said to Moses, go in peace.*

19 In *v.* 19, an additional communication from the Lord to Moses is recorded: *And the Lord said to Moses in Midian, go, return to Egypt; for all the men who were seeking your life are dead.* Various improbable explanations of the time and purpose of this communication have been suggested. Apparently, the Bible wishes only to inform us that after Moses had returned from Mount Horeb to the land of Midian (the name of this country is expressly emphasized in the text), and, having received his father-in-law's permission, had made ready to proceed on his journey, he was told by the Almighty, that he could go without any anxiety concerning the sentence of death that Pharaoh had passed upon him when he had sought (to this the expression *who were seeking* alludes) to slay Moses (ii 15). The intention is to indicate that Moses' objections and hesitations mentioned earlier in the section did not flow from any fear for his personal safety, for he had already prepared himself to go to Egypt before he learnt that this danger had passed.

20 Now that he knows that he is no longer in jeopardy, he resolves to bring his family with him. Expressions like *And Moses took his wife and his sons* usually occur in the Torah when the migration of an entire family from one place to another under the leadership of the head of the family is spoken of; they are idioms that have their root in the Canaanite literary traditions, and parallels have been found in the Ugaritic writings. See my observations on this point in my commentary on Genesis, xi 31.

The definite article in the sentence, *and set them upon the* [E.V.

an] ass, expresses general definition, that is, upon the particular ass on which he set them. Also the specific mention of the setting upon the ass in the description of the start of the journey has its origin in an old literary usage, which is already commonly found in Ugaritic texts. See my remarks on this subject in the Epstein Jubilee Volume, pp. 1–7 (= *Tarbiz*, XX, 1950 [Hebrew]).

The plural *sons* is somewhat difficult, for till now only one son had been mentioned (ii 22), and below, in *v*. 25, we find *her son*, in the singular, as though Moses and Zipporah had just one son. Possibly the ancient spelling here was בנה *bnh*, which could be read either as singular or plural, and the singular was actually intended; when, however, the Scribes introduced the present spelling, they wrote בָּנָיו *bānāw* ['his sons'] (the Septuagint, too, has the plural), because they thought that the two sons spoken of in xviii were already born.

The sense of the words *and he returned to the land of Egypt*, which precede the narration of the events that befell Moses and his family on the way, is 'in order to return to the land of Egypt', or (and this is the more likely explanation) the intention is first to state the fact generally and thereafter to go into details. This method is commonly followed in Biblical diction. Compare, for example, Genesis xxviii 10 ff.: to begin with it is related, 'And Jacob went out from Beersheba and went to Haran*', and afterwards we are told what happened to him in the course of the journey, before he came to Haran.

Moses did not forget to take the rod in his hand, as he had been enjoined: *and Moses took the rod of God in his hand*. On the expression 'rod of God' see my note above, in my commentary to *v*. 17.

21 *And the Lord said unto Moses*, etc. This statement is to be understood as a warning given at the moment of action. The ancient epic poem narrated, it seems, that, apart from being briefed in his mission generally, and in addition to the primary instructions recorded above, Moses was also given at Horeb, or in Midian, specific directions in regard to the entire course of his undertaking in all its aspects, including the ten plagues; and Scripture, with fine artistic understanding, avoids detailing them all here, in order not to weaken the impression that the account given later of Moses' deeds is due to make on the reader. At this stage, when Moses

---

* Usually rendered in the English versions: *toward Haran*. Tr.

sets forth on his journey, the word of the Lord comes to him as if to summarize allusively all the directives, to remind him of them, and to stress the main points. The Torah does not refrain from citing here this communication with its summary allusions, because it can in no way lessen the effect of the narratives that follow, but, on the contrary, it is calculated to arouse the readers' interest and curiosity in what will subsequently be recounted. *When you go back to Egypt*, that is, at this moment when you are about to start on your journey with a view to returning to Egypt — thus the Lord says to Moses — *see*, take heed of all that I have told you so far, and remember *all the portents which I have put in your hand*, in order that you may be ready to perform them: *so that* [literally, 'and'] *you may do them before Pharaoh*. These portents are not the signs given to Moses, which are mentioned in paragraph three (*vv.* 2–9), for Moses was commanded to perform these before the children of Israel, and not before Pharaoh. The reference here is to the story of the תַּנִּין *tannīn* ['serpent', 'large reptile'] (vii 8–12), which is actually called a portent (*ibid. v.* 9), and to the ten plagues, to which this term is also applied (vii 3; xi 9–10; and so, too, several times in other books.)

But I — so the Lord continues to speak — *will harden* [literally, 'make strong'] *his heart, and he will not let the people go*. Here arises, so at least it would appear at the first blush, a difficult problem, which the exegetes, and especially the medieval philosophers, have struggled hard to resolve. It may be formulated thus: If it is the Lord who makes strong (or hardens) the heart of Pharaoh, the latter cannot be blamed for this, and consequently it is unethical for him to suffer retribution. A similar question may be asked with regard to iii 19: 'And I know that the king of Egypt will not give you leave to go.' If the Lord knows *a priori* how Pharaoh will act, it follows that it is impossible for the latter to do otherwise; in that case, it is unjust that he should be punished for his actions.

When we come to consider these two questions, we must first of all realize that we are not dealing here with philosophical issues such as the relationship between the free will of man and God's prescience, or the justification of reward and punishment for human deeds that God himself brought about. The Torah does not seek to teach us philosophy; not even what is called religious philosophy. When the Torah was written, Greek philosophy had not yet been thought of; and Greek logic was likewise non-existent.

Moreover, the Torah does not address itself to the thinkers but to the entire people, and it expresses itself in language understandable to the masses and adapted to the thinking of ordinary folk. Hence we must not consider here the elucidation of the aforementioned philosophical problems as such, but only to explain the meaning of the passages and to understand the Torah's intentions — what it wishes to convey to us.

As regards iii 19, the matter is very simple if we view it in proper perspective. In the period of the Pentateuch, people were not yet conscious of the contradiction that is to be observed between God's foreknowledge of events and the responsibility imposed upon man for his deeds; and if in general they were aware of the inconsistency, they resolved it simply and superficially, holding that God's prescience was only His capacity to discern the nature of His creatures and to know that a certain person in a given situation would behave in accordance with his nature and attributes in a specific manner. That, apparently, is the intention of the Bible in iii 19.

As for the hardening of Pharaoh's heart, we must bear in mind three things, if we wish to understand the purport of the passages properly:
(a) The first is the way in which ancient Hebrew expresses itself. In early Hebrew diction, it is customary to attribute every phenomenon to the direct action of God. Of a barren woman it is said that 'the Lord had shut up her womb' (i Sam. i 5); of an accident in which one person kills another unintentionally, it is said that 'God brought it opportunely into his hand' (Exod. xxi 13), and the like. Every happening has a number of causes, and these causes, in turn, have other causes, and so on *ad infinitum*; according to the Israelite conception, the cause of all causes was the will of God, the Creator and Ruler of the world. Now the philosopher examines the long and complex chain of causation, whereas the ordinary person jumps instantly from the last effect to the first cause, and attributes the former directly to God. This, now, is how the Torah, which employs human idioms, expresses itself. Consequently, the expression 'but I will harden his heart' is, in the final analysis, the same as if it were worded: but his heart will be hard. In the continuation of the narrative, sentences like 'And the Lord hardened the heart of Pharaoh' (ix 12, *et al.*) alternate with others like 'And Pharaoh's heart was hardened' (vii 13, *et al.*); they can be interchanged because their essential meaning is identical.

(b) The second point: Pharaoh sinned in that he imposed a hard bondage on the children of Israel, and decreed that their infant sons should be destroyed; for this he was punished, not on account of his hardness of heart. Had he immediately granted the request of Moses and Aaron, he would have gone forth free and suffered no penalty, which would not have been just. Thus his hard-heartedness serves as a means of inflicting upon him the punishment of the plagues — a punishment that he deserved for his earlier sins — and of proving to the world that there is a moral law, and a Judge who requites every man according to his deeds.
(c) The third point: Not only is it nowhere stated that Pharaoh was punished for his abduracy, but it is also to be noted that nowhere does the Bible say that his intransigeance was accounted to him an iniquity. Our passage becomes perfectly clear when we compare it with the statement, couched in terms similar to those applied to Pharaoh, in Deut. ii 30: 'But Sihon king of Heshbon would not let us pass by him; for the Lord your God hardened his spirit, and made his heart obstinate, that He might deliver him into your hand, as appears this day.' Sihon's conduct in defending courageously the land of his dominion was certainly not sinful; it was only a means used by the Lord to accomplish His plan, which had been conceived from the outset in accordance with the principles of justice, which demanded that the iniquity of the Amorites should be punished and the merits of the Fathers of Israel rewarded.

Thus, if we take cognizance of these three points, and read the passages according to their simple meaning, and according to the reasoning of their period, and not in the light of concepts that came into existence at a later epoch, we shall see that in the final analysis there is no problem or difficulty here, and that everything is clear in the light of the original ideology of the Israelites.

The rest of the Divine statement refers to the consequences that Pharaoh's obstinacy will bring in its train. Since his heart will remain hard and he will refuse to let Israel go, it will ultimately be necessary, in order to compel his consent, to bring upon him the last plague, the plague of the first-born. Then you, Moses, will threaten Pharaoh with this terrible plague, which will directly

22 affect his own family, too, *and you shall say to Pharaoh: Thus says the Lord* (the customary opening formula used by envoys in the ancient East when delivering their master's message), and you shall indicate to him that this punishment is inflicted upon him

EXODUS IV 22

on the principle of measure for measure. *Israel is My son, My first-born*, yet you, Pharaoh, detain the people considered by Me as My first-born son; and although I have sent Moses to you,
23 *and I have said unto you, let My son go, that he may serve Me*, you have not agreed, *and you have refused to let him go*, your desire being that he should serve you and not Me. Therefore justice demands that you shall suffer retribution in respect of your son, your first-born, measure for measure; in the words of the Bible: *behold, I will slay your son, your first-born.* With the mention of the last plague, which is destined to be decisive and to force Pharaoh to liberate the Israelites, the summary Divine communication, which speeds Moses at the start of his journey, comes to an end.

FIFTH PARAGRAPH

THE ENCOUNTER AT THE LODGING PLACE

(IV 24–26)

24 This paragraph has served as the focal point of all kinds of fanciful expositions and a variety of views and conjectures concerning the ancient conception of the God of Israel. We must endeavour to interpret it according to its simple sense.

This paragraph does, in truth, contain much that is strange and obscure. It is strange, for instance, that at the very time when Moses is journeying for the purpose of fulfilling the task assigned to him by the Lord, the Lord Himself should seek to slay him. Even more surprising is the fact that there is no clear indication in the text of the cause of the incident. This apart, there are also a number of expressions, like חֲתַן דָּמִים *ḥăthan dāmīm* ['a blood-bridegroom'] or מוּלת *mūlōth* ['circumcised'], whose meaning is in doubt.

However, three things that can help us to understand the paragraph are clear. The first is the fact that a certain resemblance is discernible between the episode narrated here and that described in the section of Balaam with regard to the angel of the Lord, 'who placed himself in the way for an adversary against him', after the Lord had already granted him permission to go. The appearance of the angel can only be understood as a final warning to Balaam, when he set forth on his journey, and as a new reminder of the injunction that only the word that the Lord would speak unto him should be spoken. It may be that our paragraph also comes to tell us of a last warning of this kind, intended to supplement the final directives that had been given to Moses prior to his departure from Midian (*vv.* 21–23). The nature of the warning will be clarified in the exposition that will soon follow.

Secondly, our paragraph is undoubtedly linked (contrary to the view of most modern exegetes) with the paragraph before it and the one after. This is borne out by an expression like *and sought to* kill him, which recalls the earlier statement in *v.* 19: 'for all the men are dead which sought your life'; by the word וַיִּפְגְּשֵׁהוּ *wayyiphgᵉšēhū* ['and met him'], which recurs in the identical form in *v.* 27; and more particularly by the mention of Moses' son in *v.* 25 — his first-born son, as we have explained — which forms a parallel to 'My son, My first-born' in *v.* 22, and to 'your son, your first-born' in *v.* 23. The connection to be found between the verses that speak of first-born sons will become immediately apparent in the subsequent annotations.

The third point is that the pivot of the whole story is the circumcision of the child, from which it follows that the primary purpose of the paragraph is undoubtedly related to the importance of this precept.

According to our narrative, Moses' son was not circumcised at the proper time; the reason for this is explained by what is stated in Jos. v 2–7 in regard to the sons of the generation of the wilderness who were not circumcised during the wanderings. When Moses led his people in the desert he did not give heed to the observance of this commandment, and Scripture does not condemn the omission. It would consequently appear that, according to the accepted view, wayfarers were exempt from circumcision, on account of the danger involved. There was likewise a tradition concerning Moses' son, that he was not circumcised at due time, either because, when he was in Midian, a sojourner in a strange land, Moses was also deemed a wayfarer, or because the child may have been born a few days before the family left Midian, and the eighth day after his birth fell when they were on the way. Here it is written, *And it came to pass on the way* [בַּדֶּרֶךְ *badderekh*], and בַּדֶּרֶךְ *badderekh*, be it noted, is precisely the expression that occurs three times in the aforementioned paragraph in Joshua (*vv.* 4, 5, 7). And behold, when Moses was *at the lodging place*, at night, that the Lord met him, that means, that he contracted a severe illness (on the Hebrew usage that attributes every event to the direct action of God, see my remarks above, p. 56); it was so severe as to jeopardize his life: *and sought to kill him.* Zipporah then formed a plan for saving her husband's life. She had already learnt from Moses of the importance of circumcision, which was regarded by the Israelites (irrespective of the original significance of the rite of circumcision in the history of Eastern religions) as a sign of the covenant between Israel and the Lord — that is, as a token of man's dedication to the service of his God — and she thought that although, being wayfarers, they were exempt from circumcising their son, yet it was proper that a person who was journeying on a special mission given him by the Lord should go beyond the strict letter of the law and act with greater stringency. Therefore, she arose and circumcised her son.

25 She used a flint knife: *Then Zipporah took a flint, and cut off the foreskin of her son,* just as Joshua in his day circumcised the children of Israel with knives of flint. Thus the ancients were accustomed to use stone implements for every sacred rite, owing to the conservatism inherent in the sphere of worship. Even when men had learned to make metal tools and to use them in everyday life, they still continued to employ flint instruments for ritual purposes, in order not to deviate in such matters from the traditions of their fathers and forefathers. The Egyptians, too, were accustomed to use flint knives for circumcision.

Thereafter, Zipporah *made* the foreskin *touch* Moses' *feet*, as though to say: Let the one take the place of the other. Just as the first-born son sometimes suffers on account of his father (this is the link with the preceding paragraph), so shall the shedding of a few drops of the blood of Moses' first-born son, which consecrates the infant to the service of the Lord, serve as an additional and decisive consecration of his father to the Lord's mission. She thought (so the ancient tradition understood the matter) that Moses' sickness was a warning given at the moment of action to remind him that from now on he must be wholly dedicated to the fulfilment of his mission, with all his soul and capacities, to the point, if need be, of giving his life for the cause. At that moment Zipporah turned to Moses *and said* to him, *Surely a blood-bridegroom are you to me,* meaning, I am delivering you from death — indeed, I am restoring you to life — by means of our son's blood; and your return to life makes you, as it were, my bridegroom a

EXODUS IV 26

second time, this time a blood-bridegroom, a bridegroom acquired through blood. And immediately *He let him alone* — the Lord let go of Moses, that is, the illness abated, and Moses was saved.

26   In the last sentence, *Then she said, 'A blood-bridegroom'*; *with regard to the circumcised*, there is to be seen, as has already been suggested, a reference to, and explanation of (in accordance with the system of interpreting names), the expression 'blood-bridegroom', which was apparently used as a designation for the circumcised infant, and corresponds to expressions like 'bridegroom of the Torah',[1] 'bridegroom of Genesis',[2] 'bridegroom of the jubilee'[3] (our phrase should not be explained on the basis of the Arabic ختن‎ *ḥatana*, which signifies 'to circumcise', for it is more likely that this connotation is only a secondary sense, deriving from the custom of circumcising the groom before the wedding). The appellation 'blood-bridegroom' had its origin, according to this interpretation, in the episode and words of Zipporah. There is no need to read, as some scholars have proposed, *they said* instead of *she said*, or לַמּוּלִים *lammūlīm* in place of לַמּוּלוֹת *lammūlōth* ['in regard to the circumcised']. The termination ת־ *-ōth* [which is the normal feminine plural ending] is to be explained as a plural of the type found in לָקוֹחוֹת *lāqōhōth* ['buyers'; here the feminine termination refers to males], and the like.

The obscurity of the paragraph is possibly the result of a process similar to that which we postulated with regard to 'the rod of God' (p. 51), and also in respect of the episode of 'the sons of God and the daughters of men' in Gen. vi 1–4, namely, that there existed, before the Torah was written, a detailed tradition on the subject, which told the story at length (possibly as part of an epic poem on the exodus from Egypt; of this we shall speak soon). But in view of the fact that the saga in question was unduly anthropomorphic — more so than is customary in the Pentateuch — the Torah did not wish to prolong the account, but curtailed it drastically. Owing to this abridgement, the details of the narrative were left obscure and enigmatic.

---

[1] The one called to the reading of the concluding portion of the Pentateuch on *Simhat Torah* ['the day of the Rejoicing of the Torah'].
[2] The one called to the reading of the opening section of the Bible on *Simhat Torah*.
[3] One who celebrates an anniversary, e.g. his 25th, 50th, or 60th anniversary.

SIXTH PARAGRAPH

MOSES AND AARON BEFORE THE CHILDREN OF ISRAEL

(IV 27–31)

This paragraph comes, as it were, to sum up and unify all the elements of the previous paragraphs and to integrate them into a single, general conclusion.

27 The Lord appeared to Aaron in Egypt (apparently in a vision of the night), *And the Lord said to Aaron*, in accordance with the Divine statement made earlier to Moses (iv 14): *Go into the wilderness to meet Moses*. Aaron did as he was commanded; he was told to go, *and forthwith he went*. He encountered Moses in the middle of the way between Midian and Egypt: *and met him in the mountain of God* — an indication that this meeting was not accidental, but had been designed by Heaven. The reference to the wilderness and the mountain of God forms a parallel with the opening verse of the first paragraph (iii 1). The use of the word וַיִּפְגְּשֵׁהוּ *wayyiphgᵉšēhū* ['and met him'], which is identical with the word employed in the preceding paragraph, is intended by Scripture as a word-play: there [in the earlier passage] the encounter was fraught with danger, here with happy consequences.

After the two brothers, who were meeting again after a long period of separation, had given expression to their joy and affection (*and kissed him*), Moses informed Aaron of the mission with which God had entrusted him, and of the signs that he had been autho-
28 rized to perform: *And Moses told Aaron all the words of the Lord, wherewith he had sent him, and all the signs wherewith he had charged him*. Thereafter they journeyed together to Egypt, where they assembled the elders of Israel in conference, as Moses had been commanded (iii 16: 'Go, and gather the elders of Israel
29 together'): *And Moses and Aaron went and gathered together all the elders of the children of Israel*. They did so in accordance with the injunction given to Moses (iv 15–16) to associate Aaron
30 with his mission, and to put the words in his mouth: *And Aaron spoke*, before the elders and before a general assembly of the people summoned immediately after, *all the words which the Lord had spoken unto Moses* (the stem דָּבַר *dābhar* occurs three times in succession for emphasis) *and Moses did the signs*, to wit, the signs of the rod, the leprosy, and the turning of the water into blood,

EXODUS IV 31

in the sight of the people. And just as above (*vv.* 1–9) the verbs *believe* and *hearken* recur a number of times, and it is stated that Moses was assured that on account of the signs the Israelites would believe and hearken, so, too, here the Bible repeats these two verbs, and declares immediately after the reference to performing 31 the signs in front of the people: *And the people believed, and they heard*, etc. They heard and believed *that the Lord had remembered the children of Israel*, as Moses had been charged to tell them (iii 16), *and that He had seen their affliction*, in accordance with what Moses had been informed (iii 7), and with what is implied in the opening passage of this section (ii 25: 'And God saw the children of Israel'), and in several passages in the continuation of the section (iii 8–9, 16–17). Furthermore, the people *bowed down and prostrated themselves* as a token of thanksgiving to the Lord their God. The section comes to an end with this scene which shows us the luminous picture of the people bowing and prostrating themselves in gratitude to the Lord for the heartening tidings that Moses and Aaron had announced in His name and as His envoys.

Also in this section (ii 23—iv 31), whose main theme is the mission of Moses, there is discernible a numerical symmetry based on the number seven. The division of the section into seven parts (the prologue in Heaven, and thereafter six paragraphs) follows naturally from the division of the themes and the formal ending of a number of the paragraphs. The same applies to the reiteration of words that are characteristic of the episodes narrated in the section. We have already noted above (p. 32) that the stem רָאָה *rā'ā* ['see'], used to describe the Lord's perception of the affliction of the children of Israel and His manifestation to Moses at Horeb, occurs repeatedly at the beginning of the section, and at the seventh occurrence it is emphasized by the addition of the absolute infinitive. Thereafter it is employed another seven times, and in the summary verse of the concluding passage a final echo of it is heard in the sentence, *and that He had seen their affliction*. The stem שָׁלַח *šālaḥ* ['send'], which refers to the mission, is found seven times in iii 10–20, another seven times in iv 4–23, and finally once more in the summary paragraph, iv 28. The stem דָּבַר *dābhar*, which is typical of the verses dealing with Moses' third objection and the Divine answer thereto (iv 10–17), occurs, as I have already indicated (p. 52), seven times in those verses (the compound ex-

63

pression דַּבֵּר יְדַבֵּר *dabbēr yᵉdhabbēr* ['he can speak well'] is, as usual, counted as one occurrence only), and there are echoes of it in the final paragraph (a simple allusion in *v.* 28, and a triple echo in *v.* 30). The noun *mouth*, which, too, is characteristic of Moses' third doubt, is likewise found seven times in those verses. The verb הָלַךְ *hālakh* ['go'], which plays a significant role in the last paragraph not only in recalling what had previously been stated, but also in the narration of new events mentioned there for the first time, is used fourteen times, twice times seven, in the entire section.

SECTION FOUR

THE FIRST ATTEMPT AND ITS FAILURE

CHAPTER V, VERSE 1 — CHAPTER VI, VERSE 1

FIRST PARAGRAPH

MOSES AND AARON BEFORE PHARAOH

(V 1–5)

Chapter V

1 The opening sentence of the section, *And afterward Moses and Aaron came*, is worded in a form that was traditional in Canaanite literature for the commencement of new sections. In Ugaritic poetry sections often begin in this manner: Afterward so-and-so came, or: Afterward so-and-so and so-and-so came.

The Torah does not state in this instance, as we find so often later on, that Moses and Aaron were commanded by God to go to Pharaoh. Although, generally speaking, Moses had been commissioned, yet he had not so far been given definite instructions concerning the time at which he must begin his work and appear before Pharaoh. As for Aaron, he had, up to the present, been enjoined only to address the children of Israel, and not to speak to Pharaoh. Possibly Scripture intends to convey that Moses and Aaron came to Pharaoh on their own initiative, and thus acted precipitately. Since they did not wait for a specific instruction and an opportune moment, their attempt was abortive, and served only to aggravate the situation. This account of initial failure in the execution of their mission heightens the dramatic tension of the narrative, and lends added emphasis to their subsequent success, which is described in the sections that follow.

Also the wording of the speech delivered by Moses and Aaron does not conform to the directives given to Moses (iii 18). In this respect, too, they showed signs of undue haste. They used the formula customarily employed by both Israelites and Gentiles when an envoy delivered the message of his master, which commenced with the phrase, 'Thus says so-and-so', without paying heed to the possible effect of their words on the mind of Pharaoh.

EXODUS V 1

They presented themselves before Pharaoh proudly, like emissaries and plenipotentiaries of *YHWH* ['the Lord'], and proclaimed that they spoke His words, not taking into account the fact that Pharaoh was unacquainted with the name *YHWH*. That apart, they used the honoured name of their people, Israel, without considering that Pharaoh was accustomed to employ a more humble appellation — Hebrews. After the introductory statement, *Thus says YHWH, the God of Israel*, they immediately went over to the imperative, without any preparatory explanation: *Let My people go, that they may make a pilgrimage unto Me in the wilderness*.

Pharaoh's reaction was characteristic of a proud and powerful king, who, according to the Egyptian tradition, considered himself a god, and was so regarded by his subjects. With overweening haughteur he rejoins: *Who is YHWH that I should hearken unto His voice to let Israel go?* Who is this Deity whom you mention and of whose name I have never heard till today? How can you imagine that I shall let Israel go because this Divinity demands this of me? I shall give you my reply in unambiguous terms — seriatim: Firstly, *I do not know YHWH; and moreover* — that is, secondly — *I will not let Israel go*.

2

After receiving this harsh reply, Moses and Aaron employed milder terms, similar to those of the message with which Moses had been charged (iii 18). They no longer spoke as ambassadors of *YHWH*, but as representatives of their brethren. They did not again mention in their opening remarks the name *YHWH*, which was unknown to Pharaoh, or the name of Israel, which had an unpleasant sound for Pharaoh: *They said, the God of the Hebrews has lighted upon us*, etc. The expression 'the God of the Hebrews' was quite comprehensible to Pharaoh, and now he could not retort regarding the name: *I do not know* [it]. The intention of Moses and Aaron was to say to him, as it were: If you do not know His name, it is of no consequence; what is important is the fact that He is the God of the Hebrews. Furthermore, they do not use the language of command now but of request: *Let us go, we pray, three days' journey into the wilderness, and sacrifice unto YHWH, our God;* and they give reasons for this request: *YHWH, our God, appeared unto us* (the word נִקְרָא *niqrā'* ['lighted', 'chanced'] is acutally written with an *'Āleph*, but its signification is that of נִקְרָה *niqrā* [with *Hē'* at the end] above, in iii 18, the difference being orthographic only, in accordance with the practice of interchanging the spelling of *Lāmedh–'Āleph* and

3

66

Lāmedh–Hē' verbs), and we are afraid *lest*, if we fail to honour Him properly, *He fall upon us with pestilence or with the sword*.

However, Pharaoh's wrath was not assuaged, and he replied in even harsher language than before, which contained not the slightest hint of reconsideration, but only arrogant rebuke. *And the king of Egypt said unto them*, in words that stressed the glory of his majesty: *Wherefore do you, Moses and Aaron, cause the people to refrain from their labours?* the word *wherefore* is used here as an expression of reproach and censure: he reproves them for causing his slaves, by these demands, to refrain from the tasks assigned to them. Moreover he adds, with arrogant presumption, that they themselves are obliged to do work, and they may not abstain from it. What do you think, that, because you are Moses and Aaron, the adopted son of my daughter and his brother, you can desist from the labour? You, too, belong to the enslaved people: *get you to your burdens*.

In *v*. 5 there occurs, for the second time, the clause: *And Pharaoh said*. The verb *said*, which is repeated here, is to be understood, in the light of the method of exposition I suggested above with regard to iii 14 (p. 38), not as introducing a new statement, but as explaining the inner meaning of the words explicitly uttered in the speech prefaced by the preceding *said*. Proof of the correctness of this view is to be seen in the fact that *said* is not followed here by *unto them* as in *v*. 4. The inner intent in the depths of Pharaoh's heart, a thought that he was ashamed to express openly, was this: *Behold, the people of the land are now many*, that is, now I am glad to see that I have many slaves, who are engaged in my service and bring me much benefit, *and you cause them to desist from their burdens* — and you, with your worthless talk, make them stop their work and so cause me great loss.

SECOND PARAGRAPH

EDICT UPON EDICT

(V 6–9)

After his conversation with Moses and Aaron, Pharaoh takes measures calculated, in his view, to prevent the enslaved Israelites from paying heed to the propaganda of the two brothers; possibly it might even induce them to oppose it, since it brought upon

6 them only added trouble**s**. *And the same day Pharaoh commanded* — forthwith, on the same day, in order to show clearly that this was the outcome of the request made by Moses and Aaron — *the taskmasters* — the Egyptian slave-drivers — *of the people, and their foremen* — that is, the expert workers from among the Israelites, who were appointed to direct the labours of their brethren (compare
7 v. 14) — *saying, you shall not continue* (תֹּאסִפוּן *thōʾsiphūn*, which normally means 'you shall gather', stands here for תוֹסִיפוּן *thōsīphūn*, 'you shall continue') *to give the people straw to make bricks, as heretofore*. The Egyptians were accustomed to make bricks from the mud of the Nile, which is essentially a mixture of clay and sand, differing in their proportions according to locality; when the amount of clay was too great or too small, they used to mix chopped straw with the mud, so as to give the mixture proper cohesion. Until that day (*heretofore*) the people were provided with straw
8 for their work; but from now on *let them go and gather straw for themselves*. Notwithstanding, the daily number of bricks that was imposed upon them in the past must not be decreased: *And the number of bricks which they made heretofore, you shall lay upon them; you shall not diminish aught thereof*. In a word: more work!

And the reason for his decree was the heartless and superficial one that the enslavers of men customarily advance, and with which the Israelites and other oppressed peoples have been familiar throughout the generations: *for they are idle; therefore* — because they are lazy and work-shy — *they cry, saying, Let us go and sacri-*
9 *fice to our God*. Hence I decree: *Let heavier work* still *be laid upon the men, that they may labour therein*, and be occupied therewith continually; *and let them not regard lying words* — the heavy nature of the work and their constant preoccupation with it will leave them no time or desire to listen to the foolish tales that Moses and Aaron tell them. In his arrogance, he applies the expression *lying words* to what the previous section termed *the words which the Lord had spoken* — an antithesis not unlike that which is discernible between Pharaoh's query, 'Who is *YHWH*, that I should hearken unto His voice?' and the attitude of the children of Israel, who *hearkened* and believed what was told to them in the name of the Lord.

In v. 9 a play upon words is clearly to be seen: יַעֲשׂוּ *yaʿăśū* ['labour'] — יִשְׁעוּ *yišʿū* ['regard']. The reading of the ancient versions and the Samaritan Pentateuch, which, in accordance with their usual practice, harmonize the two parts of the verse and read יִשְׁעוּ

yišʿū in both, is not to be preferred. In the word יַעֲשׂוּ *yaʿăśū*, which comes towards the end of this paragraph, there is observable a parallel to the word מַעֲשֵׂיהֶם *maʿăśāw* ['their works'], which occurs near the end of the preceding paragraph.

THIRD PARAGRAPH

THE NEW BURDEN IMPOSED ON THE PEOPLE

(V 10–14)

10 *Immediately after Pharaoh had issued his decree, the taskmasters of the people and their foremen went out* from the palace to inform the Israelites of the edict. *And they spoke to the people, saying, Thus says Pharaoh*, etc. The customary formula with which messengers introduce the words of their senders is repeated here in parallelism with the statement in *v.* 1: 'Thus says *YHWH*, the God of Israel.' The command of Pharaoh, who is deemed a God in Egypt, is arrogantly announced in language similar to that in which Moses and Aaron proclaimed the words of the Lord.

His injunction is: *I will not give you straw*; therefore, *you*, your-
11 selves, *Go, get you straw*. Your request was (*v.* 3): 'Let us go, we pray you'; go, therefore, as you requested, but your going shall not be such as you desire; go, not to serve your God and to offer sacrifices to Him, but to do the service of the king of Egypt. And get you straw *where you can find it*, that is, the responsibility will be yours; it will not be the concern of the administration. Bend all your energies to secure the straw, *for naught of your work shall be diminished*. Do not think that you can do this work wholly or in part in place of your former labour; the whole of your previous task remains obligatory, and the new assignment is in addition thereto.

12 The hapless slaves were compelled to bear the new burden. *So the people were scattered abroad throughout all the land of Egypt* — in all directions, in a desperate attempt *to gather* at least *stubble*, which should serve them *for straw* — instead of the straw, which was unavailable. They returned at a late hour with a small bundle
13 of stubble in their hands, *And the* Egyptian *taskmasters were urgent*, pressing them, *saying* make haste, *fulfil your works, your*

EXODUS V 13

daily tasks, today the same as any other day, according to the amount imposed upon you, *as* was the quota *when there was straw* ⟨given to you⟩ (these words are added, as a gloss, in the ancient versions and in the Samaritan Pentateuch).

But the implementation of the taskmasters' demand was beyond the bounds of possibility. Consequently, since the work was not completed either on the first or second day, the unfortunate serfs were punished: *And the foremen of the children of Israel were beaten* — the expert workers *whom Pharaoh's taskmasters had set over them* to direct the work and to be responsible for it — *and asked*, in cruel reprimand, *Why have you not fulfilled your prescribed amount in making bricks as heretofore* [literally, 'both yesterday and the third day'], *both yesterday and today*. The phrase 'yesterday and the third day' is used in Hebrew not literally, but in a general, figurative sense to signify 'in the past'; hence it does not contradict the statement that immediately follows, to the effect that yesterday the work had not been completed.

In this paragraph, too, we find, towards the end, a noun from the stem עָשָׂה *'āśā* ['do', 'make'] — מַעֲשֵׂיכֶם *ma'ăśēkhem* ['works'] (*v*. 13) — in parallelism to the words derived from this stem that occurred at the close of the first and second paragraphs.

FOURTH PARAGRAPH
THE COMPLAINT OF THE FOREMEN
(V 15–19)

15 This paragraph commences with the word וַיָּבֹאוּ *wayyābho'ū* ['... came'] in contrast to the preceding paragraph, which begins with the word וַיֵּצְאוּ *wayyēṣe'ū* ['... went out']: *Then the foremen of the children of Israel came* before Pharaoh to complain about the situation, *and cried unto Pharaoh* concerning the wrong done to them. Although their complaint is courteously phrased, it contains a bitter protest. They commence with the word *Why*, with which Pharaoh began when he reprimanded Moses and Aaron (*v*. 4), but the words that follow express only polite blame: *Why do you deal thus with your servants?* We are your servants, who are faithful to you and devoted to your service (the expression

your servants occurs three times in their speech, as though it was their intention to emphasize it); then why do you act in this way
16 towards your faithful servants? *No straw is given to your servants,* nevertheless: *Bricks, they* — the slave-drivers — *say to us, make* (to understand the order of the words we must bear in mind that the sense of the verse is: Regarding the straw, it is not given to your servants; and regarding the bricks, the slave-drivers say to us, make them according to the prescribed amount). *Now behold, the result is that your servants are beaten,* although they are not at fault, וְחָטָאת עַמֶּךָ *wᵉḥāṭā'th 'ammekhā*. The last words are not quite clear; but apparently the text wishes to convey that the foremen intended to say: But it is you who are at fault, or, it is you who have been at fault (the *Wāw* of *wᵉḥāṭā'th* not being consecutive; cf. וְהֶאֱמִן *wᵉhe'ĕmīn* ['And he believed'] in Gen. xv 6; וְהֶחֱרִישׁ *wᵉheḥĕrīš* ['and (Jacob) held his peace'] *ibid.* xxxiv 5); but out of respect to the king they changed the wording and said that it was his people who were at fault. The form חָטָאת — which is feminine [3rd pers. sing., perfect], despite the fact that the word עַם *'am* ['people'] is nearly always treated as a masculine noun (with the exception of Jud. xviii 7, and Jer. viii 5, on account of the influence of the near-by feminine nouns), and that the afformative is אתָ- *-ā'th*, which is found only rarely in the third person [fem. sing. perfect] of *Lāmedh-'Āleph* verbs instead of the normal termination אָה- *-'ā* — possibly indicates that the intention of the foremen was to say וְחָטָאתָ אַתָּה *wᵉḥāṭā'thā 'attā* ['but it is you who are at fault (2nd pers. masc. sing.)], but out of deference they did not complete the first word, and added *'ammekhā* ['your people'; the clause should now be rendered: 'but it is your people who are at fault'].

In his reply, Pharaoh reiterated his catch-phrase, and emphasized
17 it still further by repeating the word 'idle': *But he said, you are idle, you are idle; therefore you say, Let us go and sacrifice to the Lord.* After this preliminary observation, he states the conclusion:
18 *And now,* since such is the case, it is my duty to heal you of the ailment of laziness. You say, *Let us go;* so shall it be: *Go* — not to sacrifice to the Lord, but do the service that I put upon you: *Go, work.* The conditions of service shall be those that I have laid down, without any modification: *for no straw shall be given to you, yet you shall deliver* [literally, 'give'] *the same number of bricks.* The repetition of the verb 'give' underlines the antithesis: what devolves upon me, I shall not give; but you shall give what devolves on you.

19   Such was Pharaoh's answer. *And the foremen of the children of Israel saw them* [אֹתָם *'ōthām*] — that is, themselves — *in evil* — in an evil and grievous plight, since they were under no misapprehension as to the significance of Pharaoh's reply. It meant *to say, in simple language: You shall not diminish aught from your bricks, your daily task.* The word רָע *rā‘* ['evil'] may contain, as has been suggested, an allusion to the name *Re‘* the chief deity of the Egyptian pantheon, as though to express two thoughts simultaneously: they saw themselves in an *evil* [רָע *ra‘*] plight because they had been delivered into the hands of the worshippers of the god *Re‘*. Possibly the reference is to Pharaoh himself, who was regarded as the incarnation of the god *Re‘* in human form.

FIFTH PARAGRAPH

THE ENCOUNTER WITH MOSES AND AARON

(V 20–21)

20   The tension felt already in the earlier paragraphs continues to grow. It chanced that the foremen *met Moses and Aaron, who stationed themselves to meet them* (apparently, Moses and Aaron were preparing themselves to have another audience of Pharaoh), *as they came forth from Pharaoh* after the painful interview described above. The bitter grief that they felt roused in them, as Pharaoh had hoped, feelings of resentment against the two brothers who were the cause of it all. They were so overwrought that they could not restrain themselves from assailing them, that is, from turning to them in anger and upbrading them (not without purpose does the Bible use the word וַיִּפְגְּעוּ *wayyiphge‘ū* [which can mean 'attacked' as well as 'met'] and not וַיִּפְגְּשׁוּ *wayyiphgešū* ['met'], which could imply even a friendly meeting, as in iv 27). What are these men doing in the vicinity of the king? They come to

21   do us harm, not good. *And they said unto them, The Lord look upon you, and judge*: you told us that the Lord had seen our affliction; if only, in truth, He would see what is being done to us through your fault, and would judge you as you deserve, *because you have brought us into ill odour*, that is, you have caused us to be scorned and contemned, as idle and faithless slaves, *in the eyes of Pharaoh, and in the eyes of his servants* (עֲבָדָיו *‘ăbhādhāw*,

which has here the connotation not of 'slaves' but of 'ministers', 'counsellors'), to such an extent as *to put a sword in their hand to slay us*.

The expression 'to bring someone into ill odour' acquired at an early period a metaphorical sense, and its original signification was so far forgotten that it was possible to connect it with the phrase *in the eyes of*, although an odour does not affect the eyes.

The words of the foremen are reminiscent of what Moses and Aaron said to Pharaoh (*v.* 3). You, Moses and Aaron, asked Pharaoh to let us go lest the Lord *fall upon* us with pestilence or *with the sword*; but, in actuality, you have brought it about that *the sword* of Pharaoh and his servants should be drawn against us, and that we should be compelled *to fall upon* you with angry reproaches.

SIXTH PARAGRAPH

MOSES' REMONSTRANCE AND THE LORD'S REPLY

(V 22 - VI 1)

The tension reaches its climax. Moses, too, is disillusioned and reproachful, not because Pharaoh had refused to concede his request, for he was prepared for that from the outset, but because he had learnt that his initial action had brought fresh calamity upon the heads of his oppressed brethren. He forgoes the second audience that he had intended to ask of the king, and turns to his God. In the bitterness of his soul he dares to reproach the Lord in words of despair. *And Moses returned to the Lords*: leaving the noisy city, and seeking solitude in a quiet place, he turned to Heaven, *and said, Lord* (אֲדֹנָי *Ădhōnāy*, the name used when addressing God), *Why hast Thou brought evil upon this people* — this dear, unfortunate people? For what reason hast Thou brought added evil upon it? *Why is it that Thou hast sent me?* What good hast Thou achieved by my mission? Behold, *since I came to Pharaoh to speak in Thy name*, Pharaoh *has brought* even greater *evil upon this people*; *and Thou*, although Thou didst say to me (iii 8), 'I have come down to deliver them', *hast done nought to deliver Thy people* — Thine own people, whom Thou hast called 'My people' (iii 7, and elsewhere). Such daring questions, only a man like Moses, after he had overcome his doubts and completely dedicated his whole life to the fulfilment of his exalted mission, could permit himself to ask.

Chapter VI

1 He is immediately vouchsafed an encouraging answer that confirms the promises given to him at first. *And the Lord said to Moses, Now* — in the near future — *you shall see what I will do to Pharaoh*; you shall see *that by a strong hand* — on account of My strong hand (see my comment on iii 19) — *shall he let them go*; nay more, *by a strong hand* — namely, of Pharaoh and his people — *shall he drive them out of his land* — not only will he permit them to go, but he will compel them to do so. This is how the expression 'by a strong hand' should be interpreted in the second half of the verse: first, because it is difficult to suppose that the same phrase would occur twice in a parallelism with the identical significance; secondly, on account of the similar verse (rightly indicated already by Rashi): and the Egyptians were urgent [literally, 'were strong'] upon the people, to send them out of the land in haste (xii 33).

At the conclusion of this paragraph there is discernible a parallel to the expressions of 'doing' [e.g. make, labour, works] with which a number of other paragraphs in this section conclude. This represents not merely an external parallelism but also an inner nexus with the ideas that find expression in the text. Pharaoh constantly insists on the *works* [מַעֲשִׂים *maʿăśīm*] and service of the Israelites; he says (*v.* 4): 'Wherefore do you, Moses and Aaron, cause the people to refrain from their *works* [מִמַּעֲשָׂיו *mimmaʿăśāw*]?; thereafter (*v.* 9): 'Let heavier work be laid upon the men, that they may *labour* [וְיַעֲשׂוּ *wᵉyaʿăśū*] therein'; and in his name the taskmasters proclaim (*v.* 13): 'Fulfil your *works* [מַעֲשֵׂיכֶם *maʿăśēkhem*], your daily tasks.' In contrast to all this, the Judge of the whole earth, who comes to punish the wicked person according to his wickedness, measure for measure, declares: 'Now you shall see what I *will do* [אֶעֱשֶׂה *ʾeʿĕśe*] to Pharaoh'.

The structure of the section is complete and symmetrical. It begins with verses marked by poetic rhythm (the words of Moses and Aaron in *v.* 1, and Pharaoh's reply in *v.* 2), and it ends with verses characterized by the same feature (Moses' expostulation in *v.* 23, and the Lord's answer in vi 1). Its six paragraphs are interconnected by parallelisms and repetitions with some of which we have already dealt, and others we shall discuss in the following lines. The words indicating the principal concepts of the section occur seven times, namely, the noun לְבֵנִים *lᵉbhēnīm* ['bricks'] together with the verb לָבֵן *lābhan* ['to make bricks']; expressions of 'doing', and of 'going'. The explicit mention of the number *three* in v. 3 (*three days' journey*) points to the importance of the treble occurrence of expressions in the sections for the sake of emphasis; thus we find the stem שָׁלַח *šālaḥ* ['to let go'] thrice in the first two verses, and an echo of it in the last paragraph; three times 'Let us go (and) sacrifice'; three times תְּמוֹל שִׁלְשֹׁם *tᵉmōl šilšōm* ['heretofore']; three times נִרְפִּים *nirpīm* ['idlers']; three times the verb גָּרַע *gāraʿ* ['diminish']; and three times terms connected with 'evil' and 'bringing evil' [the substantive רַע *raʿ* and the verb הֵרַע *hēraʿ*].

SECTION FIVE

PRELUDE TO SUCCESSFUL ACTION

CHAPTER VI, VERSE 2 — CHAPTER VII, VERSE 7

FIRST PARAGRAPH
THE LORD'S DECLARATION
(VI 2–9)

After the Lord's encouraging answer Moses was again at peace; 'his heart was firm, trusting in the Lord.' Shortly afterwards (what time elapsed, the Bible does not tell us), the word of the Lord came to him, apprising him, in a solemn and detailed declaration, of what He will do in order to liberate the people of Israel and to bring them to the land that had been promised to their ancestors.

2 *And God spoke unto Moses* — this is the beginning of the Section — *and said unto him, I am YHWH*. Thus the declaration opens with the words *I am YHWH*. Such a formula was customary in the ancient East in the declarations of kings, when proclaiming their deeds and might, as their inscriptions testify. The text on the stele of Mesha king of Moab commences: 'I am Mesha, son of Chemosh [......], king of Moab, the Dibonite'. So, too, begins the inscription of Yehawmilk, king of Byblos: 'I am Yehawmilk, king of Byblos', etc. [tr. *ANET*, p. 502 a]; of Kilamuwa king of Y'dy: 'I am Kilamuwa, the son of Hayya. Gabbar became king of Y'dy', etc. [tr. *ANET*, p. 500 b]; of Azitawadda, which was recently discovered: 'I am Azitawadda, the blessed of Baʻl, the servant of Baʻl', etc. [tr. *ANET*, p. 499 b]; and so forth. In our passage the king of the universe announces His purpose and the amazing plan of action that He proposes to carry out in the near future, and, in accordance with its usual practice, the Torah employs the language of men, and commences the declaration in keeping with the opening formulae of the proclamations of human kings. The scholars who saw in this verse the revelation of a new Name previously unknown failed to pay attention to four things:

(a) It was the established custom of Eastern monarchs to begin their proclamations with the formula, *I am so-and-so*, even though their name was well known to every one.

(b) If the purport of the verse had been as the aforementioned scholars supposed, the text would have read, *My name is YHWH*, not *I am YHWH*.

(c) The phrase *I am YHWH* occurs very frequently in the Bible, particularly in the section קְדֹשִׁים *Qᵉdhōšīm* ['you shall be holy' (Lev. xix 1 ff.)] and in the Book of Ezekiel, and obviously it is impossible to understand it as an oft-repeated proclamation that the name of the God of Israel is *YHWH*, or as an expression of constantly re-iterated recognition that this is His name.

(d) This formula is again found three times in the continuation of our paragraph (*vv.* 6, 7, 8), and these instances cannot possibly be regarded as a revelation of the Tetragrammaton.

The opening formula *I am YHWH* serves also, as we shall see at once in the commentary on the next verse, to draw attention to the connotation of the Tetragrammaton, which is explained in the Torah, as we have noted (see above, on iii 14–15), to mean: He who is with His creatures, and He who is constantly the same, that is, He is true to His word and fulfils His promises. I am *YHWH*, and My action shall be in keeping with My name. A similar interpretation attaches to the phrase *I am YHWH* wherever it occurs in the Bible; it comes to link the statute or the promise with the attributes of God implied in the name *YHWH* — the attributes of One who sees to it that the moral law is observed, and fulfils, with absolute faithfulness, what He promises or what He announces beforehand by His prophets. In the Book of Ezekiel we even find the complete formula: 'I the Lord have spoken and have done it' (xvii 24; xxii 14; xxxvi 36); so, too, in Num. xiv 35: 'I the Lord have spoken, surely this will I do.'

The opening words of the verse are *wayᵉdhabbēr 'Elōhīm*, and not *wayᵉdhabbēr YHWH*, for stylistic reasons: either to avoid the tautology, *And YHWH spoke... I am YHWH*, or to give greater emphasis to the Tetragrammaton in the declaration that heads the Divine communication.

3 The announcement in *v.* 3 is also to be explained on the basis of usages current in the ancient East. The text states: *And I appeared unto Abraham, unto Isaac and unto Jacob as* אֵל שַׁדָּי *'El Šadday* ['God Shaddai'], *but by My name YHWH I was not known* [לֹא נוֹדַעְתִּי *lō nōdhaʿtī*] *to them*. Although many scholars have inferred from the wording that the verse derives from a document accord-

ing to which the Patriarchs did not use the name *YHWH*, and consequently the passage has become one of the fundamental pillars of the documentary hypothesis, yet in this case, too, we can say that if this had been the intention of the text it would have been phrased differently. The verse would have read, 'but My name *YHWH* I did not make known', or 'but My name *YHWH* was not known to them', and not as in the present text, 'I was not known to them.' The ancient versions, which render as though it were written, 'I did not make known', do not point to a different reading from that of the Masoretic text; they are merely giving their interpretation of the verse, since its form appeared to them obscure. It is precisely the more difficult text that is to be preferred in accordance with the rule of *lectio difficilior*. This aside, the antiquity of the Masoretic reading is attested by Ezek. xx 9–10, which forms part of a paragraph that is undoubtedly dependent on our paragraph: 'But I wrought for My name's sake, that it should not be profaned in the sight of the nations, among whom they were, in whose sight I made Myself known [נוֹדַעְתִּי *nōdhaʿtī*], so as to bring them forth out of the land of Egypt. So I caused them to go forth out of the land of Egypt, and brought them into the wilderness.' The correct meaning, again, of our passage becomes clear, as I have stated, when we examine the traditional usages of the ancient East. The people of the Orient used to attribute to each of their gods a variety of names and qualities, and they associated with each designation specific concepts and characteristics. In the Egyptian texts, for example, it is stated that a certain deity is accustomed to do one kind of work under such a name, another kind of work under a different appellation, and a third task under yet another title, and so forth. Compare also Psa. lxviii 5: 'Extol Him that rides upon the skies, whose name is יָהּ *Yāh* ['Lord'].' With the name שַׁדַּי *Šadday* ['Shaddai'] (be its etymology what it may; see in this connection my article in the Encyclopaedia Biblica [Hebrew], Vol. I, pp. 290–292) the Israelites were wont to associate the idea of the Divinity who rules over nature and bestows upon mankind fertility, as we can see from every verse in the Pentateuch, in which this name occurs; for example, Gen. xvii 1–2: 'I am El Shaddai ...and I will multiply you exceedingly'; *ibid.* xxviii 3: 'And El Shaddai bless you, and make you fruitful, and multiply you'; *ibid.* xxxv 11: 'I am El Shaddai. Be fruitful and multiply: a nation and a company of nations shall be of you'; see further *ibid.* xlviii 3–4; xlix 25 (in Gen. xliii 14 there is also a reference to bereavement, as though the Power that bestows fruitfulness acts at times to annul it; so, too, in Ruth i 20–21). This enables us to understand the text before us clearly: I revealed Myself (God declares) to Abraham, Isaac and Jacob in My aspect that finds expression in the name Shaddai, and I made them fruitful and multiplied them and gave them children and children's children, but by the name *YHWH* (the word שְׁמִי *šᵉmī* ['My name'] is to be construed here as an accusative of nearer definition, and signifies 'by My name'), in My character as expressed by this designation, I was not known to them, that is, it was not given to them to recognize Me as One that fulfils His promises, because the assurance with regard to the possession of the Land, which I had given them, I had not yet fulfilled. Although one of the attributes connected with the Tetragrammaton — the attribute of being with His creatures — was fulfilled also in the Patriarchs, yet in the implementation of the meaning of this name — namely, that He is One who carries out His promises — God was not known to the Fathers of the nation. If we interpret *v*. 3 in this way, we shall also clearly understand the connection between it and what is narrated subsequently in the rest of the paragraph.

4–5 Verses 4 and 5, both of which begin with the word וְגַם *wᵉgham* ['and also', 'moreover'], point to two parallel statements: on the one hand, *I have established*, etc., and on the other, *I have heard*, etc. I discussed the signification of the idiom 'to establish a covenant' in my commentary on Gen. vi 18, where I showed that it was not identical with that of the expression 'make [literally, 'cut'] a covenant', as most commentators are accustomed to suppose, particularly modern exegetes, who regard the use of the two different terms as a sure indication of divergent sources. The expression 'to establish a covenant' connotes the fulfilment of a covenant that has already been made. The Lord says: Let it be known to you, Moses, that *I have established My covenant*, which I made *with them*. The words 'with them' belong not to the verb 'established' but to the substantive 'covenant', as is shown by ii 24: 'And God remembered His covenant with Abraham, Isaac and Jacob.' The covenant was a promise (on the use of the word covenant in the sense of a unilateral promise, see my note on Gen. vi 18) *to give them* — that is, the Patriarchs and their descendants — *the land of Canaan, the land of their sojournings, wherein they sojourned.* This assurance I have established, I have given it permanent validity, it exists before Me constantly. Even though the Patriarchs were not granted to witness its realization themselves, yet in My sight it was always existent. *Moreover* — apart from this — *I have heard the groaning of the children of Israel, whom the Egyptians keep in bondage.* For these two reasons I have arisen, *and I have remembered My covenant* — I have resolved to put it into effect now. It is as though there was explicitly revealed to Moses what transpired in the Court on high, as the Torah has already described it for us (ii 24) in almost identical words: 'And God heard their groaning, and God remembered His covenant with Abraham, with Isaac, and with Jacob.'

6 *Therefore* — so the Divine voice continues to speak to Moses — *say unto the children of Israel* according to these words that I speak to you. In the same way as I began My proclamation to you with the formula *I am YHWH*, so shall you commence with these words the declaration that you will deliver to them in My name: *I am YHWH*, who is with you and who fulfils through you the promise given to your ancestors. Then you shall tell them the good news of what I am about to do on their behalf.

The Divine action for the benefit of Israel is described in seven clauses, each of which begins with a verb in the first person, the
6-8 verbs being linked together by *Wāw* consecutive: *and I will bring out — and I will deliver — and I will redeem — and I will take — and I will be — and I will bring — and I will give.* Of these the first three (v. 6) refer to the liberation; the middle two (v. 7) establish the mutual relationship between the Lord and Israel; the last two (v. 8) appertain to the acquisition of the Land.

First it is stated, *and I will bring you out from under the burdens of the Egyptians*; in this we hear an echo of what we have read earlier, to wit, the expressions 'bring out' (iii 10, 11, 12) and 'burdens' (i 11; ii 11; v 4, 5). This is followed by, *and I will deliver you out of their bondage*; here, too, we are reminded of the references to 'deliverance' (iii 8; v 23), and to 'bondage' [עֲבוֹדָה *'ăbhōdhā*, rendered also: 'service', 'labour', 'work'], which occurred a number of times in the first section, and again in ii 23; v 9, 11; vi 6. The third sentence deals with the liberation: *and I will redeem you with a stretched out arm, and with great judgements.* These expressions have not occurred previously (except that of 'judgement' in other contexts), but they are due to occur often later on. Many poetic passages of the Bible speak of the Lord's mighty arm as the means used for bringing Divine retribution on the wicked and for delivering the righteous from their hand (Isa.

li 9: 'Awake, awake, put on strength, O arm of the Lord; awake, as in the days of old, the generations of long ago. Was it not Thou that didst hew Rahab in pieces', etc.; Psa. lxxxix 10 [Heb., *v.* 11]: 'Thou didst crush Rahab like a carcass; Thou didst scatter Thy enemies with Thy mighty arm'; *ibid. v.* 13 [Heb., *v.* 14]: 'Thou hast a mighty arm; strong is Thy hand, and exalted is Thy right hand'; compare Deut. xxxiii 27); apparently this expression was commonly used in the ancient epic poems that have not come down to us. The 'great judgements' are the righteous acts of the Judge of the whole earth, who requites the wicked man according to his wickedness, and delivers from his hand the righteous who are subjected to his yoke.

The liberation becomes the basis of the relationship between the Lord and Israel: *and I will take you to Me for a people,* 'a treasure from among all peoples' (xix 5–6); and in parallelism with this: *and I will be* [וְהָיִיתִי *wᵉhāyīthī*] *to you a God* (another reference to the Tetragrammaton, the stem of which is הָוָה — הָיָה *hāyā* — *hāwā* [to be]), that is to say, that you will revere Me, *and you shall know that I am YHWH your God,* and you shall not be like Pharaoh who said, 'I do not know *YHWH*' (v 2), but you shall recognize Me and know that I am *YHWH,* and as My name is so am I — One who is with you and fulfils His word, *who brings you out from under the burdens of the Egyptians* (in accordance with the first of the liberation clauses).

I shall bring you up from this land, and I will bring you in unto the land, concerning which I lifted up My hand — that is, I swore — *to give it to Abraham, to Isaac and to Jacob* (the mention of the names of the Patriarchs links the end of the Divine communication with the beginning): *and I will give it to you for a heritage* — not only shall I bring you unto the land, but I shall give it to you for an overlasting possession.

Finally, like one who signs an authorization or accepts responsibility for something, the Lord repeats the formula with which He opened His address: *I am YHWH,* and My name shall be your assurance that My promises will be fulfilled. This reiteration forms another nexus between the conclusion of the Divine communication and its beginning, as well as its middle verses.

The entire declaration, by its elevated diction, which approximates to poetic rhythm, by its triple (we may even say, quadruple) iteration of the solemn formula *I am YHWH,* by its seven expressions of promise, which succeed one another like hammer blows, as well as by the threefold mention of the word 'land' and of its being given [to the Patriarchs or their descendants], leaves a profound impression worthy of the exalted nature of the theme.

9 Moses did as he was enjoined: *And Moses spoke so* — according to the words that the Lord put in his mouth — *to the children of Israel*; but although the Israelites had believed him and hearkened to his voice when he brought them the first tidings, this time they did not give ear: *but they did not hearken unto Moses*. After their disappointment at the failure of the initial attempt to liberate them, followed by the intensification of the bondage, they were disheartened and despondent, and they found no consolation in what Moses told them in the name of the Lord, *because of dejection* [literally, 'shortness'] *of spirit and hard work* — because they were dispirited (קֹצֶר רוּחַ *qōṣer rūaḥ* ['shortness of spirit'] is a Hebrew and also Ugaritic idiom signifying a state of depression) and their work had been made even harder than before.

Again Moses' path is obstructed. Such is the usual fate of every one who engages in an enterprise of vast importance, which is, at the same time, beset with difficulties: he experiences moments of triumph and also of reverse; but his true greatness is seen when he does not permit the hour of defeat to divert him from his path or cause him to despair of ultimate success.

SECOND PARAGRAPH

MOSES AND AARON ARE COMMANDED TO GO
TO PHARAOH

(VI 10–13)

10-11 Although at the moment the children of Israel are not inclined to listen to Moses' words and to derive comfort therefrom in their trouble, the work cannot stop on account of this. The time has arrived to turn direct to Pharaoh, without delay: *And the Lord spoke to Moses, saying, Go in, speak to Pharaoh king of Egypt, that he let the children of Israel go out of his land.*

However, the apathetic attitude of the people again arouses doubt in Moses' mind. In his humility, he bases his objection on his lack of eloquence, and he expresses the fear lest this oratorical inadequacy should bring about the failure of his mission to

12 Pharaoh: *And Moses spoke before the Lord, saying, Behold the children of Israel have not hearkened unto Me; how then shall Pharaoh hear me, who am of uncircumcised lips?* This is not (as most modern exegetes are accustomed to think) a duplication of a doubt voiced by Moses in Horeb; it represents, as we often find in narratives of this kind, a recurrence of a situation similar to one that existed before, but in a different degree. At first Moses was afraid that his brethren, the children of Israel, would not listen to him; this doubt he had conquered, and it was shown in actual practice that, with the help of Aaron, it was possible for him to win the confidence of the people (iv 31). But now a new situation had arisen: after their yoke of servitude had been made heavier, the people lost faith in him and would not hearken to him any longer; thus when he received the Divine command to come and speak to Pharaoh — to speak, it will be noted — he again began to doubt his oratorical capacities in a new and more drastic form than at first. If he had no success with his own people, how much less successful was he bound to be with Pharaoh.

Thereupon the Lord's answer came to set his mind at ease. When he first doubted whether he would achieve success with his people, the Divine reply put his fears at rest with the assurance that his brother Aaron would be able to speak to the people in his name; and so it actually happened. Now, too, God spoke to him in the same vein: in his mission to Pharaoh he would again have the support of Aaron. So far Aaron had not been given the task of appearing before Pharaoh, only before the children of Israel; now he

13 was charged also to speak to Pharaoh: *And the Lord spoke to Moses and to Aaron* — to both of them alike — *and gave them a charge* — both of them — not only *to the children of Israel*, but also *to Pharaoh king of Egypt*, in order that by their combined efforts they might achieve their aim *to bring the children of Israel out of the land of Egypt.*

THIRD PARAGRAPH

THE GENEALOGY OF MOSES AND AARON

(VI 14–27)

This paragraph is regarded by many scholars as a foreign element in the narrative, which interrupts the sequence of events. But they overlooked the fact that contemporary European patterns of thought differ from those of the Orient in antiquity. In a modern book possibly (I stress the word 'possibly') the genealogy of Moses and Aaron would have been presented in its proper place, above, when the birth of Moses is spoken of. But to the way of thinking prevailing in the ancient East, which was not meticulously insistent on chronological order, it seemed, as we have already stated, that there the genealogical data would have tended to divert our attention from the exalted principal theme; nor were they needed at that moment, and hence they were not furnished. But here, after the dramatic tension of the narrative had subsided, and the rise of Moses and Aaron to a position of social distinction as the representatives of the people of Israel before the Egyptian state had been recounted, it was desirable to devote a few lines to their genealogical status among their own people, so that the reader might know in detail who these men were and what place they occupied among the tribes of Israel. Even in a modern book it might conceivably not have been inappropriate to introduce here a digression, that left the central topic for a moment in order to deal with this subsidiary matter, and to have returned subsequently to the main subject at the point at which the account was interrupted. The pedigree given here mentions before the sons of Levi — the tribe of Moses and Aaron — also the sons of Reuben and the sons of Simeon. This is not due to the fact that the beginning of the genealogical roll of all the tribes of Israel was mechanically transcribed here, as many exegetes have conjectured. Such a theory is improbable, for we see that for the Levites in particular, and even more especially for the family of Moses and Aaron, we are given details that are wanting in the case of the other tribes, thus proving that the paragraph was specifically written for the present narrative. The aim was to show not only the status of Moses and Aaron within the tribe of Levi, but also the position of the Levitic tribe among the people of Israel, namely, as the third tribe after the tribes comprising the descendants of Jacob's first two sons.

EXODUS VI 16–25

The sons of Reuben and of Simeon are mentioned here with the utmost brevity — just by name — only such details being given as are necessary to indicate the position of the tribe of Levi, whereas the latter is dealt with at length.

14-15 The paragraph begins: *These are the heads of their fathers' house*, that is, of Moses and Aaron referred to in the preceding paragraph. These words form the superscription of the entire paragraph; thereafter it is stated: *the sons of Reuben the first-born of Israel*, etc. The sense is: in order to show clearly the position of the fathers' house of Moses and Aaron it is proper to begin by mentioning the names of those who preceded them in the genealogical register of Jacob's sons. On these names see my forthcoming commentary on Gen. xlvi;* here there is no need to discuss them in detail. The expressions *these are the families of Reuben* and *these are the families of Simeon*, which form the conclusion of v. 14 and v. 15 respectively, imply, as it were: These are the families of the tribes referred to, but we shall not deal with them further. After this, in an explicit and detailed statement,

16-25 we are told: *And these are the names of the sons of Levi according to their generations*. In regard to Levi we are given not only the names of the sons, as in the case of Reuben and Simeon above, but also the names of the grandsons and great grandsons, and even further down the generations, as far as was necessitated by factors that we shall discuss later. Even in respect of these names there is no need to enter into details, and it will suffice to examine two problems that pertain to the actual content of the section, and more especially one of them, namely, the chronological question.

The problem is this: It is stated here (v. 16): *and the years of the life of Levi were a hundred thirty-seven years*; thereafter (v. 18): *and the years of the life of Kohath were a hundred and thirty-three years*; and later still (v. 20): *and the years of the life of Amram were a hundred and thirty-seven years*. But these figures do not agree with the statement in xii 40: 'Now the time that the children of Israel dwelt in Egypt, was four hundred and thirty years', nor even with the round number of 400 years mentioned in Gen. xv 13. The difficulty is formulated in Rashi's commentary as follows: Kohath was one of the company that went down to Egypt; if you add up all his years and the years of Amram

---
* Owing to the untimely demise of the author, this part of the commentary was not written. *Tr.*

and the eighty years of Moses, you will find that they do not come to four hundred; moreover, many of the years of the sons are included in those of the fathers [i.e. the sons and the fathers were contemporaries for many years. The author summarizes here Rashi's annotations to Gen. xv 13 and Exod. xii 40]. The well known explanation that the period of four hundred years, or four hundred and thirty years, is to be reckoned from the time of Isaac's birth or of the 'Covenant between the Pieces' is Midrashic; likewise the addition found in the Samaritan Pentateuch and in the Septuagint in Exod. xii 40 (the Samaritan reads: 'in the land of Canaan and in the land of Egypt'; the Septuagint: 'in the land of Egypt and in the land of Canaan', supplemented in several MSS by: 'they and their ancestors') reflects a similar Midrashic exegesis. According to the simple meaning of the Biblical text, the passages in question have to be explained differently.

As I have already shown in my commentary on Genesis, the numbers given in the Torah are mostly round or symbolic figures, and their purpose is to teach us something by their harmonious character. I also explained there (especially in Part I, *From Adam to Noah*, pp. 251–264) that these numbers are based on the sexagesimal system, which occupied in the ancient East a place similar to that of the decimal system in our days. The chronological unit in this system was a period of sixty years, which the Babylonians called a *šūš*. One *šūš* consists of sixty years, and two *šūš* of a hundred and twenty years — a phrase that is used by Jews to this day. In order to convey that a given thing continued for a long time, or comprised a very large number of units, a round figure signifying a big amount according to the sexagesimal system was employed, for example, 600, 6,000 600,000 or 300, 3,000, 300,000; or 120, 360, 1,200, 3,600, and so forth. I further demonstrated there that if it was desired to indicate a still larger amount, these figures were supplemented by seven or a multiple of seven. The number 127, for instance (Gen. xxiii 1; Esther i 1; viii 9; ix 30), was based on this system. Now there was a tradition among the Israelites that the time that the children of Israel dwelt in Egypt lasted 430 years, that is, 360 (6 × 60) and another 70: an exceedingly long time, comprising six units of sixty years, and another seventy years — ten times seven. Apart from this, there was also a tradition among the Israelites that four generations lived in Egypt, and that the fourth generation returned to the land of Israel (Gen. xv 16: 'And in the fourth generation they shall come

EXODUS VI 16–25

back hither'), and it was not easy to reconcile the two traditions. Our paragraph seeks to achieve such a reconciliation, and to harmonize the two traditions. There are four generations: (a) Levi; (b) Kohath; (c) Amram; (d) Aaron, who was privileged to go forth from Egypt and to come as far as the borders of the Promised Land. As for the total of years, we must not deduct the years of the sons that coincided with those of the fathers, but we must add together the figures given in the text here exactly as they are. We are permitted to calculate in this way for two reasons:
(a) Each generation endured the burden of exile throughout the time of its exile, and its distress was not diminished by the fact that it was shared by another generation during a certain portion of that period; hence in computing the total length of exile suffered, one is justified to some extent in reckoning the ordeal of each generation in its entirety.
(b) A similar and parallel system was used in the chronological calculations of the Mesopotamians. In the Sumerian King List dynasties that were partly coeval, one reigning in one city and another elsewhere, are recorded consecutively, and are reckoned as if they ruled successively. Consequently, if we add up the years that these dynasties reigned, we shall arrive at a total that is actually the sum of the periods of their kingship, although it will exceed the time that elapsed from the commencement of the first dynasty to the end of the last.

If now we take the sum of all the figures in our paragraph (137 + 133 + 137), and add thereto the 83 years of Aaron (vii 7), the first-born of the fourth generation, the total will be 490; and, upon deducting from it (in order to allow for the time that Levi and Kohath dwelt in the land of Canaan before they emigrated to Egypt) one unit of time, to wit, sixty years, we obtain exactly a period of 430 years, which is the number recorded in xii 40.

Following is the second problem: Why are there mentioned in the genealogy of the tribe of Levi all those — and only those — whose names are found here? The Rashbam [Rabbi Samuel B. Meir] already suggested the correct solution of this problem, namely, that Scripture was concerned to present to us at this stage all the Levites who would subsequently be mentioned in the Torah, so that on reading their names later we should know who they were and what their status was within their family. See the details in the commentary of the Rashbam — For the designation *the sister of Nahshon* in *v*. 23, note my comments on Gen. x 21.

The pedigree concludes with the formula, *These are the heads of the fathers' (house)of the Levites according to their families*, which is a kind of recapitulation of the opening formula, *These are the heads of their fathers' house* in v. 14.

Finally, there come two verses that clearly explain the object of
26 the paragraph: *These are that Aaron and Moses, to whom the Lord said, Bring out the children of Israel from the land of Egypt according to their hosts* — that is: These men, who are recorded in this list by the name of Aaron and Moses, are the same Aaron and Moses to whom the Lord assigned the exalted task of liberating the children of Israel from bondage and of bringing them forth from the land of Egypt, not like slaves who flee from their master's house, but
27 as a free people that goes on its way in ordered hosts. *These are they that spoke to Pharaoh king of Egypt* — it is they who stood before the great king in order to carry out this task, namely, *to bring out the children of Israel from Egypt*. And again, as a final summing up: *These are that Moses and Aaron*. In v. 26, which comes immediately after the genealogical roll, the text mentions the older brother before the younger; but here, after reference has been made to the mission, precedence is given to the younger brother, since it is upon him that the responsibility for the fulfilment of the mission mainly rests.

FOURTH PARAGRAPH

THE NARRATIVE IS RESUMED

(VI 28–30)

After dealing exclusively with the genealogy of Moses and Aaron, which temporarily interrupted the main course of the narrative, the Bible returns to its primary theme, and in order to make the resumption of the story clear, it briefly refers to what had been
28 stated in the verses preceding the digression. *And it came to pass*, as you have already heard. What transpired *on the day when the Lord spoke to Moses in the land of Egypt* was as follows: *the Lord*
29 *spoke to Moses, saying, I am YHWH* — that is, the Lord delivered to Moses the proclamation that begins and ends with this formula (*vv*. 2–8), and thereafter He said to him: *Speak to Pharaoh king of Egypt all that I speak to you* (as stated in *vv*. 10–11); then Moses

EXODUS VII 2

30 voiced his doubt (mentioned in *v.* 12): *And Moses said before the Lord, Behold, I am of uncircumcised lips; how then shall Pharaoh listen to me?* After we have again picked up in this way the temporarily severed thread of the story, the narrative can continue on its course. In the next paragraph, we shall be told in detail the Lord's answer to Moses' doubt, which above, in *v.* 13, was given only in a summary form.

FIFTH PARAGRAPH
DETAILED INSTRUCTIONS TO MOSES AND AARON
(VII 1–5)

Chapter VII

Replying to Moses' doubt, which was stated in the preceding verse in the words, 'Behold, I am of uncircumcised lips; how then shall Pharaoh listen to me?', the Lord deals with his objections seriatim.

1 He begins in a paternal tone: *See*, my son, consider the matter well, and you will be convinced that all your anxieties can be easily set at rest. Regarding your first fear, that you are of 'uncircumcised lips', let me put you at ease at once: you have no need to do much speaking, for *I have made you a god to Pharaoh*. You will not only be a god vis-à-vis your brother Aaron (iv 16) — that is, you will instruct him what to say, just as God instructs His prophets — but I have also made you a god before Pharaoh. Although Pharaoh is himself considered a deity, he is nevertheless accustomed to hear the prophets of Egypt address him in the name of their gods; now you will appear before him as one of the divinities, who do not speak directly but through their prophets, *and Aaron your brother shall be your prophet*, and he will speak in your name to Pharaoh. These words possibly contain a bitter ironic reflection on the Egyptian deities who 'have a mouth yet do not speak.'

But you, Moses, will transcend the gods of Egypt in that you
2 will not be wholly dumb: *You shall speak all that I command you —* words few in number but decisive in content you will be able to speak, and you will utter them at My command; *and Aaron your brother shall speak to Pharaoh*, delivering speeches before him whenever required, *and he will let go —* that means to say, so that he may let go — *the children of Israel from his land.*

EXODUS VII 3

As for the second part of the objection that you, Moses, raised before Me, saying, 'how then shall Pharaoh listen to Me?', do not fear. Pharaoh will certainly not listen to you, but this is of no consequence. On the contrary, this is one of the points of My plan: *And I will harden Pharaoh's heart* (see my observations on this subject above, in the commentary to iv 21), and his obduracy will be instrumental in bringing upon him the retributions he deserves for the enslavement of the Israelites and the murder of their infant sons. *And I will multiply*, for the purpose of this punishment, *My signs and My portents in the land of Egypt*. Do not, therefore, be concerned if you do not immediately receive a positive reply, *and Pharaoh will not listen to you*; for it is actually as a result of his refusal to grant your request, that I shall arise *and lay My hand on Egypt, and bring forth*, in the end, *My hosts* (see on vi 26), *My people the children of Israel, out of the land of Egypt by great judgements* (see on vi 6). It is true that Pharaoh said that he did not know *YHWH* (v 2), but then he and his people will learn to recognize Me, *and the Egyptians shall know that I am YHWH*, when they behold my acts, *when I stretch forth My hand upon Egypt* to inflict punishment upon the oppressors, *and when I bring out* (this is how Hebrew syntax requires that the word וְהוֹצֵאתִי *wᵉhōṣēʾthī* [literally, 'and I shall bring out'], which is coordinated with the preceding infinitive, should be understood) *the children of Israel from among them.*

CONCLUSION OF THE SECTION

(VII 6–7)

These two verses conclude the section by stating two things. First, that the commission was carried out: *And Moses and Aaron did as the Lord commanded them*. The particulars of their actions will be recounted at length in the next section, but at this stage the Bible tells us that exactly as they were enjoined *so they did*. Furthermore, we are informed of the age of Moses and Aaron at that fateful hour of their life and of the life of the people of Israel: *And Moses was eighty years old, and Aaron eighty-three years old, when they spoke to Pharaoh.* It is a common feature of Biblical narratives for the age of their heroes to be stated at the time when some momentous event befalls them; and particularly this, or a similar, formula is used, and often, as in our case, it comes at the end of the account. So, for example, we read in Gen. xvi 16, at the end of the story of the birth of Ishmael: 'And Abram was eighty-six years when Hagar bore Ishmael to Abram'; similarly *ibid.* xvii 24–25, at the end of the section on Circumcision: 'And Abraham was ninety-nine years old, when he was circumcised in the flesh of his foreskin. And Ishmael his son was thirteen years old, when he was circumcised in the flesh of his foreskin'; and likewise *ibid.* xxv 26; xli 46, and so forth.

At this point a question arises. From what was narrated earlier (ii 11 ff.) it would appear that Moses was a young man when he fled from Egypt, for it is stated at the beginning of the story: *when Moses had grown up, that he went out to his brethren*; whereas here we find him an old man of eighty. What did Moses do throughout this long period? We know that the later Haggadah fills the void with all kinds of wonderful tales about the journeys, battles and victories of Moses, and possibly these stories contain a very old nucleus of narrative that formed part of the tradition of the early generations, and which may have been included in the epic poem that antedated the Pentateuch, as I conjectured above; only the Torah did not incorporate it into its narration on account of its exaggerated Haggadic character and because it was not important to its theme. However, it may have alluded to the length of time that had elapsed in the words, 'And it came to pass in the course of those *many* days' (ii 23), as I have noted above (p. 28).

The basic idea of this section is speech. On the one side, the Lord speaks to Moses and Aaron; and on the other, we have the utterances of human beings. Consonant with customary usage, there occur seven words, derived from the stem דָּבַר *dābhar*, that refer to Divine communications and another seven that describe human discourse.

SECTION SIX

THE PLAGUES

CHAPTER VII, VERSE 8 — CHAPTER XI, VERSE 10

This section forms the focal point of the Biblical account of the bondage and liberation, describing seriatim, the Divine acts that brought retribution on Pharaoh and his servants because of the enslavement of the Israelites, and, in the end, compelled them to let Israel go free from the midst of their people.

In this section there are particularly apparent traces of the ancient epic poem to which I have already referred several times. Apparently this poem recounted the story of each plague at considerable length and in detail, whilst the Biblical prose narrative gives us a shortened, summarized account. However, there remain here and there, even in the Scriptural story — especially in less abbreviated paragraphs, like that describing the hail — relics of poetic phrases, rhythm or parallelism, which testify that they had their origin in a poetic version. I shall point out these poetic vestiges in the continuation of my commentary, and I shall draw attention to a number of bantering and satirical expressions found in the section, which may also derive from the ancient epic poem. Epic poetry was intended primarily to be chanted before the general public, and the masses are particularly fond of jocular and ironic observations.

The passages dealing with the Egyptian plagues are harmoniously and consummately constructed. In order to understand the plan and form of this structure we must pay attention to the following two facts:

(a) The first nine plagues are divisible, as the Rashbam already pointed out in his annotations on vii 26, into three cycles, each of which comprises three plagues. In each cycle, the first and second plagues come after Moses has warned Pharaoh; the third comes without warning. Furthermore — as Isaac Abravanel noted, in addition, in his commentary — before the first plague of each cycle Moses is commanded to stand in the morning before Pharaoh in the open, whereas before the second he is told to come before Pharaoh, that is, to appear

PROLOGUE

THE PRESENTATION OF CREDENTIALS

(VII 8–13)

8–9 Moses and Aaron make ready to appear before Pharaoh, in accordance with the command that the Lord had given them. This audience will serve to give them accreditation and recognition in the sight of Pharaoh and his servants as the envoys of *YHWH*, like the interview at which the emissary of a human king presents his credentials to a foreign monarch, to whom he is sent on a mission. The credentials of God's messenger will consist of performing a sign or wonder that is beyond the powers of a human being. Undoubtedly, Pharaoh would insist that Moses and Aaron should show him a wonder of this nature, just as he was accustomed to make such a demand from the prophets of his own deities. Hence Moses and Aaron are given detailed directives as to what they should do to satisfy Pharaoh's request: *And the Lord spoke unto Moses and unto Aaron, saying When Pharaoh shall speak unto you, saying, Give for yourselves* — to confirm your words — *a portent, then you,* Moses, shall turn, *and shall say unto Aaron, Take your rod, and cast it down before Pharaoh,* and I decree now upon this rod: *that it may become a crocodile.*

Aaron's rod is distinguished from that of Moses, and is not called 'the rod of God' (see on iv 17), but this miracle is very similar to the first sign delivered to Moses to perform before the children of Israel, namely, the transformation of his rod into a serpent. In place of the serpent [נָחָשׁ *nāḥāš*], which is more suited to the desert, where the sign was given to Moses, we have here a תַּנִּין *tannīn*, that is, a crocodile, which is more in keeping with the Egyptian environment.

10 And so it happened: *Moses and Aaron went in to Pharaoh, and they did so, as the Lord had commanded*; and when Pharaoh demanded that they should produce for themselves a wonder, Moses issued his order to Aaron, *and Aaron cast down his rod before Pharaoh and before his servants, and,* forthwith, without Aaron's uttering a word or performing any act, *it became a crocodile.* Pharaoh's servants are expressly mentioned here, in order to

11 prepare us for what immediately follows: *Then Pharaoh also called* ('Pharaoh also', as Moses had done with respect to Aaron) *for the wise men and the sorcerers, and they also* — these wise men

EXODUS VII 12

and sorcerers — namely, *the magicians of Egypt*, ('they also', imitating the marvel of Aaron's rod), *did the same by their secret* 12 *arts. For they cast down every man his rod, and they became crocodiles.*

In the formulation of these sentences, and even more so in the following clause, *but Aaron's rod swallowed up their rods*, there is clearly noticeable the intention to emphasize the difference between Aaron's feat and that of the Egyptian magicians (on the word חַרְטֻמִּים *ḥarṭummīm* [rendered here 'magicians'] see my forthcoming commentary on Gen. xli).* 'The wise men' [חֲכָמִים *ḥăkhāmīm*] — most cunning [מְחֻכָּמִים *mᵉḥukkāmīm*] binders of spells (compare Psa. lviii 5 [Hebrew, *v*. 6]) — are the same as 'the sorcerers', who make use of magic and achieve their purposes by means of לְהָטִים *lᵉhāṭīm* ['secret arts'], that is, by their mysterious incantations (the stem of לְהָטִים *lᵉhāṭīm* is לוּט *lūṭ* ['enwrap'; hence 'secret', 'mysterious'] with interpolated *Hē*', like אִמָּהוֹת *'immāhōth*' ['mothers'] in Hebrew; אֲבָהָת *'ăbhāhāth* ['fathers'] in Aramaic; *bhtm*, the plural of *bt* [= Hebrew בַּיִת *bayith* 'house'] from the stem *bwt*, in Ugaritic). Magic played an important role in the life and cult of the Egyptians, just as it did in the life and cult of the peoples of Canaan and of Mesopotamia (it seems that the stem כשׁף *kšp* in Hebrew [from which the terms for sorcery, sorcerers etc. are derived] is borrowed from Akkadian). An act of magic is actually an attempt to achieve a given object outside the laws of natural causation, which would otherwise be impossible. The magician believes that he has the power — or others believe so — to compel, by his acts and utterances, the forces of nature and the demons, and even the gods, to do his will. Obviously, there is no room for such views in Israel's religion. The laws of nature were established by the Creator, and it is impossible for a human being to change them in any way; *a fortiori* it is unthinkable that a man should be able to force God to do anything contrary to His will. Consequently, the Torah is absolutely opposed to all forms of magic (see, for example, Deut. xviii 9 ff.); and sometimes the Bible uses the term 'sorcery' as a derogatory designation for idolatry, which is closely linked to magic (see, for instance, ii Kings ix 22). In the narrative before us we observe, on the one hand, Aaron, who, after casting his rod to the ground, does nothing and says nothing, but only waits that the Lord his God, who rules over nature according to His will,

* The author died before the publication of this section of his commentary. *Tr.*

EXODUS VII 12

should do that which He wishes; and, on the other hand, the magicians, who can change their rods into crocodiles only by means of their magical and secret arts. Israel's superiority is underlined by the denoument, when Aaron's crocodile swallowed the crocodiles of the magicians. There is undoubtedly here an element of irony and satire.

We have already noted (pp. 46 f.) that Egypt was familiar with the story of the magician, a skilled artificer, who formed a crocodile out of wax and by his magic arts gave it life. The Bible narrative seeks to show that nothing that the Egyptian magicians were able to do was beyond the power of the servants of the Lord. The latter, however, did not make use of magic but relied upon the will of God, if He desired the wonder. Nay more, it lay within the power of Israel's God to nullify all the works of the magicians.

13 But Pharaoh's heart, notwithstanding, was not softened. *And Pharaoh's heart was hardened* — it remained hard as before — *and Pharaoh did not listen to them* — to Moses and Aaron — *as the Lord had spoken*, for He told them at the outset (*v.* 4): 'But Pharaoh will not listen to you.' It may well be that our text has 'to them' instead of 'to Moses and Aaron' in order to recapitulate [in indirect speech] the precise wording of *v.* 4.

Since the interview concluded with Pharaoh's refusal, the only course left was to continue to act in accordance with the original plan, and to inflict on Pharaoh and his people the plagues that would punish them for the bondage of Israel and impel them, step by step, to the decision to free the enslaved people. How these plagues were brought upon them, will be narrated in the continuation of the section.

FIRST PARAGRAPH

BLOOD

(VII 14–25)

The Divine communication to Moses begins with a statement of
14 fact: *Pharaoh's heart is stubborn* (apparently כָּבֵד *kābhēdh* [literally, 'heavy; rendered 'stubborn'] is either the participle or an adjective, but not the perfect), and *he refuses to let the people go*. The reference to Pharaoh's heart and its stubbornness at the beginning of

this first paragraph links it to the end of the prologue, namely, the preceding verse (*v.* 13), which states: 'And Pharaoh's heart was hardened.'

Such being the existing situation, that Pharaoh's heart is obdurate and that he declines to let the people go, there is no other way but to begin to implement the programme of the plagues.

15 To this end Moses is instructed: *Go to Pharaoh in the morning*, at the time when he leaves his palace to take his usual stroll by the river. *Lo, he goes out to the water* (the use of the word הִנֵּה *hinnē* ['Lo'] before a participle without the pronoun הוּא *hū*' is normal in Biblical diction: compare, for instance, Gen. xxiv 30; xxxvii 15; xxxviii 24; xli 1, and numerous other examples. Possibly the ancient pronunciation was הִנּוֹ *hinnō* ['Lo he']); *and you shall stand to meet him* — uprightly, unawed by the king's presence. The phrase that indicates the venue, *by the river's brink*, recalls the use of the identical expression earlier (ii 3); in both cases the moment is one of incipient redemption. Even the verb, 'you shall stand', employed here recalls the verb, 'took her stand', that occurs there (ii 4). *And the rod which was turned to a serpent shall you take in your hand*: not the rod of Aaron that was changed to a crocodile, but Moses' rod (iv 2–4),

16 *And you shall say to him*, as a warning: *YHWH, the God of the Hebrews, has sent me*, before now, *to you saying, Let My people go* (there is a word-play here שְׁלָחַנִי *šᵉlāḥanī* ['has sent me'] — שַׁלַּח *šallaḥ* ['let go']) *that they may serve Me in the wilderness* — serve Me and not you, for they are My servants, not yours. *And, behold, hitherto you have not listened* (as is stated at the end of the prologue, *v*. 13). Therefore, I come to deliver to you a further message

17 in the name of Him that sent Me: *Thus says YHWH: By this you shall know*—you who at first said, 'I do not know *YHWH*' — *that I am YHWH; behold I* — Moses (the boundaries between the Sender and the messenger are, as it were, somewhat blurred) — *will smite with the rod that is in my hand upon the waters which are in the Nile, and they shall be turned to blood*. The Nile, which gives to the land of Egypt its fertility, is regarded by the Egyptians as a god, nevertheless you will see, Pharaoh, that at the command of my God, who is truly God and has dominion over all things, I shall smite this 'divine' creature, after which its nature will degenerate and its waters will cease to be a source of blessing to Egypt as usual. The meaning is not that the water would actually become blood, but that it would resemble blood in its colour and appear-

ance. This is a phenomenon that occurs from time to time in the Nile; due to the presence of a great quantity of minute fungi and other red vegetable matter, or tiny insects of reddish hue, its water turns red and becomes unfit to drink. Similarly, the other plagues are also not actual deviations from the laws of nature, but brought about by the use of natural phenomena at the opportune moment and on an unusually large scale, until it becomes clearly evident that they have a specific significance.

The striking with the rod is not regarded here as a magical act, for Moses does not assert that he himself turns the water into blood; he only declares in the name of the Lord that the water will be changed at the will of the Lord, which is not, of course dependent on the movement of the rod. The act of smiting with the rod is intended —

(a) to indicate the commencement of the portent, which thereupon takes place in accordance with God's will, which Moses had previously announced.

(b) to symbolize actual 'striking', wherewith the Lord strikes Egypt and its gods (compare *v.* 25: 'after the Lord had smitten the Nile').

18 Moses has further to tell Pharaoh: *And the fish that is in the Nile shall die* — owing to the changes in the water — *and the river shall stink, and the Egyptians shall weary themselves* — that is, they will be unable (thus in *v.* 21 and *v.* 24: '[they] could not') *to drink water from the Nile*, both because the character of the water will change, and because the dead fish will make it even more malodorous.

Nor was that all. Just as Moses smote the main stream of the Nile, so Aaron would symbolically smite the remaining waters of Egypt. This is not a repetition of the previous story in a new form, as many expositors have supposed, but a new episode the purpose of which is to convince Pharaoh that the announcement previously made to him would not only be fully implemented, but even ex-
19 ceeded. This is the wording of the command given to Moses: *Say to Aaron, Take your rod, and stretch out your hand over the waters of Egypt, over their canals* (the rivers and canals [literally, 'Niles'] are the aqueducts and branch-streams of the Nile), *over their pools, and over their reservoirs, that they may become blood.* The Bible does not, of course, mean to say that Aaron was to tour the whole land of Egypt for this purpose, but that, standing in his place, he would wave his rod to and fro in different directions,

and in those directions to which he would point with his rod the water would turn to blood. As a result of all this, *there shall be blood in all the land of Egypt* (on the use of the word *all* in a hyperbolical sense, see below). The expression at the end of the verse, *in* [= on] *wood and in stone* means: 'even on wood and on stone', but it is not quite easy to understand to what the wood and stone refer. Vessels of wood and stone were uncommon in Egypt at that time; other explanations that have been suggested are improbably. When, however, we consider the fact that the term 'wood and stone' usually signifies idols in the Bible, and that the Egyptian priests used to wash the images of their gods in water every day early in the morning, we may possibly conjecture that the sense of the passage is that even the water that was poured that very morning over the idols turned to blood, thus providing another example of mockery at the expense of the Egyptian deities. With regard to the use of the preposition *Bēth* in the sense of *on*, compare viii 3 [Hebrew vii 29]: 'and the frogs shall come up both upon you, and upon your people, and upon all your servants.'

20 *And Moses and Aaron did so* — each of them — *as the Lord commanded*; *and he* — Moses — *lifted up the rod, and smote the waters that were in the Nile*, etc.; *and all the waters were turned,*
21 etc. *And the fish that was in the Nile died*, etc., *and the Egyptians could not*, etc. — after Moses' smiting. Furthermore, *and the blood was throughout all the land of Egypt* — after Aaron had stretched forth his hand with his rod; exactly as the Lord had spoken.

However, the magicians of Egypt tried their strength this time,
22 too: *And the magicians of Egypt did the same with their secret arts*: In those directions towards which Aaron had not stretched forth his hand, pure water was left, and these the magicians transformed into blood by their secret arts (here the word בְּלָטֵיהֶם *bᵉlāṭēhem*, 'secret arts', is spelt without a *Hē*' [after the *Lāmedh*], not as in *v.* 11). In this detail, also, there is an element of derision. What did the wise men of Egypt achieve by their efforts? They added plague upon plague! But Pharaoh was satisfied with the fact that his magicians were able to perform, with their magic arts, similar wonders to those shown by Moses and Aaron: *and Pharaoh's heart was hardened, and he did not listen to them*; *as the Lord had spoken* (the exact wording of the concluding verse of the prologue
23 is repeated here; see my commentary on *v.* 13). *And Pharaoh turned and went into his house, neither did he set his heart even to this* — he did not discern the fundamental difference between

EXODUS VII 23

the performance of the magicians and the marvel that Moses and Aaron had wrought.

After completing the account of the audience, the Bible adds a brief note on what the Egyptians were compelled to do in order to drink water. *And all the Egyptians dug* ('all' here, too, is hyperbolical) *round about the Nile for water to drink; for they could not,* etc. — a graphic picture that is also not free from satire.

25 So the position remained for a full week: *And seven days were fulfilled, after the Lord had smitten the Nile.*

The number seven, which is expressly mentioned in v. 25 (*seven days*), serves also to emphasize the principal word in the paragraph, namely, *Nile*, which occurs fourteen times in the course of the paragraph — twice times seven.

SECOND PARAGRAPH

FROGS

(VIII 1–15 [Hebrew, VII 26–VIII 11])

Chapter VIII

When the week came to an end, the word of the Lord came again to Moses: *And the Lord spoke to Moses, Go in to Pharaoh* — right into his house (this provides the nexus with the preceding paragraph, which relates, at the end, that Pharaoh 'went into his house'). There, in the midst of his magnificent palace, where he dwells like a god, you will once again declare My words before him: *Let My people go, that they may serve Me* (see above, on v. 16). *And if you refuse to let them go, behold, I will plague all your borders with frogs.* In the formulation of the warnings given in connection with the plagues, we usually find הִנֵּה אָנֹכִי *hinnē 'ānōkhī* ['behold I'] followed by the participle, and the verb changes from plague to plague. In connection with the first plague it is said: 'behold, I will smite' (and above already, in iv 23, we read: 'behold, I will slay'), and here: 'behold, I will plague.' Other variations will appear further on.

The episode of the frogs also corresponds to normal Egyptian phenomena. Every year after the inundation of the Nile, the number of frogs in the receding waters is enormous. Also in this

EXODUS VIII 4 [Heb. VII 29]

case, therefore, the Bible has in mind an endemic affliction of the country, which occurred that year on an exceptional scale and at the right conjuncture. The explanation current in the Middle Ages that by these frogs crocodiles are meant is certainly incorrect, for crocodiles would not make their home in human beds, ovens and kneading-bowls (viii 3 [Hebrew, vii 28]), and cannot easily be gathered in heaps (viii 14 [Hebrew v. 10]).

The Egyptians attributed to the frogs, which swarmed in the waters in countless numbers, a divine power, and regarded them as a symbol of fertility. One of the goddesses of the Egyptian pantheon, Ḥeḳet, the spouse of the god Khnum, who is depicted in the form of a woman with a frog's head, was held to blow the breath of life into the nostrils of the bodies that her husband fashioned on the potter's wheel from the dust of the earth (see above, on i 16). The Pentateuchal narrative intends to convey that Israel's God alone rules the world, and that He only bestows on His creatures, according to His will, the power of fertility, and that these frogs, which were considered by the Egyptians a symbol of fecundity, can be transformed, if He so desires (and particularly as a result of their overabundant prolificacy), from a token of blessing to one of blight.

3 [28] *And the Nile shall swarm with frogs*, at the will of Him who said in the days of creation, 'Let the waters swarm with swarms of living creatures' (Gen. i 20), *and they shall go up* out of the water in their multitudes, and they shall even come into places where they are not normally found, even into the palace of the king and his innermost chambers: *and they shall come into your house, and into your bedchamber, and upon your bed*, despite the precautions of your attendants. Likewise, they shall come into *the houses of thy servants*, and, needless to say, *upon your people*, that means, into the houses of your people, although frogs are fond of wet and cold places, they will be found — so great shall their number be — even *in your ovens*, which are kindled for the baking of bread, and *in your kneading-bowls*, in which the dough becomes warm and leavened. Nor is this all. The frogs will be so numerous and daring that they will even climb up people's legs, even up the legs

4 [29] of his majesty himself: *and the frogs shall climb up both upon you, and upon your people, and upon all your servants* (on the expression — עָלָה בְּ- *'ālā b^e*-— ['climb up'] compare Cant. vii 9: 'I will climb up [אֶעֱלֶה *'e^{e}ĕle*] into the palm-tree'). The mocking satire is obvious. Here the word צְפַרְדְּעִים *ṣ^{e}phard^{ee}îm* is masculine (so,

101

EXODUS VIII 4 [Heb. VII 29]

too, *vv.* 13–14 [Hebrew, *vv.* 9–10]), although normally it is feminine.

Moses did as the Lord commanded him (this is self-understood, and in Biblical narrative prose there is no need to mention the execution of such a command explicitly, when the sequel makes this clear), and came to Pharaoh and told him what the Lord had said. Pharaoh, however, remained obdurate, and Moses and Aaron departed from him (this is definitely shown by *v.* 8 [Hebrew, *v.* 4]: 'Then Pharaoh called for Moses and Aaron'). Subsequently the word of the Lord came again to Moses, and enjoined him to do what he had previously announced to Pharaoh (*v.* 5 [Hebrew, *v.* 1] continues the narrative; it does not duplicate it, as many exegetes have supposed): *And the Lord said unto Moses, Say unto Aaron, Stretch forth your hand with your rod over the streams over the canals, and over the pools* (a parallelism with the preceding paragraph, vii 19), *and cause frogs to come up upon the land of Egypt.* This time, too, as in the case of the first plague, the announcement made at the outset would not only be fully implemented, but it would even be exceeded; not only shall the frogs come up from the Nile proper, but also from all its streams and canals and reservoirs. Aaron did so: *And Aaron stretched out his hand —* with his rod *— over the waters of Egypt —* in various directions *— and the frogs came up and covered the land of Egypt.* This hyperbolic expression comprehends everything, and there is no necessity to reiterate the details listed in *vv.* 3–4 [Hebrew, vii 28–29]. Needless to say, the meaning is not that it was all accomplished in a moment. According to rabbinic Haggadah, this plague also lasted seven days, like the first. Possibly, this was also stated in the ancient tradition. Gradually, village after village, city after city, street by street, house by house, room by room, everything became filled with frogs in the course of a few days. Then Pharaoh began to fear and called the magicians to take action.

They did do something; but their action was not a cure for the plague. *And the magicians did the same by their secret arts —* just as they did after Moses' proclamation *— and they brought up the frogs —* additional frogs *— upon the land of Egypt.* They may have boasted, saying to Pharaoh: Behold, we, too, can do what these foreigners have done. But without doubt Pharaoh was not pleased with his magicians; he was not asking for a supplementary plague, but for a cure of the affliction. But this was not within their power.

Then Pharaoh was compelled to turn to Moses and Aaron. The

proud king had no option but to recall the men whom he had previously banished from his presence with the harsh words: 'Get you to your burdens' (v 4), and ask them to pray for him: *Then Pharaoh called for Moses and Aaron, and said, Entreat YHWH* (so speaks now he who had insolently declared: 'I do not know the Lord' [v 2]), *that He take away the frogs from me and from my people*, whereupon I shall accede to your request, *and I will let the people go that they may sacrifice to YHWH*. Pharaoh begins and ends his speech with the name of *YHWH*. He is humble now, or seems to be so.

⁹ Moses' reply is characterized both by dignity and complete trust in his God. He knows that the Lord is ready to receive penitents, and if Pharaoh is truly humble, as would appear from his words, the Lord will certainly grant his supplication; and if he is not sincere, the Lord will assuredly prove to him that He is all-powerful. Therefore, *Moses said to Pharaoh, Have this glory over me*; my trust in my God is so great that I may leave to you the glory of chosing the time (for the meaning of the idiom הִתְפָּאֵר עַל *hithpā'ēr 'al* [literally, 'glorify oneself'; rendered here: 'Have this glory over'] compare Jud. vii 2; Isa. x 15; other interpretations are also possible, like that of Tur-Sinai [Torczyner]: 'to cast lots'): *against what time shall I entreat for you, and for your servants, and for your people, that the frogs be destroyed from you and your houses*; until *they remain in the Nile only*? However, Moses had received no previous instructions for this; hence he chooses his words carefully, and does not enquire when the frogs should be removed, but against what time he should pray for them to be taken away. Pharaoh is quick to reply and fixes the earliest possible time: *And he said* — instantly — *against tomorrow. And Moses said* forthwith, *According to your word be it; that you may know that there is none like the Lord our God*. He then adds in detail: *And the frogs shall depart from you, and from your houses, and from your servants, and from your people; they shall remain in the Nile only* (the recapitulation emphasizes that it will actually happen as he had promised to ask of the Lord).

¹² After this solemn promise, *Moses and Aaron went out from Pharaoh* to pray in solitude. *And Moses cried to the Lord* — an expression used specifically for prayer for deliverance from danger (compare, for example, xiv 15; xvii 4); for Moses' mission was in great danger if his prayer *concerning the frogs which he had appointed for Pharaoh* were not answered, that is, according to the custo-

mary interpretation, concerning the frogs with which the Lord had smitten Pharaoh, or possibly: concerning the time of the removal of the frogs that Moses had fixed for Pharaoh. His prayer was heard: *And the Lord did according to the word of Moses* (the treble use of דָּבָר *dābhār* ['word'] is noteworthy: Moses says to Pharaoh: 'according to your *word*'; he prays עַל דְּבַר *'al d^ebhar* [literally, 'on the word of'; rendered: 'concerning'] the frogs'; and the Lord does 'according to the *word* of Moses'); *and the frogs died* (another example of צְפַרְדְּעִים *s^ephard^{ee}īm* ['frogs'] used as a masculine noun [this is shown by the masculine form of the Hebrew verb 'died']); first they disappeared *from the houses*, where they had entered last, then *from the courts*, and finally even *from the fields*, and remained only in the Nile. *And they* — the Egyptians — *piled them* (again the frogs are masculine), that is, the dead frogs, *in heaps* (similar expressions are found in Jud. xv 16, and in the Ugaritic Tablet, I* AB, line 19; in all these citations, the reference is to dead bodies); *and the land stank*, just as the Nile had become malodorous on account of the dead fish (vii 18, 21). Moses and Aaron had not made the savour of the Israelites stink, as the foremen had accused them (v 21), but only the waters and the land of the Egyptians.

However, Pharaoh's submission was only a pretence, for the sake of deliverance from an evil plight. When the frogs were removed, *and Pharaoh saw that the respite had come*, that is, relief from the affliction, *he* immediately *made his heart stubborn*, denied his promises, *and did not listen to them* — to Moses and Aaron — *as the Lord had spoken* — the identical wording found at the end of the preceding paragraphs.

THIRD PARAGRAPH

GNATS

(VIII 16–19 [Hebrew, *vv.* 12–15])

The third plague came, as we stated earlier, without warning. Pharaoh deserved this treatment because at the time of the previous plague he had given a false promise and had not kept his word.

Since Pharaoh is not given a warning in this instance, Moses was at once commanded to turn to Aaron: *Say to Aaron, Stretch*

EXODUS VIII 18 [Heb. 14]

out your rod, etc. Emphasis is given here to the word-play between the verb נְטֵה *nᵉṭē* ['stretch out'] and the substantive מַטֶּה *maṭṭe*, which is formed from the same stem; whereas in *v.* 17 [13] the sentence is given in full: 'and Aaron stretched out [וַיֵּט *wayyēṭ*] his hand with his rod [מַטֵּהוּ *maṭṭēhū*]', and so, too, in other passages. The Bible is fond of such variations; there is no need, therefore, to emend the text and to approximate it to that of *v.* 17 [13] on the basis of the Septuagint and the Samaritan Pentateuch, since it is the customary practice of these versions to harmonize the verses. This time Aaron is commanded to smite the dust of the earth: *and smite the dust of the earth, that it* — the dust — *may become* כִּנִּים *(kinnīm) throughout all the land of Egypt.*

What these כִּנִּים *kinnīm* were, is not precisely clear. Undoubtedly, they were insects, but apparently not those called by this name today [i.e. 'lice']. Since they issued from the dust of the earth, and the dust brought them upon man and beast, it appears that they were capable of flying and had wings. Perhaps some kind of fly or gnat is meant, for they, too, are an endemic affliction of Egypt (possibly it was the kind called by the Egyptians *ḥnms*).

17 [13] *And they* — Moses and Aaron — *did so*, that is, Moses spoke to Aaron, *and Aaron stretched out his hand with his rod, and smote the dust of the earth, and there were gnats* (הַכִּנָּם *hakkinnām*: this form interchanges with that of כִּנִּים *kinnīm* [the normal plural]; it has a collective significance, and hence, as in Arabic, it is connected with a verb in the feminine) *upon man, and upon beast.* The verse concludes with a hyperbolic general statement: *all the dust of the earth became gnats throughout all the land of Egypt.*

18 [14] The sentence, *And the magicians did so with their secret arts to bring forth gnats, but they could not*, is, on the face of it, difficult. If they did so, then they could, and if they could not, then they did not do so. Many forced explanations have been advanced, but they are improbable. Possibly we may be able to find a solution to the paradox if we examine the narrative in Gen. xl concerning the dreams of the chief butler and the chief baker. After Joseph had said to the butler: 'Within three days Pharaoh will lift up your head, and restore you to your office' [*v.* 13], he begins to tell the chief baker: 'Within three days Pharaoh will lift up your head'...... [*v.* 19], and at the first blush we understand (and so the poor butler was likely to understand) the meaning of the words in the sense of the identical words that Joseph had said to the baker, but he goes on to say, 'from off you', whence we learn

retrospectively that the sense of the earlier expression was different from what it appeared to connote at first. The same obtains here. In the two preceding paragraphs it is stated, 'and the magicians did the same', signifying that they achieved similar results to those obtained by Moses and Aaron; and when we read the *ipsissima verba* in our verse, we think that ostensibly this is also the meaning of the words here, to wit, that the magicians likewise succeeded in their efforts *to bring forth gnats* from dust of the earth. But when we subsequently read, *but they could not*, we learn retrospectively that the meaning of the words, *And the magicians did the same... to bring forth* is different from what we at first supposed. The sense is this: *And the magicians did the same* — just as Moses and Aaron endeavoured to carry out their work faithfully, so the magicians on their part made every effort to do their work, as it were, faithfully, by means of their secret arts, in order *to bring forth the gnats* — that is, to destroy them — *but they could not*. This makes the continuation of the passage clear: *and the gnats were upon man and upon beasts* — as they were before, so they also remained after all the efforts of the magicians.

19 [15] Thereupon the magicians were perplexed: *Then the magicians said unto Pharaoh, This is the finger of God*. They admit that there is a power here greater than theirs; and that Moses and Aaron are not working with their own capacities, as they, the magicians, are doing, but that they are the agents of a Higher Power which a human being cannot oppose. But their admission is only a partial acknowledgement. They do not say, 'the finger of *YHWH*', but only the finger of God. They do not yet concede the Divinity of *YHWH*, but merely acknowledge that there is manifested here some unnamed Divine Power. Nor do they say 'the hand of God', but just 'the finger of God', that is, they do not admit that it is a real act of God, such as a man performs with his hand, but only that it is a token or subsidiary form of assistance such as a person can render with one finger. Some time ago, several scholars thought that in an Akkadian letter discovered at Taanach there was to be found an expression signifying 'the finger of *Aširat*', which was used in the sense of 'the work of the goddess Asherah'; but it has now been established that the text has to be read and interpreted differently.

Although the magicians made a partial admission, Pharaoh did not change his attitude; *and Pharaoh's heart was hardened*. This paragraph also ends, like the earlier ones, *and he did not listen to them; as the Lord had spoken*.

FOURTH PARAGRAPH

SWARMS OF FLIES

(VIII 20-32 [Hebrew, vv. 16-28])

20 [16] Here the second cycle of the Egyptian plagues begins, and the injunction given to Moses is similar to that given to him in connection with the first plague and of the first cycle: *And the Lord said to Moses, Rise up early in the morning, and stand before Pharaoh; lo, he comes forth to the water; and say to him once again: Thus says the Lord, Let My people go, that they may serve Me.* Apart from delivering the renewed demand in My name, you shall tell him that it is in his own interest to fulfil the request:
21 [17] *Else, if you will not let My people go, behold, I will send swarms of flies upon you, and upon your servants, and upon your people, and into your houses* (note the word-play: שַׁלַּח *šallaḥ* ['let go!', *Pi'el* imperative] — מְשַׁלֵּחַ *mᵉšallēaḥ* ['let go', *Pi'el* participle] — מַשְׁלִיחַ *mašliaḥ* ['send', *Hiph'il* participle]).

What exactly the עָרֹב *'ārōbh* [rendered: 'swarms of flies'] was is uncertain. As a rule the word is explained to mean a 'mixture' (the Rashbam's interpretation that it is connected with זְאֵבֵי עֶרֶב *zᵉ'ēbhē 'erebh* ['evening wolves'] is unacceptable), that is, different kinds of creatures mingled together — beasts of prey, according to one view; tiny parasites according to another. Since it is stated that the *'ārōbh* would be sent upon human beings and into houses, and that the houses would be full of them, the second explanation appears preferable. This interpretation, which regards the *'ārōbh* as parasites, like the gnats of the preceding plague, fittingly completes the division of the ten plagues into pairs, which we discussed in the introduction to this section (pp. 92 f.). The expression, *the land was ruined* (v. 20), is quite understandable even when applied hyperbolically to insects, and, *a fortiori*, the term 'devouring' used in Psa. lxxviii 45: 'He sent among them swarms of flies, which devoured them' is appropriate.

The *'ārōbh* will be sent in swarms, and not only *shall the houses of the Egyptians be filled with swarms of flies*, but also *the ground on which they are.* 'They' refers to the Egyptians, not to the houses (as the word is customarily understood), for the text seeks to emphasize, by repeating the word עָלֶיהָ *'ālehā* ['on which', 'where'; see next verse], the distinction that the Lord will make between

the ground on which they — the Egyptians — are and that on which
22 [18] the children of Israel live. *But on that day* — on which the swarms of flies are sent — *I will set apart the land of Goshen, where My people dwell* — the differentiation will be for their good — *so that no swarms of flies shall be there*. This discrimination will also serve another purpose: *that you may know that I am the Lord in the midst of the earth*, and that throughout the whole earth everything
23 [19] is done according to My will. *And I will put* thereby a *division* [literally, 'ransom'] — that is, a distinction — *between My people and your people*. Nor shall the matter be delayed: *By tomorrow shall this sign be*, namely, this wonder.

Here, too, as in the second paragraph, the Bible does not state explicitly what is self-understood, to wit, that Moses did that which he was enjoined to do, and that Pharaoh did not change his attitude. But this is obvious from what is subsequently stated about the coming of the plague in accordance with the announcement.
24 [20] First there is a general statement, *And the Lord did so* — as Moses had said to Pharaoh; thereafter follow the particulars: *there came great swarms of flies into the house of Pharaoh and into his servants' houses* (with some variations, as usual, from the wording in *v.* 21 [Hebrew, 17]), *and in all the land of Egypt the land was ruined by reason of the flies*.

The verb תִּשָּׁחֵת *tiššāḥēth* ['was ruined'] is the 'future' [imperfect] of narration, that is, it has a past signification. Ancient Hebrew did not distinguish, especially in poetic diction, between the tenses, as in modern Hebrew. Possibly this is one of the indications that the Torah made use of the ancient epic poem.

When Pharaoh saw that the severe plague was destroying his land, he endeavoured to find deliverance from it. But since he had already learned that his magicians, and even his gods, did not have the power to put an end to the plagues, he felt it neces-
25 [21] sary to turn to the Lord's envoys. *Then Pharaoh called Moses and Aaron, and said, Go, sacrifice to your God...*; from this opening statement it might have appeared as if he acceded to their request. But he added the words, *within the land*, which restricted the meaning of the preceding concession and almost nullified his consent. Moses immediately replied trenchantly and clearly: *It*
26 [22] *would not be right to do so* (a word-play between נָכוֹן *nākhōn* ['right'] and כֵּן *kēn* ['so'] is discernible here), *for we sacrifice to the Lord our God the abomination of the Egyptians*, that is, the animals that we offer up are deemed sacred by the Egyptians —

EXODUS VIII 29 [Heb. 25]

symbols of their gods. The phrase 'the abomination of the Egyptians' can be explained in two ways: (a) that the sacrifice of the sacred animals would appear an abominable thing in the eyes of the Egyptians; (b) that the word *abomination* could be a derogatory term for idols — we sacrifice the Egyptians idols. This being the case, Moses continues, *behold* (הֵן *hēn* = הִנֵּה *hinnē*) — picture to yourself— *we shall sacrifice the abomination of the Egyptians before their eyes* — here, within the land, according to your behest — *will they not stone us?* — can there be any doubt that they will stone us? However, we stand by our request to go forth from here: 27 [23] *We must go three days' journey into the wilderness and sacrifice there to the Lord our God as He will command us* — as He himself will enjoin, not as you say to us.

Thereupon Pharaoh was compelled, in order to achieve his object, to broaden the terms of his assent. But he is still anxious to save face, and he endeavours to preserve his dignity by the manner in which he phrases his answer and by the addition of a 28 [24] condition. He says: *I* [אָנֹכִי *'ānōkhī*] (the pronoun which is superfluous before the verb, comes to emphasize his majesty and to stress that all depends upon him) *will let you go, to sacrifice to the Lord your God in the wilderness*, but the question of the three days' journey he passes over in silence, and adds a restriction: *only you shall not go very far away*, as though to show that it is still he who decides. In consideration of his consent, he concludes with the request: *Make entreaty for me* — pray to your God to withdraw the swarms of flies from me.

Moses agrees to pray. But he, too, maintains his dignity, and 29 [25] begins by saying: *Behold, I am going out from you* (if you use אָנֹכִי *'ānōkhī* ['I'] then I shall do likewise) *and I will pray to the Lord that the swarms of flies may depart from Pharaoh, from his servants, and from his people tomorrow*.

He states at the outset that the withdrawal of the flies will take place very soon, but to avoid the impression that he is bowing to the wishes of the king and relying on the promise given him at this moment, he, too, adds a reservation. You (Pharaoh) said *only*; I say the same: *only let not Pharaoh play false again* — after the removal of the plague — *by not letting the people go to sacrifice to the Lord*. He now speaks in the third person, not in the second as he began, in order not to show disrespect by qualifying his words directly to the king, and in order, also, to lend greater weight to the point.

³⁰ [26] And so he did: *And Moses went out from Pharaoh and prayed to the Lord*; and this time, too, the Lord granted his prayer: *And* ³¹ [27] *the Lord did according to the word of Moses* — in accordance with his promise to Pharaoh (compare above, v. 13 [Hebrew, v. 9]). The general statement is now followed by a detailed account: *and removed the swarms of flies from Pharaoh, from his servants, and from his people; not one remained.*

But, notwithstanding that his request was fulfilled, Pharaoh did not keep his word: *But Pharaoh hardened his heart this time also*, and though he had said, 'I will let you go', *he did not let the people go*. The conclusion resembles the ending of the three preceding paragraphs, but it differs in omitting the words 'and did not listen to them', since Pharaoh's recalcitrance reaches a new peak here: he himself had said, *I will let you go*, but in fact *he did not let the people go.*

In this paragraph, too, an interesting use of the number seven is discernible: the principal word '*ārōbh* ['swarms of flies'] occurs in it seven times.

FIFTH PARAGRAPH

PEST

(IX 1-7)

Chapter IX

With a view to preparing the fifth plague, which is the second in the second cycle, Moses was given instructions in the same terms as for the preparation of the second plague in the first cycle:
1 *Go in to Pharaoh* — go right in to his palace — *and tell him* there, a second time: *Thus says the Lord, the God of the Hebrews, Let My people go, that they may serve Me*. Likewise on this occasion tell him that it is in his own interests to agree to let the children of
2 Israel go: *For if you refuse to let* them *go, and still hold them*, you will be punished, measure for measure, and the hand of the Lord
3 will take hold of all that belongs to you: *behold, the hand of the Lord will fall upon your cattle which are in the field*, etc. This time not just the finger of God will manifest itself, as your magicians said, but the whole hand of the Lord, in its full might. The participle

הוֹיָה *hōyā* [literally, 'be'; rendered here: 'fall'], which occurs at the beginning of the announcement as a new variation of the verb for 'sending a plague' (see on viii 2 [Hebrew, vii 27]), contains an allusion to the original signification of the Tetragrammaton, which is derived from the stem הָיָה — הָוָה *hāyā–hāwā*. After the general statement, *upon your cattle which are in the field*, particulars are given: *upon the horses, the asses, the camels, the herds, and the flocks*. The exact period when the camel was domesticated is still a matter of dispute among experts in this subject, but all are agreed that there were domesticated camels in Egypt in the time of Moses.

The action of the Lord's hand would take the form of an outbreak, among the cattle of Egypt, of a *very severe pest* — a terrible pestilence that would kill the animals. In this instance, too, the possessions of the Israelites would be differentiated to their advantage:

4 *But the Lord will make a distinction* (the use here of an expression similar to that found in viii 22 [Hebrew, v. 18] serves to link this paragraph to the one preceding) *between the cattle of Israel and the cattle of Egypt, so that nothing shall die of all that belongs to the children of Israel*. The word דָּבָר *dābhār* ['thing'; rendered: 'nothing'], the use of which here may appear surprising, since living creatures and not inanimate articles are spoken of, has been introduced for the sake of the word-play, דֶּבֶר *debher* ['pest'] — דָּבָר *dābhār* ['thing']. For the same purpose, the Bible employs *dābhār* three times in three consecutive verses; nor is it without reason that there occurs in *v.* 1 the variant וְדִבַּרְתָּ *wᵉdibbartā* ['and speak', 'and tell'] instead of וְאָמַרְתָּ *wᵉ'āmartā* ['and say'] above (viii 1 [Hebrew, vii 26]).

5 *And the Lord set* — through Moses, of course — *a time, saying, Tomorrow the Lord will do this thing in the Land*, and the *thing* [דָּבָר *dābhār*] is none other than the pest [דֶּבֶר *debher*]. Again we have a variation here: in the previous paragraph the fixing of the following day for the commencement of the plague occurs as part of the Lord's communication to Moses, whereas in this paragraph the fact that the Lord set this time is mentioned as an incident in the framework of the story.

6 And as it was announced beforehand even so it happened: *And on the morrow the Lord did this thing; all the cattle of the Egyptians died*. The word *all*, like similar examples that we have noted elsewhere, is used hyperbolically, for in subsequent plagues the cattle of the Egyptians is again referred to. The differentiation was also fulfilled: *but not one of the cattle of the Israelites died* (possibly

this, too, is an exaggeration). On the parallelism between the perfect and imperfect of the same verb (וַיָּמָת *wayyāmoth* [imperfect with *Wāw* consecutive] — מֵת *mēth* [perfect; both verbs are rendered: 'died']), see my Commentary on the Book of Genesis, Part I, *From Adam to Noah*, p. 27.

7 *And Pharaoh sent* to investigate what had happened in the land. The children of Israel, he would not *let go* [*Pi'el* of שָׁלַח *šālaḥ*]; but in order to receive news of what had taken place, he *sent* [*Qal* of the same verb] his servants. *And behold* — so the taskmasters who investigated the matter reported to him — *not so much as one of the cattle of the Israelites was dead*. In the preceding verse אֶחָד *'ekḥādh* ['one'] is used; here we have עַד אֶחָד *'adh 'eḥādh* [literally, 'up to one'; rendered: 'so much as one']; the Egyptian taskmasters greatly emphasize the fact. Nevertheless, the king does not give way: *But the heart of Pharaoh was stubborn, and he did not let the people go*. The end of our paragraph resembles that of the preceding paragraph. Possibly, here, too, there was a reason for this formulation, namely, the intention to underline the antithesis between the *sending* of the taskmasters and *refusal to let the children of Israel go* [literally, 'send away'].

SIXTH PARAGRAPH

BOILS

(IX 8–12)

8 Also prior to the sixth plague, which is the third of the second cycle, no warning was given, in the same way as there was no forewarning for the third plague of the first cycle. The Torah relates at once: *And the Lord said to Moses and Aaron, Take to you your two hands full of soot from a furnace*, etc. Why they had to take soot from a furnace we are not told, and at first it seems a strange thing to do. But we must bear in mind that the furnace is a factory where work is done by means of fire, and *inter alia* it is a kiln for burning bricks. Although prior to the Roman period, the Egyptians used mainly sun-dried bricks (adobe), yet the making of fired bricks was also practised by them. Particularly in buildings of the nineteenth dynasty — to which Rameses II, the Pharaoh of the oppression (see above, p. 11), belonged — and also of the

twentieth dynasty, fire-baked bricks have often been found. Now it was stated earlier that brick-making was one of the severe tasks imposed upon the Israelites in Egypt (i 14), even constituting their primary work (v 7-19), and apparently the two things — the labour and the plague — were interconnected. The smoke of the kiln is quickly dispersed in the air; and sooner or later the bricks are taken outside the factory; but the soot continues to cling to the walls of the kiln, at once an indication and a symbol of the hard work of the toilers. Hence it was in accord with poetic justice that the soot, which had been created, as it were, by the sweat of the enslaved people should inflict punishment on the bodies of the enslavers.

There is no difficulty to be seen in the fact that both Moses and Aaron were commanded to take their two hands full of soot from a kiln, whereas afterwards it is stated only, *and let Moses throw it toward heaven* — Moses alone — *in the sight of Pharaoh*, without a word being said as to what Aaron should do with his two hands full of ash. Apparently we must picture the episode to ourselves in the following manner: both of them were to come to the kiln, and both were to take two handfuls of soot from a furnace, and put it into a box or the like, in order to bring it before Pharaoh, for one may not come before Pharaoh with sooty hands; and when they would be in Pharaoh's presence, Moses would throw the soot from the vessel toward heaven. Proof of this is to be found in Lev. xvi 12: 'And he shall take a censer full of coals of fire from the altar before the Lord, and two handfuls of sweet incense beaten small; and he shall bring it within the veil'. It is obvious that if both hands of the priest were full of incense, he could not hold the censer; the meaning, then, must be (compare Yoma V 2) that the priest would fill both his hands with incense and then put it in the pan.

9 When Moses would throw the soot heavenward, it would become scattered in the air: *And it shall become fine dust over all the land of Egypt, and become*, when this dust settles *on man and beast, boils breaking out in sores, throughout all the land of Egypt*. Boils are an endemic affliction of Egypt (Deut. xxviii 27: 'the boils of Egypt'), a disease that spreads over the whole body (*ibid. v.* 35: 'with grievous boils... from the sole of your foot to the crown of your head'; Job ii 7: 'with loathsome sores from the sole of his foot to the crown of his head'); apparently it is to be identified with the disease called today 'small pox'. The word

113

שְׁחִין *šᵉḥin* ['boils'] is formed from the stem שָׁחַן *šāḥan*, which signifies 'to be hot', and may sometimes denote a single pustule found in one spot on the body (Lev. xiii 19: 'in the place of the boil'; similarly in ii Kings xx 7; Isa. xxxviii 21); but our paragraph speaks of 'boils breaking out in sores', that is, of an eruption over the whole body in the form of pustules [of small pox].

10 Moses and Aaron did as the Lord bade them: *So they took soot from a furnace, and stood before Pharaoh* — out of doors, after he had gone out of his palace — *and Moses threw it toward heaven,* and as the Lord said so it came to pass: *and it became boils of sores breaking out on man and beast.* There is a variation in the wording here ['boils of sores breaking out' instead of 'boils breaking out into sores', as in *v.* 9], the meaning being: boils consisting of sores [i.e. small pox pustules] that spread over the bodies of man and beast. The magicians, who accompanied Pharaoh, were not only unable to remove the disease from the land of Egypt, but they were unable to protect themselves. They, too, were smitten

11 with boils, and were compelled to leave the place: *And the magicians could not stand before Moses because of the boils.* There is a clear progression noticeable in the narrative with regard to the magicians: to begin with, when the first plagues were brought upon Egypt, the magicians endeavoured to perform the same kind of portents, even though the Egyptians did not benefit thereby; when the third plague occurred — the plague of gnats — they realized that all their efforts were in vain and they were forced to acknowledge the finger of God; subsequently, when new plagues were inflicted on Egypt, they looked on in silence; now they could not even stand silently. Although Moses and Aaron stood their ground (*v.* 10), yet the magicians were unable to stand before them, *for the boils were upon the magicians, and* so they were *upon all the Egyptians.*

Nevertheless, Pharaoh's heart remained as stubborn as at first:
12 *But the Lord hardened the heart of Pharaoh, and he did not listen to them; as the Lord had spoken to Moses.* Here the conclusion reverts to the phrasing found in the paragraphs of the first cycle.

SEVENTH PARAGRAPH

HAIL

(IX 13–35)

At this point, the third cycle commences; and as at the beginning of the two preceding cycles, so on this occasion, too, Moses is
13 commanded to stand before Pharaoh in the morning: *Then the Lord said to Moses, Rise up early in the morning and stand before Pharaoh*. The magicians could not stand before Moses, but Moses was able to stand with proud bearing before the king, and not merely to reiterate his demand in the Lord's name and to declare: *Thus says the Lord, the God of the Hebrews, Let My people go, that they may serve Me*, but to threaten him with even worse consequences than
14 before: *For this time* — in the cycle of plagues beginning now, and in the climactic plague that will follow it — *I will send all my plagues upon your heart, and upon your servants and upon your people.* If you will not *release* My people, I shall *release* upon you — measure for measure — all My plagues, terribly severe plagues, which will go straight to your heart and to the heart of your servants and people (hinting at the last plague, the plague of the first-born), *that you may know* — you who said, 'I do not know the Lord' (v 2) — that there is none *like Me* [כָּמֹנִי *kāmōnī*] *in all the earth* (הָאָרֶץ *hāʾareṣ*, which here connotes 'the world' [not 'land']: there is none like Me among your gods, and I alone can perform deeds that have not their like in any part of the world. Two parallels to this expression at the beginning of our paragraph are found in the continuation (v. 18: 'such as [כָּמֹהוּ *khāmōhū*] had not been in Egypt', etc.; v. 24: 'such as [כָּמֹהוּ *khāmōhū*] had never been in all the land of Egypt', etc.); similar examples will be found further on (x 14: 'before them there was no *such* [כָּמֹהוּ *kāmōhū*] locusts as they, etc.'; xi 6: '*such as* [כָּמֹהוּ *kāmōhū*] there has never been, nor shall be *like it* [וְכָמֹהוּ *wᵉkhāmōhū*] any more'). After the division of the Sea of Reeds, the children of Israel will proclaim in their song (xv 11): 'Who is *like Thee* [כָּמֹכָה *khāmōkhā*], O Lord, among the gods? Who is *like Thee* [כָּמֹכָה *kāmōkhā*], majestic in holiness, terrible in glorious deeds, doing wonders?'

Since the third cycle is severer and more decisive than the earlier ones, the account of the plagues that it comprises is longer and fuller than that of the preceding plagues. Even in regard to the

third plague of the cycle, which comes without warning, the text is not as terse as it was with reference to the third plague of the first and second cycles. In the same way, Moses' address to Pharaoh is more expansive than formerly. He begins with a preliminary
15 explanation, in the Lord's name, of his actions: *For* — had I wished it — *by now I should have put forth My hand* — I should long ago have put forth My hand with its full might (again the verb שָׁלַח *šālaḥ* [literally, 'send'; rendered: 'put forth'] is used; and once more mention is made of 'the hand of the Lord' as in *v.* 3) — *and struck you and your people with pestilence* — I should have smitten both you and your people, and not your cattle alone; and had I done so, you would have perished, you and your people:
16 *and you would have been cut off from the earth.* But I did not wish to do this; not because My power — Heaven forfend! — is inadequate; nor because you are undeserving of such a punishment, but for an entirely different reason: *for this purpose have I maintained you alive, to show you*, more clearly, *My power, so that My name may be declared in all the earth*, that is, in order that you may learn a lesson from the final plagues, and that, together with you, the rest of humanity throughout the world may be instructed.

The concluding phrases of the three consecutive verses 14, 15, 16 (*in all the earth* — *from the earth* — *in all the earth*) parallel one another, the first and the last of these — the beginning and end of the sequence — being completely identical. The mention of the plague of pestilence in *v.* 15 serves to link this paragraph with the fifth; whilst the word הֶעֱמַדְתִּיךָ *heʿĕmadhtīkhā* [literally, 'caused you to stand'; rendered: 'maintained you alive'] in *v.* 16 establishes a nexus between our paragraph and the sixth (*v.* 10: *and stood*; *v.* 11: *stand*).

After this explanation, Moses continues to speak in the Lord's
17 name as follows: *You are still* — even now, despite the number of plagues that you have suffered — *exalting yourself against My people* — you are still elevating yourself and rising up against them in ever greater measure (for this use of the preposition *Bēth* [בְּעַמִּי] *bʿammī*, 'against My people'] compare Micah vii 6: 'the daughter rises up against her mother [בְאִמָּהּ *bhʿimmāh*]' and similar passages) — *and will not let them go.* Therefore I am about to inflict upon you — making the punishment fit the crime — retri-
18 bution from on high downwards: *Behold, tomorrow at this time* [כָּעֵת *kāʿēth*, literally, 'at the like time'] *I will rain down very heavy hail.* The time was also fixed beforehand, so that it should

EXODUS IX 20-21

be manifest on the morrow that it was not a chance occurrence. The expression 'very heavy' corresponds to that in *v.* 3: 'a very severe pest' (כָּבֵד מְאֹד *kābhēdh mᵉʾōdh* in both passages).

The hail, a phenomenon that occurs in Egypt only at rare intervals, will be so severe, as to merit the description: *such as never has been in Egypt from the day it was founded until now.* These concluding words, as well as the final clause of *v.* 24 ('since it became a nation'), resemble expressions that were in common use in Egyptian. In a document, for example, from the time of Thothmes III it is written: 'More than all the things that were in the country since it was founded.' The word הִוָּסְדָה *hiwwāsᵉdhā* ['was founded'], which is spelt here without a *Mappīq* in the final *Hē'*, and is preceded by the word הַיּוֹם *hayyōm* ['the day'] with the definite article, is certainly not the infinitive. Possibly, the Masoretes intended a rare form of the *Niphʿal* perfect, just as we find, in the case of the absolute infinitive, the form הִקָּטֹל *hiqqāṭōl* alongside the form נִקְטֹל *niqtōl*. The Samaritan Recension, in order to remove the difficulty of the rare form, reads: לְמִיּוֹם הִוָּסְדָה *lᵉmiyyōm hiwwāsᵉdhā* ['from the day it was founded'].

19 *Now, therefore* — in view of all this, Pharaoh is given good advice, so that the plague may not harm people, nor the cattle that escaped the plague of the pest: *Send, get your cattle and all that you have in the field into safe shelter.* You do not wish to *let* the children of Israel *go*, but in your own interests and in the interests of your people you will surely *let* a notification *go out* to your servants that they should get their cattle and the labourers working in the field into safe shelter (the stem of הָעֵז *hāʿēz*, 'get into safe shelter', is עוּז *ʿūz*, Arabic عوذ *ʿwdh*); *for every man and beast that will be found in the field* will suffer calamity: *the hail shall come down upon them, and they shall die.* The reference to man and beast provides a link with the preceding paragraph (*vv.* 9–10).

So far the words of the Lord, which were delivered by Moses, of course, to Pharaoh. In *vv.* 20–21 we are told what the servants of Pharaoh did or did not do after they had learnt of the Divine announcement. In both verses, contrary to the usual order followed in Biblical narrative, the subject precedes the predicate, in order to emphasize that what some did others did not do, as we find, for example, in Gen. xiii 12: '*Abram* dwelt in the land of Canaan, while *Lot* dwelt among the cities of the valley and moved his
20-21 tent as far as Sodom.' A certain section, *those who feared the word of*

117

EXODUS IX 20–21

the Lord among the servants of [עֲבְדֵי *'abhdhē*] *Pharaoh* — these were the minority (compare v. 30) — *made their slaves* (עֲבָדָיו *'ăbhādhāw*: here actual slaves are meant, i.e., the servants of Pharaoh's servants) *and their cattle flee into the houses*; whereas the rest, *who did not regard the word of the Lord*, were unconcerned *and left their slaves and their cattle in the field.*

Now the following day Moses was commanded to indicate by 22 a signal when the plague would begin. *And the Lord said to Moses, stretch forth your hand upon heaven* — that is, to heaven, toward heaven — *that there may be hail in all the land of Egypt, upon man and beast* — that is, of those who did not regard the word of the Lord — *and every plant of the field throughout the land of* 23 *Egypt.* And so Moses did: *Then Moses stretched forth his rod toward heaven* (following the normal Biblical practice, the wording in this verse varies from that in v. 22; in the Septuagint, which always endeavours to harmonize the verses, 'hand' instead of 'rod' is found here also); *and the Lord sent thunder* [literally, 'gave voices'] *and hail*, etc.

In poetic diction 'the voice of the Lord' means thunder (Psa. xxix 3: 'The voice of the Lord is upon the waters; the God of glory thunders'), and the idiom נָתַן קוֹל *nāthan qōl* ['give voice'] is, in particular, frequently used in this sense (ii Sam. xxii 14; Psa. xviii 13 [Hebrew, v. 14]; xlvi 6 [Hebrew, v. 7]; lxviii 33 [Hebrew, v. 34]; and so forth). This expression was inherited from the Canaanite literary tradition, which is known to us both from the Ugaritic texts, where we read that Baal 'gives voice' from heaven, and also from the El-Amarna letters written in Akkadian (*nadânu rigma*). Apparently this is one of the linguistic relics of the epic poem pertaining to the Exodus, which, as I have stated earlier, predated the Torah.

The second object, 'hail', even though the verb נָתַן *nāthan* ['give'] is not particularly suited to it, is joined here to the first object, 'voices', in accordance with the rhetorical usage called by the Greeks 'zeugma'.

In addition to thunder and hail, our passage also mentions lightening: *and fire ran down to the earth*; compare: Psa. xviii 13 [Hebrew, v. 14]: 'The Lord also thundered in the heavens, and the Most High uttered His voice, hailstones, and coals of fire'. This seems to be a traditional poetic portrayal of a severe storm; in this description, as well as in the rare verbal form תִּהֲלַךְ *tihălakh* [literally, 'went'; rendered: 'ran down'] (compare Psa. lxxiii 9 in the Hebrew) instead of the usual form תֵּלֶךְ *tēlēkh*, there are still to be seen traces of the epic poem referred to.

The verse continues: *And the Lord rained hail upon the land of Egypt* — the sentence is not redundant, even after it has been stated that 'the Lord sent thunder and hail'. To begin with the text speaks of what the Lord prepared in heaven, causing thunder to be heard and bringing forth hail from His storehouses ('the storehouses of the hail' in Job xxxviii 22); thereafter we are informed that this hail was rained down specifically upon the land of Egypt. In *v.* 24 the third stage is reached; the hail and the fire of the lightning reach the earth: *So there was, upon the face of the land of Egypt, hail, and fire flashing continually in the midst of the hail*, and the hail was, as had been announced at the outset, *very heavy, such as had never been in all the land of Egypt since it became a nation* (see *v.* 18 and my annotations thereto). The phrase אֵשׁ מִתְלַקַּחַת *'ēš mithlaqqaḥath* [literally, 'fire taking hold of itself'; rendered: 'fire flashing continually'] is found also in Ezekiel i 4, where, too, a storm is described. The fire of lightning is termed מִתְלַקַּחַת *mithlaqqaḥath* ['taking hold of itself'] because it does not travel in a direct line, but in zigzag fashion, as though it took hold of itself, every now and again, to turn back or to turn aside.

After the phenomenon has been depicted, a description is given of the results produced: *The hail struck down everything that was in the field throughout the land of Egypt, both man and beast*, who had been left in the field (*v.* 21); *and the hail struck down every plant of the field, and shattered every tree of the field* — that is, shattered its branches. On the use of the imperfect and perfect of the same verb (וַיַּךְ *wayyakh* — הִכָּה *hikkā* [both translated, 'struck']) to form a parallelism see *v.* 6 and my commentary thereon. The word כָּל *kol* ['all', 'every'], which occurs five times in succession (*vv.* 24–25), is used here, too, in a hyperbolic sense, not literally; further on reference will still be made to the plants of the field and the fruit of the trees (ix 32; x 5, 12, 15). The substantive שָׂדֶה *śādhe* occurs three times in *v.* 25, and in each instance the expression כָּל [וְאֶת־]וְאֵת (*wᵉ*)*'ēth* [or: *wᵉeth*] *kol* ['and (followed by the sign of the defined accusative) all'] comes before the preceding word:

'ēth kol ăšer baśśādhe	אֵת כָּל־אֲשֶׁר בַּשָּׂדֶה
wᵉ'ēth kol 'ēśebh haśśādhe	וְאֵת כָּל־עֵשֶׂב הַשָּׂדֶה
wᵉ'eth kol 'ēṣ haśśādhe	וְאֶת־כָּל עֵץ הַשָּׂדֶה

This is certainly not coincidental: we hear three mighty blows, as it were, one after the other.

Although the hail brought disaster on the land of Egypt, yet one
26 region remained tranquil and secure. *Only in the land of Goshen, where the children of Israel were, there was no hail.* In the account of the plague of hail and its consequences אֶרֶץ מִצְרַיִם *'ereṣ Miṣrayim* ['land of Egypt'] occurs five times, once we find the word אַרְצָה *'arṣā* ['to the earth'], and in the seventh reference [to אֶרֶץ *'ereṣ*, 'land', 'earth'] mention is made of אֶרֶץ גֹּשֶׁן *'ereṣ Gōšen* ['land of Goshen'], enjoying quiet and security, a picture that recalls the Seventh Day, the day of rest, which comes after the six days of hard work imposed on mankind.

The news of what was happening in the land reached Pharaoh's
27 palace and alarmed the king. *Then Pharaoh sent* (this time he did *send* [the same Hebrew stem as for 'let go']) *and called Moses and Aaron*, and confessed to them according to the customary confessional formula: *I have sinned*. But he still remains arrogant, and declines to acknowledge his earlier and primary sins; hence he adds: *this time*, as though he had no other sin on his conscience except his refusal on this occasion. He also adds a few words of a legalistic nature, as though to stress that, in the final analysis, it is only an issue between plaintiff and defendant, and it is only a question of deciding which of the two is in the right. *The Lord is in the right* — I admit now that He is justified in requiring me to let His people go — *and I and my people*, who refused to fulfil this demand, *are in the wrong* [רְשָׁעִים *rešāʿīm* is used here not in the sense of 'wicked', but in the legal connotation of 'those who are not right in their contentions'].

28 On this basis Pharaoh asks: *Entreat the Lord; for there has been enough of this thunder* [literally, 'voices of God'] *and hail*. His words contain an element of pride: Let the thunder and hail cease, for what I have heard and seen of them suffices me. He does not refer to the thunder as 'the Lord's voices' but as 'God's voices'; he regards it generally as a Divine phenomenon, but not as the specific act of *YHWH*, the God of Israel. However, he promises that if the storm will come to an end, he will no longer refuse: *I will let you go, and you shall stay no longer* [literally, 'not continue to stay']. — Pharaoh's words contain an echo of the Divine speech at the beginning of the paragraph: he also says *this time*, just as he was told, *For this time* (v. 14); and he also says לַעֲמֹד *laʿămōdh* [literally, 'to stand'; rendered: 'stay'], in the same way as it was said to him, הֶעֱמַדְתִּיךָ *heʿĕmadhtīkhā* [literally, 'I have caused you to stand'; translated: 'let you live'] (v. 16).

120

EXODUS IX 31–32

Moses' reply is characterized on this occasion, too, by refinement and nobility of expression. *As soon as I have gone out of the city* — when I can find solitude and direct my thoughts to Heaven — *I will stretch out my hands to the Lord* — to pray to Him in accordance with your request — *and then the thunder will cease, and there will be no more hail* (here, too, there is an archaic, poetic form, יֶחְדָּלוּן *yeḥdālūn* ['cease'; note the older and fuller termination with paragogic *Nūn*], and also poetic parallelism); all this I shall do *that you may know that the earth is the Lord's* (compare v. 14), and that it is He who makes the hail rain down, and likewise stops it, according to His will. Only to achieve this end, which has not yet been accomplisehd, shall the storm cease; not for your sake, nor yet for our sake, for — thus Moses continues to speak so that Pharaoh should not suppose that he (Moses) believes, in all innocence, in his assurances — I know that in your heart you are not yet humbled, nor are the great majority of your servants as yet in humble mood: *But as for you and your servants, I know that you do not yet fear* [this is the meaning of טֶרֶם תִּירְאוּן *ṭerem tīreʾūn*, not 'you will not yet fear'], *before the Lord God*. Although you are afraid of the severity of the plague, and also generally of the Divine power, nevertheless the Lord God, the God whom we designate by the name *YHWH*, you have still not recognized and you still do not fear.

So far the words of Moses. Now, before it is narrated that Moses prayed and that conformably with his prayer the hail ceased to come down, the Torah states what, at that moment, was the extent of the damage that the hail had already caused to the crops. These verses contain a number of rare poetic words and forms, a poetic rhythm and chiastic parallelism — all, apparently, in conformity with the text of the ancient epic poem. On the placing of the subject before the predicate see above, on vv. 20–21. *The flax* — an important plant in Egypt for making cloth — *and the barley* — which was used for the making of cheap bread for the slaves and the poor — *were ruined* (נֻכָּתָה *nukkāthā* [literally, 'smitten'], in the *Puʿal* conjugation instead of the usual *Hophʿal*; compare the *Hiphʿīl* in v. 25), *for the barley was in the ear* — it had already reached the stage of forming new ears — *and the flax was* גִּבְעֹל *gibhʿōl* — that is, *in bud* — *But the wheat and the spelt were not ruined, for they are late in coming up* [אֲפִילֹת *ǎphīlōth*] — they had so far grown only tender shoots, which on account of their smallness were not damaged, and even if they were affected could easily recover. The best bread was made, of course, from wheat, but even spelt was used, both in Egypt and in Canaan, for the making of bread. There have been discovered in Egypt in modern times, remains of spelt bread; and the Ugaritic texts testify that the Canaanites used to offer up spelt loaves as meal-offerings to the gods.

33 This was the situation at the time of the conversation between Pharaoh and Moses. *So Moses went out from Pharaoh* (recapitulation with a few variations, as usual), *and stretched out his hands to the Lord; and the thunder and the hail ceased, and* even ordinary *rain, no longer poured upon the earth.* The word מָטָר *māṭār* ['rain'] occurs here without the definite article, since it was not mentioned previously. The occurrence of the verb נִתַּךְ *nittakh* ['poured'] is another example of a poetic usage.

34 Pharaoh, however, did not fulfil his word. *But when Pharaoh saw that the rain* (now הַמָּטָר *hammāṭār*, with the definite article, since it has been mentioned before) *and the hail and the thunder* (in reverse order this time) *had ceased, he sinned yet again* [literally, 'continued to sin'] the very sin that he had confessed a little while earlier when he declared, 'I have sinned' (v. 27). The danger having passed, his fear also passed away; and he who had promised that the children of Israel would not *continue* to stay (v. 28), now *continued* to sin, *and he hardened* [literally, 'made heavy'] *his heart, he and his servants*, even as the hail was heavy. The conclusion is similar to the endings of the preceding paragraphs: *So the heart of Pharaoh was hardened, and he did not let the children of Israel go, as the Lord had spoken through Moses.* On the schematic repetition of the words שָׂדֶה *śādhe* ['field'] and אֶרֶץ *'ereṣ* ['land', 'earth'] in the description of the storm we have already commented. It should now be added that in the entire paragraph שָׂדֶה occurs seven times, and בָּרָד *bārādh* ['hail'] fourteen times, twice times seven.

EIGHTH PARAGRAPH

LOCUSTS

(X 1–20)

Chapter X

1 In the story of the eighth plague, which is the second in the third cycle, Moses is commanded, *Go in to Pharaoh*, just as he was

enjoined to do before the second plague of the first cycle and of the second cycle. Here a reason is added: you must go again to Pharaoh and inform him of a new plague, *for I have hardened his heart and the heart of his servants, that I may put these signs of Mine* — the fearful plagues of the third cycle — *in his midst*, that is, in the midst of his country, so as to inflict upon him and upon his people the punishment due to them for enslaving the Israelites and destroying their infant sons in the waters of the Nile, and, at the same time, to educate the people of Israel: *and that you may tell* — the verb here in the second person does not refer to Moses only, but to the whole of Israel — *in the hearing of your son and of your sons' son how I have dealt ruthlessly with the Egyptians* — bringing retribution on them according to their wickedness — *and what signs I have set among them* (the verb שִׂים *śim* ['set'] is used as a variant for שִׁית *śith* ['put'] above); *and that you may know* — all of you, O children of Israel — *that I am the Lord*, who is with you in your affliction and fulfils His word.

2

The rest of the Lord's communication to Moses is not expressly stated, but we can infer it from what we are subsequently told (*vv.* 3ff.) that Moses and Aaron said to Pharaoh in the Lord's name. To avoid repeating the words, the Bible cites them only when reporting that they were conveyed to Pharaoh, and it is self-understood that they were uttered by Divine command, just as in the paragraphs that follow the opposite method and quote the words of the Lord when they are communicated to Moses, it is obvious that Moses subsequently delivered the message to Pharaoh as directed (see above, on viii 5, 24 [Hebrew, *vv.* 1, 20]).

3 *So Moses and Aaron went in* (Aaron always accompanied Moses, but he is explicitly mentioned here in order to emphasize the fact that he, too, was subsequently expelled from Pharaoh's presence [*v.* 11], and consequently he was included among those to whom Pharaoh was compelled to express his penitence: 'I have sinned against the Lord your God, and against you' [*v.* 16]) *to Pharaoh, and said to him, Thus says the Lord, the God of the Hebrews, How long will you refuse to humble yourself before Me?* The question implies a severe rebuke: you should have acceded to My demand, but you did not; how long do you intend to remain rebellious? The perfect מֵאַנְתָּ *mē'antā* ['refuse'] has not a past signification here; it denotes something that had already happened in the past and is continuing in the present and will occur again

in the future. The sense is: How long will you go on behaving in this way? Again I warn you and repeat My demand: *Let My people go, that they may serve Me.* It will be better for you to let them go, *For if you refuse to let My people go, behold, tomorrow I will bring locusts into your country, and they* — the locusts — *shall cover 'the eye' of the land* — that is, the appearance (Rashi), the face, of the land — *so that no one can see the land* — that is, the face of the ground covered with locusts. It is similarly related in Num. xxii 5, that the king of Moab said concerning the people of Israel: 'they cover the face of the earth'; possibly the intention there is to compare the people to the locusts.

The locusts will destroy all the vegetation: *and they shall eat the residue* of the herbage of the field, such as the wheat and the spelt (ix, 32), *which remains to you from the hail, and shall eat every tree* — all that is left on the tree — *which grows for you out of the field.* The locusts will even enter into the houses (it happened, for example, in Israel [Palestine] in the year 1865, that the locusts in their multitudes invaded the houses by way of the windows and doors): *and your houses shall be filled, and the houses of all your servants, and the houses of all the Egyptians; as neither your fathers nor your grandfathers have seen, from the day they came on earth to this day* (this expression, which recalls similar phrases in ix 18, 24, as well as the reference to the hail, provides a link with the preceding paragraph).

When Moses and Aaron finished speaking, they did not wait for a reply, for it was clear to them from the first that this time, too, Pharaoh would not consent. *Then he turned* — that is, Moses, and Aaron with him — *and went out from Pharaoh.*

Pharaoh's servants, who remained in his presence after the departure of Moses and Aaron, counselled him to adopt a conciliatory attitude. They, too, like Moses and Aaron, began with the question, *How long?*, but out of respect for the king, they blamed the trouble on the other side: *And Pharaoh's servants said to him, How long shall this matter be a snare to us? Let the men go, that they may serve the Lord their God* — let them do what they wish according to the requirements of their religion. *Do you not yet know* — have you not yet understood — *that Egypt is ruined* — that our country will be ruined if such plagues continue to come upon it? The word טֶרֶם *ṭerem* ['not yet'] also forms a parallelism with what Moses said in the previous conversation (ix 30).

The king does not dare oppose the advice of his counsellors, and he endeavours to forestall the calamity, something that he has never tried to do before. He issues an order, *And Moses and Aaron were brought back to Pharaoh:* he then addresses them in terms that seem to imply assent to their request: *Go, serve the Lord your God.* But he is not yet willing to agree completely; hence he adds a question that is in effect a condition: *but who are they that shall go?* I wish to know precisely who among you will be going, for I shall give permission for this journey only to such as I approve.

Moses answers at once proudly, not as a slave speaking to his master, but as one power replying to another, and rejects any condition or restriction. A poetic rhythm and solemn tone are discernible in his words: *We will go with our young and our old; we will go with our sons and daughters and with our flocks and herds, for we must hold the Lord's feast.* We shall all go, and we shall take our entire families with us, and also our cattle, for we must hold the Lord's feast; and in accordance with our will, not yours, we shall act. Moses does not yet declare expressly that the Israelites wish to leave Egypt never to return, but this intention is clear from his words; and Pharaoh understands this well, but he, too, does not react to it openly. It is a case of diplomatic bargaining: neither side explicitly declares its real aims, but disguises them by other statements; yet each one fully understands what is in the mind of the other side. On this verse, or on its poetic source, Hos. v 6, apparently, depends: 'With their flocks and their herds they shall go to seek the Lord'.

Pharaoh responds to Moses' declaration with harsh words, charged with bitter irony: *So be the Lord with you, as I will let you go, and your little ones,* that is, may the help of your God be as far from you as I am far from giving you permission to go forth with your little ones. In the continuation of the narrative, we notice an ironic retort to his irony; in the end, he will let them and their children go, and so the Lord will actually be with them.

The word טַף *ṭaph* [rendered: 'little ones'], which sometimes, when the women are mentioned in addition, denotes the children specifically (so, for instance, Gen. xxxiv 29; xlv 19; xlvi 5, and so on), at other times includes the women together with the children. This is the case, for example, in Gen. xliii 8: 'Both we, and you, and also our טַף *ṭaph*'; *ibid.* l 8: 'only their טַף *ṭaph*, their flocks, and their herds were left in the land of Goshen'; and so forth. In this way the word is to be understood here, and also further on.

EXODUS X 10

Pharaoh continues to speak, and says: *Look, for there is evil* [רָעָה *rāʿā*] *before you* — take heed, for if you urge me overmuch, evil is in store for you. Possibly here, too, as has already been suggested, an allusion is to be detected to the god *Reʿ*, the sun-deity, the head of the Egyptian pantheon. The sense is: know that the power of my god will oppose you (in rabbinic Haggadah: 'there is a star called *Rāʿaʾ*; see above, on v 19; cf. xxxii 12). *Not so*, as you have said: *We will go with our young and our old*, etc., but as I say: *Go now, the men among you* only, without the women and the children and the cattle; *and serve the Lord* — you, the men, will carry out the order of your service.

Pharaoh does not expressly say that he does not permit the people to leave the country for good; he confines himself to the diplomatic request made by Moses: *for that is what you desire* — this is the only request that you have submitted to me. However, he understands Moses' real purpose, and in his reply he hints at his own intention. As for the advice of his counsellors, he accepts it at its face value and not in accordance with its true purport. They said: *Let the men* [אֲנָשִׁים *ʾănāšīm*] *go*, and meant, by this word, the entire people; but he pretends that he understood it in its restricted sense, namely, הַגְּבָרִים *haggebhārīm* ['men', 'males']. Of this point, too, an echo may be heard in the subsequent narrative, which relates that what actually happened was as Moses, not Pharaoh, had said (xii 37): 'And the children of Israel journeyed from Rameses to Succoth, about six hundred thousand *men* on foot, *besides women and children.*'

When he finished speaking, Pharaoh gave orders that Moses and Aaron should be ejected out — literally so — from the palace hall: *And he* — whoever he was — *drove them out* — that is, they were driven out —*from Pharaoh's presence*. The ancient translators who rendered the text as if the reading were, וַיְגֹרְשׁוּ *wayeghorešū* ['and they were driven out', *Puʿal* plural, instead of *Piʿēl* sing.], were only interpreting the word, and using a grammatical construction that was idiomatic in the language of the translation. Similarly, the Samaritan Pentateuch, which reads וַיְגֹרְשׁוּ *wayeghorešū* merely seeks to make the passage clearer by rewording it in conformity with later Hebrew usage.

Since in respect of the main issue Pharaoh still refused to give his assent, it was only right to implement what had been predicted in *vv.* 4 f. Therefore, *The Lord said to Moses, Stretch out your hand over the land of Egypt for the locusts* — in the matter of the locusts — *that they may come up* — so that the locusts may come up at the signal of your hand — *upon the land of Egypt, and eat every plant in the land,* or, more exactly, since very little only was left of the vegetation of the land after the hail, *all that the hail has left.*

13 Moses did as he was enjoined: *So Moses stretched forth his rod* (in *v.* 12 we find, *your hand*; we thus have a variation here, as above) *over the land of Egypt, and the Lord led an east wind upon the land* (the wind is an important factor in the migrations of the swarms of locusts; but it was not actually the east wind that brought the plague, for the locusts do not come to Egypt from the east, but from the south, from the Sudan; east wind thus denotes here a fierce wind in general, as in Job xv 2: 'Should a wise man answer with windy knowledge, and fill himself with the east wind?'; or in Hos. xii 1 [Hebrew, *v.* 2]: 'Ephraim herds the wind, and pursues the east wind') *all that day and all that night* — to allow sufficient time for the locusts to arrive from a distant country (the plagues, as we have stated, were not contrary to nature, but a wondrous and amazing utilization of natural phenomena), and, behold, at the time predetermined there came to pass that which had been foretold: *and when it was morning* — the morning of the following day — *the east wind had brought the locusts.* There now follows a detailed account of the plague, which recapitulates, with some variations, what had been stated earlier: *And the locusts came up*
14 *over all the land of Egypt, and rested* — in accordance with their habit of resting when, fatigued after a long journey, they find land covered with vegetation — *in the whole territory of Egypt.* These swarms of locusts were *very heavy,* just as the pest and the hail had been 'very heavy'. Although locusts are an endemic plague of Egypt, it was far severer than usual on this occasion: *before them there were no such locusts as they, neither after them shall be such* (a traditional hyperbole, which occurs in similar form
15 in Joel ii 2). *For they* — the locusts — *covered the face* [literally, 'eye'] *of the whole land, so that the land was darkened* — that is, the face of the land became black on account of the locusts that were on it (the expression 'darkened' contains an anticipatory allusion to the plague of darkness that followed — *and they ate all the plants in the land and all the fruit of the trees which the hail had left.* The hail did, indeed, leave something, but after the locusts *not a green thing remained,* neither tree nor plant of the field, through all the land of Egypt.

Even before the general destruction of all the vegetation, mentioned at the end of *v*. 15, Pharaoh hastened, when he saw the multitude of locusts that had settled on the land of Egypt, to
16 turn to Moses and Aaron in the hope of saving something: *Then Pharaoh called Moses and Aaron in haste, and said, I have sinned against the Lord your God, and against you*. Once again he confesses in accordance with the customary formula, declaring: *I have sinned*; but now his confession is more comprehensive. He no longer adds the qualification, *this time* (ix 27), and he acknowledges that he sinned not only against the Lord, but also against Moses and Aaron, when he expelled them from his presence. Nevertheless, he preserves his dignity, and at the end of his speech — the
17 conclusion begins, as usual, with the word וְעַתָּה *wᵉʿattā* ['and now'] — he does not go so far as to ask his subjects' forgiveness, nor does he say: 'forgive [plural], I pray you, my sin', but in an impersonal manner, he requests: *forgive* [singular], *pray, my sin*, as if to say: let my sin be forgiven (the Samaritan Recension adds a *Wāw*, reading שאו *śᵉʾū* ['forgive you', imperative plural], in order, as usual, to simplify the text). There will be need to forgive his sin *only this once*; thereby Pharaoh hints indirectly that he will no longer refuse, but only indirectly, so that Moses should not react by expressing his distrust. His words end with the customary request: *and entreat the Lord your God* — that He may be willing — *only to remove this death upon me*. He says רַק *raq* ['only'], just as he had previously said אַךְ *'akh* ['only', 'but']: there will be no further need to intervene in this way in the future.

Since Pharaoh's words consisted only of confession and supplication, there was no necessity for Moses to reply; nor, in fact
18 did he reply. *So he went out from Pharaoh, and entreated the Lord.*
19 This time, also, the Lord granted his prayer: *And the Lord turned a... west wind* — He changed the direction of the wind from a south-north course to a west-east course (רוּחַ־יָם *rūaḥ yām* [literally, 'wind of the sea'; rendered: 'west wind'] corresponds to the customary expression used by the inhabitants of Canaan, which has the sea on its west side); *a very strong* [חָזָק *ḥāzāq*, mas. sing.] *west wind* (רוּחַ *rūaḥ*, occurs here as a masculine noun) — just as the locusts' invasion of Egypt had been helped by the force of the south wind, so now the west wind removed them from the country: *and the wind lifted the locusts and thrust them* — that is, cast them, and sank them — *into the Sea of Reeds* — east of Egypt; and consequently *not a single locust was left in all the territory of*

Egypt. There may be a preparatory allusion here to what will subsequently be stated concerning the host of Pharaoh, who also sank in the Sea of Reeds, 'and not so much as one of them remained' (xiv 28). Even if we assume that the Sea of Reeds [יָם סוּף *Yam Sūph*] in chapters xiv–xv is not actually the same as that mentioned here (on this see further on), the parallelism remains valid.

Once the locusts disappeared, Pharaoh did not keep his word. 20 *But the Lord hardened Pharaoh's heart, and he did not let the children of Israel go*. Again the same ending.

NINTH PARAGRAPH

DARKNESS

(X 21–29)

Like the third plague of every cycle, so also this plague comes 21 without warning. *Then the Lord said to Moses, Stretch out your hand toward heaven* (compare ix 22) — as a signal for the commencement of the plague — *that there may be darkness over the land of Egypt*. The reference apparently is to a sand-storm; the sand coming from the wilderness will fill the air, so that it will be possible almost to feel it: *a darkness to be felt*.

This plague will demonstrate how great is the Lord's power against the gods of Egypt: when the God of Israel wills it, the sun, which is regarded by the Egyptians as the chief deity, will be hidden and unable to shine upon its worshippers; and if the conjecture that the word רָעָה *rāʿā* in v. 10 alludes to the Egyptian sun-god be correct, the plague of darkness may be viewed as an immediate reaction to Pharaoh's remarks.

22 *So Moses stretched out his hand toward heaven and there was thick darkness* (this phrase indicates the density of the darkness) *in all the land of Egypt three days* — the entire period of the sand-23 storm. *They did not see one another* — and even the lighting of lamps did not help on account of the thickness of the sand in the atmosphere — *nor did any rise from his place for three days* — on account of the danger of walking in the darkness. *But all the children of Israel had light where they dwelt*, because the storm did not reach the land of Goshen.

Pharaoh understood, although he had not been forwarned about it, that this, too, was a plague inflicted on him by the God of Israel. *Then Pharaoh called Moses* — that is, after the three days of darkness — *and said, Go, serve the Lord*. Once more his opening words give the impression that he is prepared to grant the request, and once again he immediately adds a reservation that nullifies the value of the consent: *only let your flocks and your herds be stayed* — that is, remain behind. He wanted a pledge as surety for the return of the Israelites to be left in Egypt. Although he adds: *your little ones also may go with you*, and thereby enlarges somewhat the scope of the permission that he granted at the time of the locusts (*vv.* 8–10), yet the prohibition not to take out the flocks and herds sufficed for his purpose.

25 Moses replies in his customary manner. Just as Pharaoh commenced the broadening of his sanction with the word גַּם *gam* ['also'], so Moses begins his reply with the same word. You spoke as though you were making an important concession to us; let me tell you, then, that not only is it no concession on your part to let our children go, but it is our right and not a matter for discussion; and not only do I not acquiesce in your reservation regarding our flocks and herds, but I go further and declare that in the end you will give more than you now refuse to concede. *You must also let us have* of your sheep and oxen to slaughter as *sacrifices and burnt offerings, that we may make* them oblations *to the Lord our God* (compare xii 32: 'and bless me also!'). It is
26 self-understood that *our cattle also must go with us* — all of them; *there shall not be left* in Egypt a *hoof* — not one foot (a hyperbolical expression, meaning: not a single animal of our cattle shall be left behind); *for thereof* — from our cattle — *must we take to serve the Lord our God*; and we need all our cattle, for *we do not know* — we cannot tell beforehand — *with what we must serve the Lord* — what we shall require for our sacrifices — *until we arrive there* — at the place of worship. The diplomatic negotiations still continue: Moses' answer leaves no doubt whatsoever as to his refusal to leave any pledge in Egypt; but to the idea of the pledge, which is not consonant with national dignity, he does not make the slightest reference, just as Pharaoh did not allude to it explicitly.

27 *But the Lord hardened Pharaoh's heart, and he* — Pharaoh — *would not let them go* with their flocks and herds as Moses had insisted. Here we find the expression, 'he would not' — that is,

he did not agree to — 'let them go', and not just that he did not let them go, as in previous paragraphs, because now Pharaoh had reached the stage of diplomatic bargaining over the detailed conditions under which the Israelites would be permitted to leave, only in the end he did not agree to specific demands on which Moses took an inflexible stand.

Not only did Pharaoh not give his assent, but he was angry with Moses, and expelled him from his presence with sharp words 28 and fearful threats: *Get away from me; take heed to yourself: never see my face again; for in the day you see my face you shall die.* However, Moses was neither afraid nor dismayed, and gave Pharaoh 29 a fitting rejoinder: *You have spoken well* — you are right in what you say, for *I will not again* come of my own volition to this palace, and I shall ask no more to *see your face*, not because of your threat to me, but because of mine to you. The nature of this threat, and why Moses was in a position to make it, we shall learn in the next paragraph.

TENTH PARAGRAPH

THE WARNING REGARDING THE PLAGUE OF THE FIRST-BORN

(XI 1–8)

Chapter XI

Moses' announcement reported in *vv*. 4–8 is doubtless the continuation of the speech that begins at the end of the preceding paragraph, in *v*. 29. The preceding verses, 1–3, are to be understood as a parenthetic explanatory note.

1 When we read here, *And the Lord said to Moses*, we cannot imagine that an actual revelation of the Lord in the presence of Pharaoh and his servants is meant. In all the passages preceding and following this paragraph, solitude is a prior condition of every Divine communication, and it is inconceivable that an extraordinary revelation should be referred to in the simple, customary terms: *And the Lord said to Moses*. It is also difficult to suppose that the paragraph was misplaced here, for its subject-matter is well-suited to our theme; nor can we readily understand the verb וַיֹּאמֶר *wayyō'mer* ['and... said'] as a pluperfect (he had already said pre-

viously), for a pluperfect of this kind is not found in Biblical narrative prose. On the other hand it is true that nothing new is stated here; all the matters mentioned here were already known to Moses from the day that he received the preliminary instructions relative to the entire series of plagues and in particular to the last plague (see above, on iv 21-23). Hence it appears that the intention of the passage is to indicate only what was taking place at that moment in Moses' mind. When Moses heard Pharaoh's dire threat, he recalled the directives that were given him long ago concerning the tenth and decisive plague, and he felt that the time for their implementation had now arrived. It seemed to him as if that Divine announcement was reiterated at that moment, and as if the Lord reminded him then that the plague that was soon to come would be the last: *Yet one plague more I will bring upon Pharaoh and upon Egypt; afterwards he will let you go hence* (compare iii 20: 'after that he will let you go'); and then, *when he lets you go* — as soon as he makes up his mind to do so — he will let you go entirely, without any reservation; it will be a total expulsion: *he will drive you away completely* (compare vi 1: 'for with a strong hand he will send them out, yea, with a strong hand he will drive them out of his land'). At the same time Moses remembered what he had been told (iii 22) with regard to the preparations for the exodus, the time for which was now approaching: *Speak now in the hearing of the people, that they ask, every man of his neighbour and every woman of her neighbour, jewelry of silver and of gold*. Although it might at first seem out of place in the present context, this matter is referred to in our passage because in the established tradition (compare iii 21-22; xii 35-36) it is linked with the idea of finding favour in the eyes of the Egyptians, which is important for the understanding of our paragraph; for immediately after the sentence, *And the Lord gave the people favour in the sight of the Egyptians,* follows the statement: *Moreover, the man Moses was very great in the land of Egypt, in the sight of Pharaoh's servants and in the sight of the people* of Egypt. This explains how Moses was able to speak to Pharaoh as he did.

After this explanatory note comes the stern proclamation of Moses to Pharaoh, continuing his reply to the king cited above (x 29). In the recesses of his soul, Moses felt that the spirit of the Lord stirred him, and that it was the Lord who was speaking through him; hence he began: *Thus says the Lord,* and continued to speak in the Lord's name in the first person. *About midnight*, when the day of retribution arrives, *I will go out*, like a king issuing forth to do battle with his foes, *in the midst of Egypt*, whereupon a terrible plague will come upon Egypt, *and all the first-born in the land of Egypt shall die*, from the highest to the lowest, *from the first-born of Pharaoh who sits upon his throne* — that is, who is due to sit upon his father's throne after the latter's death, or who is now enthroned as prince — *even to the first-born of the maid-servant who is behind the mill*. This expression, 'the maid-servant behind the mill', is common in Egyptian literature in the sense of 'the poorest of the poor' (it occurs, for example, in the opening section of the instructions of Ptah-Hotep). Thou hast said that I, Moses, shall die on the day that I see your face; However, I declare to you in the name of my God that I shall not die, but all the first-born of Egypt will die, and even your first-born son shall perish. Not only the first-born of human beings shall die, but also *all the first-born of the cattle*, even the first-born of the animals to which you attribute a divine character, like the bulls of Apis and the cows of Hathor; then you will realize that I execute judgements upon all the gods of Egypt. *And there shall be*, on that night, *a great cry through all the land of Egypt, such* — on such a scale — *as there has never been, nor ever shall be again* (the reading suggested in the Masoretic note, כָּמֹהָ *kāmōhā* ['like her', 'such as', which would agree with the feminine noun צְעָקָה *ṣeʿāqā* ['cry'], to which it refers] instead of כָּמֹהוּ *kāmōhū* [literally, 'like him'; rendered: 'such as'], is intended only to ease the construction of the verse, and is not to be regarded as original). So it will happen throughout all the land of Egypt, except one region, the place where the Israelites dwell; there there will be neither calamity nor cry. *But against any of the children of Israel shall not a dog whet his tongue* — not a dog's bark or sharpening of his tongue will be heard against the Israelites, nor even against their cattle — *against man or beast*. The purpose of all this being *that you may know what distinction the Lord makes between the Egyptians and Israel*. Then, on that terrible night, *all these your servants* — all your ministers who stand around you now in this hall — *shall come down to me* — to my house (at this point Moses speaks in his own name) to beg me to go out of Egypt with all my people. I shall have no need to see your face again in order to present my request to you; it is you Egyptians who will present your request to me. It is not I who will come to prostrate myself before you; they shall come *and prostrate themselves to me, saying, Get out, you and all the people that are at your feet* — who follow you, that is, the entire people—just as I have said: 'We will go with our young and our old; we will go with our sons and daughters and with our flocks and herds.' *And after that* — after the retribution that you deserve for your ruthlessness towards us shall have come upon you (compare אַחֲרֵי־כֵן 'aḥărē khēn [rendered: 'afterwards'] in v. 1) — *I will go out* with the people that are at my feet.

So Moses concludes his speech, which is characterized by a lofty style, in part poetic; and with the last word אֵצֵא 'ēṣē' ['I will go out'] he brings to mind what he had said in the Lord's name (v. 4): 'I will go out [יוֹצֵא yōṣē'] in the midst of Egypt.'

As soon as he had finished speaking, Moses turned away abruptly *and went out from Pharaoh* (again the verb יָצָא yāṣā' ['go out'] *in hot anger* — not like one who is banished from the king's presence, but as one who no longer wishes to stand in his presence, and leaves of his own accord in fierce anger.

EPILOGUE

(XI 9–10)

These two verses are considered by many commentators as redundant or misplaced. But they can easily be explained as a summary and epilogue of the Section of the Plagues.

In the following section not only the course of events will change, but also the background and the *dramatis personae.* Till now the central theme was the negotiations conducted by Moses and Aaron on the one hand, and Pharaoh and his servants on the other, in Pharaoh's palace or its environs. But henceforth the principal hero of the drama will be the people of Israel in its totality, and the perspective will be enlarged. Moses and Aaron will no longer be sent to Pharaoh but to the Israelites, in order to prepare them for the exodus and to implement it; nor will they be enjoined again to perform acts for the purpose of bringing the plagues, for the last plague will take place of its own accord, through the instrumentality of the angel of the Lord. Since the episode about to be narrated represents a new theme, and one, moreover, of fundamental importance, it is desirable that before reading this

EXODUS XI 10

account we should look back for a moment, and review generally the events that have taken place thus far, as well as the situation obtaining at the conclusion of those events. This review is provided for us in the verses under consideration. From the very outset
9 the Lord had told Moses: *Pharaoh will not listen to you*, and his abduracy will continue *that my portents may be multiplied in the land of Egypt*, so that both Pharaoh and his servants and the child-
10 ren of Israel may learn the lesson thereof. *And Moses and Aaron did all these portents before Pharaoh* — as was narrated in detail above — *and the Lord hardened Pharaoh's heart, and he did not let the children of Israel go out of his land* (the usual formula has been supplemented by the phrase *out of his land*, in order to round off the epilogue with appropriate fullness). So the position remained, without any amelioration, after the ninth plague. But now, in the next paragraph, it will be narrated how the situation underwent a fundamental transformation when the Lord brought the tenth plague upon Pharaoh and Egypt — the plague of the firstborn.

In several paragraphs of this section we have already observed a numerical schematism that finds expression in the mention of the name of a plague seven times (swarms of flies, locusts), or fourteen times (hail). The tendency towards numerical patterns based on the number seven and on the sexagesimal system is observable throughout the section. In the first cycle, the names of the plagues occur 21 times — three times seven (blood 5 times, frogs 11, gnats 5) and with the paragraph pertaining to the crocodile (3 times), 24 — twice times twelve; in the second cycle 12 times (swarms of flies 7, pest 1, boils 4); in the third cycle 24 (hail 14, locusts 7, darkness 3); in all 60 times. All this can hardly be fortuitous.

SECTION SEVEN

THE EXODUS FROM EGYPT

CHAPTER XII, 1–42

FIRST PARAGRAPH

INSTRUCTIONS ON THE OBSERVANCE OF PASSOVER IN EGYPT

(XII 1–13)

Chapter XII
After the completion of the preceding section there is an interval, which is followed, as stated, by a transformation in the character of the narration; the story changes its aspect, assuming a new form. Pharaoh is forgotten, and so are his servants; Pharaoh's palace and the entire environment in which we found ourselves throughout the whole of the preceding section disappears, as it were, from our sight. The epic now has its centre in the midst of the people of Israel, and the commands given to Moses and Aaron are directed towards the Israelites. What has to be done vis-à-vis Pharaoh, the Lord will do. Moses and Aaron must concern themselves only with their people. The first injunction they receive is to prepare for the day of redemption, which is due to come soon.

On the first day of the first month of the new year — that is, at the beginning of a new period of time in human life — God communicates to them joyful tidings; the new calendar period marks a new historic epoch in the life of Israel. *And the Lord* 1 *spoke to Moses and Aaron in the land of Egypt, saying*, etc. The Torah states explicitly that the communication took place in the land of Egypt in order to make it clear that the directives given at first (*vv*. 2–13) were only of a temporary character, valid only in Egypt, at that particular time, and not for later generations. Only thereafter, in *vv*. 14–20, are regulations laid down for the observance of the festival of Passover for all time.

2 The word of the Lord begins: *This month* — this renewal of the moon [חֹדֶשׁ *ḥōdheš*, rendered 'month', means literally, 'new moon'] —

is for you the beginning of the months — the beginning of the lunar renewals of the year; *it is the first month of the year for you.* According to the plain meaning of the text, this is not a positive precept to commence the year with the month of Nisan; for if that had been the intention, the Bible would have written, יִהְיֶה *yihᵉye* ['it shall be'], or יְהִי *yᵉhi* ['let it be'], לָכֶם *lākhem* ['for you'] (instead of הוּא לָכֶם *hū' lākhem* ['it is for you']). We have here a statement of an existing fact, serving as a prefatory note to what follows. In the ancient East there existed two different systems relative to the commencement of the year. According to one system, the year began in spring, in the month of Nisan, and according to the other it began in autumn, in the month of Tishri (this word actually means, *beginning*). Here it is assumed that the Israelites in Egypt started to count the months of the year from Nisan, and the sense of the verse is: You are now beginning to count a new year; now the new year will bring you a change of destiny.

3 Therefore you, Moses and Aaron, *Speak to all the congregation of Israel, telling* them what they must do in order to prepare for their change of destiny and for their liberation from the bondage of Egypt. *On the tenth day of this month* — on the tenth day after the new moon, a distinguished day according to the ancient division of the month into three parts comprising ten days each, and paralleling to the tenth of Tishri, which is the Day of Atonement and the day of the proclamation of the year of the Jubilee and of liberty — they shall begin their preparation and *take to them* (on the use of the verb לָקַח *lāqaḥ* ['take'] in this sense, see my commentary on Gen. vii 2) *every man a lamb according to their fathers' houses* — that is, every man who is the head of a 'father's house' shall take a lamb for his house; and to make it clear that 'father's house' is not used here in the widest signification of the term, the text adds, by way of explanation, *a lamb for a house* — for one family, in the restricted connotation

4 of the word. *And if* the number of the members of *the household be too small for a lamb* — that is, if it be a household incapable of consuming a complete lamb in one night — then *a man and his neighbour next to his house* — be it propinquity of relationship or place — *shall take according to the number of souls* — that is, they should share the expenses according to the number of persons. Generally speaking the passage concludes, *according to what each one can eat you shall make your count for the lamb.* Furthermore, the

5 requisite characteristics of the lamb are stated: *Your lamb shall*

be without blemish [literally, 'whole', 'sound'], *a male, a year old*; but it can be of different species: *from the sheep and from the goats* — that is, or from the goats — *you shall take* it.

    The passover has partly the character of an oblation and partly that of a family sacrifice. It may be conjectured that it is connected with an ancient custom of offering up sacrifices of sheep at springtime, but here, in a commentary on the Book of Exodus, it is not our concern to inquire into the primary origin of the festival ceremony, or to examine the course of its history; our function is to explain the purport of the text. It is clear that the Torah gives a new form and meaning to an ancient observance. The significance attached by the Torah to the passover offering we learn from *v.* 27, which states that in post-Exodus observances of Passover the lamb would be a memorial to the fact that the Lord passed over the houses of the children of Israel when He smote the Egyptians. In agreement with this interpretation, the lamb of the Egyptian Passover served as a substitute for the lives of the Israelite first-born on the day that the Lord sent the destroyer to smite the first-born of Egypt. This apart, the blood of the passover sacrifice may also be regarded, like the blood of the circumcision (see above on iv 24–26, and compare below, *v.* 48), as a symbol of the dedication of the lives of the children of Israel to their God, and of their readiness to shed their own blood, too, in His service, should this be necessary. It is also possible that the Bible intends to convey that it was through the merit of this very dedication that the Israelite first-born were saved when the plague came upon Egypt.

    The lamb that was held in readiness from the tenth day was to 6 be kept for four days: *and you shall keep it until the fourteenth day of this month*, and on the fourteenth they were to slaughter it: *and the whole assembly of the congregation of Israel shall kill it* (the children of Israel are called *congregation* in *v.* 3, and here *assembly of the congregation*, as though to say that, even though they dwell in different places, they become integrated into a single assembly by their united and simultaneous act of worship) *between the two evenings* — that is, toward the evening of the full moon.
7 *Then they shall take of the blood* of the slaughtered lamb, *and put some of it on the two doorposts and the lintel* — not, apparently, on account of the particular importance of these places in ritual-worship, for the latter ascribes greater significance to the threshold than to the lintel, but for the purpose of external indication (com-

pare v. 13) — *upon the houses wherein they shall eat it* — the sacrifice. This would betoken that these belonged to people dedicated to the God of Israel. The doorposts and the lintel are naturally suited to bear the sign of the person dwelling in the house, and such is the custom to this day. *And they shall eat the flesh* of the lamb *that night* — the evening of the fifteenth — *roasted in the fire.* In this respect the Israelite passover sacrifice marked an innovation, for according to the ancient custom the flesh of the spring sacrifice was eaten raw or half-boiled; the intention here was to abolish the idolatrous character of the ancient rite. With the flesh they had to eat *unleavened cakes* — bread in its earliest form, which was also preserved as a permanent feature of the Israelite ritual in accordance with the conservative character of all sacred observances (compare above, on iv 25), when there is no special reason for making changes, such as that which caused a modification of the manner in which the flesh was prepared for the repast. It is further stated: *with bitter herbs they shall eat it*; an anticipatory allusion to the eating of bitter herbs is already found in the previous narrative (i 14): 'and made their lives bitter with hard service', etc.

9 Expressly Scripture warns: *Do not eat any of it raw or boiled with water,* so as to forbid its being eaten according to the pagan custom mentioned above; *but* eat it *roasted in the fire,* and in order to avoid the possibility of any part of it being consumed unroasted, the text adds that all of it must be roasted at the same time: *its head with its legs and its inner parts.* The period fixed for eating

10 it: *And you shall let none of it remain until the morning,* and the commandment to burn that which is left over: *but that which remains of it until the morning you shall burn in the fire,* accord

11 with sacrificial law. The statement in *v.* 11: *In this manner you shall eat it: your loins girded, your sandals on your feet, and your staff in your hand; and you shall eat it in haste,* implies that the Israelites must be ready to set out on their journey at any moment during that night.

The passage concludes with the sentence: *It is the Lord's passover.* In order to understand this formula, we must assume that, apparently, *passover* was already an established and previously-known term, just as *Sabbath* was a well-entrenched and familiar word prior to the Torah's injunction concerning the observance of the seventh day; and in the same way as the Torah gave a new form and meaning to the Sabbath day, sanctifying it to the Lord — 'it is the Lord's sabbath' [Lev. xxiii 3] — so the Bible also gave to the Passover festival, as we have seen, a new aspect and significance, and dedicated it to the Lord: *It is the Lord's passover.*

Thus shall the children of Israel prepare themselves; and even as they will do their part, so shall the Lord do His, in accordance with the announcement (xi 4 f.) that Moses had made to Pharaoh: 12 *For I will pass through the land of Egypt that night, and I will smite all the first-born in the land of Egypt, both man and beast; and on all the gods of Egypt I will execute judgements* (see above, on ix 5): *I am the Lord* — and in Person I shall execute judgements on the Egyptian gods, for they are no-gods. As for you, O children 13 of Israel, *the blood shall be a sign for you, upon the houses where you are* (see above, on v. 7); *and when I see the blood, I will pass over you* (an allusion to the name *Passover*, linking the new meaning of the festival with its ancient name) *and there shall be no plague for a destroyer upon you*—that is, no destructive force or destroying angel shall have the power to harm you, *when I smite the land of Egypt.*

So concludes the paragraph that cites the first part of the Divine communication. Note should be taken of the poetic parallelism in *v.* 2, and also of the occurrence, seven times, of references to *eating* — an important aspect of the sacrificial rite.

SECOND PARAGRAPH

DIRECTIVES FOR THE OBSERVANCE OF PASSOVER IN THE FUTURE

(XII 14–20)

This paragraph contains the second part of the Divine communication, which enjoins the children of Israel to bring to mind, year by year, in all generations, the story of the exodus from bondage 14 to freedom: *And this day shall be for you a memorial day, and you shall keep it as a festival to the Lord; throughout your generations you shall observe it as an ordinance for ever.* It is self-understood, and therefore it is not stated here explicitly, that this festival of remembrance will include a re-enactment of the essential elements of the Passover celebration in Egypt, that is, the Passover offering will be slaughtered, roasted and eaten together with unleavened cakes and bitter herbs, and that the time of its incidence shall be the evening of the fifteenth of the first month. Only the new points that are to be added to the observance of Passover in future generations are stressed. In the first place, the festival will not be confined to one day only, but will be observed for a full week, that is, a complete series of days (seven being the number of perfection); similarly, the eating of unleavened cakes, which in the case of the Egyptian Passover was limited to the night of the fifteenth (on *v.* 39, see below), will likewise continue for an entire

15 week: *Seven days you shall eat unleavened cakes.* Furthermore it is added: *surely on the first day you shall put away* [literally, 'cause to cease'] *leaven out of your houses* — that is, you must see to it, that leaven shall cease, be absent from your houses, and not be therein, even on the first day, *for if any one eats what is leavened that person shall be cut off from Israel*; and the period of this prohibition shall be *from the first day until the seventh day.* It is

16 further stated: *On the first day there shall be to you a holy assembly, and on the seventh day a holy assembly* — that is, at the beginning and at the end of the festival week you shall gather yourselves together for holy services, and on these two days *no work shall be done in them* (the verb יֵעָשֶׂה *yēʿāśe* ['shall be done'] is masculine because it refers to the word כָּל *kol* ['all']), except what is requisite for the preparation of food: *but what every one must eat, that only may be prepared by you.*

Although the paragraph deals primarily with ritual regulations, it is not formulated with the brevity and terseness characteristic of statutory laws. Rather it is marked by an expansive and elevated style that appertains to literary language (see particularly, *v.* 16). Hence it is not surprising that in *vv.* 17–20 the text recapitulates the whole subject. From the aspect of their content, these verses contain a renewed injunction concerning the observance of the festival precepts, added stress being laid on their reason and a supplementary explanation being given of their details; from the point of view of form, they constitute a parallelism, which provides a new formulation of the theme in different words, in accordance with the prevailing literary method used in the ancient East for the purpose of emphasis and confirmation. The parallelism embraces every detail, following the order of the preceding verses. Verse 17 corresponds to verse 14, and in its two members, both of which begin with the verb וּשְׁמַרְתֶּם *ūšᵉmartem* ['and you shall observe'] — an echo of the word מִשְׁמֶרֶת *mišmereth* [literally,

EXODUS XII 17

'charge', 'keeping', rendered: 'and you shall keep'] in *v.* 6 — there
17 twice occurs the expression *this day*, used in *v.* 14: *And you shall observe the feast of unleavened cakes, for on this very day* — mentioned earlier — *I brought your hosts out of the land of Egypt* (on *your hosts* compare above, on vi 26); *therefore you shall observe this day, throughout your generations, as an ordinance for ever* — exactly as in *v.* 14. Verse 18 parallels the first part of *v.* 15, fixing the time
18 more precisely: *In the first month, on the fourteenth day of the month at evening, you shall eat unleavened cakes* (on the formula *the fourteenth day at evening* in the sense of the post-Biblical expression 'on the evening of the fifteenth', see my Commentary on the Book of Genesis, Part I, *From Adam To Noah*, pp. 28–30), *until the twenty-first day of the month at evening*. Verse 19 repeats,
19 with some variations, the second and third parts of *v.* 15: *For seven days no leaven shall be found in your houses* (and to this end shall you put it away, *v.* 15); *for if any one eats what is leavened* (מַחְמֶצֶת *maḥmeṣeth*, a more comprehensive term in place of חָמֵץ *ḥāmēṣ* ['what is leavened'] used above), *that person shall be cut off from the congregation of Israel, whether he is a sojourner or a native of the land*. The inclusion of the sojourner in the prohibition of eating what is leavened is in antithesis to the injunction in *v.* 48 concerning the Passover offering, which the sojourner is forbidden to eat until he is circumcised. At the end, in *v.* 20, there is a general parallelism to the whole theme, constituting a formal conclusion that summarizes the prohibition of eating that which is leavened
20 and the commandment to eat unleavened cakes: *You shall eat nothing leavened; in all your dwelling places you shall eat unleavened cakes*. In this paragraph, too, there are seven references to eating.

THIRD PARAGRAPH

THE INSTRUCTIONS ARE CONVEYED TO THE PEOPLE AND PASSOVER IS CELEBRATED IN EGYPT

(XII 21–28)

21 Moses made haste to fulfil the Lord's commands: *Then Moses called all the elders of Israel, and said to them* — in order that each one should give instructions to the families under his charge:

Draw out and take for yourselves lambs according to your families, and kill the passover lamb. The formulation here is abbreviated, and without doubt the Torah intends to convey that Moses told the elders all the details that were given to him, directed them how, and when, to take the animal, explained what was meant by צֹאן *ṣō'n* ['flock'; rendered: 'lambs'], how to understand the term 'according to your families', when to slaughter, and what was the connotation of passover; but there was no need to repeat all the details, since the reader is already familiar with the whole subject. On the other hand, additional particulars are mentioned here, which were not recorded above, either because there Scripture wishes to omit such matters as were not part of the primary theme, or because we are given here directions added by Moses for the sake of greater clarity. Above it was stated in general terms (v. 7): 'Then they shall take of the blood and put it on the two door posts and the lintel', and here Moses explains how to take it and

22 how to apply it: *Take a bunch of hyssop,* which is well adapted for sprinkling the blood, since the large number of stalks on it collects the fibrin, and thus prevents the blood from coagulating; *and dip* the bunch of hyssop *in the blood* of the lamb *which you will receive in a basin,* at the time of slaughtering, *and touch the lintel and the two doorposts* — by means of the hyssop — *with the blood which is in the basin.* He further adds: *and none of you shall go out of the door of his house until the morning* — so that you may be ready to journey when you are given the signal, in accordance with the injunction in v. 11. He also tells them what is due to happen that

23 night: *For the Lord will pass through to strike down the Egyptians; and when He sees the blood on the lintel and on the two doorposts, the Lord will pass over the door* (a word-play, פֶּתַח *pethaḥ* ['door'] — פָּסַח *pāsaḥ* ['pass over']), and will *not allow the destroyer* — will not permit the destroying angel — *to enter your houses to strike you down.* Thereafter Moses gives the elders general directions concerning the observance of Passover in the future. Just as the word וּשְׁמַרְתֶּם *ūsᵉmartem* ['and you shall observe'] was said to him

24 twice in v. 17, so he uses the word twice to them: *And you shall observe* [וּשְׁמַרְתֶּם *ūsᵉmartem*] *this thing* — the festival of Passover —

25 *as an ordinance for you and for your sons for ever. And when you come to the land which the Lord will give you, as He has promised, you shall keep* [וּשְׁמַרְתֶּם *ūsᵉmartem*] *this service.* Instead of the hard service that you rendered unto Pharaoh and the Egyptians, you shall keep the service of the Lord your God. Moses does not

instruct the people, at this stage, in the regulations for the future observance of Passover, not even in summary form, because the time is not appropriate for this. He contents himself with a passing reference to the continuation of the custom of offering the passover sacrifice in the future; the rest he will tell the people subsequently (xiii 3 ff.). For the time being he merely adds that it will be the duty of every father in Israel to remind his children of the
26 events of that fateful night: *And it shall come to pass, when your*
27 *children say to you, What do you mean by this service? you shall say, It is the sacrifice of the Lord's passover* (compare the end of v. 11, and my commentary *ibid.*), *for He passed over the houses of the people of Israel, in Egypt, when He struck the Egyptians down but spared our houses.*

And when the elders of the people heard these things from Moses, and the rest of the people from the elders, and they realized that the hour of liberation was approaching, they lifted their hearts up in gratitude to the Lord, *and the people bowed their heads and prostrated themselves —* as an expression of thanksgiving. Needless
28 to say, they acted according to the instructions given to them: *Then the children of Israel went and did as the Lord had commanded Moses and Aaron; so they did.*

At this point there is a break in the narrative. We have learnt that the Israelites did as the Lord had commanded them, and prepared themselves for the great events that were about to take place. We now eagerly await the resumption of the story in the continuation of the Biblical account.

FOURTH PARAGRAPH

PLAGUE OF THE FIRST-BORN

(XII 29–32)

The style becomes more elevated; the hour of decision has arrived.
29 *And it came to pass at midnight* — between the fourteenth and the fifteenth, when all the children of Israel were prepared for the approaching events — *that the Lord smote all the first-born in the land of Egypt, from the first-born of Pharaoh who sat on his throne to the first-born of the captive who was in the dungeon* — in prison, where the captives were compelled to do hard labour,

particularly the grinding of corn in the mill (compare xi 5) — *and all the first-born of the cattle* — exactly as Moses had announced 30 to Pharaoh. *And Pharaoh rose up in the night* — the proud king is forced to rise from his bed at night (an unroyal procedure) — *he, and all his servants, and all the Egyptians, and there was a great cry in Egypt* — this, too, was in accord with Moses' forewarning 31 (xi 6) — *for there was not a house where one was not dead. And Pharaoh called for Moses and Aaron by night* — despite his pride and warning to Moses never to see his face again (x 28), he is now compelled to humble himself and to summon to his palace the very men whom a little while ago he had banished therefrom. And all this at dead of night, for time is pressing and he dare not wait till morning. In three consecutive verses the first clause ends with the word *night*, like a threefold echo stressing the terror of that wonder-frought moment: *And it came to pass at midnight — And Pharaoh rose up in the night — And he called for Moses and Aaron by night.*

It was no idle remark that Moses made to Pharaoh (xi 8): 'And all these your servants shall come down to me, and prostrate themselves to me,' etc. So, in truth, it happened: Pharaoh's servants came running to him that night and summoned him and his brother to come before Pharaoh and hear his words of submission from his own lips. When they appeared before him, Pharaoh spoke to them tersely and jerkily, in words [in the Hebrew] of one or two syllables only, like one seized by a terrible dread, who cannot speak calmly: *Rise up, go forth from among my people, both you and the children of Israel; and go, serve the Lord.* Only after he had uttered his assent to their going forth, or more accurately, the command to go, is he able to breathe normally and to utter longer words. He adds: *according to your word* — as you, not I, have said. He now withdraws all his previous restrictions, one by one, even to the last and lightest of them 32 (x 24: 'only let your flocks and your herds be stayed'): *Take your flocks and your herds, as you have said* — as you, and not I, have said (here he again makes the point that he is nullifying his will before theirs) — *and be gone*! And realizing that only from Israel's God, and through the merit of Israel's prayer, can blessing come upon him after his capitulation, just as punishment came upon him on account of his sins, he concludes: *and bless me also*. At the very end there is a word of blessing. The first meeting of the old patriarch Israel with the king of Egypt was marked by benison

(Gen. xlvii, 7, 10: 'and Jacob blessed Pharaoh'), and the last encounter of the leaders of Israel with the king of Egypt concludes with blessing. Possibly the Bible wished to allude thereby to what God had said to Abraham when he was first chosen (Gen. xii 3): 'and in you will be blessed all the families of the earth.'

FIFTH PARAGRAPH

PREPARATIONS FOR THE EXODUS

(XII 33-36)

Just as Pharaoh and his servants had hardened their hearts not to let the Israelites go free, so they were now equally determined to let them go: *And the Egyptians were urgent with the people to send them out of the land in haste* (how the position had changed since Pharaoh first voiced his concern [i 10], lest anything happen to enable the Israelites to go up 'out of the land'!), *for they said* — that is, thought —, *We are all dead men*, if we continue to enslave the Israelites.

The particulars given in *v.* 34 concerning the dough and the kneading bowls that were tied up in the garments of the children of Israel and placed on their shoulders appear at first strange and unnecessary. But it is possible to understand the reference if we assume that the intention of the verse is to prepare us for what we shall subsequently be told, in *v.* 39, about the dough that did not become leavened. In the directions regarding the observance of Passover in Egypt mention is made of the eating of unleavened cakes on the night only, but not on the following day. Since the Israelites ate only unleavened cakes at night, they had no leaven when they left: *So the people took their dough before it was leavened*; but they wanted to eat fresh leavened bread when they reached their first stopping-place. Hence they took with them *their kneading bowls bound up in their mantles,* in order that the dough should become leavened more quickly through being tied up in the mantles, and they put them on *their shoulders*, so that the warmth of their body should help on the process. Subsequently it will be stated in *v.* 39 that all this proved insufficient, and that also on the morrow the Israelites ate only unleavened cakes. The purpose of this narrative is to link the future observance of Passover, which

EXODUS XII 38

prolongs the eating of unleavened bread beyond the first night, with what happened at the exodus from Egypt.

35 Another matter is recorded here, namely, that before their departure *The children of Israel did as Moses told them, and they asked of the Egyptians jewelry of silver and of gold, and clothing;* 36 *and the Lord* (on the position, in the Hebrew, of the subject before the verb both in *v.* 35 and in *v.* 36, see above, on ix 20–21) *gave the people favour in the sight of the Egyptians, so that they let them have what they asked. Thus they despoiled the Egyptians* (for the explanation of this incident, see above, on iii 21–22).

SIXTH PARAGRAPH

THE EXODUS

(XII 37–42)

The place where the Israelites were concentrated prior to their departure from Egypt was Rameses, the last of the store-cities that they had built for Pharaoh (i 11), and from there they set out 37 on their way: *And the children of Israel journeyed from Rameses to Succoth.* Succoth was a border town, named in Egyptian *Ṯkw.* Here the name appears in a Hebrew or Hebraized form. Apparently it was situated at the *tell* called by the Egyptians today Tell el-Maskhuta.

The verse does not give the exact number of those who went out of Egypt; it states the figure only approximately: *about six hundred thousand on foot.* Six hundred thousand is a round number based on the sexagesimal system, and indicates a very large multitude. In order to enhance the impression of this high figure still further, the Bible adds that this includes only *the men*, besides the טַף *ṭaph* — that is, apart from the women and children (see above, on x 10), all of whom likewise left Egypt, and not as Pharaoh had said when he first began to incline towards submission: 'Go now the men among you' (x 11), but as Moses had declared: 'We will go with our young and our old; we will 38 go with our sons and daughters', etc. (x 9). *A mixed multitude also went up with them* — a motley mob who were not of Israelite origin. Apparently the correct view is that which regards the expression עֵרֶב רַב *'ērebh rabh* ['mixed multitude'] as a single

147

EXODUS XII 38

word, from the stem עָרַב 'ārabh, formed by the repetition of the last two radicals, like פְּקַח־קוֹחַ pᵉqaḥ-qōaḥ ['opening of eyes' (Isa. lxi 1)], (לַ)חְפֹּר פֵּרוֹת (la)ḥpōr pērōth [read: לַ חֲפַרְפָּרוֹת (la)ḥăphar-pārōth, 'moles' (Isa. ii 20)], and especially the word הָאסַפְסֻף (hā)'saphsuph ('rabble'; Num. xi 4), which also designates the mixed multitude that went up from Egypt with the Israelites. The children of Israel brought with them, needless to say, all their cattle: *and flocks and herds, even very much cattle.*

When they reached their first halting-place, they tried to prepare good bread, leavened bread (see above, on v. 34), but they were 39 unsuccessful. *And they baked the dough which they had brought out of Egypt,* but they were able to make of it only *unleavened cakes, for it was not leavened* — the dough had not yet had time to become leavened — *because they were thrust out of Egypt and could not tarry* and leaven the dough, *neither had they prepared for themselves any provisions* of other bread, or of leaven.

Now, at the conclusion of the section, the Bible bids us look back at the length of the prolonged exile in Egypt, which 40 has now come to an end: *Now the time that the children of Israel dwelt in Egypt was four hundred and thirty years.* I have dealt with this number and its relationship to the other chronological data above, in my annotations to vi 16–26. I explained there that the figure is to be understood as indicating a very long interval of time, in accordance with the customary practice in the ancient East; thus it comprises a round number based on the sexagesimal system (360), with the addition of a multiple of seven (70). This was the time, Scripture tells us here, that Divine providence had determined from the first that the Israelites should stay in 41 Egypt. *And it came to pass at the end of four hundred and thirty years, on that very day* — when the period previously fixed by God came to an end — *that all the hosts of the Lord went out* (compare v. 17) — that is all the tribes of the people sanctified unto the Lord, and organized according to their hosts (see above, on vi 26) — *from the land of Egypt.* The night of the exodus from bondage to 42 freedom *was a night of watching by the Lord* — as the shepherd watches his flock at night (this sense of keeping watch at night is an old and special signification of the stem שָׁמַר šāmar in the Semitic languages) — ordained from the beginning *to bring them out from the land of Egypt.* Such *is this night unto the Lord,* and as such it must be *a night of observance* [= watching] *by all the children of Israel throughout their generations* — that is, a night on which the

Israelites will observe the holy charge ['watching', 'observe' and 'charge' are all from the same root שָׁמַר *šāmar* in Hebrew] of the service of the Shepherd and Redeemer of Israel.

So the section draws to a close, with a twofold repetition of the expression for 'watching' or 'observance' [שִׁמֻּרִים *šimmūrīm*], which we have already encountered [the words are different, but the stem is the same] once at the beginning (v. 6: לְמִשְׁמֶרֶת *lᵉmišmereth* [literally, 'charge'; rendered: 'you shall keep it']); then twice in v. 17 (וּשְׁמַרְתֶּם *ūšᵉmartem* ['and you shall observe']); and twice again in vv. 24–25 (in this case, too, וּשְׁמַרְתֶּם *ūšᵉmartem*); in all there are seven references, which are intended to emphasize the principal thought that the Lord is the keeper of Israel. Similarly, the expressions *this (that) day* and *(this) that night* occur seven times in the section; and fourteen times we find the word *house (household)*, referring to the houses of the Israelites over which the Keeper of Israel kept watch. Proof that this is not fortuitous is to be found in the text itself, which expressly mentions the number seven and its multiples a number of times (vv. 15, 19: 'seven days'; vv. 15, 16: 'the seventh day'; vv. 6, 18: 'the fourteenth day'; v. 18: 'the twenty-first day'), and adds seventy to the round number 360 in vv. 40–41.

APPENDIXES TO THE SECTION

(XII 43–XIII 16)

Two appendices are attached to the section of the Exodus from Egypt, which deal with ritual laws connected with the subject, namely, laws relating to the Passover, laws of the first-born, and other precepts that were ordained for all time as a memorial to the departure from Egypt.

FIRST APPENDIX

THE ORDINANCE OF PASSOVER

(XII 43–50)

43 This addendum begins after the formula, *And the Lord said to Moses and Aaron*, with the words, *This is the ordinance of the*

Passover, which serves as a rubric to the collection of regulations that follow. This ritual compendium was intended to be learned by heart, and its form is adapted to assist memorization. It contains seven laws, formulated with legal brevity and precision, and each one ends with the pronominal suffix [masc. sing.] of the third person (וֹ–ō). The first three regulations, and also the last, conclude with the words, *shall (may) eat of it* or *then shall he eat of it*; the three remaining laws end with the words, *of it* [בּוֹ *bō*] — *it* [אֹתוֹ *'ōthō*] — *keep it* [לַעֲשֹׂתוֹ *la'ăśōthō*; literally, 'to do it']. The regulations are as follows:

(a) *No foreigner shall eat of it.* This is the main rule, namely, that participation in the Passover sacrifice is restricted to Israelites.

44 (b) *But every slave*, who is *a man* — that is, a male — *that is bought for money, when you have circumcised him* — thereby joining him to the congregation of Israel — *then he may eat of it.*

45 (c) *A settler or hired servant* — who actually dwells among the children of Israel, but has not joined them — *shall not eat of it.*

46 (d) *In one house shall* the flesh of the sacrifice *be eaten; you shall not carry forth outside the house* any portion *of the flesh; and you shall not break a bone of it.*

47 (e) *All the congregation of Israel* — without exception — *shall keep it.*

48 (f) *And when a sojourner shall sojourn with you, and will keep* — that is, will wish to keep — *the passover to the Lord, let all his males be circumcised, then he may come near and keep it.*

(g) Then, after his circumcision, *he* — the sojourner — *shall be as a native of the land.* However, till such time as he is circumcised, he will be subject to the law of every uncircumcised person, *and no uncircumcised person shall eat of it* (on the connection between the commandment of circumcision and that of passover, see my note above, on xii 5).

After the ordinance of the Passover, apropos of the last regula-
49 tion, a general law in regard to the sojourner is prescribed: *There shall be one law for the native and for the sojourner who sojourns among you* — if he joins the heritage of Israel.

50 Finally, there comes the customary formula: *And all the children of Israel did as the Lord commanded Moses and Aaron; so they did.*

SECOND APPENDIX

THE LAWS OF THE FIRST-BORN AND A MEMORIAL TO THE EXODUS

(XII 51–XIII 16)

Verse 51 serves to connect this appendix to the section of the Exodus from Egypt. It recapitulates the previous narrative and summarizes it in words that, on the one hand, parallel xii 41, and,
51 on the other, *v.* 3 below: *And it came to pass* — in accordance with what we were told above — *on that very day* — which had been predetermined — *that the Lord brought the children of Israel out of the land of Egypt by their hosts* (see my comments on xii 41), and consequently the following precepts were given to Israel.

Chapter XIII

In the Lord's communication to Moses, which is introduced by
1 the usual formula, *And the Lord spoke unto Moses saying*, the commandment concerning the sanctification of the first-born is given in general outline only. The details will be mentioned in Moses' address to the people (*vv.* 12 ff.). Without doubt Scripture intends us to understand that they were all given to Moses by the Almighty, but that they are not recorded here in order to avoid repetition (see my remarks on this literary procedure in my commentary on
2 x 2). At this stage only the general principle is stated: *Consecrate to Me all the first-born*, that is to say, *whatever is the first to open the womb among the children of Israel, both of men and of beast* — owned by an Israelite; the firstborn from among these *is Mine*.

After this comes Moses' address to the people, which is divided into two parts. The first part, which extends to the end of *v.* 10, comprises detailed regulations for the observance of Passover in the future, concerning which Moses had so far given only general instructions (see above, on xii 24–25). The passage begins with the word *Remember*, in keeping with what God had said to Moses
3 (xii 14): 'And this day shall be for you a memorial day'. *Remember* – for all generations to come — *this day, in which you came out from Egypt, out of the house of bondage*; and remember that you succeeded in coming out only on account of the fact *that by strength of hand the Lord brought you out from this place*; and just as on the night before the liberation and on the following day you did not eat anything leavened, so, too, in the future, as an annual me-

4 morial of this fact, *no leavened bread shall be eaten. This day you go forth, in the month of Abib,* which renews your life even as it revives the life of all nature; and you go forth in order to come to
5 the Land of Promise: *And it shall be when the Lord brings you into the land of the Canaanites, the Hittites… which He swore to your fathers to give you, a land flowing with milk and honey* (there recur here, with some variations, the expressions announcing the good tidings concerning the possession of the land that are found above, iii 8, 17), *that you shall continue to celebrate the festival of Passover, and you shall keep this service in this month.* You have departed from the house of bondage, and the yoke of the hard work that you were forced to do in Egypt has been removed from your neck; in its stead you will perform this pleasant service, the service of the Lord your God, and in His honour you will
6 celebrate the festival of Freedom. *Seven* additional *days* — apart from the first night of the festival — *you shall eat unleavened cakes, and on the seventh day* of this week, there shall be again *a festival*
7 *to the Lord.* You are not only enjoined that *Unleavened cakes shall be eaten for seven days,* but also that *no leavened bread shall be seen with you, and no leaven shall be seen with you in all your territory.* Similarly you are commanded not only to remember,
8 but also to remind your children: *And you shall tell your son on that day* — on the day of the festival of freedom — *saying, It is because of this* — the fact that we the children of Israel will dedicate our lives to His service — *that the Lord did for me* [literally, 'to me'] — that is, the Lord wrought on my behalf — *when I came out of Egypt.* And in order to preserve the memory of your exodus from bondage to freedom by the hand of the Lord, you shall make for yourself a sign that shall serve as a reminder. In *v.* 9, the subject
9 of the verb וְהָיָה *wᵉhāyā* ['and… shall be'] is the sentence at the end of the verse: *that with a strong hand,* etc., whilst the words, *so that the law of the Lord may be in your mouth,* constitute a parenthetic statement (in *v.* 16, which is similar to this verse, these words do not occur). *And this thing shall be to you as a sign on your hand and as a remembrance* — that is, a memorial — *between your eyes (so that the law of the Lord may be in your mouth),* to wit, *that with a strong hand the Lord has brought you out of Egypt.* The sign on the hand recalls the 'strong hand'. Of the form of the sign and the memorial the text gives us no details; according to Talmudic interpretation, as is well known, the reference is to the precept of the phylacteries. The expression *between your eyes* certainly means op-

posite the part between the eyes, that is, on the forehead, which is the Talmudic interpretation of the phrase, and also the signification that the corresponding expressions have in Ugaritic and Syriac. *The law of the Lord* referred to in this verse connotes the entire body of precepts connected with the service of the Lord, which you undertook to keep when you dedicated your life to Him on being redeemed from the house of bondage, and which will ever be near to your heart and soul, if you will remember constantly the day when you went forth out of the land of Egypt.

The first part of Moses' oration concludes with another reference to the duty of observance, which, as we have seen, is the basic theme of the section of the Exodus from Egypt, and with the repetition of the word *ordinance*, which occurs (*v.* 43) in the rubric of
10 the first appendix: *You shall therefore observe this ordinance at its appointed time from year to year* [literally, 'from days to days'].

The second part of Moses' address contains detailed regulations appertaining to the first-born (see above, on *v.* 2). The formulation of this part corresponds to that of the first. Its opening sentence is
11 like *v.* 5, with certain variations: *And it shall be when the Lord brings you into the land of the Canaanites, as he swore to you and your fathers, and shall give it to you*, that, when you have settled
12 in your land, *you shall cause to pass over all that first opens the womb* [רֶחֶם *reḥem*], among human beings, *to the Lord* — you shall transfer it from your possession to the Lord's — *and likewise all that first opens the womb* [שֶׁגֶר *šegher*] *of your cattle, which you shall have* (a beast's רֶחֶם *reḥem* is apparently also called שֶׁגֶר *šegher*); if these first-born, be they of people or cattle, are *males*, they shall be transferred *to the Lord*. This 'causing to pass over' meant originally, in the tradition of the ancient East, to offer as a sacrifice; but it is characteristic of the Torah that when it accepts or confirms one of the customs of the neighbouring peoples, it introduces innovations therein, giving it a new *raison d'être*, and imbuing it with new significance. This also applies to the law of the first-born. The custom of offering them on the altar continued to obtain only in regard to clean domestic animals; in the case of unclean beasts, there took place, instead, redemption
13 by a clean animal or the breaking of its neck: *Every firstling of an ass you shall redeem with a lamb, or if you will not redeem it you shall break its neck*. To the human first-born, of course, only the law of redemption applies: *Every first-born of man among your sons you shall redeem*. The new reason is the deliverance of

EXODUS XIII 13

the Israelite first-born at the time of the plague, when the first born of Egypt were destroyed. This explanation is given, in parallelism
14 with *v.* 8, in the form of an answer to the son's question: *And it shall be when your son asks you in time to come, saying, What is this?* — what is the significance of the laws of the first-born? — that you shall answer: *you shall say to him, By strength of hand the Lord brought us out of Egypt, from the house of bondage* (paralleling
15 *v.* 3 and *v.* 9); *and it came to pass, when Pharaoh hardened* — when Pharaoh hardened his heart and refused — *to let us go*, that punishment came upon him from the hand of the Lord: *the Lorf slew all the first-born in the land of Egypt, both the first-born od man and the first-born of cattle. Therefore I sacrifice to the Lord all the males that first open the womb* — of the clean cattle — *but all the first-born of my sons I redeem.* Verse 16 corresponds to *v.* 9, and is almost identical with it, except for a few variations:
16 *And it shall be as a sign on your hand, and as frontlet-bands between your eyes*, namely, *that by strength of hand the Lord brought us out of Egypt*. For the exposition of the verse, see above, on *v.* 9. The etymology of the word טוֹטָפֹת *ṭōṭāphōth* ['frontlet-bands'], which takes the place here of the word זִכָּרוֹן *zikkārōn* ['memorial'] in *v.* 9, is not clear; but it is certain that it denotes a sign or mark placed, as a memorial, on the forehead, like the frontlets with which women adorn themselves (Tractate Shabbat, vi 1).

SECTION EIGHT

THE DIVISION OF THE SEA OF REEDS

CHAPTER XIII, VERSE 17—CHAPTER XV, VERSE 21

FIRST PARAGRAPH

THE JOURNEY IN THE WILDERNESS

(XIII 17-22)

After the two ritual appendixes, the Torah resumes the narration of events. In order to provide a link with the preceding narrative, the Bible begins with a brief reference to the last episode related before the appendixes: *And it came to pass, when Pharaoh let the people go*. After this allusion, it is possible to continue the story and to describe what happened subsequently.

The first matter dealt with here is the direction taken by the children of Israel. Three routes were possible: one to the northeast, the other to the southeast, and the third in between. The first was the route known as 'the way of the sea' along the Mediterranean sea-coast; this was the military road of the Egyptians, which they used on their expeditions northward. The middle course lay in the direction of Beersheba and the Negeb, which leads to the heart of the land of Caanan *via* the territory of the Philistines — not the Philistines who settled in the southern Shephelah in the twelfth century B.C.E., but those tribes of related stock, who apparently preceded them and made their home in Gerar and the surrounding area (on this subject, see my book *From Noah to Abraham*, pp. 206-208). The southeast route, towards the peninsula of Sinai, would not bring the migrants nearer to the land of Canaan, but on the contrary would take them further away from it. Yet it was precisely this direction that was chosen out of the three. The first was certainly unsuitable, since the Egyptians guarded the main road effectively by means of an organized garrison force that was stationed at each of the posts *en route*; to have travelled along that road would have meant not liberation from Egypt, but, on the contrary, putting one's neck more firmly under the Egyptian yoke. Hence there is not the slightest reference in the text to this

155

EXODUS XIII 17

route. Regarding the intermediate direction, it is stated here: *that God did not lead them by way of the land of the Philistines* — that is, by the route that crosses the land of the Philistines (the word *way* means here 'through', '*via*') — just *because it was near*, and would have brought the Israelites to the land of Canaan too soon. The reason for this was: *for God said* — that is, thought that there was cause to fear—*Lest the people repent* of their desire for freedom (note the word-play: וְלֹא נָחָם *wᵉlō' nāḥām* ['did not lead them'] — פֶּן יִנָּחֵם *pen yinnāḥēm* ['lest… repent']) *when they see war* — if they reach the border of the land of Canaan after only a few days and will have to fight its inhabitants when their morale is still low as a result of their servitude — *and return to Egypt* — and they will prefer to return to their hard labour, so long as they do not have to face the hazards of battle. Bearing out this very fear, it is narrated in Num. xiv 4 that, when the children of Israel approached the land of the Negeb and learnt from the spies how strong the inhabitants were, and saw the danger of war to be imminent, they said: 'Let us choose a captain, and go back to Egypt.'

18 For this reason the southeastern direction was chosen: *But God led the people round* by a long circuitous route that passed *by the way of the wilderness* — through the wilderness — toward *the Sea of Reeds* and the peninsula of Sinai. This agrees with what Moses had been told at the outset, namely, that, when they left Egypt, the Israelites would serve God at Mount Horeb, which is Sinai (iii 12). As will be seen later, the Sea of Reeds mentioned here is one of the lakes to the north of Suez.

Recently it has been suggested that the meaning of the passage is that God did not lead the people by 'the way of the sea', which leads to the land of the Philistines in the Shephelah and is consequently called *the way of the land of the Philistines*, but that He led them actually along the Mediterranean sea-coast, north of that road, in which case the Sea of Reeds is Lake Sirbonis, which is close to the Mediterranean. This conjecture is improbable, because the proximity of this route to the military road would have been a danger to the people, as we have already explained, and also for other reasons that we shall discuss in the continuation of our commentary (after our annotations to xiv 29; and in our notes on xvi 13; xvii 8).

The Torah further indicates that *the children of Israel went up out of the land of Egypt* חֲמֻשִׁים *ḥămūšīm* — that is, on the basis of the Arabic, in proper military formation [translate: 'in orderly array']. They went not like a mob of slaves escaping from their masters, in confusion and disorder, but well organized, in conformity with the statement above that they went forth 'by their hosts'.

So efficient was the organization that even at that most fateful and difficult moment Moses did not forget the promise that earlier generations had made to Joseph before his death: *And Moses took the bones of Joseph with him; for he* [Joseph] *had solemnly sworn the children of Israel, saying, God will surely remember you; then you must carry my bones up with you from here.* The *ipsissima verba* of Joseph, recorded in Gen. l 25, are repeated here with the addition of the words *with you*, which parallel the words *with him* in the first part of the verse; this literal repetition explains why the name *'Elōhīm* ['God'] and not *YHWH* ['Lord'] occurs in these verses. Joseph employed the name *'Elōhim* for the reason given above, at the end of my commentary to chapter i; and since his words are quoted exactly, the name *'Elōhīm* is used also in the preceding sentences, in order to avoid the impression that there is a difference between Joseph's God [*'Elōhīm*] and the Lord [*YHWH*], who brought Israel out of Egypt, and, contrariwise, to emphasize that 'the Lord He is God.' Once the point had been made clear, the text can revert, from *v.* 21 onwards, to its customary use of the Tetragrammaton.

In accordance with the route selected, the children of Israel turned, when they left Succoth (xii 37), towards the wilderness: *And they moved on from Succoth, and encamped at Etham, on the edge of the wilderness* — that is, at the last station of the inhabited country adjoining the wilderness. It is not stated how long they stayed at Succoth; it may have been a day, or possibly more. Similarly, we are not told how long the journey from Succoth to Etham took. The identification of the site of Etham is in doubt. Some hold that it was the castle called in Egyptian *Ḫtm n Ṯrw* an important border station (today, Tell Abu-Seifeh); but this identification appears to be incorrect, for this fortress was actually on the main maritime road, which the Israelites certainly did not take. See further, on the identification of Etham, my annotations to xiv 1–2. — This verse occurs in almost identical form in Num. xxxiii 6: *And they moved on from Succoth, and encamped at Etham, which is on the edge of the wilderness*; and in general, this formula, 'and they journeyed (= moved on) from so-and-so place and encamped in so-and-so place', is the customary way of describing the journeyings in the wilderness.

EXODUS XIII 21

Although the Israelites were travelling in a country that they did not know, they had no reason to fear that they would go astray in the desert. Just as caravan guides in the wilderness are accustomed to carry in front of their caravans certain signals to guide the caravans in the right direction, smoke signals by day and fire
21 signals by night, so it is narrated here that the *Lord*, the Shepherd and Guide of Israel, *went before them by day in a pillar of cloud to lead them along the way* (here, at the end of the paragraph, the verb נָחָה *nāḥā* ['lead'], used in the opening verse, recurs), *and by night in a pillar of fire to give them light*. In the continuation of the narrative (xiv 19) the pillar that went before the Israelite camp is called 'the angel of God', but here the act is attributed to the Lord Himself, since 'a person's agent is as himself', a principle that applies even to the Almighty. With the help of these pillars it was possible for the people *to travel by day and by night* — that is, either by day or by night, as required. This guidance by the pillars
22 was continuous: *The pillar of cloud by day and the pillar of fire by night did not depart* from *before the people* (the expressions *by day* and *by night* occur three times for emphasis).

The style of the entire paragraph is poetic and elevated, and, particularly in the closing verses, a poetic rhythm is noticeable. Possibly one may detect here traces of the ancient epic poem on the exodus from Egypt, which I have already mentioned a number of times. It may also be that this paragraph, or its source, was the inspiration of several Biblical passages that depict the ultimate redemption in terms of the first redemption, for example, Micah ii 13: '[they will break through and pass the gate] going out by it; and their King will pass on before them; the Lord at their head'; Isa. lii 12: 'For you shall not go in haste, and you shall not go in flight, for the Lord will go before you', etc.; and so, too, another passage, which, although referring to another subject, uses similar phraseology, to wit, Jos. i 8-9: 'This book of the law shall not depart out of your mouth (compare *v.* 9 in our chapter), but you shall meditate on it day and night... for then you shall make your way prosperous... for the Lord your God is with you wherever you go.'

SECOND PARAGRAPH

THE ENCAMPMENT BY THE SEA OF REEDS

(XIV 1–4)

Chapter XIV
After the Israelites had reached the edge of the wilderness, and had encamped some time at Etham (here, too, it is not stated how long their stay there lasted, and also in this case it may have been a single day or longer), Moses was commanded by the Lord to
1-2 change their route slightly: *that they turn back* [וְיָשֻׁבוּ *wᵉyāšūbhū*] (compare וַיָּשֻׁבוּ *wayyāšūbhū* ['then they turned back'] in Gen. xiv 7) — that is, let them turn round and not continue to travel in a south-easterly direction, which would bring them into the desert, but let them make a detour in a south-westerly direction and return to the edge of the inhabited country. The site where they are enjoined to camp is specified in detail: *and encamp in front of Pi-hahiroth, between Migdol and the sea, in front of Baal-zephon; you shall encamp over against it, by the sea.* The sea mentioned here is the same as that called further on 'the Sea of Reeds' [יַם־סוּף *Yam Sūph*]. This name usually denotes in the Bible the Red Sea, and so the ancient commentators and translators understood it here, but apparently in our passage it is the designation of one of the marshes or lakes near the Red Sea; see Rashi on xiii 18: 'סוּף *Sūph* means a marsh in which reeds grow.' The most probable interpretation is that the Bible refers here by this name to one of the Bitter Lakes north of Suez, and more particularly to the largest of them, which in ancient times may have been connected, at least periodically, to the Red Sea, and could have been considered a part of it and called by the same name. Not long ago, a French scholar, Captain Bourdon, carried out investigations in the area, and came to the conclusion that it is actually this lake that is called 'the Sea of Reeds' in our section. He identifies Etham with a station north of this lake; it is referred to in the Itinerary of Antonine by the name of *Serapaeum*, and today, too, this is the name of the local railway station. According to this view, the words *that they turn back* mean that after staying in Etham, which is north of the Lake, the Israelites would go back a little way, and skirt the western shore of the lake until they reached the place of their new encampment. There, on the west of the lake, there is still to be seen the

EXODUS XIV 1-2

ruins of a tower, one of the towers situated on the borders of Egypt, which is apparently to be identified with Migdol [which means 'tower'] of our verse. Bourdon also quotes an Egyptian papyrus, a kind of itinerary, that comprises a list of geographical names; among these are recorded, after the designations of the lakes, the names of four towers, one of which is the Tower of Baal-zephon. The latter is the appellation of one of the Canaanite deities ('Al'iyn Ba'al of the Ugaritic texts, who dwells in the heights of the North [צָפוֹן *ṣᵉphōn* (zephon) signifies 'north'], which the Canaanites introduced also into Egypt, and apparently this tower was called after the temple of Baal-zephon, which was close by. Possibly this is the tower mentioned here by the name Migdol next to the name Baal-zephon. Bourdon thinks that it is possible to find in the aforementioned papyrus also a name resembling Pi-hahiroth, but this identification is doubtful. Be this as it may, the remaining data suffice as a basis for the assumption that our passage refers to the aforementioned lake and to the tower called in the papyrus the Tower of Baal-zephon. Accordingly, the meaning of our text will be: Let the children of Israel encamp on the stretch of land between the tower and the sea, in front of the temple of Baal-zephon. Encamp opposite that temple, on the sea, that is, close to the bank of the lake.

When the report of the Egyptian police concerning the return of the Israelites to inhabited territory after they had already reached the edge of the desert will be brought to Pharaoh, he will begin

3 to wonder: *For Pharaoh will say of the children of Israel* — that is, he will think regarding the Israelites — *They are perplexed in the land* — they are bemused wherever they are — and *the wilderness has shut for them* the route, like a barrier that cannot be crossed. These thoughts will lead to the hardening of Pharaoh's heart after it had become softened on the night of the plague of the first born, and he will decide to pursue the children of Israel:

4 *And I will harden Pharaoh's heart, and he will pursue them*, and as a result of the punishment that will be inflicted on Pharaoh and his men in the course of their pursuit, *I will get glory over Pharaoh and all his host; and the Egyptians shall know* — both Pharaoh, who had said at first (v 2): 'I do not know YHWH ['the Lord']', and his people, who did not yet 'fear the Lord God' (ix 30) — *that I am the Lord*. In this communication Moses receives tidings, as yet obscure and without details, concerning the final punishment of Pharaoh and his servants, and the deliverance of the Israelites

from their hand. And they — the children of Israel — *did so*, and went back and encamped in the place appointed for them. Thus the paragraph concludes with a picture of the people encamped according to its tribes near the Sea of Reeds, tranquil and trusting in the Lord and in Moses his servant.

THIRD PARAGRAPH

THE PURSUIT BY THE EGYPTIANS

(XIV 5–8)

Now the Bible leaves the children of Israel encamped by the sea and transports us to Egypt and Pharaoh's palace, so that we may learn what happened there since the first day after the night of the exodus of the Israelites.

5 *And the king of Egypt was told*, by his police and officers, *that the people had fled*. This took place, it seems, on the fifteenth of the month, for in the second half of the night, the children of Israel went forth from Rameses (compare Num. xxxiii 3, which is dependent on our narrative or a common source), and on the same day they reached Succoth, and, without doubt, on that very day Pharaoh's officers delivered to him their report on the subject. From what the police saw, they clearly recognized that this was not a temporary departure with a view to returning after a short time, but a permanent exodus; hence they told the king *that the people had fled*. The exodus from Egypt, which the Israelites regarded as a liberation from bondage and an emergence into freedom, appeared to the Egyptians merely as the escape of slaves from their masters. Similarly, Jacob's departure from Laban's house is termed in the Book of Genesis an act of flight whenever it is referred to from the viewpoint of Laban. Since the Egyptians were now considering the loss that they had suffered by the termination of the Israelites' service, they were distressed that they had permitted them to leave. *The mind of Pharaoh and his servants was changed toward the people*; when they were terror-stricken they urged the Israelites to go forth, but now the position was changed: *and they said, What is this we have done, that we have let Israel go from serving us*. With a view to bringing them back to their service,
6 Pharaoh issued an order of mobilization: *And he made ready his*

chariot — that is, his chariots of war [the word 'chariot' is to be understood as a collective] — *and his people* — his army — *he took with him* (we have a word-play here: עַמּוֹ *'ammō* ['his people'] — עִמּוֹ *'immō* ['with him']). The general statement is now followed by
7 particulars to indicate what he took: *and he took six hundred picked chariots* — six hundred is a round number based on the sexagesimal system (see my comments on xii 37, 40), and together with them also *all the other chariots of Egypt* (the word *all* is a hyperbolic expression indicating a great quantity, as we have already observed a number of times) *and* שָׁלִישִׁים *šālīšīm* — that is (according to the signification of the word *tlt* in the Ugaritic texts), 'chariot-warriors' — *on all of them* — on each chariot.

The issue and implementation of the mobilization order took, of course, several days, and in the meantime the Israelites journeyed from Succoth to Etham, and from Etham to a station on the Sea of Reeds; and when Pharaoh was apprised of the return of the Israelites to settled country and of their encampment by the sea,
8 that which had been foretold to Moses happened (*vv.* 3–4): *And the Lord hardened the heart of Pharaoh king of Egypt and he pursued the children of Israel* — on the assumption that they were perplexed in the land and that the desert barred their way. However, it was not as Pharaoh imagined: *for the children of Israel* were not perplexed in the land, *but were going out with a high hand* (compare again Num. xxxiii 3) — that is, with bold mien and complete confidence. A fitting ending to the paragraph.

FOURTH PARAGRAPH

THE MEETING OF THE TWO HOSTS

(XIV 9–14)

9 The opening words, *And the Egyptians pursued them*, serve to link this paragraph to the one preceding at the point prior to the parenthetic note at the end of *v.* 8, which states that the children of Israel went out with a high hand. The narrative then continues: *and overtook them encamped at the sea,* for it was easy for the soldiers mounted on chariots to overtake quickly the people who were proceeding at a leisurely pace. From what is subsequently stated it is clear that 'overtake' is not to be understood literally,

EXODUS XIV 11

but means simply that they drew near enough to see them. This proximity was quite sufficient to inspire the Israelites with dread, for it was *all Pharaoh's horses and chariots and his horsemen and his army* who were pursuing them, and they had already reached the very area where the Israelites were encamped, *by Pi-hahiroth, in front of Baal-zephon* (compare v. 2). The phrasing of this verse derives apparently from the language of the Song of the Sea (xv 1: 'the horse and his rider'; ibid., v. 4: 'Pharaoh's chariot and his host'; ibid., v. 9: 'I will pursue, I will overtake'; compare also v. 19, which follows the Song: 'the horses of Pharaoh with his chariots and his horsemen'). As for the reference to the horses and chariots, which are particularly stressed in both passages, and are mentioned before the army, we shall see the reason for this emphasis further on.

The two narrative threads of the preceding paragraphs meet and become entwined here: the first and second paragraphs speak of the journey of the children of Israel; paragraph three deals with the pursuit of the Egyptians; here we learn of the two hosts coming together in one place.

10 In that narrow terrain Pharaoh's host approached swiftly: *And Pharaoh drew near. And the children of Israel lifted up their eyes* (a stereotyped formula in the Canaanite literary tradition, as is evidenced in the Ugaritic writings), *and behold* — they saw a terrifying vision — *Egypt was marching after them* with hostile intent. Although the children of Israel were armed (xiii 18), yet they had with them their women and children and old folk, and they were certainly unable to withstand an organized army; hence their alarm: *and they were in great fear*. In front of them the sea, and behind them the army of the foe; no human power was able to save them. Then they turned to the Lord for help: *and the children of Israel cried out to the Lord*.

The psychological reaction of the Israelites was typical of the usual fickleness of the masses who willingly obey their leaders when things go well, but are quick to rise up against them in time

11 of calamity and danger: *And they said to Moses, Is it because* [הֲמִבְּלִי *hămibbᵉlī*, literally, 'Is it without'] *there are no graves in Egypt that you have taken us away to die in the wilderness*? Is it because there is a dearth of graves in Egypt (compare ii Kings i 3, 6, 16: 'Is it because [הֲמִבְּלִי *hămibbᵉlī*] there is no God in Israel?'; Ecclesiastes iii 11: 'yet so that [מִבְּלִי *mibbᵉlī*] man cannot find out', etc.) that you have brought us out from there so that we should

163

die in the wilderness? *What is this you have done to us, in bringing us out of Egypt?* Why have you done us evil by bringing us from there here? The parallelism between this question of the Israelites and the question of the Egyptians in *v.* 5 ('What is this we have done?' — 'What is this you have done?') is significant. At this fateful moment both peoples regret what they have done; as yet they do not understand that it is all the work of Providence.

12   The children of Israel further ask Moses: *Is not this the word that we spoke to you in Egypt, saying, Let us alone that we may serve the Egyptians?* This question appears surprising at first, for we have not read previously that such words were spoken to Moses. Nor is the purport of the protest of the Israelite foremen (v 21) identical with that of the words uttered now. However, from a psychological standpoint the matter can easily be explained. In the hour of peril the children of Israel remember that remonstrance, and now it seems to them that it was of a sharper character and flowed from their foresight, and that the present situation justifies it, for death awaits them at this moment in the desert. Without doubt *it would have been better for us to serve the Egyptians than to die in the wilderness.*

But Moses is not dispirited, either by the danger or the censure of his people. He answers with courage and unmitigated faith in
13 God's help: *Fear not, stand* firm and confident *and see* — you have nothing to do but to see — *the salvation of the Lord which He will work for you today* — this very day, without your having to wait — *for* — on this point I can assure you — *the form in which you see the Egyptians today* — as threatening and frightening enemies — *you will see them again no more for ever.* The antithetic parallelism between seeing salvation (*and see*) and seeing the Egyptians (*you see* — *will see them*), and the threefold occurrence of the verb *to see* are certainly not accidental (cf. *vv.* 30–31); so, too, the alliteration of the three words commencing with ʿ*Ayin* (עוֹד ʿ*ōdh* ['again'] — עַד ʿ*adh* ['until, for'] — עוֹלָם ʿ*ōlām* ['ever'] is not fortuitous.

14   The closing words of Moses recall his opening assurance: *The Lord will fight you* (compare in the Song of the Sea, *v.* 3: 'The Lord is a man of war'), *and you have only to be still* — to be silent and put your trust in Him, and He will act.

Moses is fully confident in the Lord's salvation, although he does not yet know in what manner it will come. The reader waits with wondering eagerness to learn what will happen now. The next paragraph will provide the answer that he is awaiting.

FIFTH PARAGRAPH
THE WAY OF SALVATION
(XIV 15–18)

15 *The Lord said to Moses, Why do you cry to Me?* The word מַה *ma* [rendered: 'why'] may have the normal interrogative meaning here, or even a negative connotation, like the Arabic ما *mā*, that is 'Do not cry to Me.' We may assume that Moses also took part in the prayer mentioned in *v.* 10 ('and the children of Israel cried out to the Lord'); now he is told that there is no need to continue praying; the time for action has arrived. *Speak to the children of Israel that they should journey* — that they should go forward, without fear or anxiety. Although they see in front of them the Sea of Reeds, and it appears to them an impassable barrier, yet I say, 'that they should go forward'; the sea shall not impede their way.

The commencement of this paragraph parallels that of paragraph two ('Speak to the children of Israel that they turn back and encamp' — 'speak to the children of Israel that they journey'). Note should also be taken of what I stated above (on xiii 20) in regard to the frequent parallelism between *and they journeyed* (= moved on) and *and they encamped*.

16 *And you*, Moses, after giving the order to move forward, do this: *Lift up your rod and stretch out your hand over the sea* — as a sign that it is I who will what is about to happen — *and divide it*; as soon as you give this signal the waters of the sea will be divided, as though you had done this, and thereby a ford will be formed, *and the children of Israel will go on dry ground through the sea*. How the dividing of the Sea of Reeds is to be understood according to the simple meaning of the text, we shall explain later.

17–18 The statements contained in *vv.* 17–18: *And I, behold, I am about to harden the hearts of the Egyptians... And the Egyptians shall know that I am the Lord*, etc. corresponds to what was said to Moses in *v.* 4. There are only a few changes in the wording here, necessitated by the altered circumstances. These are mainly: (a) instead of *And I will harden* we have here, *and I, behold, I am about to harden*, because the act is about to be performed at once; (b) in place of *Pharaoh's heart* we read here *the hearts of the Egyptians*, because not only Pharaoh but all his men will behave bravely when they go into the midst of the sea; (c) the announcement made to Moses in *v.* 4 in general terms begins to receive at least partial clarification now in the words, *and they shall go in after them.* But even at this stage it is not explicitly stated what will happen.

The pronoun *I*, which is emphasized at the beginning of *v.* 17, parallels the pronoun *you*, which is stressed at the commencement of *v.* 16. An echo of the expression at the end of *v.* 17, *and I will get glory over Pharaoh and all his host, his chariots and his horsemen*, is heard in *v.* 18, *when I have gotten glory over Pharaoh, his chariots, and his horsemen.* This echo gives a formal ending to our paragraph.

SIXTH PARAGRAPH

THE ISRAELITES PASS THROUGH THE MIDST
OF THE SEA

(XIV 19–22)

This paragraph depicts for us, in an exalted and poetic style, a sublime scene, which is the climactic act in the liberation of the children of Israel.

19 The first word וַיִּסַּע *wayyissaʽ* ['and moved'] parallels the word וְיִסָּעוּ *wᵉyissāʽū* ['that they journey', 'go forward'] at the beginning of the preceding paragraph, as though the action of the angel of God signified: 'Look at me, and do likewise.' *Then the angel of God moved* — he was, as will be explained in the continuation of the verse, the pillar of cloud *that went before the host of Israel, and he went behind them.* In the evening, after standing all day as a signal before the host, the cloud did not, as hitherto, disappear, but passed from the front to the back of the host, to separate the Israelites from the pursuing Egyptians. The second half of the verse, which parallels the first half, elucidates what is meant by the angel of God: *and the pillar of cloud moved from before and stood behind them.* The expression *stood* instead of *went*, used previously, signifies that the pillar of cloud [after its change of position] remained stationary, not moving from its new site; and again the point is
20 further clarified in *v.* 20: *coming between the host of Egypt and the host of Israel* — it entered in between, so as to conceal the movements of the Israelites from the Egyptians. *And there was*

the cloud and the darkness — and so, facing the Egyptians, the heavens remained all night covered with cloud; darkness was spread over them, because the light of the moon was not visible to them from behind the clouds. However, in front of the host of the Israelites there was the pillar of fire as usual: *and it lit up the night.* As at the time of the ninth plague, so now it was dark for the Egyptians, but all the children of Israel had light before them. *And the one came not near the other all night* — the Egyptians were unable, throughout the night, to come nearer to the Israelite encampment, and remained immobilized in their place.

21 Moses did what the Lord had commanded him: *Then Moses stretched out his hand over the sea,* at the beginning of the night, *and the Lord caused the sea to go by a strong east wind all night* — that is, He caused a strong wind to blow throughout the night ('east wind' is not to be taken literally, see above, on x 13), and this strong wind caused the sea to go (the connotation of the verb וַיּוֹלֶךְ *wayyōlekh* ['caused to go'] we shall explain immediately below) — *and made the sea dry land, and the waters were divided* (compare in *v.* 16: 'and divide it'). Here, also, as we have already seen in xii 29–31, the word *night* occurs at the end of three consecutive sentences (and in the last two instances: *all night*) to emphasize the miraculous character of that moment: *and it lit up the night — and the one came not near the other all night — by a strong east wind all night.*

In order to understand the purport of the Biblical account of the division of the Sea of Reeds, we must bear in mind the natural conditions prevailing in the area. The following phenomenon is a common occurrence in the region of the Suez: at high tide, the waters of the Red Sea penetrate the sand, from under the surface, and suddenly the water begins to ooze up out of the sand, which had hitherto been dry; within a short time the sand turns to mud, but the water continues to rise and ultimately a deep layer of water is formed above the sand, the whole area becoming flooded. This was once experienced by Napoleon I, when he toured that neighbourhood; when he set out he passed, without difficulty, over dry land, but on his return he found the place covered with water, and his position became dangerous. The same thing has happened in that region to tourists in our own day; they were compelled to return by boat over the water that covered the area where but a few hours earlier they had travelled on foot. The reverse sometimes happens when the Red Sea is at low tide; the water covering the sand gradually diminishes and finally disappears, and in the part that, several hours earlier, was covered by water suddenly dry land appears. Now in the vicinity of the Great Bitter Lake, which as we have seen above is to be identified with the Sea of Reeds of our narrative, there is a zone where such, or similar, phenomena are particularly liable to occur on a large scale. Between the southern third of the lake, and the remaining two thirds to the north, the lake narrows, and in the strait thus formed the water is not as deep as in the southern and northern parts, and the bed of the lake is firmer. Against this natural background the Biblical account can easily be understood.

I have no wish whatsoever to rationalize the Biblical story. The narrative clearly intends to relate a miraculous event, and whoever attempts to explain the entire episode rationally does not in fact interpret the text but projects his own ideas in place of those expressed by Scripture. But we should endeavour to understand how our text pictures the wondrous happening of which it tells, and what is the natural basis of the miracle described, for it is clear that the Torah does not imply that laws of nature were changed but that a wonderful use was made of those laws. The miracle consisted in the fact that at the very moment when it was necessary, in just the manner conducive to the achievement of the desired goal, and on a scale that was abnormal, there occurred, in accordance with the Lord's will, phenomena that brought about Israel's salvation. An exceptionally low tide at the Red Sea was liable to reduce the waters of the Sea of Reeds considerably, and the east wind blowing violently all night could have dried up the little water left in the narrow channel of the lake, where the bed of the lake is highest and hardest. North and south of the strait, the waters of the Sea of Reeds remained, but in the middle a ford was created. In this way we can understand the passage: *and the Lord caused the sea to go* — that is, destroyed it, made an end of it, in accordance with the meaning of the stem هلك *hlk* in Arabic — *by a strong east wind all night, and made the sea dry land* — in the middle — *and the waters* of the sea of Reeds *were divided* into two lakes, one to the south and one to the north.

22 *And the children of Israel went* — in the second half of the night, when the way was opened before them — *into the midst of the sea on dry ground* — on the bed of the strait that had become dry — *the waters being a wall to them* (hyperbole) *on their right hand and on their left* — north and south of the ford.

Jewish exegesis has found seventy-two letters in each of the three verses 19, 20, 21. But it is difficult to imagine that this was the original intention, since the spelling in ancient times was more defective than that fixed by the Masoretes. Be this as it may, it is clear that the three verses are of the same length and have a similar rhythm.

SEVENTH PARAGRAPH

THE DISCOMFITURE OF THE EGYPTIANS

(XIV 23–25)

When the Israelites had reached the eastern bank of the Sea of Reeds, the cloud rose, and the Egyptians saw the children of Israel standing opposite them, and the way before them open. The Egyptians thought that the phenomenon that permitted the crossing by the Israelites would still continue, and that they, too, would be able to cross the danger point quickly. Hence *the Egyptians pursued, and went in after them* (compare v. 17: 'and they shall go in after them') — all of them in a great rush — *all Pharaoh's horses, his chariots and his horsemen.*

But the strong wind that was blowing all night turned into a terrible hurricane when the Egyptians were passing through the midst of the sea: *And it came to pass in the morning watch that the Lord looked down* [וַיַּשְׁקֵף *wayyašqēph*] *upon the host of the Egyptians through a pillar of fire and cloud* — that is, they saw the heavens become clouded and illumined by lightning (the verb הִשְׁקִיף *hišqīph* ['look'] means as a rule looking down from above, and consequently the reference is to celestial phenomena; and the words *a pillar of fire and cloud* do not denote the well-known pillars that went in front of the Israelite host, since they occur here without the definite article) *and discomfited* — by means of this hurricane — *the host of the Egyptians* (compare Psa. xviii 14 [Hebrew, v. 15]: 'And He shot forth lightnings, and discomfited them'; so, too, ii Sam. xxii 15: 'lightning, and discomfited them'). In the meantime the Red Sea was no longer at low tide but at high tide, and the water began to well up from the ground of the crossing and turned it to mud. This explains the words of our text: *and He removed their chariot wheels* — the wheels of the chariots got stuck in the mud, and as a result of the efforts of the horses to continue to run, they were torn off the chariots. *And He made them drive heavily* — that is, even the chariots that were not dismembered were unable to advance swiftly, but moved heavily. In general the Egyptian host was not able to pull away from the narrow ford, which the Israelites had crossed without difficulty a few hours earlier. Then the Egyptians recognized that a superhuman power was protecting the Israelites, and attempted, unsuccessfully, to retreat and escape. *And the Egyptians said, Let us flee from before Israel; for the Lord fights for them against the Egyptians.* The last words, which conclude the paragraph, parallel in their form and content the words of Moses in *v.* 14, at the end of the fourth paragraph: 'The Lord will fight for you.' What Moses had foreseen from the first because of his strength of faith, the Egyptians realized after the event. Then the promise given to Moses was fulfilled (*v.* 18): 'And the Egyptians shall know that I am the Lord.'

EIGHTH PARAGRAPH

THE PUNISHMENT OF THE PURSUERS

(XIV 26–29)

26 *Then the Lord said to Moses, Stretch out your hand over the sea* (a parallelism with *v.* 16, at the beginning of the fifth paragraph) *that the water may come back upon the Egyptians, upon their chariots and upon their horsemen* (the words *that... may come back* parallel the same words in *v.* 2 at the beginning of paragraph two). The waters will return to their place, over the Egyptians who cannot move from there. This will be the final retribution, measure for measure, for the casting of the infant sons of the Israelites into the waters of the Nile (i 22).

27 *So Moses stretched forth his hand over the sea*, and the water, which had already turned the ground beneath the Egyptian host to mud, rose higher and higher, and the ford on which the Egyptians stood was flooded not only by the water that oozed out of the ground, but also by the waters of the two parts of the lake, from the south and the north, which likewise rose and came pouring from opposite directions: *and the sea returned to its wonted*

flow when the morning appeared, and there was again a single lake as before. *As the Egyptians were fleeing against it* — were endeavouring to flee from the waves that were pouring over them from both sides, but without success. *And the Lord shook off the Egyptians in the midst of the sea* — the waves of the sea that were sweeping violently over the crossing dragged the Egyptians from their place and threw them into the deeper waters to the north and south; this is the meaning of the word וַיְנַעֵר *way*ᵉ*na*ʿ*ēr* [rendered: 'And... shook off'], which signifies 'throwing downward' (compare Job xxxviii 13: 'that it might take hold of the skirts of the earth, and the wicked be shaken out of it'; see also Neh. v 13). The waters rose still higher, growing greatly in strength and
28 covering everything: *And the waters returned* (compare *v.* 26) *and covered the chariots and horsemen, even all the host of Pharaoh that went in after them into the sea* (although there was no prior mention of the children of Israel near this sentence, the pronoun 'them' is sufficient to indicate them, because the expression *that went in after them* repeats the words *and went in after them* that occurred above [*v.* 23]); *not so much as one of them remained.*

In order to end on a happy note, the text repeats what was stated in *v.* 22, with a few changes of formulation including the placing of the subject [in the Hebrew] before the verb in order to emphasize the antithesis between the Egyptians and the Israelites:
29 *But the children of Israel* — that is: as for the children of Israel, they, as stated, *walked on dry ground through the sea, the waters being a wall to them on their right hand and on their left* — a clear parallel between the end of this paragraph and that of the sixth paragraph.

Those who hold the view that the route taken by the children of Israel when they went out of Egypt was along the shore of the Mediterranean Sea, have to identify the Sea of Reeds with Lake Sirbonis (see above, on xiii 18). But the attempts made to explain our passage on the basis of the testimonies in our possession concerning the nature of this lake have not proved successful, for the descriptions in these testimonies do not fit the details of the Biblical narrative.

NINTH PARAGRAPH

THE DELIVERANCE

(XIV 30–31)

30 Verses 30–31 provide a concluding summary of what had been narrated in the previous paragraphs. *Thus the Lord saved Israel —* as was related in detail above — *that day* (compare *v.* 13: 'and see the salvation of the Lord which He will work for you today') *from the hand of the Egyptians; and Israel saw the Egyptians dead upon the seashore.* The day before, Moses had said to the Israelites that they would not again see the Egyptians as they saw them then, that is, as pursuing and threatening enemies; now they did indeed see the Egyptians again, but not as they had seen them the day before — they saw them as men powerless to harm. The repetition of the verb 'to see' is certainly not accidental.

31 Even more so, the further repetition of the words *And Israel saw* at the beginning of *v.* 31 cannot be considered fortuitous, nor the threefold occurrence of *Israel — Egypt* (*Israel... from the hand of the Egyptians — and Israel saw the Egyptians — and Israel saw... which the Lord did against the Egyptians*). What Moses had promised the Israelites was fulfilled: they saw the salvation; they saw the Egyptians dead upon the seashore; and they saw *the great hand —* the great work (the Bible uses the word *hand* here in antithesis to *the hand of the Egyptians* in the preceding verse) *which the Lord did against the Egyptians.* Having seen, they also feared: *and the people feared the Lord —* that is, they were filled with reverence towards God — *and they believed in the Lord —* that He would also save them in the future — *and in His servant Moses.* Although they had spoken harsh words to Moses in the hour of danger, yet now they realized that they ought to have complete faith in him.

My observations above regarding the poetic character of the first paragraph (xiii 17–22) apply also to the other paragraphs. The poetic rhythm discernible in many verses, the frequent parallelism found in them, the points of correspondence between one paragraph and another, the rare and poetic expressions, and the resemblance to many other Biblical passages (for example, Isa. li 10; Ezek. xxviii 2, and so forth), which point to a common origin, all indicate that our section is dependent on a poetic source. Ap-

EXODUS XV 1

parently, our text borrowed a great deal from the ancient epic poem on the Exodus from Egypt. But the Bible also had another poetic source (in this instance, not epic but lyric), namely, the Song of the Sea. This source is cited *in extenso* in the tenth paragraph.

TENTH PARAGRAPH

THE SONG OF THE SEA

(XV 1–21)

Chapter XV

1 The Song of the Sea is set here in a framework that links it to the narration of the events. It is preceded by the formula, *Then Moses and the children of Israel sang*, etc., which resembles the wording found in Jos. x 12 ('Then spoke Joshua', etc.), which serves to connect the excerpt taken from the Book of Jashar with the narrative.

The poem is divisible, as several scholars have already noted (particularly Dillmann and Müller), into three strophes (*vv.* 1–6; 7–11; 12–16) and an epilogue (*vv.* 17–18); at the end of each of the three strophes certain words are repeated to mark the conclusion (*Thy right hand, O Lord — Thy right hand, O Lord* in *v.* 6; *Who is like Thee? — Who is like Thee?* in *v.* 11; *till... pass by — till... pass by* in *v.* 16). It may be added that before the repetition there is, in each strophe, a simile (*v.* 5: *like a stone*; *v.* 10: *as lead*; *v.* 16: *as a stone*).

In form the poem is a psalm, such as we find in the Psalter, and it may be classified as an Ode of Triumph. The rhythm is mainly quaternary (for example: *I will síng to the Lórd, for He has triumphed glóriously*), but in part ternary (for example: *This is my Gód, and I'll praíse Him*); only in exceptional cases is there a line with only two beats (for instance: *The Lórd is His náme*). A long word may be considered to have two beats. [It should be borne in mind that the observations appertain to the Hebrew text, the English translation does not adequately reflect the majestic rhythm and diction of the original poem].

The first strophe serves as a general introduction. First, it sets forth the theme: *I will sing to the Lord, for He has triumphed gloriously*;

EXODUS XV 1

the horse and his rider He has thrown into the sea. For poems to begin with an expression like *I will sing* [אָשִׁירָה 'āšīrā] is a common feature both of Eastern and Western poesy. In Ugaritic poetry the identical word is found (with defective spelling *'ašr*, at the beginning of the epithalamium to *Nikkal* and *Yarikh*). The first part proclaims at the outset that his song is a song to the Lord, in honour of the Lord. In the pagan odes of triumph, the glory of the victory is ascribed to the conquering king, but here there is not a single word of praise or glory given to Moses; these are rendered to the Lord alone. The same applies to the Song of Deborah: 'bless the Lord.'

Why the poet uses the expression גָּאֹה גָּאָה *gā'ō gā'ā* ['He hath triumphed gloriously'], and why he mentions the horse first will be clarified later. For the significance of רָמָה *rāmā* ['He has thrown']; and so, too, of יָרָה *yārā* ['He cast'] and טֻבְּעוּ *ṭubbeʿū* ['are sunk'] in *v.* 4, and of יָרְדוּ בִמְצוֹלֹת כְּמוֹ אָבֶן *yāreḏhū bhimeṣōlōth kemō 'ābhen* ['they went down into the depths like a stone'] in *v.* 5, see my observations above on וַיְנַעֵר *wayenaʿēr* ['and shook off'] (xiv 27).

After the statement of the theme, Israel acknowledges and proclaims that he derives all his strength from his God alone. *The Lord* [*Yah*] *is my strength and help* [זִמְרָת *zimrāth*] — this last word is to be understood as זִמְרָתִי *zimrāthī* ['my help'], the final *Yōdh* having been omitted in the spelling, and possibly even in pronunciation, on account of the following *yōdh*; it signifies not 'melody', 'song', but 'power', 'help' (ذمر *dhmr*). *And He has become my salvation* — it is from Him that my salvation came. The whole of this sentence is cited in its exact form, or nearly so, in Isa. xii 2, and Psa. cxviii 14.

This, and no other, is my God — the God whom I acknowledge as my Lord and whom I wish to serve with all my heart and soul — *and I will glorify Him* [וְאַנְוֵהוּ *weʾanwēhū*] — uplift Him in my song (نوه *nwh* — 'to be high'); *He is my father's God* — as Moses was informed (iii 6 ff.) — *and I will exalt Him* — a clear parallelism with *weʾanwēhū*. *The Lord is a man of war* — Moses had told us that the Lord would fight for us (xiv 14), but now we see in truth that He is a man of war, a Warrior. *The Lord* (*YHWH*) *is His name* — Moses explained His name to us, to wit, that it signifies He who is with His creatures, and assures and keeps His promises (iii 14–15), but now we recognize that His name befits Him and He befits His name. We realize all this, because we have seen with our own eyes that *Pharaoh's chariots and his host He cast into the sea, and*

EXODUS XV 10

his picked chariot warriors (on these two words, see above on
xiv 7) are sunk in the Sea of Reeds. The floods cover them — did
cover them (xiv 28) — and they went down into the depths like a
stone. The verb יְכַסְיֻמוּ y^{e}khasyūmū [literally, 'they (will) cover
them'] has a past sense, like most of the verbs of this poem that
are in the imperfect.

At the end of this strophe, the poet turns ardently to his God
and declares: Thy right hand, O Lord, glorious in power, Thy right
hand, O Lord, shatters the enemy.

In the second strophe, the poet describes in detail the event to
which he made passing references in the first strophe. He begins:
And in the greatness of Thy majesty (גְּאוֹנְךָ g$^{e'}$ōn^{e}khā, which forms a
parallelism with גָּאֹה גָּאָה gā'ō gā'ā ['He has triumphed gloriously']
at the beginning of the opening strophe) Thou didst break down
Thy adversaries — Thou didst humble the pride of those who rose
up against Thee; Thou sendest forth Thy fury — Thou didst send
forth against them, like a destroying angel, Thy burning fury, and
it annihilated them, like a flame of fire consuming stubble: it consumed them like stubble. Then in language most appropriate to the
theme: And at the blast of Thy nostrils — by the east wind that
Thou didst cause to blow — the waters piled up — that is, hyperbolically, the waters stood like a heap on both sides; the floods
stood up in a heap [נֵד nēdh] — the waters, which are naturally
fluid, stood firm as though they were a heap, a mound of earth
(ندّ nadd in Arabic), or as if the deeps congealed in the heart
of the sea — as though the waters of the deeps in the midst of the
sea were turned to solid ice. By means of these miracles, the Lord
brought retribution upon the wicked according to their wickedness.

At first they had been proud and boastful of their strength: The
enemy said — he thought to himself that he would have no difficulty
in carrying out his plan: I will pursue, and immediately I will
overtake, and forthwith I will divide the spoil (note the alliteration
of five consecutive words commencing with 'Aleph); my soul shall
have its fill of them — my desire, my lust, will be satisfied by the
spoil that I shall take from them. It will suffice that I will draw
[literally, 'empty'] my sword — that I will take it out of its scabbard
— and instantly my hand shall possess them [תּוֹרִישֵׁמוֹ tōrīšēmō] —
shall acquire them for me again as slaves (the usual interpretation
'destroy them' is improbable, since this was not the intention of
the Egyptians). But Thou didst blow with Thy wind (corresponding
to 'And at the blast of Thy nostrils' in v. 8), and immediately the

175

sea covered them (paralleling 'the floods cover them' in *v.* 5, which, like this verse, is near the end of the strophe), and *they sank as lead in the mighty waters* (forming a parallelism with the continuation of *v.* 5: 'they went down into the depths like a stone').

This strophe also concludes like the first with a glowing apostro-
11 phe to the Lord: *Who is like Thee among the gods, O Lord?* — Who can be compared to Thee from among the pagan deities, and particularly among the divinities of Egypt, who were unable to deliver their devotees? — *Who is like Thee, glorious in holiness* (corresponding to 'glorious in power', at the end of the first strophe), *fearful in praises* — fearful in Thy works, which are worthy of praise — *doing wonders?*

The third strophe describes the consequences of the event. On
12 the one hand, the enemy was destroyed: *Thou didst stretch out Thy right hand* (forming a parallelism with 'Thy right hand' at the end of the first strophe, and possibly also with Moses' stretching out his hand over the sea), and at once *the earth swallowed them* — that is, Sheol swallowed them (the word אֶרֶץ *'ereṣ* ['earth', 'land'] like *erṣitu* in Akkadian and *'arṣ* in Ugaritic, sometimes serves as a designation for Sheol [the underworld]); and on the
13 other hand, *Thou didst lead in Thy steadfast love the people whom Thou hast redeemed* — this people whom Thou didst redeem, Thy first-born son, whom Thou didst ransom in accordance with the law of redemption — and him *Thou didst guide by Thy strength to Thy holy abode* — Thou didst direct him to Thy holy place in Mount Sinai as Thou didst announce to Moses beforehand (iii 12). It may be that the word נָוֵה *nāwe* ['abode'] here, in the second verse of the third strophe, is in parallelism with וְאַנְוֵהוּ *wᵉ'anwēhū* ['and I will glorify him'] in the second verse of the first strophe. When news of the miracles that took place here will reach the neighbouring
14 peoples, they will be greatly afraid: *The peoples heard, they trembled* — especially those whose land we are due to enter, or near to whose borders we must pass — *pangs seized on the inhabitants of Philistia* — these are the Philistines in the vicinity of Gerar (see above, on
15 xiii 17). *Then were the chiefs* [אַלּוּפֵי *'allūphē*] *of Edom dismayed* — the heads of the people of Edom, who bear the title אַלּוּף *'allūph* ['chief'] (Gen. xxxvi) — *the mighty men of Moab, trembling seizes them; all the inhabitants of Canaan melted away* (the similar ex-
16 pression in Jos. ii 24 derives from this verse). *Terror and dread fall upon them; because of the greatness of Thy arm, they are as still as a stone, till Thy people pass through, O Lord, till the people*

pass through whom Thou hast purchased — the people that became Thy people after Thou didst acquire them through Thy work of redemption, and Thou didst prevent the Egyptians from enslaving them again as they had wished (see above, on 'my hand shall possess them', in *v.* 9). The comparison with stone, which already occurred in *v.* 5, is repeated here, as though to emphasize that the power of the Lord, which made the Egyptians go down into the depths like a stone, would in future petrify all Israel's enemies. The description of the peoples who are turned to stone until the people of Israel pass through them parallels the description of the waters that piled and stood like a heap in order that Israel might pass through them. The clause *the people... whom Thou hast purchased* at the end of this strophe corresponds in form and meaning to *the people whom Thou hast redeemed* at the beginning of it.

The third strophe having stressed the immediate consequences, the verses of the epilogue direct our gaze to the distant outcome in the future. *Thou wilt bring them in* — the children of this people whom Thou hast purchased — *and plant them in the mountain of Thy inheritance* — in the mountainous country that Thou hast chosen for Thyself as the land of Thy inheritance (compare Psalms lxxviii 53–54: 'And He led them safely, and they feared not; but the sea overwhelmed their enemies. And He brought them to His holy border, to the mountain, which His right hand had gotten') — till they reach *the place* which *Thou hast made for Thy abode, O Lord*, that *sanctuary, O Lord,* which *Thy hands have established* (paralleling 'in holiness' in the second strophe, and 'Thy holy abode' in the third strophe). It cannot be deduced from here that the song (or these verses) was composed after the construction of the Temple, for without doubt the Israelites intended, even before entering the Land, to build therein a sanctuary to the Lord their God.

18 The poem ends by proclaiming the Kingdom of Heaven: *The Lord will reign for ever and ever.*

In order to understand why the song concludes with this proclamation, and in general if we wish to comprehend the whole poem properly, our investigations must go beyond its confines. First, we must consider the other Biblical passages that refer, in poetic form, to the division of the Sea of Reeds. These passages regard the phenomenon not only as a mighty act of the Lord against Pharaoh and his host, but also as an act of might against the sea, which was compelled to submit to His will. The prophets and the poets (so, too, at a later period, rabbinic exegesis) link the episode with the ancient myths appertaining to the revolt of the sea against his Creator in the cosmic beginning, to the rebellion of Rahab, the prince of the sea, and his allies the sea monsters, and to the crushing of the revolt by the Lord's mighty power, as though the ancient miracles were renewed for the deliverance of Israel. It will suffice to mention as an example, Isa. li 9–10: 'Awake, awake, put on strength, O arm of the Lord; awake, as in days of old, the generations of long ago. Was it not thou that didst cut Rahab in pieces, that didst pierce the dragon? Was it not thou that didst dry up the sea, the waters of the great deep; that didst make the depths of the sea a way for the redeemed to pass over?'

These Israelite myths are derived from similar myths that were current among the neighbouring peoples concerning the war waged by one of the great gods against the deity of the sea. The famous Babylonian story about the war of Marduk against Tiamat is but one example of an entire series of similar narratives. Similarly in the Ugaritic texts, it is narrated regarding Baal the god of Heaven that he fought against Mot the god of Sheol and against the latter's confederates, namely, the Prince of the Sea and the Judge of the River and his other helpers, and he smote them and compelled them to recognize him as king of the world. Among the Israelites, of course, legends in the form of a war between the gods had no place; the traditionary material that was current in the lands of the East was given by Israel an aspect more in accord with their ethos, to wit, the aspect of a revolt by the sea against his Creator. There are numerous allusions to this myth in the prophetic and poetic literature of the Bible, and also in the pseudepigrapha and rabbinic legends. On the basis of these allusions, I advanced the theory, in my Hebrew essay on 'The Epic Poetry of Israel' (in $K^eneseth$, dedicated to H. N. Bialik, Vol. viii, pp. 121–142), that in very ancient times there was composed in Israel an epic poem on this theme, and I endeavoured to reconstruct the contents of this poem. I shall give here, in very brief summary, a general outline of the subject-matter of the poem according to my reconstruction (the sources on which I have based my reconstruction I have cited in detail in the aforementioned essay).

In their sagas the poets of Israel told (I cite in italics the expressions, attested by the references found in Biblical literature, that were definitely used by the poets) of *the work of the Lord*, and

EXODUS XV 1–18

of *the wonders that He wrought in days of old*, when he created the world. Then *arose Rahab, the prince of the sea*, with his great strength, and not content with the portion that the Sovereign of the universe had allotted him, he exalted himself so as to conquer the whole world. On the side of the rebellious sea, who was designated in the poem by the terms תְּהוֹם *tᵉhōm* ['deep'], תְּהוֹם רַבָּה *tᵉhōm rabbā* ['great deep'], צוּלָה *ṣūlā* ['ocean-deep'], מְצוּלָה *mᵉṣūlā* ['depth'], מְצֹל(וֹ)ל(וֹ)ת *mᵉṣōlōth* or *mᵉṣūlōth* ['depths'], מַיִם רַבִּים *mayim rabbīm* ['many waters'], מַיִם כַּבִּירִים *mayim kabbīrīm* ['mighty waters'], מַיִם אַדִּירִים *mayim 'addīrīm* ['majestic waters'] and the like, stood the *rivers*; the waters of the sea and the rivers *rose up and exalted themselves* against the will of the Creator, they *roared*, and caused *a mighty voice* to be heard, a voice of *uproar*. They had *hɛlpers* in their revolt: *Leviathan the fleeing serpent, Leviathan the twisting serpent, the dragon* or *dragons*. But *the anger of the Lord was kindled* against the rebels, and He appeared against them as *One riding* upon *'ărābhōth, riding upon His horses,* upon His *chariots of salvation,* which are the clouds of the sky. *He rebuked His enemies, those who rose up against Him, with the thunder of His voice,* and *He fought* against them *with His right hand* and *with His mighty arm*, and the weapons in His hand. *They writhed* and *trembled* and fled at the sound of *the Lord's rebuke*. The Lord put, as a muzzle, *a rope of rushes in the nose* of Leviathan; and He *played with him*; and He *wounded, hewed, pierced, cleft, exterminated Rahab* and *his helpers*; He *disturbed* and *stilled* the waters of the sea; He *cleft* the sea in two; He *cleft* the rivers; He *made dry* [הֶחֱרִיב *heḥĕrībh*] and *dried up* [הוֹבִישׁ *hōbhīš*] the waters of the sea and the rivers that had gone outside their bounds; He *placed a bound for the sea which it cannot pass*; He *trod upon the high places of the sea*; and after subduing all the rebels He *reigned* and was acknowledged as *King* over the whole world.

The Biblical allusions to this subject are found only in the writings of the prophets and poets, but not in the Pentateuch. The reason for this is clear. Even in the Israelite version of these myths, there still remained certain elements that betrayed an alien spirit, and therefore, while it was possible to use them as poetic similes and metaphors in the utterances of the prophets and in poetry, where it is customary to employ similitudes and figurative language, this was not the case with the Torah, which weighs every word and refrains from citing anything that cannot be understood literally. On the contrary, the Torah voices at times a protest against these myths. It narrates, for instance, that God said: 'Let the waters be gathered together under the heavens into one place, and let the dry land appear. And it was so.' The sea is not a creature with an independent will, which can oppose, as it were, the will of the Creator. It is only like clay in the hands of the potter, which receives the form that the potter wishes to give it (see on this, and on the creation of the dragons [or sea monsters] in Gen. i 21, the annotations in my book *From Adam To Noah*, pp. 35-39, 49-51).

However, even though the Torah did not accept anything of the *content* of the legends pertaining to the revolt of the sea and its helpers, in so far as the *form* is concerned, traces of these myths are discernible in the Pentateuch. Already in chapter xiv the emphasis given to the *horses* and *chariots* of the Egyptians, — an emphasis that is repeated in several other passages of the Bible — and particularly the mention made of the horses before the horsemen and soldiers, are to be explained as a continuation of the literary tradition relating to the hostile forces that were unable to stand before the One riding upon the clouds, who revealed Himself against them, in the words of Habakkuk (iii 8), upon His horses and chariots of victory. So, too, the verb *divide* (xiv 16, 21), the expression *dry ground* [or *dry land*] (xiv 16, 22, 29), the description of the Lord as a Warrior (xiv 14, 25), and possibly also the expression of *salvation* [or *saving*], are elements belonging to that tradition, and they likewise recur again in the Bible with reference to the division of the Sea of Reeds. These elements are more numerous, needless to say, in the poetic language of the Song of the Sea. However, this poem also does not expressly connect the division of the Sea of Reeds with the revolt of the sea, as the two events are linked together in Isa. li 9-10; and if it had established such a nexus, the song would not have been incorporated into the Torah. But vestiges of the literary tradition are clearly noticeable in the phrases and figures of speech throughout the poem. We shall easily be convinced of this, if we compare its language with that of the reconstruction that I have given above.

It begins with a reference to the *exaltation of the Lord*, who prevailed over the *rising-up* of the sea: although the sea *rose up* [גָּאָה *gā'ā*], yet *He rose higher still* [גָּאֹה גָּאָה *gā'ō gā'ā*, rendered above: 'He has triumphed gloriously']. Immediately thereafter, in the same verse, mention is made of *the horse* and *his rider*, and in *v.* 2 the words *strength* and *salvation* are used; in *v.* 3 the Lord is designated a *man of war* — that is, one who fights with might against his foes; in *v.* 4 there is further reference to the *chariots*; in *v.* 5, the *floods* [literally, 'deeps'] and the *depths* are mentioned; *v.* 6 speaks of *the right hand of the Lord glorious* [literally, 'mighty'] *in power* (although 'the breakers of the sea are mighty, yet mightier still is the Lord on high', as the psalmist says in Psa. xciii 4); and again reference is made in *v.* 7 to *the majesty* [literally, 'exaltation'] of the Lord, and in the same verse to the *fury* of the Lord, and in *v.* 8 to the blast of His *nostrils*; we are told there of the waters of the sea that stood within the bounds set for them by the Lord when He divided them in two; in the same verse the word *floods* recurs; the expression *mighty* [translated above, 'majestic'] *waters* is used, and, in contradistinction, the Lord is described as '*majestic* [literally, 'mighty'] in holiness'; He is further depicted as *doing wonders*; in *v.* 14 reference is again made to the fact that the enemies *trembled* and that *pangs seized on them*, and in *v.* 16 to the fact that because of the greatness of the Lord's *arm* they are *still*; and after mention has been made in *v.* 17 of what the Lord *made* and of what *His hands* established, the song closes in *v.* 18, like the epilogues in the ancient epic poems, with a reference to the Lord's reign: *The Lord will reign for ever and ever.*

The poem is followed by the final portion of its framework (*vv.* 19–21).

Verse 19 indicates the reason for the song of Moses and Aaron, by repeating expressions that had occurred in ch. xiv, as though it were a continuation of the initial words of the framework (*v.* 1):

19 'Then Moses and the children of Israel sang'... *For when the horses of Pharaoh with his chariots and his horsemen went into the sea,* etc. (here, too, the horses are mentioned first, followed immediately by the chariots, and only at the end are the horsemen mentioned; see on this above). The verse consists of three clauses, each of which ends with the word *sea*: *For when the horses of Pharaoh with his chariots and his horsemen went into the sea — the Lord brought back upon them the waters of the sea — but the children of Israel walked on dry ground in the midst of the sea.*

In *vv.* 20–21, we are told how the song was accompanied by
20 instrumental music. *Then took Miriam* — who is mentioned here for the first time by her name, and hence also by her title of honour, *the prophetess*, and also by her formal epithet, *the sister of Aaron*, in accordance with the system in which the eldest brother

181

is recognized as the head of the family [fratriarchy] (see my commentary on Gen. x 21) — *a timbrel in her hand* — in order to accompany the singers with the music of the timbrel (compare Psa. lxviii 25 [Hebrew, *v.* 26]: 'the singers in front, the minstrels last, between them maidens playing timbrels') — *and all the women* — not actually all, but many of them — *went out* — from their place, so as to stand in the midst of the choir — *after her, with timbrels and with mᵉḥōlōth* — holding timbrels and *mᵉḥōlōth*. The last word does not denote 'dances' but musical instruments like the timbrels. Compare particularly for the expression *went out*, Jer. xxxi 3: 'Again you shall adorn yourself with timbrels and go forth with the *māḥol* of the merrymakers; so, too, i Sam. xviii 6, and elsewhere. *And Miriam* — with her companions — *sang antiphonally*, with the Israelite men: *Sing to the Lord for He has triumphed gloriously; the horse and his rider He has thrown into the sea* — as a refrain at the end of each strophe.

SECTION NINE

THE TRAVAILS OF THE JOURNEY

CHAPTER XV, VERSE 22 — CHAPTER XVII, VERSE 16

FIRST PARAGRAPH

THE WATERS OF MARAH

(XV 22–27)

After crossing the Sea of Reeds, the Israelites turned to the wilderness: *Then Moses led Israel onward from the Sea of Reeds, and they went into the wilderness of Shur* [שׁוּר *Šūr*] — possibly so called on account of the שׁוּר *Šūr* or wall, that is, the fortified wall that apparently stood on the border of Egypt. *And they went three days in the wilderness.* Three days is a usual period of time mentioned in the literary tradition of the East, representing a sequence of several days, which, although somewhat long, was shorter than the perfect unit of a week. *Inter alia*, and more particularly, a series of three days is commonly found in narratives of long journeys; so, for example, in the Epic of Gilgameš, in the story of the journey of Gilgameš and Enkidu to the Forest of Cedars; and also in the Ugaritic Epic of Keret, in the account of Keret's journey to the land of King Pabel; in the Bible compare (apart from Num. xxxiii 8, which deals with the same subject as our paragraph) Gen. xxii 4; Num. x 33; Jos. ix 17; ii Sam. i 2; ii Kings ii 17; and so forth. *And found no water* — in the course of the three days; *And when they came to Marah* — after the period mentioned, and found water there, *they could not drink the water of Marah, because it was bitter* — on account of the large quantity of salts that it contained; *therefore the name of it* — of that site — *was called* — by people in general, even before this — *Marah* [i.e. 'Bitterness']. The determination of the site of Marah is in dispute and uncertain. The most probable conjecture is the one that identifies it with ʿAin Ḥawwârah, a pool of bitter water situated about three days journey from the Bitter Lakes. The name Marah occurs three times in the passage, for emphasis, corresponding to the period of three days, which underlines the length of time during which they found no water.

EXODUS XV 23

The Israelites then experienced something similar to that which befell the Egyptians during the period of the first plague, when *they could not drink the water of the Nile* (vii 24); and thereby the Lord taught them a lesson, as we shall see further on.

24 *And the people murmured against Moses* — for having led them there — *saying, What shall we drink?* — What can we drink? or, We cannot drink (see on xiv 15); and you, Moses, are to be blamed
25 for this. *And he* — Moses — *cried to the Lord* (compare xiv 10); *and the Lord showed him a* particular *tree*, the nature of which is to absorb the salt in the water and thus sweeten it. This property is found, according to the testimony of travellers, in one of the varieties of local brier. *And he* — Moses — *threw* this tree *into* the vessels in which they had put *the water, and the water became sweet* — so that the Israelites were able to drink it.

The expression *and the Lord showed him* indicates the intention of the narrative. It was desirable that immediately after their liberation the children of Israel should learn the great truth that they need instruction and guidance from Heaven. For this reason the Lord let them journey from the Sea of Reeds as Moses saw fit (*v.* 22: 'Then Moses led Israel onward', etc.), and they went astray in the wilderness and suffered from lack of water until they received instruction (*and the Lord showed* him*) from the Almighty, and as a result of this direction they obtained drinkable water. The realization of the need for *instruction** from the Lord prepares the people spiritually for the acceptance of the yoke of the *Torah** and precepts.

On this basis we can understand the rest of the verse: *There set He them* — in this manner — *a statute and an ordinance* — a preliminary introduction to His statutes and ordinances — *and there He proved them* — by the severe trial of the lack of water, He taught them that the Lord is able to save them even from extreme danger, if
26 only they remain loyal to His precepts. *And He* — Moses — *said* — drawing the moral of the episode — *If you will diligently hearken to the voice of the Lord your God, and do that which is right in His eyes, and give ear to His commandments and keep all His statutes* — then, and only then — *I will put none of the diseases upon you which I put upon the Egyptians* — such as boils or this trouble of lack of water to drink — *for I am the Lord your healer* — and just

---

* From the stem יָרָה *yārā*, which in the *Hiph'il* conjugation means 'to teach, instruct'. *Tr.*

EXODUS XV 27

as I have now healed the water, so I will protect you from all sickness.

The passage dealing with the healing of the water by Elisha draws upon our narrative (see ii Kings ii 19–22); there, too, we find *and he threw*, as well as the verb *to heal*).

After encamping at Marah, the children of Israel again journeyed, 27 *And they came to Elim* — this time it is not stated that Moses led them, and apparently we are to understand that they came there under the Lord's guidance in the manner described in xiii 21 — *where there were twelve springs of water and seventy palm trees* — the Lord brought them to one of the desert oases that are blessed with an abundance of water and fertility; *and they encamped there by the water* — a suitable site for encampment (compare Psa. xxiii 1–2: 'The Lord is my shepherd... He leads me beside waters of rest'). The numbers are round figures: the first — twelve — is based on the sexagesimal system, and the second — seventy — on the special importance attaching to the number seven. The identification of the site of Elim is also a matter of dispute; it is generally considered that the reference is to *Wady Gharandel*, in the west of the Peninsula of Sinai, where to this day an abundance of water, palm trees, tamarisks and acacias are to be found.

A number of word-plays are manifest in this paragraph. In verse 25: וְשָׁם נִסָּהוּ......שָׁם לוֹ שָׁם *šām šām lō... wešām nissāhū* ['There set He them... and there He proved them'], the word שָׁם *šām* occurs, once with a slight change of pronunciation, three times; in *v*. 26 again, a number of words contain the letters שמ- *š(ś)m-*: שָׁמוֹעַ תִּשְׁמַע *šāmōa' tišma'* ['you will diligently hearken'], וְשָׁמַרְתָּ *wešāmartā* ['and keep'], שַׂמְתִּי *śamtī* ['I put'], אָשִׂים *'āśīm* ['I will put']; and in *v*. 27: וְשָׁם....שָׁם *wešām... šām* (שָׁם *šām*, שָׁם *šām*, or שמ- *š(ś)m-* occur seven times; compare also שִׁבְעִים תְּמָרִים *šibh'īm temārīm* ['seventy palm trees']. Furthermore, in the first verse of the paragraph we find the word מִיָּם *miyyam* ['from the Sea'], and thereafter six times (in all seven times) the same letters with different vocalization: מַיִם *mayim* or מָיִם *māyim* ['water']; as though to say: from the peril of the Sea of Reeds to the safe dwelling-place by the waters of the wells of Elim.

SECOND PARAGRAPH

THE MANNA AND THE QUAILS

(XVI 1-36)

Chapter XVI

Chapter xvi is one of the most difficult chapters in our Book. The following problems are particularly perplexing:

(a) The Sabbath Day and the prohibition to do work on it are spoken of as matters that are already known, although the children of Israel had not yet heard the commandment concerning the Sabbath contained in the Ten Commandments. It is true that the Decalogue enjoins: '*Remember* the sabbath day', as if the children of Israel were already familiar with the essential principles of the Sabbath; but here, too, in ch. xvi, the matter is not reported as a first instruction.

(b) We find here the expression *before the Lord* (*vv.* 9, 33), and more clearly, *before the Testimony* (*v.* 34), although the Tabernacle was not yet in existence.

(c) The complaint about the dearth of food is surprising, since it was stated earlier (xii 38) that the Israelites had 'flocks and herds, even very much cattle', and further on (xviii, 3), too, reference is made to their cattle.

(d) The concatenation of the episode of the quails with the manna is strange.

(e) Moses announces in *v.* 8 that which he was told only subsequently by the Almighty (*vv.* 11-12). There are also many other problems pertaining to details of the text.

With a view to solving the difficulties, many complicated hypotheses have been advanced on the assumption that fragments from various sources have been joined together in our chapter by a process of repeated editing. But these conjectures aim only at determining the pre-history of the narrative, and make no attempt to interpret the chapter before us, or to understand the intention of the redactor who gave it its final form. To my mind, however, it is precisely this task, which is as a rule neglected, that constitutes the primary task of the expositor of our book; for this reason I shall devote particular attention to it. Needless to say, I shall also endeavour to trace the phases of the tradition that preceded the present text, but this will serve only as a means to understanding the text.

EXODUS XVI

In the first instance, we must bear in mind that the Torah does not seek to provide us with an objective itinerary of the journeying of the Israelites in the wilderness, nor does it record history for its own sake. Its aim is purely didactic, and for this purpose it utilizes the traditions that were current among the Israelites. Verse 35 ('And the children of Israel ate manna for forty years, till they came to an inhabited [or, a habitable] land', etc.) shows that the chapter in its present form was written after the Israelites had entered a settled country. At that time there undoubtedly existed numerous stories about the happenings that befell the generation of the wilderness; some of these were incorporated in the Book of Exodus, some were included in other books of the Pentateuch, and some were never recorded in any book. Out of the store of these traditions the Torah chose what it desired for the achievement of its purpose.

The arrangement of the narratives in the Torah is certainly not in the 'sequence' required by the Greek ways of thinking to which we are accustomed today. Rather does it follow the thought processes of the ancient East, which are not generally in accord with those of the Greek and modern writers. Chronological order, for instance, which takes precedence in the techniques of Greek and modern literature, is not of such importance in the ancient Eastern writings; the rabbinic sages, already, noted that there is no 'early and late' in the Torah. But this does not mean that the Pentateuchal arrangement is arbitrary; there are rules and methods. I have already shown (in my lecture at the Congress of Jewish Studies, Jerusalem 1947, and elsewhere) that one of the methods is to arrange the subject-matter on the basis of association — both thematic and verbal association.

The contents of chapter xvi and ch. xvii 1–7 are arranged in accordance with this principle. After the story of Marah there immediately follow the two episodes of the manna and the quails, which were selected from the stock of traditionary tales because of both kinds of association — of content and of language. In all three narratives mention is made of the murmurings of the Israelites on account of the lack of vital things, such as water and food, and of the provision of the people's needs by the Lord; and in all three there occur characteristic expressions of *proving* (xv 25: *and there He proved them*; xvi 4: *that I may prove them*; xvii 2: *why do you put... to the proof*; ibid., *v.* 7: *Massah* ['Proof']... *and because they put... to the proof*), and of *murmuring* (xv 24; xvi 2, 7, 8, 9, 12;

xvii 3). The lessons that the Torah desires to inculcate are emphasized and confirmed by the threefold narration of similar stories, which is also a technique commonly employed in the Pentateuch, as I have shown in many parts of my commentary on the Book of Genesis, and in my book called *The Documentary Hypothesis*, English translation, pp. 78–83.

In order to knit them together, these narratives were arranged in the framework of a partial itinerary of the desert wanderings. Not *all* the stations recorded by tradition are mentioned (in Num. xxxiii other encampments, omitted here, are mentioned), but the few suffice to form a concatenated series of events.

The narrative of ch. xvi, when it formed part of the pre-Torah tradition, was an isolated and independent story — one of the many tales dealing with incidents of the desert — and belonged to the period subsequent to the Revelation at Mount Sinai and the erection of the Tabernacle, or perhaps, better still, was not connected with any particular date, but together with the other stories concerning the generation of the wilderness, it was placed, as it were, in a unitary historical stratum, without detailed chronological perspective. The Torah took the chapter as it was, without concerning itself with particulars, such as the mention of the Sabbath and the Tabernacle, which those who are accustomed to Greek ways of thought are liable to find surprising, but not so those used to 'organic' thinking (for this concept see, J. Heinemann, *Darkhē Hā'aggādā* (Hebrew), pp. 8–9). At all events, the text has been worded with care, and an effort has been made to efface discrepancies. Thus, for example, the Torah does not explicitly state the place and date of the episode. Although place and date are mentioned in the 'frame' verse (*v.* 1), yet immediately afterwards it is said that the incident happened 'in the wilderness'. This phrase, which at first appears redundant, and has led to various far-fetched conjectures, seeks to convey that the occurrence took place in the wilderness generally, in some place that need not be indicated exactly, somewhere in the desert. Neither the place nor the time is important, only the theme is significant. Similarly in the rest of the narrative, the formulation is invariably guarded, as will be explained later on.

After these prefatory notes, we can go on to the detailed exposition of the text. In this we shall try to elucidate the problems that we have so far left unexplained, and, *inter alia*, the confusion existing in certain verses. This is due, apparently, to changes in-

EXODUS XVI 3

troduced in the ancient tradition; but it is worthwhile attempting to clarify the underlying intention of the present wording.

1 Although the encampment at Elim was comfortable and pleasant, yet the children of Israel could not stay there long; it was necessary to resume the journey. Therefore, *They set out from Elim* and entered the wilderness. *And all the congregation of the children of Israel came to the wilderness of Sin, which is between Elim and Sinai* — that is, as far as we can judge, the desert area south or south-east of Elim — *on the fifteenth day of the second month after they had departed from the land of Egypt*; this was the fifteenth of Iyyar, and the fifteenth, being the period of the full moon, was a suitable time for the people to travel in the desert.

2 In the wilderness they began to feel the dearth of food, *And the whole congregation of the children of Israel murmured* (וַיִּלּוֹנוּ *way-yillōnū* [*Niph'al*] is the *Q*ᵉ*rē*;* the *K*ᵉ*thībh*** is וַיָּלִינוּ *wayyallīnū* [*Hiph'īl*]) *against Moses and Aaron in the wilderness* (for the significance of the last word, see above, at the end of the prefatory notes to this paragraph). The word *whole* is not to be taken literally; here, too, as we have seen several times before, it is a hyperbolical generalization; this apart, the complete expression, *the whole congregation of the children of Israel*, is only a continuation of the use of the formula that occurred in v. 1 and will recur later on. Those of the Israelites who possessed cattle certainly had no reason to complain about the lack of food; but we may easily assume that there were not a few among the people who had no cattle, whilst actual bread, such as they were accustomed to eat in Egypt, none of them had. The murmuring on this occasion was
3 more formidable than that at Marah: *and the children of Israel said to them* — to Moses and Aaron — *would that we had died by the hand of the Lord* — that is, a natural death — *in the land of Egypt, when we sat by the fleshpots, when we ate bread to the full.* This exaggeration is well understandable from a psychological viewpoint, for people are inclined to forget past troubles when faced with new ones, and to picture the past to themselves as far better than it was in fact. Would that we had been granted to die in Egypt — they now contend — seeing that our present fate is worse than natural death, *for you have brought us out into the*

---

* Masoretic marginal reading.
** Reading of the text. See note on v. 7.

wilderness to kill this whole assembly with hunger. Again a clear exaggeration.

The Israelites craved for two things: for *meat* ('when we sat by the fleshpots') and for *bread* ('when we ate bread to the full'). Against this background it is possible to understand the connection between the story of the manna and that of the quails: since they longed for meat, they were given the quails; and since they yearned for bread, they were given manna. Both episodes — that of the manna and that of the quails — are closely linked from the commencement of the narrative, and cannot be separated; and apparently they were already interconnected in the ancient tradition: just as the quails are mentioned here apropos of the manna, so in Num. xi the manna is mentioned apropos of the quails.

4   In *v.* 4 it is related that the Lord said to Moses: *Behold, I will rain bread from Heaven for you,* etc. The implication, apparently, is that as soon as the children of Israel began to complain, Moses prayed to the Lord (compare xv 25), and that this was the Lord's answer to his prayer: this time, too, the Lord would provide His people's needs. What kind of bread would be rained down from heaven is not yet expressly stated, but the assurance is already given that this blessing would not be bestowed once only, but would continue also in the future: *and the people shall go out and gather a day's portion every day.* Also in this instance God's gift is associated with a test of, and instruction to, the people: *that I may prove them* — the meaning is: in a way (not: in order) that I may test them and see *whether they will walk in My instruction or not.* The
5   probe will be in connection with the Sabbath: *And it shall come to pass on the sixth day, when they prepare what they bring in,* etc.

On the ancient nexus between the traditional narrative concerning the manna and the observance of the Sabbath, see my remarks above, in the introductory notes to this paragraph. There I explained how the tradition originally placed the episode in the period after the Revelation at Mount Sinai and the erection of the Tabernacle. Here I shall add only that the formulation of the passage is intended to ease the difficulty arising from the fact that the Sabbath is mentioned prior to the story of the Decalogue. The narrative is so worded that it can be taken to refer not necessarily to the precept in the Ten Commandments but merely to the ancient tradition, with which the patriarchs of Israel were already acquainted, and which related to a time unit of seven days and its termination on a day that was differentiated from the six preceding days. In the poetic tradition of Mesopotamia, which was certainly known to the patriarchs, who emigrated from there, and similarly in the poetic tradition of the Canaanites, with which the patriarchs were undoubtedly familiar from the time that they settled in the land, every important work is described as being accomplished in the course of six days, and as attaining its completion, or conclusion, or culminating in the emergence of a new and important situation on the seventh day. The Israelite tradition already depicted in this way the work of Creation: six days of creative activity and a seventh day of rest. On the basis of their knowledge of all this, the Israelites could have understood such statements as are made here concerning the difference between the seventh day and the six preceding days, and regarding the sanctification of the former to the Lord. At the commencement it is said: *And it shall come to pass on the sixth day, when they prepare* — with all the requisite culinary preparations, such as cooking and the like — the heavenly bread *that they bring in* to their tents, *that* the bread that they bring in to their tents on the sixth day *will be twice as much as they gather daily*. They were not yet told why they were to bring in twice as much bread on the sixth day, nor why they had to prepare it all on that day, but on the basis of the aforementioned traditions they expected an important innovation to take place on the seventh day, and when they saw that the change consisted in the fact that on this day the Lord did not rain bread, and that they had no need to go out to gather it or to put themselves to the trouble of preparing it, they learned from this experience what would be the law of the seventh day among the Israelites. This practical lesson was likely to leave a much deeper impression on them than if they were enjoined merely in an abstract form: Six days shall you work and on the seventh you shall refrain therefrom.

We must also bear in mind that in Mesopotamia, the original home of the patriarchs of Israel, there was a specific day in the month called Sabbath; the name was therefore already known to the Israelites, although the character of the Mesopotamian Sabbath was considerably different from that of the Israelite Sabbath. We shall deal with this point specifically later, in our commentary on xx 8.

After Moses and Aaron had heard the promise regarding the raining of bread from heaven, they turned to the people and said
6 to them: *At evening* — immediately, before this day is out (they

were able to rely on the words הִנְנִי מַמְטִיר *hinenī mamṭīr* [literally, 'Behold, I am about to rain'; rendered: 'Behold, I will rain'], since the participle after הִנֵּה *hinnē* ['Behold'] denotes an action that is due to be performed in a very short time) *you shall know that* it was actually *the Lord who brought you out of the land of Egypt*, and not we as you said (*v.* 3); and He acts in accord with

7 His name, which signifies, 'He that is with His creatures'. *And in the morning* — tomorrow morning — (they were able to presume this from the statement made to Moses: 'a day's portion every day'), *you shall see the glory of the Lord*, who performs miracles for your sake. The meaning is not that just in the evening they would know that it was the Lord who brought them out from Egypt and precisely in the morning they would see the glory of the Lord, but that, in accordance with one of the idiomatic usages of Biblical parallelism, both in the evening and morning they would know that it was the Lord who brought them out from Egypt, and both in the evening and morning they would see the Lord's glory. All this, Moses continues to declare, you will know and see, *because He has heard your murmurings* — because He has received your requests favourably (this is how the verb שָׁמַע *šāma'* ['hear'] has to be understood in this verse — in the sense of expressions like 'hear a prayer' etc. — and not, according to the customary interpretation, that the murmurings had reached the Lord's ears and that He regarded them as an affront to His glory). The complaints are *against the Lord*, for only He can implement your wishes, not we: *For what are we that you murmur against us* (here we find the reverse of what we observed in *v.* 2: the *Kethībh* is תִּלּוֹנוּ *tillōnū* [*Niph'al*] and the *Qerē* is תַלִּינוּ *tallīnū* [*Hiph'īl*; but the meaning in both cases is the same: 'you murmur']; the Masoretes wished to introduce variety into the readings).

8 After this we read a second time: *And Moses said* [the first time in *v.* 6]. As I explained above, on ch. iii 14, when there is a repetition like *And... said — And... said* with reference to the same subject, only the first *said* introduces the actual words spoken, whereas the second *said* merely elucidates the inner purport of these words. This also obtains here. And it is precisely because the sentence is only explanatory that it is incomplete and its first part is not expressly stated. The text comes to tell us that Moses' underlying intention was to state: all that I tell you, namely, 'At evening you shall know... and in the morning you shall see', etc., will receive its implementation *When the Lord gives you in the evening flesh to*

eat and in the morning bread to the full, etc. Although Moses had not yet heard what would be given and when it would be given, for these particulars were not told to him till later (*vv.* 11–12), yet he was able to draw the necessary inferences. Since the Lord had told him that He was willing to grant the requests of the Israelites, Moses understood that it was the Lord's will to give them the two things for which they craved — both the *flesh* and the *bread* — and without doubt it was His desire that *they should eat to the full,* in accordance with their nostalgic references to the past. Furthermore, he understood that when God promised to rain לֶחֶם *leḥem* [translated, 'bread'], He used the word in its widest signification, including also meat (in Arabic لحم *laḥm* means specifically 'flesh'). Moses surmised that as their daily ration they would receive bread, which was given to them each day in Egypt, and that it would be supplied in the morning, since he was told that on the sixth day they should prepare it for the Sabbath, and hence there would necessarily have to be time to do this during the day. It followed, therefore, that the thing that would be given forthwith in the evening as a non-recurring gift would be the flesh, which was not an article of daily diet. So Moses thought to himself, but he did not tell the people his thoughts explicitly. Further on, in *vv.* 11–12 it is stated that the Lord agreed with Moses' thought, just as we are told above, viii 5–9, 25–26, that Moses fixed a time for Pharaoh, and that the Lord consented and did as Moses asked.

In the same way as the first part of *v.* 8 explains the inner significance of Moses' words cited in *v.* 6 and in the first part of *v.* 7, so the second part of *v.* 8 elucidates the underlying meaning of what Moses said in the second half of *v.* 7, by a considerable expansion of his statement: *because the Lord has heard your murmurings which you murmur against Him* — actually against Him and not us — *for what are we? Your murmurings are not against us but against the Lord.*

Then Moses turned to Aaron, who is accustomed to speak to
9 the people in his name, and said to him: *Say to the whole congregation of the children of Israel* (again the same formula as at the beginning of the paragraph): *Come near before the Lord* — that is, look in gratitude (compare, *they looked toward* in *v.* 10) toward the cloud that is in front of the camp and represents the Lord — *for he has heard your murmurings* — for he received your requests
10 and is about to fulfil them. *And it came to pass, as Aaron spoke to the whole congregation of the children of Israel* (once more the

same formula) *that they looked toward the wilderness* — in the direction in which they were journeying, towards the heart of the desert, towards the place where the pillar of cloud stood, — *and behold, the glory of the Lord appeared in the cloud.* The meaning of these words is clarified by what we are subsequently told in xxiv 15–17: 'and the cloud covered the mountain. And the glory of the Lord dwelt on Mount Sinai, and the cloud covered it... now the appearance of the glory of the Lord was like a devouring fire on the top of the mountain.' The Israelites saw, as it were, the appearance of fire in the midst of the pillar of cloud, and they recognized in this vision the presence of the Lord and His paternal desire to promote their welfare. It is possible that, in the ancient form of this tradition, the connotation of the expression *before the Lord* was 'toward the tabernacle'. But the text before us is worded in a form that allows us to understand it in the way that I have explained: toward the pillar of cloud, which faced the wilderness.

The Lord gave assent to Moses' thoughts, and said to him:
11-12 *I have heard the murmurings of the children of Israel*, therefore *speak to them, saying* — explicitly, that which you have already been thinking to yourself: *At twilight you shall eat flesh, and in the morning you shall be filled with bread* (the words used by the people in *v.* 3 are again repeated); *then you shall know* — as a result of this — *that I am the Lord your God.*

13 And so it happened: *And it came to pass in the evening, that quails came up* — from the horizon; compare the expression: 'He it is who makes the vapours rise at the end of the earth' (Psa. cxxxv 7; also Jer. x 13) — *and covered the camp.* Quails are migratory birds (*Coturnix coturnix*) and usually fly in vast numbers in autumn from the cold northern countries to the warm lands of the south, returning in spring from the southern to the northern regions. When they reach land, after a day of prolonged travelling over the sea, they are exhausted and rest from sheer fatigue on the ground, and it is quite easy for people to capture them by hand, If we bear in mind the date at the beginning of the 'framework', in *v.* 1 (on this hypothesis see above), namely, the fifteenth of Iyyar, we shall see that this is actually the season when these birds migrate from south to north, and probably the quails reached at this time the shore of the Peninsula of Sinai after a protracted flight over the waters of the Read Sea. In Num. xi there is another narrative about the quails, in a form similar to the story in this paragraph.

EXODUS XVI 14

The sequence of the passages in the existing text implies that two separate incidents are intended, one of which occurred in the first year and the other in the second year, at the same season (Num. x 11: 'in the second month, on the twentieth day of the month') and in the same area (according to the view that the Israelites travelled along the shore of the Mediterranean sea, the narrative does not fit the season, for the quails come there from the northern countries in autumn). Since this is a usual occurrence, the Bible does not speak of it at length, and mentions the quails with the definite article, as something generally known and clear. When the multitudes of quails came and covered the camp, it was easy for the Israelites to seize many birds and to eat flesh to the full. In this way the first promise was fulfilled, to wit, that on the same evening they would eat meat that would rain down, as it were, from heaven.

When morning came, they did not at first realize that anything extraordinary had happened: *and in the morning there was* — as usual — *a layer of (the) dew* (again the definite article is used, because this is a well-known and normal phenomenon) *round about the camp*. But after a little while the sun warmed the air,

14 *And the layer of dew went up* — the dew evaporated and what was hidden beneath it stood revealed. The verb וַתַּעַל *watta'al* ['came up', 'went up'], which is repeated here in a different sense (but in a form identical with that used in *v*. 13 in connection with the quails) to create a word-play, clearly proves that our text does not consist of fragments derived from two diverse sources, but that it forms a single sequence. As the layer of dew continued to rise, the children of Israel looked, *and behold, upon the face of the wilderness* — upon the ground of the desert in the area round about their tents — there was a *finely-formed substance revealing itself* (מְחֻסְפָּס *meḥuspās*; in Ugaritic the verb *ḥsp* is used in the sense of the Biblical stem חָשַׂף *ḥāśaph* ['uncover', 'reveal']), and this substance was *fine as hoar-frost* — was composed of innumerable fine grains like those of hoar-frost lying *on the ground*.

Here begins the account of a miracle, the story of the coming down of the manna in the wilderness. Like most of the miracles narrated above, it, too, was based on a local phenomenon of nature, but was exceptional in regard to scale and details (see my notes above, on the division of the Sea of Reeds). The natural background of the wonder, according to S. Bodenheimer, who investigated the matter in the Sinai Peninsula a few years ago, is the fact that certain kinds of aphides, which habitually live on the numerous tamarisk trees of the region, exude from their bodies the superfluous sugar that they absorb from the trees, in the form of drops that dry in the hot desert air and become minute whitish or yellowish globules. These globules fall to the ground, where they remain till the ants arrive, after the early hours of the morning, and collect them, or until human beings gather them. The Arabs call them *mann*, or *mann as-samā*, 'manna of heaven' (compare 'the grain of heaven', Psa. lxxviii 24; and 'bread from heaven', *ibid.*, cv 40). Similar excretions of other insects are to be found in other countries, particularly in Iraq, and these are likewise called *mann* in Arabic. The miracle narrated in our text consists only in the enormous quantity of the manna and in the special circumstances attending its manifestation.

15 *And the children of Israel saw* — that is, and when the children of Israel saw the thing (on the syntactic construction see above, on ii 2) — then *they said to one another, What* [מָן *mān*] *is it? For they did not know what* [מַה *ma*] *it was*. Here the Torah gives us an 'etymological' explanation of the word *manna*. In the ancient Canaanite tongue, which was spoken by the Israelites in the early generations, the word *mn* was also used in the sense of *what*, as the El Amarna letters and Ugaritic poetry testify. To the question of the Israelites Moses replies: *It is the bread which the Lord has given you* [לָכֶם *lākhem*] *to eat* [לְאָכְלָה *leʾokhlā*], as I told you yesterday. The wording of the sentence recalls the passage in Gen. i 29: 'Behold, I have *given you* every plant yielding seed... *you* [לָכֶם *lākhem*; literally, 'to you'] *shall have them for food* [לְאָכְלָה *leʾokhlā*; literally, 'to eat']. He who concerned Himself since the days of Creation to provide sustenance for His creatures, concerns Himself, in the same way, to provide it now.

The parallelism with the story of Creation is continued later on, in connection with the Sabbath.

16 Moses also added, in the Lord's name, detailed instructions: *This is what the Lord has commanded: Gather of it, every man of you, as much as he can eat; you shall take an omer apiece, according to the number of the persons whom each of you has in his tent*. These directions, which resemble those concerning the passover sacrifice (xii 4–5: 'according to what each can eat... you shall take it'), were not expressly mentioned in the words of the Lord; apparently the text implies that although they were given to Moses by the Almighty, yet there was no need to state them twice (see above, on x 2), or that the Lord's injunction goes only as far as the

words, *as much as he can eat*, and that Moses added the rest as his own directives for the implementation of the commandment
17 (compare above, on xii 21). *And the children of Israel did so* — as Moses had told them — *and they gathered, some more some less* —
18 *each one according to the number of persons in his tent. But when they measured it with an omer* — according to Moses' direction — *he that gathered much had nothing over* — that is, he that gathered much did not gather more than was warranted by the persons of his house — *and he that gathered little had no lack* — he that gathered little did not take less than required by the number of persons in his family; *each gathered according to what he could eat.*
19 Moses also gave another instruction to his people: *Let no man leave any of it till the morning*; since it was enjoined (*v*. 4), 'and gather a day's portion every day', they must rely on this promise. But there were some people of little faith there, who did not trust
20 the promise: *Notwithstanding, they did not listen to Moses; and some* (this is also the subject of the preceding clause: 'Notwithstanding, they did not listen') *left part of it till the morning*. However, their concern for the future did not avail them: *and it* — the manna — *bred worms and it became foul*. Possibly the reference is to the ants, who came to gather the manna in the tents (the Arabs who gather the manna call these ants to this day by a name signifying 'worms'). *And Moses was angry with them* — because of their lack of faith and indiscipline; but after this incident the Israelites were obedient:
21 *And they gathered it* — the manna — *morning by morning, each as much as he could eat* — in the early hours of the morning, for thereafter, *when the sun grew hot* וְנָמָס *wᵉnāmās* — possibly the last word is not to be rendered 'it melted', but *it became loathsome* (like the word נָמֵס *nāmēs* [usually translated, 'rejected', 'worthless'] in i Sam. xv 9), on account of the ants that swarmed on it a few hours after sunrise.
22 *And it came to pass that on the sixth day* the quantity of manna on the ground was greater than on the previous days. The Israelites regarded this as an opportunity to gather more than usual, and so they actually did: *they gathered twice as much bread, two omers apiece*. At first Moses told them nothing about this, in order that the lesson that they would learn from their experience should, as I have explained earlier, make a greater impression upon them. *And all the chieftains of the congregation came* — the heads of the fathers' houses of the Israelites, when they saw that the people
23 were gathering more than usual — *and told Moses. And he* —

Moses — *said unto them*: Let them gather today twice as much bread, for *This is what the Lord has spoken* — when He informed me of this matter. Know, and make known to the people, that *Tomorrow is a day of cessation, a holy sabbath to the Lord* — a day of cessation from all work in honour of the Lord, and therefore: *what you will bake* — whatever you wish to bake together with the manna — *bake* — today — *and what you will boil* — of, or with, the manna — *boil* today, *and all that is left over* of today's meals, even if it is uncooked, *lay by for you to be kept* [לָכֶם לְמִשְׁמֶרֶת *lākhem lᵉmišmereth*] — again words that recall the passover sacrifice (xii 6: *And you shall keep it* [לָכֶם לְמִשְׁמֶרֶת *lākhem lᵉmišmereth*]) — *till the morning* — and do not be afraid that it may become foul.

24 *So they laid it by*, namely, that which was left, *till the morning, as Moses bade them*; *and it did not become foul, and there were no worms in it* — the *contretemps* described in *v*. 20 did not recur.

25 *And Moses said*, on the seventh day, *Eat it today* — namely, whatever remains over from the baked or cooked or raw food — *for today is a sabbath unto the Lord*, and just as the Lord abstained from work on the seventh day after the six days of Creation, so He will also abstain today, and will not rain for you bread from heaven; *today you will not find it* — you will not find the manna — *in the field*. In accordance with the usual formulation of the Sabbath laws (for example xx 9–10: 'Six days you shall labour, and do all your work; but the seventh day is a sabbath to the Lord your God'; xxiii 12: 'Six days you shall do your work, but on the seventh day you shall desist'; xxxiv 21: 'Six days you shall work, but on the

26 seventh day you shall desist') he added: *Six days you shall gather it; but on the seventh day, which is a sabbath, there will be none.*

However, on this occasion, too, they did not all listen to Moses.

27 *And it came to pass that on the seventh day* (although the story had already reached the seventh day in the preceding verses, yet, since a new episode begins here, it was proper to employ an expression corresponding to the commencement of the previous narration. 'And it came to pass that on the sixth day', in *v*. 22) *there went out* some *of the people to gather, and they found none*, as Moses had told them: 'today you will not find it in the field.' This time the act of indiscipline was worse than that recounted in *v*. 20, and therefore the Bible does not just speak of Moses' anger but

28 of the Lord's rebuke. *And the Lord said to Moses* that he should

29 speak to the people in His name as follows: *How long do you refuse to keep My commandments and My laws? See!* — with your

own eyes, since the manna is not on the ground this day as you have seen it (v. 15) on the previous days — *that the Lord has given you the sabbath*; consequently, have no fear, either now or in the future, that, because you will refrain from working on the seventh day, you will lack food, for (compare the assurance with regard to the seventh year in Lev. xxv 20–21) *therefore on the sixth day He gives you bread for two days*. Although God *has given* you the sabbath, yet He *gives* you beforehand bread for two days. Therefore *remain every man of you in his place, let no man go out of his place* to gather the manna *on the seventh day* (note the assonance: שַׁבָּת *šabbāth* ['sabbath'] — שְׁבוּ *šᵉbhū* ['remain'] — שְׁבִיעִי *šᵉbhīʿī*
30 ['seventh']). The people accepted this commandment: *and the people abstained from work on the seventh day*, just as God did not work on the seventh day.

So far the story of the manna. Attached to it incidentally are several notes on matters connected with the manna, which belong mainly to a period subsequent to the episode related above.

The first note deals with the naming of the manna for all time:
31 *Now the house of Israel called* — that is, not only the children of Israel living at the time, but the whole house of Israel throughout the generations — *its name* — the name of the bread that they ate in the generation of the wilderness — *manna* (compare v. 15).

The second note describes the characteristics of the manna: *it was like coriander seed*, that is, that in its round shape and in its size, which is twice that of a pea, it resembles the seed (so it is generally designated, although it is actually the fruit) of the plant called גַּד *gadh* ['coriander'] in the Bible, כֻּסְבָּר *kusbār* in the Mishnah, and in botanical terminology, *Coriandrum sativum*. Its colour was *white, and the taste of it was like wafers made with honey*, a food eaten to this day by the Bedouins and known by this name also in Arabic.

The third note relates what was done, after the erection of the Tabernacle, to perpetuate the memory of the manna (again the formulation, in the form of an appendix that belongs to a later period, is intended to remove the difficulty arising from the fact that the
32 *Testimony* is mentioned at this stage). *And Moses said* to the people: *This is what the Lord has commanded* (paralleling vv. 16 and 23): *Let an omerful of it be kept throughout your generations* (Samaritan Pentateuch, in order to ease the construction of the text, reads מִלְאוּ *milᵉʾū* ['fill (an omer)'] instead of מְלֹא *mᵉloʾ* ['fulness (an omer']), *that they* — those generations — *may see*, as you have

199

seen, *the bread with which I fed you in the wilderness, when I brought you out of the land of Egypt.* With a view to implementing this
33 command, Moses said to Aaron: *Take a jar, and put an omer of manna in it, and place it before the Lord*, that is, before the Ark of the Testimony, *to be kept throughout your generations.* Aaron
34 did *As the Lord commanded Moses, and Aaron placed it before the Testimony, to be kept.* The Bible uses three times, for emphasis, the word לְמִשְׁמֶרֶת *l^emišmereth* ['to be kept'] found in *v.* 23 (and prior to that already, in connection with the passover sacrifice, in xii 6), and twice also the verb הִנִּיחַ *hinnīaḥ* ['place', 'lay by'] that occurs *ibid.*

The fourth note brings us to a still later period, to the time after the first Passover celebrated by the Israelites in the land of Canaan
35 in the days of Joshua: *And the children of Israel ate the manna forty years, till they came to an inhabited* [or, *a habitable*] *land; they ate* only *the manna* instead of bread (but the meaning of the verse is not, needless to say, that the manna was their sole food throughout the period of their wanderings in the wilderness; their cattle provided them with both meat and milk, and the murmuring mentioned in Num. xi emanated from those who had no cattle), *till they came to the border of the land of Canaan,* as is stated in Jos. v 11.
36 The fifth note fixes the size of the omer: *Now an omer is the tenth part of an ephah,* that is, approximately three and a half litres [six and a half pints].

THIRD PARAGRAPH

THE WATERS OF MERIBAH

(XVII 1–7)

Chapter XVII

This is the third narrative in the series dealing with the provision, by the Lord, for the needs of the Israelites in the wilderness.

The story begins with the customary formula used in describing the journeyings in the desert: 'and they journeyed... and they
1 camped.' *And all the congregation of the children of Israel journeyed* (this, too, as we have seen, is a stereotyped formula) *from the wilderness of Sin* (xvi 1) *by their stages* (which there was no need to

200

EXODUS XVII 3

list here in detail, in the way they are enumerated in Num. xxxiii 12-14) *according to the commandment of the Lord* — not as Moses saw fit, but according to the directions of the Lord, who wished to demonstrate to them, for the third time, His power to help — *and they camped at Rephidim,* apparently an oasis in the desert, which it is difficult to identify exactly; *but there was no water for the people to drink.* They had hoped to find water there, but the waters of the wady failed at that time, in a manner reminiscent of the scene depicted in Job vi 15-20. On this occasion the circumstances were worse than those described in the two preceding narratives. At Marah the children of Israel found bitter water, and thereafter they suffered in the wilderness from restriction of diet; but now the supreme calamity of desert travellers befell them — complete lack of

2 water. This time they were not content merely to murmur, but *the people strove with Moses,* that is, the Israelites rose up against him as opponents in a quarrel, who claim what is due to them: *and they said,* in their dispute with him, *Give* [תְּנוּ *tᵉnū*, plural] *us water to drink;* you and Aaron (there is also another reading תְּנָה *tᵉnā* ['Give!'] in the singular, found in several MSS, as well as in the Samaritan Pentateuch, the Septuagint and the Peshiṭta) have brought us out of Egypt, and consequently you have an obligation to give us water according to our needs. *And Moses said to them, Why do you strive with me? Why do you put the Lord to the proof?* (on the meaning of the word מַה *ma* ['why?' or 'not'] see above, on xiv 15; xv 24); your quarrel with me has no justification. I brought you out of Egypt at the Lord's command; your contentiousness shows your lack of faith in Him, and that you have come, as it were, to test 'whether the Lord is in our midst or not' (*v.* 7). It is, indeed, right that He should put you to the proof (xv 25; xvi 4), but not (Heaven forfend!) that you should prove Him. Moses' words prepare the way for the etymologies of the names appearing in *v.* 7.

3 Verse 3, *And the people thirsted there for water,* etc., tells us nothing new; nor is it another recension of the narrative. It gives us, in accordance with the established literary practice, a detailed account after the general statement in *v.* 2, explaining the nature of the charges levelled by the people against Moses. In conformity with Biblical style, which prefers coordinate rather than subordinate clauses, the sentence, *And the people thirsted there for water,* is to be understood as a subordinate clause, to wit: Since the people thirsted for water, they complained against Moses, etc. It was neces-

sary to reiterate the gravity of the situation, because the narrative had been interrupted by the reference to Moses' reaction. *And the people murmured against Moses, and said, Why did you bring us up out of Egypt, to kill me and my children and my cattle with thirst?* The singular pronoun *me* follows the plural *us*, in order to make it possible to give special emphasis to the suffering of the children; for if the text read *us*, the children would also have been implied. There is a clear parallelism here with xvi 3.

4 Moses prayed: *So Moses cried to the Lord*, (compare xiv 10; xv 25), *saying, What shall I do with this people?* I am at a loss to know what to do with this people (the demonstrative pronoun contains an undertone of grievance against the people); *they are almost ready to stone me* — they have risen up against me and very nearly have reached the point of stoning me to death. It is not without reason that the text above states, *the people strove with Moses*, and not *against Moses*; the people voiced their complaints against Moses, and Moses voiced his against the people. The contention was reciprocal.

The Lord's reply to Moses is on a lofty and majestic plane; He does not intervene in the strife between the people and Moses, neither in regard to the people's allegations against Moses, nor in respect of his counter-charges against the people. His attitude is that of a father whose children are in distress, and in their distress an altercation breaks out between them; he pays no attention to the wrangling, but endeavours only to deliver his children from their
5 trouble. Thus God says to Moses: *Pass on before the people* — that is, proceed further in the wady, in the direction indicated by the pillar of cloud, and go in front of the rest of the people (for the expression 'pass on before so-and-so' compare Gen. xxxii 16 [Hebrew, v. 17], 21 [Hebrew, v. 22]; xxxiii 3), *and take with you some of the elders of Israel*, who shall act as witnesses, *and take in your hand the rod with which you struck the Nile, and go*, till I give you
6 a signal. Now the signal shall be as follows: *Behold, I will stand* — that is, My pillar of cloud shall stand — *before you there on the rock at Horeb*, near the place where I first revealed Myself to you in the bush; and *you shall strike the rock* with your rod even as you struck the Nile (the word הִכִּיתָ *hikkītha* [rendered first: 'you struck', and then: 'you will strike'] occurs twice in consecutive sentences, once in a bad sense and once in a good sense, as though to say: 'I kill and I make alive; I wound and I heal'), *and water shall come out of it, that the people may drink*; but whereas the striking

of the Nile signalized that there would be insufficient water to drink, the striking of the rock would indicate the reverse.

In this paragraph, also, a marvel is described that has its basis in a natural phenomenon; and again we have to make the same observation as we made in connection with the miracles recorded above, and especially with regard to the division of the Sea of Reeds (pp. 167 f.). Several commentators have already mentioned a similar occurrence in our own time, namely, that on the mountain called by the Arabs Jebel Musa ('the Mountain of Moses'), which is identified in their tradition with Mount Sinai, there was suddenly opened up a stream of running well water through the breaking of a thin layer of rock. Not long ago, too, an English officer saw with his own eyes, in a wady in the southern part of the Sinai Peninsula, a company of the Sudanese camel corps digging in the gravel heaped up by the side of a cliff in order to discover the source of the water that was dripping between the pebbles, when suddenly, after a hard knock with an axe that broke the outer face of the cliff, numerous cavities were revealed in the stone, from which an abundance of water began to gush.

Moses went up the slope of the wady, and reached the rock at Horeb, which was apparently the site whence in normal times the waters of the wady, now temporarily arrested, used to flow. *And Moses did so* — as he was commanded — *in the sight of the elders of Israel*, and water issued from the rock in abundance. The stream of the wady began to flow as usual, and its waters reached the encampment of the people, and they drank their fill thereof.

7 The paragraph concludes with etymologies: *And he* — that is, one — *called the name of the place*, in which the people camped, *Massah* ['Proof'] *and Meribah* ['Contention']. It is possible that the names antedated the incident, and the verse comes only to tell us that these names are suited to this district, since they are in keeping with what happened there to the Israelites, and allude, so to speak, to that episode, *to the contention of the children of Israel* with Moses *and to their putting the Lord to the proof* with their complaints, which were tantamount, as it were, to their *saying*, Let us test and see: *Is the Lord among us or not?* With these words the passage reverts to the beginning of the narrative (v. 2), and reiterates what was stated at the commencement of the story.

An incident similar to this one, which took place at the outset of the Israelite itinerary in the wilderness, is described in another part of the Torah (Num. xx 1–11), dealing with the end of the wanderings. From the literary viewpoint, this provides an interesting example of the symmetry that the Biblical style is fond of achieving by means of parallelism between the beginning and the conclusion of its narrations; and from a thematic standpoint, we may see in this duplication the intention to substantiate emphatically the tradition concerning the providential care that the Lord gave to the needs of His people in the wilderness, from the first to the last stage of their travels.

FOURTH PARAGRAPH

WAR WITH THE AMALEKITES

(XVII 8–16)

The purpose of this paragraph is to show that just as the Lord was concerned to deliver the children of Israel from every danger to which they were subjected by the forces of inanimate nature, even so He was concerned to deliver them from the power of human beings who rose up in hostility against them after they had been saved from the hands of the Egyptians.

8 Amalek was a Bedouin people, who led a nomadic existence in the desert south of the land of Canaan, as is evidenced by Scripture in Gen. xiv 7, which mentions the country of the Amalekites as being in the proximity of Kadesh, and in other passages that speak of Amalek as dwelling in the region of the Negeb (Num. xiii 29; xiv 25, 43); but it is not to be inferred from here that Rephidim was near to Kadesh. On the contrary, it is stated here, *And Amalek came*, that means to say, that they were not settled there but came from a distance. Since they occupied the approaches to the land of Canaan from the south, and undoubtedly they had heard that the Israelites were marching in that direction, they wished to forestall trouble by sending a detachment of soldiers to attack the Israelites at the commencement of their journey. According to the tradition reflected in another passage of the Torah (Deut. xxv 18: 'and cut off at your rear all who lagged behind you') the first action taken by this troop was to attack the rearguard of the Israelite host, the weak and the weary who were unable to defend themselves. It is stated here, *and fought with Israel*, and not *against Israel*,

because the general statement of this verse refers also to the counter-attack by Israel, which will be mentioned in detail later (compare above, v. 2: 'the people strove *with Moses*' — implying reciprocal contention, as I have explained). The site of the battle was at *Rephidim*.

Moses, being advanced in years, was unable to go forth to battle at the head of the people; hence he handed over this task to Joshua: 9 *And Moses said to Joshua, Choose for us men* who are strong and fit to do battle, *and go out, fight against Amalek*. Although Joshua has not yet been mentioned in the Book of Exodus, yet his name was known in the Israelite tradition, and the reader would easily understand who was being referred to. Hence it was possible to cite here the exact words of the source (possibly the epic poem on the Exodus from Egypt) without any additional explanation.

Furthermore, Moses told Joshua that he, too, would play his part: *tomorrow*, when you go forth to fight, *I will stand on the top of the hill* that overlooks the battlefield, *with the rod of God in my hand* to hearten you by recalling the miracles of the Lord that were wrought by the signals of the rod, and to ask of the 10 Lord to renew His wonders on your behalf. *So Joshua did as Moses told him*, choosing men and going forth with them *to fight against Amalek, and Moses*, together with *Aaron and Hur* (Hur also has not yet been mentioned in the Book of Exodus, but the reference to him can be explained in the same way as that to 11 Joshua) *went to the top of the hill. And it came to pass that* (וְהָיָה $w^eh\bar{a}y\bar{a}$: the perfect with *Waw* denotes here continued action in the past), *whenever Moses held up his hand* with his rod, the Israelite fighters were encouraged and rallied, *and Israel prevailed*; on the other hand, *whenever he lowered his hand*, and the Israelites saw him exhausted, their strength also ebbed, *and Amalek prevailed*. But Moses, although he was still strong and mighty of spirit, was 12 unable to stand continuously with his hands uplifted: *and Moses' hands grew heavy* (כְּבֵדִים $k^ebh\bar{e}dh\bar{\imath}m$, masc. plur. although the Hebrew word for 'hands' is fem.; but possibly this is an archaic grammatical form with the dual termination and should be vocalized כְּבֵדַיִם $k^ebh\bar{e}dhayim$); *so they* — Aaron and Hur — *took a stone and put it under him, and he sat upon it, and Aaron and Hur held up hands, one on one side, and the other on the other side; so his hands were steady* (literally, 'steadiness'; compare expressions like, 'Now the whole earth was [rendered: 'had'] one speech', in Gen. xi 1) *until the going down of the sun* — until darkness put an end to the fighting.

EXODUS XVII 13

13 So Israel prevailed and won a victory: *And Joshua disabled Amalek and his people* (that is, his army) *with the edge of the sword.*

If we bear in mind that, apparently, both this paragraph and the one about Amalek in Deut. xxv 17–19 are derived from a common source, namely, the epic poem on the Exodus from Egypt, we can posit that there was a word-play in that poem between the word הַנֶּחֱשָׁלִים *hanneḥĕšālīm* [Deut. xxv 18: 'who lagged behind'] at the beginning of the account and the word וַיַּחֲלֹשׁ *wayyaḥălōš* ['disabled'] at the end. Although Amalek had sought to exploit the weakness of those who lagged behind, yet ultimately, with the help of the Lord, Joshua prevailed over him and disabled him and his people with the edge of the sword.

Notwithstanding Amalek's failure, the existence of such an enemy on the southern border of the Land could become a source of permanent danger to Israel in the future. Hence Israel regarded Amalek as his eternal foe, and considered his destruction a national duty, till king Saul fulfilled it. In the light of this situation we can understand the significance of *vv.* 14–16:

14 *And the Lord said to Moses, Write this* — what happened now and what I am about to tell you ('that I will utterly blot out', etc.) — *as a memorial in the book* (the definite article expresses general definition: in the book in which you will write, that is in a special book of memorial for the purpose; possibly the meaning of the word סֵפֶר *sēpher* here is 'inscription' — a memorial inscription) *and recite it in the ears of Joshua*, that is, apart from writing it down, teach it to Joshua by heart, so that it may be preserved for generations both in writing and orally. Write and deliver to Joshua the promise: *that I will utterly blot out the remembrance of Amalek* — that is, Amalek's name — *from under heaven.* It is self- 15 understood that Moses did so. *And Moses built an altar* on that very site, as a memorial to the events that had occurred there — possibly he engraved the inscription upon it, if the word סֵפֶר *sēpher* is to be understood in the signification suggested above — *and called the name of it* — of the altar — *the Lord* [*YHWH*] *is my banner*, that is: Let this altar be a witness that the Lord, who is symbolized by the rod of God in my hand, was a banner to us on the hill, and a source of courage until salvation and victory 16 were achieved. *And he* — Moses — *said,* כִּי יָד עַל כֵּס יָהּ *kī yādh ʿal kēs Yāh. The Lord will have war with Amalek from generation to generation.* This poetic verse is apparently quoted word for word from the epic poem that was the source of the paragraph.

EXODUS XVII 15

The first part is obscure, but it seems to me that it should be interpreted as follows: Truly (כִּי *kī*), this altar shall be a *hand* [monument], that is, a memorial pillar, to the Lord's plan (כֵּס *kēs* being from the stem כָּסַס *kāsas*, 'count', 'reckon') to blot out Amalek's memory. To this end the Lord will have war with Amalek from generation to generation, until the memory of Amalek is blotted out from under heaven.

It is possibly not fortuitous that the word *hand* occurs in this paragraph, in both its meanings, seven times.

PART TWO
THE TORAH AND ITS PRECEPTS
A Commentary on Exodus XVIII-XXIV

SECTION ONE

ISRAEL IS WELCOMED AS ONE OF THE NATIONS OF THE WORLD

CHAPTER XVIII, 1–27

With fine artistic understanding, the Torah prefaces the account of the central theme of this part of the Book of Exodus with a prologue, the purpose of which is to prepare the reader's mind for the narrative that follows. So far we have read stories about the travails of the journey and the difficulties encountered by the Israelites through natural causes and human hostility. But now, at the beginning of the second part, it was fitting that we should be told of a gesture of sympathy and esteem for the people of Israel shown by an important person, one of the leaders of the neighbouring peoples, who was able to understand and to honour the unique and wonderful destiny of the children of Israel, and came to congratulate the new people, which was now entering the family of nations. We are prepared here, as it were, for what is to be stated in the next chapter (xix 5–6) concerning the election of Israel as 'a people of special possession' from among the nations of the earth; whilst the reference in this introductory passage to the statutes and teachings of God (*vv.* 15 f.) serve to prepare us for what will subsequently be related regarding the giving of the Torah to the people of Israel.

This section constitutes an antithesis to what is narrated at the end of the preceding part with regard to the war with the Amalekites. Ibn Ezra noted this already, and on the basis of this antithesis he sought to reconcile the chronological difficulty arising from the fact that the section has been placed here although its historic setting belongs to a later period than that of the episodes recorded in the following chapters (*v.* 5 reads: 'into the wilderness where he was encamped, at the mountain of God'; whereas, only later, at the commencement of ch. xix, is it stated that the Israelites journeyed from Rephidim and came to the wilderness of Sinai and encamped there before the mountain).

According to my theory concerning the evolution of the tradition and the arrangement of the sections, we have to envisage the matter in the following way:

There was current among the Israelites, as we learn from i Sam. xv 6, a tradition that told, on the one hand, of the Amalekite raiders who attacked the Israelites during the exodus from Egypt, and, on the other, of the tribe of the Kenites, close neighbours of Amalek, who took no part in this act of aggression, but, on the contrary, were sympathetic towards the Israelites. Conformably with this, when the traditional stories concerning the generation of the wilderness came to be written down, the section narrating the episode of Jethro, who belonged to the tribe of the Kenites, was placed in juxtaposition to that of Amalek, in order to emphasize the fundamental difference between the attitudes of the two tribes toward the children of Israel, a difference that left a very profound impress on the Israelite mind. I have already indicated above, in my introductory remarks to ch. xvi (pp. 186 ff.), that in general the association of subjects, and even verbal association, was a more important factor in the arrangement and linking of sections than the chronological sequence.

Even the formulation of the two sections in the form before us is intended to underline the antithesis between the two episodes. Above (xvii 8) it is stated: 'And Amalek *came* and *fought* with Israel', and here (*vv.* 5, 7): 'And Jethro, Moses' father-in-law, *came...* and they asked each other of their *welfare* [literally, 'peace']'; in the previous narrative (xvii 9) it is written: '*Choose* for us men' — a selection for war, whereas in our passage (*v.* 25) it is recorded: 'And Moses *chose* able men' — a selection for judgement and peace; there (xvii 12) we are told of Moses: 'and he *sat* upon it' — upon the stone to pray for the victory of his people in battle, and in our section it is said (*v.* 13): 'Moses *sat* to judge the people.' There are also other parallels: 'and Moses' hands *grew heavy*' (xvii 12) — 'for the thing is too *heavy* for you' (xviii 18); *stand* (xvii 9) — *stand* (xviii 14); *until the going down of the sun* (xvii 12) — *till* (the) *evening* (xviii 13, 14); *tomorrow* (xvii 9) — *on the morrow* (xviii 13); *war... from generation to generation*, at the end of the section on Amalek (xvii 16) — 'and all this people also will go to their place in *peace*', at the conclusion of Jethro's speech (xviii 23). With the close of the first part of our book, the calamities — the travails and the dangers — also come to an end; the people now find themselves in a position of tranquillity and security, from which it can rise on eagles' wings and become worthy of witnessing God's manifestation.

FIRST PARAGRAPH
JETHRO'S VISIT
(XVIII 1–12)

Chapter XVIII

The passages that previously mentioned Jethro's name and position (chapters ii–iv) are now far behind us; in the meantime, narratives of great importance, which diverted the reader's mind from Jethro, have intervened. Hence, when the Bible resumes his story here,

1 it tells us again in detail who he was. *Now Jethro*, who was *the priest of Midian*, a man of importance among his people, and who was also *Moses' father-in-law*, closely related to the leader of the children of Israel, *heard of all that God*, the Divine Power that rules the world, the knowledge of whom is shared by all peoples, *had done for Moses*, his dearly beloved son-in-law (for this reason he is mentioned first) *and for Israel his people* — Moses' people; and more particularly he heard this: that *YHWH* — that God whom the Israelites designate by this name — *had brought Israel out of Egypt*. The fact that the narrative begins with the name אֱלֹהִים *'Elōhīm* ['God'] and continues to use this name and not the Tetragrammaton, except for verses that seek to emphasize specifically the name of Israel's God, proves that there is no substance in the conjecture of a number of scholars that it was from the Kenites that the Israelites learned to know the name of *YHWH*.

2 Upon hearing these reports, *Jethro, Moses' father-in-law arose and took Zipporah* his daughter, *Moses' wife* — with a view to bringing her to Moses — *after he had sent her away*. The words *after he had sent her away*, which appear to refer to something already known, pertain apparently to one of the incidents recounted by the Israelite tradition, which were well known to the people, but which were not incorporated in the Torah because they were not germane to its purpose. It may be assumed that this tradition related that when the decisive phase of the execution of his task drew near, Moses sent his wife and his sons to her father's house, in order to be free of family responsibilities at that fateful hour, but intending to return and fetch them after the fulfilment of his mission. Possibly this story was told in detail in the epic poem that was current among the people, and the Torah, which did not include it among its narratives because it was the private concern

213

of Moses, made a passing allusion to it here, since this would suffice for any one who was already familiar with the account given in the poem. *After he had sent her away* — the episode that is common knowledge.

3 *And her two sons* Jethro took with him, *of whom the name of the one was Gershom for he said, I have been a sojourner in a foreign land* (compare ii 22). It is not without reason that the text deals with the sons' names and their etymologies at length. The explanations of the names are relevant to our theme. When his first son was born, Moses said: *I have been a sojourner in a foreign land*, which to him as an Egyptian (the designation applied to him by the daughters of the priest of Midian) was an alien country; at that time, it would seem, he prophesied without realizing what he was prophesying, but at this juncture his words acquired a wider significance. Now that he was bringing his people to the Promised Land it was manifest to him that even the land of Egypt was a foreign country to him and that he had been a sojourner there (the text specifically states, *I have been*, in the past, but now I am no longer a sojourner). The word גֵּר *gēr* ['sojourner'] in particular is used, even as God had said to Abraham (Gen. xv 13): 'that your descendants will be sojourners in a land that is not theirs'; and as the brothers of Joseph had said to Pharaoh (Gen. xlvii 4): 'We have come to sojourn in the land.' The connection with our subject is even clearer in the explanation of the second son's name. Moses' words imply, apparently, that this son was born shortly after Moses' return to Egypt, and that Moses called him by a name expressive of his joy at the fact that he was able to return to Egypt without fear of the death-sentence that had been passed
4 on him at the king's command: *and the name of the other, Eliezer* [signifying: 'God is my help'], *for the God of my father*, the God who revealed himself to me at Horeb with the words, 'I am the God of your father' (iii 6), *was my help, and delivered me from the sword of Pharaoh*. This statement of Moses' is well suited to our chapter, which uses the expression 'delivered' a number of times, and once in particular in connection with Pharaoh (v. 8: 'and how the Lord had delivered them'; v. 9; 'in that He had delivered them out of the hand of the Egyptians'; v. 10: 'who has delivered you out of the hands of the Egyptians and out of the hand of Pharaoh').

Now, since Moses had reached a place not far from where Jethro dwelt (compare iii 1, which comes to mind on account of

EXODUS XVIII 9

the similar expressions that occur in this verse), Jethro wished to go and welcome him without waiting for Moses to come to him. He set out and came, with Zipporah and her sons, to Moses' encampment:

5 *And Jethro, Moses' father-in-law, came with his sons and his wife to Moses in the wilderness where he was encamped*, that is, near to *the mountain of God* (this is how the mountain is designated above, iii 1, and our verse iterates what is stated there).

6 *And he said to Moses* — when Jethro arrived at the gateway of the camp, he sent, through one of the guards, the following message to Moses: *I your father-in-law Jethro am coming to you* (the Samaritan Pentateuch and the Septuagint read: הִנֵּה *hinnē* ['behold'] instead of אֲנִי *'anī* ['I'], in conformity with Gen. xlviii 2, so as to facilitate the comprehension of the text), *and your wife* is coming with me, *and her two sons with her.*

7 *And Moses went out* from his tent and went to the entrance of the camp *to meet his father-in-law, and prostrated himself* as a gesture of honour and as an expression of gratitude for his having brought him his wife and sons; *and he kissed him, and they asked each other of their welfare*, in accordance with the eastern custom obtaining to this day among the Arabs, which requires the guest and the host to begin their conversation with explicit questions and answers regarding their well-being and that of each member of the family, and the welfare of all that they have; *and they went into the tent* — they entered Moses' tent for serious discussion.

8 *Then Moses told his father-in-law* all the details of the happenings of which the latter had received general reports: *all that the Lord had done* (here Moses is speaking; hence the Tetragrammaton is used and not the generic name אֱלֹהִים *'Elōhīm* ['God']) *to Pharaoh and to the Egyptians for Israel's sake* (not for his sake, Moses emphasizes, but on account of the people), *and also all the hardship that had come upon them in the way* after the exodus from Egypt — the pursuit of the Egyptians, the division of the Sea of Reeds, the lack of water, the dearth of food, and the war with Amalek — and how everything ended happily: *and how the Lord delivered them.*

9 *And Jethro rejoiced*; he had already rejoiced over the general reports that he had heard at first, but now his joy was even greater in view of the particulars that Moses told him *concerning all the good which the Lord had done to Israel*, etc. (וַיִּחַדְּ *wayyiḥad* [rendered: 'rejoiced'] is an expression of 'joy'; the Septuagint translation of the word, ἐξέστη — 'he shuddered' — is not based, as many believe, on a different reading like וַיֶּחֱרַד *wayyeḥĕradh* ['he trem-

215

bled'], but on the midrashic interpretation cited in B. Sanhedrin 94 b: 'he [Jethro] felt like cuts in his body' [חִדּוּדִין *ḥiddū-dhīn*, translated 'cuts', is a word-play on וַיִּחַדְ *wayyiḥad*]. The words at the end of the verse, *in that he had delivered them out of the hand of the Egyptians*, are a repetition to give emphasis to the thought and to establish the nexus, referred to above, with the clause: 'and delivered me from the sword of Pharaoh' (v. 4).

10 *And Jethro said, Blessed be YHWH* ['the Lord']— that is, praise and thanks be to the God whom you call by the name of *YHWH* (for the connotation of the word בָּרוּךְ *bārūkh* [rendered 'blessed'] as an expression of praise and thanks, compare Gen. xiv 20: 'and blessed be God most High, who has delivered your enemies into your hand') — *who has delivered you* — you Moses and your brother Aaron — *out of the hand of the Egyptians and out of the hand of Pharaoh* — who threatened to put you to death (x 28) — and *who* likewise *has delivered the people from under* the burden of bondage at *the hand of the Egyptians*. The threefold use of the expression *delivered* is intended for emphasis; the omission of the last clause in the Septuagint, although accepted by many scholars, is only due to lack of understanding.

11 Continuing his speech, Jethro says: *Now I know* — I recognize now — *that the Lord*, your God, *is greater than all the other gods* כִּי בַדָּבָר אֲשֶׁר זָדוּ עֲלֵיהֶם *kī bhaddābhār 'ăšer zādhū 'ălēhem*. All the various interpretations and emendations that have been proposed with regard to these obscure words are improbable. Perhaps the word *gods*, which occurs in the verse, is to be regarded as the subject of the verb זָדוּ *zādhū* ['act proudly', 'boast'], and the sense is: precisely (this is the meaning of the word כִּי *kī* below, in xxxii 29: 'precisely [כִּי *kī*] because every man was against his son and against his brother') in respect of these things of which the gods of Egypt boasted, for example, the divine power of the Nile, the divine light of the sun, the divine might of the sea, He is greater *than they* [עֲלֵיהֶם *'ălēhem*], and His power exceeds their power, and He executed judgements on all the gods of Egypt. [The clause should be rendered: 'excelling them in the very things to which they laid claim'].

12 *And Jethro, Moses' father-in-law, took* (the customary term for preparing animals for sacrifice; compare Gen. viii 20; xv 9–10, and many similar instances) *a burnt offering* — a holocaust — *and sacrifices* — peace offerings in the eating of which the sacrificer and his relatives and friends partook — *to God* — in honour of the God of Israel, who is here designated by the generic name

'*Elōhīm* and not by the Tetragrammaton, in order to inform us that although Jethro recognized the supremacy of *YHWH* over the other deities, he did not entirely accept the faith of Israel (the rabbinic sages, however, considered him an actual proselyte), and he regarded the Lord as only one of the gods. As the Rabbis noted (Sifrē Num. § 143, and parallel passages): 'In connection with none of the sacrifices mentioned in the Torah is אֱלֹהִים *'Elōhīm* or אֱלֹהֶיךָ *'Elōhekhā* ['your God'] or שַׁדַּי *Šadday* ['Almighty'] or צְבָאוֹת *Ṣᵉbhā'ōth* ['Hosts'] mentioned, but only the Specific Name — יְ-הֹ *YHWH*'; yet here we observe an exception to the rule. Apparently this anomaly is intended to emphasize that the sacrificer was an alien, who, despite his declaration in the preceding verse, had not yet attained to the knowledge of the Lord in all its purity and perfection. It is not stated whence Jethro took the animals for sacrifice, since this detail was not of importance; perhaps we are to understand that he took them from the sheep and the oxen that he brought with him, or that he bought them from an Israelite or one of the mixed multitude. *And there came*, apart from Moses, also *Aaron and all the elders of Israel to eat bread* — that is, to partake of the holy meal and to eat of the flesh of the peace-offerings — *with Moses' father-in-law before God*, to wit, at the entrance of the Tent of Meeting, which had already been erected before Jethro's visit (on the arrangement of the sections, which is not in accord with the chronological order, see the introductory notes to this section).

SECOND PARAGRAPH

THE ADVICE TO APPOINT JUDGES
AND ITS ACCEPTANCE

(XVIII 13–26)

This paragraph tells of the appointment of Israelite judges in accordance with the counsel given by Jethro to Moses. Possibly this was the form of the judicature of the Kenite tribe, and a similar organization was established among the Israelites. In essence the story is repeated in Deut. i 9 ff., but there the details are different; Jethro is not mentioned, and it is stated that Moses consulted the people on the subject. The divergences are due to the different contexts of the two narratives. Here the aim is to focus attention on the relations between Jethro and the people of Israel; hence Jethro's initiative and advice are dealt with in detail, the implementation of the advice is mentioned only briefly, and there was no need to inform us whether Moses consulted the people or not. In Deuteronomy, on the other hand, Moses' words are cited when he summarizes briefly, at the end of the wanderings in the wilderness, the history of the events that have occurred; it was only necessary, therefore, to recall the manner in which the new judicial system was established, and the directives that were given to the judges, which still retained their validity, and there was no reason to state who was the initiator of the idea.

Throughout the paragraph, the Bible uses the name *'Elōhīm* and not the Tetragrammaton, for this is the usual procedure in conversations with non-Israelites, so long as there is no intention to make an express distinction between the God of Israel and the heathen deities.

13 *And it came to pass on the morrow* — after Jethro's arrival — *that Moses sat to judge the people*. The meaning is not that he did so every day, but that that particular day happened to be one of those appointed for the reception of the people, and Moses was sitting as judge and teacher, and whoever had a dispute with his fellow, or wished to receive instruction from Moses, came to him. Since Jethro's counsel appertained specifically to judicial procedure, it is stated here briefly, *to judge the people*, whilst the instruction given by Moses is mentioned as it were incidentally only later. *And the people stood about Moses*; he alone was seated in accordance with the custom of judges, and they stood before him *from morning till evening* — clearly an exaggeration, for this was impossible without a break, however slight. The element of exaggeration is even more obvious in *v.* 14: 'and all the people stand about you from morning till evening' — in the present tense, that is, Jethro is speaking at a time when evening had not yet arrived.

14 *And when Moses' father-in-law saw all that he was doing for the people* (the word *all* is used here, too, in a general, hyperbolical sense), that is, he saw to what great trouble Moses put himself on behalf of the people. The phrasing is intended to form a parallelism between the beginning of this paragraph and the commencement of the first paragraph (*v.* 1): first he heard all that God had done for Israel; now he sees all that Moses is doing for Israel.

He, Jethro, *said*, to Moses, *What is this thing that you are doing for the people?* A general, preliminary question with which to open the discussion. *Why do you sit alone*, without any one to assist you, *and all the people stand about you from morning to evening*, and are fatigued thereby? There recur here, with the usual variations, the expressions used in the preceding verse.

The exegetes have found the interpretation of *vv.* 15-16 extremely difficult. It seems to me, however, that Moses' words are to be understood as follows:

15 I act thus, *Because the people come to me to inquire of God*, and this inquiry can take one of two forms: first, a judicial form:
16 *when they have a matter* — that is, a judgement, a dispute — the matter *comes to me, and I judge between a man and his neighbour*. Secondly, when they come to ask for instruction and guidance, and I answer in God's name, *and I make them know the statutes of God and His directions*. The word דָּבָר *dābhār* [rendered in *v.* 14: 'thing'], which occurs in the initial question of Jethro, is repeated, but in a different sense [in *v.* 16 it is translated: 'matter'], in Moses' reply. In the continuation of his speech, Jethro uses the word a
17 second and even a third time: *The thing that you are doing is not*
18 *good*. There is reason to fear that *you will wear yourself out* [נָבֹל תִּבֹּל *nābhōl tibbōl*] — you will become weak and ill (the stem נָבַל *nābhal* is akin to נָפַל *nāphal* ['fall']) — *both you and this people that I see here with you; for the thing that you do is too heavy for you* — is more than you can endure — *you cannot perform it alone* (re-
19 peated from *v.* 14). *Now* (an expression introducing the conclusion) permit me to give you good advice: *Listen to my voice wherewith I will give you counsel, and God be with you* to approve my counsel and to help to implement it.

The formulation of Jethro's advice has also been subjected to different interpretations. To me it seems that the import of the passage is that Jethro understood Moses' observations in accordance with his pagan conception, and regarded them not as two forms of inquiry of God, as I have interpreted them, but as three unrelated matters, and on this basis he replied as he did. The words, *you be for the people in front of God*, can well be explained in the light of the practice of the heathen priests, who came before the idols to offer the petitions of the worshippers, such as a request for healing from sickness or for deliverance from any trouble. This then is how Jethro's counsel is to be understood: The aspects of your work that you alone can perform, continue to do by yourself; but these only. *You be for the people* — on behalf of the people — *in front of God* — before your God to pray to Him on their behalf — *and you* by yourself *bring the words* — that is, the petitions of your people — *to God*. I understand that you cannot delegate this work to any one else, and therefore you must do it in person. Similarly you must carry out yourself the task of instruction and guidance: *and warn them* — the people — *of the statutes and the directions, and make them to know the way wherein they should walk, and the work they should do* — that is, you shall guide them religiously and morally. But the judicial duties, at least the greater part of them, you can hand over to others. *And you* will confine yourself to one facet only of judicial work, namely, that *you will see*, that is, choose (both in Hebrew and in Ugaritic, expressions of 'seeing' are used in the sense of 'choosing'; compare, for instance, Gen. xli 33: 'Now therefore let Pharaoh see a man discreet', etc.; see also below, *v.* 25, which parallels this verse: 'And Moses chose') *from all the people* — from all sections of the people without restriction — *men of worth* — that is, men of fine qualities of character (compare, 'a woman of worth', in Prov. xxxi 10) — *such as fear God, men of truth* — seekers of truth, who realize that the task of the judge is none other than to give true judgement — *who hate unjust gain*, having not only the negative quality that they do not accept bribes, but also the positive attribute that they hate bribery and all kinds of unjust gain; *and place* them *over them* — over the Israelites — to serve as *rulers of thousands, rulers of hundreds, rulers of fifties, and rulers of tens* — these numbers are not to be interpreted with mathematical exactitude, but as various ranks of rulers, one senior to the other. *And let them* — these rulers — *judge the people at all times* — in all normal cases: if the dispute affects a family, it should be brought before a ruler of ten; if a wider circle, it should be tried by a ruler of fifty or of a hundred; and if a still larger group is involved, the case should be judged by a ruler of a thousand. Only the most important and most difficult cases are to be brought to you: *and it shall be, that every great matter they shall bring to you, but every small matter they shall decide themselves* (here, too, the word דָּבָר *dābhār* [rendered: 'matter'] occurs twice). *And lighten for yourself* the burden in this way, *and they*, these rulers, *shall bear* it *with you*. Finally, Jethro sums up and concludes his advice as follows: *If you do this thing* (again the word דָּבָר *dābhār* [rendered: 'thing'], and once more in a different connotation), *and God so commands you* — that is, if your God will sanction this thing and will command you to implement it — then *you will be able to stand* up to the tasks entrusted to you, *and all this people also* (a repetition of the expression in v. 18, with the addition of the word *all*) — all these men, who now came crowding before you in such great numbers, and wait so long for their turn — *will go to their place in peace* — will come easily and simply and in proper order to the correct place to have their cases tried.

24 *So Moses listened to the voice of his father-in-law* — just as the latter had said (v. 19), 'listen to my voice'— *and did all that he had said*. And after this general statement comes a detailed account,
25-26 which repeats Jethro's words with a few changes, as usual: *And Moses chose men of worth out of all Israel* ('you will see [= choose] from all the people men of worth'), *and made them heads over the people* ('and place over them'), *rulers of thousands*, etc. — the exact words of Jethro — *And they judged the people*, etc. — almost the *ipsissima verba* of Jethro, with slight changes (the omission of *and it shall be*, of *every*; *hard* instead of *great*; יְבִיאוּן *yᵉbhī'ūn* in place of יָבִיאוּ *yābhī'ū* [both mean, 'they shall bring']; יִשְׁפּוּטוּ *yišpūṭū* for יִשְׁפְּטוּ *yišpᵉṭū* [both mean, 'decide']). Similar variations and changes are found in the repetitions of the Ugaritic texts.

CONCLUSION OF THE SECTION

(XVIII 27)

The meeting comes to an end, and the entire account of the episod of
27 Jethro is now concluded. *Then Moses let his father-in-law depart* [וַיְשַׁלַּח *wayᵉšallaḥ*]— he gave him permission to go, and accompanied him on the first part of the journey (compare Gen. xviii 16: 'and Abraham went with them to set them on their way [לְשַׁלְּחָם *lᵉšallᵉḥām*]') *and he*, Jethro, *went his way to his own country*.

In this section, too, the literary features that we have already pointed out in the previous sections are clearly noticeable, namely, parallelism and numerical symmetry.

The parallelism between the beginning of the first paragraph (v. 1) and the commencement of the second paragraph (v. 14) was indicated above. It may further be noted that an expression of 'sending away' occurs at the beginning and the end of the section

EXODUS XVIII 27

(*v.* 2: 'after he had sent her away'; *v.* 27: 'let... depart [literally, 'sent away']'); the verb *took* is found at the commencement and conclusion of the first paragraph (*v.* 2 and *v.* 12); reference is made to שָׁלוֹם *šālōm* ['peace', 'welfare'] in the middle of the first paragraph (*v.* 7) and also in the middle of the second (*v.* 23); וַיִּשְׁמַע יִתְרוֹ *wayyišmaʿ Yithrō* ['Now Jethro heard'] (*v.* 1) corresponds to וַיִּשְׁמַע מֹשֶׁה *wayyišmaʿ Mōše* ['So Moses listened'] (*v.* 24); the recurrence of expressions of *deliverance* we have mentioned before.

The numerical schematism has a special character in this section; it is now mainly based on the number ten. The word דָּבָר *dābhār* ['word', 'thing', 'matter'] occurs again and again in different meanings, particularly in the dialogue between Moses and Jethro, and finally even in the narrative; in all it is found ten times in the singular and once in the plural. Possibly this decade is to be regarded as a preliminary allusion to the *Decalogue* [עֲשֶׂרֶת הַדְּבָרִים *ʿăśereth haddᵉbhārīm*], which is to form the main theme of the next section. Other sets of ten are also discernible in the section: the verb עָשָׂה *ʿāśā* ['do'] occurs ten times, beginning with 'that God had done' in *v.* 1; likewise the verb בּוֹא *bō*' ['come'], commencing with 'And Jethro... came' in *v.* 5. Since *Jethro*'s name appears seven times, as is usual in the case of characteristic words of a given section or paragraph, and the designation *Moses' father-in-law* is found thirteen times, we arrive at a total of twenty references — twice times ten.

SECTION TWO

THE REVELATION AT MOUNT SINAI

CHAPTER XIX, VERSE 1—CHAPTER XX, VERSE 21

Now begins the most sublime section in the whole Book. The theme of this section is supremely significant, playing a role of decisive importance in the history of Israel and of humanity as a whole. And as befits a passage treating of so exalted a subject, the diction rises above the level of prose, and even assumes, at times, poetic aspects in its form, qualities and poetic rhythm.

FIRST PARAGRAPH

THE PREPARATIONS

(XIX 1–15)

Chapter XIX

Already in the opening verses, although their purpose is only to inform us of the place and time of the event, an elevation of style is observable. According to the usual diction of Biblical narrative prose, it would have been possible to write, 'And it came to pass that in the third month after their exodus from Egypt the children of Israel journeyed from Rephidim and came to the wilderness of Sinai and encamped there', or the like. This would have been simple prose; what we have before us is poetry. Even if we read the passage merely according to the accents, we shall immediately notice the poetic rhythm of its composition. The rhythm of each of the first two verses [in the Hebrew] is: 2:2:2 || 2:2 (the expressions *children of Israel* and *wilderness of Sinai*, which signify respectively a single concept, are each counted as one beat). The subsequent verses are similarly constructed.

1   The passage begins, *On the third* חֹדֶשׁ *ḥōdheš*, without preceding וַיְהִי *wayᵉhī* ['And it came to pass'], and without any link with the previous text, as though to notify us that here begins a theme that stands alone, that is unique, that requires the reader to forget

EXODUS XIX 1

almost everything else and concentrate his full attention on what he is about to be told now.

The word חֹדֶשׁ *ḥōdheš* means here, in accordance with its usual signification in ancient Hebrew, 'new moon'. On the day of the new moon, which marks the commencement of a new period of time in the life of nature, on the third new moon *after the children of Israel had gone forth out of the land of Egypt*, after this momentous event, which deserves to serve as the starting-point for dating, *on that* very *day, they*, the children of Israel, *came into the wilderness of Sinai*. The words *on that day*, which parallel *On the third new moon*, re-emphasize that the Israelites came to this place at the commencement of a new period of time, as though to indicate that the event that is due to take place there was so important that no other happening could precede it in that interval of time. Had this event been second chronologically, it might have been regarded as of secondary importance.

The mention of the third new moon is not unintentional. Since the exodus from Egypt, the last two weeks of Nissan and four weeks of Iyyar had passed, and we are now in the seventh week. Since seven was considered the number of perfection, seven days constituted, according to the customary conception of the ancient East, a given unit of time, while seven weeks formed a still higher unit; and just as after six days of labour the seventh day brought rest and the enjoyment of the results of that labour, so after six weeks of the travails of journeying the seventh week brought a sense of exaltation and of drawing nearer to the world Divine. Although the Torah does not state the exact day on which the Revelation on Mount Sinai occurred, and only the later tradition connects the Festival of Weeks with the commemoration of the giving of the Torah, yet it is obvious that this tradition corresponds to what, if not expressly stated in Scripture, is at least alluded to therein by inference. Perhaps the Torah did not wish to link the word of God with a given day in the way that natural phenomena are bound to time, but, if not directly, then indirectly it tells us something about the date of the Revelation on Mount Sinai. We shall devote further discussion to this point later.

At the end of this verse already we are informed, *they came into the wilderness of Sinai*; and only subsequently, in v. 2, as an explanatory supplement, and as a detail following the general statement, are we told whence they came. Similarly it is written in Gen. xxviii 10 with respect to Jacob: 'and he went to Haran'; and only after the Bible has mentioned the place that he reached at the end of his travels, does it go back in the story and describe the particulars of the journey.

2   The detailed account in v. 2 begins: *And they journeyed from Rephidim*, where they had previously camped (xvii 1), *and came* from there *into the wilderness of Sinai, and they encamped* there *in the wilderness*. The location of the wilderness of Sinai and of Mount Sinai is in doubt. Even if we reject the view of those who set the route of the Israelites in the north and seek Mount Sinai near Kadesh Barnea, and also of those who look for Mount Sinai in the land of Midian, and we search for it in the southern part of the peninsula, called today the Sinai Peninsula, it is still impossible to determine precisely the site of the Biblical Mount Sinai. The local tradition that identifies it with Jebel Serbal or with Jebel Musa is a very late one. The text gives us no details that can help us to determine the site, and possibly this silence is not unintended. Just as the Torah did not desire to associate the theophany expressly with a specific time, even so it did not wish to link it with a definite place, so that a person should not be able to corporealize the memory of the event and declare: Here, upon this mountain, the Lord revealed Himself to the children of Israel, and from here He uttered the Ten Commandments. It is fitting that the happening should remain shrouded in the mists of sanctity.

Only this is clearly to be inferred from the passages, that the mountain called in this section Mount Sinai is the same as the one named in chapter iii 'the mountain of God' and Horeb, the latter signifying apparently 'dryness' or 'dry ground' — a suitable name for a mountain situated in the midst of the desert. The term 'the mountain of God' recurred already in xviii 5; see my introductory notes to chapter xviii.

The clause, *and there Israel encamped before the mountain*, appears to be redundant, at least in part, since it was previously stated, 'and they encamped in the wilderness.' But the import becomes clear when we pay attention to the continuation of the
3   passage, which puts the subject *Moses* before the predicate *went up* for the sake of antithesis to the preceding statement (on this construction see above, my annotation to ix 20–21), the sense being: although the people encamped there before the mountain — the well-known mountain in the wilderness of Sinai — and rested there from the fatigue of the journey, yet Moses did not rest or remain

facing the mountain [i.e. at a distance from it], because he remembered that on the day that the vision of the burning bush had appeared to him, he was told (iii 12): 'when you have brought forth the people out of Egypt, you shall serve God upon this mountain.' He had already brought the people out of Egypt, and now that he had arrived at that mountain, he immediately *went up to God*, to keep his trust; he did not wait that God should call him, but he went up before he was summoned.

Apparently the verse implies that Moses ascended early in the morning, as is usual in performing a sacred task, which must take precedence over anything else done that day. This must have taken place then on the second day of the third month.

When he went up, Moses expected that God would manifest Himself to him; and behold, suddenly he hears the Voice calling to him: *and the Lord called to him from the mountain* — from the top of the mountain. It seems that the verb *called* [וַיִּקְרָא *wayyiqrā'*] does not mean here 'summoned', but 'spoke in a loud voice', as in the expression, 'and lifted up his voice, and cried aloud ['*wayyiqrā'*]' (Jud. ix 7), a usage inherited by Israel from Canaanite poetry, which commonly used this verb to introduce the speeches of its heroes. The Voice that calls communicates to Moses what he must tell Israel in the name of the Lord.

The Divine utterance is composed in true poetic style, having the rhythm of verse and being marked by parallelism between its parts. First comes Moses' commission: *Thus you shall say to the house of Jacob, and tell the children of Israel*. Even this formula, 'Thus you shall say to so-and-so, and tell the son of so-and-so', or the like, is commonly found in the poetic tradition as an expression of 'commissioning', and this, too, was inherited by Israel from Canaanite poetry. We thus have here a clear example of the principle: 'The Torah uses the language of men.'

4 This formula is followed by the prefatory statement preceding the main theme. *You have seen* with your own eyes, and not just heard from afar like strangers (compare xviii 1: 'And Jethro... heard') *what I did to the Egyptians* on account of you, and by the same token you saw what I did to you for your benefit, *how I bore you on eagles' wings* to deliver you from all trouble like the eagle, which carries its young upon its wings (a simile that occurs with greater detail in Deut. xxxii 11: 'Like an eagle that... spreads out its wings, takes them, bears them on its pinions'), *and brought you to Myself*, to the appointed place that I specified when I

spoke to Moses. Since you have already been given proof of My dominion over the world and of My love for you, you can understand the value of the message that I am sending you.

This message begins with the word וְעַתָּה $w^{e\,\text{‘}}att\bar{a}$ ['Now, therefore'], which usually introduces the conclusion after the prefatory statements. The conclusion is a proposal, to wit, that Israel should make a covenant and be chosen as 'a people of special possession' on condition that they accept certain obligations: *if you will listen diligently to My voice* — if you will obey what I am due to command you — *and keep My covenant* — if you will be faithful to the covenant that I intend to make with you — then *you shall be My special possession out of all the peoples* — from among all the peoples of the earth, who are all Mine. I am not your God alone, but the God of the whole world; I am not like the gods of the land of Egypt whence you went forth, nor like the deities of the land of Canaan whither I am bringing you; these divinities, even according to their worshippers, have dominion over their own people only; whereas I am the God of all the peoples: *for all the earth is Mine*, that is, all the peoples of the earth (compare Gen. xi 1: 'Now the whole earth had one speech and a single language'). But if you will agree to My proposal, I shall choose you specifically for the fulfilment of an exalted spiritual task: *and you shall be to Me a kingdom of priests* — a people comprised wholly of priests, a people that will occupy among humanity the place filled by the priests within each nation — *and a holy nation* — a nation dedicated entirely to the service of the Godhead, in the same way as priests are consecrated thereto. The proposal envisages a bilateral covenant, giving Israel an exalted position among the peoples in lieu of the acceptance of a special discipline.

At the end, there is a solemn, concluding formula: *These are the words which you shall speak to the children of Israel.*

So Moses came to the camp, that is, he came down from the mountain and returned to his brethren, *and called the elders of the people* — summoned them to him — *and set before them* — proposed to them — *all these things which the Lord had commanded him* to propose. Needless to say, each of the elders brought the proposal before the fathers' houses that were subject to his authority. They all answered affirmatively: *And all the people answered together* — all were of one mind and spirit — *and said, all that the Lord has spoken we will do* — we are prepared to accept the proposal and do whatever we are called upon to do. *And Moses brought* back the words of the people to the Lord; the verb brought back [וַיָּ֫שֶׁב *wayyāšebh*] is used in the sense of replied [תְּשׁוּבָה *tᵉšūbhā* = 'a reply'], for the proposal was in the nature of a question that required an answer. This implies that Moses again ascended Mount Sinai, apparently early in the morning on the following day, that is, on the third day of the month, in order to seclude himself, and thus draw near, through this seclusion, to the Divine sphere and receive additional instructions on the basis of the people's affirmative reply.

9 The directions given to Moses begin as follows: *Lo, I am coming to you in a thick cloud*. Just as I brought you to Me so that you should come near to Me, so shall I come and draw near to you — and particularly to you, Moses — but you will see no form, for I shall be concealed in a thick cloud, as though in a disguise that the eye of man cannot penetrate. The purpose of My coming to you will be *that the people may hear when I speak with you*; as they have already seen with their eyes (v. 4), so they shall now hear with their ears. *And may believe you also for ever* — the trust that they reposed in you after their salvation through the division of the Sea of Reeds (xiv 31: 'and they believed in the Lord and in His servant Moses') will endure for ever. In these words God apprises Moses that the first phase of the making of the covenant will consist in His speaking with Moses to inform him of the fundamental principles upon which the covenant will be based, and that the entire people will hear His words when He speaks with Moses. *Then Moses told the words of the people to the Lord*; in order not to dwell on unnecessary details, and not to distract the reader's attention from the theme proper, the Bible uses here summary language, and does not state expressly that Moses conveyed the Lord's words to the people and that they agreed. All this is self-understood; compare my observations above, in my commentary on viii 1, 20. After the people had expressed their consent and readiness to hear themselves the word of the Lord, Moses again ascended Mount Sinai in order to receive fresh instructions in view of the people's willingness. If we assume that this ascent also took place early in the morning on the following day, we thus arrive at the fourth day of the month.

The parallelism between the end of *v.* 9 and that of *v.* 8, and the threefold reference to Moses' ascent of the mountain, conform to the customary stylistic devices of the ancient narrative literature. Likewise the change from *he brought back* to *he told* is in keeping with this literary method, and is also suited to the subject-matter, for it was only after God's proposal that a 'reply' was requisite, but not so in *v.* 9.

Agreement having been achieved between the two sides both in respect of the making of the covenant and the manner of commencing the ceremony, nothing remains now but to prepare for the ceremony itself. This will not be an everyday occurrence, but an event completely transcending the plane of ordinary life; hence it is necessary that the children of Israel should prepare themselves for it in a unique manner. On this occasion, therefore, Moses is 10 enjoined: *Go to the people and consecrate them* — prepare them by the observance of sanctity and purity — *today and tomorrow, and let them wash their garments*, for it is not seemly to come before the King in unclean dress; moreover, the cleanness of the 11 clothes would symbolize the inner purity of the soul. *And let them be*, in this way, *ready* — prepared and expectant — *for the third day* — that is, for the day after tomorrow — *for on the third day the Lord will come down upon Mount Sinai in the sight of all the people*, and all the people will see with their own eyes the thick cloud that signalizes the Divine Presence. For the importance of a series of three days, see above, the annotations to xv 22.

If the text implies, as seems likely (see above, on *v.* 9), that these words were spoken to Moses on the fourth of the month, then the words *today and tomorrow* in v. 10 indicate the fourth and the fifth, and consequently the day of the Revelation was on the sixth of the month, which marked the end of the seventh week after the exodus of the Israelites from the land of Egypt. The later tradition that links the Festival of Weeks with the Day of the Revelation on Mount Sinai agrees, apparently, with the actual meaning of the text.

The theophany described here does not imply the effacement of the boundaries between the Divine and human spheres. On the contrary, the Torah emphasizes again and again that this 12 barrier can by no means be demolished: *And you shall set bounds for the people*, etc. This is one of the new concepts taught by the Torah relative to the beliefs of the peoples of the ancient East. They considered the forces of nature as gods, and just as there is a direct relationship between man and the natural phenomena around him, so it is possible to imagine a direct association between man and the deities. It will suffice to mention Gilgameš of Mesopotamian mythology, who contemptuously rejects the requests of the goddess Ištar, who solicited him in the manner in which Potiphar's wife appealed to Joseph; or the goddess Anath of Ugaritic mythology, who sits down to eat and drink with Aqhat the son of Daniel, and asks him, unsuccessfully, that he should present her with his bow and arrows. The Torah conception rises to a loftier level: the Godhead is not bound to nature, but stands above and outside it, and everything in nature, even the most powerful natural elements, are merely creatures formed by his word. To this end, it is stated here: *And you shall set bounds for the people round about* (the reading of the Samaritan Pentateuch, 'And you shall set bounds about *the mountain*', is intended, in accordance with the practice of this recension, to harmonize this verse with v. 23; see my commentary *ad locum*) — tell them that it is impossible for them to break through the barrier between them and Me, and that they must remain round about the mountain and not draw near to it — *saying, Take heed that you do not go up into the mountain or touch the border of it*; the least contact is forbidden. Obviously, there is a symbolic significance to this, for otherwise the notion of touching the mountain with the hand (v. 13) would be quite bizarre. Whoever will attempt to break through the boundary will pay for it with his life: *whoever touches the mountain shall be surely put to death.*

13 *No hand shall touch it* — the mountain (the threefold reference to touching is for emphasis) — *but he shall surely be stoned or shot* from a distance, since also those who come to punish him are prohibited from touching the mountain. *Whether beast or man, he shall not live*, and you must take heed that even your cattle do not enter the area of the mountain. Only *when the ram's horn sounds a long blast* — when the signal marking the conclusion of the Revelation is given by a long note of the horn (compare Jos. vi 5) — *they shall come up into the mountain* — they shall be permitted to ascend. It will be Moses' duty, of course, to see to it that the signal is given at the proper time.

14 Moses did what he was enjoined to do: *So Moses went down from the mountain to the people, and consecrated the people; and they*
15 *washed their garments. And he said to the people, Be ready for the third day*, etc. In the account of the implementation of the command, the words of the injunction are reiterated as usual. But Moses further adds, not as a thematic supplement of his own, but as a detailed instruction in elucidation of the concept of sanctification: *do not go near a woman.*

SECOND PARAGRAPH

THE ELEMENTS OF NATURE IN COMMOTION

(XIX 16–19)

The people prepares, and waits with yearning for the third day.
16 *And it came to pass on the third day*, on the day determined beforehand, *when it was morning, that* unusual phenomena occurred: *There were thunders* [literally, 'voices'] *and lightnings, and a dense cloud upon the mountain* — a fearful storm burst forth: the heavens were covered with clouds; flashes of lightning and peals of thunder, in great number, filled the sky. This storm announced the theophany. We have already seen earlier, in our commentary on ix 23 (p. 118), that Biblical poetry is accustomed to describe thunder as 'the voice of the Lord', an expression that continues the literary tradition of the Canaanites, who believed that thunder was actually the voice of Baal. But the 'voices' in this verse are not 'the voice of the Lord', according to the customary expression in poetry. The voice of the Lord will be referred to later on, and its meaning there will be 'the sound of words', the utterance of speech, as when human beings converse with one another. But here the 'voices', accompanied by lightnings, are simply thunder-claps, which are mentioned as a natural occurrence, as one of the mighty phenomena of nature that presage the approach of the Lord of the universe. Similarly it is stated in the narrative of i Kings xix 11–13, when God manifested Himself to Elijah on Mount Horeb; 'but the Lord was not in the wind... not in the earthquake... not in the fire; only in the still small voice' did Elijah perceive the word of the Lord. The wind and the earthquake and the fire were only phenomena announcing the theophany that followed in tranquillity, as befitted the glory of God. Nor are we to suppose, as do many exegetes, that the episode in the Book of Kings stands in contrast to the narrative in this section; on the contrary there is a fundamental parallelism between them. Even the strong wind in the story of Elijah is alluded to here, for the expression, *and the sound of a horn exceedingly loud*, does not really refer to the note of a horn [שׁוֹפָר *šōphār*] (called in *v.* 13 יֹבֵל *yōbhēl*, 'ram's horn'); it signifies the strong wind that blows violently through the gorges between the mountains, rending the air with a great noise like the sound of a horn.

The storm frightened the people, as storms that occur in the

17 region of mountains usually do: *and all the people that were in the camp trembled*. But in Moses' heart there was no fear: *And Moses brought the people out to meet God* (also from the expression, *to meet God*, we can see that the preceding phenomena were not yet the theophany, but only the signs announcing God's advent). The Israelites went forth *from the camp* and went as far as they were permitted to go, *and they took their stand at the foot of the mountain*. There they stood and waited.

They stood waiting quietly, but the forces of nature were not 18 yet still; on the contrary they became increasingly turbulent: *and Mount Sinai was all wrapped in smoke* (here, too, as in v. 3, the subject precedes the predicate to express contrast), *because the Lord descended upon it in fire; and the smoke of it went up like the smoke of a kiln, and the whole mountain trembled greatly* (compare the word *trembled* in v. 16). Also these details concerning the smoke and the fire and the quaking of the mountain belong to the literary tradition of theophany descriptions. It is possible that the creation of this tradition was originally influenced by the observation of volcanic activity; but there is no reference here, as many have supposed, to volcanic phenomena. The most recent geographical investigations have shown that there are no volcanoes in the regions that merit consideration in our attempts to identify Mount Sinai; furthermore, the fire of volcanoes goes upward and does not descend from the sky. In this verse the description of the storm still continues: the smoke is the mist rising from the mountains; the fire is that of lightning, which is regarded as accompanying God in His descent from heaven; and the trembling of the mountain (only the mountain is referred to, and not the ground on which the people stood) is not an earthquake, but a tremor due to the force of the crashing thunder. Another phenomenon, too, 19 continues and grows stronger and stronger: *And the sound of the horn* — the howling of the wind blowing among the mountains, which resembled the sound of the horn — *grew louder and louder*. Nevertheless, despite all the tumult of the tempest, it was possible to conduct a dialogue between God and Moses: *Moses kept speaking*, normally, *and God kept answering him with a voice* — He was answering him with a loud voice so that it was possible for Moses to hear His words clearly in the midst of the storm. The word בְּקוֹל *b^eqōl* ['with a voice'] corresponds exactly to the Ugaritic word *gm* (*g* = voice; *m* at the end of the word = *b-* [at the beginning: 'with'], which is commonly found in epic poetry when the poet tells us that one of the gods was speaking in a loud voice.

The nature of the dialogue is stated in the next paragraph.

THIRD PARAGRAPH

THE FINAL INSTRUCTIONS

(XIX 20–25)

20 This paragraph begins: *And the Lord came down upon Mount Sinai*. Although God's descent was already referred to in *v.* 18, yet this was done incidentally, in a subordinate clause, as the cause of natural phenomena, and therefore it was necessary to revert to it in a principal and independent sentence, as befits a main theme that is basic to the subsequent narrative, and to elucidate its particulars. The first is: *to the top of the mountain*. This establishes that there, at the summit of the mountain, was the scene of the theophany, in contrast to the foot of the mountain (*v.* 17), where the people stood. The second detail is that from there, from the mountain top, the Lord called to Moses: *and the Lord called Moses to come up to the top of the mountain* — in the direction of the mountain top — *and Moses went up* as he was commanded. It is not stated that he ascended to the top of the mountain, since it is impossible for a human being, be he even Moses, to attain to
21 the place of the Divine Presence. *And the Lord said to Moses*, as he was ascending and was half-way up: *Go down and warn the people*; I summoned you for this purpose, namely, to enjoin you to warn the people *lest they break through* the bounds and draw nigh *to the Lord to gaze, and many of them perish*. This admonition may appear superfluous after the statement in *vv*. 12–13, and the Bible itself points this out to us in the words of Moses in *v.* 23. Since, however, it is cited thus, and Moses' observation is set aside, it follows that the whole episode was recorded with full intention. The purpose may be twofold: (a) to stress still further the thought that the boundary between the two spheres, the human and the Divine, is not to be effaced; (b) that it was necessary to repeat the warning at the crucial moment when the Revelation was about to take place (see Mekhilta). It may also be added that the triple reference to an important subject (*vv*. 12–13; 21–22; 24) accords with a common literary practice.

At this stage there is also mentioned a detail that had not been expressly stated at first, but it was desirable to indicate it now in
22 order to avoid any possible misunderstanding: *And also let the priests*, although as a rule, they are the men *who come near to the Lord* to perform the sacred service (here the Bible speaks of priests, a designation that was not in use till later; but the reference may be to the first-born), *sanctify themselves*, too, that is, let them observe special sanctity and take care not to enter the restricted area, *lest the Lord break out upon them* — measure for measure: if they will break through the boundary, the Lord will break out upon them.

Moses is surprised at the repetition of the warning, and observes:
23 *The people cannot come up to Mount Sinai; for Thou Thyself didst charge us* already, *saying, Set bounds about the mountain and consecrate it*. Although it is stated above, in *v.* 12, 'And you shall set bounds for *the people*, and not, 'And you shall set bounds about *the mountain*' (only the Samaritan Recension, which is accustomed to harmonize the Biblical passages, reads there, too, *the mountain* on the basis of this verse), yet this is not a difficulty. The reading *the people* in *v.* 12 is corroborated by the continuation of the passage, in which the people are addressed ('Take heed that you do not go up into the mountain', etc.); but Moses gives here the substance and not the *ipsissima verba* of the Lord's injunction, in accordance with customary literary usage; and the meaning is identical, since the demarcation applies equally to both.

24 Moses' statement is rejected sharply: *Go down* — do what I have commanded you, and do not query my orders; go down and warn the people, and then ascend again: *and come up, you and Aaron with you*, as far as the place appointed for you, *but do not let the priests and the people*, as stated, *break through to come up to the Lord, lest He break out against them.*

25 *So Moses went down to the people*, as he was commanded, *and told them* what he was enjoined to tell. Thereafter, of course, he ascended to the place that was assigned to him, and Aaron came up with him. This is self-understood, and there is no need to narrate it explicitly (compare my note above, on *v.* 9). The time has come for our whole attention to be devoted to the Decalogue.

Now all is still. There is no further mention of thunder, or lightning, or the sound of the horn, or of anything similar. All the forces of nature remain tranquil, and everything bespeaks the Divine glory. And out of the amazing stillness that prevailed after the fearful storm are heard the words of the Lord, who speaks to His people and makes known to them the fundamentals of His Torah*.

Our detailed exposition of this chapter has shown that the whole chapter can be explained simply as a single sequence, and that there is no reason to regard it as a collection of fragments derived from various sources, as many modern commentators have supposed. The name 'Elōhīm occurs several times (vv. 3, 17, 19) in place of the Tetragrammaton, in order to indicate, also by this variation, that the Lord [YHWH], who chose Israel, is the God of the entire world, and that the whole earth belongs to Him (v. 5).

In this chapter there recur a number of times words from the stem דָּבַר dābhar ['speak'; the noun דָּבָר dābhār means 'word']. The Torah's purpose is to prepare its readers for the giving of the Decalogue. And the fact that the number of these words in the present chapter and the introductory verse at the beginning of chapter xx is precisely ten, as in chapter xviii, this is certainly not accidental.

FOURTH PARAGRAPH

THE DECALOGUE

(XX 1–17)

We now reach the climax of the entire Book, the central and most exalted theme, all that came before being, as it were, a preparation for it, and all that follows, a result of, and supplement to, it.

Till recently, the prevailing view among exegetes was that the Decalogue, even in its original and shortest form, was a product of later development in the culture of Israel, and that it is based on the teaching of the Prophets. According to the view of many commentators, there are discernible in it even traces of the conditions under which the Israelites lived after the destruction of the First Temple. Today, as a result of the study of the ethical teaching of the ancient East, and especially of the 'negative confession' of the Egyptian Book of the Dead (circa fifteenth century B.C.E.)

---

* I. e., 'Teaching', 'Instruction'. *Tr.*

and the Mesopotamian penitential texts in the *Šurpu* series (of the same period or slightly later), the opinion is gaining ground that there is nothing in the essential content of the Decalogue that could not have been expressed in the generation of Moses, and that therefore it should be attributed to Moses in its original form, which contained only short, lapidary sentences like: I am the Lord your God — You shall have no other gods — Remember the sabbath day — Honour your father and your mother, and so on and so forth; whilst all the rest, according to this view, is to be considered merely as accretions that accumulated in the course of time, particulary under the inspiration of the Book of Deuteronomy. But the very premise that to Moses' generation may be attributed only such concepts and ideas as were already in existence at that period, or can be regarded as conforming to the actual conditions of life at the time, is based on the preconception that there is no possibility in the world of introducing daring reforms, and that no fundamental innovation or spiritual revolution may be assumed without a prior process of gradual evolution. Like all prejudgements, this, too, has no justification from the viewpoint of pure science. If we wish to assess the Decalogue without bias, we must recognize that, relative to the ideas prevailing among the peoples of the ancient East, we are confronted here with a basically new conception and a spiritual revolution.

The basically new conception consists, in the first instance, in the completely transcendental view of the Godhead. This breaks entirely new ground even vis-à-vis the trend (usually associated with the name of the Egyptian king Akhenaten or with a certain circle that preceded him or formed his *entourage*) to acknowledge the dominion of one god, namely, the sun-disc, called Aten. But Aten is still a body and force in nature, and the Egyptian king is his incarnation in human form, whereas the God of Israel is outside and above nature, and the whole of nature, the sun, and the moon, and all the hosts of heaven, and the earth beneath, and the sea that is under the earth, and all that is in them — they are all His creatures which He created according to His will. We have already dealt with this point in our commentary on chapter xix, and we have seen there that in the Torah's view there is an absolute barrier between the Creator and the created, which no creature in the world can transcend.

From this speculative concept flows a new practical corollary, to wit, that God cannot be depicted by any material form whatsoever, for every form resembles a natural object, and cannot even remotely accord with the absolute, transcendental character of the God of Israel.

Also with regard to the Sabbath, a vital transformation was effected. As will be explained in detail later, the name of the Sabbath and the association of this name with a given day were already known in the Orient before the people of Israel came into being, but among the Israelites the Sabbath assumed a new character and significance, and became a new and original institution.

For these innovations, which constituted a revolutionary reformation, it was necessary to give reasons. It was not possible to introduce such important changes without explaining and clarifying them. Hence the commandments pertaining to these subjects had to be somewhat longer. In the case of prohibitions like 'you shall not kill', 'you shall not commit adultery', 'you shall not steal', there was no need to give a reason, because they are principles without which no organized society is able to exist, and they were already accepted by all civilized peoples. They could therefore be articulated in lapidary, absolute form. But the position was different in regard to the earlier commandments; hence it is not to be presumed that all the reasons given in connection with them were added later; they were needed in their own time and place.

Groups of precepts, containing ten commandments each, are found in other parts of the Pentateuch, and that has given rise to a problem that has occupied an important place in Biblical study. Many exegetes have held the view that the original Decalogue is not that of chapter xx, but a different series of ten commandments, namely, the practical precepts in ch. xxxiv 14–26. This view, after being alluded to in ancient times, in a Greek book dating from the end of the fifth century C.E., was advanced in a youthful work of Goethe's; and since Wellhausen agreed with it and gave it a scientific basis, it enjoyed popularity, and until recently was widely accepted among Biblical scholars. Its primary basis was the theory held by historians of religion and culture that ritualism antedated the development of ethical principles. Seeing that the ten precepts in ch. xxxiv are entirely ritualistic, while the commandments of ch. xx are almost wholly of a moral character, it followed that the decalogue of ch. xxxiv was the earlier. Today this argument does not carry so much weight. Even if we concede the premise that the ritual code precedes the ethical in the development of human culture, the assumption applies only to the primitive stages of cultural history; today, however, it is definitely known that the generation of Moses was by no means a primitive age, but had behind it centuries and even millennia of highly developed civilization. Furthermore, it may be stated that the whole question of the relationship between ritual and ethics falls away once we clearly comprehend the text before us.

To achieve this understanding, attention must first be drawn to an error of method committed by most exegetes in dealing with this subject. They treated the Decalogue as an isolated document, as an independent unit. But by taking a literary passage out of its context we debar ourselves from understanding it. The Ten Words* were handed to us in a given framework, and they cannot be considered outside it. They occur here in the story of the making of the Covenant between the Lord and Israel, the covenant proposed to Israel, according to xix 5–6. This covenant, as we have seen, implies mutual obligations: the people undertake *to listen to the voice of the Lord*, that is, to obey His commandments, *and to keep His covenant* — an expression synonymous with the preceding phrase, which connotes to fulfil the terms of the covenant, these being none other than His commandments; and, in return, the Lord agrees to treat them as a people who are His special possession among the peoples of the earth, and to make them a *kingdom of priests*, who perform His service in the midst of mankind, and a *holy nation*, sanctified by their special relationship to God and by the observance of a particular discipline. The conditions of the covenant, that is, the Lord's precepts, which are obligatory upon Israel, will be explained in a later section, from xx 22 to the end of chapter xxiii, which includes both ritual and ethical commandments (if it be permissible to employ these modern expressions and establish a dualism that was certainly not felt in Moses' time), and also precepts pertaining to social life, whose character we shall discuss later. All these commandments are presented in the form of a communication from the Lord to Moses, who acts as an intermediary between Him and the people in the making of the covenant. The precepts are preceded by the Decalogue in the form of an address by God to the entire people. Thus the Ten Words are not the substance of the covenant, nor its conditions, but the introduction to it. Before the particulars and terms of the

---

* A more accurate term than Ten Commandments; see Deut. iv 13; x 4; and compare p. 251. *Tr.*

covenant are conveyed by the intermediary, God Himself makes a prefatory declaration that establishes the basic principles on which the covenant will be founded. The declaration sets forth: (a) what must be the relationship of the Israelites to the Lord their God as the Chosen People; (b) what must be their relationship to one another as human beings.

Regarding the relationship to God, only duties of the heart are spoken of, without any reference to ritual worship; and even the precept of the Sabbath has here a negative aspect of cessation from work as a testimony to the creation of the entire world by the Lord. But this silence with regard to ritual does not imply its negation. The system of worship belongs to the conditions of the covenant, which Moses will subsequently announce. They will comprise, *inter alia*, the ritual commands of ch. xxxiv 14–26, for in the final analysis these are no more than a revised version of what is stated here in ch. xxiii 10 ff. They are not mentioned in the Decalogue, because they do not fit into the context of a general declaration concerning the fundamental principles underlying the covenant, whose details and terms are to be explained later.

We have already seen the nature of the new ideas comprised in this part of the Decalogue, which constitute, as stated, a radical revolution in the religious conceptions of the ancient East. No less significant are the innovations in the second part, pertaining to the commandments between man and man. Although prohibitions like 'you shall not kill', 'you shall not commit adultery', 'you shall not steal', 'you shall not bear false witness', were already known to, and accepted by, non-Israelites as well, and their essential substance remains unchanged, yet they are characterized by three new features:

(a) First of all, the absolute form of these prohibitions, which lifts them above all circumstances and every accident of detail. When the conditions of the covenant and the other precepts of the Torah would be proclaimed, particulars and definitions and restrictions would be cited in accordance with the requirements and circumstances of life, and different penalties would be prescribed relative to the different contingencies. Then the instances in which a given prohibition does or does not apply would be specified; a distinction would be drawn between wilful murder and unwitting homicide, and between the punishment of the one crime and the other; the concept of adultery would be defined and its penalty stated; different categories of theft would be distinguished and various penalties for the various types fixed; and so on and so forth. All this would come afterwards, but here, in the ten Words, the principle was established with unqualified absoluteness. We find here none of the wordiness and confusion that characterize the 'negative confession' of the Egyptians, nor the mixture of grave transgressions with all kinds of absurdities and superstitions that we find in the Mesopotamian texts. The difference is that between the absolute and the contingent.

(b) The second innovation consists in the very inclusion of these prohibitions in the preliminary statement of principles, which forms the preamble to the covenant proper. The formulation of the content and conditions of the covenant is preceded by a solemn declaration concerning the primary obligations resting on a man towards his fellow, which accords these duties equal status with those that man owes to his Maker.

(c) The commandment *you shall not covet* marks yet another new and exalted concept. The exact signification of the verb חָמַד *ḥāmadh* [rendered: 'covet'], which is in dispute, we shall discuss fully in the continuation of our commentary, where it will be shown that its correct connotation is 'to yearn for', 'desire'. It is the fundamental duty of a man not only to refrain from committing adultery with his neighbour's wife and from stealing what belongs to his fellow, but also not to yearn for another person's wife or property. This very desire is a grave sin against the principles of the Divine declaration. The meaning, apparently, is not only that the longing may lead to criminal action, which should necessarily be prohibited as a preventive measure, but that the yearning itself constitutes a trespass, in thought if not in deed.

Such is the lofty ethical plane of the Decalogue. And it was right that this declaration, which forms the preamble to the covenant between Israel and his God, should become the foundation of the spiritual life of all mankind, in accordance with the promise: 'in you will be blessed all the families of the earth.'

Later on we shall discuss the different recensions of the Decalogue and its division. But first we must interpret the verses in detail. This we shall now proceed to do.

Chapter XX

1 Amid the stillness that fell upon the mountain and its environs, when the storm had abated, the people hear the words of God: *And God* — the God of the whole earth, according to the general

meaning of this name — *spoke all these words* that follow, *saying*:

2   *I am the Lord your God*, etc. This verse contains no command, only a proclamation announcing the speaker. We have already seen in our annotations to vi 2, that in this manner, by announcing their names, the Eastern kings were accustomed to begin their solemn declarations respecting their deeds, as the inscriptions that have reached us testify; and so, too, the King of the universe commences His declaration to man — in man's own style: *I*, the Speaker, am called *YHWH*, and *I am your God* specifically. Although I am the God of the whole earth (xix 5), yet I am your God in the sense that you recognized Me and sanctified your life to My service, and I am also your God in the sense that, in consideration of this sanctification, I have chosen you to be the people of My special possession from among all the peoples of the earth (xix 6); and it is I *who brought you out of the land of Egypt*, not just bringing you forth from one place to another, but liberating you *from the house of bondage*. Hence it behoves you to serve Me not out of fear and dread, in the way that the other peoples are used to worship their gods, but from a sense of love and gratitude.

And bear in mind that I shall not tolerate your associating with Me any other god from among the divinities of the peoples round
3   about you: *You shall have no other gods* (the text does not read, לֹא יִהְיוּ *lō' yiheyū* [literally, 'there shall not be', plural [rendered: 'have no'], but לֹא יִהְיֶה *lō' yiheye*, in the singular, in order to emphasize the prohibition of associating even one god; nor does the Bible say אֵל אַחֵר *'ēl 'aḥēr* ['another god', singular], but אֱלֹהִים אֲחֵרִים *'ĕlōhīm 'ăḥērīm* ['other gods', plural], so as to make it clear that not only is it forbidden to associate one deity but all the deities in general, whoever they may be) *in front of Me* — before Me, when I am present (compare Gen. xi 28: 'in the presence of [literally, 'in front of'; rendered: 'in the lifetime of'] his father Terah'), and you must know that at any time and in any place that you turn to another god, I am there.

The expression *other gods* became a regular, stereotyped term for the gods of the gentiles, who are no-gods. Every deity apart from the Lord is *another* god. The adjective *other* came to assume in Hebrew the signification of something strange or bizarre, something that is other than it should be (compare Mekhilta II, Tractate *Baḥodesh* ['In the [third] month'], ed. Lauterbach, p. 239: '*Other gods*: who act like strangers [literally, 'who are other'] towards those who worship them; cf. also the byname 'other' applied to Elisha b. Abuyah).

4 And, even in general, even without the association of other gods, *You shall not make yourself*, for the service of God, any *image*, any carved object, such as is commonly found among the heathen peoples, *or any likeness* whatsoever, of anything *that is in heaven above, or that is in the earth beneath, or that is in the water under the earth* — in a word, of any created thing in the world. The absolute prohibition of any likeness emanates, as we observed above, in the introductory notes to this paragraph, p. 236, from the absolute transcendental conception of the Godhead. This is not a primitive, aniconic attitude, like that of the tribes who have not yet attained the cultural level that enables them to make images and likenesses; for a people that had lived a long time in the land of Egypt, this primitive period belonged to the distant past of several centuries earlier. There is a deliberate antithesis here to a practice already existent in the world, particularly in Egypt. Possibly, it was just because of the Israelites' residence in Egypt that a powerful counterblast was issued against the worship of icons and other representations; possibly, it was just in Egypt that there was aroused the feeling of opposition to this worship that was widespread there. The theriomorphic figures, (that is, those that were partly fashioned in the form of cattle or beasts), and even more so the obscene representations of the fertility gods like Min, and sometimes even Amon, were undoubtedly regarded as detestable by the Israelites. The Torah seeks to confirm and preserve these feelings in Israel.

5 *You shall not prostrate yourself to them* — to any created thing, or their images and likenesses, or to the 'other gods' referred to in v. 3 — *or serve them* (תָעָבְדֵם *thoʿobhᵉdhēm*; the vocalization of the first two letters with *Qāmeṣ-ḥāṭūph* [short *Qāmeṣ*] instead of *Pathaḥ* is intended to express contempt — like the pointing עֲשְׁתֹּרֶת *ʿaštōreth* for *ʿastereth* [the substituted vowels being those of בֹּשֶׁת *bōšeth*, 'shame'] — as though to indicate that the worship of idols does not merit the honourable name of 'service' but a distorted form of it ['servitude', so to speak, rather than 'service']); *for I, the Lord your God*, who speaks to you this day, *am a jealous God*, and if you, O Congregation of Israel, will act towards Me like a faithless wife (the simile comparing the love between the people of Israel and their God to the love of a wife for the husband of her youth is well known), a spirit of jealousy will pass over

Me, and you will suffer severe punishment for breaking My covenant. Know, furthermore, that *I visit the iniquity of the fathers upon the children to the third and fourth generation*, if these children and children's children are also *of those who hate Me*, and, on the other hand, *I show lovingkindness to thousands* — not just to four generations, the period of punishment of those who hate Me, but to thousands of generations — *of those who love Me and keep My commandments*.

In regard to the fearful threat of punishment that will be inflicted upon the children and children's children, various apologetic interpretations have been advanced, which it is not possible to accept. It has been suggested, for example, that we should see here an allusion to the transmission of parental qualities to the character of the children and children's children, but this is merely a modernization of the verse; it has also been proposed that the statement should be understood as a postponement of the retribution in order to provide an opportunity for repentance, but this explanation does not fit the context, since the passage speaks of the Divine attribute of justice not of mercy; and there are other expositions of this kind. The difficulty exists, however, only for those who overlook the fact that the verse, in its simple signification, is directed to the entire nation as a single entity in time throughout its generations. Since a man, and particularly an Israelite, grieves over the tribulation of his children and grandchildren not less — nay, even more — than over his own affliction, the Bible issues a warning, so as to keep man far from sin, that in the course of the nation's life it is possible that the children and grandchildren will suffer the consequences of the iniquities of their father and grandfather. On the other hand, the text moves our hearts to love the Lord by the assurance that the beneficent results of their love will endure in the life of the nation and be bestowed upon the children and the children's children and upon their descendants up to thousands of generations. Thousands of generations, or even a thousand generations (Deut. vii 9), is so long a period that it is equivalent to saying: to the end of all generations.

The injunction in verse 7 is likewise connected with the preceding commandment. *You shall not take up the name of the Lord your God for unreality*, that is, you shall not use the name of the Lord for any valueless purpose, not just for a false oath, as it is usually interpreted (this is only a particular instance, whereas this is not the place for particulars), but in general for any worthless practice, in connection with which the gentiles mention the names of their gods, such as incantations, sorcery, divination, and the like, *for the Lord will not hold him guiltless who takes His name for unreality*, and for this sin, too, the Lord will impose severe punishment, even if an earthly court will be unable or unwilling to punish the sinner.

The precept of the Sabbath is included in the Decalogue because of its primary purpose, which is to recognize and attest that the Lord is the Creator of the world. Were it not for this underlying thought, which links the sabbath to a basic idea in the relationship between the children of Israel and God, this commandment would have no place here, just as it would be out of place to include here the other specific holy days, or even the detailed rules for the observance of the sabbath, apart from the general principle of abstaining from all labour.

On the concept of the hebdomad in the ancient East, see my observations above, in my annotations to xvi 5. I have also referred there to the Mesopotamian sabbath, which I discussed at length in my commentary on Gen. ii 3. There will be no need to repeat here all that I have stated there; it will suffice to mention briefly the main points. The name *Šabattu* or *Šapattu* was applied by the Babylonians and Assyrians to the day of the full moon, the fifteenth of the month, which was especially dedicated to the worship of the moon-god and of related deities. Also the seventh, fourteenth, twenty-first and twenty-eighth days of the month, which likewise have a particular significance in the Mesopotamian calendar, are similarly important for the pre-history of Israel's sabbath; they are connected with the four phases of the moon, and are seven days apart, except for the seventh of the month, which comes eight days after the twenty-eighth day of the preceding month, if that month was defective [i.e. consisted of 29 days], or nine days thereafter if that month was full [i.e. comprised 30 days]. All these days, both the day of the full moon and the other days enumerated above, were considered days of ill luck, on which it befitted a man to fast, to abstain from pleasures, and to avoid performing important works, for they would not succeed. The Israelite sabbath was instituted, it seems, in antithesis to the Mesopotamian system, and its character is completely original. It is not the day of the full moon, nor any other day dependent on the lunar phases; it is the seventh day in perpetual sequence, independent and freed from all connection with the signs of heaven. It is not a day

EXODUS XX 11

appointed for the worship of the host of heaven, but a day consecrated to Him who created the host of heaven, just as He created all the other parts of the universe; not a day of fasting and of misfortune, but a day of rest and benison (see *v.* 11 below: 'therefore the Lord blessed the sabbath day'; and similarly Gen. ii 3); not a day on which no tasks of importance are to be performed for fear that they will fail, but a day on which man rises above the need for the hard work that he is called upon to do on other days for his livelihood, and thereby he becomes like God, who rested and was refreshed after the creation of the world.

On account of all these changes, the Israelite sabbath assumed an entirely new and original form, an immeasurably higher and nobler character than that of its precursors, and became the treasured possession of Israel and of all the peoples who received it from them.

8 The formulation of the text is in keeping with all this: *Remember the sabbath day*, with which you are already familiar; but remember it so as *to keep it holy*, that is, to exalt it above the everyday plane
9 of life (holiness connotes separateness and sublimity). *Six days you shall labour, and do all your work*—all work requisite to your subsis-
10 tence do during the first six days of the week; *but the seventh day shall be a sabbath sanctified to the Lord your God*, to His glory and to the remembrance of His work as the Creator of the world, and in it *you shall not do any work*, neither you nor any of those who belong to you. At this point a series of seven categories of living beings is listed, which serves to underscore the number seven, on which the sabbath is based: (i) *you*; (ii) *or your son*; (iii) *or your daughter*; (iv) *your bondman*; (v) *or your bondmaid*; (vi) *or your cattle*; or even one who, although not actually dependent on you, is nevertheless bound to you because he dwells with you, namely, the seventh in the series: (vii) *or your sojourner who is in your gates* — within your gates — that is, within your cities. Since the basic principles underlying the Decalogue were not intended for the fleeting moment, but for all time, their formulation was not adapted to the temporary situation of the generation of the wilderness, who were tent-dwellers, but to the anticipated circumstances of the near future, when Israel would be settled in the Promised Land and dwell in its cities.
11 All this is enjoined upon you, *because in six days the Lord made heaven and earth, the sea, and all that is in them* — all three parts

of the world that the peoples, who are your neighbours, assign to three different gods and to a certain extent identify them with these three deities; and after the Lord had created His world and saw that everything was 'very good', He had only to enjoy His creation and to rejoice over His works: *and He rested the seventh day. Therefore the Lord blessed the sabbath day* — He blessed it and made it a source of blessing to man — *and hallowed it* — He uplifted it, raising it high above the level of the other days. Hence it is also your duty to sanctify the sabbath, just as the Lord did, and to rest thereon even as He did. Rise on this day above the plane of ordinary activities, liberate yourself from the burden of work of the six preceding days, and dedicate it not to your body but to your soul, not to material things but to things of the spirit, not to your relationship to nature, but to your relationship to the Creator of nature. Thereby you will imitate the ways in which the Lord your God works, and you will bear constant witness to the fact that He alone created the whole world in all its parts, and that He is not to be identified with any portion of the world or with any of the forces of nature, but He transcends the sphere of nature.

Verse 12, which enjoins the honouring of father and mother, marks a transition from man's duties towards God to his duties towards his fellow men. Parents are human, and as human beings they belong to the category of 'your neighbour', but, on the other hand, they are partners of the Creator in bringing you into the world (compare B. Qiddushin 30 b), and consequently you have 12 a duty to honour them: *Honour your father and your mother*, just as you honour your Creator. On this basis it is possible to understand the reason for the reward promised in connection with this precept: *that your days may be long in the land which the Lord your God is giving you*. The reward is determined on the principle of measure for measure: if you will honour the one who is the source of your life, you will be vouchsafed long life upon earth.

13-15 In regard to the three prohibitions: *You shall not kill — you shall not commit adultery — you shall not steal*, we have already stated above (pp. 239 f.) that actually there is nothing new in their substance, for in every civilized society, murder, adultery and theft are accounted forbidden acts; and yet even these verses contain something unusual: (a) first of all, their absolute form, without object or complement, without definitions or qualifications, without particulars or conditions, like the enunciation of fundamental, abstract and eternal principles, which transcend any condition or circumstance, detailed definition or restriction; (b) the incorporation of these principles in the Divine preamble to the Deed of Covenant as apodictic imperatives and statutes sanctified by the sanctity of their Legislator, as a fundamental basis and central pillar of the life of humanity according to the Creator's will.

16 Similar observations apply to the prohibition in *v.* 16: *You shall not answer* — that is, testify — concerning any matter pertaining *to your neighbour*, testimony contrary to the truth, as a *false witness*. Here, too, the prohibition is expressed absolutely, although not in so lapidary a form as that of the previous prohibitions. Here the complement (*pertaining*) *to your neighbour* has been added, in order to emphasize, apparently, that although false evidence is not an act that directly hurts one's neighbour or what belongs to him, as do murder, adultery and theft, it nevertheless injures him at least indirectly, through the influence that untrue testimony is liable to exert on the decision of the judge. Take heed of the fact that if you bear false witness you will cause unjustified injury to your fellow and hurt him.

Exegetes are not agreed as to the scope of the concept רֵעֶךָ *rēʿăkhā* [literally, 'your fellow'; rendered: 'your neighbour'] in the Pentateuch. Some hold that wherever רֵעֶךָ *rēʿăkhā*, or אָחִיךָ *'āḥīkhā* ['your brother'], or עֲמִיתֶךָ *ʿămīthᵉkhā* ['your fellow, associate'] occurs the reference is limited to the children of Israel; whilst others maintain that these expressions include all mankind. These two views — the first as well as the second — are not always free from the taint of preconceived ideas. The first may be due to the theological dogma that refuses to concede that Israel's Torah had already reached the level of the highest ethical teaching; while the second may flow from the apologetic tendency of Jewish scholars. If we examine the relevant passages objectively, without any prejudgement, we shall see that the truth lies midway. There can be no doubt that in a number of passages the terms *rēʿăkhā*, *'āḥīkhā*, *ʿămīthᵉkhā*, refer to Israelites; this is true even of the sublime precept in Lev. xix 18: 'but you shall love your neighbour [*rēʿăkhā*] as yourself', which parallels the beginning of the verse: 'You shall not take vengeance or bear any grudge against the sons of your people.' But in the continuation of the very same chapter (*v.* 34) it is expressly stated: 'The stranger [גֵּר *gēr*; literally, 'sojourner'] who sojourns with you (that is, the alien, according to the signification of the word גֵּר *gēr* in the Bible), shall be to you as the home-born among you, and you shall love him as yourself.' This being the case, all men are implied. The statutes of the Torah are intended for the people of Israel in its own land, and in the Israelite society of the Land of Israel there were only two classes of people, Israelites and strangers, and if both are included in the precept, all human beings are included. When Israelites dwell in exile in another country, then all the inhabitants of that land are included in the term 'your neighbour', as we learn from the phrase employed in Exod. xi 2: 'every man of his neighbour and every woman of her neighbour.' There 'his neighbour' and 'her neighbour' are Egyptian men and women: every Egyptian man is the neighbour [i.e. fellow] of every Israelite, and every Egyptian woman is the neighbour of every Israelite woman. Here, in the Decalogue, which is concerned with general principles and not with particular instances, the expression *your neighbour* is certainly used in a universal sense.

17   The precise meaning of לֹא תַחְמֹד *lō' thaḥmōdh* [rendered: 'You shall not covet'] is also the subject of dispute. Many consider that it connotes practical action: you shall not do anything in order to acquire what belongs to your neighbour. This opinion bases itself on passages like Exod. xxxiv 24: 'For I will dispossess nations before you, and enlarge your borders; neither shall any man desire your land', etc; Jos. vii 21: 'then I coveted them, and took them'; Micah ii 2: 'They covet fields, and seize them; and houses and take them away' [in all these verses the verb חָמַד *ḥāmadh* (rendered: 'desire', 'covet') is used]. However, it is precisely these passages that show that the correct meaning is different. In Exod. xxxiv 24 the intention is to set the minds of the festival pilgrims at rest, so that when they are far from their estates they should not be concerned about their possessions. In order that they should have no anxiety, and that the assurance should be complete, the Bible expresses itself in emphatic terms: not even a single person shall *desire* your land — even the thought of taking your land for himself will not enter his mind. As for the verses in Joshua and Micah, it is just the expressions *and took them — and seize them — and take them away* that prove that the verbs וָאֶחְמְדֵם *wā'eḥmᵉdhēm* [translated: 'then I coveted them'] — וְחָמְדוּ *wᵉḥāmᵉdhū* [rendered: 'they covet'] are not synonymous with them, but connote the stage anterior to the action. Compare Prov. xxxi 16: 'She considers a field and buys it.' Similarly, in the Phoenician inscription of king Azitawadda (iii line 14) the verb *yḥmd* ['covet'] stands in antithesis to the verb that signifies the actual deed (line 15: *ysʿ* ['removes']) and it is preceded by the word *'p* ['even'], which

indicates the emphatic character of the statement. Furthermore, if the negative precept לֹא תַחְמֹד *lō' thaḥmōdh* signified a prohibition of action, it would be a superfluous repetition of 'You shall not commit adultery' and 'You shall not steal.' Therefore it appears that the correct interpretation is, in accordance with the usual signification of the stem חָמַד *ḥāmadh*, that the verb is an expression of desire and yearning of the heart. All peoples acknowledge that it is forbidden to commit adultery or steal; but here the commandment goes further, and it is specifically enjoined as one of the fundaments of social life according to God's will: it is even forbidden to desire in one's heart another's wife or property. Desire is the first step, liable to lead to the second — adultery, theft, and possibly even murder. It already disturbs one's spiritual peace, and must therefore also be prohibited. This interpretation is given in the Pentateuch itself in the second recension of the Decalogue, which reads וְלֹא תִתְאַוֶּה *wᵉlō' thith'awwe* ['You shall not long for'] (Deut. v 21; Hebrew, v. 18)] in place of the second *lō' thaḥmōdh*.

The number of things that may not be coveted, like the list of those who are obliged to rest on the sabbath, totals seven. First in the series is a general term, *your neighbour's house*, which includes the house and all that is in it (the expression 'tent of your neighbour' is not used, since here, too, as we have noted in the case of the sabbath, the Bible has in mind not the temporary situation of the desert wanderers, but the hoped-for position in the near future). The general statement is followed by detailed examples, with the repetition of the prohibition, (1) *you shall not covet*: (2) *your neighbour's wife*; (3) *or his bondman*; (4) *or his bondwoman*; (5) *or his ox*; (6) *or his ass*; and in the end (7) a final general expression to include all the things that were not specifically mentioned: *or anything that is your neighbour's*.

The Decalogue concludes with the words *your neighbour's*, forming a parallel, as it were, to the opening statement: *I am the Lord your God*.

The central thought in the first part is the love of the Lord — 'and you shall love the Lord your God' — and in the second, the love of man — 'but you shall love your neighbour as yourself.' The two sections parallel each other, and the two loves correspond to, and complement, one another.

As we know, there is more than one recension of the Decalogue. In Deut. v 6–21 [Hebrew, 6–18], there occurs a version that differs

THE DECALOGUE

somewhat from that recorded here in the Book of Exodus. Yet a third recension exists in the Nash Papyrus, which was discovered in Egypt in 1902. This papyrus apparently gives us the Decalogue according to the text that was in common use among the Jews of Egypt (for example, the order of the commandments that it follows, 'You shall not commit adultery' — 'You shall not kill' — 'You shall not steal', is that found in the writings of Philo of Alexandria and in several MSS of the Septuagint, as well as in a few quotations in the New Testament); mainly it corresponds to the formulation found in the Book of Exodus, with a few variations in form, which mostly follow the version in the Book of Deuteronomy. However, since this is a late recension, the main problem is that of the relationship between the two different versions of the Eretz-Israel text, which served as the basis of the Masoretic text. The differences between the two recensions before us are of two kinds: differences of form and of content. The divergences of form can be classified as follows: (a) the addition or omission of the *Wāw* copulative; (b) the substitution of synonymous expressions, like *Remember — Observe*; *insincere* [שָׁוְא *šāw'*] *witness — false* [שֶׁקֶר *šeqer*] *witness*; (c) variations in the order of the words; (d) extension for the sake of particularization: *or your cattle* in Exodus; *or your ox, or your ass, or any of your cattle*, in Deuteronomy. Changes in content are found in two places: (a) in the reason given for the precept of the sabbath; (b) in stating the reward for honouring father and mother.

The problem of the relationship between the two recensions is not difficult to solve if we do not regard them as isolated documents standing by themselves, as most commentators are accustomed to do, but consider them in their context. In the Book of Exodus it is narrated that the Lord proclaimed the Decalogue to the people of Israel at the Revelation on Mount Sinai; whilst in the Book of Deuteronomy we are told that Moses reminded the people, after forty years, of what happened at the time. Now according to the customary literary usage followed both in the Bible and in the other literatures of the ancient East, when someone's utterance is cited and subsequently it is related that someone else referred to it, the statement is not repeated in the *ipsissima verba*, but certain variations and changes are introduced (see my observations above, on xix 23). In Gen. xxiv, when Abraham's servant speaks in the house of Bethuel, he does not quote his conversation with Abraham, or his talk with Rebekah, in the identical form recorded earlier in that chapter. The same obtains in our case; when Moses reminds the people of God's words, he does not repeat them exactly. Hence, there is no reason for surprise at the changes in form; on the contrary, it would be surprising if everything were iterated with complete exactitude. As for the two modifications in the substance of the Decalogue, in connection with the sabbath and in regard to the honouring of parents, it should be noted that just in these two instances, and in them only, Moses says: *as the Lord your God commanded you*, as if to allude to the fact that although the commandments were formulated in a given way, he is not quoting the precise words.

Another question to be considered is that of the division of the Ten Words. The number is expressly stated in the Bible, and is not to be doubted (Exod. xxxiv 28; Deut. iv 13; x 4: 'the ten words'*). It was fixed apparently as an aid to memorization, so that the Ten Words could easily be counted on the fingers of the hands. We have already seen that there is an allusion to the Decalogue in the occurrence ten times of the stem דבר *dbr* in ch. xviii, and another ten times in the narrative of the Revelation at Mount Sinai (xix 1 – xx 1). However, there are different views about the way in which the 'statements' should be divided. The traditional Jewish division, which is already found in the Tannaitic Midrashim (Mekhilta de Rabbi Ishmael, ed. Lauterbach, II, pp. 262–264; Mekhilta de Rabbi Simon b. Yohai, ed. Hofmann, p. 113; and in several other passages), is as follows: (1) *I am the Lord your God*; (2) *You shall have no other gods*; (3) *You shall not take up*; (4) *Remember the sabbath day*; (5) *Honour your father and mother*; (6) *You shall not kill*; (7) *You shall not commit adultery*; (8) *You shall not steal*; (9) *You shall not bear false witness*; (10) *You shall not covet*. Another division, which regards *I am the Lord* and *You shall have no other gods*, as the first statement, is alluded to in Siphrē Num. (ed. Horowitz, p. 121, on Num. xv 31). Similarly, Philo of Alexandria and several Christian scholars combine *I am the Lord* with *You shall have no other gods*, and list the Ten Words thus: (1) *I am... you shall have no other gods*; (2) *You shall not make yourself*; (3) *You shall not take up*, etc. Other Christian exegetes join *I am the Lord* with *you shall have no other gods* and *You shall*

---

* עֲשֶׂרֶת הַדְּבָרִים *ʿăsereth haddᵉbhārīm*. The author notes here that the later Hebrew term דִּבְּרוֹת *dibbᵉrōth* is the plural of דִּבֵּר *dibbēr* ['statement'] (not דִּבְּרָה *dibbᵉrā*), a synonym of דִּבּוּר *dibbūr*, which is the more common form in the singular. *Tr.*

THE DECALOGUE

not make yourself, and divide *You shall not covet* into two. Also the superlinear vocalization of several MSS of the Masora unites, as it were, into one verse, *I am the Lord*, and *You shall have no other gods* and *You shall not make yourself*. In the MSS emanating from the school of Ben Asher, a small space, almost similar to that which marks a closed section, has been left between the two clauses commencing with the words, *You shall not covet*. However, the simple sense of the text favours the division mentioned first.

CONCLUSION OF THE SECTION

(XX 18–21)

This concluding paragraph does not merely come to relate what occurred after the proclamation of the *Decalogue*, but to describe the reaction of the people to the Revelation as a whole. The beginning of *v.* 18, where the subject precedes the predicate, stating 18 וְכָל הָעָם רֹאִים ... *wᵉkhol hā'ām rō'īm*... ['and all the people saw'] and not וַיַּרְא כָּל־הָעָם *wayyar' kol hā'ām*... [literally, 'and saw all the people'], which is the normal construction in consecutive narration, shows that this verse does not describe an action that took place subsequent to the events described above, but something that happened simultaneously (compare my notes on ix 20–21, xix 3, 18). It reverts to the awe-inspiring phenomena that heralded the theophany, which are recorded earlier (xix 16), and what is there described objectively is now depicted anew from the aspect of the subjective reactions of the people to these phenomena, in order to prepare the way for the expression of similar feelings on the part of the people towards the Revelation itself (*v.* 19). Earlier it was stated: 'there were thunders and lightnings, and a dense cloud upon the mountain, and the sound of a horn exceedingly loud'; whereas here our gaze is directed towards the people. *Now all the people* — what were they doing at that time? *They were seeing* (more exactly: they were seeing and hearing, only the verb רָאָה *rā'ā* ['see'] may be used in the general signification of perceiving with the senses; furthermore we have here an example of zeugma, that is, the use of one verb that is suited to only some of the objects exactly, but not to all; see above, on ix 23) *the thunderings and the flames*, that is, the lightnings, *and the sound of the horn and the mountain smoking; and the people saw* — that is, and when the people saw all these phenomena (the verb *to see* is repeated here, because its first occurrence, *were seeing*, is now far removed on account of the long list of objects intervening) — *and they swayed* — they retreated in panic on account of their terror (xix 16: 'and all the people that were in the camp trembled [or, were terrified]') — *and they stood afar off*, at the end of the camp farthest from the mountain, and only after Moses had heartened and reassured them was it possible for him to bring them forth from the camp to meet God and to make them stand at the foot of the mountain (xix 17). If they were so frightened by the natural phenomena, how much greater was their dread on hearing the Divine speech! When, therefore, Moses returned to them after they had listened to the Decalogue from God, the

19 Israelites submitted to him a request: *And they said to Moses, You speak to us*, from now on, *and we will hear* from your mouth the commandments of God, *but let not God Himself speak to us* further, *lest we die*.

Moses hastened once again to encourage the people and to assure
20 them that there was no reason to be afraid: *And Moses said to the people, Do not fear* (compare xiv 13); *for*, it is not to slay you, Heaven forfend!, but *to prove you* — whether you will follow His teaching, or not — that *God has come, and that the fear of Him* — not dread but reverence — *may be before you, that you may not sin*.

21 Nevertheless, Moses sought to fulfil their request: *And the people stood afar off*, that is, the people remained far from the mountain, in the midst of their camp, *but Moses* (here, too, the subject precedes the verb to express antithesis to the subject of the preceding clause) *drew near to the thick cloud where God was* to receive the rest of his teachings.

No surprise need be felt at the fact that in this paragraph the name *'Elōhīm* ['God'] and not *YHWH* ['Lord'] occurs. Since our passage still forms part of the proclamation of the Decalogue, which was given in the name of the God of the whole earth, as is emphasized at the beginning of chapter xix and chapter xx, the Bible uses here, too, the generic appellation *'Elōhīm*.

What directives Moses received from 'the thick cloud where God was' will be stated in the next section.

SECTION THREE

STATUTES AND ORDINANCES

CHAPTER XX, VERSE 22—CHAPTER XXIII, VERSE 33

After the prefatory declaration, which sets forth in ten statements the basic principles on which the deed of covenant between the Lord and Israel was founded, had been proclaimed to the latter, Moses is given the terms and details of the covenant, so that he may make them known to his people.

The whole section is presented in the form of a long and comprehensive communication by the Lord to Moses. It begins with 22 the formula: *And the Lord said to Moses*, which serves as a caption for the entire section right to the end; thereafter, at the beginning of the next section (xxiv 1), there comes another formula similar to it: 'And to Moses He said.'

Since the theme is now one that pertains essentially to Israelites, Scripture uses here the Tetragrammaton and not the name ʾ*Elōhīm*.

THE EXORDIUM

INTRODUCTORY OBSERVATIONS

(XX 22b—26)

The formula introducing the Lord's words to Moses, *Thus you shall say to the children of Israel*, is a solemn injunction resembling the one we encountered earlier (xix 3), and which we discussed in our commentary *ad locum*.

The Divine communication, which Moses is charged to deliver to the people, takes as its starting point the episode of the Revelation at Mount Sinai, and on this basis it sets forth, in its introductory words, the principles of the Israelite worship. It begins: *You have seen for yourselves*, that is, you have felt, recognized (on the general signification of the stem רָאָה *rāʾā* ['see'], see above, v. 18) *that from heaven* — not face to face, but from the top of the mountain, which reaches to the heart of heaven, from the Divine sphere, which is separated from the human plane — *I have talked with you*, and you have perceived no form, only a voice. Not only does the content of this verse connect the Divine communication with the Sinaitic Revelation, but its wording emphasizes the nexus; the opening words, *You have seen for yourselves*, are identical with the commencement of the communication in xix 4 ff., while the expression, *I have talked with you*, recalls the conclusion of the preceding section (*v.* 19: 'You speak to us... but let not God speak to us').

23 Since I have spoken with you from afar, and you have seen no likeness, you must necessarily learn from this that *You shall not make gods of silver to be with Me* (this was apparently the original division of the verse, though contrary to the accents), *nor shall you make for yourselves gods of gold*. Each of the two expressions 'with Me' and 'for yourselves' appertains, according to the rules of parallelism, to both parts of the verse. The punctuation, by accents, of the Masoretes (*you shall not make with Me* — absolutely, anything at all) was intended perhaps to avoid the interpretation that idols that were not made of silver and gold were permissible.

This verse is not redundant even after the prohibition in the Decalogue. There the general principle is stated forbidding the making of any likeness, whereas here particular examples of the law are given. Even if the aim be to honour the God of Israel (*with Me*), and even if such precious metals as silver and gold be used, with which other nations do honour to their gods, you may not make any divine image. Even the most exquisite ornamentation cannot serve as a fitting symbol of the Invisible God.

Even the worship in My honour should not resemble the ornate ritual of the gentiles, who build elaborate altars to their gods, 24 but should be very simple: *An altar of earth you shall make for Me*, a modest altar of clods of earth like those of the earlier generations (compare, for example, the ancient altar discovered at Megiddo, which is made of lumps of earth enclosed by stones and rubble), *and sacrifice on it* — on this simple altar — *your burnt offerings and your peace offerings*, that is, all the oblations that you will sacrifice to Me (burnt offerings and peace offerings are the two principal categories of sacrifices), namely, the oblations of *your sheep* and the oblations of *your oxen*. The fourfold emphasis on the word *your* connotes as it were: Know that it is not I (God) who have need of sacrifices, but you alone require them, in order to express your feelings towards Me. The sacrifices are your sacrifices.

Furthermore, do not imagine that I am connected, like the gentile gods, with a given locality; on the contrary: *in every place where I cause My name to be remembered I will come to you and bless you.* This verse has been made the subject of countless conjectures. The prevailing opinion among scholars regards it as establishing the principle that the worship of the Lord is permitted everywhere, in opposition to the view that finds expression in the Book of Deuteronomy, to wit, that Divine worship should be centralized in one place only, the place chosen by the Lord. This interpretation treats the verse as though it were detached from its setting, after the manner of the homiletical glosses of the rabbinic sages, who disregard the framework of the Scriptural passages, and explain every verse as a separate entity. From the viewpoint of method, such an approach is scientifically indefensible; nothing can be studied outside its context. As for the passage under discussion, we must not lose sight of the fact that it belongs to the narrative following immediately after the story of the Revelation at Mount Sinai, and is to be understood only against that background. The people were privileged to witness the theophany on Mount Sinai, but they are on the point of departing from there soon, in order to continue their journey in the wilderness, and they may possibly imagine that in leaving the mountain of God they are also going away from God. To avoid their entertaining such thoughts, it is stated here that the Lord is not exclusively connected with this mountain or with any other place. *In every place* [כָּל־הַמָּקוֹם *kol hammāqōm*] (for this expression, and the definite article of *hammāqōm*, compare Gen. xx 13: 'At every place [*kol hammāqōm*] to which we come, say of me, He is my brother') *where I cause My name to be remembered*, that is, wherever I shall permit My name to be mentioned and service to take place in My honour (the Peshitta reads 'you cause My name to be remembered' instead of 'I cause My name to be remembered', apparently with the intention of making the meaning of the verse clearer); or, possibly, a better interpretation would be: wherever I reveal Myself (since revelation through speech begins with the mention of the speaker's name, as I indicated above, on vi 2 and on xx 2), *I will come to you and bless you.* Another point to which attention should be paid is the fact that throughout this paragraph one altar only is spoken of, which indicates that even in this passage it is intended that worship should be centralized in one place.

25 *And if* in the future, when you come to the Promised Land, which is a country of mountains and rocks, and you will be able to use stone as much as you wish, *you make Me an altar of stone, you shall not build them* — the stones — as *hewn stones*, that is, stones beautifully dressed, but you shall build the altar of plain, whole stones (Deut. xxvii 6) in their natural state, as they are found on the ground; *for if you wield your tool upon it* — on the stone, to chisel it, you remove thereby its natural form from it, and *you profane it* from being used in the structure of My altar.

26 *And you shall not go up by steps to My altar*, as is done on many of the heathen altars, like those that have been found in Petra and the surrounding area, and like the one at Megiddo that I have mentioned above. This, too, is undesirable adornment; furthermore, it is desirable to refrain from this in order *that your nakedness be not exposed on it*. Possibly the verse intends to oppose the practice of certain peoples in the ancient East, like the Sumerians for instance, whose priests on account of the conservatism that is customary in matters of worship, used to perform every ritual ceremony in a state of nakedness. Likewise the Egyptian priests, and even the Egyptian king when he officiated in the sanctuary, used to wear only a linen ephod, a kind of short, primitive apron. The Israelite sense of modesty cannot tolerate such customs, and, as an added precaution, it further requires (xxviii 42) that the priests should wear drawers to cover their naked flesh, and these drawers *shall reach from the loins to the thighs*.

THE LEGAL PARAGRAPHS

Chapter XXI

After the introductory statements, which set out the principles of Israelite worship, the Divine communication proceeds to give Moses a series of judicial regulations. The general superscription to the
1 entire series is: *Now these are the ordinances which you shall set before them*, that is, which you shall present and propose to them. The covenant has not yet been made, and everything is said in the form of a proposal.

It is self-understood that in order to comprehend and evaluate

THE LEGAL PARAGRAPHS

these legal paragraphs, it will be necessary to compare the collections of statutes of the ancient East, which were discovered in recent times. Likewise the judicial and economic documents, which have also been found in our times in great numbers, can be of help to us.

These are the codes of the ancient East that are thus far known to us (bibliographical details relative to them will be given in the notes at the end of the book):

(A) Sumerian and Akkadian Laws of Babylonia:

1. The laws of the city of Ešnunna, in Akkadian, promulgated apparently in the twentieth century B.C.E. They were discovered in two copies in Tell Harmal, excavated by the Iraq Directorate of Antiquities, one copy in 1945 and the other in 1947, and were first published by A. Goetze in 1948.

2. The laws of Lipit–Ištar king of Isin, in Sumerian, from the nineteenth century B.C.E. Excerpts of this code, comprising about a third of the entire collection, were found by Francis R. Steele among tablets from Nippur in the possession of the University Museum at Philadelphia. Steele first announced his discovery in 1947, and published the excerpts in 1948. He found and published another excerpt in 1950. Previously there were known only brief extracts of Sumerian laws in the *ana ittišu* series and in fragmentary tablets from Nippur, and were published in part by A.T. Clay in 1915, and partly by H. J. Lutz in 1919.

3. The laws of Ḫammurabi king of Babylon, who reigned, according to the chronology that appears most correct today, at the close of the eighteenth century and the beginning of the seventeenth B.C.E. The code belongs to the end of his reign, and may therefore be dated round about the year 1690. This code, which is inscribed on a big stela, was discovered in Susa, by the excavations of a French expedition, between December 1901 and January 1902, and first published by V. Scheil in 1902. There were also found a number of fragmentary copies of this text, and with their help it is possible to restore a part of the seven columns that were erased from the big stela. Thus the code is known to us almost in its entirety. It seems that Ḫammurabi utilized earlier Sumerian and Akkadian law-codes, like those mentioned above in Nos. 1–2.

4. Excerpts from later Babylonian laws found in one of the tablets in the possession of the British Museum. The whole tablet was first published by F. E. Peiser in 1889.

(B) Assyrian Laws:

5. Short legal extracts are found among the tablets belonging

THE LEGAL PARAGRAPHS

to the Assyrian settlements in Cappadocia, which were discovered particularly in the twenties of this century. It appears that these tablets were inscribed in the second half of the nineteenth century or in the beginning of the eighteenth B.C.E.

6. Collections of Assyrian laws (from Middle Assyria) were discovered in several tablets in excavations by Germans in the ruins of the city of Ashur in the years 1903–1914, and were first published by O. Schroeder in 1920. They belong, apparently, to the fourteenth century B.C.E., approximately.

(C) Hittite Laws:

7. A large body of Hittite laws, dating apparently from the fourteenth century B.C.E., was unearthed in Boğazköy in two principal tablets and in several secondary fragments, and were first published by F. Hrozný in 1921 and 1922.

Legal and economic documents in thousands and tens of thousands were found in various places. In relation to our subject, it is worth noting in particular the large collection that was discovered in the years 1925–1931 at Yorgan Tepe near Kirkuk (ancient Nuzu, fifteenth century B.C.E.) and the other big collection found in 1935 and onward in Tell Hariri (ancient Mari, eighteenth to seventeenth centuries B.C.E.).

An examination of the codes and documents clearly proves that there existed in the countries of the East a legal tradition that was unitary in its basic elements and principles. It had its roots in Mesopotamia, whilst its branches extended northward and westward, due to the spread of the Mesopotamian culture. From the time of the first publication of the Ḥammurabi Code, much research and writing have been devoted to the comparative story of the Pentateuchal laws and those of the Eastern peoples, and the Torah ordinances have also independently become the subject of considerable investigation and many publications; see on this the bibliographical notes that I shall provide at the end of the volume. Great importance attaches to the entire range of this research; but earlier scholars have still left room for additional study. Hence it is not out of place to summarize here briefly some of the results of my investigations, in so far as these can contribute to the exegesis and comprehension of this section.

In the first place, let us endeavour to establish the character of the Biblical laws in general, for so far their nature has not been sufficiently understood.

The legal tradition of the ancient East was, in all its branches, secular, not religious. The sources of the law were on the one hand usage — *consuetudo* — and on the other, the king's will. In all the aforementioned codes we observe that the law does not emanate from the will of the gods. Although the bas-relief on the top of Ḥammurabi's stele, which shows the king standing before the god Šamaš, was at first explained to mean that the king was receiving the code from the hands of that deity, yet it is now clear, from a study of the prologue and epilogue of the code, that this interpretation is incorrect. Possibly scholars were influenced by their recollections of Scripture. The sculpture on the stele represents only a ritual ceremony, in which the king pays homage to Šamaš. From the introduction and conluding words of the code, it is clear that it is Ḥammurabi who enacts the laws. He turns to the gods only to ask them to give a good reward to him that will keep his statutes, and to inflict severe punishment on the one who will annul or transgress them. In general, moreover, none of the aforementioned codes contains any law pertaining to the rituals of worship or to other religious matters; and their content is wholly secular. For religious subjects specific, separate manuals were composed, like the Hittite Instructions on the duties incumbent on the priests and the temple officials (even this body of instructions, in so far as it is possible to judge despite the fact that the beginning of the text is missing, was not promulgated in the name of the gods themselves).

Now it is possible to show that also among the Israelites, during the whole period preceding the destruction of the First Temple, the sources of the official law were the secular statutes of the ruling authorities and accepted usage; whereas the Torah laws were regarded as religious and ethical requirements directed to the collective and individual conscience. Although Israelite governmental codes, like those of the Mesopotamian kings, have not come down to us, yet we are permitted to posit that such codes existed at the time. Clear indications of the existence of secular law among the Israelites are to be found in the Bible. It will suffice, for example, to cite the following references:

(a) In i Sam. xxx 24–25 it is related that David established a rule for the division of the spoils of war, and it is stated there: 'And from that day forward he made it a statute and an ordinance for Israel to this day.'

(b) Not without cause does the prophet (Isa. x i) inveigh against 'those who decree iniquitous decrees, and the writers who keep writing oppression.' The formulation of the statement precludes the assumption that it refers, according to the usual interpretation, to judicial sentences. It is worth noting that the text specifically refers to written legislation.

(c) In Jer. xxxiv 8 ff. it is narrated that after the men of Jerusalem had entered into a covenant 'that every one should set free his bondman, and every one his bondwoman, being a Hebrew man or a Hebrew woman', in accordance with the Torah precept, and after they had carried out the terms of the covenant, they turned around and took them back and brought them into subjection as bondmen and bondwomen. It is obvious, that they would not have been permitted to bring them back to a state of servitude, had not the existing law given them the right to do this. It would seem that the state law of the time made no provision for the Hebrew slave to be freed after a given number of years, and whoever acquired a Hebrew slave acquired him for ever. The Torah law, whose existence at the time is not in doubt, since the covenant was based upon it, was regarded as an ethical precept that was left to a person's conscience in the name of religion. The covenant that was made on the initiative of king Zedekiah did not mean the enactment of a new civil law, but only a moral obligation, which the princes and the people accepted voluntarily, in order to fulfil the Torah precept. Had the king desired to promulgate a statute in this regard, there would have been no need for a covenant to have been made between the parts of the calf. His intention was doubtless to arrange a solemn religious ceremony to mark the acceptance of the obligation of the commandment that was ordained in the name of the Lord.

Similarly there are references in the Bible to the existence of recognized legal usage. Thus, for example, the Torah mentions the bride money [מֹהַר *mōhar*] of virgins as something well-known and fixed (Exod. xxii 16): 'he shall pay money equivalent to the bride-money for virgins'; compare also the reference in Ruth iv 7: 'Now this was the custom in former times in Israel concerning redeeming and exchanging', etc.; and the story narrated in i Kings ii 28 f. concerning Joab, who fled to the tent of the Lord and caught hold of the horns of the altar in order to escape execution, in accordance with the custom obtaining throughout the world, which granted the right of asylum in temples — a practice that the Torah seeks to abolish in the case of murder (Exod. xxi 14; see my commentary *ad locum*.).

THE LEGAL PARAGRAPHS

It may also be assumed that the law of Israel was an offshoot of the general legal tradition that was current, as we have stated, throughout the ancient East. But the statutes of the Torah are not to be identified with Israel's secular legislation. Only in the time of Ezra were the laws of the Torah accepted as the laws of the country, by the consent of the people and its leaders. When we come to compare the Pentateuchal statutes with those of the neighbouring peoples, we must not forget, as the scholars engaged in this field of study usually do, the difference in character between them: the laws of the neighbouring peoples were not decreed on behalf of the gods, but on behalf of the kings; whereas the laws of the Torah were not promulgated in the name of the monarchy, nor even in the name of Moses as the leader of Israel, but are religious and ethical instructions in judicial matters ordained in the name of the God of Israel. Every section, whether its subject-matter be legal or purely religious, is prefaced by the stereotyped formula: *And the Lord spoke to Moses*, saying, or a similar sentence (in Exod. xx 22: *And the Lord said to Moses*).

'Religious and ethical instructions in judicial matters' is the correct definition of the legal passages of the Torah. These instructions are of three kinds:

(a) Those that introduce amendments in the existing legal tradition;
(b) those that oppose or invalidate particular aspects of this tradition;
(c) those that confirm, in the name of religion, other aspects that are deemed worthy of express corroboration even in the name of the religion of Israel.

These directions are based, therefore, on the premise that there are already in existence legal usages and secular statutes, and that the rulers have the right to enact more laws, only the Torah sets bounds to this right from a religious viewpoint.

Hence, the legal sections of the Pentateuch should not be regarded as a code of laws, or even as a number of different codes, but only as separate instructions on given matters. This fact explains why the Torah does not deal at all with several subjects that constitute basic legal themes: for example the laws of marriage, apart from forbidden relations and the reference to the marriage-price of virgins, which occurs incidentally; or with the laws of divorce, which are also mentioned only incidentally in order to forbid, on moral grounds, that a divorced woman who has married another man should return to her first husband. Although the codes of the Eastern kings are also incomplete and do not include every branch of law, yet, when they deal with a given subject, they enter into all its details, and are not content with a few chance, unrelated notes. See further, on the Torah system, my remarks on the laws of theft (xxi 37–xxii 3), and on xxii 15.

Another important distinction between state legislation and the Torah laws is to be seen in the fact that the form of the latter is not always that of a complete statute. They do not always state the penalty to be imposed on the transgressor; sometimes only an absolute command or prohibition is enjoined as an expression of the absolute will of the Lord. Alt already has rightly recognized that the absolute apodictic form of statutes is of Israelite origin, in contradistinction to the casuistic form, which is common also to the other peoples (with this form I shall deal later).

Contrariwise, sometimes the Torah adds the reason for the law, from the religious or ethical point of view, unlike the codes mentioned above, which give no reasons. It would be superfluous to state further that in the Pentateuch are to be found, as is well known, religious and ritual regulations alongside legal ordinances without differentiation, which is not the case, as we have seen, in codes of the neighbouring nations.

The Torah's ethical intent creates further disparity. The entire concern of the aforementioned codes is to determine what is due to a person according to the letter of the law, according to abstract justice, whereas the Torah seeks on many an occasion, to go beyond strictly legal requirements and to grant a man what is due to him from the ethical viewpoint and from the aspect of the love a man should bear his fellow, who is his brother, since both have One Heavenly Father.

In view of the fact that the Torah statutes are only notes on the existing laws, we should feel no surprise at the fact that their style and usual phraseology resemble those of the prevailing legal traditions. One of the similarities, recognized already some time ago, is to be found in the casuistic formulation, which begins by setting out a given case (if such-and-such an instance [*casus*] occurs), and thereafter states what the law is in that particular case. In the Pentateuch, the primary case is introduced mostly by the word כִּי *kī* ['when', 'if'], whilst the various conditions, that is, the secondary circumstances within the framework of the principal case, are generally prefaced by the word אִם *'im* ['if']. Also in regard to the selection of cases to be considered from among the large number of possible cases, there are to be discerned traces of the legal tradition, which was accustomed to deal with certain typical instances. There is no need to add that in the third category of Torah notes, the group which affirms existing laws, the resemblance is not limited to the form only, but is to be found also in the actual substance of the statutes.

Chapters xxi–xxiii of the Book of Exodus are usually designated *The Book of the Covenant*, on the basis of verse 7 in ch. xxiv. But it is doubtful if this expression there indicates particularly these chapters; possibly, it has another meaning (see my annotations *ad locum*). It follows, needless to say, that the countless theories that have been advanced regarding this 'Book of the Covenant', its relationship to the other parts of the Pentateuch, its structure, and the process of its composition, are no more than conjectures. But this is not the place to discuss all these problems; I intend doing so elsewhere. Here I wish only to determine the correct interpretation of the passages in their present form, and this interpretation will constitute the primary basis of our discussion of these problems. I shall preface my exposition, however, with two additional observations:

(a) The subject-matter of the chapters is not presented systematically. The various topics are arranged on the principle of analogy and association, a feature with which I have already dealt in my introductory remarks on the passage concerning the manna and the quails (above, pp. 187 f.). In the case of each paragraph, I shall explain the reason for the juxtaposition of the texts.

(b) I shall endeavour in my commentary to establish the original meaning of the verses, that is, their primary purport at the time when they were first written. Although Jewish law continued to develop through the ages, and the traditional interpretation, based on rabbinic exegesis, reflects in respect of many verses the later evolution of the Halakha, in accordance with the conditions of life prevailing in the Talmudic period, yet the Rabbis themselves taught that no Biblical passage loses its primary signification. It is of value, therefore, to endeavour to delve to the original sense of the text according to its simple meaning.

FIRST PARAGRAPH

THE LAWS OF THE HEBREW SLAVE

(XXI 2–6)

This paragraph prescribes, according to the later *Halakhah*, the regulations pertaining to the Israelite, in contradistinction to the 'Canaanite', slave, that is, the non-Israelite bondman. This is consonant with the social conditions existing in the rabbinic age. Already in the time of Jeremiah, the term *Hebrew slave* was identical with that of *Jewish slave* (see Jer. xxxiv 9: 'that every one should set free his bondman, and every one his bondwoman, being a Hebrew man or Hebrew woman; that none should enslave them, even a Jew his brother'). But the actual sense of the verse in this paragraph, which is undoubtedly very old (later on, too, we shall note signs of antiquity in these legal paragraphs), corresponds to the conditions of life obtaining in early times and uses the expression *Hebrew slave* in its primary signification, which included not only Israelite slaves, but a wider category of bondmen. We have already seen above, in our annotations to i 15, that designations similar to the word עִבְרִי *'ibhrī* [rendered: 'Hebrew'] (*Ḫabiru* or *Ḫapiru* in Akkadian; *'pr* in Ugaritic and Egyptian) denote a certain social class. We also mentioned there:

(a) the documents from Nuzu, which indicate by the above Akkadian appellation, in general, people of alien origin who are employed mostly as slaves or servants;

(b) the Egyptian documents, where the aforementioned Egyptian term signifies people who are made to do compulsory labour in the service of Pharaoh. This is also not the proper place for a detailed discussion of the complicated question of the relationship between these designations and the name עִבְרִי *'ibhrī*; it will suffice to note the fact that it was particularly when they were foreign slaves in Egypt that the Israelites were specifically called Hebrews, just as Joseph already was described in Egypt as *a Hebrew man* [usually rendered: 'a Hebrew'], *a Hebrew youth* [usually translated: 'a young man, a Hebrew'], or actually *a Hebrew slave* [rendered: 'Hebrew servant']. Apparently the connotation of this expression in our section comprises all the members of this class, which was called in the Eastern countries by the appellations corresponding to עִבְרִי *'ibhrī*. These statutes, whose aim is to grant certain rights to the Hebrew slave, say, in effect, to the Israelites: you have been *Hebrew slaves* in Egypt, and, therefore, you must act with love and compassion towards the people who are *Hebrew slaves*, even as you were, irrespective of their racial origin. It is self-understood that, if the 'Hebrew slave' is an Israelite, it is all the more incumbent on you to treat him lovingly and compassionately, but the law is the same for all 'Hebrew slaves', for they are all your brethren in misfortune.

Possibly it is not accidental that these legal sections commence particularly with the laws of the Hebrew slave. It corresponds, as it were, to the first verse of the Decalogue, which reminds the children of Israel that the Lord *brought them out from the house of bondage*. Just as you *went out* free, for nothing, from the house of bondage, so shall every Hebrew slave *go out* free, for nothing, from your homes after he has served you a number of years.

2 *When you* — an Israelite — *buy*, as a bondman, a man who belongs to the category called *a Hebrew slave*, that slave *shall serve six years, and in the seventh he shall go out free, for nothing*, that is, without having to pay any redemption money. On the importance of a series of seven units of time, see above, in our commentary on xvi 5, xix 1, xx 8. The Hebrew slaves of Nuzu were apparently slaves for life (although there is also a different view); the Torah, on the other hand, enacts that the Hebrew slave shall serve only a limited time, and thereafter he shall be a free man. This is one of the amendments that the Torah affected in the existing law on ethical grounds. In the Ḥammurabi Code (§ 117) a fixed period of service (three years) is laid down only in the case where a Babylonian freeman sells, on account of debt, his wife, or his son, or his daughter. This kind of sale is dealt with by the Torah in the next paragraph.

3 *If he* — the Hebrew slave — *comes* to your house בְּגַפּוֹ *bᵉghappō*, that is, alone, with the corner of his coat only [גַף *gaph* is understood by the author to mean 'wing', 'corner'] (compare Gen. xxxii 10 [Hebrew, *v.* 11]: 'for with only my staff I crossed this Jordan; and now I have become two companies'), *he shall go out alone* from your house after six years; *if he comes in married*, and his wife is a Hebrew slave like himself (such cases are cited in the Nuzu documents), *then his wife shall go out with him*. The term 'Hebrew slave' in *v.* 2, according to the plain meaning of the verse, includes also the bondwoman, and the law in regard to her is the same as that for the male slave. In the next paragraph a special

4 case is referred to, and it is governed by a special law. *If his master gives him a wife* — one of his female slaves — *and she* — this woman — *bears him sons or daughters, the wife and her children shall be her master's,* even when the seventh year arrives, *and he shall go out alone,* and he shall have no right to obtain the manumission of
5 his wife and children without paying a ransom. *But if the slave shall declare,* in a case where his master has not given him a wife, *I love my master,* and have no desire to leave his house; or, where his master has given him a wife, he says, I love *my wife and my*
6 *children,* and, therefore, *I will not go out free,* then his master shall *bring him to 'God'* (originally the word *'ĕlōhīm* in the ancient legal tradition of the East undoubtedly denoted the idols standing in the court of justice; among the Israelites the expression remained a stereotyped term signifying the place of the court), *and he shall bring him to the door or the doorpost,* not on account of any magical significance attaching to the door or the doorpost, according to the usual explanation of the ceremony, but simply to provide a wooden support on which the ear can be suitably rested for boring; *and his master shall bore his ear through with an awl,* in order to mark it with the sign of servitude, because from now on he will be a slave in the full sense of the word (the Ḥammurabi Code rules that the ear of a slave who rebelled against his master was to be cut off); *and he shall serve him for ever,* that is, all the days of his life (compare in Ugaritic *dʿlm,* 'of ever', that is, an everlasting slave).

In this paragraph, after the principal case that is introduced by the word כִּי *kī* ['when', 'if'], four secondary cases are cited, prefaced by אִם *'im* ['if'] or וְאִם *wᵉ'im* ['and if']. The same, we shall find, obtains in the next paragraph.

SECOND PARAGRAPH

THE LAWS OF THE BONDWOMAN

(XXI 7–11)

According to later Jewish law, this paragraph appertains to a minor, and states the laws governing her case in detail. The original meaning of the passage, however, appears to be as follows:
7 *And when a man,* an Israelite, *sells his daughter* — who was not

EXODUS XXI 7

born a Hebrew slave, but was free till now — *as a bondwoman in the house of another Israelite, she shall not be subject to the same law as for male slaves, and therefore she shall not go out as do the male slaves*, spoken of in the previous paragraph. This statute was enacted for the benefit of the girl; since the bondwoman is not just a servant, but also becomes the concubine of her master or of one of his sons, her status is that of a married woman, and as such she is permitted to remain in her husband's house all her life just like her mistress, the legal wife in the full sense of the term. The Torah took pity on her and granted her a greater privilege than that of manumission at the end of a given time (according to the Code of Ḥammurabi, as we have seen, the girl is set free, in such circumstances, after three years).

8 If a man finds some indecency in his legal wife, he is permitted to write her a bill of divorce and to send her out of his house (Deut. xxiv 1), but the girl under consideration, since she was not legally married, does not require a divorce. Therefore, *if* her master finds her indecent, and *she does not please her master, who has designated her for himself* (the K^{e}thībh* is לֹא *lō'* [which normally, but not here, means 'not'], but the Q^{e}re** is לוֹ *lō*['for him(self)']; for the K^{e}thibh לֹא *lō'*, with an 'Āleph, that is, for the use of the letter 'Āleph as the sign of a long final vowel, compare the spelling in the Dead Sea Scrolls), that is, he appointed her as a concubine for himself, *then he shall let her be redeemed* — he shall permit her to redeem herself and go free, and this alone shall be the way of terminating the relations between them. He shall not be able to sell her to strangers: *to a foreign people*, that is, to a strange family (the word עַם *'am* ['people'] is used here in an archaic significance) *he shall have no power* [literally, 'dominion'] *to sell her, thus dealing faithlessly with her*, because such selling would be an act of treachery towards one whom he took to wife. An ethical reason is given here for the Torah statute.

9 And if he does not appoint her for himself, but *he designates her for his son, he shall deal with her as with a daughter* — she shall be in his house, as one of the daughters of the family.

10 If her master, after appointing her for himself, *takes another wife to himself* in addition to her, he is not permitted to infringe the rights of the concubine whom he took to himself first; and, therefore, *he shall not diminish her food* [שְׁאֵרָהּ *š^{e}ērāh*, literally,

---

* The text as it is *written*.
** The marginal Masoretic recommendation that is *to be read*.

'her flesh'], *her clothing or her quarters* [עֹנָתָהּ *'ōnāthah*] — he shall not reduce her food [*še'ērāh* is apparently an old term for food, connected with the ancient custom among nomads of making meat their staple diet; compare Arabic لحم *laḥm* = 'flesh' [whilst in Hebrew לֶחֶם *leḥem* = 'bread']), or her raiment, or the conditions of her abode (this appears to be the real meaning of the word *'ōnāthah*, and not as later tradition interpreted it: times of cohabitation).

11   *And if these three things* — the normal food, clothing and quarters — *he* — the man who designated her for himself — *does not do for her* [i.e. give her], and thereby breaks his obligations to her, his right as her husband is annulled, *and she shall go out for nothing, without payment of money.*

This paragraph, which has been placed here, after the paragraph dealing with the Hebrew slave, on account of the similarity of themes, also begins by stating a principal case, commencing with the word וְכִי *wᵉkhī* ['And when'], and thereafter there are cited here, too, four secondary cases, introduced by the word אִם *'im* ['If'] or וְאִם *wᵉ'im* ['And if']. In all there are ten subsections on the laws of slavery in these two paragraphs, a number that aids memorization, like the number of the Ten Words (Decalogue).

THIRD PARAGRAPH

CAPITAL OFFENCES

(XXI 12–17)

The Torah wishes to affirm and establish the principle, in the name of Divine law, that human life is sacred, and whoever assails this sanctity forfeits his own life — measure for measure. This principle is linked to a religious concept referred to already in Gen. ix 6: 'Whoever sheds the blood of man, by man shall his blood be shed; for in the image of God was man made.' Conformably with this
12 maxim, the Torah prescribes here in legal form: *Whoever strikes a man so that he dies shall be put to death.* However, the life of the slayer is also sacred, and therefore it is forbidden to put him to death if he took his fellow's life unintentionally, an accident having
13 occurred: *But if he did not lie in wait*, that is, he did not attack

with the intent to kill (i Sam. xxiv 11: 'though you lie in wait for my life to take it'; compare also the legal term 'lying in wait' in Num. xxxv 20–25), *but God*, the impersonal Godhead (the text does not read: 'and I'), that is, fate, chance, something that is beyond human control (similar expressions are also found in the Code of Ḥammurabi, for instance, in § 249), *brought him opportunely into his hand* — an expression implying an accident — *then I will appoint for you a place to which he may flee*, and there he will be secure from the vengeance of the avenger of blood. The Torah's purpose is to amend the primitive practice of blood vengeance, and also to oppose the principle reflected in the Code of Ḥammurabi, § 229, according to which one who causes the death of another, even unintentionally, must be put to death. But let it be clear that the refuge can protect only one who killed unwittingly; but no place of asylum, even the sanctuary precincts, can save one who

14 killed purposely: *But if* (the initial *Wāw* in the Hebrew is antithetic) *a man willfully attacks another to kill him with* עָרְמָה *ʿormā*, that is, with prior intent (possibly our word is to be connected with the word עָרְמָה *ʿormā* in Prov. viii 5, 12, the meaning of which approximates to 'understanding' [usually rendered: 'prudence']; or it may be linked with the Arabic stem عرم *ʿrm*, which means 'to be an enemy', or 'to have evil intentions against someone'; compare the word *enmity* in the parallel passage in Num. xxxv 21–22; and *ibid. v.* 23: 'though he was not his enemy, and did not seek his harm'), even *from my altar you shall take him, that he may die*. It was a widespread custom, both in Eastern and Western countries, and accepted also in Israelite usage (i Kings ii 28 ff.; see on this point above, p. 261), that whoever entered a sacred place was saved from all punishment, even if he had killed a person willfully. The Torah abolishes this practice in the case of deliberate murder; the sanctity of the temple cannot override the sanctity of human life.

15 *Whoever strikes his father and mother*, that is, his father or his mother, even if the assault is not fatal, so that the case does not come under the ruling of *v.* 12 (here it is not stated, as above: 'so that he dies') *he shall surely be put to death*. In § 195 of the Code of Ḥammurabi it is ordained that he who strikes his father should have his hands cut off. The Torah, which sets greater store by the precept of honouring father and mother, is stricter in its legislation, by including the mother as well as the father and by the penalty it imposes. See also *v.* 17.

16 *Whoever steals a man and sells him, or* — the same applies if,

EXODUS XXI 17

when a person steals a man — *he is found in his possession* (the meaning of the *Wāw* of וְנִמְצָא *wᵉnimṣā'* [literally, 'and he is found'] is the same as that of the *Wāw* of וְאִמּוֹ *wᵉ'immō* ['and his mother'] in v. 15 and v. 17 [i.e. it connotes 'or']) *shall surely be put to death*. It was necessary for this law to be confirmed by the Torah, because such an incident is related concerning Joseph's brethren, and one might possibly have thought that the Torah did not take a severe view of such an offence.

7 Finally, the penalty of death is laid down even for a minor offence against one's father or mother: *Whoever dishonours* [מְקַלֵּל *mᵉqallēl*, usually rendered: 'curses'] *his father or his mother shall surely be put to death* (compare Lev. xx 9; Prov. xx 20; xxx 11). The word מְקַלֵּל *mᵉqallēl* does not connote here specifically cursing. The original signification of the stem קלל *qālal* is the opposite of כבד *kābhēdh* with reference to weight [the former stem means 'to be light', the latter 'to be heavy']. Also in their figurative sense the two stems are antonyms. Compare, for example, i Sam. ii 30: 'for those who honour me I will honour [אֲכַבֵּד *'ăkhabbēdh*], and those who despise me shall be lightly esteemed [יֵקַלּוּ *yēqāllū*];' or ii Sam. vi 22: 'I will make myself yet more contemptible [וּנְקַלֹּתִי *unᵉqallōthī*] than this... I shall be held in honour [אִכָּבֵדָה *'ikkābhē-dhā*].' In Ugaritic texts the stem *qll* is commonly found in parallelism with the stem *kbd* to denote the conduct of one who *humbles himself* and bows down before a great god and *honours* him. It appears, therefore, that this verse applies the term 'מְקַלֵּל *mᵉqallēl* [rendered: 'whoever dishonours'] his father or his mother' to one who commits any act contrary to the honour due to parents.

In this paragraph are enumerated five cases carrying the penalty of death, beginning with the gravest crime: (a) whoever strikes a man so that he dies; (b) the law applies even if the assailant seeks refuge in the precincts of the sanctuary; (c) whoever strikes his father or mother; (d) whoever steals a man; (e) whoever dishonours his father or mother. In the next paragraph five cases of bodily injury will be cited, the first of which is connected with the present paragraph, namely, the case of the one who strikes another and the victim does not die but keeps his bed.

Just as the laws of slavery were placed at the head of the ordinances as a parallel to the commencement of the Decalogue (*out of the house of bondage*), so the laws of murder come after them to correspond to the beginning of the second part of the Decalogue (*you shall not kill*).

FOURTH PARAGRAPH

LAWS APPERTAINING TO BODILY INJURIES

(XXI 18–27)

18 The first law begins: *And when men quarrel*, but the quarrel is not the primary consideration; the main point is, *and one strikes the other*, only the statute pictures the case as it normally happens, and as a rule one person does not hit another unless they have a dispute. With whatever it is that he strikes him, *with a stone or with his fist*, that is, with weapons or with his hands alone (the word *stone* is apparently an archaic expression, which remained unchanged since the period in which weapons were made of flint), if the assault does not cause a fatality, *and* the injured person *does not die, but* becomes ill as a result of his wound and *keeps*
19 *his bed*, if after a time *he rises again* from his bed *and walks abroad*, be it even *with his staff* only, and *a fortiori* if he completely recovers, *then he that struck him shall be exempt* from capital punishment, and shall *only* be liable to pay for his injury, that means, for the loss of time and medical attention: *he shall pay for the loss of his time, and shall have him thoroughly healed*.

Since the penalty of the assailant is only to pay for the enforced idleness and medical care, no distinction is made between the one who strikes wittingly and the one who does so unwittingly; even he that acted unwittingly does not discharge his liability with less. Furthermore, at the time of the quarrel it is difficult even for the two contestants to distinguish between intentional and unintentional injury, and for the judge it is even harder to differentiate between the two after a lapse of time. In the Hittite Laws, § 10, it is ordained, without any distinction between wilful and unwitting injury, that if one man hits another and the victim keeps his bed, the assailant is obliged to provide the one who was struck with a person who shall work in his stead until he recovers, and to pay the cost of healing, as well as a fine of six shekels of silver. In § 206 of the Ḥammurabi Code the penalty of payment for healing is imposed if the assailant swears that he had no intention to cause an injury. The text reads as follows: 'And if a man shall strike another in a quarrel and wound him, he shall swear that he struck him unintentionally and he shall pay the doctor.'

20 *And when a man strikes his male or female slave with a rod*, the

customary instrument for punishing slaves, *and he dies* immediately as a result of the beating *under his hand, he shall surely be punished*. The slave, too, is a human being, he, too, was created in the Divine image, and whoever assails the sanctity of his life shall be answerable for it and be put to death. This is an important innovation introduced by the Torah: the law that declares (v. 12): 'Whoever strikes a man so that he dies shall be put to death', applies even to one who beats his slave. This law is stated here in order to

21 mention an exception to it: *But if* the beating with the rod did not kill the slave under the hand of his master, and the slave *survives a day or two, he is not to be punished* — his master is not to be put to death. His master is also a human being, and his life must also be protected if absolute justice does not demand the forfeiture of his life; now this man did not actually kill his slave, but only caused his death indirectly, and he has already received material punishment through the loss of his property, *for he*, the slave, *is his money*. Therefore, he shall not be put to death. The expression *a day or two* means 'a day or more'; it was necessary, however, to add the words *or two*, for if the text had only *a day*, one might have thought that if he survives more than a day he shall surely be punished (a similar example is found in Deut. xix 15: 'only on the evidence of two witnesses, or of three witnesses, shall a charge be sustained').

When two men quarrel and seek to strike each other, it may happen accidentally that by their impetuous and violent movements they will push and hurt someone else. If another man is hurt, the one who caused the injury is, in general, subject to the same law as one who strikes his opponent in a quarrel, in accordance with the provisions of *vv.* 18–19. But possibly the injury will be of a particular kind, of a type commonly dealt with in the legal tradition of the ancient East, to wit, injury inflicted on a woman with child, which causes a miscarriage.

A number of laws on this subject are found in the law-codes of the neighbouring peoples. These are, as far as we know today, as follows:

(a) In the excerpts of Sumerian laws, published by A. T. Clay in 1915, there occur two clauses that prescribe the penalty for one who hurts (apparently accidentally) and for one who strikes (apparently intentionally) a woman with child, so that there is a miscarriage. The penalty is to be a monetary payment: ten shekels in the first case, and a third of a mina in the second instance.

It is not stated expressly to whom he must pay this money, but it is clear, that he has to pay it to the woman's husband.

(b) According to the Code of Ḥammurabi, § 209–210, the assailant is obliged, if the woman is a lady, a seignior's daughter, to pay ten shekels for the fetus; and if the woman dies as a result of the beating, the daughter of the offender shall be put to death. According to § 211–214, the one who strikes, if the woman belongs to the social class of the *muškēnum* [rendered in ANET, p. 175, 'commoner'], or if she is a bondwoman, is liable to a monetary payment, even if she dies from the assault.

(c) The Middle Assyrian Laws (§ 21) ordain that if the woman is a lady, the punishment of the assailant shall not be merely a monetary payment but also a flogging and a month's labour in the king's service. This clause speaks only of miscarriage, but makes no reference to the case where the woman dies. In § 50 it is prescribed that if the woman is a commoner, [the wife of the assailant] shall be treated (so it appears that the lacuna in the tablet has to be completed) as he treated her, and he shall compensate (if the fetus dies; so I think it should be interpreted) with 'life' for the fetus; and if the woman dies, the assailant shall be put to death, and he shall compensate (if the fetus also dies, according to my interpretation) with 'life' for the fetus. In the continuation of this clause and in § 51–52, several special cases are dealt with, but the meaning of the details is in dispute (*inter alia*, a certain distinction is made between a male and a female fetus), but this is not the place to enter into these problems.

(d) § 17–18 of the Hittite Laws impose on the one who strikes a monetary penalty for miscarriage. The case where the woman dies is not mentioned there.

In the Pentateuch there is no special law referring to the case of one who strikes a pregnant woman wilfully. Nor was there any need for it, since this contingency is included in the injunction of *v.* 12, if the woman dies, and in the case described in *vv.* 18–19, if she does not die but keeps her bed. Only the law of the one who strikes a woman with child unintentionally is stated, in order to introduce innovations and amendments in it. These innovations and amendments are as follows:

(a) No differentiation is to be made on the basis of the social class of the woman; all human beings are equal.

(b) The punishment is to be inflicted only on the man who causes the injury, but not on any one else; his daughter or his wife is not to be punished for his deed, as the Mesopotamian laws ordained. (c) The penalty of the offender is to be determined according to the Torah principles. We shall deal with this point later in the detailed annotations on the formulation of the passage.

22 The statute commences, *And when men strive together*, etc., in order to give an example of accidental injury to a pregnant woman, and here, too, as we saw above, the law presents the case realistically. Details follow: *and they hurt* unintentionally *a woman with child* — the sense is, that one of the combatants, whichever of them it be (for this reason the verb translated 'and they hurt' is in the plural) is responsible — *and her children come forth* [i.e. there is a miscarriage] on account of the hurt she suffers (irrespective of the nature of the fetus, be it male or female, one or two; hence here, too, there is a generic plural as in the case of the verb 'they hurt'), *but no mischief happens* — that is, the woman and the children do not die — the one who hurt her *shall surely be punished* by a fine, *according as the woman's husband shall lay* — impose — *upon him*, having regard to the extent of the injuries and the special circumstances of the accident; *and he* who caused the hurt *shall pay* the amount of the fine to the woman's husband *with judges*, in accordance with the decision of the court that will confirm the husband's claim and compel the offender to pay compensation, for it is impossible to leave the determination of the amount of the fine to the discretion of the husband, and, on the other hand, it is not within the husband's power to compel the assailant to pay

23 if he refuses. *But if any mischief happen*, that is, if the woman dies or the children die, *then you shall give life for life, eye for eye*, etc.: you, O judge (or you, O Israel, through the judge who represents you) shall adopt the principle of 'life for life', etc.

This principle implies, according to the Rabbis, that one who takes a life must pay the value of the life, and one who blinds an eye must pay the value of the eye, and so forth, and the apologetically inclined commentators have endeavoured to show that this was the meaning of this formula even in ancient Hebrew. But this is impossible. It is not feasible that the meaning of the word 'eye' should be 'the value of the eye'. Undoubtedly this formula denotes the archaic legal principle called in Roman law *talio*: 'as he has disfigured a man, he shall be disfigured' (Lev. xxiv 20). This archaic doctrine, which is based on the view that the punishment must fit the crime, measure for measure, is still reflected in the Code of Ḥammurabi, which ordains, for instance, in § 196: 'if a seignior destroy the eye of a seignior, his own eye shall be destroyed'; and in § 200: 'If a seignior knock out the tooth of a seignior of his own rank, his tooth shall be knocked out.' Only if the victim belongs to the class of *muškēnum* ['a commoner'] does the law of Hammurabi impose upon him only the payment of a mina of silver for the blinding of an eye (§ 198), or a third of a mina for the loss of the tooth (§ 201). But already in the Code of Ešnunna, which is earlier than that of Hammurabi, mention is made only of monetary compensation — a mina of silver for destroying an eye, and half a mina for knocking out a tooth (§ 42) — and not of corporal punishment. The Hittite Laws also prescribe only fines (§ 7 f.). Here, in the Book of Exodus, the *talio* formula is used as in the ordinances of the Hammurabi Laws that pertain to the striking of a member of the aristocratic class. But two difficulties arise:

(a) It is incomprehensible why one who hurts a pregnant woman accidentally should be liable to the death penalty in the case of a fatality, although earlier, in *v.* 13, it was stated that whoever killed a person unintentionally is not to be put to death.

(b) It is strange that in the law concerning the person who injures a woman with child mention should be made of eye, and tooth, and foot, and burn, and wound, and stripe, which are not germane to our theme. To solve the second problem, it is necessary to assume that a stereotyped formula is cited here, and since the first part of it, which bears on the case of a fatality — *life for life* — has been quoted, the formula is given in its entirety. This premise enables us also to find a way of solving the first problem. If this wording is stereotyped, we may take it for granted that it is an ancient formula that at first actually expressed the principle of *talio* in its literal sense, and it remained crystallized in its original form even after the introduction, in the course of the development of the legal tradition, of the reform found in the laws of Ešnunna and in the Hittite Code, and monetary compensation took the place of the ancient corporal punishment. The case is similar to what we have already noted in regard to other archaic expressions that were preserved in the legal phraseology, like *flesh* (*v.* 10), which signifies food in general, or *stone*, which (*v.* 18) denotes all kinds of weapons. The payment is a form of ransom that takes the place of the bodily punishment prescribed by the ancient system. It is what is called in legal terminology a settlement, that is, a compromise arrangement made by the two sides between themselves, generally with the confirmation of the court. Theoretically, he who blinds another's eye should be sentenced to have his own blinded; only he is permitted to give a ransom in order to save his eye. According to Num. xxxv 31 it is only from a wilful murderer that it is forbidden to accept ransom; this implies that in all other instances the taking of a ransom is permitted. So apparently we have to understand, in the Assyrian laws cited above, the payment of 'life' (literally, 'lives'; the plural has a singular meaning, to wit, 'a life'), for if the assailant is put to death because the woman who was struck died, it is impossible to add thereto that the offender should die a second time for the death of the fetus; thus the meaning of the 'life' that he has to pay for the death of the fetus can only be this, that before he is executed on account of the woman's death, he must pay her husband the value of the life of the fetus. Possibly the intention of the Ḥammurabi laws is to stress that for blinding the eye of a 'man' [rendered above: 'seignior'] of the upper class, or for knocking out his tooth, it is not sufficient to pay merely the amount given in compensation for a similar injury done to a *muškēnum* ['commoner'], and rightly the one who causes the injury should lose his own eye or tooth, and if he wishes to give a ransom, he must give a much bigger ransom, whatever is laid upon him. I shall deal with the other parallel passages in the Pentateuch, when, *Deo volente*, I come to them. I would only note at this stage that also in Deut. xix 21, in the law of false witnesses who are subject to the law of retaliation, we find the full formula: 'it shall be life for life, eye for eye, tooth for tooth, hand for hand, foot for foot', although bodily injuries are not spoken of there; but since the beginning of the formula was cited — *life for life* — the whole formula is quoted verbatim, and its purport is simply that the punishment that was due to be meted out to the accused should be imposed on the false witnesses.

This being so, the meaning here in our paragraph of the expression *life for life* is that the one who hurts the woman accidentally shall be obliged to pay her husband the value of her life if she dies, and of her children if they die. The citation of the opening words of the formula drew after it the entire continuation, although not

24 germane to our subject: *eye for eye*, *tooth for tooth* (these two organs are specifically mentioned, as a rule, in the legal tradition of the
25 East), *hand for hand, foot for foot, burn for burn, wound for wound, stripe for stripe*.

Since eye and tooth were mentioned in *v*. 24, the law of the liberation of the slave on account of his eye and tooth is stated at this

26 point: *And when a man strikes the eye of his bondman or the eye of his bondwoman, and destroys it, he shall let the slave go free for his eye's sake.* In § 199 of the Ḥammurabi's Code it is written that if a man destroy the eye of another man's slave, he shall pay [his master] half the price [of the slave]. A similar penalty is prescribed in the Hittite Laws, § 8, for one who strikes another man's slave. In neither of these two codes is anything said with regard to one who blinds the eye of his own slave; apparently, they did not ordain any punishment for such a person, in addition to the loss he caused himself by reducing the value of his slave. But the Torah took pity on the slave: if his master strikes his eye and destroys it, the assailant shall be punished in that his slave shall go free, for nothing. And not only for the loss of an important organ like an eye shall the slave go free, but even for the loss of one
27 tooth: *And if he knocks out the tooth of his bondman, or the tooth of his bondwoman, he shall let him go free for his tooth's sake.* This statute is sufficient to ensure that slave owners take care not to beat their slaves ruthlessly.

The paragraph contains five cases of bodily injury caused by beating (*vv.* 18–19, 20–21; 22–25; 26; 27), just as the previous paragraph comprised five cases of capital offences. In all they constitute a series of ten cases, a number intended to assist the memory, as we stated before.

FIFTH PARAGRAPH

THE OX AND THE PIT

(XXI 28–36)

In the legal tradition of the ancient East, goring by an ox was the typical example of damage caused by cattle or domestic animals. In the ancient laws of Ešnunna there is mentioned, together with this case, the instance of a person being bitten by a mad dog. In the Code of Ḥammurabi only goring by an ox is cited; and the same obtains in the Torah, which deals with the subject in order to make certain amendments to the law.

28   *And when an ox gores a man* (although the word *man* is not defined, it is preceded by the particle אֶת *'eth* [sign of the definite accusative],

EXODUS XXI 30

in order that we should not construe the words to mean: 'an ox of a man') *or a woman, and* the man or the woman *dies, the ox shall surely be stoned* (a Biblical innovation, according to the principle in Gen. ix 5: 'and surely for your own blood I will require a reckoning; of every beast I will require it'), *and its flesh shall not be eaten* (the prohibition of food on religious grounds is also something new); *but the owner of the ox shall be clear*. Also in the laws of Ḥammurabi, § 250, there is no claim, in such an instance, against the owner of the ox. On the use of the particle אֶת *'eth* in a passive clause (יֵאָכֵל אֶת *yē'ākhēl 'eth* 'shall… be eaten'), see also xxvii 7.

All this applies to an ox that is not a habitual gorer. But if the ox has been accustomed to gore, the responsibility rests on the owner, if he did not take precautions with regard to it. In the Code of Ešnunna, where no mention is made of an ox that gores for the first time, it is stated in § 54: 'If the ox is known to gore habitually, and the authorities have warned the owner, but he did not cut off its horns, and it gored a man and killed him, the owner of the ox shall pay two thirds of a mina of silver.' A similar enactment is found in § 251 of the laws of Ḥammurabi: 'If a seignior's ox was a gorer, and the village elders informed [the owner] that it was a gorer, but he did not cut off its horns or tie up his ox, and that ox gored the son of a seignior (the reference, apparently, is to any freeman) and killed him, he shall give one-half mina of silver.' The case of an ox that gored a slave is dealt with in § 252; see on this below. The Torah employs the traditional terminology in describing the case, but determines the penalty according to

29 its own principles: *But if the ox has been accustomed to gore in the past*, that means, it has already gored but has not killed any one, and therefore was left alive, *and its owner has been warned by the authorities, and he did not take precautions with regard to it* [literally, 'and he did not keep it'] in one of the ways indicated in the aforementioned laws, that is, he did not dehorn it or tie it up (compare Baba Qamma iv 9: 'if its owner tied it [the animal, to a fence] by the reins') *and it kills a man or a woman, the ox shall be stoned*, in accordance with the principle enunciated in Gen. ix 5, *and its owner shall also be put to death*, that means, since he is responsible for the death of a person, rightly he should die, as stated in Gen. ix 6, but, since he did not cause his death wil-

30 fully, he may redeem himself by a ransom: *If a ransom is laid on him, then he shall give for the redemption of his life whatever is laid upon him by the order of the court.*

279

EXODUS XXI 31

31   Verse 31, *whether it* — the habitual gorer — *gores a son, or it gores a daughter, he shall be dealt with according to this same rule*, seeks to abolish the legal tradition that demanded that, if a man caused the death of another man's son, his own son should be put to death (see, for example, § 230 of the Code of Ḥammurabi, which ordains that if a builder erects a house and the building collapses and kills the owner's son, the builder's son shall be put to death).

32   *If the ox* — a habitual gorer — *gores a bondman or a bondwoman, the owner of the ox shall give thirty shekels of silver to his master*, that is, he shall give to the master of the bondman or bondwoman the usual price of a slave as compensation. This corresponds to § 252 of the Ḥammurabi Code, which prescribes in such a case the payment of one-third mina of silver to the slave's master. *And the ox shall be stoned*, in accordance with the rule laid down in Gen. ix 5, because the slaves, too, were created in the Divine image.

Also the case of the pit, as a typical exemplar of damage, is commonly found in the legal tradition of the ancient East (the Hittite Laws, § 146–147; the Neo-Babylonian Laws, § 3), but so far no statute has been found concerning the case of an ox or an
33   ass that fell into a pit, except in the Bible. *And when a man leaves a pit open* — a pit that has already been dug, which he fails to cover after opening it — *or when a man digs a* new *pit and does not cover* it, *and there falls into it* a domestic animal, such as
34   *an ox or an ass*, and dies, then *the owner of the pit shall pay* the price of the animal that died; *he shall give back money to its owner* in lieu of the ox or the ass, *and the dead beast shall be his*, and thus he will be paying full compensation, which is the difference between the price of the living animal and that of the carcass. It is impossible to tell whether the Torah has introduced any innovation here, or it simply comes to confirm the existing law, since there is no known parallel to this particular statute.

35   But there exists an exact parallel to *v.* 35: *When one man's ox hurts another, and it* — the injured ox — *dies*, then *they shall sell the live ox and divide the price of it; and the dead beast also they shall divide*, and in this way the owner of the ox that gored will pay for half the damage. The Pentateuch confirms here the tradition known to us from § 53 of the Laws of Ešnunna: 'When an ox gores another ox and kills it, both ox owners shall divide the price of the ox and also the value of the dead ox.' The law of the ox that

EXODUS XXII 1 [Heb. XXI 37]

gores habitually is found in the above-mentioned Mesopotamian laws only in the case where the death of a human being has been caused; but the Torah differentiates between an ox that does not habitually gore and a habitual gorer even in the case of one ox goring another. *Or it is known* — that is, but if it is known (similar terms are used also in the Laws of Ešnunna in regard to the habitual gorer) *that the ox has been accustomed to gore in the past* — its master being aware of the fact — *and its owner did not take precautions with regard to it* [literally, 'and he did not keep it'], in one of the ways mentioned earlier, its master *shall surely pay ox for ox* (this formula, too, — 'ox for ox' — occurs frequently in the legal tradition of the East in connection with injuries involving cattle), *and the dead beast shall be his*, that is, he shall pay full compensation.

In this paragraph we have first a series of five cases in connection with an ox that gores a man (*vv.* 28-32), like the groups of five statutes in the preceding paragraphs, and then a series of three cases in which an ox is the victim (*vv.* 33-36). The verses of the second series are linked together by the repetition of the expression *and the dead beast shall be his* at the end of *v.* 34 and the end of *v.* 36. There is also a parallelism between the series of five cases and the series of three: [the owner] *shall give thirty shekels of silver to his master* (*v.* 32) — *he shall give back money* [literally, 'silver'] (*v.* 34).

Our paragraph was placed here on account of the parallelism between it and the preceding paragraph. In the latter, in *v.* 22, it is stated: *according as the woman's husband shall lay upon him, and he shall pay* [literally, 'give'] *as the judges determine*; and in our paragraph, in *v.* 30, it is written: If *a ransom is laid upon him, then he shall give for the redemption of his life whatever is laid upon him.*

SIXTH PARAGRAPH

LAWS OF THEFT

(XXII 1-4 [Hebrew, XXI 37-XXII 3])

The Torah cites these laws in order to oppose the system of the legal tradition reflected in the laws of Ḥammurabi, according to which a thief was sentenced to death if he had not the means to pay

EXODUS XXII 1 [Heb. XXI 37]

(Code of Ḥammurabi, § 8), or if he stole by breaking in (*ibid.*, § 21). In accordance with the principle of the sanctity of human life, the Torah had compassion on the thief's life. It annulled the penalty of death in the case of the thief who was unable to pay, and substituted for it the penalty of being sold into slavery. It also protected the thief found breaking in, and limited this protection only out of its even more justified concern for the life of the owner.

Chapter XXII

1 [37] *When a man steals an ox or a sheep, and kills it or sells it*, and hence the stolen beast is no longer found in his possession when he is caught, he must pay a bigger fine than the twofold restitution that is imposed on him, if the theft is found in his possession (xxii 4 [Hebrew, *v.* 3]). The reason for the distinction is possibly this: if the owner of the animal is able to recover his own beast, which is dear to him, it is sufficient for the thief to add another beast like it, but if the thief is unable to restore the stolen animal, he must give the owner additional compensation. *He shall pay five oxen for an ox, and four sheep for a sheep* — less for a sheep than for an ox, possibly because the rearing of sheep does not require so much, or such prolonged, effort as the rearing of herds.

The logical continuation of *v.* 1 [Hebrew, xxi 37] is *v.* 4 [Hebrew, *v.* 3], which prescribes the penalty for stealing a beast, if it is found in the thief's possession, that is, if he neither killed nor sold it. If the Torah's purpose were to draw up a code of laws, we should have to assume that the verses here are in disorder. But in the light of my explanation that the legal sections of the Pentateuch are only religious and ethical directions on judicial subjects, it is possible to understand the order of the verses before us. The Torah cites in the first verse and in the last verse of the paragraph the provisions of the existing Israelite law, and in the middle, immediately after beginning to state the laws of theft, it interpolates its directives, which are intended to protect both the life of the house owner and the life of the thief, in accordance with the Torah's principles.

2 [1] These directives commence: *If a thief is found digging through*, at night-time, *and he is struck so that he dies, there shall be no bloodguilt for him* — for the householder who killed him, for it is a rightful presumption that a thief caught breaking into premises is prepared to murder the owner in order to save himself; hence if the owner struck him it was only an act of self-defence. But, 3 [2] on the other hand, *if the sun has risen upon him*, that is, the thief

EXODUS XXII 4 [Heb. 3]

was caught in the day-time, it can be taken for granted that the proprietor was not in danger and he had no need to kill in order to protect himself, and therefore *there shall be bloodguilt for him* — the householder — and he is deemed a murderer. It is self-understood, that if witnesses were to testify that the killing in the night was not necessary, or was necessary in the day-time, the law would be different; only the Bible presents the case in usual circumstances. In order to protect the householder's life, it declares that he does not commit a capital offence if he kills the thief that is found breaking in at night; and in order to protect the thief's life, it prescribes that if the owner kills him in the day-time, he shall be regarded as a murderer. The penalty of the thief who is caught during the day, even if he is found breaking in, shall only be that *he shall surely pay*, but on no account is he to be put to death; *if he has not* sufficient to pay, *then he shall be sold for his theft*, and with the price paid for him shall be paid the sum imposed on him; but in this case, too, he shall not be sentenced to death.

After the explanatory notes, which are given, as it were, in parenthesis, comes the second part of the law, which apparently antedated the Torah, namely, the continuation of *v*. 1 [Hebrew, xxi 37]:

4 [3] *If the theft is found in his possession*, that is, the stolen beast, irrespective of what animal it is, *whether it is an ox or an ass or a sheep*, provided only it is still *alive, he shall pay double*, that is, what he has stolen and another like it. The law of twofold payment for the theft of chattels is referred to incidentally later on, in *v*. 7 [Hebrew, *v*. 6].

This paragraph, too, contains a group of five cases: the first case, with which the subject opens and which is introduced by the word כִּי *kī* ['when']; and thereafter four special instances, each of which is prefaced by the word אִם *'im* ['if'].

The parallelism with the preceding paragraph is discernible in the mention of ox, sheep and ass, and in the recurrence of the expression *he shall pay*.

SEVENTH PARAGRAPH

DAMAGE BY GRAZING AND BURNINNG

(XXII 5–6 [Hebrew vv. 4–5])

The two subjects dealt with in this paragraph are also juxtaposed in the Hittite Code (§ 105–107), and possibly they were linked together in the legal tradition. There is clearly noticeable here a word-play in the use of the verb בָּעַר *bāʿar* in two different senses ['graze' and 'burn'] and in its proximity to the substantive בְּעִיר *bᵉʿīr* ['cattle', 'beast']. Although it is possible that the sages of the Mishnah read יַבְעֶה *yabhʿe* for יַבְעֶר *yabhʿer* [both verbs meaning: 'causes to be grazed over'] in v. 5 [Hebrew, v. 4], and hence the derivation of the term מַבְעֶה *mabhʿe* ['damage done to crops'], which is commonly used in Mishnaic Hebrew (compare also the continuation of the verse in the Samaritan recension), yet there is, in any case, a great similarity also in the sound of the two verbs בָּעָה בָּעַר *bāʿā* and *bāʿar*. The use of word-plays, which will be found again in other parts of these laws (see in the Hebrew, xxii 9, 12, 24; xxiii 2, 5), was intended to aid the memory.

5 [4] After the opening clause, *When a man causes a field or vineyard to be grazed over*, the text itself explains the meaning of the verb יַבְעֶר *yabhʿer* [rendered: 'causes to be grazed over'], to wit, *or lets his beast loose* (the initial *Wāw*, translated 'or', is explicative) — that is, lets his sheep or his herd loose (accordingly, the verb יַבְעֶר *yabhʿer* is either a denominative from the noun בְּעִיר *bᵉʿīr* ['beast'], or the causative conjugation [*Hiphʿīl*] from the stem בָּעַר *bāʿar*, which in the intensive conjugation [*Piʿēl*] signifies 'to lick up, eat grass') and the cattle feeds *in the field of another* man (according to rabbinic exegesis, the verb וְשִׁלַּח *wᵉšillaḥ* ['and lets loose'] implies damage by the animal's foot [i.e. trampling], while the verb בָּעַר *biʿēr*, which follows, refers to damage by the tooth [i.e. grazing]), *he shall make restitution from the best of his own field and of his own vineyard* to the owner of the field that was damaged. Hittite law (§ 107) imposes on the owner monetary payment, whilst the Ḥammurabi Code (§ 57) enjoins compensation in kind. The Torah regards the subject not only from the legal aspect but also, and particularly, from the ethical point of view, in keeping with the words of the prophet (Isa. iii 14): 'It is you who have devoured the vineyard, the spoil of the poor is in your houses', and insists

EXODUS XXII 7 [Heb. 6]

that in this case, too, the punishment should be in accordance with the principle of measure for measure, and that the penalty should be severe; restitution must be made from the choice land, from the best part of the field and the best part of the vineyard of the one responsible for the damage.

Since the Torah cites this law, it also mentions the law relating to one who kindles a fire, which is connected with the preceding ordinance by virtue of the similarity of theme and vocabulary:

6 [5] *When fire breaks out* from the place where it was kindled, *and catches in thorns*, which easily burn, and spreads to another man's field, *so that stacked grain or the standing grain or the field is consumed*, the man *who kindled the fire* in his own property, and did not take care to prevent its spreading, *shall make full restitution* for the damage.

In this paragraph, too, a formal parallelism is to be discerned with preceding paragraphs, created by the expressions, *shall pay — shall surely pay* [also rendered: 'shall make full restitution'].

EIGHTH PARAGRAPH

FOUR CLASSES OF BAILEES

(XXII 7–15 [Hebrew *vv.* 6–14])

According to the plain meaning of the text, the Torah does not expressly differentiate between an unpaid and a paid bailee, as later Jewish law, in the period of the Talmud, does. It distinguishes only between the custody of articles and that of cattle. But this very differentiation shows that the rabbinic view, which interprets *vv.* 7 f. [Hebrew, *vv.* 6 f.] to refer to an unpaid custodian and *v.* 10 [Hebrew, *v.* 9] to a paid keeper, agrees essentially with the actual sense of the passage, for generally one who has charge of articles receives no pay, since such custody does not entail exertion, whereas one who looks after cattle is, as a rule, a shepherd, who is paid for his continuous labour.

The Torah cites these ordinances in order to introduce changes, as we shall see later, with regard to the law of lost property, which is connected with that of custody.

7 [6] · The first case: *When a man delivers to his neighbour money or*

285

EXODUS XXII 7 [Heb. 6]

goods to keep, and the deposit *is stolen out of the house of the man* with whom it was left, *if the thief is found, he* — the thief — *shall pay double* to the owner of the articles stolen, in conformity with the penalty prescribed in v. 4 [Hebrew, v. 3] with regard to the theft of cattle. But *if the thief is not found*, and consequently the depositor cannot receive twofold compensation, *then the owner of the house*, that is, the depositary, who is thus designated, *bêl bîtim*, also in the Code of Ḥammurabi (§ 125), *shall come near to God* (for the signification of this expression see above, on xxi 6), in order to take an oath and thereby be exempt from any payment, *if* it is true that *he did not put his hand to his neighbour's goods*. It is not possible to construe the words אִם לֹא שָׁלַח *'im lō' šālaḥ* [rendered: 'if he did not put'], etc., as an oath, for in that case the text would have read אִם שָׁלַח *'im šālaḥ* ['that he did not put'] and not אִם לֹא שָׁלַח *'im lo' šālaḥ* ['that he did put']. It is obvious that if he does not swear, he is obliged to pay for the loss. It is similarly stated in § 125 of the Ḥammurabi Code, that if the theft occurred on account of the negligence of the depositary, he must compensate the depositor.

8 [7]

In the preceding clause of the Ḥammurabi Code it is laid down that if the depositary denies that the property was left in his custody, and the depositor proves his claim by witnesses, the depositary shall pay double. With this ruling, v. 9 [Hebrew, v. 8] is in agreement; it ordains: *For every breach of trust* — not only in respect of a deposit of money or goods, but also in regard to anything that is subject to breach of trust or negligence, such as the custody of animals — *whether it is for ox, for ass, for sheep*, or in connection with the safekeeping of any articles, for example, *for raiment*, and so, too, *for any kind of lost thing* that is found, and generally for anything *which* its owner recognizes, and *says, This is it*, in all such matters, *the case of both parties shall come before God* (we have already explained this term above, on xxi 6), and then the man *whom God shall condemn* (here, too, it is an archaic expression, meaning: whom the Divine judgement, passed by the judges in God's name, will condemn), *shall pay double to his neighbour*. If the judges find that the depositary or the one who found the lost property put his hand to his neighbour's goods, or was negligent in looking after it, they shall impose on him twofold payment; but if they find that the owner of the deposit or of the lost-property brought a false charge against his fellow, they shall fine him double as compensation to the accused. The Code of Ḥammurabi (§ 124

9 [8]

EXODUS XXII 13 [Heb. 12]

and 12b) likewise imposes double payment on the depositary who denies receiving the deposit, and on one who brings a false charge against his neighbour by accusing him of denying a deposit. But the penalty for one who is guilty of the misappropriation of lost property is death (§ 9), and the same punishment is meted out to one who falsely accuses another of this crime (§ 11). But the Torah, in accordance with its principles, wished to spare human life, and consequently amended the ancient law, and ordained, even for offences involving lost property, only twofold payment as in the case of deposits.

10 [9] Thereafter follow the laws appertaining to a keeper of cattle, that is, a herdsman, who, as a rule, receives payment: *When a man delivers to his neighbour an ass or an ox or a sheep or any beast*, in general, *to keep, and* the ass or the ox etc. *dies* of its own accord, *or is maimed* of its own accord, *or is carried away*, by raiders (note the assonance נִשְׁבַּר *nišbar* ['broken', 'maimed'] נִשְׁבָּה *nišbā* ['carried away', 'captured']), *without anyone seeing it* — that 11 [10] is, there are no witnesses who saw what happened — then *an oath by the Lord shall be between them both*, that is, the keeper shall swear (here the Bible drops the archaic expression and uses an Israelite term, *an oath by the Lord*) that he did not appropriate the beast himself, *if* it is true that *he did not put his hand to his neighbour's property* (on this expression see above, on *v*. 8 [Hebrew, *v*. 7]; *and its owner shall take* what remains, if anything is left, such as the dead or maimed animal, *and* the keeper *shall not pay him* anything. In other words, a paid bailee is exempt from making restitution in the event of an accident. But he is not exempt in the case of theft, since it was his duty to guard the deposit against 12 [11] theft. *But if it is stolen from him* — from his custody, because he failed to look after it properly — *he shall make restitution to its owner*, in the event of the thief's not being found, for if the thief 13 [12] is found, the thief must pay double. *If it is torn by beasts, let him bring it as evidence* — let him bring as evidence whatever he can deliver from the beast that tore it in pieces, such as 'two legs or a piece of an ear' (Amos iii 12), and then he shall be exempt from payment even without an oath; *he shall not make restitution for what has been torn*, for this, too, is a case of accident. If, however, he is unable to deliver anything from the raiding beast, he shall clear himself by taking an oath in accordance with *v*. 11 [Hebrew, *v*. 10]. The word עֵד *'ēdh* ['witness', 'evidence'] contains a play on, and a reference to, עַד *'adh*, which means *prey*. Also

287

EXODUS XXII 13 [Heb. 12]

in the Code of Ḥammurabi (§ 263–267) the shepherd is liable for breach of trust but exempt in the case of accident.

14 [13] At the end come the laws relating to borrowing and hiring. *If a man borrows anything of his neighbour* — be it an ox or any other animal — *and it is maimed or dies, if its owner*, that is, the lender, *is not with it*, the borrower *shall make full restitution* for **15** [14] the damage; he is liable even in the case of accident. But *if its owner was with it, he shall not make restitution*, since the responsibility is shared by them. *If* the ox or any other animal *is hired*, that is, its owner hired it out, and the person that uses it pays a hiring fee to its owner, the hirer is exempt in the case of accidental injury, since the loss suffered by the owner of the animal *is reckoned* [literally, 'comes'] *in its hire*. The animal's owner receives a fee for each day's use, and therefore his loss is counterbalanced by his gain. Also in the Code of Ḥammurabi (§ 249) the hirer is not liable for accidental damage, only he must take an oath.

In this paragraph כִּי *kī* ['when'] occurs twice, and אִם *'im* ['if'] six times, forming together with the two occurrences of כִּי *kī* in the preceding paragraph, a complete series of ten. The expressions *shall pay* or *make restitution*, and *shall make full restitution*, link our paragraph to those preceding.

NINTH PARAGRAPH

THE LAW OF THE SEDUCER

(XXII 16–17 [Hebrew *vv.* 15–16])

Since the previous paragraphs cited many cases involving monetary payments, this paragraph, which speaks of an offence punishable by a fine, namely, the seduction of an unbetrothed virgin, is also given a place here. This provides one of the most convincing proofs that it is not the intention of these paragraphs to furnish us with a complete code, even relatively speaking; for since it is stated, *who* **16** [15] *is not betrothed*, it follows that if she is betrothed, the law is different; similarly, from the use of the word *seduces* — that is, he persuades the girl and she consents, it is to be inferred that if he forces her against her will, the law is not the same. The opportunity to cite these various statutes will occur in another book of the Pentateuch

EXODUS XXII 18 [Heb. 17]

(Deut. xxii 23–29), just as they are dealt with in the law-codes of the neighbouring peoples. It is clear, therefore, that we have here only a solitary note, and not a systematic citation of laws on this subject.

The note is worded as follows: *If a man seduces a virgin who is not betrothed, and lies with her, he shall give the bride-money for her, and make her his wife*, that is, he is obliged to marry her, and to pay her father the usual bride-money for virgins. This is a moral obligation resting on him, and he may not evade it; but, on the other hand, the girl's father is not compelled to give her to him for a wife. It is possible that her father will not consider

17 [16] him a fit person for his daughter, in which case, *if her father utterly refuses to give her to him*, the seducer is nonetheless obliged to pay her father the bride-money: *he shall pay money equivalent to the bride-money for virgins*. According to § 56 of the Middle Assyrian Laws, which treat of such a case, the seducer must pay a third bride-money (which some interpret as threefold the usual amount, and others as a third of the sum), and the father of the bride is permitted to do to her what he wishes, which the commentators explain to mean that he has the right even to kill her. The Torah, needless to say, gives the father no such powers.

TENTH PARAGRAPH

STATUTES AGAINST IDOLATROUS CUSTOMS

(XXII 18–20 [Hebrew, *vv*. 17–19])

We have here a series of three statutes that impose the death penalty. Each one is formulated in its own way: *you shall not permit to live — shall surely be put to death — shall be utterly destroyed*. The factor common to the three transgressions under consideration here is that they are all connected, directly or indirectly, with idolatry and its usages. All three ordinances are connected, therefore, with the hard struggle waged by the religion of Israel against the worship of idols.

18 [17] The first statute is directed against the practice of magic: *You shall not permit a sorceress to live*. On the use of magic in the life and worship of the peoples of the ancient East, see what I have stated above, on p. 95. It is true that 'black' magic, whereby the

289

EXODUS XXII 18 [Heb. 17]

sorcerer seeks to harm another person, is, of course, forbidden, even among the gentiles, and in the Eastern law-codes the death penalty is ordained for one who practices it and for one who falsely charges his neighbour with this practice (Ḥammurabi Code, § 2; Middle Assyrian Laws, § 47), but in Israel no distinction was made between permitted and prohibited magic. Every magical act, even for a purpose that is not evil, is forbidden, since it constitutes an attempt to prevail over the will of God, who alone has dominion over the world. Thus it is not without reason that in Israel the concepts of magic and idolatry were identified. Jezebel's efforts to spread the worship of the Tyrian Baal among the Israelites is termed by Jehu harlotries and sorceries (ii Kings ix 22); and the prophets mention sorcery as typical of gentile life (see, for example, Nahum iii 4; Isa. xlvii 9, 12–13). Here, in the absolute form of the statute, unqualified and unrestricted, there is felt the overpowering desire to uproot all magic from Israel, in whatever form: 'You shall not permit... to live.' Similarly, in Deut. xviii 10: 'There shall not be found among you....' Such things have no right to exist in Israel.

The sorceress only is mentioned here, and not the sorcerer, because women were particularly associated with magical practices, and the Bible speaks of things as they are. But there can be no doubt that the Torah does not intend to differentiate between man and woman in this regard.

19 [18] The second statute: *Whoever lies with a beast shall be put to death*. These despicable practices were sometimes connected with magic, and there are many references to them in pagan mythology. In Ugaritic poetry it is narrated that Baal had intercourse with a cow in order to be saved magically from the death that awaited him as a result of the devices of Mot the king of the netherworld; and in the epic of Gilgameš there are references to the relations of the goddess Ištar with various animals.

The word כָּל *kol* ['all'; rendered: 'whoever'] in this verse appears, at first sight, redundant and surprising. Even more surprising is the fact that it occurs also in the parallel passages: 'And you shall not lie with any beast and defile yourself with it' (Lev. xviii 23); 'If a woman approaches any beast', etc. (Lev. xx 16); 'Cursed be he who lies with any kind of beast' (Deut. xxvii 21). There is undoubtedly a motive behind it. We shall understand this motive when we consider the Hittite laws, which differentiate between one kind of beast and another. They impose the death penalty on whoever lies with certain animals (§ 187, 188, 199 lines 16–18),

EXODUS XXII 21 [Heb. 20]

and exempt from all punishment one lying with other animals (§ 199, lines 20–22; § 200, lines 23–25). Therefore the Torah emphasizes that there is no distinction whatsoever, but *whoever* defiles himself with such things shall be put to death.

20 [19] The third ordinance enjoins the death penalty on any one who offers sacrifices to idols: *Whoever sacrifices to other gods shall be banned, that is*, shall be put to death and destroyed, irrespective of the god to whom the offering is dedicated, *save to the Lord [YHWH] only*. On the vocalization of the *Lāmedh* [with *Qāmeṣ*] in the word לָאֱלֹהִים *lā'ĕlōhīm* ['gods'] see my commentary on Gen. iii 17 (*From Adam To Noah*, pp. 166–167).

This group of three laws was given its place here on account of the association between the word *lies* [שֹׁכֵב *šōkhēbh*] here and the word *lies* [וְשָׁכַב *wᵉšākhabh*] in the preceding paragraph.

ELEVENTH PARAGRAPH

LOVE AND FELLOWSHIP TOWARDS THE POOR AND THE NEEDY

(XXII 21–27 [Hebrew, *vv*. 20–26])

Since the preceding paragraph contained drastic laws against alien customs, the Bible wishes to indicate at once that this opposition is directed only against the customs, and not against the foreigner. On the contrary, it is forbidden to wrong or oppress the stranger:

21 [20] *You shall not wrong a sojourner or oppress him, for you were sojourners in the land of Egypt*. The reason given is purely ethical: you yourselves suffered as sojourners in a strange land, and you know the soul of the sojourner; therefore, take heed not to embitter the life of the sojourner living in your midst just as you did not wish the Egyptians to embitter your lives when you dwelt among them. The text uses the expression *oppress him*, because it was stated above that it was particularly *oppression* that the Israelites were made to endure in Egypt: 'and I have seen the oppression with which the Egyptians oppress them' (iii 9). Compare on the subject xxiii 9; Lev. xix 34; Deut. x 19.

The admonition designed to protect the sojourner led, through the association of ideas, to other admonitory precepts in the interest of other social groups who resembled the sojourner in

EXODUS XXII 21 [Heb. 20]

that they, too, were defenceless before aggressors, namely, widows and orphans, who are usually mentioned in the Bible together with sojourners: *You shall not afflict any widow or orphan*. This prohibition is followed by a warning, couched in prophetic diction, that severe retribution, measure for measure, will be meted out to anyone transgressing the injunction. The particle *if* at the beginning of v. 23 is used here as in oath-formulae: Evil shall come upon you, *if you do afflict him*, that is, everyone who belongs to the class of sojourners, widows and orphans (compare, for singular masculine that refers to certain categories expressly mentioned earlier, xxi 26, 27, 32, 34; xxii 7, 9 [Hebrew, vv. 6, 8]; and numerous other examples). Take heed not to afflict him, *for, if he*, the afflicted one, *cries out to Me, I will surely hear his cry*, just as I heard your cry when the Egyptians afflicted you (iii 7), *and My wrath will burn* against you, *and I will slay you with the sword* of your enemies, *and your wives shall become widows and your children fatherless* — measure for measure.

22 [21]

23 [22]

24 [23]

There are also other weak members of society, namely, the poor, who need to borrow from their wealthy brethren. On them, too, the Torah took particular pity: *If you lend money to any of My people with you who is poor* (a word-play: עַמִּי 'ammī ['My people'] — עִמָּךְ 'immākh ['with you']; do not forget that the poor man *with you* [עִמָּךְ 'immākh] is the son of *My people* [עַמִּי 'ammī]), *you shall not be to him as a creditor*, who demands repayment of the money due to him with the full rigour of the law, and, needless to say, *you shall not exact interest from him*. Furthermore, *If ever you take your neighbour's mantle in pledge*, as security for his debt, *before the sun goes down you shall return it* [masc.] *to him*, that is, the pledge (here, too, the masculine is used [notwithstanding that the Hebrew word for 'mantle' is feminine] in conformity with the sense, though not in accord with grammar). Although you are permitted, by the strict letter of the law, to take a pledge and to retain it in your possession till the time of repayment, yet the Israelite ethic imposes on you the duty to return it to your poor brother before he has need of it. The motivation is moral, going beyond the letter of the law: *for that* — the mantle — *is his only covering, it is his mantle for his body; in what shall he sleep at night*, to protect himself against the cold, if you do not restore it to him? *And it shall come to pass, when he cries to Me* against you, because you retain his mantle when he is suffering from the cold, *I will hear, for I am compassionate*.

25 [24]

26 [25]

27 [26]

EXODUS XXII 28 [Heb. 27]

There is a clear parallelism between the two parts of this paragraph: *for if he cries out to Me I will surely hear his cry* in v. 23 [Hebrew, v. 22]; *and it shall come to pass, when he cries to Me* in v. 27 [Hebrew, v. 26]. This parallelism links the two parts together and integrates them into a single unit. This unit has been placed here because it contains the word יִשְׁכָּב *yiškābh* [literally, 'shall he lie'; rendered: 'sleep'] in v. 27 [Hebrew, v. 26], which corresponds to שֹׁכֵב *šōkhēbh* ['lies'] in v. 19 [Hebrew, v. 18] of the preceding paragraph, and to וְשָׁכַב *wešākhabh* ['lies'] in v. 16 [Hebrew, v. 15] of the paragraph before that.

TWELFTH PARAGRAPH

REVERENCE TOWARDS GOD AND THE LEADERS OF THE COMMUNITY

(XXII 28–31 [Hebrew, vv. 27–30])

After there have been cited in the previous paragraph the duties resting on an Israelite towards those lower than himself in the social scale, we are given here the precepts he is called upon to observe towards those above him. Apart from this principal nexus, there is also another link between the two paragraphs, which is immediately discernible in the opening sentence: *You shall not revile* [from the stem קלל *qālal*] *God*. This admonition includes every utterance or act that detracts from the Divine glory, and is to be understood in the same way as we explained the injunction against 'dishonouring' [also from the stem *qālal*] parents (xxi 17); more particularly it refers to cursing God, which is thematically connected with the cry of the poor mentioned at the end of the preceding paragraph, since the person who suffers trouble and calamity is liable to fall into this sin. Compare Isa. viii 21: 'and it shall come to pass that, when they [literally, 'he'] are hungry, they will be enraged and will curse their king and their God'; Job ii 9: 'Curse God, and die.' Hence an admonition is given here: the oppressed may cry out to God against their oppressors, but let them take great heed that they do not curse God. Similarly, they must take care not to curse those in authority: *nor curse a ruler of your people*. Compare, for this, i Kings xxi 10: 'You have cursed God and the king'; also the aforementioned verse in Isa. viii 21.

EXODUS XXII 29 [Heb. 28]

29 [28] Verse 29 [Hebrew, *v.* 28] also deals with a matter related to the honour due to God; possibly it was inserted at this particular point on account of the resemblance between the word תְאַחֵר *theʾaḥēr* ['you shall... delay'] and תָאֹר *thāʾōr* ['curse'] in the preceding verse. מְלֵאָתְךָ וְדִמְעֲךָ *meleʾāthekhā wedhimʿākhā* [rendered: 'from the fulness of your harvest and from the outflow of your presses'] are archaic expressions that were preserved unchanged in the legal terminology: מְלֵאָה *meleʾā* [literally, 'fulness'] signifies 'produce' (Num. xviii 27; Deut. xxii 9), and refers here to the sacred gifts from the produce of the land, such as the first fruits; דֶּמַע *demaʿ* is a noun of doubtful etymology, and apparently denotes the heave-offering [*terūmā*, 'the priest's share of the crop']. The traditional interpretation of *you shall not delay* is that it is forbidden to change the order of the separation of the sacred gifts, to postpone the earlier offering or anticipate the later; for example, to give the Second Tithe before the First Tithe, and the like (Mekhilta, ed. Lauterbach, iii, p. 153). According to its plain meaning, the expression seems to have a more general connotation. The brevity of the injunction indicates that it is only an allusion, and the archaic phrasing shows that it belongs to an ancient tradition that expressed itself in a terse and lapidary style. In order to understand the precept and its significance, we must consider the Hittite Instructions on the duties of the priests and the temple attendants that we have already mentioned above. In § 15 and in § 18 of these Instructions, there is a detailed and lengthy exposition (ten lines in § 15, and twenty-two lines in § 18) of the obligation resting on the shepherds, the herdsmen and the farmers who work on the temple estate, to bring the calves, the lambs and the goats to the temple promptly at the correct time, without any delay; so, too, the first-fruits must be brought promptly at the right time, without delay, before any one eats of them, even the high officials of the temple, who are in charge of the shepherds and farmers; the first enjoyment of the offerings is reserved for the gods. The punishment for anyone transgressing this commandment is analogous to the Hebrew *kārēth* ['extinction'] for him and all his household. Apparently a similar tradition also existed among the Israelites (although without the penalty of *kārēth*), and it is to this tradition that this archaic verse refers.

Here, too, as in the Hittite Instructions, the law of the first-born is connected with that of the first-fruits of the produce: *The firstborn of your sons you shall give to Me*. This command is also

EXODUS XXII 31 [Heb. 30]

formulated in a stereotyped, archaic style, which was preserved in its original form, even though among the Israelites the practice had certainly been introduced of redeeming the first-born of man (compare xiii 13, etc.), and hence the sense of the injunction is: Rightly you should give him to Me as a sacrifice on My altar, but in actuality you shall redeem him and give the priest a substitute for him. Moreover, *You shall do likewise with your oxen and with your sheep*, namely, you shall give Me, in this case without the right of redemption, every first-born that is born to you among your herds and your sheep. *Seven days it* — the first-born of cattle — *shall be with its mother* — a complete week, a complete unit of time — and then *on the eighth day you shall give it to Me*, that is, to the priest who attends to My service.

The ordinance of the first-born sons, who were consecrated to God, brings to mind the idea of the election of the people of Israel, who are designated the *first-born son* of the Lord (iv 22), and were chosen to be 'a kingdom of priests and a *holy* nation' (xix 6), consecrated to the service of their Creator. Hence v. 31 has been given a place here in order to remind the children of Israel of the duty resting upon them to conduct themselves in a manner worthy of sanctified people, and befitting the glory of Him who chose them and called them to His service. *Holy men you shall be to Me*; the ending of the injunction recalls the conclusion of the two preceding verses: *you shall give to Me — you shall give it to Me — you shall be to Me*. And because of the nobility of your mission you must behave like noblemen, not only from the spiritual aspect, but also in the sense that you cultivate fine habits and maintain the self-respect due to your calling. Therefore, do not make yourselves despicable by eating objectionable things, such as *flesh* that you may find *in the field* (note the assonance: בָּשָׂר *bāśār* ['flesh'] — בַּשָּׂדֶה *baśśādhe* ['in the field']), namely, flesh *that is torn* — that means to say, flesh of an animal that a predatory beast has torn (the word טְרֵפָה *ṭᵉrēphā* [translated: 'that is torn'] is used here as a noun). *You shall cast it to the dogs*; this is food fit for dogs and not for a people wholly consecrated to the Lord.

295

THIRTEENTH PARAGRAPH
JUSTICE TOWARDS ALL MEN
(XXIII 1–9)

Chapter XXIII

Till now the Torah spoke of the precepts of love and compassion, which the Israelite is duty-bound to observe towards people who are unprotected and without means, and of the honour that he must show towards his superiors. Now the Bible issues an admonition concerning a virtue that must be practiced towards all people, namely, that of *justice*.

1 *You shall not utter a groundless report*, that is, you shall not go about as a tale-bearer, spreading calumny and falsehood about your fellow. It follows, *a fortiori*, that you shall not bring untrue reports before the court. *Put not your hand with the wicked* — if you are summoned to testify in court, do not join the litigant that is wicked in the legal sense, namely, that is wrong in his claims, so as to give evidence in his favour and defeat the ends of justice; *to be a witness of violence*, that is, a false witness (compare my annotations to the word חָמָס *ḥāmās* [literally, 'violence'; rendered: 'unrighteousness'] in Gen. vi 11). Signs of alliteration are noticeable in this verse, in the frequent occurrence of *Šīn* and *Śīn*. The use of two words of negation, first לֹא *lō*' and then אַל *'al* [both mean 'not'], is apparently due to fondness for variation.

2 *You shall not follow a multitude to do evil*: if you see many tending in their views or their acts in a wrong direction, do not go with them, even if they constitute the overriding majority; endeavour to swim against the tide, if it flows towards evil. Particularly, take heed in this regard when giving evidence before the court (in this verse, too, as in the preceding one, the general prohibition is followed by a particular admonition with regard to conduct in court). *Nor shall you answer* — do not testify — *in a suit*, in a dispute between one person and another, wrong testimony, *to turn aside after a multitude* who give such evidence, in a way that will cause this testimony *to incline* the judgement unjustly. Here, also, there is a play upon words: לִנְטֹת *linṭōth* ['to turn aside'] — לְהַטֹּת *lᵉhaṭṭōth* ['to incline, wrest judgement'].

Even out of compassion for an indigent person, you are for-
3 bidden to pervert judgement: *nor shall you favour a poor man in*

EXODUS XXIII 5

his suit. When you sit in the seat of judgement, and you have to adjudicate between a poor and rich man, needless to say you are forbidden to turn aside from the path of justice for the benefit of the rich man, but know that you are prohibited to deviate from the way of justice even in the interests of the poor man. Everywhere, and at all times, 'justice and only justice you shall follow.' Compare Lev. xix 15: 'You shall not respect the person of the poor, nor favour the person of the great; but in righteousness shall you judge your neighbour.' The verb *favour*, which is used in Leviticus with reference to the great, is used here in regard to the poor.

There now follows a series of three verses that have been placed here for reasons of association, as we shall explain later, in our commentary on *v.* 6.

4   The first verse begins: *When you meet your enemy's ox or his ass going astray,* do not withhold your help from it, thinking to yourself that the matter is no concern of yours, but *you shall surely bring it back to him.* Your enemy is also your brother, and it is your duty to do to him as you would wish to be done by. Here, too, as in *v.* 3, the line of thought is: this, needless to say that. The verse refers to your enemy; the case of your friend is taken for granted; but you are forbidden to differentiate between them. In the parallel admonition in Deut. xxii 1–3, the general expression *your brother* is used.

5   So, too, *When you see the ass of one who hates you* — and needless to say of one who loves you (in Deut. xxii 4: *your brother*) — *lying under its burden, you shall cease to forsake* [עֲזֹב *ăzōbh*] *him,* that is, you shall refrain from leaving your enemy in perplexity. On the contrary, עָזֹב תַּעֲזֹב *ʿāzōbh taʿăzōbh with him* — you shall arrange, together with him, the load on the ass's back. There is a play here between the two verbs, which have acquired in Hebrew an identical form, although their derivations and significations are different. עָזַב *ʿāzabh*, with original *Zayin*, means 'to forsake', and is spelt in Arabic عزب *ʿzb*; whilst עָזַב *ʿāzabh*, with a *Zayin* that derives from ד׳ *dh* (Arabic ذ *Dhāl*), means 'to arrange', and is from the same stem as the noun מַעֲזִיבָה *maʿăzībhā* ['pavement'; see Jastrow, *Talmud Dictionary, s.v.*], and the verb וַיַּעַזְבוּ *wayyaʿazᵉbhū* ['paved' or 'repaired'] in Neh. iii 8, corresponding to South Arabian *ʿdhb* and Ugaritic *ʿdb*. Possibly the two Hebrew verbs were differently pronounced, and the quip was clear in the ancient Hebrew pronunciation: Do not *forsake* [תַּעֲזֹב

taʿăzōbh], but, on the contrary, *arrange the load* [בֹ׳עֲדַ *taʿădhōbh*].

6 Verse 6, *You shall not pervert the justice due to your* אֶבְיוֹן *'ebhyōn* [usually rendered: 'poor'] *in his suit*, appears, at first, surprising, since it was already stated in *v.* 3: 'nor shall you favour a poor man', and it seems an unnecessary repetition. But we may presume that the word אֶבְיוֹן *'ebhyōn* here is not the usual word meaning poor and needy, but another substantive from the stem *'b(h)* — *'by* ابی *'by*, found in other Semitic languages, and possibly originally also in Hebrew, which means 'to refuse, be unwilling'. Accordingly, the noun denotes here an 'opponent', 'adversary', and is a synonym of the nouns אֹיֵב *'ōyēbh* ['enemy'] and שֹׂנֵא *śōnē'* ['one who hates']. This signification makes it easier to understand the use here of the pronominal suffix, second person, (ךָ- *–khā*), which would not have been justified if אֶבְיוֹן *'ebhyōn* had been employed in its usual connotation (the position is different in Deut. xv 11: 'to your brother, to your needy and to your poor, in the land'). If this be so, we have here a prohibition corresponding to the two preceding admonitions: when you are called upon to adjudicate between your enemy and someone else, do not pervert the judgement against your enemy, because he is your enemy. The three verses of this group thus contain three synonyms, *your enemy — one who hates you — your adversary*, just as in the three verses 17–19 of chapter xxii we find three synonyms for the death-penalty.

This series of three verses has been placed here for reasons of association in respect of both form and content: regarding form, it will be seen that the last verse resembles *v.* 3; as far as the content is concerned, it will be observed that the purport of the third prohibition, not to wrest the judgement of one's enemy, is connected with the main theme of the paragraph, to wit, that *justice* shall be done to all men.

There now follows another sequence of three verses, which are linked together by the assonance marking the closing words [in the Hebrew] of their initial clauses: תִּרְחָק *tirḥāq* ['keep far'] — תִּקַּח *tiqqāḥ* ['you shall take'] — תִּלְחָץ *tilḥāṣ* ['you shall... oppress']. Since the three verses form a single unit, they are cited *in toto*, even though their contents have in part been stated earlier. In order to present what is new in them, that which is not new is also included.

7 The opening injunction of *v.* 7, *Keep far from a false charge*, is in essence similar to the beginning of *v.* 1; and the continuation of the verse contains an admonition directed to the judges similar

EXODUS XXIII 9

to that given in the continuation of *v.* 1 to the witnesses. *And do not slay the innocent and the righteous* — do not bring destruction, by your unjust sentence, upon the innocent and righteous in the judicial sense of these terms, that is, upon the one who is in the right and deserves to be free of all punishment. For the verb הָרַג *hāragh* ['slay'], in the sense of causing someone great loss, compare passages like Prov. vii 26: 'For many a victim has she laid low; yea, all her slain are a mighty host.' You, O judge, must pay heed to this, *for* you should know that if you, in your court, will declare the righteous [i.e. the one who is in the right] guilty and acquit the wicked [i.e. the one who is in the wrong], *I*, in my court, *will not acquit the wicked*, and if you pronounce a wrong judgement and become thereby wicked in My sight, you will not be held innocent by My court — a punishment befitting the crime, emphasized by alliterative word-play.

8 Verse 8 is also directed to the judge: *And you shall take no bribe* — you shall accept no gift whatsoever from either of the two parties to a suit, or from the accused before the court, *for* you must know that *a bribe blinds the clear-sighted, and perverts the words of the righteous*; and even if you are sure that you are clear-sighted and the bribe will have no influence on you, in the end you will be blinded by the bribe, and even if you were consistently righteous till that moment and it is also your desire to remain righteous in the future, yet perforce the words of your decision will be perverted on account of the bribe that you accepted. This verse is marked by poetic rhythm and parallelism, and the entire saying is repeated almost verbatim in Deut. xvi 19: 'for a bribe blinds the eyes of the wise, and perverts the words of the righteous.' It appears that this was a popular dictum of the tradition of the 'Sages'. Compare also Ecclesiasticus xx 29.

9 The law of *v.* 9, *And a sojourner you shall not oppress*, etc., was already cited earlier (xxii 21 [Hebrew, *v.* 20]) in a similar form, together with its reason, nevertheless it is repeated here, and with it, in like wording, also the motivation, *for you know the heart of a sojourner, for you were sojourners in the land of Egypt*, because the complete group of three verses, which was already in existence independently, was cited as a whole, and also because this verse in particular marks the transition to the next paragraph, as we shall see forthwith.

FOURTEENTH PARAGRAPH

THE SACRED SEASONS

(XXIII 10–19)

Till now the text dealt with positive and negative precepts that are valid at all times; now we have a series of precepts that are to be observed at given times, commandments that apply to seasons that are specifically dedicated to the service of the Lord, and are intended to remind the Israelites of the covenant that the Lord made with them, and of the duty resting upon them to be faithful to this covenant.

The first precepts of this group appertain to the seventh year and the seventh day (*vv.* 10–12), and the verses in which they are formulated conclude with the mention of the *sojourner* preceded by the verb נָפַשׁ *nāphaš* [*Niph‘al*: 'be refreshed'] (*v.* 12: 'and the son of your bondwoman, and the sojourner, may be refreshed') — a parallelism that connects the first part of this paragraph with the conclusion of the preceding paragraph, which speaks of the *sojourner* and *the heart* [נֶפֶשׁ *nepheš*, literally, 'soul'] *of a sojourner* (*v.* 9). We may also possibly detect a link between the two paragraphs in the phrase אֶבְיֹנֵי עַמֶּךָ *'ebhyōnē 'ammekhā* ['the poor of your people'] in *v.* 11, which recalls the words אֶבְיֹנְךָ *'ebhyōn\u1d49khā* [rendered: 'your adversary'] in *v.* 6, although the meaning of the word אֶבְיוֹן *'ebhyōn* is different apparently in the two passages.

The importance attached by the peoples of the ancient Orient to sequences of seven units of time, and the innovation introduced in Israel with regard to resting on the seventh period, we have already discussed above, in our commentary on xvi 5, xix 1, and xx 8. Here the Torah speaks of a series of seven years. Verse 10 does not stand alone, but serves as an introduction to the commandment in *v.* 11. The sense of this passage is as follows:

10 Although throughout *six years you shall sow your land and gather in its yield,* you shall not do so in the seventh year: *but* (the *Wāw* is
11 antithetic) *the seventh year,* — that is, but in regard to the seventh year (*casus pendens*) — *you shall let it* — the land — *rest, and leave it* — that is, you shall not sow it nor gather in its produce, but you shall leave it to itself — *and the poor of your people shall eat* the produce that it will yield of itself. This crop will not be your private property nor of any other person; it shall be ownerless, so that

the poor who have no inheritance of field or vineyard may have the benefit thereof, *and what they* — the poor — *leave, the wild beasts may eat*, for the animals are also the Lord's creatures, and they, too, have a share in His bounty. And as you will do with your field of produce, sowing it for six years and letting it rest on the seventh, *you shall do likewise with your vineyard, and with your olive orchard*; you shall not tend them in the seventh year, and the fruit that they yield in this year shall be ownerless, and shall be given to all such as wish to enjoy it, be they the poor or wild beasts. For the expression כֵּן תַּעֲשֶׂה *kēn taʿăśū* ['You shall do likewise'], compare above xxii 30 [Hebrew, v. 29], Deut. xxii 3, etc. It was possibly a common formula in the legal language of Israel.

On the reference to precepts pertaining to the Land of Israel in this section, see my observations above, in my annotations to xx 10.

This paragraph, the last of those dealing with ordinances and statutes, thus parallels the first, which speaks of the Hebrew slave (xxi 2–6); in both paragraphs reference is made to six years of labour and to release from work in the seventh year. Every Israelite resembles the Hebrew slave in this respect, that he, too, shall work for only six consecutive years, and after this period he also shall be freed, in the seventh year, from the yoke of hard toil.

In the same way as he is released from the burden of his hard work for a year after the entire series of six years, so he is liberated from the burden of his hard service for one day after the complete sequence of six days. Indeed, *six days you shall do your work* — but only six days — *yet* (the *Wāw* is antithetic) *on the seventh day you shall desist* — you shall cease from all work (on the verb שָׁבַת *šābhath* [rendered: 'desist'] and its negative signification 'not to do any work', and also the allusion it contains to the term יוֹם הַשַּׁבָּת *yōm haššabbāth* ['the Sabbath day'], see my commentary to Gen. ii 2, *From Adam to Noah*, p. 63) — *that there may rest*, together with you, every creature that you compel to work for you during the six week-days, such as *your ox and your ass*, and that there may also rest *and be refreshed* with you *the son of your bondwoman* — the slave who works in your service — *and the sojourner*, who dwells with you and who finds himself, while in your midst, in the unhappy position of one who sojourns in a foreign land. Here, too, the parallelism, as well as the rhythm, of Biblical poetry is discernible.

On account of its fundamental importance, the Sabbath day was already referred to in the Decalogue; here it is mentioned in its proper place, in the series of days dedicated to rest and the service of the Lord.

Verse 13 is connected with what was stated concerning the sojourner in the preceding verse, and twice in the previous paragraph. I have indeed commanded you to act towards the sojourners with love and fellowship, but do not forget what I have told you in 13 regard to their religion and cult: *And in all things that I have said to you take heed; and make no mention of the name of other gods*, that is, solemn mention in worship and when taking an oath, and possibly also in general speech, as a precaution; *nor let it* — their name — *be heard out of your mouth* — an iteration of the thought in different words.

14 You must, in truth, take heed to avoid all that is linked with idolatrous worship, but agricultural festivals, such as the Canaanites celebrate unto their gods, you, too, may observe in honour of your God, although your outlook will be different and the form of the celebration will not be the same. *Three* רְגָלִים *reghālīm* [literally, 'feet'] — that is, *three times*, in accordance with the parallel in *v.* 17: 'three times in the year', and according to the signification of the word in Num. xxii 28, 32, 33 (it is only in a later period that the word *reghālīm* acquired, on the basis of our verse here, the meaning of 'pilgrimage festivals'; also the noun פַּעַם *pa'am* [rendered in *v.* 17: 'times'] originally meant 'foot') — *you shall keep a feast unto Me in the year*. The verb חָגַג *ḥāghagh* [translated: 'keep a feast'] means originally, as in Arabic, 'to go round, encircle, dance a sacred dance with circular movement'; hence the connotation of a festival in general, and more particularly of a pilgrimage to the temple.

These festivals are referred to here in general terms, without any details concerning the way in which they were to be observed, since this observance was still a matter for the distant future. The particulars would be given only after a time; see on this my commentary on Lev. xxiii, when it is published*. But, in any case, some reference to the subject was necessary even here, in order that it should not be thought that the prohibition in *v.* 24, 'nor do according to their works', includes also the observance of the agricultural festivals.

---

* Unhappily, owing to the untimely demise of the author, this part of his commentary was never completed. *Tr.*

The first of these festivals is the Feast of Unleavened Cakes.
15 *The feast of unleavened cakes* — although the Canaanites also observe it, *you*, too, *shall keep* it (the object comes before, and not after, the verb to express antithesis: you should, indeed, in general eschew the pagan ritual, but nevertheless keep the festival of unleavened cakes), and for *seven* festive *days* (here, too, there is a sequence of seven days) *you shall eat unleavened cakes, as I commanded you* (xii 15) — as a memorial to the exodus from Egypt, and this will be the new significance with which you will imbue this festival and this custom — *at the appointed time in the month of Abib*. The new motivation for the celebration of your festival, which will differentiate it from the Canaanite feast, will be this: *for in it*, in the month of Abib, *you came out of Egypt. And none shall appear before Me empty-handed*, when you come to My sanctuary to celebrate this festival, but you shall bring with you the firstlings of your flocks and your herds (see xxxiv 18–20).
16 The second festival is that of the harvest: *And the feast of harvest, of the first-fruits of your work, of what you sow in the field* — the festival of the first-fruits of the produce of your land, that, too, you shall celebrate, although it is also common to the Canaanites. On the customs of the Canaanites, see further below. In the parallel passage (xxxiv 22) this festival is designated 'the feast of weeks'; see the commentary there.

The same applies to the third festival, namely, *the feast of ingathering*, which you shall celebrate *at the going out of the year* — at the end of the agricultural year — *when you gather in your work* — the fruit of your labour in the receding year — *out of the field* into the storehouse. This celebration was also observed among the Canaanites, as is evidenced by Judges ix 27: 'And they went out into the field, and gathered the grapes from their vineyards and trod them, and held festival, and went into the house of their god, and ate and drank.'
17 *Three times in the year*, at these three festivals, *shall all your males appear before the Lord, YHWH*, in His sanctuary, wherever it may be. Nothing is said here concerning the site of the sanctuary. The name אָדוֹן *'ādhōn* ['Lord'] is used here in antithesis to the name *Baal* ['master', 'lord']. The Canaanites observe festivals similar to these so as to express their thanks to the god that they designate *Baal*, and to ask him also for the gifts of the fruit of the earth in the future; but do not you turn to this fictitious *Baal* ['lord'], but to the true אָדוֹן *'ādhōn* ['Lord'], namely, *YHWH*, your God.

EXODUS XXIII 17

There is no mention here of 'the day of blowing the horn' or of 'the day of atonement', but this silence is no proof that these days had not yet been instituted in this early period. Our passage deals solely with agricultural festivals akin to the agricultural feasts of the Canaanites, and this is not the place for extraneous matters.

The last two verses of the paragraph lay down certain regulations in regard to the agricultural festivals. These are:

18 (a) *You shall not offer, with* [עַל *'al*, literally, 'on'] *leavened bread, the blood of My sacrifice*, that is, 'My blood-sacrifice' (for this construction compare passages like Isa. i 16: 'remove the evil of your doings from before My eyes', that is, 'your evil doings'; Isa. xxxvii 24: 'and I felled the height of its cedars', that is, 'its tall cedars'). According to the plain meaning of the text, the reference here is not specifically to the Passover sacrifice, for it is obvious that that must not be slaughtered with leavened bread. The injunction, according to its simple sense, includes all sacrifices with the exception of the thanksgiving offering, concerning which it is prescribed (Lev. vii 13): 'With [עַל *'al*] cakes of leavened bread he shall bring his offering' (this passage clearly shows that the word *'al* in such circumstances signifies *with*). Now this is a basic rule of the Torah, that apart from the leavened bread of the thanksgiving offering and the two loaves [Lev. xxiii 17], which belong to the priests and not to the altar, it is forbidden to offer cereal oblations with leaven (Lev. ii 11): 'No cereal offering which you bring to the Lord shall be made with leaven; for you shall burn no leaven nor any honey as an offering by fire to the Lord.' The Canaanites used to offer honey to their gods, as we are informed by the Ugaritic texts (*nbt* = נֹפֶת 'honey from the comb'), and possibly also by one of the Carthage inscriptions (if the word *npt* there does indeed mean 'honey'). They were likewise, it seems, accustomed to offer leavened loaves (except, perhaps, on the spring festival) in accordance with their agricultural civilization. The Egyptians regarded honey as the special food of the gods, and also of the king, who was likewise deemed a god. The Torah is opposed to the sacrificial practices customary among the neighbouring peoples, in order, it may be, to preserve the desert tradition as far as possible, and perhaps because fermentation by leaven and honey was considered a sign of corruption, and consequently as something unfit to be offered on the altar.

(b) *Or let the fat of My feast remain all night until the morning.*

EXODUS XXIII 20

The purpose of this prohibition may have been to prevent the sacred meal continuing till morning, and thereafter providing an opportunity for riotous and unchaste behaviour. In the parallel passage (xxxiv 25) we find, *the sacrifice of the feast of the passover*, instead of *the fat of My feast*; see my annotations *ad locum*.

19 (c) Although *the first of the first-fruits of your ground*, that is, the best and choicest of the first-fruits of your ground, *you shall bring* into *the house of the Lord your God*, just as the Canaanites bring the first-fruits to the house of their gods, yet *you shall not boil a kid in its mother's milk* according to the heartless custom that they practise on their festival of first-fruits. Maimonides already conjectured that the prohibition of boiling a kid in its mother's milk was intended to keep the Israelites away from idolatrous customs, but he had no proof that the gentiles actually practised such things. Now we know from the Ugaritic texts that the Canaanites prepared such a dish particularly at festal ceremonies pertaining to the fertility of the soil. In the Ugaritic tablet on 'The gods pleasant and beautiful' it is written (line 14): *ṭb[ḫ g]d bḥlb 'annḫ bḫm'at* 'boil a kid in milk, a lamb in butter.' The custom of boiling small cattle in milk has been preserved to this day among Bedouins.

EPILOGUE OF THE SECTION

(XXIII 20–33)

Just as the ordinances and statutes were preceded by a form of prologue (xx 22–26), so they are followed here by an epilogue, in which the children of Israel are promised in the Lord's name protection and success, provided they will remain unfailingly faithful to the covenant. Similar opening and closing remarks are also found in the codes of Ḥammurabi and Lipit-Ištar.

20 The initial words, *Behold I send an angel before you*, do not imply a being distinct from God. In ancient thought-processes the line of demarcation between the sender and the sent is liable easily to be blurred; in the final analysis the angel of God is simply God's action. From another part of the Bible we learn what is meant by an angel of the Lord being sent before one. In Gen. xxiv 7 Abraham says to his servant: 'The Lord, the God of heaven... He will send His angel before you', but in the continuation of the

EXODUS XXIII 20

narrative there is not the slightest reference to an actual angel accompanying the servant; it is only related that the Lord prospered his way; and the servant says (*ibid.*, *v.* 27): 'As for me, the Lord has led me in the way.' Compare also *ibid., vv.* 40, 48, 56. It is clear from that passage, therefore, that the angel stands only for the guidance and help of the Lord. Similarly it is stated in Num. xx 16: 'and sent an angel and brought us forth out of Egypt'; but above (xiv 19) the Bible designates the pillar of cloud 'the angel of God.' Hence the words under discussion here mean only: I will guide you and prosper you. In the continuation of the passage, at the end of *v.* 22 and also further on, it is clear that the reference is to the actions of God Himself. On the relationship between this verse and what is stated in chapters xxxii–xxxiii, see my commentary there.

The sending of the angel will serve *to guard you* [לִשְׁמָרְךָ *lišmorekhā*] from all evil and to lead you *on the way and to bring you*, at the end of your journey on this road, *to the place which I have prepared* for you (cf. iii 8: 'to the place of the Canaanites', etc.).

21 *Give heed* [הִשָּׁמֶר *hiššāmer*, literally, 'be guarded'] *to him*; just as he comes to guard you, so you must guard yourself not to transgress his words, which are My words (this recurrence of the verb שָׁמַר *šāmar* ['keep', 'guard'] corresponds to its twofold use in the preceding paragraph, *vv.* 13–15: תִּשָּׁמֵרוּ *tiššāmerū* ['take heed'] — תִּשְׁמֹר *tišmōr* ['you shall keep']). *Do not rebel* [תַּמֵּר *tammēr*] *against him* (the stem of תַּמֵּר is מָרַר *mārar*, which is akin to מָרָה *mārā* ['rebel']; possibly there is a word-play here on the verb הִשָּׁמֶר *hiššāmer*) *for he will not pardon your transgression; for My name is in him*. All the theological concepts that the expositors have attached to this passage with reference to the function of angels, their nature, and their relation to God, and the like, are completely foreign to the simple meaning of Scripture. In the Biblical conception, there is no precise distinction, as I have explained, between the Lord and His angel, and this is clearly indicated by the expression, *for My name is in Him*. The connotation of the words *My name* is, 'I in My glory', and the sense is: I Myself reveal Myself to you through him, and I and he are the same.

22 So shall you observe to do his bidding, *for only if you hearken attentively to his voice*, namely, of My angel who speaks to you in My name, *and do all that I say* (a repetition of the thought in different words, and another clear indication of identity: the voice of the angel is what I say) — only if you fulfil this condition will I

protect you through My angel — *and will I be an enemy to your enemies* — I shall be a foe to your foes and your foes will be Mine — *and an adversary to your adversaries* (here, too, the thought is iterated in different words).

23 Take heed also in another matter: כִּי *kī, when*, at the time that, *My angel goes before you*, as stated at the beginning of *v.* 20, *and brings you*, as we are informed at the end of that verse, *to the place which I have prepared*, that is, to the Amorites, and the Hittites, and the Perizzites, and the Canaanites, the Hivites, and the Jebusites, *and I blot him out*, that is, I blot out the entire group [hence the singular, 'him'] of these peoples, then take heed: *you shall not* 24 *prostrate yourself to their gods* — the gods of these peoples — *nor serve them*, as I commanded you at the revelation on Mount Sinai (on the grammatical form of the verb תָּעָבְדֵם *thoʿobhedhēm*, see my note on xx 5), *nor do according to their works* — the works of these nations in the service of their gods — *but*, on the contrary, *you shall utterly overthrow them* — the works mentioned above, that is, the works of their edifices and their altars, which they have built unto their gods — *and break in pieces their pillars* — the 25 stelae that they have erected in honour of their gods. *And you* [plural] *shall serve* none but *the Lord your* [plural] *God, and He* — and not Baal to whom the Canaanites attribute the fertility of the soil and the abundance of water — *shall bless your* [singular] *bread and your* [singular] *water* (the change from plural to singular, which occurs a number of times in these verses, is common in Biblical Hebrew and particular in poetic style; it breaks the monotony of the oft-repeated recurrence of the same termination). 26 *And I will take away* (another variation; this time it is a change of person [i.e. from third to second person], which is also common in poetic diction) *sickness from the midst of you* (compare xv 26; Deut. vii 15). Similarly, I shall remove from your midst every case of infertility: *None shall cast her young* [literally, 'show abortion'] *or be barren* — incapable of conceiving, either among human beings or cattle — *in your land* — in the land to which I shall bring you, and which will become your possession. Compare Deut. vii 14, which occurs in the paragraph in which we have already found one parallel to our paragraph, and whose ending, in *v.* 16, is similar to that of our paragraph: 'there shall not be male or female barren among you, or among your cattle.' Likewise, *the number of your days* — the days of each one in your midst — *I shall fulfil*.

Even after you enter the borders of your land, I will grant you My help against your foes, just as I will help you throughout the course of your journey in the wilderness. *I will send My terror before you*, an expression corresponding to that of sending the angel mentioned in *v.* 20, which refers to the terror as a kind of vanguard marching in front of the host (compare xv 16: 'Terror and dread fall upon them'), *and I will throw into confusion*, by means of this terror (a word-play: אֵימָתִי *'ēmāthī* ['My terror'] — הַמֹּתִי *hammōthī* ['I will throw into confusion']), *all the people against whom you shall come, and I will make all your enemies turn their backs* [literally, 'the back of the neck'] *to you*; they will flee before you because of My terror, and you will seize them by the back of their necks when you pursue them. *And I will send the hornet before you* — it, too, I shall send as a spearhead before your host. The hornet, which is also mentioned in Deut. vii 20, and Jos. xxiv 12, is nothing but unreasoning dread, panic, synonymous with the word for terror (a repetition of the thought in different words; for this, too, compare the aforementioned verse of the Song of the Sea: 'Terror and dread fall upon them'). This is apparently the correct interpretation of hornet, for the Arabs to this day call panic resulting in mass flight by a word signifying 'hornet'. *And it* — this hornet — *will drive out the Hivite, the Canaanite and the Hittite, from before you*. Here one people from each pair of those enumerated in *v.* 23 is mentioned for the sake of brevity, and also in order to avoid too great an interval between the word וְגֵרְשָׁה *weghēreshā* ['will drive out'] and the word מִלְּפָנֶיךָ *millephānekhā* ['from before you'], with which it is syntactically connected. *I will not drive him out*, that is, the Canaanite and the other peoples (on the accusative pronoun *him* in the singular, see my annotations above to xxii 23 [Hebrew *v.* 22], and compare the expression 'I blot him out' in *v.* 23) *from before you in one year, lest the land become desolate* — lest it happen that you are unable to settle quickly in all the areas fit for settlement and the desolation in the midst of the land will be great, *and the wild beasts multiply against you* in the forsaken and desolate places. This is what I shall do: *Little by little I will drive them out from before you, until you are fruitful* and increase, and are able to occupy, with your numerous offspring, all the districts, *and you possess the land through its length and breadth. And I will set your bounds from the Sea of Reeds to the Sea of the Philistines* — from Elath, which is by the Red Sea, up to the Mediterranean Sea (or according to

Tur-Sinai [Torczyner] as far as the Sea of the Shephela, which is the Dead Sea), that is, the borders of your land will reach as far as the sea on both sides, 'from sea to sea' as it is expressed in Amos viii 12 and Psalms lxxii 8 (compare also Micah vii 12) — *and from the wilderness*, in the south, *to the River*, the Euphrates, in the north. This is the ideal extent of the inheritance of Israel, which was attained in the days of David. Such will be your territory, *for I will deliver into your hand* — into your power — *the inhabitants of the land* who dwell there now, *and you shall drive them out before you*. The expulsion of the inhabitants of the land is not only a promise, but also a command that is imposed upon the people of Israel, in order that they should not learn to act as they do. Therefore, *you shall make no covenant with* [literally,

32 'to'] *them or with their gods*. The making of a covenant here does not mean a reciprocal undertaking, but signifies, as we can infer from the syntactic construction with prefixed *Lāmedh* [לָהֶם *lāhem*, 'to them'] and not with the particle אֶת *'eth* ['with'], the amnesty granted by a conqueror to the conquered. Such an amnesty you shall not grant them, because it would imply, or, sooner or later, lead to, the adoption of a similar attitude *to their gods*. Therefore,

33 *they shall not dwell in your land* — do not permit them to continue to dwell in the land when it becomes yours, but drive them out, *lest they make you sin against Me* in *that you will serve their gods*. You must give heed to this danger, *for* such a sin *will be a snare to you*, and bring you to ruin and destruction. The term *snare*, used with reference to the danger of serving the strange gods of the land, occurs frequently in the Bible; hence it appears that it was a traditional expression for this concept (compare Deut. vii 16; Jos. xxiii 13; Jud. ii 3; viii 27; Psalms cvi 36). Here the epilogue reverts to a theme that forms part of the prologue (xx 23).

In these verses of the epilogue, as is customary in concluding passages, the diction becomes elevated and approximates to the style of poetry. They are marked by poetic rhythm, parallelism, phraseology and even grammatical forms (like וְגֵרַשְׁתָּמוֹ *wᵉghēraš-tāmō*, 'and you shall drive them out' in *v.* 31). Similar characteristics are found at the end of the law-codes of the gentile kings.

SECTION FOUR

THE MAKING OF THE COVENANT

CHAPTER XXIV, 1–18

FIRST PARAGRAPH
THE INSTRUCTIONS GIVEN TO MOSES
(XXIV 1–2)

Chapter XXIV

In the preceding chapters we were informed of the things that Moses was commanded to tell the people, and of the ordinances that he was enjoined to place before them; now comes the command appertaining to Moses in particular. For this reason the comple-
1 ment, *And to Moses*, precedes the verb אָמַר *'āmar* ['He said'], in order to give it emphasis. The meaning is as follows: And as for what Moses himself had to do, this is what the Lord said to him: After you have delivered all My words to the people, and have arranged, in accordance with these directives, the ceremony of the making of the Covenant, come up again to Me; the purpose of the ascent will be explained to him later (*v.* 12). To begin with, *Come up to the Lord* — in the direction of the top of the mountain, where the Lord had revealed Himself to Israel — *you and Aaron, Nadab and Abihu*, the first two sons of Aaron, whom the Torah has already introduced to us in the genealogy of the family of Moses and Aaron (vi 23), *and seventy of the elders of Israel*, a perfect representation of the people by a number that symbolizes perfection (i 5), *and prostrate yourselves* — all of you, both the leaders and the representatives of the people, in order to express the people's gratitude to the Lord for His having vouchsafed them a deed of covenant, and in order to accept the yoke of His kingdom upon the people. But this prostration must take place only *afar off*, when you are still a distance away from the summit of the mountain. From there onward, Moses alone
2 will be privileged to ascend: *And Moses alone shall come near* [וְנִגַּשׁ *w^eniggaš*] *to the Lord*, to the place of His theophany, as he was also vouchsafed the right to approach before now (compare

the word נִגַּשׁ *niggaš* ['drew near'] above, xx 21); *and they* — Aaron, his sons and the elders — *shall not come near* there, *and the people shall not come up* at all *with him*, but shall remain standing at the foot of the mountain. Verse 2 is worded in the third and not the second person, because those who accompanied Moses were also enjoined to let him go up by himself.

SECOND PARAGRAPH

DETAILS OF THE AGREEMENT RELATIVE TO THE MAKING OF THE COVENANT

(XXIV 3–8)

3 Moses carried out his charge: *And Moses came* from the mountain, upon which he was still standing after his ascent described in xx 21, *to the camp, and told the people all the words of the Lord, and all the ordinances*, that is, all that is written in our text from xx 22 to xxiii 33, *and all the people answered with one voice, and said, All the words which the Lord has spoken we will do*, that is, they accepted, by solemn declaration, all the ordinances, and instructions, and admonitions that they had heard from Moses.
4 *And Moses wrote all the words of the Lord* — all that he had told his people orally he recorded in writing on parchment or papyrus, or possibly on a stone tablet, as a document that would serve as a testimony for future generations.

And Moses *rose up early in the morning* of the following day, for the implementation of an important matter of this kind may not be delayed till after other things have been attended to on that day, *and built an altar* — an altar of earth according to xx 24 — *at the foot of the mountain* (compare xix 17), *and* erected *twelve pillars, according to the twelve tribes of Israel* (on the use of the verb to *build*, which is suited exactly only to the object *altar* but not to the other object, *pillars*, see above, on ix 23, and on xx 18). In the ceremony to be performed, the altar will represent the glory of the Lord, whilst the pillars will represent the tribes of Israel; the two contracting parties will stand facing each other.
5 *And he*, Moses, *sent the young men of the children of Israel*, that is, the first-born youths who were still ministering as priests (see my commentary on xix 22), *and they offered* on the altar *burnt*

offerings, and sacrificed peace offerings of oxen to the Lord (compare xx 24: 'and sacrifice on it [on the altar of earth] your burnt offerings and your peace offerings'). The two coordinated verbs וַיִּשְׁלַח...וַיַּעֲלוּ *wayyišlaḥ... wayyaʿălū* ['and he sent... and they offered'] connote 'and he sent to offer', like analogous instance in ii 5: 'and sent her handmaid to fetch it' [literally, 'and she fetched it']. Particular emphasis is given to the fact that the sacrifices were offered to the Lord, in agreement with xxii 20 [Hebrew, *v.* 19]: 'Whoever sacrifices to other gods shall be banned [i.e. put to death], save to the Lord [*YHWH*] only.' *And Moses took half of the blood* of the sacrifices, *and put it in basins*, in order to throw it afterwards against the people or against the pillars that represented the people (*v.* 8), *and half of the blood he threw against the altar.* The throwing of half of the blood of the offerings against the altar, which represented the Lord, and half on the people, or that which represented them, signifies a joining together of the two contracting parties (*communio*), and symbolized the execution of the deed of covenant between them.

6

Between one blood-throwing and the other, the content of the covenant was finally and solemnly ratified by Moses' reading from the Book of the Covenant and by the people's expression of consent. By the term *the book of the covenant* Scripture intends, according to the customary interpretation today, to indicate chapters xxi–xxiii (see above, p. 264). But this explanation encounters several difficulties:
(a) It was superfluous to repeat on this day what Moses had actually told the people, according to *v.* 3, on the preceding day.
(b) It is not expressly stated that what Moses read was what he had spoken according to *v.* 3, nor what he had written according to *v.* 4.
(c) If the Book of the Covenant was a written record of all the words of the Covenant, it would have been necessary to include not only the ordinances but also, and in particular, the essence of the covenant, namely, the proposals advanced in xix 5–6, and the fundamental principles contained in the Decalogue.

Consequently, the term *the book of the covenant* is to be explained in one of these two ways: (a) that it denotes a short general document, a kind of testimony and memorial to the making of the covenant, that is, a written declaration that the people undertook to listen to the voice of the Lord and to keep His covenant (xix 5), and that in return the Lord chose them to be a people that is His special possession out of all the peoples, a kingdom of priests and a holy nation (*ibid.*, *vv.* 5–6); or (b) it indicates a detailed and explicit document that included everything, namely, the contents of chapter xix, the Decalogue and the entire Divine utterance from xx 22 to xxiii 33. From the reiteration of the words דְּבָרִים *dᵉbhārīm* ['words'], דִּבְרֵי *dibhrē* ['words of'], דִּבֶּר *dibber* ['has spoken'], the first alternative seems the more probable.

7 It is narrated here that Moses took this book in his hand: *Then he took the book of the covenant, and read* it *in the hearing of the people; and they,* the children of Israel, *said, All that the Lord has spoken*, in accordance with what we heard from Him and from you, *we will do, and we will hear*, that is, so we will do and obey (compare xxiii 21: 'and hearken to his voice'; *ibid., v.* 22: 'But if you hearken attentively to his voice and do all that I say'). There-
8 after *Moses took* what was left of *the blood*, that is, the second half, *and threw it upon the people* — perhaps on the pillars that represented the twelve tribes of Israel — *and said*, in order to supplement the symbolic action with an explicit declaration of the meaning of the symbol: *Behold the blood of the covenant which the Lord has made with you in accordance with all these words*, which are written in this book that I read before you.

The solemn repetition of the word וַיִּקַּח *wayyiqqaḥ* ['and he took'] at the beginning of each of three consecutive verses indicates three important phases in the ceremony of the making of the Covenant: the throwing of the blood at the beginning and at the end, and in the middle the reading from the document of the Covenant and the assent of the people.

THIRD PARAGRAPH

IN AUDIENCE WITH GOD

(XXIV 9–11)

After the completion of the ceremony and the making of the Covenant, the representatives of the people are vouchsafed, as it were, the privilege of being received in audience by the King of the universe, who chose them and their service.

9 *Then Moses and Aaron, Nadab and Abihu, and seventy of the elders of Israel went up*, in conformity with the command recorded

EXODUS XXIV 9

in *v.* 1, and they came to a given place on the slope of the mountain, in order to prostrate themselves there from afar, and there they
10 were vouchsafed a vision of God: *and they saw the God of Israel*, etc. The sentence *and they saw the God of Israel* is at first surprising, for expressions so corporeal are uncommon in the Torah. But in the ultimate analysis the statement here differs only in the active form of the verb רָאָה *rā'ā* ['saw'] from what is stated in many passages in the passive, for example: 'and behold, the glory of the Lord appeared [literally, 'was seen']in the cloud' (xvi 10); or in the form of a noun-clause [in the Hebrew], such as *v.* 17 below: 'Now the appearance of the glory of the Lord was like a devouring fire on the top of the mountain in the sight of the people of Israel.' But even here the sentence is worded with care; it is not stated, 'and they saw *YHWH*', using the name that belongs specifically and exclusively to the Lord All-glorious Himself, but only *and they saw the God* ['*Elōhīm*] *of Israel*, employing the generic appellation that denotes any Divine phenomenon; nor is there any reference to the likeness itself that they saw, but only to what they saw beneath God's feet, recalling the words of the prophet (Isa. vi 1), who described the vision that he beheld in these terms: 'I saw the Lord sitting upon a throne, high and lifted up; and His train filled the temple.' He, too, did not use the Tetragrammaton, only the designation אֲדֹנָי '*Ădhōnāy* ['Lord']; nor did he describe more than the throne and the train. The meaning is that they saw the likeness of the appearance of light or of fire, *and under His feet* they saw *as it were a tile* [or 'brick'; this is the literal signification of לְבֵנָה *lᵉbhēnā*] — something resembling *paved work* of sapphire stone, which symbolizes the heavens by its blue colour, like the firmament that Ezekiel saw beneath the Throne of Glory (Ezek. i 22) — *and like the very heaven*, that is, like the appearance of the sky, its hue (compare Lam. iv 7: 'they were actually [usually rendered: 'in body'] more ruddy than coral'), *for purity* — for brightness. The description is duplicated here by the use of different similes, in accordance with poetic diction. A poetic tradition is reflected also in the last word, לְטֹהַר *lᵉṭōhar* ['for purity'], which is derived from the stem טהר *ṭhr*, which is commonly used in Ugaritic poetry to signify the brightness of the sapphire. The simile is employed apparently to indicate that the divine sphere is above heaven, that is, higher than the world of nature.

Although the seeing of a vision of God was deemed fatal for a person unworthy of this privilege, no evil befell the representatives

11 of the people: *And on the nobles of the children of Israel* — on those men who were the noblemen and chosen ones of the children of Israel, and were worthy that God should reveal Himself to them, *He put not forth His hand*; *and they beheld God* (here, too, we have the generic designation *'Elōhīm*, that is, they saw a Divine vision), and, nevertheless, *they ate and drank* at the sacred meal of the peace offerings when they returned to the camp. Perhaps there is an allusion here to the fact that Aaron and his sons and the elders did not attain to the spiritual level of Moses, who was privileged to come nearer than they to the sphere of the Godhead and to rise higher than they above normal human life; for during the forty days of his stay on Mount Sinai 'he neither ate bread nor drank water' (xxxiv 28; compare Deut. ix 9, 18).

FOURTH PARAGRAPH

MOSES' ASCENT

(XXIV 12–18)

12 *And the Lord said to Moses*, after Moses' return together with Aaron and his other companions to the camp: *Come up to Me on the mountain*, as he was enjoined already in *v.* 2; the time to ascend has now arrived, so he is again exhorted at the moment when he is due to set out. *And be there* — remain there, on the mountain, a considerable time — *and I will give you*, whilst you are there, *the tables of stone, and the instruction* [תּוֹרָה *tōrā*] *and the commandment*, that is, the tables of stone inscribed with the instructions and commandment, *which I have written to instruct them*; these are, as will be explained subsequently (xxxiv 28), the Decalogue. Just as they were proclaimed by God, so their writing must necessarily be the writing of God, graven upon the tables (xxxii 16).

13 *So Moses rose up with his servant Joshua*, who accompanied him in order to minister to him during the period that he would have to wait until God called him to ascend to the top of the mountain, and he would rise above the plane of everyday life, and would no longer need food and drink. Possibly the text means that Joshua set up a tent on the slope of the mountain, and there they both dwelt. In this way Moses fulfilled the command that was given him: *and Moses went up into the mountain of God.*

After it has been stated in general terms that Moses went up into the mountain, we are given details of the ascent, in accordance with the literary method of first making a general statement, and thereafter mentioning the particulars. *And to the elders he said*, before leaving the camp: *Abide here for us* — wait here for us, namely, for Joshua and me — *until we come to you again*; *and, behold, Aaron and Hur are with you* to act in my stead; *whoever has a cause, let him go to them. Then Moses went up*, after he had given these instructions to the elders, *into the mountain* — but at first only as far as a given place on its slope (here it is not written 'the mountain of God'), together with Joshua, *and the cloud*, heralding the approach of God, *covered the mountain*.

Now come three verses that bring the entire section to a solemn close. They portray in elevated, poetic diction the theophany on Mount Sinai and Moses' approach to the site of the Divine manifestation on the top of the mountain. The initial word וַיִּשְׁכֹּן *wayyiškōn* ['and dwelt'] gives here, at the end of the section, a preliminary inkling of the subject of the next section, to wit, the work of the מִשְׁכָּן *miškān* ['the dwelling-place (of God), Tabernacle'], and a nexus is thereby formed between the two sections — not just an external, but also a thematic, connection, as we shall explain later. *And the glory of the Lord dwelt upon Mount Sinai, and the cloud covered it*, that is, continued to cover it, *six days* — days of spiritual preparation for Moses — *and the voice of God called to Moses on the seventh day out of the midst of the cloud.* On the concept, frequently encountered, of an action continuing for six consecutive days until the outcome is reached on the seventh, see my remarks above, pp. 190 f. At the same time that the Divine call was heard by Moses, *the appearance of the glory of the Lord* was *like a devouring fire on the top of the mountain in the sight of the children of Israel*, and they all saw with their own eyes the appearance of the fire, which was the appearance of the glory of the Lord. *And Moses* alone *entered the cloud*, while Joshua remained in his place on the slope of the mountain. In the cloud Moses was hidden from the eyes of the people; *and he* — Moses — *went up into the mountain* — to its summit — *and Moses was on the mountain*, as he had been enjoined (*v*. 12: 'and be there'), *forty days and forty nights*.

PART THREE
THE TABERNACLE AND ITS SERVICE
A Commentary on Exodus XXV-XL

SECTION ONE

DIRECTIONS FOR THE CONSTRUCTION OF THE TABERNACLE

CHAPTER XXV, VERSE 1—CHAPTER XXXI, VERSE 18

In order to understand the significance and purpose of the Tabernacle, we must realize that the children of Israel, after they had been privileged to witness the Revelation of God on Mount Sinai, were about to journey from there and thus draw away from the site of the theophany. So long as they were encamped in the place, they were conscious of God's nearness; but once they set out on their journey, it seemed to them as though the link had been broken, unless there were in their midst a tangible symbol of God's presence among them. It was the function of the Tabernacle [literally, 'Dwelling'] to serve as such a symbol. Not without reason, therefore, does this section come immediately after the section that describes the making of the Covenant at Mount Sinai. The nexus between Israel and the Tabernacle is a perpetual extension of the bond that was forged at Sinai between the people and their God. The children of Israel, dwelling in tribal order at every encampment, are able to see, from every side, the Tabernacle standing in the midst of the camp, and the visible presence of the Sanctuary proves to them that just as the glory of the Lord dwelt on Mount Sinai, so He dwells in their midst wherever they wander in the wilderness. This is the purport of Scripture (xxv 8), when it states: 'And let them make Me a Sanctuary, that I may dwell in their midst.' This is also the significance of the clear parallelism between the last sentences of the preceding section, describing how the Divine Presence dwelt upon Mount Sinai, and the closing passage of our Book, which depicts, in like terms, how the Divine Presence abode in the Tabernacle (see below, my annotations to the concluding verses). Further on we shall explain in detail how the very design of the Tabernacle was able to inspire the people with the confident feeling that the Lord was present in their midst.

According to the view that prevailed among Bible critics, without serious opposition, until recently, the Tabernacle never existed. The sections speaking of it belong, in their view, to various strata of the Priestly Code (P), and were written in the period of the Second Temple; and the whole account is only an imaginary picture created by the priests of those generations on the basis of memories of Solomon's Temple. Today there is an increasing tendency, particularly on the part of scholars engaged in studying the archaeology of the ancient East, to assume that we have here, at least in its essential features, an ancient and trustworthy tradition. But there is still room for further research, and my subsequent remarks, in the following lines, will be devoted to such additional investigation.

In dealing with this subject, just as in my exposition of other parts of Exodus, my chief aim will be to interpret and explain the words of the text. In any case, it is obvious that a thorough elucidation of the text should help to shed light on the historical problem, too. I wish to approach my task without any prejudgement, and allow the Bible to speak for itself.

Before I begin to explain the passages in detail, it appears to me necessary to make a few preliminary observations.

In the first instance, we must consider the purpose of the sections dealing with the construction of the Tabernacle. In the same way as the narrative portions of the Pentateuch are not intended to teach history for its own sake, but to give, by the narration, religious or ethical or national instruction, so these sections do not aim to provide a disquisition on the antiquities of Israelite worship in their minutest detail, but to instruct us in the fundamental idea of the presence of God in the camp of Israel, and to give a comprehensive description of whatever is considered conducive to the achievement of this object, in other words, of whatever is capable of leaving on the reader's mind the desired impression. I do not wish to convey thereby that the text is in any sense allegorical; all the numerous and varied proposals that have been advanced with a view to interpreting the construction of the Tabernacle allegorically have no value in so far as the plain meaning of the Scriptural passages is concerned. I merely desire to indicate that, in order to attain its goal, the Torah utilized various means conformable to the spirit of ancient times, and that *inter alia* it employed the principle of numerical symmetry, which greatly appealed to those generations. These sections cite figures that are mentioned only for the sake of achieving such symmetry, which is based partly on the decimal system and partly on the number seven and the sexagesimal system, as will be explained in detail further on. This note will suffice to remove a number of difficulties that have been raised and have brought many exegetes to the conclusion that the plan of the Biblical Tabernacle was incapable of practical implementation.

And another point. In keeping with its aim, the Torah was not concerned to state explicitly all the particulars that would have been necessary if its intention had been to describe the Tabernacle and its appurtenances with complete exactitude, and to afford adequate guidance to anyone wishing to fashion a tabernacle and its equipment according to their design. Much of what is essential for this purpose is not in the Book. Hence the attempts made to reconstruct the Tabernacle and its vessels in detail mostly lack a proper basis. It is very interesting to note that, in the very passages where the lack of details in the text is most noticeable, it is stated that the Lord showed Moses the likeness of the object that he had to make, as though Scripture intended to say that whatever is not explicitly mentioned in the description of the articles was shown to Moses by Heaven in a vision. We must be careful, therefore, not to supply from imagination what is not expressly found in the text, nor to draw inferences in regard to the historical problem from the incompleteness of the Biblical descriptions.

We can find aid for the elucidation of the texts and their purport on the one hand in the archaeological discoveries made in the Land of Israel and in the neighbouring countries, and on the other hand in what we can learn concerning the customs and concepts of antiquity from the literatures and documents of the peoples of the East, for it is particularly through our knowledge of the world in which the early generations of Israelites lived that we are able to understand their own feelings and the impression they were likely to gain from what met their gaze. The study of these documents will enable us also to comprehend a number of things that the commentators have found difficult, and to solve formidable problems such as the combination of the boards, which are elements of a permanent structure, with the curtains, which are features of a tent designed to be moved from place to place.

Similarly we can be assisted by the detailed descriptions in the *Baraitha On The Erection Of The Tabernacle* and in the parallel passages in Talmudic literature; but we must not resort to these sources without caution, since much of what is stated there is based on a haggadic interpretation of the verses, which is unrelated to their real sense, and much else reflects the later conditions obtaining in the Second Temple.

THE TABERNACLE

Very important for the understanding of the subject is the oft-repeated statement that the Lord showed Moses the pattern of the Tabernacle and of its appurtenances (xxv 9, 40; xxvi 30; xxvii 8; Num. viii 4). It means that Moses saw in a prophetic vision the Divine Dwelling-Place in heaven, and it was incumbent upon him to erect in the midst of the camp of Israel a tabernacle [literally, 'dwelling'] designed like the one that he saw in his vision, an earthly sanctuary corresponding to the heavenly sanctuary. The two concepts, to wit, that of seeing the design in a vision and that of the correspondence between the terrestrial and the celestial sanctuaries, are not confined to these sections only. In the Book of Ezekiel likewise there is discernible the resemblance between the Chariot that the prophet saw and the כַּפֹּרֶת *kappōreth* ['propitiatory' or 'covering'] of the cherubim upon the ark, and later on in the book we are told of the vision of the model of the sanctuary that was to be built in the future. In the Book of Chronicles (i Chron. xxviii 19) it is stated that the plan of Solomon's Temple was 'by the writing from the hand of the Lord.' The idea frequently encountered in the Talmud that the Temple at Jerusalem faced the Temple in heaven is certainly not a new notion invented by the Sages, but an ancient tradition on the subject in their possession.

Similar ideas, despite the fundamental differences in the conception of God and His relationship to man, are found also among the gentiles. In cylinder A of Gudea it is narrated that the god Ningirsu showed Gudea, in dreams of the night, the likeness of the sanctuary that he had to build, and he delivered to him a sketch of the structure. The Babylonians, who gloried in the magnificent temple of Marduk, called *Esagila*, in their city, believed that it was situated opposite the celestial *Esagila*.

Since the Torah uses human terminology and addresses itself to human beings, it is not surprising that it prescribed for the generation of the wilderness things that were consonant with the concepts and thought-modes of that period, making only such changes as were required by the spirit of the Israelite faith. When we examine the literature of the time and the region, we find a similar picture, apart from the aforementioned modifications, to that described here in the Bible.

When the Canaanites speak of the dwelling-place of *El*, the father of the gods, and of the abodes of the other deities, they designate them *tabernacle* or *tent*, the very two terms employed in the Pentateuch; nor are they just two words that signify *taber-*

THE TABERNACLE

nacle and *tent*, but they are actually *mškn* and *'hl*, letter for letter the same as in Hebrew. It is narrated, for example, in the Ugaritic epic of King Keret, that *El* and the other gods came to his wedding celebration to bless him with fertility and prosperity, and thereafter they returned to their dwelling-places: 'The gods proceed to their tents, the family of *El* to their tabernacles' (Tablet III K, iii, 18-19; similarly in the epic of Aqhat (Tablet II D, v, 31-33). Even if we grant that archaic poetic expressions are used here, which figuratively connote a habitation and an abode in general, nevertheless they show that the Canaanites originally pictured to themselves the cosmic dwelling-place of their deities in the form of a tent or a tabernacle. Nor is this all. The tabernacle of the Canaanite El is made of *boards*, the actual term found in the Pentateuch (*the boards of El* are mentioned a number of times in Ugaritic poetry), and these boards were erected on *pedestals* (Tablet V AB, v, 17), like the boards of the Biblical Tabernacle. Hence we need feel no surprise, as do most exegetes, at the integration of a tent with boards in the Pentateuchal descriptions; the combination presents no difficulty.

What we have stated concerning the general design of the Tabernacle can be said also in regard to the sacred appurtenances within it; they, too, conform to the ideas of the time. In one of the Ugaritic poems, which speaks in particular of the building of the cosmic temple of Baal, the articles of furniture prepared for this fane are described (Tablet II AB, ii, 1 ff.). These are: a throne; a footstool; a lamp, a chest of drawers; a table with all its utensils; and a bed. The chest and the bed are necessary according to idolatrous theology, which portrays the gods as resembling human beings in their requirements. Baal needs a bed to lie upon; and he requires a chest with many drawers to put his garments and other articles in. Needless to say, there is no place for all this in Israelite doctrine, and such furniture did not exist in the Israelite Tabernacle. But it did have a throne, to wit, the *kappōreth* of the cherubim with outstretched wings, who form with their outspread pinions a throne for the Lord who sits on the cherubim and is invisible to the eye (on this topic, see further on); the ark beneath the *kappōreth* is the Lord's footstool (on this, too, see below); whilst the lamp and the table and its vessels constitute a perfect parallel to the gentile appurtenances. With regard to the golden altar, it is mentioned in this section only as an addendum at the end, and does not belong to the main theme.

THE TABERNACLE

This correspondence to the concepts of early antiquity proves beyond doubt that the composition of the sections dealing with the construction of the Tabernacle cannot be attributed to the period of the Second Temple. The priests of that age could not know the notions prevailing among the ancient generations. An important corollary follows from this in regard to the historical problem; if the subject-matter of the text fits the generation of the wilderness, there is no reason to doubt its historicity.

FIRST PARAGRAPH

THE CONTRIBUTION TO THE TABERNACLE

(XXV 1–9)

Chapter XXV

1 *And the Lord spoke to Moses* — whilst the latter was still on Mount Sinai, as is stated at the end of the preceding section (xxiv 18) — delivering a long and detailed address that continues as far as xxx 10, and is supplemented by a series of additional directions extending to xxxi 17. The first and main communication begins:
2 *saying, Speak to the children of Israel*, for it is desirable that the entire people should take part in the fulfilment of this precept, *that they take* [וְיִקְחוּ *wᵉyiqḥū*] *for Me a contribution* — that they set aside in My honour a portion of their possessions. The verb לָקַח *lāqaḥ* ['take'] occurs frequently in the Bible in this or a similar sense, in connection with the preparation of a sacrifice or gift for the Lord (see above, on xviii 12); regarding the expression *for Me*, compare particularly Gen. xv 9: 'Bring Me [literally, 'for Me'] a heifer three years old', etc. This precept shall not be an obligatory but a voluntary act, according to each man's liberality: *from every man whose heart makes him willing* — that is, from every one who wishes, whether he be rich or poor, whether he give much or little — *you shall take* — [תִּקְחוּ *tiqḥū*, pl.] you and your associates who will assist you and help to implement the commandment — *My contribution*, to wit, the offering that is *for Me*, as was stated at the beginning of the verse. Here the verb לָקַח
3 *lāqaḥ* is used in another sense, namely, *to receive. And this is the contribution that you shall take from them* — from the children of Israel — that is: These are the kinds of things that you may

receive for the purpose of this precept (again the noun *contribution* is used and again the verb *take*; each word occurs three times).

First, the metals are mentioned: *gold, silver and bronze*. The age in which silver was rarer and more precious than gold was already past; hence gold is mentioned first, as the most valuable metal. The use of iron in the generation of the wilderness was still a novelty, and new things are not to be used for sacred purposes, in accordance with the principle of conservatism obtaining in ritual tradition (see above, on iv 25); for this reason no mention is made here of iron.

4 After the metals, materials used in spinning and weaving are mentioned; to begin with, four different kinds required for the making of sumptuous vestments. Three of them are types of wool (not flax, as some thought), and one a special sort of linen. The first stuff is תְּכֵלֶת *t*ᵉ*khēleth*, that is, wool dyed the colour of that name, to wit, a dye extracted from a species of shell-fish found in abundance in the sea, by the coasts of the Mediterranean, and especially by the shores of Phoenicia and the Land of Israel. The dyers used to prise open the shell-fish whilst they were still alive (compare B. Shabbat 75a), and the transparent liquid secreted from their glands acquired in sunlight a *deep violet* colour — this is תְּכֵלֶת *t*ᵉ*khēleth*. The second is אַרְגָּמָן *'argāmān*, wool dyed *dark red* (πορφύρα *purpura*), which they manufactured by the addition of certain ingredients to the dye *t*ᵉ*khēleth*. The third is wool dyed תּוֹלַעַת שָׁנִי *tōla'ath šānī* [literally, 'worm of scarlet'; rendered: 'scarlet'], a colour that derived its name from the fact that it was extracted from the body of a worm [*tōla'ath*] — coccida, to be exact — of the genus *Kermes* (one of the species of this genus being designated *Kermes biblicus*). The substantive שָׁנִי *šānī* is derived from the stem שנה־שני *šn(h)-šny*, meaning 'to shine, flash' (compare سنو *snw* in Arabic ['to shine']). This colour, as well as wool so dyed, is called in Hebrew both by the one word שָׁנִי *šānī* ['scarlet'] and by the designation שְׁנִי (הַ)תּוֹלַעַת *š*ᵉ*nī (hat)tōla'ath* [literally, 'scarlet of (the) worm'], and in the late Hebrew of Chronicles [ii Chron. ii 6, 13; iii 14] by the name כַּרְמִיל *karmīl* ['crimson, carmine'], in Arabic قرمز *qirmiz*, a Persian loan-word; thence all the corresponding European names are derived. After the three varieties of wool comes שֵׁשׁ *šēš*, in Egyptian *šs*, apparently the term for very fine threads of flax, suitable for weaving the most delicate garments. In Hebrew this material is also called בּוּץ *būṣ*, as in Akkadian (whence βύσσος, *byssus*). These costly

materials are followed by a coarser stuff, namely, *goats*, that is, goats' hair, called in the Talmud נוֹצַת עִזִּים *nōṣath ʿizzīm* [literally, 'goats' feathers'].

So far raw materials have been mentioned, which can assume different forms in accordance with the wishes of the craftsman. Now, in *v.* 5, three things of a different character are listed. First, two kinds of material that can be used as they are: *rams' skins dyed red, and the skins of* תְּחָשִׁים *tᵉḥāšīm*. These are possibly *dolphins* [*tuḥas* in Arabic], which are common in the Red Sea, or a kind of sea-cow, the *dugong*, which is likewise frequently found in the Red Sea. The skin of these creatures is very strong, and till a few generations ago, the sandals of the Bedouins in the Peninsula of Sinai were mostly made of them. Compare also Ezek. xvi 10: *and I shod you with* תַּחַשׁ *taḥaš* [sing. of plural given above]. After the skins, comes wood, which requires only to be sawed and planed in order to be made into planks. עֲצֵי שִׁטִּים *ʿăṣē šiṭṭīm* ['Shittah trees'] are different species of the genus Acacia, which grow abundantly in the Arabah, and generally south of the Land of Israel.

The purpose for which all the materials mentioned so far were to be used will be explained in the paragraphs that follow. On the other hand, in *vv.* 6–7, the Bible specifies, together with the material, the use to which it was to be put. This difference is not accidental, but stems from the nature of the things. When gold is referred to, one immediately knows what is meant; the same applies to deep violet wool, or rams' skins dyed red, and the like. But when oil is mentioned, it is not yet clear which kind of oil is intended — edible oil, or oil for anointing and washing (cf. שמן רחץ =*šemen raḥaṣ* ['oil of washing'] in the the Samaria Ostraca), or any other kind of oil; when spices are spoken of, we still need to know if the reference is to spices used for seasoning, or for fragrance, or for some other object; this is also the case with the stones for setting. Further details are necessary. Hence it is stated that the children of Israel should bring *oil for the light, spices for the anointing oil and for the incense of fragrant powders*, etc. What the light, the oil of anointing and the incense of fragrant powders are will be elucidated later, just as the purpose of the previous materials will be clarified. In addition, they must bring שֹׁהַם *šōham* [usually rendered: 'onyx'] *stones*, called *sându* or *sâmtu* stones in Akkadian (see my commentary on Genesis, *From Adam to Noah*, pp. 77, 120), and various *stones for setting*, both onyx and other gems, *for the ephod and for the breastpiece.* Subsequently the nature of the ephod and the breastpiece will be explained.

The omission of the *Wāw* conjunctive in v. 6 and at the beginning of v. 7 is a stylistic variation of no importance; in the parallel verses (xxxv 8–9) the *Wāw* is there. Verse 6 is missing in most of the Septuagint MSS; this may be due to the fact that the translators skipped from the word שִׁטִּים *šiṭṭīm* ['acacia'] to the word סַמִּים *sammīm* ['fragrant powders'], since both words have the same ending; or to the fact that they thought this verse superfluous, because oil is spoken of in detail later, in xxvii 20. But actually it is not redundant; it was essential to mention here the entire range of materials, without exception.

It was not impossible for these materials to be in the possession of the Israelites. Some of them, like the metals and precious stones, they could have brought with them from Egypt; and not without purpose were we told earlier of the jewelry of silver and of gold that they received from the Egyptians before leaving. They had an abundance of wool and rams' skins, since they possessed 'very much' cattle (xii 38); there was a plentiful supply of acacia trees locally; it was not difficult to acquire dugong skins in the neighbourhood; whilst other things, such as dyes, oil, spices and the like, could be purchased from the caravans passing through the area. For the working of the metals, they were able to utilize the services of the members of the neighbouring Kenite tribe.

The object for which the Israelites were to bring the contribution of the Lord is stated in v. 8: *And let them make Me*, with the aforementioned contribution, *a sanctuary*, a structure sanctified and dedicated to Me (the Bible does not say, 'And let them make Me a tabernacle [literally, 'a dwelling-place'], for God has no need of a tabernacle in which to dwell; it is only Israel that requires a Divine Tabernacle), and when they look at this sanctuary, which will be erected in their camp, they will become conscious of My presence. *That I may dwell in their midst*, in the same way as they have already seen My glory dwell on Mount Sinai.

You, Moses, see here on Mount Sinai the likeness of the heavenly sanctuary, now behold, *According to all that I show you concerning the pattern of the tabernacle, and of all its furniture* (on this vision see my observations above, in the introductory notes to this section), *even* [literally, *and*] *so you shall make it* — you and the children of Israel. The *Wāw* conjunctive ['and'] of וְכֵן תַּעֲשׂוּ *wᵉkhēn taʿăśū* ['and so you shall make it'] has perplexed many commentators, but it presents no difficulty. It can be explained in one of the following two ways: (a) It is an idiomatic Hebrew usage to add at times the *Wāw conjunctive* before the apodosis; compare, for example, Num. i 19: 'As the Lord commanded Moses, and so did he number them in the wilderness of Sinai'; (b) (Everything shall be) according to all that I show you... and so you shall make it. Also the verse quoted above from Numbers may be explained in this way.

SECOND PARAGRAPH

THE ARK AND THE KAPPŌRETH

(XXV 10–22)

After the general introduction regarding the contribution to the Tabernacle, the Divine communication deals separately with each of the holy articles that are to be placed within the Tabernacle and kept there. The articles are described here before the Tabernacle itself, because they are of primary importance, and their sanctity is greater than that of the Tabernacle. The Tabernacle serves to protect them; but they do not serve the Tabernacle. The holiest of them — the ark and the *kappōreth* — which were to be placed in the holy of holies, are dealt with first.

10 The commandment to make the ark begins with the word וְעָשׂוּ *weʿāśū* ['And they shall make'] — and not with the word וְעָשִׂיתָ *weʿāśīthā* ['And you shall make'], which is the usual formula employed subsequently — in order to establish a link with the verb וְעָשׂוּ *weʿāśū* ['And let them make'] in v. 8, the thought being: And let the children of Israel make Me a sanctuary in the following way: let them make, first of all, an ark, etc. The Samaritan Recension and the Septuagint, which are accustomed to harmonize the verses, read also here 'And you shall make'.

The word אָרוֹן *'ārōn* [rendered: 'ark'] denotes here a kind of chest or box.* It was to be made of the wood of *acacia trees*, which grow in the vicinity, as we have stated, and its dimensions

---

* In the Hebrew text, the author notes that אָרוֹן *'ārōn* has not the same signification in the Bible as in modern Hebrew. Its present meaning, a piece of furniture in which scrolls of the Torah are placed in Synagogue, evolved from the use of the expression אֲרוֹן הַקֹּדֶשׁ *'ărōn haqqōdheš* ['holy ark'], on the basis of the tradition that a Torah scroll was kept in the ark in the Temple. *Tr.*

were to be: *two cubits and a half shall be its length, and a cubit and a half its breadth, and a cubit and a half its height.*

After the first sentence, which is in the third person and in the plural for the reason mentioned, the text can continue in the
11 second person [sing.]: *And you shall overlay it* — to enhance its dignity and beauty — *with pure gold,* that is, refined gold, and there shall be a twofold overlay: *within and without shall you overlay it.* From archaeological finds in Egypt we learn that wooden furniture was covered with gold in one of these two ways: either hammered plates of gold were attached to the wood by means of small nails, or thin leaves of gold were glued to a fine layer of plaster spread over the wood. Here, apparently, the first method is intended, since, if the second method were used, the overlay would not hold very long, especially inside the ark, where the two tables of stone were to be kept. *And you shall make upon it a moulding of gold round about* — an adornment in the form of a garland of flowers or leaves running right round the four sides of the ark on the outside, bisecting its height, and resembling in its form a similar adornment that was to be made for the table and its frame and for the altar of incense; all the sacred appurtenances were to be fashioned in
12 the same style. *And you shall cast for it* — for the ark, that is, to handle it therewith, and so that they are attached to it — *four rings of gold, and put* the rings *on its four feet* (פַּעֲמֹתָיו *paʿămōthāw*; not 'its four corners', as the word is usually explained) — short feet, measuring a few finger-breadths, whose purpose was to prevent the ark from resting directly on the ground. The original meaning of the word פַּעַם *paʿam* [the sing., without suffixes, of the aforementioned Hebrew word] is 'foot' (see above, on xxiii 14), and the plural termination of nouns appertaining to members of the human body, when used figuratively of a part of an object, is ־וֹת *-ōth*, like the word יָדוֹת *yādhōth* [literally, 'hands'; translated: 'tenons'] (xxvi 17), the plural of יָד *yādh* ['hand'], when employed in a metaphorical sense, and like the noun כְּתֵפוֹת *kᵉthēphōth* ['shoulder-straps'] (which also occurs later [xxviii 7 ff.]), the plural of כָּתֵף *kāthēph* ['shoulder'], when used in a figurative signification. *And two rings,* that is, the rings shall be so arranged (the *Wāw* rendered 'and', is explicative) that two rings shall be *on the one side of it* — on one of the shorter sides of the ark — *and two rings on the other side of it.* The rings were made for the purpose of inserting in them the בַּדִּים *baddīm*, long poles, that were placed on the shoulders of those who carried the ark, whenever it was

13 necessary to move it from one place to another: *And you shall*
14 *make poles of acacia wood, and overlay them with gold. And you shall put the poles into the rings on the sides of the ark, to carry the ark by them.* When the ark was being carried, one of its longer sides was in front, and the two cherubs on the *kappōreth* were borne forward, one next to the other, and thus the ark was placed in the most holy place — the two cherubim alongside each other,
15 one on the right and the other on the left. *The poles shall remain in the rings of the ark* — constantly, and not just when the ark was carried. *They shall not be taken from it* — from off the ark, whereas the poles of the other sacred vessels were not fitted onto them permanently, but only when they were moved from one place to another in the course of the Israelites' journeys. The reason for the distinction is, apparently, the fact that the ark was due to be carried not only when the camp as a whole was on the move, but also in connection with solemn processions, like those described in Jos. iii 3 f.; vi 4 ff.; and consequently, it was fitting that whatever was necessary to its transportation should always be ready. The poles were, so to speak, an inseparable part of the ark, which was intended always to be carried. The meaning of the words *and shall put in its poles* in Num. iv 6 we shall discuss when we come to that passage*.
16 *And you shall put to the ark* — inside it — *the testimony* — the tablets of the testimony, the tablets on which the Decalogue is inscribed (xxxiv 28), and which are called *testimony* because they testify to the covenant that was made between the Lord and the children of Israel — *which I shall give you,* when I conclude My communication (xxxi 18), as I have already apprised you (xxiv 12).

Since the *kappōreth* of the cherubim, which was placed upon the ark, connotes, as it were, the throne of God, as we shall explain later, it follows that the ark, which is beneath the throne, is a kind of footstool of God. Now it is by this very designation — *His footstool* — that several verses allude to the ark; compare Psa. xcix 5: 'Extol the Lord our God, and prostrate yourselves at His footstool! Holy is He!'; *ibid.*, cxxxii 7-8: 'Let us go to His dwelling; let us prostrate ourselves at His footstool! Arise, O Lord, and go to Thy resting place, Thou and *the ark of Thy might*'; so, too, David said according to i Chron. xxviii 2: 'I had it in my heart

---

* Unfortunately the author died before he was able to write his commentary on the Book of Numbers. *Tr.*

to build a house of rest for the ark of the covenant of the Lord, and for the footstool of our God.' Apparently, also in Lam. ii 1 the reference is to the ark: 'and He has not remembered His footstool in the day of His anger' (according to the usual interpretation, the reference is to the Temple as a whole). But the prophet who raised his gaze to still greater heights and saw God's sanctuary throughout the universe, likened the earth to God's footstool, and declared: 'Thus says the Lord: Heaven is My throne and the earth is My footstool', etc. (Isa. lxvi 1).

The conception of the ark as the Lord's footstool enables us to understand why the tables of the covenant were placed within it, and to realize that the conjectures of many modern exegetes, who thought that inside the ark were not the tables but sacred stones (kinds of fetishes, or idols, and the like), are without foundation. It was the custom in the ancient East to deposit the deeds of a covenant made between human kings in the sanctuaries of the gods, in the footstool of the idols that symbolized the deity, so that the godhead should be a witness to the covenant and see that it was observed. Thus, for example, in a letter from Ramses II king of Egypt to the king of Mira, it is stated that the document of the oath whereby he obligated himself to keep the terms of his covenant with the king of the Hittites was placed beneath the feet of *Tešub* the god of the Hittites (in the temple of *Tešub*, of course, in the land of the Hittites); similarly, the document of the oath of the king of the Hittites to keep that agreement was placed beneath the feet of the sun god, to wit, the Egyptian god *Re'* (needless to say, in the land of Egypt), in order that the great deities should be witnesses thereto. This custom makes it clear why the testimony to the covenant made between the Lord and Israel was enshrined in the ark. Among the Israelites there was no image to symbolize the God of Israel, but there was His footstool, and therein the testimony of the covenant was placed and preserved.

If the question be asked, why the tables, which comprise the principles of the Covenant and the basic precepts incumbent on the Israelites, were lying in an enclosed place, and were not exhibited before the people, it can easily be answered that there were undoubtedly copies of the Decalogue engraven on stone, or written on parchment or papyrus, available for the people to see, and that it was only the original testimony that was put in the ark for safe keeping.

The tables, which were certainly not very large (of their size we shall speak later), lay side by side, apparently, inside the ark, one to the right and one to the left, and were wrapped in linen, so that when the ark was carried the writing engraven on them should not be rubbed away, nor the inner overlay of the ark impaired.

Having told us what was to be placed within the ark, the Torah
17 speaks of the thing that has to be placed on top of it: *Then you shall make a* כַּפֹּרֶת *(kappōreth) of pure gold*, etc. The word *kappōreth* is explained by some to mean *covering* (Arabic كفر *kfr*, 'to cover'), because the *kappōreth* used to cover the ark; whilst others connect it with the word כִּפּוּר *kippūr* ['atonement'], since it was particularly associated with the service of the Day of Atonement (Lev. xvi 2, 13–15). In the final analysis the etymology is the same, since even the word *kippūr* signifies the covering up of iniquity, as the thought [though a different verb is used for 'cover'] is expressed in Psa. xxxii 1: 'Blessed be he whose transgression is forgiven, whose sin is covered.' But it is a basic and correct principle not to rely unduly, when seeking to ascertain the nature of a given matter, on the etymology of its name, because the signification of names changes continually with the passage of time, and sometimes bears but remote resemblance to its original derivation. If we wish to understand the true nature and significance of the *kappōreth*, we must examine the rest of the passage.

The dimensions of the *kappōreth* are specified as follows: *two cubits and a half shall be its length, and a cubit and a half its breadth*, that means, it shall be a slab of gold, whose measurements will correspond to the length and breadth of the ark. Upon it are to be
18 two figures of cherubim: *And you shall make two cherubim of gold: of hammered work shall you make them*, that is, you shall make them by beating with a hammer on a plate of gold, each one being upon one *of the two ends of the kappōreth* (the numeral שְׁנֵי *šᵉnē* ['two' masculine], which occurs here before a feminine noun, and so, too, several times later, can be used for both masculine and
19 feminine also in Ugaritic). More specifically: *And make* (the *Wāw* ['and'] is explicative) *one cherub on the one end, and one cherub on the other end; all of one piece with the kappōreth shall you make the cherubim on its two ends*, that is, both the *kappōreth* and the *cherubim* should be made together, of hammered work, out of a single plate of gold.

The Torah does not describe the form of the cherubim. This indicates that it was well known and required no elucidation. In

Ezekiel chapter x, the creatures that carry the Divine chariot, upon which rests the throne of glory, are called *cherubim*. According to the description given in the vision recorded in chapter i, they are winged creatures with four faces — the face of a man, of a lion, of an ox and of an eagle. Ezekiel's vision is based on the traditional view, which regarded the clouds of the sky as the chariot of God, and consequently applied to the Deity the designation, *He who rides upon* עֲרָבוֹת *'ărābhōth* (Psa. lxviii 4 [Hebrew, *v.* 5]), that is, 'He who rides upon the clouds.' The Canaanites believed the clouds to be the chariot of Baal in the literal and material sense of the term, and they designated Baal *rkb 'rpt*, which is the equivalent of the Hebrew רֹכֵב עֲרָבוֹת *rōkhēbh 'ărābhōth* ['He who rides upon the clouds']. The Israelites inherited the appellation from the Canaanites in a figurative sense, as a poetic expression. The cherubim are regarded as an embodiment of the winds, which blow in the sky and drive the clouds of the chariot from place to place. Thus it is written in Psa. xviii 10 [Hebrew, *v.* 11]: 'He rode on a cherub, and flew; yea, He came swiftly (ii Sam. xxii 11: 'He was seen') upon the wings of the wind', and according to the rules of poetic parallelism the wings of the wind are identical with the wings of the cherubim. We find similar examples in other Biblical passages, which I have already discussed elsewhere (see the bibliography at the end of the book). The *kappōreth* is specifically called 'chariot' in i Chron. xxviii 18. In the Divine visions that appeared to Ezekiel, he saw 'the likeness of a throne' above the chariot, and above the throne 'the appearance of the likeness of the glory of the Lord.' Since in the thought processes of the ancient East the boundary between the symbol and the thing symbolized, and likewise the distinctions between the different parts of the symbol, were liable to be easily blurred, in the end the chariot is identified with the throne, and even the wings of the cherubim are regarded as identical with the throne, and not without reason is the Divine designation *who is enthroned on the cherubim* used particularly when the Bible refers to the ark, which carries upon it the *kappōreth*. Thus it is stated in i Sam. iv 4: 'and brought from there the ark of the covenant of the Lord of hosts, who is enthroned on the cherubim'; and in ii Sam. vi 2: 'the ark of God, whereupon is called the Name, even the name of the Lord of hosts who sits enthroned on the cherubim' (compare i Chron. xiii 6).

A figure resembling somewhat the Israelite cherub was that of the Mesopotamian *kâribu*, an imaginary creature that mediated between man and the godhead, and brought man's prayers before the deity. It was depicted as a composite creature, with wings, a human head and the body of an ox, or in other forms combining elements of the body of a man or an ox or a lion or an eagle. In Egypt the form of the sphinx was prevalent, which had the body of a lion with a human head; similarly the representation of a winged lion with a human head was a widespread feature of the art of Syria and the land of Canaan. But on the *kappōreth* there was not sufficient room for two images of quadrupeds, and it appears that the cherubim on it were erect figures, like the cherubim of Ezekiel's visions and those of Solomon's Temple. So, too, according to Talmudic tradition, the cherubim on the *kappōreth* resembled youths (B. Ḥagiga 13 b). Similar figures, of winged boys or girls, are found in great number in the Egyptian paintings and reliefs, and also in the Land of Israel, for instance, among the ivory ornaments, the product of Phoenician art, which were found at Megiddo and Samaria. These figures, which were widespread in the ancient East, and the prevailing concept that the deity stood or sat upon wild beasts or cattle, we shall discuss again later, in the commentary on the making of the golden calf.

20 Although the appearance of the cherubim is not described in the text, particular mention is made of the outspread wings: *And the cherubim shall spread out their wings on high*; and their outstretched wings would be, so to speak, a throne for God — an empty throne on which God, invisible to the human eye, would sit. It is just the empty seat that clearly indicates that God has no likeness whatsoever, for in the very place of His enthronement no representation was to be seen. On the idea of the vacant throne see further below, in my annotations to *v.* 22. Apart from serving this purpose, the cherubim would be *overshadowing the kappōreth with their wings*, that is, they would protect and guard the *kappōreth* and the ark beneath it with their wings, which formed a kind of canopy. This corresponds to the ancient tradition that relates that the task of the cherubim of the Garden of Eden was *to guard*. This detail of the ancient tradition we learn from the passage in Ezek. xxviii 14–16, which applies to the cherub in the Garden of Eden the ephitet סוֹכֵךְ *sōkhēkh* [literally, 'overshadowing, screening'; rendered: 'guardian'], the same term as is used here in Exodus [סֹכְכִים *sōkhᵉkhīm*, translated: 'overshadowing'] (compare also i Kings viii 7; i Chron. xxviii 18), and from the narrative in Genesis, where, although the Torah transfers the guarding of the Garden

EXODUS XXV 20

from the cherub to Adam, in conformity with its usual tendency to tone down miraculous stories as much as possible (Gen. ii 15: 'And the Lord God took the man and put him in the garden of Eden to serve and *to keep*'), it nevertheless still uses the expression 'to guard' with reference to the cherubim at the end of the story of the Garden of Eden (*ibid.* iii 24: 'and at the east of the garden of Eden He placed the cherubim... *to guard* the way to the tree of life'). See further, on the subject of the cherubim, my commentary on the Book of Genesis, Pt. I (*From Adam To Noah*), pp. 74–75, 174–176.

Thus, the figures of the cherubim allude to two things at the same time: on the one hand, they symbolize by their outspread wings the throne of God in heaven, and on the other, they recall the garden of Eden, the place where Man dwelt when he was free from sin, and they link thereby the *kappōreth* to the idea of the atonement of sin, the main intent of the priest's service before the *kappōreth* on the Day of Atonement.

With their — the cherubs' — *faces one to another* — that is, they both faced towards the middle of the *kappōreth* — yet *toward the kappōreth shall the faces of the cherubim be*, that is, they shall look downwards, out of reverence, in order not to gaze upon God who is enthroned upon their wings, just as the Seraphim seen by Isaiah covered their faces with two of their wings (Isa. vi 2), and in the same way as Moses hid his face when he beheld the vision of the burning bush, *for he was afraid to look at God* (iii 6).

From all that was stated above, we clearly see how great was the significance attached to the *kappōreth*, and why the 'most holy place' was also called *the room of the kappōreth* (i Chron. xxviii 11).

Nevertheless, it is not to be assumed, as several exegetes have done, that the *kappōreth* was considered an independent object, separate from the ark. There is a close connection between the ark and the *kappōreth*; they are like two components of one thing, and cannot exist apart. Without the *kappōreth* the ark would remain open at the top, and the tables uncovered, unless we assume that the ark had another cover, something which is not stated in the text and seems unlikely; whilst without the ark the *kappōreth* would lack a base, and the throne a footstool. Although each part has its own significance, yet they are jointly a single object. Understandably, therefore, the entire composite structure, the ark with the *kappōreth* upon it, is called in many passages

335

simple 'ark'. We can also comprehend why the same paragraph deals here with both parts, commencing with the ark, continuing

21 with the *kappōreth* and reverting to the ark at the end: *And you shall put the kappōreth on top of the ark* — to rest thereon and to close it — *and to the ark* — inside it — *you shall put*, as stated in v. 16, *the testimony that I shall give you* — a repetition intended to emphasize here the fact that the *kappōreth* and the wings of the cherubs protect the tables of the testimony. We should also note the recurrence of the verb נָתַן *nāthan* ['give'] signifying: I shall *give* you the testimony, and you shall *give* [i.e. place] it inside the ark.

The function of the *kappōreth* and of the wings of the cherubim

22 as the throne of God is clearly alluded to in v. 22: *And there I will meet with you*, that means, I shall appoint for you a meeting with Me there, when you will stand before the ark and the *kappōreth* (compare also xxix 43; xxx 6), *and I will speak with you from above the kappōreth, from between the two cherubim that are upon the ark of the testimony* — it is designated by this name here because the tables of the testimony are kept therein — *of all that I will give you in commandment for the children of Israel.*

THIRD PARAGRAPH

THE TABLE

(XXV 23–30)

Also in regard to the Table, the religion of Israel made fundamental innovations, and introduced important changes in the usage current in the ancient East. Among the neighbouring peoples the table, which was used for serving the offerings to the gods, played an important role in the worship. There is no need to consider here the primitive systems predating this custom, nor the process of its development; it will suffice for us to glance at the ritual procedures current in the age of the Torah. In Mesopotamia they would arrange on the table (*paššûru*) the foods that had been prepared as a meal for the gods, such as boiled or roasted flesh, placed in dishes or plates, loaves of bread, jars of wine, milk and honey, and various kinds of fruit, recalling the tables set before kings. The Egyptians practised similar customs in the worship of their gods, and the other peoples of the countries of the East did likewise. In the Bible, too, there is a reference to this usage in the rebuke administered by the prophet to those 'who set a table for Fortune' (Isa. lxv 11). The practice was based on the belief that the gods, who, like human beings, also needed food, actually ate and drank, in some traditionary manner, the foods and the drinks that were put before them, like a king who eats and drinks of the repast that his servants have set before him on his table.

The ritual use of the table continued also among the Israelites, but not without innovations and changes consonant with the character of Israel's faith. In the Israelite view it was not only inconceivable to associate concepts of eating and drinking in their material sense with the conception of Divinity, but it is related even of a human being like Moses that when he drew near to the Divine sphere 'he neither ate bread nor drank water' (Exod. xxxiv 28; Deut. ix 9, 18). Hence, the function of the table in the Israelite sanctuary is not like that of the table in the idolatrous shrines. The parts of the sacrifices that were set aside for God were not prepared by boiling or roasting, and were not placed in dishes or plates upon the table, but were burned on the altar, in the sanctuary courtyard, as though the only way to bring them near to the Deity was to turn them into vapours and odour, exceedingly fine matter and without substance, which are dispersed in the air and ascend heavenward. The dishes on the table, mentioned in *v.* 29, remain empty, just as God's throne on the *kappōreth*, stands empty. The same applies to the libations. The priests of the heathen nations, when they offered libations, would pour out the liquid from a large jar into a smaller vessel, like a slave filling his master's cup, or they would pour it on the ground. But among the Israelites, the wine was poured on the flesh that was being burned on the altar, and thus the wine, too, was vaporized in the heat of the fire, and its fumes and fragrance would ascend heavenward. The vessels for libation standing on the table, which are also mentioned in *v.* 29, likewise remained empty. The same applied also to the bread; the portion of the cereal oblations intended for the Lord was also consumed on the altar. The 'bread of the Presence' referred to in *v.* 30 was given to the priests to eat (Lev. xxiv 5–9), and was kept on the table for a complete week in order that the priests who ministered to God should have the privilege of eating from God's table. Thus the table and the empty vessels upon it were only a symbol.

EXODUS XXV 23

Ezekiel went a step further. In his Temple there is no table, and only the altar of incense bears that name (Ezek. xli 22; xliv 16; the tables mentioned *ibid.*, xl 39 are only ordinary boards); nothing is set before the Lord except what is burned in His honour. Also in the Book of Malachi, the altar is called 'table' (Mal. i 7, 12).

23 The paragraph begins with the expression, *And you shall make*, which is the usual formula after the commencement of the preceding paragraph: *And you shall make a table of acacia wood* according to the following measurements: *two cubits shall be its length, a cubit its breadth, and a cubit and a half its height*. Possibly it is not fortuitous that the measurements mentioned in this and the previous paragraphs total fourteen cubits, twice times seven.

24 *And you shall overlay it with pure gold*, so that it may fittingly serve in the temple of the King of the universe, *and you shall make for it a moulding of gold round about*, resembling, and corresponding to, the moulding of the ark (see above, on *v.* 11). The text does not specify where the moulding should be placed; apparently, it was intended that this adornment should be made on the surface of the table, near its edge on its four sides, like the ornamentation on the tables of the temples discovered in Eastern countries.

25 *And you shall make for it a frame* of wooden boards that should join the legs of the table together about half-way down, to give them added firmness; of this, too, we have examples among the relics and portrayals found in the ancient East. And the width of the boards of the frame shall be a *handbreadth* (טֹפַח *ṭōphaḥ* = טֶפַח *ṭephaḥ*, two different forms of the same word) *round about*. *And you shall make a moulding of gold to its frame round about*: another decoration similar to the one on the sides of the ark and on the surface of the table. Needless to say, the frame was also to be covered with pure gold, and likewise the feet of the table; every part of the table is included in the injunction of *v.* 24: 'And

26 you shall overlay it with pure gold.' *And you shall make for it* — for the table (the expression *and you shall make for it* occurs three times consecutively) — *four rings of gold, and put the rings on the four corners at its four legs*. The legs of the table were apparently square — at least their upper portion (the lower part may have been round) — and thus each one had four edges; the 'corners' are

27 the outer edges. *Close to the frame*, that is, at the same height at which the boards of the frame were affixed, there *shall the rings be*, and serve *as holders for the poles* (לְבָתִּים לְבַדִּים *lᵉbhāttīm lᵉbhaddīm* —

28 a word-play) *to carry the table. And you shall make the poles of acacia wood, and overlay them with gold,* as in the case of the poles of the ark (v. 13), *and the table shall be carried with these.* These staves were not permanently fixed in the rings like the staves of the ark, but were put in their places only when the table had to be carried.

29 *And you shall make its dishes* — these were, according to the simple meaning of the text, vessels similar to those in which the priests of the pagan temples put the portions of meat for the meals of the gods; but in the Israelite sanctuary the dishes were to remain empty, a symbol only — *and its cups* [כַּפֹּתָיו *kappōthāw*] — apparently, dishes of a smaller type (compare, in connection with the sacrifices of the leaders mentioned in Num. vii: 'one golden cup [כַּף *kaph*] of ten shekels, full of incense'), which were likewise empty — *and its* קְשׂוֹת *q^eśāwōth* — apparently *beakers* for libations (in Ugaritic poetry the word *qš* is used in parallelism with *ks*, the Hebrew כּוֹס *kōs* ['beaker']) — *and its* מְנַקִּיֹּת *m^enaqqiyyōth* — a noun from the stem נקה-נקי *nq(h)–nqy*, whose root meaning is 'to pour out, offer a libation', from which evolved the general signification of 'offering an oblation' in Akkadian and Syriac, and the connotation of 'cleanness, innocence' in Hebrew, that is, the state of a thing after the removal of its impurity, both in the material and spiritual sense. The name מְנַקִּיֹּת *m^enaqqiyyōth* [translate: 'chalices'] preserves the original signification of the stem, the explanation of which immediately follows: *with which to pour out*, that is, with which the libations are to be poured out. The words *with which* refer not only to the chalices but also to the beakers [both are included in the termination of בָּהֵן *bāhen* (literally, 'with them')], as we clearly see from the different order of the words found later (xxxvii 16): 'and its chalices and its beakers with which to pour libations', and from the text in Num. iv 7: 'and the chalices and the beakers for the drink offering.' Also the beakers and the chalices remained empty as long as they were on the table, and when the priest wished to use them for pouring out libations, he brought them out from the sanctuary to the court, where he filled them with wine, subsequently pouring from them the wine upon the flesh that was on the altar-fire; there were no libations inside the sanctuary (xxx 9). *Of pure gold you shall make them*, namely, all the vessels that are on the table. In antiquity it was customary also in private houses to leave the vessels on the tables permanently, unlike the present practice of putting them

away in cupboards and arranging them upon the tables only at meal time. In the description of the furniture of Baal's palace in Ugaritic poetry it is said of the table, *dml'a mnm*, signifying that it was full of vessels (or, according to another interpretation, that it was full of everything).

30 Although the vessels were empty, the table was not completely empty. After speaking of the vessels, the Torah continues: *And you shall set the bread of the Presence on the table before Me always.* Many interpretations have been proposed regarding the expression לֶחֶם פָּנִים *leḥem pānīm* [rendered here: 'bread of the Presence']. According to the simple meaning of the text it appears that the signification of the term is explained immediately afterwards by the word לְפָנַי *lᵉphānay* ['before Me'], to wit, it is bread that is placed *before* God, bread whose primary ritual function is only to be set continuously before the Divine Presence within the precincts of the sanctuary as a symbol, being replaced periodically by fresh bread and consumed by the priests (Lev. xxiv 5–9).

FOURTH PARAGRAPH

THE LAMPSTAND

(XXV 31–40)

The lamps (v. 37), from which emanates the light, constitute the essential part of the lampstand*. The ancient lamp was an oil lamp, its design changing somewhat in different periods. The most ancient and simplest form of it was a kind of small, round saucer, made in terracotta, the rim of which was pinched together at one point so as to form a spout, from which protruded the top of the wick that was dipped in the oil of the saucer. In order that the light of the wick, which burnt at the point of its protrusion from the spout, might cast its light down on whatever a person wanted to see, it was necessary to place the lamp on an object that was high enough for the purpose, and to position it in such a way that the object on which it was standing should not obscure the flame

---

* In the Hebrew text, the author notes here that in our passage, as in the rest of the Bible, and also in the Mishnah and Talmud, the meaning of the word נֵר *nēr* [rendered: 'lamp'] is quite different from its signification in contemporary Hebrew — 'candle'. Tr.

of the wick below. Hence, the idea was not hard to conceive of designing a more perfect form of lamp, namely, a lamp and stand joined together. Already in the Late Bronze age there were in use in the Land of Israel and in Syria, together with the simple lamps of the type described above, also composite lamps, such as those, for example, that were found at Taanach and Ugarit; these are made in terracotta and shaped at the top like a large round saucer, which serves as a receptacle for oil, with a number of spouts all around its rim, mostly *seven*, in each of which it is possible to place and to light a wick. Beneath the saucer, the vessel narrows so as to provide a hold by which it can easily be grasped, and at the bottom it broadens out again and forms a base that can rest on a flat surface. There have also been found in Syria and in the Land of Israel saucers, belonging to the Late Bronze and Early Iron periods, that have seven spouts but no base. In strata appertaining to the Early Iron age there have still been discovered — for example, at Beth-shean and Megiddo — metal pedestals designed to carry a lamp. They consist of an upright shaft at the top of which is a ledge on which a lamp can be placed; below, the shaft divides into three feet, which are all joined at their lower end to a ring that rests firmly on the ground. The lampstand of the Tabernacle combined the features of two lamp forms: the number of the lamps is seven as in the saucer-type of lamp, and the branches are of metal as in the case of the lamps of Beth-shean and Megiddo. An earlier example of it may have existed already in the age of the Patriarchs, if an engraving depicting seven branches on two Assyrian seals found in Cappadocia may be interpreted as a lampstand. At all events, it is clear that there is no reason to assert, as several scholars have done on the basis of the date that they assign to these verses, that there was no seven-branched lampstand in existence until the fifth or fourth century B.C.E.

The description of the lampstand in this paragraph comprises a number of particulars but does not give all the details. That apart, many of its terms are extremely obscure. Consequently, numerous explanations, of varied and peculiar kinds, have been proposed in respect of each detail, and any one wishing to reconstruct the lampstand is compelled to resort to conjectures and to no small measure of imagination. As for the bas-relief on the Arch of Titus in Rome, the Talmudic sources and the description of Josephus Flavius, they are all based on the design of the lampstand in the Second Temple, and hence the data they provide may be applied to the Tabernacle lampstand only with considerable reservation. In the following lines, we shall endeavour to explain the passage according to its simple sense and in the light of the archaeological finds pertaining to that period. Following our usual practice, we shall not cite the various interpretations that have been advanced, but give our own explanation only.

31 The lampstand was made, as befitted a royal sanctuary, entirely of pure gold: *And you shall make a lampstand of pure gold. Of hammered work shall the lampstand be made*, that means to say, the lampstand is not to be made in separate sections, subsequently joined together, but it must be fashioned entirely in one piece, after the manner of beaten work (see above, on *v.* 18), out of a single plate of gold. (The Masoretes, who as a rule use defective spelling, preferred the word תֵּיעָשֶׂה *tēʿāśe* ['shall... be made'] to be written *plene* [with a *Yōdh*] in order to obviate the reading תַּעֲשֶׂה *taʿăśe* ['you shall make']). So shall all the parts of the lampstand be made together — both *its* יָרֵךְ *yārēkh* [literally, 'thigh'] *and its* קָנֶה *qāne* [literally, 'reed', 'stem']. The word יָרֵךְ *yārēkh*, a borrowed term primarily signifying human thighs, is used here as a collective noun, denoting the feet into which the central shaft branched at the bottom, after the style of the feet of the lampstands discovered at Beth-shean and Megiddo, and includes also the base, perhaps a round base like the bases of the excavated lampstands. The term קָנֶה *qāne* ['stem'] likewise has here a collective sense, and denotes all the branches of the lampstand, both the central shaft and the six branches emanating from its sides. All these parts — 'thigh' and branches — were to be fashioned as a single piece from the beginning of their construction. Also their ornaments, the *cups, knobs and flowers* of the lampstand (on these adornments see below) *shall be out of it* — they shall all be made of the same plate of gold as the branches of the lampstand, not separately and subsequently affixed to the branches.

32 *And there shall be six branches going out of its sides*, that is, from the sides of the central shaft, which is the primary feature of the lampstand's design: *three branches of the lampstand out of one side of it and three branches of the lampstand out of the other side of it* — seven in all. The general shape imitates a natural object: the stem or stalk of a plant with paired branches at the sides, which are all turned upwards. The ornamentation is also of floral design.

33 This is how they are described: *three* גְּבִיעִים *gᵉbhīʿīm* — three

EXODUS XXV 36

decorations in the form of a cup or beaker (Gen. xliv 2 ff.) — מְשֻׁקָּדִים *mᵉšuqqādhīm* — shaped like an almond-blossom — shall be made *on one branch*, and every cup shall consist of two parts: (a) *a knob*, that is, the receptacle* at the base of the almond-blossom, which contains the ovary (the word כַּפְתֹּר *kaphtōr* ['knob'] is an expansion of the word כֶּתֶר *kether* ['crown'], which denotes in general anything round); (b) *and a flower* — in the restricted sense of the term; what is called 'corolla'. The same shall be made on the other branches: *and three cups made like almond-blossoms on the other branch, a knob and a flower; so for the six branches going out of the lampstand*. The flower of the uppermost cup, which stood at the top of each branch, was to serve as a support for one of the lamps (compare the Mishna, Kelim 11: 7: 'the branches of a lampstand are not susceptible to uncleanness, but the flower and the base are susceptible'; Oholoth 11: 8: 'If a lampstand stood in the cistern of a house, and its flower projected'). The other two cups
34 were below it, along the length of the branch. *And on the lampstand*, that is, on the central shaft, *four cups made like almonds*, and hence four sets of *their knobs and flowers*. The uppermost cup was to be at the top of the shaft, like the topmost cup of the other branches; two cups were to be made at the same height as the two lower cups in the six side branches; and a fourth cup was apparently to be formed on the part of the central shaft extending between the point where the feet radiated and the place where the first branches diverged. There were also to be other ornaments on the
35 middle branch: *and a knob*, that is, the bulging of the shaft in the form of a ball, *under the two branches* — precisely beneath the point where the pair of branches issue, one on each side — *out of it* — out of the central shaft, which is often called just lampstand. The phrase is repeated twice more: *and a knob under the two branches out of it, and a knob under the two branches out of it*, that is, one knob under each pair of branches, *for the six branches going out*
36 *of the lampstand*. The first part of v. 36, *their knobs and their* קְנוֹת *qānōth shall be out of it*, has been regarded as difficult by many exegetes, because they thought that the word וּקְנוֹתָם *ūqᵉnōthām* means the same as וּקְנֵיהֶם *ūqᵉnēhem* ['and their branches']. But the correct interpretation is different; the sense of the sentence is as follows: also the knobs of the branches, that is, the knobs beneath the point where the pairs of branches go out, shall be made of it,

---

* Other views are: 'flower-bud'; 'calyx'. *Tr.*

343

of the lampstand, of the same plate of gold, and so, too, their קָנוֹת *qānōth*, which is the plural of קָנֶה *qānā* and not of קָנֶה *qāne*. Now קָנֶה *qānā* is the joint, the point at which the side branches radiate from the central shaft; in this case, too, the construction must not take the form of uniting segments but of beating out — *the joints of the branches shall likewise be of one piece with it* (the lampstand). This is also the meaning, apparently, of the word קָנֶה *qānā* (without *Mappīq Hē*) in Job xxxi 22: 'and my arm be broken from the joint [מִקָּנֶה *miqqānā*].' To sum up: the entire lampstand and all its adornments were to be *wholly one piece of hammered work of pure gold*.

37 The text now proceeds to speak of parts that are not joined to the lampstand. First, the lamps: *And you shall make its lamps, seven*. The lamps are not to be visualized as affixed to the lampstand, but as resting on the flowers at the top of the branches, and capable of being removed from there daily when trimmed. On their shape, see what I have written above, in the introductory notes to this paragraph. The number seven is placed at the end for emphasis, נֵרֹתֶיהָ שִׁבְעָה *nērōthehā šibh'ā*], which is contrary to the usual construction, שִׁבְעָה נֵרֹתֶיהָ *šibh'ā nērōthehā* or שִׁבְעַת נֵרֹתֶיהָ *šibh'ath nērōthehā* ['its seven lamps']. The emphasis is due not only to the importance of the number seven, but also to the fact that it has not yet been stated that a lamp would be placed upon each branch, and only here is the matter alluded to: and you shall make its lamps, and they shall be seven, like the number of the branches, one upon each branch. It is not stated of what material the lamps are to be. Gold is prescribed earlier and also later, but nothing is mentioned here. Apparently it was not intended that the lamps should be of gold but of terracotta or of copper. In Solomon's Temple the lamps, too, were made of gold (i Kings vii 49). וְהֶעֱלָה *weheʿĕlā* [literally, 'and he shall bring up']: the construction is impersonal — one shall bring up *its lamps*, that is, bring up their flame, kindle them; or possibly the meaning is that one shall lift up the lamps in order to put them on top of the branches. *So as to give light on the side of its face*: this is not an instruction regarding the order of the sanctuary service, for this is not the place for such directives. The sense is: When the attendant 'brings up' [i.e. kindles or puts in position] its lamps, he must so arrange them that their spouts and the wick-heads protruding from them should face towards the front of the lampstand, towards that which stands opposite it, that is, towards the table, so that the flames should

illumine that side without hindrance, and the lamps' shadows should fall at the back of it, towards the wall.

38   Other articles not attached to the lampstand: וּמַלְקָחֶיהָ *ūmal-qāḥehā* [translate: 'and its snuffers'] these are a kind of tweezers used for taking out the old and burnt-out wicks and putting new ones in their place. וּמַחְתֹּתֶיהָ *ūmaḥtōthehā* [render: 'and its trays'], receptacles in which the wicks removed by the tweezers were taken outside [the sanctuary] and thrown away; possibly, they were also used for the lamps when taken to be cleaned outside the Tabernacle It may be assumed that these trays corresponded to the כּוּז *kūz* mentioned in the Mishnah. All these utensils were also to be made of *pure gold*.

The weight of all the gold required for the making of the candelabrum and its utensils was to be a talent, that is, three thousand
39   shekels (xxxviii 24 ff.): *Of a talent of pure gold shall it be made, with all these utensils.*
40   *And see* — you, Moses — the picture of the lampstand and its utensils that I show you, in order that you may include the details that have been omitted in the description of the articles, *that you make them after the pattern for them, which is being shown you* here *on the mountain.*

FIFTH PARAGRAPH

THE TABERNACLE AND THE TENT

(XXVI 1–14)

Chapter XXVI

The stem שָׁכַן *šākhan*, from which the noun מִשְׁכָּן *miškān* ['dwelling-place', 'tabernacle'] is derived, means 'to dwell or make one's abode' in general; but its primary and specific meaning is 'to stay somewhere temporarily or for a short time.' It will suffice to note such verses as Deut. xxxiii 20: 'couches [שָׁכֵן *šākhēn*] like a lion'; Micha iv 10: 'for now you will go forth from the city and dwell [שָׁכַנְתְּ *šākhant*] in the open country'; or Psa. cxxxix 9: 'If I take the wings of the morning and dwell [אֶשְׁכְּנָה *'eškᵉnā*] in the uttermost parts of the sea'; and similar passages. More particularly it signifies the temporary residence of the desert nomads in their tents, who are consequently called 'they who dwell in tents' (Jud.

viii 11). The word מִשְׁכָּן *miškān* serves as a synonym of אֹהֶל *'ōhel* ['tent'] and is used in phrases like 'the shepherds' tents' [מִשְׁכְּנוֹת *mišk^{e}nōth*]' (Cant. i 8), and in poetic parallelism with אֹהֶל *'ōhel*, for instance, 'How fair are your tents [אֹהָלֶיךָ *'ōhālekhā*], O Jacob, your dwellings [מִשְׁכְּנֹתֶיךָ *mišk^{e}nōthekhā*], O Israel' (Num. xxiv 5). Even after the dwellings of the Israelites had become permanent structures these two synonyms continued to be used in poetic parallelism in the sense of residences generally. Thus, for example, Isa. liv 2: 'Enlarge the place of your tent [אָהֳלֵךְ *'ohŏlēkh*], and let the curtains of your habitations [מִשְׁכְּנוֹתַיִךְ *mišk^{e}nōthayikh*] be stretched out'; Jer. xxx 18: 'Behold, I will restore the fortunes of the tents of [אָהֳלֵי *'ohŏlē*] Jacob, and have compassion on his dwellings [מִשְׁכְּנֹתָיו *mišk^{e}nōthāw*]'; compare also Job xxi 28: '*the tent* [אֹהֶל *'ōhel*] in which the wicked dwelt [מִשְׁכְּנוֹת *mišk^{e}nōth*, literally, 'dwellings of'].' With the parallelism in Ugaritic poetry between *mškn* and *'hl*, used to designate the dwelling-places of the gods, I have already dealt earlier (pp. 322 f.).

The Sanctuary of the generation of the wilderness was intended to be moved from place to place, in order to accompany the children of Israel on their wanderings; hence the two names, מִשְׁכָּן *miškān* and אֹהֶל *'ōhel*, are appropriate to it, especially in their original signification, and both are frequently employed in the Bible to denote the shrine that Moses erected in the desert. Even when the Israelites had settled in their land they did not change the form of the sanctuary for a number of generations; actually, because of the conservatism that customarily prevails in religious matters they still preserved the tent and tabernacle pattern of their fane up to the time of Solomon (although it may possibly be assumed that at Shiloh structures or walls were built round the Tent). In poetic language the ancient names were even used with reference to the permanent Temple that Solomon built. Thus we find in Psa. xv 1: 'O Lord, who shall sojourn in Thy tent [בְּאָהֳלֶךָ *b^e'ohŏlekhā*], who shall dwell on Thy holy hill?'; and *ibid*. xxvi 8: 'O Lord, I love the habitation of Thy house, and the place where Thy glory dwells [מִשְׁכַּן *miškan*, literally, 'dwelling-place of'].'

In order to understand properly this paragraph and the next, we must consider the design of the tents and dwellings of the desert nomads, in so far as it is possible to study them from the pictures and reliefs that have been found in Egypt and in Mesopotamia, and from the pattern of the tents of the Bedouins in our day, which has preserved the essential features of the ancient tents.

The Bedouin tents are constructed of a number of curtains, which are woven of threads spun from black goats' hair. The spinning and the weaving, as well as the sewing together of the curtains, are entrusted to the women. The men fix wooden pillars into the ground, on which they stretch the curtains, and in order to enable the tent to withstand all kinds of winds, they make the cords taut, tying one end to the top of the tent and the other to pegs that are driven into the ground. The area covered by the tent is rectangular in shape. The ancient pictures and reliefs provide us with similar information.

The Tent dedicated to the Lord was likewise made of curtains, and specifically of black goats' hair curtains, but these served only as an outer protection against rain and wind and dust and the sun's heat. Beneath these curtains, however, that is, within the Tent, hung other curtains, graceful and decorative, the work of artists. Like the maiden in the Song of Songs, who was black as the tents of Kedar but comely as the curtains of Solomon, even so was the Sanctuary black without like the tents of the Bedouins, but made beautiful and graceful by its curtains within, as befits a Royal Dwelling-place. The pillars that supported the curtains were not crude branches of trees like those found in the tents of commoners, but were likewise artistically fashioned — of wooden boards overlaid with gold, set close to one another so as to form continuous walls, and fitted into heavy silver sockets. Its area was also rectangular in shape, but much wider and longer than the area of an ordinary tent, and it was surrounded by a court of fair dimensions.

The two synonyms, מִשְׁכָּן *miškān* and אֹהֶל *'ōhel*, can be used in a general sense to denote the structure of the sanctuary as a whole, and also in a restricted signification, as technical terms, each designating a definite portion of the shrine. In this paragraph they occur mostly in the restricted meaning: the term *miškān*, which usually indicates the entire sanctuary even when used by itself, without any supplementary word (xxv 9: 'the pattern of the tabernacle, and of all its furniture'), is applied here specifically to the beautiful interior curtains enclosing the sacred furniture, which formed the 'tabernacle' proper; whilst the word *'ōhel*, which as a rule signifies the sanctuary as a whole only when some other noun is added, as, for example, in the expressions אֹהֶל מוֹעֵד *'ōhel mōʿēdh* ['tent of meeting'] or אֹהֶל הָעֵדוּת *'ōhel hāʿēdhūth* ['tent of the testimony'], and by itself denotes the simple tents made of curtains of

347

goats' hair, is applied here to the exterior curtains of goats' hair, which formed, as it were, a second tent spread over the inner curtains. Also in our annotations to this paragraph the two nouns will be employed mainly in their narrower application.

1   In *v.* 1 the object וְאֶת הַמִּשְׁכָּן *wᵉʾeth hammiškān* ['Moreover (literally, 'And') the tabernacle'] precedes the verb תַּעֲשֶׂה *taʿăśe* ['you shall make'] for the sake of emphasis, since the word *miškān*, although it signifies here a specific part of the sanctuary, nevertheless refers back to the concept of the *miškān* occurring at the beginning of the section, as though to say: The furniture to be placed in the tabernacle having been dealt with, *the tabernacle* itself you shall make in the following way.

The tabernacle shall comprise *ten curtains*, and this is how they shall be made: the materials shall consist of *fine twined linen, and deep violet, dark red and scarlet wool* (see above, on xxv 4) woven together in such a way that the combination of the various colours in the fabric would produce the figures of *cherubim* in the manner of מַעֲשֵׂה חֹשֵׁב *maʿăśē ḥōšēbh* [literally, 'work of a thinker'], that is, מְלֶאכֶת מַחֲשֶׁבֶת *mᵉleʾkheth maḥăšebheth* [literally, 'work of thought'; rendered: 'work of skill'; cf. xxxv 33], work that implements the creative thought of the artist [translate: 'work of the designer']; so *shall you make them* (אֹתָם *ʾōthām*: masculine instead of feminine

2   pronoun [אֹתָן *ʾōthān*]). *The length of the one curtain shall be twenty-eight cubits, and the breadth of the one curtain four cubits*, and so shall be the measurements of all the other curtains; *all the curtains shall have one measure*. Why these particular measurements are prescribed will become apparent later on.

3   *Five curtains shall be coupled to one another* — sewn to each other lengthwise. The text has חֹבְרֹת *ḥōbhᵉrōth* [active participle, literally, 'joining', 'coupling'] not חֲבוּרוֹת *ḥăbhūrōth* [passive participle, 'joined', 'coupled'], because it is not just the act of sewing that the Bible has in mind, but the result of it, namely, that every curtain accompanies the others; *and the five* remaining *curtains shall* also *be coupled to one another*. In this way two sets of curtains would be formed, each one twenty-eight cubits long and twenty cubits wide. It would have been impracticable to sew all ten curtains together, because it would have been very difficult to move so heavy a weight from place to place and arrange it on the boards; the division into two halves made the work easier. The two sets could without difficulty be joined together temporarily,

by means of loops and clasps, whenever the tabernacle was erected, and they could easily be detached, by the removal of the clasps from the loops, when the tabernacle was taken down. This is
4 described in detail in the text: *And you shall make loops of deep violet on the edge of the one curtain at the extremity in the (first) set* — that is, on the edge of the curtain that comes at the extremity of one of the sets — *and likewise you shall make* deep violet loops *in the edge of the outmost curtain in the second set* (note the differences in phrasing between the first half of the verse and the second: *on the edge — in the edge; at the extremity — outmost*; בַּחֹבָרֶת *baḥōbhāreth* ['in the set', in first half] — בַּמַּחְבָּרֶת *bammaḥbereth* ['in the set', in second half]; further variations occur in the next verse, and still others in *v*. 10). Special mention is made of the number of the loops in *v*. 5 for emphasis (otherwise it would have been simple to give the number in *v*. 4, in the same way as it is incor-
5 porated in *v*. 10): *Fifty loops you shall make on the one curtain, and fifty loops you shall make on the edge of the curtain that is in the second set*. In all there shall be one hundred loops, but it is clear that a round figure based on the decimal system is intended, for the number of loops does not fit in well with the number of cubits, or of handbreadths, forming the length of the edge: (28 cubits; 168 handbreadths). And *the loops* shall be *opposite one another*: each one of the loops in the one set shall face one of the
6 loops in the other set. *And you shall make fifty clasps of gold*, each of which could fit into one of the loops on each side, *and couple the* two *curtains* bearing the loops *one to the other with the clasps, that the tabernacle may be one whole*.

The directions for the making of the curtains of the tabernacle are followed by instructions for the making of the curtains of
7 goats' hair that will be spread over them: *And you shall make curtains of goats' hair* (see above, on xxv 4, and the prefatory notes to this paragraph) *for a tent over the tabernacle* (in the aforementioned notes I discussed the two terms אֹהֶל *'ōhel* ['tent'] and מִשְׁכָּן *miškān* ['tabernacle']); *eleven curtains shall you make them* (אֹתָם *'ōthām*: again the masculine pronoun for the feminine [אֹתָן *'ōthān*]). The number of the tent curtains is one more than the curtains of
8 the tabernacle; the reason for this will become apparent later. *The length of each curtain shall be thirty cubits*, two cubits more than the length of the curtains of the tabernacle; the explanation of this difference will also be found further on. *And the breadth of each curtain four cubits; the eleven curtains shall have one measure*.

Also the curtains of the tent shall be sewn together to form two sets, for the reason stated, but since their number is odd, it will 9 not be possible for the two sets to be of equal size: *And you shall couple five curtains by themselves, and six curtains by themselves.* This being so, the breadth of one of the sets will be twenty-four cubits and of the second twenty cubits. The end of this verse, *and the sixth curtain you shall double over at the front of the tent*, will be explained below together with the other verses pertaining to the draping of the curtains over the boards. The two sets of the tent shall be joined together, like the two sets of the tabernacle, 10 in a temporary coupling: *And you shall make fifty loops* (since the number had already been stressed in *v.* 5, there was no need to do so again here; it was sufficient to mention it without special emphasis) *on the edge of the curtain that is outmost in one set, and fifty loops on the edge of the curtain* that is outmost in *the second set*. Thus we have here, too, a hundred loops. It is not stated of what kind of material these loops were to be made, although in the case of the tabernacle loops it was enjoined that they should be made of deep violet thread; possibly it was intended that these 11 loops should be made of goats' hair fibre. *And you shall make fifty clasps of bronze*, corresponding to the gold clasps of the tabernacle, *and put the clasps into the loops, and couple the tent together that it may be one whole.*

The manner of hanging the curtains over the beams is not described in the Bible, except for certain details given in *vv.* 12–13 and in the last part of *v.* 9. Many strange and diverse conjectures have been advanced on the subject, and various extraordinary attempts at reconstruction have been proposed, but the vast majority of them are fanciful and improbable. According to the reconstruction of Schick and Fergusson, for example, the curtains were stretched over very high wooden pillars, far taller than the boards, and they thus formed a lofty tent, majestic even in its imposing measurements, which was fastened to the ground by cords and pegs. But Scripture makes no reference to high pillars, or to the cords of the tent and tabernacle (only the cords of the courtyard are mentioned in the text; in regard to xxxviii 18 see my commentary *ad locum*); nor does such a magnificent structure fit the desert conditions. Others found it difficult to imagine that the richly worked curtains of the tabernacle would be covered by the goats' hair curtains, and thought that the meaning of the text was that the curtains of the tabernacle would be hung on the boards from the inside. But the difficulty that is removed in one respect crops out in another, for, if the conjecture were correct, it would not be possible to understand the purpose of the gold plating on the boards, which were wholly covered by the curtains of the tabernacle within and the curtains of the tent without. Another view is that the boards [קְרָשִׁים *q^erāšīm*] were simply frames, hollow in the middle, through the back of which the tabernacle curtains on the outside could be seen. But it is hard to suppose that the boards were not actually boards. Other theories have also been advanced.

The best explanation, however, is the simplest. We shall endeavour to arrive at such an interpretation in the lines that follow, avoiding, as far as possible, the addition of our own conjectures to the text with a view to supplementing the description, for the Bible never intended to give us complete specifications, and added in *v.* 30, which also belongs to this paragraph, the reference to Moses' vision on Mt. Sinai, in order to inform us that not all the details were given to Moses verbally, and that what was left unexplained in words was clarified by the vision that he saw.

The boards, as will be shown in the next paragraph, formed three walls ten cubits high; the southern and northern walls were each thirty cubits long, whilst the length of the western wall, at the rear of the tabernacle, was ten cubits, corresponding to the width of the sanctuary. The eastern flank, which also measured ten cubits, was left open. The curtains of the tabernacle were placed lengthwise over the tops of the boards, commencing from the east side, and passed across the width of the shrine, so as to form, in the middle, a roof over the interior of the sanctuary, and the excess in length remained hanging at both ends on the outside. Since the width of the tabernacle was ten cubits and the length of the curtains was twenty-eight cubits, nine cubits were left hanging over the boards on each side. Apparently, the extremities of the curtains hanging down were fastened at each end by clasps or loops at their edges to pegs (resembling nails) affixed to the boards; these are *the pegs of the tabernacle* referred to subsequently (xxvii 19, and elsewhere). In a similar manner the *Ka'ba* at the Arab shrine in Mecca is covered by the *kiswa* — its veil. Of the boards on both sides, which were covered on the outside by the curtains of the tabernacle, the nethermost cubit still remained bare, since the boards were ten cubits high, whilst the overhanging portion of the curtains on each side was only nine cubits long. The boards at the back of the sanctuary, on the west side, were completely covered, for the length of the shrine was thirty cubits, whereas the two sets of the tabernacle curtains were together forty cubits long; it follows that at the rear of the sanctuary there were left over ten cubits of the curtains, which covered the boards at the back from top to bottom. On the curtains of the tabernacle lay the goats' hair curtains of the tent, covering them on top and on all three sides. No difficulty is presented by the fact that their beauty remained concealed, for this covering was only on the outside, whereas in the interior the curtains, with their designs of cherubim figures, were visible on the ceiling of the sanctuary. Anyone inside the tabernacle looking upward would see the cherubim, which symbolized the celestial throne of God, and he would also see the gold clasps, in which, too, there was an allusion to the heavens, as the sages of the Talmud already realized (*Baraitha On The Erection Of The Tabernacle*, ch. ii, and parallel passages: 'and the clasps appeared in the tabernacle like stars in the sky').

The excess in the case of the tent curtains was greater than that of the tabernacle curtains, since the former were longer and their number was greater. This surplus was spread over the four sides of the tabernacle, as I shall now explain.

To the part left over on the eastern side, that is, on the side of the entrance of the sanctuary, appertains the statement in *v*. 9: *and you shall double over the sixth curtain at the front of the tent*. Apparently, the larger set of the tent curtains, comprising six curtains, was placed on the east side, and the smaller set, consisting of five curtains, was put on the west side. Hence, the curtain that is reckoned as the sixth, if one begins to count from where the two sets are joined together by the clasps, is the first on the eastern side, the one nearest to the entrance. At the point where it actually reached the entrance, *at the forefront of the tent*, it was doubled, that is, it was folded in the middle along its whole length so that two cubits of its breadth were laid above the first curtain of the tabernacle, and the two remaining cubits — to wit, the outermost — were folded back and placed beneath the same tabernacle curtain in order to cover its edge well and to give it thorough protection. Thus the clasps of the tent were not lying exactly over the tabernacle clasps (such an arrangement was liable to give trouble), but were located two cubits further towards the west.

Now the excess of the tent curtains on the western side was twelve cubits long, for the length of the two sets together came to forty-four cubits (there were eleven curtains of four cubits each), and if we deduct the two folded cubits and the thirty cubits representing the length of the sanctuary, twelve cubits were left over at the back of the shrine. Ten of these covered the boards at the rear of the sanctuary down to the ground; thus there still remained

12 two cubits concerning which it is stated in *v.* 12: *And the part that remains of the curtains of the tent, the half curtain that remains* — that is, the two remaining cubits, constituting half of the last curtain, which, like its companions, was four cubits wide — *you shall cause to hang over* (תִּסְרַח *tisraḥ*, second person, masc. sing.), on to the ground, at *the back of the tabernacle.* Compare B. Shab. 98 b: 'What did the tabernacle resemble? A woman walking in the street with her train trailing behind her.' The construction of the expression חֲצִי הַיְרִיעָה הָעֹדֶפֶת *ḥăṣi hayᵉrī'ā hā'ōdhepheth* ['the half curtain that remains'] is like that of the phrase קֶשֶׁת גִּבֹּרִים חַתִּים *qešeth gibbōrīm ḥattīm* ['the bow of the mighty is broken'] in i Sam. ii 4, that is to say, the verb in the present agrees in gender and number with the genitive [*nomen rectum*] next to it and not with the preceding word in the construct [*nomen regens*], to which it is logically related.

To the north and to the south, since the tent curtains were thirty cubits long, there were ten cubits left over on each side; these covered the nine cubits of the curtains of the tabernacle and also the bottom cubit of the boards, which the tabernacle curtains

13 did not suffice to cover. It is to this that *v.* 13 refers: *And the cubit on the one side, and the cubit on the other side, of what remains in the length of the curtains of the tent, shall hang over the sides of the tabernacle, on this side and that side, to cover it.* Apparently, the curtains of the tent were also fixed to the boards below like the tabernacle curtains (see my observations on this subject above).

14 Over the tent there was to be another cover: *And you shall make for the tent a covering of rams' skins dyed red.* To this day the Bedouins sometimes spread skins over their tents. Among gentile peoples, too, it was customary to use red, which is visible from a distance, to distinguish the sacred tents. The measurements of this covering are not stated in the Bible, and it would seem that the rams' skins did not cover the tent curtains completely. According to Rabbinic tradition the cover measured ten cubits by thirty, and it lay flat on the roof of the sanctuary. It may possibly be assumed that it also hung down a little over the walls, for otherwise it could not have been seen from a low position. And still another cover was to be made: *and a covering of dugong skins* (xxv 5)

353

above. Perhaps this cover was intended to be used as a protective container for the curtains only when in transit, during the camp's journeys from place to place, its purpose being similar to that of the dugong-skin coverings mentioned in Numbers chapter 4. In the account of the erection of the tabernacle the word מִכְסֵה *mikhsē* ['covering of'] is used in the singular (xl 19: 'And he spread the tent over the tabernacle, and put the covering of the tent above upon it'; cf. also xxxv 11); apparently the meaning there is that only the covering of rams' skins dyed red was placed over the tabernacle when it was erected.

Numerical schematism based on the decimal system is manifest in this paragraph: the curtains of the tabernacle number 10; their loops 100, their clasps 50, and each set of the tabernacle curtains is 20 cubits wide; the tent curtains are 10+1, their loops 100, and their clasps 50, whilst the width of the western set is 20 cubits.

SIXTH PARAGRAPH

THE BOARDS

(XXVI 15–30)

A number of different interpretations has been suggested with regard to the details of this paragraph; however, in accordance with the method that I have adopted in this commentary, I shall not discuss them all, but shall content myself with offering my own exposition.

The use of boards as the essential basis of the walls of a divine dwelling was well known in the neighbourhood of the Israelites, as we have observed above (p. 323); hence the word is 15 used here with the definite article: *And you shall make the boards for the tabernacle*. The material to be used for their construction was *acacia trees*, which are plentiful in the Wilderness of Sinai. In order to form the walls, the beams were to be arranged *standing up* [עֹמְדִים *'ōmᵉdhīm*], that is, in an erect and not in a lying position, and in each wall they were to be placed next to one another, without any intervening space. Their function would be the same as that fulfilled in ordinary tents by the wooden *pillars* [עַמּוּדִים *'ammūdhīm*] (by which name the Bedouins call them to this day), a

16 fact to which the word עֹמְדִים 'ōmᵉdhīm may possibly allude. *Ten cubits shall be the length of a board* — that is, its height when standing up — *and a cubit and a half the breadth of the one board*, that is, the breadth of each board. The thickness is not specified in the text; we shall discuss this point later.

In order to hold the boards firmly in place and to facilitate their erection when the tabernacle was set up and their dismantling when the tabernacle was taken down, it was necessary to make use of various devices and expedients. The first of these (others will be mentioned later) was to fix the boards onto strong pedestals.
17 This was the purpose of the *two hands* [יָדוֹת yādhōth, usually rendered: 'tenons'], that is, two vertical projections that jutted out from the lower end of each board (for the termination וֹת- -ōth see above, on xxv 12), which were made to fit into the holes of the pedestals like door hinges. Two were necessary — not one — so that the board should not be able to turn like a door on its hinge, but should remain securely fixed in its place. Two tenons like these shall there be *in the one board* — that is, in each board — *joined one to another* — parallel to each other like the rungs of a ladder; *so shall you do for all the boards of the tabernacle.*

In v. 18 the text begins to enumerate the number of boards on
18 each side, and hence it reverts to the making of the boards. *And you shall make the boards for the tabernacle* in the following quantities: *twenty boards for the south* [literally, 'to the Negeb'] *side southward*, that is, for the side of the tabernacle facing southward. Since the width of each board was a cubit and a half, the length of this side would be thirty cubits, and that would also be the length of the sanctuary. The number of pedestals — the perforated bases in each of which was to be fixed one of the two tenons of a board —
19 would be double the number of the boards: *And forty pedestals of silver you shall make under the twenty boards*, of the south side, *two pedestals under one board for its two tenons, and two pedestals under another board for its two tenons* — the repetition has a dis-
20 tributive sense. *And for the second side of the tabernacle*, which faces the *north side, twenty boards*, as in the parallel side on the
21 south. *And their forty pedestals of silver*, etc. — exactly as on the south side (for the sake of variation the words *for its two tenons*,
22 which occur in v. 19, are omitted here). *And for the rear of the tabernacle* — for the side opposite the entrance, at the inner extremity of the tabernacle — *to the sea*, that is, westward (the Hebrew tongue is fundamentally the language of Canaan, and was created

in the land of Canaan, which has the sea on *its* west), *you shall*
23 *make six boards* identical with those at the sides. *And two boards
in addition to these shall you make for the corners of the tabernacle
in the rear.* These two boards were certainly intended to buttress
the corners, but the description given of them in *v.* 24 is very
obscure, and has been subjected to various far-fetched interpretations. To me it seems that the verse should be explained as follows:
24 *And* these two boards *shall be* תֹאֲמִים *thō'ămīm* [literally, 'be twinned',
'doubled'] — that is, shall fit, *at their lower end,* the last two boards
[one at each end] of the side-walls, in other words, each one shall
have a projection below that will fit into a corresponding hole in
the last board of the adjacent wall, or, contrariwise, it will contain
a hole into which will fit the projection in the rearmost board of
the wall; *and together they shall be* תַּמִּים *tammīm* ['completed'] —
the upper end of the additional boards at the rear and the upper
end of the adjoining board in the side will end together (a word-
play: *thō'ămīm — tammīm*) — *at the top* — above, at the top of
the tabernacle (which is mentioned in the previous verse), that is,
the boards will be joined together above, exactly as beneath, by
means of a projection in one of them and an aperture in the other,
and both together will be inserted above *into the one ring,* which
will encompass both of them and clamp them together. This was
one of the customary methods used in Egypt to strengthen the
corners of wooden structures; they were braced by a copper fillet
that enclosed them like a ring. The corners of the large sarcophagus
of Amenemhet I, for instance, a Pharaoh of the twelfth dynasty,
were braced in this way, and so, too, were the corners of his coffin.
Thus shall it be with both of them — with the two additional boards
at the extremities, on each side — *they shall form the two corners.*
Each of these two boards will be permanently affixed to the last
board of the adjacent side, and will not be detached from it even
when the tabernacle is taken down. Seeing that these two supplementary boards are mentioned separately, whilst at first only six
boards are spoken of (*v.* 22), it appears that they were different
from these six boards as well as from the boards of the sides, and
were exceptional in their measurements. But since it is impossible
that there should have been any difference in the height, the divergence must have been in their width, which was to be small, for it
would not be easy to move two boards joined together at right
angles, if both were to be very wide, up to a cubit and a half. It
seems reasonable to assume that the two additional boards were

not wider than half a cubit each; accordingly the length of the western wall, in symmetrical agreement with the other measurements of the tabernacle, was ten cubits: six boards each a cubit and a half wide, making nine cubits in all, and another two boards of half a cubit on each side. Many expositors, from the time of the Talmud to our own day, in order to arrive at the measurement of ten cubits for the *interior* width of the tabernacle, came to the conclusion, on the assumption that all the boards were a cubit and a half wide, that the thickness of the boards, which is not stated in the text, was perforce a full cubit. Thus the length of the boards on the west was twelve cubits outside (eight boards of a cubit and a half each), but a cubit on each side was taken up by the thickness of the boards of the sides, which were supported by the boards at the corners, and consequently the interior was only ten cubits across. However, so great a thickness is impossible; such gigantic boards (each of which would certainly have weighed up to a thousand kilogram, approximately), even if we assume that it was possible to make them, would not have been portable, the pedestals, each of which comprised only a talent of silver (xxxviii 27), would have been unsuitable; and the proper term for them would not have been קְרָשִׁים *qerāšīm* ['boards'] but קוֹרוֹת *qōrōth* ['beams']. According to my interpretation there is no difficulty; the fact that the Bible did not specify the thickness of the boards as it did their length and width, indicates that the thickness was little and was altogether of no account. It follows that the question so much discussed by the exegetes as to whether the measurements are external or internal falls away. The difference between the outer and inner dimensions is quite small and without significance. The importance lies in the numbers mentioned in the Torah and in their symmetrical relationship.

25 The description continues: *And* the boards at the rear *shall be* altogether *eight boards and their pedestals of silver, sixteen pedestals, two pedestals under one board*, etc. Even the narrow boards at the corners were to have two tenons and be fixed onto two pedestals, so as to complete the number of one hundred (on this figure, see below).

Another device designed to secure the boards, so that they should not incline either way but stand in alignment, would be the use of
26 bars passing across them. *And you shall make bars of acacia wood,*
27 *five for the boards of the one side of the tabernacle, and five bars for the boards of the other side of the tabernacle, and five bars for*

the boards of the side of the tabernacle at the rear westward — five bars to each side. *And the middle bar* — not another bar in addition to the five, but the middle one of the five — *in the midst of the boards, shall pass through from end to end*. The manner in which the bars were arranged is a moot question. The most likely interpretation is that the bars were placed on the boards inside the tabernacle — not outside, nor were they thrust through the thickness of the boards — and that each side had two bars above, one on the right and the other on the left, and two bars below, on the right and on the left respectively, and halfway up the boards was the middle bar, which was longer and extended from one end of the side to the other. The bars, which apparently were inserted in rings attached to the boards, held the boards of each side firmly together as a single unit. How it was possible to prevent the south and north units from inclining inwards on account of the massive weight of the curtains draped over them will be shown later, in our annotations to v. 37. *And you shall overlay the boards with gold, and shall make their rings of gold for holders for the bars; and you shall overlay the bars with gold* — all that will be visible to the eye shall be of gold.

In this paragraph, too, a complete description is not given, and at the end *v*. 30 comes to tell us that the directions given to Moses were completed by the vision vouchsafed him by heaven: *And you shall erect the tabernacle* (here the term *tabernacle* is used in its comprehensive sense) *according to the plan for it which has been shown you on the mountain*.

The numbers recorded in this paragraph, or those deduceable from it directly or indirectly, evince in most cases signs of numerical symmetry based on the decimal system. The length of the boards and the height of the tabernacle are 10 cubits. The length of the tabernacle is 30 cubits, and its width 10 cubits. The length of the walls made of boards is altogether 70 cubits (seven times ten), whilst the entire perimeter of the tabernacle measures 80 cubits. The boards of the south side total 20, and their pedestals 40; the same obtains on the north side. The number of bars on each side are half of 10. The pedestals, if we include also the four silver pedestals mentioned in *v*. 32, come to 100 (see xxxviii 27).

SEVENTH PARAGRAPH

THE VEIL AND THE SCREEN

(XXVI 31–37)

The word פָּרֹכֶת *pārōkheth* ['veil'] is derived from the stem פרך *prk*, whose original meaning was to 'close', 'shut'; from it comes the Akkadian noun *parakku*, which sometimes denotes the temple and sometimes the adytum. Akin to it, as far as we can see, is also the Ugaritic substantive *prk* (the noun *prkm* that appears on one of the Phoenician inscriptions from the city of Kition in the island of Cyprus signifies something else). The Biblical *pārōkheth* was a kind of curtain [veil] or screen (it is called 'the veil of the screen' below, xxxv 12, *et al.*), which was hung inside the tabernacle so as to divide the interior into two parts, one next to the entrance and the other further in. The inner section was the Most Holy place, before which hung the veil.

The paragraph begins, as usual, with the injunction, 'and you
31 shall make' — *And you shall make a veil of deep violet and dark red and scarlet wool and fine twined linen*, like the curtains of the tabernacle; and like them *in skilled work shall he* — the artisan — *make it*, so that the combination of colours shall produce representations of *cherubim*. The expressions employed here are similar to — indeed, almost identical with — those used of the curtains (*v.* 1), with a few variations, as is customary. *And you shall put it,*
32 that is, hang it, *upon four pillars of acacia* [שִׁטִּים *šittīm*] — the language, on account of the rhythm, is elliptical for 'acacia wood' עֲצֵי שִׁטִּים *ʿăṣē šiṭṭīm*] — *overlaid with gold*, and upon them shall be *their hooks* made of *gold*, that is, small pegs shaped like the ancient letter *Wāw*, which resembled a Y, whose perpendicular shafts would be inserted into the tops of the pillars, and upon whose two tenons, which bifurcated above and projected from the pillars, the wooden pole from which the veil hung would be laid. The pillars were to be fixed *upon four pedestals of silver*, similar to the pedestals of the boards; in each pedestal there was to be a hole, into which the pillar would be wedged. The veil was to hang,
33 apparently, behind the pillars. *And you shall hang* [rendered in *v.*32, 'put'] *the veil beneath the clasps* of the curtains of the tabernacle, that is, at a distance of twenty cubits from the entrance of the tent (since there were to be five curtains in front of the clasps, and each

one was to be four cubits wide); it will thus be seen that behind the veil there would remain a space ten cubits by ten cubits and ten cubits high, and this was to be the Most Holy place. *And bring in thither*, into the area *within the veil, the ark of the testimony*. The meaning is not that the veil should be put up first and thereafter the ark should be brought to its place, for the space between the pillars would have been insufficient. Even if we assume that the pillars were slender, and their diameter no more than half a cubit, and that the first and the last pillars adjoined the boards without any intervening space, there would remain between one pillar and the other an interval of only two and a third cubits, and since the length of the ark between the staves was two and a half cubits, and to it must be added the thickness of the staves, the ark could not have passed between the pillars without extreme difficulty. The intention here is only to specify the place of the ark, not the order of the stages in the erection of the tabernacle. According to the procedure of erection, which is expressly described in chapter xl, verses 20–21, the ark, with the *kappōreth* upon it, was to be brought to its place first, and thereafter the pillars and the veil were to be put up, and they would bar the way to the removal of the ark. Properly, the ark should be shut in, and it should not be possible to take it out from its place except when the tabernacle was taken down, or in abnormal circumstances, by the removal of the pillars from their position. See further on this below, at the end of the commentary to this paragraph. *And the veil shall separate for you the holy place* — the area twenty cubits by ten in front of the veil — *from the most holy*, which was behind it.

Having been told where the ark was to be put, we are informed in vv. 34–35 of the respective places to be occupied by the other sacred articles mentioned in the preceding paragraphs. The passage begins with the word וְנָתַתָּ *wᵉnāthattā* ['And you shall put'], in order to form a series of three consecutive verses — 32, 33, 34 — commencing with this word (the difference in the termination, תָּ֫- -*tā* [in v. 34] and תָּה -*tā(h)* [in vv. 32 and 33], is merely a divergency of spelling, due to the usual tendency of the Masoretic scholars to introduce variations of this kind): *And you shall put the kappōreth*, whose function it was to rest *upon the ark of the testimony, in the most holy place* (the complement of the verb 'and you shall put' is 'in the most holy place', not 'upon the ark of the testimony').

35 *And you shall set the table outside the veil*, in the holy place, *and the lampstand opposite the table on the side of the tabernacle toward*

EXODUS XXVI 37

the south — next to the southern side, in other words, on the left side as one enters; *and the table* — the meaning is: and as for the table — *you shall put* it *on the north side*, that is, not beside the lampstand but next to the north side, on the right as one enters.

36 The entrance to the tabernacle shall not remain open: *And you shall make a screen* [מָסָךְ *māsākh*] *for the doorway of the tent* — again a curtain similar to the פָּרֹכֶת *pārōkheth* ['veil'], but it is called just מָסָךְ *māsākh*, since the name פָּרֹכֶת *pārōkheth* was reserved for the screen in front of the most holy place. The screen at the doorway of the tabernacle was also to be a fabric of *deep violet and dark red and scarlet wool and fine twined linen*, but the ornamentation on it was not to be woven like the designs on the veil and on the curtains of the tabernacle, but embroidered — *the work of the* 37 *embroiderer. And you shall make for the screen* — to hang it thereon — *five pillars of acacia* (note should be taken of the differences in the wording here, as compared with that of v. 32), *and overlay them with gold; their hooks shall be of gold*, like the hooks of the pillars of the veil (see my annotation to v. 32); and the pole lying on the hooks, from which the screen hung, was to extend as far as the first board on each side, and thus prevent the boards from inclining inwards. The screen was to hang, it seems, behind the pillars, whilst the pole, apparently, was not merely to lie on the hooks, but was to be tied to them with thongs or by some other method, so that the wind should not easily be able to shift the screen from its place. *And you shall cast for them* — for these pillars — *five pedestals of bronze*, into which to fix the lower end of the pillars. Since the screen would separate the holy place from the court, it would partly belong to the court, and hence the pedestals were to be made of bronze like the other appurtenances of the court.

The space between the pillars of the screen was narrower even than that between the pillars of the veil; consequently, the screen with its pillars formed an even more effective barrier to the removal of the ark. The ark, and the *kappōreth* upon it, would remain shut in within the tabernacle, where they would be entirely safe, for it would be impossible to take them away from their place until the tabernacle was dismantled. When an occasion would arise to bring them forth from there for an exceptional purpose, such as at the crossing of the Jordan or when the ark compassed Jericho, it would be necessary to lift the veil and to move its middle pillars apart, and similarly the screen at the doorway of the tabernacle would have to be lifted and its central pillar removed from its position — such would be the solemn opening of the entrance for a solemn occasion.

EIGHTH PARAGRAPH

THE ALTAR

(XXVII 1–8)

Chapter XXVII
The altar, on which the sacrifices were offered, occupied a central cultic position, and no shrine could possibly be without an altar. It was obvious that in the Israelite sanctuary, too, there would be an altar; hence, from the very beginning, the word is used with the definite article.

It was essential that the form of the altar should comply with two requirements, which seemingly were in conflict with each other: (a) that the altar, as stated earlier (xx 24–25), should be of earth or stone; (b) that the altar should not be of a temporary character, which would necessitate its complete rebuilding at every encampment from local earth or stone, but a permanent structure that could be transported from place to place. A compromise between the two requirements was effected in this way: the altar was made hollow, consisting of an empty frame of wood overlaid with bronze, which could easily be filled from time to time with earth or stones. This frame was to be without a top; thus its horns and sides are mentioned here, but not its top, as we find later in connection with the altar of incense (xxx 3: 'its top and its sides round about and its horns'). Hence the observation made by several exegetes to the effect that the altar described here could not have survived a single day when the fire was kindled upon it is pointless; the fire was not kindled on the bronze that overlaid the wood but upon the earth or the stones in the centre.

1 Here, too, the description begins with the words 'And you shall make': *And you shall make the altar* — with the definite article for the reason stated — *five cubits long and five cubits broad* (the measurements are given here in the accusative — and not in a separate sentence with the pronominal suffix — in order to vary the formulation from that of the preceding paragraphs), and consequently *the altar shall be square* at its base; *and its height shall be*

EXODUS XXVII 5

2 *three cubits. And you shall make the horns of it upon the four corners thereof*, in accordance with the usual custom in regard to altars in the countries of the ancient East (and not only in the East). The original significance of the horns is the subject of dispute, and is unimportant for our theme, since in Bible times the convention was already established and had existed for many generations; the Israelites retained the accepted design without concerning themselves about its prehistory. *Its horns shall be of one piece with it*, that is, they were not to be made separately and subsequently attached to the altar, but they were to be formed originally as a direct prolongation of the planks forming the sides of the altar. *And you shall overlay it with bronze* — its sides. Although the altar had no top, as was stated before, it did apparently have a bottom made of planks so as to reinforce the structure.

3 *And you shall make its pots* [סִירוֹתָיו *sīrōthāw*] — vessels with wide openings, like cooking pots or kettles — *to receive its ashes* — to empty therein the fat ashes of the sacrifices on the altar and to carry it out to the place where the ashes were poured forth — *and its shovels* [יָעָיו *yāʿāw*] (from the stem יעה־יעי *yʿ(h)–yʿy*, Isa. xxviii 17 ['will sweep away']) — that is, shovels with which the ashes were swept off the altar and poured into the pots — *and its basins* [מִזְרְקֹתָיו *mizreqōthāw*, literally, 'its tossing-vessels'] — utensils used for collecting the blood of the offerings and tossing it upon the altar, and also for other purposes — *and its forks* [מִזְלְגֹתָיו *mizle-ghōthāw*] (note the word-play: מִזְרָקֹת *mizrāqōth* — מִזְלָגֹת *mizlāghōth*) — instruments with a long handle and large prongs, used for turning over and arranging the flesh on the altar-fire — *and its fire pans* [מַחְתֹּתָיו *maḥtōthāw*, from the stem חָתָה *ḥāthā*, 'to snatch up'], with which to snatch coals of fire from off the altar. *To* [-לְ *le-*] *all its vessels* — that is, with all its vessels (the *Lāmedh* of inclusion [cf. *Gesenius' Hebrew Grammar*2, § 143e], as in Gen. xxiii 10: 'of [-לְ *le-*] all who went in at the gate of his city') — *you*
4 *shall make it of bronze. And you shall make for it* — for the altar — מִכְבָּר *mikhbār* [rendered: 'grating'] — from the same stem as כְּבָרָה *kebhārā* ['sieve'] (Rashi); its explanation follows immediately: *a network of bronze*. The place and purpose of the network will be explained later. *And you shall make upon* — next to the upper edge of — *the net four bronze rings, at the four ends thereof* — of the altar, that is, at its four corners; the use to which the rings
5 will be put will also be clarified later on. *And you shall set it* — the net — *under the ledge* [כַּרְכֹּב *karkōbh*] *of the altar beneath*: the

363

karkōbh, as we learn from an examination of the ancient altars that have been found in great numbers in Israel and in the neighbouring countries, is a kind of horizontal projection that encompasses the altar on all sides, and is situated a third or a quarter of the way down from the top; its purpose, apparently, was purely ornamental. *So that the net may reach halfway up the altar*; this, it seems, is how the clause has to be understood: the sides of the altar were not whole, but were full of apertures, especially in the lower half, in order that air might enter from below and facilitate the kindling of the fire on the altar (hence it is to be assumed that they preferred to fill the interior of the altar with stones or pebbles rather than with soil); possibly in the lower half there were only wooden laths adjoining the four corners. In order to give strength and stability to the entire structure, despite the openings, a bronze network was to encompass the lower portion of the altar, extending half way up, and through the holes of the net the air would be able to enter without hindrance.

6 *And you shall make poles for the altar, poles of acacia wood,*
7 *and overlay them with bronze; and the poles shall be put through the rings* [וְהוּבָא אֶת־בַּדָּיו *wᵉhūbhā' 'eth baddāw*] (for the use of the particle אֵת *'eth* [sign of the accusative] with a passive form of the verb compare xxi 28 וְלֹא יֵאָכֵל אֶת בְּשָׂרוֹ *wᵉlō' yē'ākhēl 'eth bᵉśārō* ['and its flesh shall not be eaten']). *So that the poles shall be upon the two sides of the altar*, not permanently, like the poles of the ark, but only *when it is carried* — in order to carry the altar by means of them, when the tabernacle is moved from place to place.
8 *Hollow, with boards* — hollow in the interior, a sort of framework of boards — *you shall make it. As it has been shown you* [literally, 'as he has shown you'] (the verb is used impersonally, in the sense: as he that showed showed you) *on the mountain* — that is, all the details that were not adequately explained to you orally — *so shall they* — who do the work — *make it.*

The place of the altar is not expressly stated here, but from the fact that this paragraph comes after the completion of the description of the interior of the tabernacle it is to be inferred that the altar was placed in the court, which was a suitable site for the burning of the sacrifices. This is also implied in the subsequent statement (xxx 18) that the laver was to be put between the tent and the altar; see further xl 6, 29.

NINTH PARAGRAPH

THE COURT OF THE TABERNACLE

(XXVII 9–19)

Just as above the structure of the tabernacle was dealt with after the Torah had described the sacred furniture that was to be placed therein, so here the description of the construction of the court follows that of the altar that was to stand in it.

The word חָצֵר *ḥāṣēr* ['court'], which can be used both as a masculine and feminine noun, denotes the area, enclosed by a partition of hangings, that surrounded the tabernacle. The curtains were hung on pillars and held fast by means of cords (xxxv 18, *et al.*), by which they were tied to bronze pegs (xxvii 19, *et al.*) fixed into the ground on each side of them. Apparently, the intention was that the hangings should be suspended on wooden poles resting on silver hooks affixed to the top of the pillars (compare my earlier observations on the hooks of the pillars of the veil and of the screen at the entrance of the tabernacle), and that they should be fastened to the pillars not only at the top but also at the bottom and in the middle; on all this see further on. On the east side of the court was to be the gate; on this point, too, see below.

9 The text describes each side of the court. *And you shall make the court of the tabernacle: on the Negeb side southward* — that is, on the south side (compare xxvi 18) — *there shall be hangings for the court of fine twined linen* — white, it would seem — *a hundred cubits long for one side* — namely, the one just mentioned, the south side. The hangings were to be sewn together in a continuous line, but their length is not specified; on their width see *v.* 18.

10 *And its pillars* — that is, of the court — *shall be twenty*, set up at intervals of five cubits, *and their pedestals twenty, of bronze*, one for each pillar. *But the hooks of the pillars and their bands shall be silver*; the shape of the hooks we have already explained above (xxvi 32), and the bands were apparently rings encompassing the pillars at different heights, one at the top and one at the bottom, and one or more in the middle, which served both as decorations and as fittings to which to tie the hangings, with the help of straps or fine cords, so that they should not be shifted from their position

11 by the winds. *And likewise for its length on the north side*, etc. —
12 exactly as stated with regard to the south side. *And the breadth of*

the court on the west side — at the back of the tabernacle — will comprise *hangings for fifty cubits* — that is, the breadth would be half the length. *Their pillars ten* — they, too, were spaced five cubits apart — *and their pedestals ten. And the breadth of the court on the front to the east* — facing the entrance of the tent — shall likewise be *fifty cubits,* but shall be divided into three sections, two at the sides, called כָּתֵף *kātheph* ['shoulder', 'side'], and one in the middle — the gate of the court. And this is how they shall be constructed: *And* [-וְ *wᵉ-*] *fifteen cubits shall be the hangings of the one shoulder* — that is (the *Wāw* at the beginning of the sentence is explicative) in one of the sections adjoining the sides of the court running lengthwise hangings covering fifteen cubits shall be put up — *their pillars three and their pedestals three,* with the usual interval of five cubits between them. So, too, on the opposite side: *And on the other shoulder* — adjoining the other side running lengthwise — there, also, *shall be fifteen hangings* — that is, fifteen cubits of hangings — *their pillars three and their pedestals three.* It follows that in the middle there would be left a third section, twenty cubits long, which would serve as an entrance to the court. There would be hung a screen, fixed only at the top, that a person entering could easily lift up and then pass through into the court: *And for the gate of the court there shall be a screen twenty cubits long, of deep violet, and dark red and scarlet wool, and fine twined linen, embroidered with needlework* — exactly like the screen at the doorway of the tent. *Their pillars* [עַמֻּדֵיהֶם *ʿammūdhēhem*] — that is, of the twenty cubits (on the masculine form of the suffix [הֶם- *-hem*] instead of the feminine [הֶן- *-hen*], compare xxvi 1, 7), or possibly the pillars of the screen are meant, and עַמֻּדֵיהֶם *ʿammūdhēhem* was written in place of עַמֻּדָיו *ʿammūdhaw* ['its pillars'] on account of the influence of vv. 12, 14, 15, and of the word וְאַדְנֵיהֶם *wᵉʾadhnēhem* ['and their pedestals'], which immediately follows (compare also *wᵉʾadhnēhem* in v. 18) — *four* — implying that also these pillars would stand five cubits apart — *and their pedestals* — that is, of the pillars — shall be *four.*

The shape of the court was thus rectangular, a hundred cubits long and fifty cubits wide, and the total number of the pillars was sixty. Each of the four pillars at the four corners is, of course counted only once in this aggregate, although actually it served both adjacent sides, in so far as it was necessary to complete the number of spaces between the pillars. In order that there should be, for example, twenty intervals of five cubits each between the pillars, twenty-one pillars are needed, but the last pillar also serves as the first of the adjoining side, and so on right round, until we reach again the first side at which we started, the first pillar of each side serving as the last pillar of the preceding side; thus in practice sixty pillars suffice exactly for sixty spaces. In this way is to be understood the arrangement of the pillars of the screen of the court gate, which the exegetes have needlessly found difficult. On the east side there are fifteen cubits of hangings on the right-hand side, fifteen cubits of hangings on the left, and twenty cubits of the screen in the middle; all this requires ten spaces of five cubits each between the pillars, and hence eleven pillars. If we take into account the ten pillars mentioned in the text as belonging to this side (3+4+3) and the pillar at one of the corners, which was already counted with the pillars of one of the longer sides, we arrive precisely at eleven. It is not to be deduced, therefore, that on account of this the screen will not be in the middle; on the contrary, it will definitely be in the centre. The fifteen cubits of hangings at the one shoulder, which require three interspaces and four pillars, are suspended on the first three pillars and on the first pillar of the screen; the screen, which needs four intervals and five pillars, hangs on its own four pillars and on the first pillar of the second shoulder, whilst the hangings of the second side, for which three spaces and four pillars are required, are suspended on the three pillars of this shoulder and on the first pillar of the adjacent side. Thus the screen is found to be exactly in the middle of the east side.

After each of the four sides of the court has been dealt with, there follows a general review of the pillars, to inform us that although the manner of attaching the screen to its pillars is not identical with that by which the hangings are secured to its pillars,

17 yet the pillars themselves are all alike: *All the pillars of the court shall be filleted with silver* — that is, adorned with bands of silver (*v.* 10) — *their hooks of silver, and their pedestals of bronze.*

The paragraph concludes with two verses that summarize it and
18 round it off: *The length of the court shall be a hundred cubits, and the breadth fifty with fifty* [בַּחֲמִשִּׁים *baḥămiššīm*] — that is, fifty in the west and also fifty in the east, if we add together the length of the 'shoulder' on each side and the length of the gate of the court — *and the height* of the pillars and the hangings (that is, their width, which becomes their height when they are suspended on the pillars) *five cubits*, and they shall be made *of fine twined linen, and their pedestals* — that is, of the pillars that support the

19 hangings — *of bronze*. The same would apply *to all* (לְכֹל *lᵉkhōl*; on this use of *Lāmedh* with a generalizing force, compare above, *v*. 3, and my annotations *ad locum*) *the instruments of the tabernacle*, that is, including all the tools necessary *for its entire construction*, such as hammers, anvils, knives, saws, and so forth, *and all its pegs* — that is, of the tabernacle (compare my note above on the manner in which the curtains of the tabernacle were put up) — *and all the pegs of the court* — all these shall be made *of bronze*.

Numerical schematism and fundamental symmetry are manifest through the whole of this description. The decimal system is the primary basis of the measurements: the length of the court is 100 cubits; the entire perimeter is 300 cubits; there are 20 pillars on each of the longer sides, and 10 on each of the shorter sides, totalling 60 in all (on this number see above); the height of the pillars and the hangings is five cubits, that is, half of 10 cubits. Possibly there are here also elements of the sexagesimal system in the aggregate of the pillars and in the extent of the perimeter.

The Torah does not state in which part of the court's area the tabernacle was to be placed. If we were to assume the principle of schematic symmetry, the prevailing theory would appear to be correct, namely, that the entrance of the tabernacle was located on the line dividing the length of the court into two equal parts: there was an area fifty cubits long in front of the tabernacle and fifty cubits from there in the other direction, allowing thirty cubits for the length of the tabernacle, and twenty behind it; there was also a space of twenty cubits on both sides — south and north — between the tabernacle and the hangings. If this was so, the ark was situated exactly in the centre of the western half of the court; and the altar, possibly, was placed in the middle of the eastern half. But there is not the slightest indication of all this in the text.

Here end the principal directions for the construction of the tabernacle. Additional instructions are added later on; we shall discuss the reasons for their insertion there when we reach the passage.

TENTH PARAGRAPH
FIRST DIRECTIONS FOR THE PRIESTHOOD
(XXVII 20–XXVIII 5)

At this point commences a series of paragraphs dealing with the priests and their service in the Tabernacle. They begin, as did the instructions for the making of the Tabernacle (xxv 2 f.), with an expression of *taking*, used actually in both meanings of the verb לָקַח *lāqaḥ* ['take']: in the sense of separating something as a contribution to the holy service (xxvii 20: 'that they take unto you clear olive oil'), and in the signification of receiving the separated object from the hands of those who make the contribution (xxviii 5: 'And they shall take the gold', etc.). The parallelism between the two series of directions is manifest.

This paragraph contains three allocutions to Moses, all of which begin with the word וְאַתָּה *weʾattā* ['And you'], followed by a verb in the imperfect or imperative. The first of these, which is repeated almost word for word in Leviticus xxiv 2–3, concerns the kindling of the perpetual lamp. Above, in the paragraph dealing with the lampstand (xxv 31–40), only its form and the arrangement of its lamps upon it are described, and in *v.* 37 (*ibid.*) the clause וְהֶעֱלָה *weheʿĕlā* [literally, 'and he shall bring up'], etc. is phrased impersonally, in the sense of 'one that brings up', whoever he may be, its sole purpose being to indicate, without digression, the place and orientation of the lamps on the branches of the lampstand. All this relates to the construction of the lampstand and the primary connection of its accessories to it. In this new paragraph, however, Scripture tells us of the way the lamps were used in the continual service of the sanctuary, day by day.

20 *And you*, Moses, hear, pray, the orders that I deliver to you in particular, and of the execution of which you must take charge. In accordance with My injunction *you shall command the children of Israel, and they shall take* — that is, that they take — of what they have, and bring *to you* — apart from the oil that they would contribute as a non-recurring gift, according to their generosity (xxv 2, 6), for the erection of the tabernacle and the commencement of its service — yet another perpetual contribution develving upon them at all times, namely, that of the *clear beaten olive oil*, made by the pounding of olives in a mortar and not by pressing

EXODUS XXVII 20

in the olive press, which would serve *for the light*, that is, *to kindle* [or 'set up... to burn'; see xxv 37]. *lamps* [נֵר *nēr*] *continually* [תָּמִיד *tāmīdh*]. The noun נֵר *nēr* ['lamp'] is used here in a collective sense: 'lamps' or 'candelabrum'. The word תָּמִיד *tāmīdh* is intrinsically capable of two interpretations: it can mean 'continuously, without interruption' — that is, the lamps would never be extinguished, either by day or by night; or it can signify 'regularly' — that is, the lamps would burn every night; on no night would its light be wanting — as in the expression עֹלַת תָּמִיד *'ōlath tāmīdh* ['continual burnt offering']. According to the plain meaning of the text, the second sense is more probable, for in *v.* 21 it is stated: 'from evening to morning'; so, too, in Leviticus xxiv 3; compare, further, Exodus xxx 7–8, and also i Samuel iii 3: 'And the lamp of the Lord had not yet gone out.' During the day there was no need for the light of the candelabrum, since sufficient light from without entered through the screen; moreover, the priests could lift up the screen and illumine the interior of the holy place. It is not to be objected that it was not possible to obtain clear beaten olive oil in the desert, for such a small quantity as that required for the kindling of the lamps could be obtained from the caravans passing through the wilderness. Furthermore, this precept was to be observed in perpetuity (*v.* 21: 'It shall be a statute for ever throughout their generations').

21 *In the tent of meeting* — that is, the Tabernacle, by which name it is several times designated from now on, on the basis of the Biblical statement (xxv 22; xxix 42–43, *et al.*) that the Lord met there with Moses and Israel — *outside the veil which is upon the testimony* — that is to say, before the ark of the testimony, as is stated above (xxvi 35) — *Aaron and his sons shall arrange it* — the candelabrum; it now becomes clear who is intended by the unnamed tender of the lamps referred to above (xxv 37). They shall arrange the candelabrum *from evening to morning* — that is, every evening so that it burns all night until the following morning — *before the Lord* — before the most holy place. This shall be a *statute for ever throughout their generations*, namely, of Aaron and his sons — a task assigned to them, as representatives of the people, *by the children of Israel*. In the following verses the ambit of their task will be enlarged and become the generalized duty of serving as priests in the sanctuary.

It should be noted that the first ritual act to be mentioned in the order of the sacred services is the kindling of the perpetual lamp before the most holy place, whereas the perpetual [daily] sacrifice is referred to only at the end (xxix 38–42). The reason for this will be explained in my commentary on the Book of Leviticus*.

Chapter XXVIII

The second of the commands given here to Moses is the appointment of Aaron and his sons as priests. Since this appointment does not flow from the will of the people but from the will of the Lord, who chooses the priests by means of Moses, the pronoun

1 וְאַתָּה *wᵉʾattā* ['And you'] is stressed also here: *And you*, Moses, in My name and at My behest, *bring near to you Aaron your brother, and his sons with him, from among the children of Israel to serve Me as priests*. The expression לְכַהֲנוֹ־לִי *lᵉkhahănō lī* ['to serve Me as priests'] occurs three times in this paragraph, at the conclusion of three sentences; undoubtedly this was intended to give it emphasis. Commentators have found considerable difficulty in elucidating the phrase on account of its strange grammatical form; and as yet no satisfactory explanation of it has been suggested. Possibly it is a fossilized archaic term, and the *Wāw* may have been added to the construct infinitive after the manner of the *Wāw* [compaginis] in חַיְתוֹ אֶרֶץ *hayᵉthō ʾereṣ* [Gen. i 24]. The meaning of the expression, however, is clear: so that they may minister in My service and worship. Bring all of them near: both *Aaron* and his sons, *Nadab and Abihu*, the first pair, and also *Eleazar*

2 *and Ithamar*, the second pair of *Aaron's sons* (vi 23). *And you shall make holy garments* — clothes that will indicate the degree of holiness — *for Aaron your brother, for glory and for beauty*, in keeping with his high office.

The third command concerns the priestly garments. Just as the appointment of the priests was to be effected by Moses in the Lord's name, even so the priestly vestments were to be made at the special behest of Moses in the name of the Lord. Hence here, too, after the brief reference to Aaron's vestments in *v.* 2, the word

3 וְאַתָּה *wᵉʾattā* ['And you'] is stressed a third time: *And you shall speak to all that are wise-hearted, whom I have filled with the spirit of wisdom* — to all the artisans skilled in the making of stately and beautiful robes, in the heart [i.e. mind] of each of whom I have implanted sagacity in his craft so that he may do his work successfully (compare xxxi 6, and several further examples there-

---

* Owing to the untimely demise of the author, this commentary was never written. *Tr.*

after) — *that they* — these craftsmen — *make Aaron's garments to consecrate him that he may serve me as a priest* — that is, garments that will symbolize his consecration for the stated office, to wit, My priesthood. *And these are the garments which they shall make for Aaron: a pouch, and an ephod, and a robe, and a tunic of chequer work, a turban and a sash*; the manner of making each of these garments is explained in detail in the next paragraph. *And they shall make holy garments* not only *for Aaron your brother*, but also *for his sons, that they may serve Me as priests*. The garments assigned for Aaron's sons are mentioned later on. *And they* — these craftsmen — *shall take the gold, and the deep violet, and the dark red, and the scarlet wool, and the fine linen*, and make therefrom the holy vestments for Aaron and his sons in accordance with the detailed instructions given in the verses that follow.

In this paragraph dealing with the priesthood of Aaron and his sons, the name of *Aaron*, which is the principal name in the passage, occurs seven times.

ELEVENTH PARAGRAPH

THE PRIESTLY GARMENTS

(XXVIII 6–43)

This paragraph, which, after the general introduction in the previous paragraph, commences the detailed description of the things to be made for the ministration in the tabernacle, opens with the words, *And they shall make*, like the paragraph that begins the portrayal of the work to be done for the construction of the Tabernacle itself (xxv 10); and here, too, the words are used to form a link with the preceding text. Above, in *v*. 5, it is stated: 'And they [the craftsmen] shall take the gold', etc.; here Scripture continues with the injunction: *And they shall make*.

The first garment mentioned here is the *ephod*. The word אֵפֹד *'ēphōdh* ['ephod'] is, apparently, derived from the stem אפד *'pd*, in the same way as אֵזוֹר *'ēzōr* ['girdle'] is formed from the stem אָזַר *'āzar* ['to gird']; this is also the origin of the substantive אֲפֻדָּה *'ăphuddā* ['ephod'] (xxviii 8, etc.). Likewise in Ugaritic we find the term *'ipd*; there is no need, therefore, to regard *'ēphōdh* as a loanword from Akkadian. It primarily denoted, it seems, a kind of simple pinafore that covered the loins; in this sense the 'linen ephod' of the ministrants at the sanctuaries is to be understood (i Sam. ii 18; xxii 18; ii Sam. vi 14; i Chron. xv 27). From this signification two secondary meanings derive: it connotes (a) an article used specifically for cultic purposes, the nature of which is not clear (Jud. xvii 5; xviii 14, 17, 18, 20; i Sam. xxi 10); (b) one of the holy garments worn exclusively by the high priest. It is in this last sense that it is employed in our paragraph. The description in the text is somewhat obscure, and a number of different explanations of the ephod and its details has been offered. Here, following our customary practice, we shall not cite the various interpretations (except for a few particulars that, for one reason or another, may call for mention), and we shall content ourselves with expounding the simple meaning of the text, in the manner we deem correct.

In the list given above, in verse 4, the pouch, which is the most important article, is mentioned first, and thereafter the ephod. But now, in describing how they were to be made, it is necessary to give precedence to the ephod, since it forms the background to the pouch. Hence our passage speaks first of the ephod, then of the pouch, and thereafter of the manner in which the pouch was to be attached to the ephod.

It is stated here, *And they make the ephod*, with the definite article, just as we find the definite article in xxvii 1 ('And you shall make the altar'), because the ephod, like the altar, was found, in one form or another, in every sanctuary, and only its design and distinctive features belonged exclusively to the Israelite shrine. It was to be made, like the curtains of the tabernacle, *of gold, of deep violet, and dark red and scarlet wool, and of fine twined linen, the work of the designer*, and, in accordance with the original signification of the word, it was to be girt about the loins of the priest (not to cover his chest, as many thought), and it was to hang down in front, whilst its two ends were joined together at the back.

7 In order to fit it closely to the priest's body, *it* — the ephod — *shall have two shoulder-pieces attached* — that is, two straps made to pass over the priest's shoulders, and sewed on to the ephod (compare xxvi 3) — *to its two edges* (regarding the use of the masculine numeral שְׁנֵי *šᵉnē* ['two'] with a feminine noun [קְצוֹתָיו *qᵉṣōthāw* ('its edges')] see above, on xxv 18) — that is, the shoulder-pieces should be sewn onto the two edges of the ephod at the back of the priest — *that it* — the ephod — *may be joined together* in this way to the shoulder-pieces. A passive verb [(וְ)חֻבָּר (*wᵉ*)*ḥubbār*, Puʿal

EXODUS XXVIII 7

perfect ('that it may be joined')] follows here an active form of the same verb [חֹבְרֹת *ḥōbhᵉrōth*, Qal participle ('joining', 'attached')], as also we find in Jeremiah xxxi 4 [Hebrew, *v*. 3]: 'Again I will build you, and you shall be built' — a construction that is common both in Hebrew and in Ugaritic. These shoulder-pieces would come up over the priest's shoulders, and then, reversing the process, would come down over his chest, and would be attached below to the

8 band of the ephod. *And the band of its attachment, which is upon it* — that is, the girdle of the ephod that attaches it to the priest's body, to wit, the upper border of the ephod, which is thicker and stronger than the rest of the garment, and is fastened at the back by means of clasps or some similar device — *shall be like the work thereof* — like the work of the ephod as a whole — *of it shall it be* [so literally] — it shall be woven as a single piece with it — *of gold, deep violet, and dark red, and scarlet wool, and fine twined linen.*

9 *And you shall take two* שֹׁהַם *šōham* ['onyx'] *stones* — that is, two of the *šōham* stones mentioned above (xxv 7) as exclusive to the ephod and pouch (still another *šōham* stone was to be used in the making of the pouch) — *and engrave on them* [עֲלֵיהֶם *ʿălēhem*] (here, too, the masculine form of the pronominal suffix is used instead of the feminine form) *the names of the sons of Israel* as

10 follows: *six of their names* — that is, of the tribes — *on the one stone, and the names of the remaining six on the other stone, according to their birth* — according to the order of the birth of Jacob's

11 sons. After the manner of *the work of an artificer in stone* — that is, a jeweller — *the engravings of a signet* — as the name of the owner of a signet is engraved upon it — so *shall you engrave the two stones with the names of the sons of Israel. Enclosed in chequered work of gold* — that is, encased in a frame of gold — *shall you make them* — the stones (again we have a masculine form for the pronoun [the pronoun אֹתָם *'ōthām* ('them') is masc., whereas the noun אֲבָנִים *'ăbhānīm* ('stones'), to which it refers, is fem.]).

12 *And you shall set the two stones upon the shoulder-pieces of the ephod* — you shall attach them in the middle of the length of the shoulder-pieces, so that they should rest on the priests' shoulders, one on each side, and serve as *stones of remembrance for the children of Israel*, a memorial and symbol that the priest ministers in the name of the tribes of Israel. This shall be the 'dominion' upon his shoulder (compare Isa. ix 5); *and Aaron shall bear their names before the Lord upon his two shoulders for remembrance.*

So far the ephod has been discussed; now we must proceed to a

description of the pouch. In between, however, occur two verses (13–14) dealing with the settings and chains to be used for attaching
13 the pouch to the ephod. *And you shall make filigree settings* [literally, 'chequered work', as in *v.* 11] *of gold*, that is, gold ornaments perforated by a hole through which an object can pass, the aperture
14 being encompassed by artistic decorations. *And two chains of pure gold, like cords* — that is, plaited chains made by twining and twisting — *you shall make them* (here, too, the masculine pronoun [אֹתָם *'ōthām*] is used instead of the feminine [אֹתָן *'ōthān*]), *of interwoven work* — in the way cords are made. — These particulars are intended to indicate that the chains must be strong, so that a heavy weight may be hung on them. *And you shall fasten the interwoven chains* — these cordlike chains — *to the settings*, that is to say, you shall pass the end of each chain through the aperture of one of the settings. What was to be done with the settings and the chains will be explained later; here only a preliminary direction is given.

Verse 15 commences to give instructions concerning the חֹשֶׁן
15 *ḥōšen* [rendered: 'pouch']: *And you shall make a* חֹשֶׁן מִשְׁפָּט *ḥōšen mišpāṭ* [rendered: 'pouch of judgement'], etc. The etymology of the word חֹשֶׁן *ḥōšen* is obscure; neither the Arabic stem حسن *ḥsn* nor the Ugaritic word *ḥšn*, which is even textually uncertain, helps us to explain it. The purpose, or purposes, of the *ḥōšen*, and the sense of the word מִשְׁפָּט *mišpāṭ* [rendered: 'judgement'] here, we shall endeavour to elucidate when we come to *vv.* 29–30. The *ḥōšen* shall be *the work of the designer* (xxvi 1); *like the work of the ephod you shall make it, of gold, deep violet, and dark red, and scarlet wool, and fine twined linen shall you make it* — it, too, shall be woven, in the style of the tabernacle
16 curtains and the ephod. *It shall be square doubled* — that is, square when it is doubled; *a span its length and a span its breadth* — after it is folded double. By being doubled it will form a kind of pocket
17 to hold the Urim and Thummim (*v.* 30). *And you shall set in it* — on its outer square — *a setting of stone* — a gold frame containing cavities in each of which it will be possible to set a precious stone — *four rows of stone*, each row containing three stones. These stones, which are mentioned by name in *vv.* 17–20, are identical with the precious or semi-precious stones that, according to the tradition reflected in Ezekiel xxviii 13, were to be found in Eden, the garden of God. The Torah, it is true, made no mention of the gems and the gold in its narrative concerning the Garden of Eden,

and, on the contrary, was opposed to this detail, indicating that it was outside the garden of Eden that gold and precious stones were to be found (Gen. ii 11–12; see my commentary *ad locum* [*From Adam to Noah*], pp. 77–79, 119–120). Nevertheless, the Torah did not refrain from utilizing, as a symbol, the tradition that was current among the people: the priest, when making atonement for the iniquities of the children of Israel, was to wear on his garments the gold and the precious stones that implicitly symbolized the situation obtaining in the Garden of Eden, when man was free from all sin. This, apparently, is the primary significance of the stones of the pouch, and although the exact identification of each stone is in doubt, our understanding of the subject, at least, is not affected thereby.

The stones of the first *row* are: אֹדֶם '*ōdhem*, a red stone difficult to identify; פִּטְדָה *piṭᵉdhā*, possibly 'topaz'; and בָּרֶקֶת, *bāreqeth*,
18 apparently 'malachite'; these are the stones of *the first row. And the second row*: נֹפֶךְ *nōphekh*, סַפִּיר *sappīr*, and יַהֲלֹם *yahălōm*, of which only *sappīr* ['sapphire'] is known; it is the blue stone whose hue
19 is like that of the heavens (xxiv 10). *And the third row*: לֶשֶׁם *lešem*, שְׁבוֹ *šᵉbhō* — the identity of both is in doubt — *and* אַחְלָמָה '*aḥlāmā*,
20 possibly the 'amethyst'. *And the fourth row*: תַּרְשִׁישׁ *taršīš and* שֹׁהַם *šōham and* יָשְׁפֵה *yāšᵉphē* — the identification of all three is doubtful (it seems, however, that the word שֹׁהַם *šōham* corresponds to the Akkadian *sâmtu* or *sându* [see above, p. 326], but it is difficult to determine with exactitude what this substantive denotes). *They shall* all *be enclosed in gold in their settings* — each stone shall be
21 fitted into a setting of gold. *And the stones shall be according to* [עַל '*al*, literally, 'on'] *the names of the children of Israel: twelve* stones *according to* the number of *their names* — that is, of the tribes — and on each of them shall be inscribed the name of a tribe; *like the engravings of a signet* (v. 11), *every one according to his name*, that is, every tribe would appear according to its name. So *shall* the twelve stones *be* correlated *to the twelve tribes*.

The symbolism of the engraving of the names on the stones of the pouch has the same significance as the engraving of the names on the *šōham* stones of the shoulder-pieces of the ephod (vv. 9 f.; compare v. 29, below); the duplication, however, should occasion no surprise, for in such matters repetition is not eschewed. To this day, it is customary in synagogues to depict the tribes in a number of illustrations: on windows, lamps, the doors of the holy ark, and the like. Moreover, the second set of engravings is not redundant: the names inscribed on the *šoham* stones face upward, and are only *before the Lord* (v. 12), and it is not easy for a person standing in front of the priest to read them. To be read easily, the names must be engraved on an upright plane confronting the eyes, like those on the priest's breast; these are not only 'before the Lord' (v. 29) but also before men.

Now the text proceeds to explain the manner in which the pouch was to be attached to the ephod. *And you shall make for the pouch* — for the pouch and in addition to it — two *chains like cords of interwoven work of pure gold*. These are the chains that have already been mentioned earlier, in the directions given in v. 14; here Scripture mentions them again (with the usual variations of form) in order to indicate specifically that they are intended to be used for the pouch. *And you shall make on the pouch* — for the pouch and in addition to it — *two rings of gold, and put* these *two rings on the two* (xxv 18) upper *corners of the pouch*, on the right and on the left, *and you shall put the two cords of gold* — that is, the two chains mentioned before, which were to be made of interwoven work — *in* these *two rings* that were to be attached *to the corners of the pouch*: you shall insert one end of each chain in one of the rings. *And the two ends of the two cords* — the other end of each one of the chains — *you shall put on the two filigree settings* — you shall insert into the hole of one of the filigree settings referred to in vv. 13–14. *And you shall put* these two settings *on the shoulder-pieces of the ephod in front*: you shall affix the filigree settings to the part of the shoulder-pieces lying on the front side, above the priest's chest. Thus, the pouch will be fastened above in the following manner: on both sides, to the right and to the left, there shall be fixed to the shoulder-pieces of the ephod golden ornaments, namely, the two filigree settings, and the pouch shall be suspended from them by two strong chains of gold. Below there will be no need to fasten it so firmly, and a slight coupling will suffice. *And you shall make* yet another *two rings of gold, and put them* (אֹתָם *'ōthām* — again a masculine pronoun [although the Hebrew for rings is feminine]) *on the two* lower *corners of the pouch, upon its edge, which is toward tne side of the ephod* — the lower edge next to the ephod — *inward*, that is to say, the rings shall be placed inside, on the inner half of the doubled pouch, upon the priest's heart, and not on the outer half. *And you shall make two* more *rings of gold, and put them* (אֹתָם *'ōthām* — once again a masculine pronoun [referring to a feminine noun]) *on the two shoulder-*

pieces of the ephod low down, in front of it — that is, upon the ends of the shoulder-pieces on the front side, below the pouch — *alongside its juncture* — close to the point where the shoulder-pieces join the band of the ephod — exactly *above the band of the* 28 *ephod. And they shall join* [or *bind*] *the pouch by its* lower *rings to the rings of* the shoulder-pieces of *the ephod with a lace of deep violet,* for below there is no need for a strong coupling like the gold chains that are necessary at the top in order to bear the full weight of the pouch, and a simple lace will suffice to ensure that the pouch *shall be* firmly fixed *upon* — above — *the band of the ephod and that the pouch* shall not come loose from the ephod.

Just as above, in the second paragraph, the Torah described the ark, and thereafter the *kappōreth* that was to be placed thereon, and finally reverted to the ark in order to give the directions for joining them together, so, too, in the present case, Scripture to begin with described the ephod, afterwards the pouch, and in the end returned to the ephod so as to set down the instructions for attaching them to each other.

By being fastened in this way to the ephod, the pouch will rest 29 securely on Aaron's breast, *and Aaron shall bear the names of the sons of Israel in the pouch of judgement upon his breast, when he goes into the holy place, for remembrance before the Lord continually.* This is one of the functions of the pouch: the priest will come before the Lord as the representative of Israel with the names of those whom he represents engraven for remembrance on the pouch that he wears on his heart. The pouch will also serve another purpose, which will be implemented by the placing of the Urim 30 and Thummim in it: *And into the pouch of judgement* — inside it, between its two folded halves — *you shall put the Urim and Thummim.* What the Urim and Thummim were we are not told; the Torah mentions them as something well known. Needless to say, nothing is said about their use; even in the next verse there is no clear indication of this. Similarly, there is nothing to be learnt from other references to them of a general character, for example, Lev. viii 8, or Deut. xxxiii 8. But there are a few passages from which we may deduce something concerning the use of the Urim and Thummim.

In the section dealing with the appointment of Joshua as leader of the people in place of Moses it is said (Num. xxvii 21): 'And he shall stand before Eleazar the priest, who shall inquire for him by the judgement of the Urim before the Lord.' In i Sam. xiv 37 after it had been stated that the priest was present with the ark of God, the Bible relates that king Saul asked counsel of God: 'Shall I go down after the Philistines? Wilt Thou give them into the hand of Israel? But He did not answer him that day.' *Ibid. v.* 38 ff. we are told that king Saul inquired again of God in order to know through whose sin it was that the answer was withheld, and he said unto all Israel: 'You shall be on one side, and I and Jonathan my son will be on the other side... And Jonathan and Saul were taken, but the people escaped. Then Saul said, Cast the lot between me and my son Jonathan. And Jonathan was taken.' In the Septuagint version the Urim and Thummim are expressly mentioned in this narrative. In i Sam. xxiii 2 ff. we read: 'Therefore David inquired of the Lord, Shall I go and attack these Philistines?... Then David inquired of the Lord again. And the Lord answered him... And when Abiathar the son of Ahimelech fled to David to Keilah, he came down with an ephod in his hand... Then said David, O Lord, the God of Israel, Thy servant has surely heard that Saul seeks to come to Keilah, to destroy the city on my account. Will the men of Keilah surrender me into his hand? Will Saul come down as Thy servant has heard?... And the Lord said, He will come down. Then said David, Will the men of Keilah surrender me and my men into the hand of Saul? And the Lord said, They will surrender you.' We further find in i Sam. xxx 7–8: 'And David said to Abiathar the priest, the son of Ahimeleh, Bring me, pray, the ephod. So Abiathar brought the ephod to David. And David inquired of the Lord, saying, Shall I pursue after this band? Shall I overtake them? He answered him, Pursue; for you shall surely overtake and shall surely rescue.' Other instances of inquiry of God, apparently by means of the Urim and Thummim, although no specific reference is made to them or to the ephod, occur in Jud. i 1–2; xx 18, 23, 27–28 (here the ark is mentioned); ii Sam. ii 1; v 19. From all these passages we learn:

1) That permission to inquire of the Lord through the priest by means of the Urim and Thummim in the pouch of the ephod was granted only to the person standing at the head of the people (Joshua; Saul; David as the head of his faction) and only on matters of public concern;

2) That the inquiry related to matters that human beings could not possibly know, for instance an issue dependent on the conscience of an individual or something belonging to the future;

3) That the question had to be so formulated as to make only

one of two answers possible: yes or no; the first matter or the second;

4) That two or more inquiries could not be made simultaneously; the answer was given to one question only (in this regard see particularly i Sam. xxiii 10–12);

5) That the reply was given by lot, as the expressions 'casting' and 'taking' indicate; this was based on the belief that the lot was not a matter of chance, but that God made his 'judgement' known thereby, namely, His decision or verdict (compare the word *dyn* in a similar sense in Akkadian, and see on this point below). Hence the expression *judgement of the Urim* in the passage cited above, Num. xxvii 21, and also the term *pouch of judgement*.

Thus it is possible to arrive at the following conclusion concerning the use of the Urim and Thummim contained in the pouch of judgement: they served as a means of inquiring of God, that is to say, of obtaining from the Deity, with the help of the priest, an answer concerning matters beyond human ken. It is also possible to assess the nature of the Urim and Thummim, and to postulate that they were two lots: one for an affirmative and the other for a negative answer; or one for the first possibility and the other for the second.

The shape of these lots it is impossible to ascertain, for there is no indication of it given in the relevant passages. The etymology of the two words cannot assist us to determine their form, because of its obscurity; all the suggestions that have been advanced, from the ancient versions up to our own times, do not go beyond conjecture. We may add that the observations we made in connection with the etymology of the word כַּפֹּרֶת *kappōreth* (see the note on xxv 17) apply also here. It must suffice for us to posit that there were two lots.

A matter that has an important bearing on our subject — one, moreover, that has escaped attention so far — is the reference in Lev. xvi 8 to the use of two lots by Aaron in the service of the Day of Atonement for the purpose of choosing between the two he-goats and determining which of them shall be for the Lord and which for Azazel. The great importance that Scripture attaches to this ceremony on the Day of Atonement for all the assembly of Israel permits us to assume that this casting of lots was also carried out by the judgement of the Urim. In any event, even if we do not make such an assumption, we have before us a clear instance of the use of two lots by the high priest.

EXODUS XXVIII 30

To know God's will and intention in important matters is a natural human desire, and the religions of the ancient East endeavoured to satisfy this yearning in various ways. In Mesopotamia the practice of divination and magic was very widespread, and whoever was about to undertake an important task did not proceed to execute it without consulting the priest who performed divination and magic (the class of priest called *bârû*), in order to learn from him the attitude of the gods. The means of divination were varied: inspecting the liver, shaking arrows (compare Ezekiel xxi 21 [Hebrew, *v.* 26]), observing the signs of heaven, examining the movements of birds, and so on and so forth. The Torah is opposed to any kind of divination or magic, and prohibits them absolutely. However, Scripture did not wish to close the door completely to this natural desire of the human heart, and contented itself with permitting the minimum (inquiry of God is allowed only to the leader of the people, and only in respect of public needs), and gave it a form devoid of divination or of magic — the form of the simplest sortilege. Only the ancient terms were preserved among the Israelites, but endowed with a new signification and involving a new approach, namely, the term to *inquire*, which continues the use of the verb שָׁאַל *šā'al* ['ask', 'inquire'], which is employed also in Akkadian, and the word מִשְׁפָּט *mišpāṭ* ['judgement'], which corresponds to the use of the substantive *dyn* [in Hebrew, 'judgement, law'], which in Akkadian signifies the answer of the gods to the question asked.

After David's time we do not find any further references to the use of the Urim and Thummim, either because it so happened that no stories on the subject, like those cited above, have come down to us, or for the reason that the children of Israel discontinued inquiring of God in this manner. The second reason may be the real one. Permission to ask the judgement of the Urim was, in the final analysis, only a concession or indulgence accorded by the Torah temporarily so as to satisfy, as far as possible, the innate yearnings of the people, and hence it does not enlarge on the subject, but mentions it so to speak, incidentally, as the secondary function of the pouch, which is ancillary to the first and primary purpose stated in *v.* 29. Subsequently, when the spiritual progress of the Israelites made it possible to desist from using this concession, the heads and leaders of the people abandoned the practice, and the Urim and Thummim remained only an honoured and hallowed relic of antiquity, without any practical function. It is possible to find evidence of this trend in the present form of the narratives about Saul and David that we have cited earlier. In i Sam. xiv 19 there is a break in the middle of the verse, and so, too, in *v.* 36, and such a break in the middle of a verse indicates, as is well known, that something that was originally in the text has been omitted from the recension before us. Thus, the express mention of the Urim and Thummim, which has been preserved in the Septuagint, was expunged from that chapter or altered. In chapter xxiii there are two further examples of a break in the middle of a verse — in *v.* 2 and *v.* 11. All this cannot be accidental; without doubt there is a definite purpose underlying the whole matter. In the Second Temple, the Urim and Thummim no longer existed, as we can infer from Ezra ii 63 and Nehemiah vii 65.

The conclusion of the theme of our paragraph is also worded cautiously, and only refers in terms similar to those of *v.* 29 to the first function of the pouch: *and they* — the names of the sons of Israel engraved upon the jewels of the pouch — *shall be upon Aaron's heart, when he goes in before the Lord; thus Aaron shall bear the judgement of the children of Israel upon his heart before the Lord continually.*

31 Beneath the ephod Aaron shall wear a robe: *And you shall make the robe of the ephod* — the robe over which the ephod is to be placed — *all of deep violet,* that is, wholly made of wool dyed the beautiful shade of תְּכֵלֶת *tᵉkhēleth,* which is the colour of the sky. The robe is of the same colour throughout in order to
32 point up the multi-hued ephod that was worn over it. *And the mouth of its head* — that is, of the robe; the upper opening in it, namely, the neck — *shall be in the midst of it* — wholly encompassed by the cloth of the robe; in other words, the robe shall not be open in front along its length, but the priest shall put his head through the hole of the flexible neck. This opening had, indeed, to be pliant in order to allow the passage of the priest's head: but at the same time it had to be strong so that it should not tear when stretched to enable the head to go through. For this purpose *it shall have a* strong *binding around its opening* [rendered above: 'mouth'], and this binding shall be made of *the work of the weaver,* that is to say, it shall not be separate to begin with and subsequently sewn onto the robe, but shall form part of the woven fabric of the garment. *It* — the robe — *shall have, as it*

EXODUS XXVIII 36

were, *the opening of a* תַּחְרָא *taḥrā'* (the usual rendering of the word, 'coat of mail', is not beyond doubt [BDB, '(linen) corselet']), לֹא יִקָּרֵעַ *lō' yiqqārēaʿ* [literally, 'it shall not be torn'], *which cannot be torn* (not: 'so that it shall not be torn', for if that were the meaning the text would have read: וְלֹא יִקָּרֵעַ *wᵉlō' yiqqārēaʿ*, with *Wāw* 33 conjunctive ['and']). *And you shall make upon its skirts* — of the coat — *pomegranates of deep violet and dark red and scarlet wool* — ball-like decorations, shaped like pomegranates, which were made of wool dyed these varied colours, the very colours of the ephod and pouch — *around its skirts*. The pomegranate form was apparently a common ornamental device, and it will suffice to mention here two examples belonging to this period: a circular pedestal of bronze found in Ugarit, under the rim of which there were decorations shaped like pomegranates suspended all round; there was also a mould found there for the making of metal ornaments decorated with a row of pomegranates hanging from them along their entire length. *And bells of gold shall you make between them* — between the pomegranates, which were also suspended from the 34 skirts of the robe *round about* in alternating order, *a golden bell and a pomegranate, a golden bell and a pomegranate*, in continuing 35 rotation, *on the skirts of the robe round about. And it* — the robe — *shall be upon Aaron for ministering, and its sound* — that is, the sound of the bells on the hem of Aaron's robe — *shall be heard when he goes into the holy place before the Lord*, for it is unseemly to enter the royal palace suddenly; propriety demands that the entry should be preceded by an announcement, and the priest should be careful not to go into the sanctuary irreverently. *And* likewise *when he comes out*, as he prostrates himself before departing, the sound of the bells, together with the act of prostration, will constitute a kind of parting blessing on leaving the sanctuary. *Lest he die* for not showing due reverence for the shrine.

36 *And you shall make a plate* [צִיץ *ṣīṣ*] *of pure gold.* The plate is not included in the list of vestments given in *v.* 4, since only the woven garments are enumerated there, whereas the plate is not a real article of apparel in the usual sense of the word. It is an adornment, made wholly of gold, and consequently it is not mentioned above, even though it is also, according to the formula used there [*v.* 2], 'for glory and for beauty.'

The original meaning of the stem צִיץ *ṣīṣ*, which is related to the stem נָצַץ *nāṣaṣ*, is to 'shine, sparkle', and hence the signification 'flower', whose colours gleam in the midst of the grass or among the branches of a tree, and hence it also denotes the brightness of a golden crown (compare Psa. cxxxii 18: 'but upon himself [on the king's head] his crown will shed its lustre'). The plate of the high priest is also a kind of crown or diadem, and later on (xxix 6, etc.) it is actually designated 'the holy crown.' But it differs from a diadem in that it does not encompass the entire head, but is placed only on the front half of it, namely, on the forehead (v. 38).

On the plate, too, an inscription is to be engraven: *and engrave on it, like the engraving of a signet*. The subject of engraving and its likeness to the engravings of signets are mentioned here for the third time (see above, v. 11, and v. 21). This threefold reference may not be coincidental but intentional, in order to emphasize the importance of that which is written and has a permanent character. The inscriptions worn on the shoulders and heart of the priest indicate that he represents the tribes of Israel, whilst the words he carries on his forehead proclaim that both he and those whom he represents, as well as all the services he performs as a priest, are completely *Holy to the Lord*. The written word takes in the Israelite worship the place assigned in the Mesopotamian and Egyptian cults to the spoken word, to the incantation and the formula uttered by the priest. Incantations and spoken formulas have a magic character, and consequently the Torah refrains from using them, and prescribes a cult that is conducted silently.

Now follow directions as to the manner of putting the plate on
37 Aaron's head: *And you shall put it on a lace of deep violet*, that means, you shall fasten the plate by a ribbon, or fine cord, of deep violet, which was apparently inserted into two holes at the two extremities of the plate, one on the right and the other on the left, *and it* — the plate — *shall* rest *on the turban* that is on the priest's head (v. 39); precisely *towards the face of the turban* — that is,
38 on the front side of the turban — *shall it be. And it shall be upon Aaron's forehead*, that is, it shall be placed on the edge of the turban and beneath it, covering Aaron's forehead, and the lace of deep violet shall go round the head and be fastened at the back so as to hold the plate firmly on the turban and on the forehead.

The plate on the priest's head corresponds to the frontlet-bands that every Israelite is enjoined to put between his eyes (see above, p. 154). There is also a parallelism between the 'lace of deep violet' on the *plate* [צִיץ *ṣîṣ*] (compare xxxix 31) and the 'cord of deep violet' [the identical expression in Hebrew] which was 'upon the *tassel* [צִיצִית *ṣīṣīth*] of each corner' of the garments of the children of Israel (Num. xv 38). They are all reminders and symbols of holiness.

And Aaron shall bear, because of the plate on his forehead, *the iniquity of the holy things, which the children of Israel shall hallow in all their holy gifts*, that is to say, he will atone for all transgressions committed in connection with the order of the service, the purity of the consecrated things, or the use of the holy gifts, for the declaration engraved on the plate will prove that everything was intended to be *holy to the Lord*, and if aught was done irregularly, the intention at least was good.

Apart from this atonement for given cases of guilt that may occur from time to time, the plate will also serve a constant purpose: *and it shall be always upon his forehead, for their acceptance before the Lord* — the plate will be a perpetual reminder that the people of Israel, represented by the priest, has dedicated itself unto the Lord and has undertaken to be a holy nation (xix 6), a thought that will be acceptable before the Lord.

After mentioning the most important vestments — the pouch, the ephod and the robe — followed by the plate, the Torah refers
39 briefly to the other garments of Aaron: *And you shall weave the tunic in chequer work of fine linen*, that means, you shall make the tunic mentioned earlier (v. 4) of fine linen fabric (that is, of fine threads of flax) worked in a pattern of chequers after the style, still usual today, of table cloths and napkins; for this reason the tunic is called in v. 4 'a tunic of chequer work.' Apparently this was the customary way of making stately tunics. Possibly Aaron's tunic should be compared to the כְּתֹנֶת פַּסִּים *kᵉthōneth passīm* ['tunic reaching to palms and soles' — BDB] worn by princesses (ii Sam. xiii 18) and by Joseph (Gen. xxxvii 3, 23). The priest was to wear the tunic beneath the robe (xxix 5; Lev. viii 7).

Aaron's head was also to be covered with fine linen: *and you shall make a turban of fine linen*. The head covering consisted of a long kerchief, which could be wrapped and wound round the head so as to give it a high and majestic shape. Furthermore, *and you shall make a sash*, a girdle fitted over the tunic, beneath the robe (Lev. viii 7). This sash shall be *the work of the embroiderer*; further on (xxxix 29) it is stated that it was made, like the ephod and the pouch, 'of fine twined linen and deep violet and dark red and scarlet wool.' Thus its manufacture was similar to that of the screen for the doorway of the Tabernacle (xxvi 36).

EXODUS XXVIII 40

The vestments of the other priests were to be like the garments of Aaron mentioned at the end, in *v.* 39, but mostly they were to
40 be simpler. *And for Aaron's sons you shall make tunics* — these, too, were to be of fine linen according to xxxix 27, but of a plain weave, without chequers; *and you shall make for them sashes* to wind round the tunic. These, since there is no robe worn over them, shall be the same as Aaron's sash, and shall also be made decoratively, embroidered, of deep violet and dark red, etc. (xxxix 29). *And caps shall you make for them* — head coverings that were not as majestic as Aaron's turban, but they, too, were *for glory and beauty.*

Moses is enjoined to attire the priests with these vestments for the purpose of delivering to them the charge of the priesthood:
41 *And you shall put them* — these garments — *upon Aaron your brother and his sons with him.* These garments shall be the external sign of their priesthood, and you shall put them upon them in order to indicate thereby that you are bestowing on them in My name the office of priesthood. You shall also perform another symbolic act at the time of their consecration: *and you shall anoint them,* namely, Aaron and his sons, with the anointing oil (see on this below, xxx 30, xl 15), *and you shall fill their hand,* that is to say, install them (an expression corresponding to this idiom, word for word, is found in Akkadian in the sense of 'installing', the original meaning being to fill the hands of the appointed person with the material for the work entrusted to him and with the tools required for executing it), *and you shall consecrate them* — you shall sanctify them for their service by means of these symbols — *and they shall serve Me as priests* — in this way they shall be enabled to minister in my worship and serve as priests unto Me.

The fact that here it is stated that all the priests are to be anointed, whilst in other passages it is said that Aaron was anointed, presents no difficulty; nor is it an indication of different sources, one of which held that the high priest alone was anointed, and the other that all the priests were anointed. The anointment is only a token of appointment, and there are different kinds of anointment for different kinds of appointment. Aaron was anointed as High Priest, and his sons were anointed as ordinary priests, just as the king, too, was anointed to mark his coronation.

There was still another thing that had to be provided for the
42 priests, apart from the holy vestments: *And you shall make for them* — both for Aaron and his sons — מִכְנְסֵי־בָד *mikhnᵉsē bhādh,*

EXODUS XXIX 1–37

linen drawers (according to xxxix 28 they were of שֵׁשׁ מָשְׁזָר *šēš mošzār*, 'twined linen thread' [rendered: 'fine twined linen']; שֵׁשׁ *šēš* is the name of the material, whilst בַּד *badh* denotes the fabric), *to cover their naked flesh* — we have already encountered an example of this kind of concern (xx 26), and we have discussed its motive, namely, to register opposition to the practice of performing religious rites in a state of nakedness, which was customary among certain peoples. *From the loins to the thighs they* — the drawers — *shall reach*, that is to say, they shall begin at the loins and extend downwards along the thighs to a point beneath his private parts, and then again cover the thighs above (that is the sense of the expression מִן — וְעַד *min* — *wᵉʿadh* [literally, 'from — and as far as']; compare: מִחוּט וְעַד שְׂרוֹךְ נַעַל *miḥuṭ wᵉʿadh śᵉrōkh naʿal* [literally, 'from a thread as far as a sandal-thong'] in Gen. xiv 23, and my commentary *ad*

43 *locum*, when it is published*). *And they* — the linen drawers — *shall be upon Aaron, and upon his sons, when they go into the tent of meeting, or when they come near the altar*, which is in the court, *to minister in the holy place; lest they bear guilt* — for, if they approach the sanctuary with lack of modesty, it shall be accounted to them as an iniquity — *and die.* This shall be *a perpetual statute for him* — for Aaron — *and for his descendants after him.*

TWELFTH PARAGRAPH

THE INDUCTION

(XXIX 1–46)

Chapter XXIX

1-37 It is recounted here (*vv*. 1–37) how Moses was given directions concerning the induction of Aaron and his sons into the priesthood. The implementation of these instructions is related, almost word by word, in Leviticus viii. This ceremony belongs to the sphere of sacrificial service, and its details can only be explained in the general framework of the laws pertaining to the offerings. I shall not, therefore, give a detailed exposition here of the verses;

---

* Owing to the untimely demise of the author this part of the commentary was not completed. *Tr.*

EXODUS XXIX 1–37

the reader will find the interpretation in my commentary to Lev. viii, when I am privileged, *Deo volente*, to publish it*.

38-42 After the directions regarding the ritual of installation, a brief allusion is made here (*vv*. 38–42) to the continual offering. For the reason stated I shall postpone the annotation of these verses until I am able to expound ch. xxviii in Numbers*, in the general context of the public sacrifices.

The last part of the paragraph, from the middle of *v*. 42 onwards, retraces its steps and seeks, as it were, to sum up and finalize the main theme of the Tabernacle by emphasizing its significance and purpose in the life of the people of Israel. After the statement that the continual burnt offering shall be offered up *at the door of the tent of meeting*, that is, on the altar in front of the door of the Tabernacle, *before the Lord*, the Divine communication, addressed to Moses, continues and confirms to him that the tent of meeting is the place where *I will meet with you* — where I shall reveal myself to you, O children of Israel, and appoint for you, so to speak, a meeting with Me (compare xxv 22, xxx 6) — *to speak to you there*, that is, when I speak to you there. In view of
43 the fact that *there I will meet with the children of Israel* (this does not revert to what is stated in *v*. 42, but provides a reason for the concluding statement of the present verse — *v*. 43 — the word *there* being emphasized), consequently *it* — the tent of meeting — *shall be sanctified by My glory*, that is to say, when I reveal Myself to you
44 therein. *And I* (emphatic) *will sanctify* — for the consecration that you, Moses, perform will be only on My behalf and serve merely as a symbol of My sanctification — *the tent of meeting*, with all that it contains, *and the altar* that stands before it; *and Aaron and his*
45 *sons I will* likewise *sanctify to serve Me as priests. And I will dwell among the children of Israel* — I shall cause My presence to abide in the tabernacle that is in the midst of Israel's camp — *and I will be to them a God*, who cares for them and protects them,
46 *And they shall know*, through seeing the tabernacle that symbolizes My presence in their midst, *that*, as I declared at the beginning of the Decalogue, which I proclaimed on Mt. Sinai, *I am the Lord their God, who brought them forth out of the Land of Egypt*, with the object *that I might dwell among them*, in order to make a covenant with them so that they shall be to Me a people, and I

---

* Unhappily the author died before he was able to write his commentary on either Leviticus or Numbers. *Tr.*

EXODUS XXX 1

shall be to them a God and cause My presence to dwell in their midst. These verses parallel, in thought and phrasing, the commencement of the section (xxv 1 ff.), and their style is distinguished by its stately rhythm and by the threefold occurrence of the stem יָעַד *yāʿadh* ['appoint'] and קָדֵשׁ *qādhaš* ['be consecrated', 'sanctify'].

Finally, as befits a king, who signs his name at the end of the declaration that he has issued, in order to validate it and accept full responsibility for its implementation, comes the solemn formula, *I am the Lord their God*, which concludes the main part of the Divine communication concerning the tabernacle of God's glory, wherein He would cause His presence to dwell among the children of Israel.

THIRTEENTH PARAGRAPH

THE ALTAR OF INCENSE

(XXX 1–10)

Chapter XXX

The position of this paragraph, having regard to the fact that the preceding paragraph concludes with verses that bring the subject to an end, may, at first, appear incongruous. Seeing that the altar of incense, as we are informed in *v.* 6, is one of the articles of furniture belonging to the Tabernacle, it appears that the paragraph pertaining to it should correctly have come above, where the rest of the tabernacle Turniture is described, namely, the ark, the *kappōreth*, the table and the lampstand. But it is impossible to assume, as most scholars do, that we have here a late and extraneous addition to the original subject, for two reasons: (a) if anyone had wished to make an interpolation of this nature, he would have inserted it in its proper place, not outside it; (b) archaeological research has proven the existence of incense altars with four horns in the Land of Israel (in the tenth century B.C.E., already in Megiddo), and although we attribute them to idolatrous shrines, it is inconceivable that such an altar should be lacking in the Israelite sanctuary; whereas in a later epoch, in the time of the Second Temple, it is out of the question that the Jews would have initiated a pagan custom.

However, the existing order is explicable in the light of the following two considerations:

EXODUS XXX 1

(a) We have already stated, in the notes prefacing this section (pp. 322 f.), that the Tabernacle was the tangible symbol of the Celestial Sanctuary, the cosmic abode of the Deity; and in order to enable the people readily to understand this symbol, it was constructed in the form that people living in the period of the Scripture passages concerned conceived a divine dwelling to have. We also observed in these notes that Israel's neighbours used to envisage a divine habitation that contained a throne, a footstool, a candelabrum, a table, and also other furniture, but no article corresponding to an altar of incense. The altar of incense was not an object that belonged to the Deity's abode but to His worship by man. Hence it is not described in chapter xxv, together with the articles of the Divine dwelling, but is dealt with here, in the first of the series of paragraphs pertaining to the order of the Tabernacle service.

(b) This paragraph does not merely contain, as do the paragraphs of chapter xxv, a description of the object concerned; its main theme, from *v.* 7 onward, is an account of the ritual to be performed on it, to wit, the continual daily service, and the special rite of the Day of Atonement. For this reason the paragraph was placed here, at the conclusion of the directions for the construction of the Tabernacle and the consecration of its priests, at the point where the Torah begins to explain the order of the service.

In chapter xxxvii, which recounts how the work of construction was carried out by Bezalel and his assistants, there is no room for differentiation between one article and another, and so the making of the altar of incense is described there together with that of the rest of the holy furniture of the Tabernacle. The substantive מִזְבֵּחַ *mizbēaḥ* ['altar'], which occurs in this passage, provides an interesting example of the semantic transformation of a word from its original signification to another. The noun is derived from the stem זָבַח *zābhaḥ* ['slaughter for sacrifice'], but there is no question of slaughtering here at all. This sacred article is designated מִזְבֵּחַ *mizbēaḥ* only because it is similar in shape to an altar, and because it is used in the sacred service in the same way as an altar.

1 The text, which opens with the words, *And you shall make an altar to burn incense upon*, immediately explains the meaning of the word *altar* here by adding the phrase, *to burn incense upon* — an altar that will be used only for burning on it the incense of spices. It too, shall be made of the wood of trees that grow in the neighbourhood like all the other wooden parts of the Tabernacle:

of acacia wood shall you make it. Its measurements shall be as
2 follows: *A cubit shall be its length, and a cubit its breadth; it shall be square,* like the altar of the burnt offering, *and two cubits shall be its height.* It, too, shall have horns, in accordance with the usual altar design (see above, on xxvii 2), and they shall not be made separately but shall be an extension of the boards of its walls:
3 *Its horns shall be of one piece with it. And you shall overlay it with pure gold, its top and its sides round about and its horns,* and only gold shall be seen on it, as in the case of the rest of the Tabernacle equipment. *And you shall make for it a moulding of gold round about* — a decoration on its sides similar to the decorations on the ark, and on the table and on its frame, so that all the vessels should be in harmony with each other, designed in a single style.
4 *And two golden rings shall you make for it; under its moulding on its two flanks;* and should you say that it is not clear to you which two sides are meant, seeing that it is square and its length and breadth are equal, know that the intention is that *you shall make* the rings *upon its two sides,* on the right and on the left of the person entering the Tabernacle. *And it* — the rings collectively — *shall be holders for poles,* which will be passed through the rings, *with which*
5 *to carry it. You shall make the poles of acacia wood, and overlay*
6 *them with gold,* like the other poles. *And you shall put it,* namely, the altar of incense, *before the veil that is in front of the ark of the testimony* — that means to say, inside the Tabernacle at a point halfway across its width, further inward than the lampstand and table, close to the veil — *before the kappōreth that is over the testimony, where I will meet with you* — these are all technical terms that have already been explained. The special mention of the *kappōreth* may be due to the fact that the priest makes atonement on the Day of Atonement both upon the *kappōreth* and upon
7 this altar (see *v.* 10). *And Aaron shall burn on it* — on this altar — *incense of spices* according to the following schedule: *every morning when he dresses* [literally, 'makes good'] *the lamps* — that is, when
8 he cleanses and trims the lamps of the candelabrum — *he shall burn it; and when Aaron kindles* [or, *sets up*] *the lamps towards evening* [literally, 'between the two evenings'], *he shall likewise burn it* — twice every day. The time of the burning of the incense was synchronized with that of the dressing and kindling of the lamps with the intention, apparently, that, owing to the pleasant fragrance of the incense, the unpleasant odour of extinguished wicks and burnt oil should not be felt. This incense shall be *con-*

tinual incense, which shall be burnt every day of the year before the Lord throughout your generations. The composition of the incense will be explained in detail further on (*vv.* 34 f.). *You shall not offer upon it* — on this altar — *strange incense* — that is, incense not prescribed in the Torah — *nor burnt offering, nor meal offering; and you shall pour no libation thereon* — throughout the year this altar shall be used only for the burning of incense (words derived from the stem קטר *qtr* ['smoke'] occur seven times in this paragraph). Only one exceptional rite shall be performed upon it once a year, namely, the putting of blood on its horns on the Day of Atonement: *And Aaron shall make atonement upon its horns once a year* (compare Lev. xvi 18; and see my annotations *ad locum** on the interpretation of the verse) *with the blood of the sin offering of atonement.* With the blood of the bull for the sin offering and of the goat for the sin offering, which are offered up *once in the year, shall he make atonement upon it,* in accordance with a statute that shall endure *throughout your generations. It* — this altar — *is most holy to the Lord*, and you are forbidden to use it for a purpose other than that mentioned here. Of the other articles of the Tabernacle it is not said that they are most holy, but with regard to the altar of incense this is nevertheless stated expressly, so that no one should suppose, since it is dealt with last, that its sanctity is less than that of the remaining vessels (compare below, xl 10, and my commentary *ad locum*).

Scripture does not explain how it was possible to burn the incense on the golden altar. It seems that the process is to be envisaged as follows: a special bowl was placed on the altar and in it the incense was burnt (see the bibliographical notes at the end of the book).

FOURTEENTH PARAGRAPH

THE HALF SHEKEL

(XXX 11–16)

This paragraph deals with the contribution of half a shekel that was imposed upon every Israelite at the time of the general census.

---

* Owing to the author's demise, this section of the commentary was never written. *Tr.*

EXODUS XXX 12

It was inserted between the paragraphs concerned with the service in the Tabernacle in order to prepare us now for what will subsequently be stated (xxxviii 25–28) in regard to the use made of these shekels in the construction of the Tabernacle. This particular place — after the paragraph dealing with the altar of incense — was chosen for the insertion of our paragraph, because of the connection between the words כֹּפֶר *kōpher* ['ransom'], לְכַפֵּר *lᵉkhappēr* ['to make atonement'], הַכִּפֻּרִים *hakkippūrīm* ['the atonement'], לְכַפֵּר *lᵉkhappēr*, which occur in it, and the words וְכִפֶּר *wᵉkhipper* ['shall make atonement'], הַכִּפֻּרִים *hakkippūrīm*, יְכַפֵּר *yᵉkhappēr* ['shall he make atonement'], which are found at the end of the preceding paragraph.

Since our passage is not as closely related to the main theme of the section as is the preceding paragraph, it is prefaced by the
11 formula that customarily procedes an isolated regulation: *And the Lord spoke to Moses saying*. The same obtains in the following paragraphs, each of which comprises a separate topic.

Regarding the census methods of the ancient East we possess today clear evidence in Akkadian documents found at Mari (eighteenth century B.C.E.), which throw considerable light on the details of the censuses recorded in the Bible. We shall cite from them here what is requisite for the elucidation of this paragraph, and then revert to the subject again later on in our commentary on xxxviii 25 ff., when we discuss the question of the atonement money and its employment for the construction of the pedestals.

12 Here it is stated: *When you take the sum* [literally, 'head'] — that means to say, when you count the total number (in Akkadian, too, *qaqqadu*, which corresponds to the Hebrew קָדְקֹד *qodhqōdh* ['crown of the head'] is used) — *of the children of Israel according to those that are numbered of them* — according to the census that you take of them (the word פְּקוּדִים *pᵉqudhīm* [literally, 'those that are numbered'] means 'census'; in Akkadian, also, the root *paqâdu* has this signification) — *then each shall give a ransom for his life to the Lord, when you number them*. In Mesopotamia the taking of a census was bound up with a religious ritual of purification, and so much importance was attached to this rite that the entire census was named after it *tebêbtu*, that is, 'purification'. This was apparently due to the fact that the census was considered a sin, implying, as it were, lack of faith in the deity; therefore it was necessary to associate it with a ceremony of atonement and cleansing from sin. The Israelite conception was similar to this,

393

hence the reference to *a ransom* that was to be given at the time of the census; it is furthermore stated, *that there be no plague among them when you number them*, that is to say, that by giving this ransom the children of Israel would be delivered from the punishment that was liable to be inflicted upon them on account
13 of the sin implicit in the carrying out of the census. *This they shall give*, for a ransom, *each one who passes over to those who are numbered* — that is, each one of the men who are included in the census: *half a shekel* — that is, silver (v. 16) weighing half a shekel (not coins, for coins did not come into existence until 700 B.C.E., and Jews, apparently, did not use them till after the Babylonian exile) — *according to the sacred shekel*, namely, the heavy shekel used for holy purposes, which was double the weight of the normal light shekel. *The shekel is twenty gerahs* (compare Ezekiel xlv 12; this is not, however, the place to deal with the complicated question of the detailed elucidation of Biblical weights). Each one shall give *half a shekel* (these words are repeated on account of the inter-
14 vening sentence, 'the shekel is twenty gerahs') *as a contribution to the Lord. Every one who is numbered in the census*, which includes every man of military age, *from twenty years old and upward* (in the Mari documents, also, we see that only the men of military age were counted in the census) *shall give the Lord's contribution*.
15 They shall all be equal in this matter: *The rich shall not give more, and the poor shall not give less* (even in the generation of the wilderness there could be found differences of wealth), *than the half shekel, when you give the Lord's contribution to make atonement for your lives*.

The contribution of the third part of a shekel that those who went up from Babylon gave (Nehemiah x 32 [Hebrew, *v.* 33]) was an entirely different matter; it was an annual offering and was not connected with a census. The scholars who thought that both contributions were of the same character, and, on the basis of this view, advanced innumerable conjectures, failed to understand the texts correctly. It is clear that 'the service of the tent of meeting', mentioned in *v.* 16, does not refer to the sacrificial service but to the construction of the Tabernacle, since it is stated that the money [literally, 'silver'] shall be 'a memorial for the children of Israel'; thus a permanent object was undoubtedly intended.
16 *And you shall take the atonement money* [literally, 'silver'] — to wit, the contribution of half a shekel given at the time of the census — *from the children of Israel, and shall appoint it for the*

EXODUS XXX 20

service of the tent of meeting — that is, you shall use it in the making of the Tabernacle (compare xxxviii 25 ff., and see my comments *ad locum*) — *that it* — this silver that went into the work of the Tabernacle — *may be a memorial for the children of Israel before the Lord, to make atonement for your lives.*

The threefold occurrence of the expression *an offering to the Lord* or *the Lord's offering*, and so, too, the triple use of the phrase *half a shekel*, and of the term *life* [נֶפֶשׁ *nepheš*, literally, 'soul'] in association with the stem כָּפַר *kāphar*, are certainly not accidental, and were intended for emphasis.

FIFTEENTH PARAGRAPH

THE LAVER AND ITS BASE

(XXX 17–21)

17 The laver is spoken of here alone, and not above, because it was not only not part of the furniture of the Divine dwelling but it was placed outside the tent, in the court, and even in the court it was not used for the holy ministration proper, but in preparation for it. Although it was also most holy (*vv*. 28–29), its use was of a secondary nature. This paragraph was inserted at this particular point on account of the parallelism between *vv*. 20, 21 — *lest they die* — and *v*. 12 in the preceding paragraph — *that there be no plague among them when you number them.*

18 *And you shall also make a laver of bronze* — a receptacle for water in the form of a round bronze vessel (the word כִּיּוֹר *kiyyōr* ['laver'] is from the stem כור *kwr*, which means 'round'), *and its base of bronze*, that is, a pedestal shaped like a hollow circle, resting on legs, into which the rim of the laver would mould fit, and which would carry the entire weight of the laver. The base was necessary in order to enable the water issuing from the taps of the laver to flow down on the hands and feet of the priests. The laver was to serve the priests *for washing, and you shall put it* inside the court of the tabernacle *between the tent of meeting and* 19 *the altar, and you shall put in it* — in the laver — *water, and Aaron and his sons shall wash their hands and their feet thereat.* Now these are the times at which the priests are obliged to wash their 20 hands and feet: *when they go into the tent of meeting* — before

395

entering the tent for whatever reason — *they shall wash with water, lest they die* because of disrespect to the sanctuary; *or* — that is to say, they shall likewise wash with water — *when they come near to the altar*, which is in the court, *to minister, to burn an offering by fire to the Lord*. This qualification — 'to minister, to burn an offering by fire to the Lord' — is necessary, because not infrequently the priests would have occasion to approach the altar in the court for a purpose other than that of ministering there, and, needless to say, they would not be obliged to wash themselves each time.

21 *So they shall wash their hands and feet* — the repetition comes to explain the nature of the washing mentioned in general terms in v. 20; thus shall they do, *lest they die. And it* — this duty to wash themselves — *shall be a statute for ever to them* — to them all; *to him* — to Aaron — *and to his seed throughout their generations*.

After the undefined expression 'for washing' used in v. 18, the verb רָחַץ *rāḥaṣ* occurs three times as the predicate of the subject *Aaron and his sons* (expressed or understood); this, too, is intended, as usual, for emphasis.

SIXTEENTH PARAGRAPH

THE OIL OF ANOINTMENT

(XXX 22–33)

22 This paragraph dealing with the anointing oil was placed here possibly on account of the connection between washing and anointing with precious oil.

Anointing with oil for the purpose of consecration was likewise customary among the neighbouring peoples, and since the practice is in no way contrary to Israel's faith, it continued also among the Israelites. In accordance with this custom instructions are here given to Moses to prepare oil to serve for anointing the Tabernacle, its vessels and the priests, as a mark of their consecra-
23 tion: *And you, take* בְּשָׂמִים רֹאשׁ *beśāmim rō'š* [literally, 'spices head'], that means to say, fine spices, 'chief spices' (Canticles iv 14 [רָאשֵׁי בְשָׂמִים *rā'šē beśāmim*, literally, 'heads of spices']), or 'the best of all kinds of spices' (Ezekiel xxvii 22 [רֹאשׁ כָּל בֹּשֶׂם *rō'š kol bōśem*, literally, 'head of all spice']), which were to be specifically the following four: (1) *of liquid myrrh* [מָר־דְּרוֹר *mor derōr*] — a resinous

exudation from the tree *Balsamodendron Myrrha* and the like, which dries on the stem of the tree in a form resembling pearls — *five hundred* units of weight, namely, sacred shekels, as we are immediately informed [in the next verse];

(2) *and of sweet-smelling cinnamon* — not actually what was called by that name at a later period, to wit, the inner bark of *Cinnamomum ceylanicum var. Cassia,* but another spice whose name in the course of time acquired the aforementioned signification — *half as much* — according to the simple meaning of the words, half the weight of the myrrh, that is, *two hundred and fifty* shekels;

(3) *and of sweet-smelling cane* — also called 'the goodly cane' (Jer. vi 20), *qanû tâbu* in Akkadian, belonging, apparently, to the genus *Cymbopogon* — likewise *two hundred and fifty* shekels;

24 (4) *and of cassia* [קִדָּה *qiddā*] — in rabbinic Hebrew קְצִיעָה *qᵉṣîʿā*; they are actually the flowers of *Cinnamomum ceylanicum var. Cassia* mentioned above — *five hundred,* all *according to the sacred shekel* [בְּשֶׁקֶל הַקֹּדֶשׁ *bᵉšeqel haqqōdheš*] (v. 13). The preposition *Bēth* [-בְּ *bᵉ*-], rendered here 'according to' is to be understood in the same way as in the expression שְׁמֹנֶה וְעֶשְׂרִים בָּאַמָּה *šᵉmōne wᵉʿeśrīm bāʾammā* ['twenty-eight cubits'; in this case English usage requires the *Bēth* to be left untranslated] in xxvi 2. In addition to these spices Moses had still to take *of olive oil a hin.* Many commentators have found it difficult to understand why the quantity of oil is so very small relative to the weight of the spices, which totals 1500 shekels. The weight of the oil is only about a quarter or a fifth of the spices taken together, and if so large a quantity of spices was put into the hin of oil, the resultant mixture would be a thick mass, not oil that could easily be poured, such as would be required for anointing the priests (xxix 7). But those who raise this objection have overlooked the fact that the entire aromatic material was not mixed with the oil, but the spices were subjected to a long and complicated process of soaking in water and boiling etc., over a period of many days, as we are informed by the Akkadian documents that describe the making of the anointing oil (see the bibliography at the end of this volume), and as is indicated also in rabbinic tradition (compare *Kerithoth* 5: 1–2; *Horayoth* 11: 2), and at the end of the distillation only the fragrance of the spices remained in the oil, not the raw material. It is to this very processing that the continuation of the text refers, when it

25 states: *and you shall make it a sacred anointing oil, a perfume of ointment–mixture, the work of the perfumer,* and as a result of this

26-28 distillation *a holy anointing oil it shall be. And you shall anoint with it* — the anointing oil — *the tent of meeting and the ark of the testimony*, etc. — in a word, all the articles of the tabernacle. Here, too, a number of exegetes found a difficulty, since they held that the limited quantity of oil could not suffice for this purpose. But they confused anointing with smearing. The verse does not mean that oil was to be spread over the entire surface of the articles of furniture, vessels, curtains and beams, but that one or two drops of the oil were to be sprinkled (Lev. viii 11) upon one end of each object; that was all (according to Talmudic tradition the anointing was done in the form of a Greek *Chi* [X]). It was further objected that the oil would spoil the beautiful curtains of the tabernacle; but this objection also falls away when we realize that the text has in mind merely the sprinkling of drops. If a small oil stain were left at the edge of the curtains, this would not be a blemish but a tangible sign that they had been properly consecrated.

29 *And you shall consecrate them* — the Tabernacle and all its appurtenances — by this anointing, after which they shall be sanctified *and be most holy*; hence *whatever touches them will become holy* (xxix 37; Lev. vi 11), that means that if any object touches them a part of their sanctity will cleave thereto, and it will be prohibited to treat it as something profane. The consecration of the priests is also to 30 be marked by anointment: *And you shall anoint Aaron and his sons, and consecrate them* in this manner *that they may serve me as priests.*

Since this oil was a token of holiness, it was to be treated as something sacred. Moses was accordingly given this admonitory 31 injunction: *And you shall speak to the children of Israel, saying, This shall be a holy anointing oil unto Me* — dedicated to Me — 32 *throughout your generations*, therefore *upon the flesh of man it shall not be poured* for secular anointing; and not only may one not use, in this way, the oil that was originally prepared for holy anointing, but it is forbidden even to make its like for profane purposes: *neither shall you make any like it, according to the composition thereof. It is holy* in itself, and therefore *it shall be holy* 33 *to you* — you shall regard it as something sacred. *Whoever compounds like it* a profane anointing oil, *and whoever puts any of it* — either of the holy anointing oil, or even of oil made according to the same recipe — *upon a stranger*, on one not entitled to priestly sanctity, he shall be liable to the penalty of *kārēth* ['cutting off']* — *he shall be cut off from his people.*

* Probably, as rabbinic tradition maintains, it was a punishment imposed by

EXODUS XXX 34

The phrase *a holy anointing oil* occurs three times in this paragraph, in order, as usual, to give it emphasis.

SEVENTEENTH PARAGRAPH
INCENSE OF SPICES
(XXX 34–38)

This paragraph corresponds to the preceding paragraph both in theme and in phrasing, and on account of this parallelism, which gives the two passages almost the character of a single section, there is lacking here the full formula, 'And the Lord spoke to Moses, saying', which marks each separate communication, and we have instead only an abbreviated statement, indicative of a

34 break within a single address: *And the Lord said to Moses.*

The directions for the preparation of the incense, the burning of which has been dealt with earlier, vv. 7–8, commence like the instructions contained in the previous paragraph (v. 23): *Take spices*, etc. Here occurs the generic term סַמִּים *sammīm* ['spices'], not בְּשָׂמִים *beśāmīm* ['fragrant spices'], for not all those mentioned here are sweet-smelling. Rabbinic exegesis, as we know, deduced that the incense was compounded of eleven spices, which was the practice followed in the time of the Second Temple. According to the simple sense of the text, which apparently accords with ancient Israelite usage, the spices named first in the list are to be identified as follows: (a) נָטָף *nāṭāph* [the stem means 'to drip'], a balsam that drips from resinous trees (*Styrax officinalis*); (b) שְׁחֵלֶת *šeḥēleth*, which is mentioned by this name in Ugaritic ritual texts, and in the form *šaḥullatu* in Akkadian texts, may be a plant, or possibly what the Talmudic sages called צִפּוֹרֶן *ṣippōren* ['nail'] (in Greek ὄνυξ; in Latin, *unguis odoratus*) the operculum of various species of molluscs of the genus *Strombus*; when burnt it gives forth a pungent odour; (c) חֶלְבְּנָה *ḥelbenā*, galbanum, a gum exuded from different species of plants of the genus *Ferula*; its odour is unpleasant, but when it is mixed with fragrant species and burnt with them, the overall effect is pleasant. The repetition of the word

---

Heaven, that is, the transgressor died before his time, leaving no children. Others consider that the term connotes excommunication, or even execution. *Tr.*

EXODUS XXX 34

spices has been interpreted in various ways and given rise to a number of conjectures. According to the plain sense of the verse, it means, apparently, that the three spices mentioned on the one hand, and the pure *frankincense* on the other, shall form the two parts of the incense, in equal weight; *of each shall there be an equal part,* [בַּד בְּבַד יִהְיֶה *badh b*ᵉ*bhadh yih*ᵉ*ye*] that is, the weight of the frankincense shall equal the combined weights of the three spices. The frankincense is not included among the spices, and constitutes by itself the basic ingredient of the incense; it is mentioned separately at the end, after the spices, in the same way as in *v.* 24 the oil is mentioned at the close of the verse after the fragrant spices. It is a resin that exudes from different species of plants of the genus *Boswellia*, and is called in Hebrew לְבוֹנָה *l*ᵉ*bhōnā* [from a stem meaning 'white'] on account of its white colour. The verb יִהְיֶה *yih*ᵉ*ye* ['shall be'] at the end of the verse is in the masculine singular because the subject is the noun בַּד *badh*, which signifies 'a part', and the meaning of the sentence is [as translated above]: 'of each shall there be an equal part.' The quantity of the spices and frankincense is not stated, unlike the amounts of the fragrant spices and anointing oil, which are given in *v.* 23, because there is a difference between the two preparations: the anointing oil mentioned earlier was to be made once and no more, whereas the incense, which was required for the daily service, was to be compounded periodically, whenever possible and whenever needed.

The first part of *v.* 35 resembles that of *v.* 25, with a few verbal variations: *And you shall make of it an incense, a perfume, the work of the perfumer.* Now the perfume was to be מְמֻלָּח *m*ᵉ*mullāḥ*, that is, 'mixed' (Targum Onkelos, Rashi) — all its parts were to be finely ground and well mixed together (the word is not to be understood in the sense of 'salted', for in this signification there was no need for the *Puʿal*) — *pure*, that is, without any impurities (Sforno), and consequently fit to be *holy*, a sacred object. This shall be the incense that is to be burnt twice daily on the gold altar according to *vv.* 7–8; in addition the incense was to be used for a special service once a year, on the Day of Atonement, as enjoined in Lev. xvi 12–13; and with reference to this latter service our text prescribes: *And you shall beat some of it very small* (the rabbinic interpretation of the precept to make the incense grains as fine as possible apparently accords with the actual meaning of the text), *and put part of it* — of the incense finely ground — *before the testimony in the tent of meeting* — within the veil — *where I shall* *meet with you*; *it* — this special incense, which is burnt in the most holy place — *shall be for you most holy.*

In parallelism with vv. 32–33, our passage, in vv. 37–38, admonishes: *And the incense which you shall make* in general, not just that which is specifically intended for the Day of Atonement, *according to its composition you shall not make for yourselves* — for your own use. *It shall be for you holy to the Lord* — you shall regard it as something dedicated solely to the Lord. *Whoever shall make any like it to use as a perfume* for his own pleasure, he shall be liable to the penalty of *kārēth* ['cutting off'; see on v. 33] — *he shall be cut off from his people.*

EIGHTEENTH PARAGRAPH

APPOINTMENT OF ARTISANS

(XXXI 1–11)

Chapter XXXI

All the directions relative to the construction of the tabernacle, supplemented by the instructions concerning the order of the service that would take place there, having been completed, we are now told of the appointment of the artificers to whom the task of construction would be assigned. The paragraph commences with the customary formula used in all Divine communications cited separately: *And the Lord spoke unto Moses saying.*

The word רְאֵה *rᵉ'ē* ['see', 'behold'] usually comes before a verb describing an action that takes place as soon as it is announced and by virtue of that announcement, for example: 'I have set you' (Gen. xli 41), 'I make you' (Exod. vii 1, etc.); 'I set before you this day' (Deut. xi 26); 'I have set you this day' (Jer. i 10), and the like. This is also the case here: *I have called by name* — that is, I appoint this day by this declaration that I address to you, and which designates the person by name — *Bezalel the son of Uri, son of Hur* (xvii 10, 12; xxiv 14; i Chron. iv 4) *of the tribe of Judah. And I have filled him with the spirit of God* — intellectual qualities that are a gift from God (it should be noted that the text does not say, 'the spirit of the Lord'), *with wisdom* — that is, expert knowledge of the techniques of workmanship and the ability to employ them — *and with understanding* — that is, the capacity to deduce one thing

EXODUS XXXI 3

from another and to find a way of solving any problem that may arise in the course of the work — *and with knowledge* — that is, the store of expertness that continues to grow relative to a basic skill as a result of practical experience — *and in all craftsmanship* — that means to say, these attributes would apply to all manner of workmanship.

Everything was to be made by human agency, in a natural way. It is true that according to the later Haggada, which seeks to magnify and glorify the grandeur and magnificence of the Tabernacle, the sanctuary was built miraculously, of its own accord; but this is not the meaning inherent in the simple interpretation of the text. On the contrary, Scripture comes, as it were, to oppose the Canaanite legends concerning the building of the temples of their gods by one of the deities themselves. The qualities attributed by the Canaanites to this divinity — *kṯr-w-ḥss*, 'skilful and understanding'; *hyn*, 'quick at his work'; *d ḥrš ydm*, 'a handcraftsman' — are here ascribed to human beings. These attributes will enable

4 Bezalel *to think thoughts*, which means to 'devise plans', and thereafter *to do* — to execute them, in all types of work: *in gold, and in silver and in bronze, and in cutting* precious *stones* for *setting*

5 in frames of gold, *and in carving wood*, and in general *to work in every craft.*

6 Bezalel was also to have a helpmate: *And I, behold, I appoint with him* (the verb נָתַתִּי *nāthattī* [literally, 'I have given', 'I have appointed'] like the verb קָרָאתִי *qārā'thī* ['I have called'] in v. 2, occurs in the perfect but has a present signification) *Oholiab* — a man whose very name, which contains an allusion to אֹהֶל *'ōhel* ['tent'], befits him and his task — *the son of Ahisamach of the tribe of Dan.* In conjunction with these master craftsmen there would also be a number of artisans working, and their skill at their work would likewise be a gift from God: *and in the hearts of all that are wise hearted I* Myself *have put wisdom.* They were given the designation *wise hearted* on account of the understanding that they ultimately acquired: they became wise of heart after the Lord had instilled wisdom into their hearts. All of them, Bezalel and every wise hearted person, shall work together, *and they shall make all that I have commanded you.* The general statement 'all that I have commanded you' is followed by particularization: *the*

7-11 *tent of meeting, and the ark of the testimony, and the kappōreth that is thereon,* etc. — a detailed list that summarizes all the articles enumerated from the commencement of the section until now.

402

EXODUS XXXI 12

This list also includes a new item, namely, בִּגְדֵי הַשְּׂרָד *bighe dhê* ['garments of'] *hasse rādh* in v. 10. The meaning of the word שְׂרָד *serādh* is obscure. The term cannot, according to the plain sense of the text, denote the holy garments of the priests, since these are mentioned immediately afterwards. Nor can it be a designation for the cloths used for covering the Tabernacle furniture during the journeys, in view of the subsequent statement (xxxv 19; xxxix 1, 41): *the garments of* שְׂרָד *serādh for ministering in the holy place*. Possibly they were the garments worn by the priests under their tunics in winter, during the service, as a protection against the cold; to wear them was not obligatory but optional, hence they are not referred to above. The expression *for ministering in the holy place* occurred previously already (xxviii 43 [where it is rendered: 'to minister', etc.]) in connection with the linen drawers, which were also not holy vestments and were prescribed for use during the sanctuary service only for reasons of decency. 'The garments of *serādh*' were apparently made of knitted [or plaited] work (the stem שרד *śrd*, or סרד *srd* in Aramaic, has a signification akin to that of סרג *srg*, and in Mishnaic Hebrew we find the occupational designation סָרָד *sārādh*, which signifies 'one who does knitted work' [or a 'net-maker']).

After the detailed list we have again a general expression, to include everything: *according to all that I have commanded you they shall do*.

NINETEENTH PARAGRAPH

ABSTENTION FROM WORK IN THE SABBATH DAY

(XXXI 12–17)

After all the directions appertaining to the execution of the work, comes the following admonition: Although I have commanded you to perform the work of the Tabernacle, do not forget that I have already forbidden you to do any work on the Sabbath day; know, then, that the construction of the Tabernacle does not set aside the Sabbath. Therefore, every Sabbath you must stop working.

12 The introductory formula of this paragraph is: *And the Lord*

said to Moses, and not: 'And the Lord spoke', etc., as is usual. This may be due to the fact that the verb *speak* immediately follows
13 at the beginning of v. 13: *And you, speak to the children of Israel saying*. Although I have commanded you to make Me a sanctuary, *nevertheless* (אַךְ *'akh*) *My Sabbaths* — all the Sabbaths that will occur in the period of the Tabernacle's construction — *you shall keep, for it*, the Sabbath, *is a sign between Me and you*, concerning the creation of the world (v. 17) and the making of the covenant (v. 16), *throughout your generations* — at all times and periods — *to know* — that you may know — *that I am the Lord who sanctifies you*, drawing you near to My holiness by this commandment, which makes the sequence of your labour and rest analogous to that of My work, when I created the world and then abstained from the work. And it would be wrong to set aside one sign of sanctity in order to expedite the completion of another sign. There-
14 fore, *you shall keep the sabbath, because it is holy unto you*, and it is forbidden to desecrate that which is holy. *Every one who profanes it shall be put to death*, for thus does the statute, which, basically, takes precedence of the injunction to construct the tabernacle, ordain: *whoever does any work on it* — the sabbath — *that soul shall be cut off from among his people*. The statute of the sabbath
15 is given in full in vv. 15–17 in the following form: *Six days shall work be done* (יֵעָשֶׂה מְלָאכָה *yēʿāśe mᵉlāʾkhā*; the verb is in the masculine because it precedes the subject), *but on the seventh day is a sabbath of entire rest* [literally, 'of desisting'], *holy to the Lord* (on all these terms and concepts see my commentary to ch. xvi and
16 the Decalogue); *whoever does any work on the sabbath day shall be put to death. And the children of Israel shall keep* (this verb is connected with the expression 'perpetual covenant' at the end of the verse: they shall keep it as one keeps an everlasting covenant) *the sabbath, to observe* [לַעֲשׂוֹת *laʿăśōth*, literally, 'to do'] *the sabbath* (a word-play: this is how it is to be kept — they shall do no work, but 'do' the sabbath; possibly the word *laʿăśōth* contains an allusion to the conclusion of the first section dealing with the sabbath, in Genesis ii 3: 'which He had creatively made [*laʿăśōth*]'), *throughout their generations* (it is to this expression that the phrase *throughout your generations* in v. 13 alludes), as one keeps *a perpetual covenant*.
17 *It is a sign between Me and the children of Israel for ever* (there is an allusion to this clause in v. 13, which states: 'for it is a sign between Me and you') — a sign for this: *that in six days the Lord made heaven and earth, and on the seventh day He abstained from*

work and was refreshed. This graceful and poetic expression *and was refreshed* serves as a fitting conclusion to the Divine communication.

It is certainly not fortuitous that expressions derived from the stem שָׁבַת *šābhath* ['abstain from work', 'desist'] (one of which is the compound expression שַׁבָּת שַׁבָּתוֹן *šabbāth šabbāthōn* [rendered: 'sabbath of entire rest']) occur seven times in the paragraph. Nor is it to be regarded as merely coincidental that the verb שָׁמַר *šāmar* ['keep'], that expressions of *holiness*, and that the term *to work* appear three times; the underlying intention is to give them all emphasis.

TWENTIETH PARAGRAPH

THE HANDING OVER OF THE TABLES OF THE COVENANT

(XXXI 18)

18 This verse informs us that after Moses had been given on Mount Sinai all the directions he was to receive (the text does not mean to imply that all the instructions have been cited here, but only such as had necessarily to be mentioned at this stage in conformity with the order and purpose of the narrative), on the last day of Moses' stay on Mount Sinai, the Lord fulfilled the promise that He had made to him at the beginning (xxiv 12), *and He gave to Moses* (the subject, the Lord, is not specifically mentioned, but is readily understood), *when He had made an end of speaking with him on Mount Sinai, the two tables of testimony* — an everlasting memorial testifying to the covenant that had been made between the Lord and Israel — *tables of stone written with the finger of God.* The text is worded with great care: Scripture does not state, 'written by the hand of the Lord', but 'written with the finger of God', in order to inform us specifically that the writing was of Divine character and had its origin in the sphere of the Godhead. The phrase *finger of God* occurred earlier already (viii 15; see my annotations *ad locum*) as a general allusion to the Divine power, and in this passage, too, it bears this sense: whoever writes uses not a single finger but a whole hand, or at least two fingers; hence the expression certainly does not refer to actual writing, and the univer-

sal designation *Elōhīm* ['God'], which is used here instead of the personal name *YHWH*, was chosen specifically in order to avoid attributing a material act of this nature to the Lord Himself.

After the two tablets had been delivered to him, Moses made ready to descend the mountain. Scripture implies that he went down in the morning, for it is stated (xxiv 18) that he was on the mountain forty days and forty nights, and seeing that he ascended as a rule early in the morning, the implication is that he came down at an early hour on the morning of the forty-first day. This is how we have to visualize the matter: on the fortieth day Moses received the tablets, and when night fell he entered a cave to rest therein, and he spent the whole night there in order to complete his descent on the morning of the following day. As for the statement in Deuteronomy ix 11 ('And it came to pass at the end of forty days and forty nights, that the Lord gave me the two tables of stone, even the tables of the covenant'), it was worded in this form only in order to repeat the customary phrase 'forty days and forty nights.'

However, before we are told that Moses came down from the mountain, we must know what happened in the meantime at the bottom of the mountain, and what the children of Israel did during the absence of their leader. This will be related in the following section.

SECTION TWO

THE MAKING OF THE CALF

CHAPTER XXXII, VERSE 1 — CHAPTER XXXIV, VERSE 35

To enable us to understand the story of the making of the calf in its general aspect and in its details, and also to explain why it is recorded at this particular juncture, between the directions for the construction of the tabernacle and the account of their implementation, several preliminary observations will be necessary.

We have already noted earlier, in our commentary to xxv 18 ff., that the *kappōreth* over the ark, and particularly the wings of the cherubim spread over it, were a kind of throne for God who sits upon the cherubim, a vacant throne for the Deity who is invisible to man. Similarly we observed there that in general the peoples of the ancient East were accustomed to portray the deities as standing or sitting upon wild beasts or cattle, such as lions, oxen or other animals. On this basis, several exegetes have in recent times put forward the view that the golden calves — that is, the golden bulls (on the meaning of the word עֵגֶל *ēghel* [literally, 'calf'] see below) — both the one made in the wilderness and the two of Jeroboam, according to the account in i Kings xii, were not originally deemed to be actual gods, but were likewise regarded as the seat of the invisible godhead. This view appears probable, especially when we bear in mind that the one who made the calf in the wilderness was Aaron, the person who had been appointed to be the priest of Israel's God. A question, however, arises here: Why did the Torah, on the one hand, enjoin that cherubim be set up in the tabernacle and, on the other, accounted the making of the calf as a grave iniquity? In answer it may be said that, despite the resemblance between the two objects, there was a fundamental difference that distinguished them. The Decalogue forbade the construction of 'a graven image, or any likeness of anything that is in heaven above, or that is in the earth beneath, or that is in the water under the earth.' The likeness of an ox, an earthly creature, is included in this prohibition; but not so the cherubim, which are imaginary beings to be found neither in the sky, or on the earth, nor in the waters. The reason for this distinction is clear:

whoever sees the representation of the cherubim, knowing that they are products of the imagination, will readily understand that they are only images, and is unlikely, therefore, to make the mistake of attributing to them actual divinity; but one who looks at a bovine statue, since he knows that there are many bulls in the world and that they are creatures of such tremendous strength and such enormous fertility that the heathen peoples considered them to possess divine attributes (the Canaanites gave the father of their gods the designation 'Bull'), is liable to err and ascribe to that likeness, and even to living oxen, a divine character and to worship them as deities. In the view of Scripture, Aaron's intention, when he made the calf, was only to fashion a vacant throne for the Godhead, like the throne of the cherubim, which, at this very time, Moses had been commanded to make. He made the calf in order to satisfy the need of the multitude to see at least a tangible symbol of the Deity's presence, the same need that the Torah sought to gratify when it permitted the cherubim and even enjoined their construction. He thought that the prohibition of the Decalogue referred only to prostrating oneself to idols and serving them ('you shall not prostrate yourself to them or serve them'), and he did not realize that the prohibition to make them, which is expressly stated by itself, was a kind of 'protective fence' to prevent the general populace from falling into error and being guilty of prostration to and worship of images. It was certainly not the intention of the Bible to convey that Aaron actually committed the sin of idolatry, for in that case it would have been impossible for the Torah itself to relate that Aaron was chosen to be priest in the Lord's sanctuary and to become the Father of the priesthood throughout the generations. The Bible merely wishes to imply that Aaron sinned in that he did not take into account the need for a preventive measure and the possibility of error on the part of the masses, an error that actually materialized when the people saw the calf and acted as they did. Possibly it is also part of Scripture's intention to demonstrate the need for a 'fence' in order to safeguard people from transgression.

The story recorded in i Kings xii concerning the two golden calves that Jeroboam made is undoubtedly related to our section. This is evidenced by the declaration made by Jeroboam (*ibid. v.* 28): 'Behold your gods, O Israel, who brought you up out of the land of Egypt', which parallels the words of the people in the present section (xxxii 4): 'These are your gods, O Israel, who brought you up out of the land of Egypt!' Noteworthy is also the fact that the names of Jeroboam's two sons, Abijah and Nadab (i Kings xiv–xv), correspond to the names of the two elder sons of Aaron, Nadab and Abihu, who offered strange fire and died before the Lord (Leviticus x 1–2). On this basis the theory was advanced that not only our section, but also the narrative about Nadab and Abihu, was written after the partition of Israel from Judah as an allusion to Jeroboam's action. It is difficult to accept this hypothesis, since the declaration cited above, 'Behold your gods (or, These are your gods), O Israel, who brought you up out of the land of Egypt', is apposite to the theme of our section, which speaks of the period immediately following the exodus from Egypt, but is not suited to the age of Jeroboam. On the contrary, it is more feasible that the story of the calf made by Aaron was already widely known at the time of the division of the kingdom, and that Jeroboam, in his endeavour to alienate his people from the sanctuary at Jerusalem, which was built in accordance with the Mosaic tradition and contained the *kappōreth* of the cherubim, wished to link himself to the opposite doctrine. To this end, instead of the cherubim of Jerusalem, Jeroboam placed in his sanctuaries calves like the one that Aaron made in the wilderness, and proclaimed in regard to them the very words that the Israelites had used on that occasion. As a clear and continual indication of his views and tendencies he named his two sons after the sons of Aaron, who, according to tradition, conducted their service in a manner opposed to the Mosaic rite, which was still in force in the Jerusalem Temple. The influence of our section on the narrative in the First Book of Kings is discernible also in other respects:

1) The statement in i Kings xii 31, 'and he appointed priests from among all the people, who were not of the Levites', is an allusion to the attitude of the Levites in the episode of the calf (xxxii 26).

2) In i Kings, as here, reference is made to a feast, an altar, and to sacrifices.

3) In both passages prayer is spoken of in similar, unusual terms: i Kings xiii 6, 'Implore now the Lord your God', which parallels Exodus xxxii 11, 'And Moses implored the Lord his God.'

The long and detailed narrative, which concludes with the attainment of forgiveness, begins with this prayer of Moses. Its length and details are not unintended: in this story the Torah seeks to inculcate its teachings concerning punishment, atonement and forgiveness, and also the functioning of the Divine attributes of justice and mercy. When we consider the motive of the story, we shall be able to comprehend its particulars and various subdivisions, and we shall be convinced that there is no need for all the theories advanced to explain the length of the account on the basis of the assumption that a number of fragmentary sources and later additions have been fused together here.

Now we shall also be able to understand why our section was inserted at this point. After the establishment of the covenant between the Lord and the Israelites, the people were commanded to construct the tabernacle, which was symbolic of the Divine Presence in the midst of the camp, and contained the ark, which testified by its tablets to the covenant that had been made. However, since the children of Israel had committed the sin of the calf and had thereby broken the covenant, the latter was annulled. For this reason Moses shattered the tables that bore witness to the covenant, and the injunction to erect the tabernacle was likewise rescinded. Only when the people had obtained forgiveness was the covenant renewed, and the tablets were reinscribed like the first which had been broken, and permission was again granted to execute the work of the tabernacle. In view of this, the proper place of our section is precisely here, after the directions that had first been given regarding the construction of the tabernacle and had subsequently been revoked because of the episode of the calf, and before the account of the implementation of the instructions, which was possible only after the attainment of pardon. A dramatic concatenation of events!

This section contains key words that recur again and again, like continuing echoes, which leave a deep impression on the reader's mind, namely, the verb יָדַע *yādhaʿ* ['know'] and the noun פָּנִים *pānīm* ['face', 'before']. In particular these words are found in greatest concentration in the eighth paragraph (xxxiii 12–23), which cites the dialogue between Moses and the Lord. Also the expression, *to find favour in the Lord's sight*, occurs a number of times in the same paragraph, and recurs once again in the following paragraph (xxxiv 9); the repetition of this phrase is likewise evidence of a special purpose. We shall discuss these and other repetitions in the continuation of our commentary.

FIRST PARAGRAPH

AT THE FOOT OF THE MOUNTAIN

(XXXII 1–6)

Chapter XXXII

The story commences with a reference to the mood of the people, who were waiting longingly for Moses to descend the mountain,
1 and in the end despaired of ever seeing him again. *And the people saw,* that is, since the people realized (a co-ordinate clause, in accordance with ancient Hebrew diction, in place of a subordinate clause that would have been expected in modern usage) *that Moses delayed* [literally, 'caused shame', i.e., disappointed, was late] *to come down from the mountain,* and since they feared that he might never return, they considered it necessary to put in his place someone or something that would lead them in the wilderness; *and the people gathered themselves together to Aaron,* in a spirit of contention and rebellion (compare, 'And they gathered themselves together to [i.e. against] Moses and Aaron', in the account of Korah's rebellion, in Num. xvi 3, and in the narrative of 'the waters of Meribah' ['Contention'], *ibid.* xx 2), *and they said to him, Up* — a very emphatic imperative — *make us gods, who shall go before us* — prepare for us a godlike image that shall show us the way in which we must go, as Moses, your brother, did until now in the name of the Lord — *for as for this Moses, the man that brought us up out of the land of Egypt,* and brought us thus far, *we do not know what has become of him.* This happened, according to our text, which follows immediately upon the statement, *when He had made an end of speaking with him* (xxxi 18), on the fortieth day after Moses had ascended Mount Sinai. He had not told them when he would return (xxiv 14); so they waited for him a number of weeks, and on the fortieth day they gave up hope.

From the stylistic point of view it is noteworthy that there are seven references to bringing up out of the land of Egypt in this section (xxxii 1, 4, 7, 8, 11, 23; xxxiii 1).

Aaron, who was not as resolute as Moses, was unable to withstand the rebellious people, and seeing that after all they did not demand a substitute for the God of Israel, but only a surrogate for Moses, he did not reject their request completely, but gave
2 them a non-committal answer that could gain him time. *And*

Aaron said to them, Take off the rings of gold which are in the ears of your wives, your sons, and your daughters, and bring them to me.

3 But the attempt at procrastination was unsuccessful: *And all the people* (the word *all* expresses, as usual, hyperbolical generalization) made haste and *took off the rings of gold which were in their ears*. Not only did the men take off the rings that were in the ears of their wives and children, but they also removed the rings in their own ears, *and brought them to Aaron*, even as he had requested: 'and bring them to me.' Then Aaron had no alternative

4 but to continue along the course upon which he had started: *And he received* the rings *at their hand* and commenced to work.

In order to understand the details of the subsequent narrative, it is necessary to pay attention to the method of making images of silver and gold in antiquity (see the bibliography at the end of the book): first they would make a wooden model, and then overlay it with plating of precious metal. The existence of the inner core of wood, which formed the greater part of the idol, serves to explain *v.* 20, which relates that Moses burnt the calf and ground it to powder; whilst the gold plating, which was made by melting down and casting the metal (in this case, the earrings), elucidates the word מַסֵּכָה *massēkhā* ['molten image'] in *v.* 4 (compare Isaiah xxx 22: 'Then you will defile your silver-covered graven images and your gold-plated molten images [מַסֵּכַת *massēkhath*]'). In order to sculpture the finest details on the gold plating, such as the eyes, the hair and the like, artistic work required a sharp and delicate instrument, namely, a graving tool. This, then, is the meaning of the verse: *and he fashioned it* — the gold — *with a graving tool*, producing by means of this instrument an exact likeness, *and made it*, when his work was complete, *a molten calf* — a calf overlaid with molten gold.

The word עֵגֶל ['calf'] is not a pejorative term for an ox, as many surmised. It denotes a young ox, an ox in the full vigour of its youth. עֶגְלָה מְשֻׁלֶּשֶׁת *'eghlā mᵉšullešeth* (Gen. xv 9) means 'a heifer three years old.' It is likewise a designation applied to an animal that produces much milk (Isa. vii 21–22), or that works at ploughing and threshing (Jud. xiv 18; Jer. *l* 11; Hos. x 11). In Psalm cvi 19–20, the words עֵגֶל *'ēghel* and שׁוֹר *šōr* ['ox'] occur in parallelism to each other in reference to the very episode of the golden calf that the Israelites had made in the wilderness. In Ugaritic, too (Tablet I* AB, *V*, line 18), we find in juxtaposed parallelism the words *prt* and *'glt*.

Although Aaron intended only to present the people with a palpable symbol, a kind of empty throne, as stated above, the Israelites went astray after the concrete representation, and treated it as an actual deity, *and they said, These are your gods, O Israel, who brought you up out of the land of Egypt!* Not without reason is the plural used here, *These... brought* [plural] *you up.* Scripture does not attribute to the children of Israel the fooliish dea that it was the calf that had just now been fashioned that brought them up from the land of Egypt; they could not possibly have forgotten what Moses had caused them to see and hear in the name of the Lord. The meaning of this proclamation is that they regarded the calf as an emblem of the Lord, and they considered this emblem itself worthy of divine honour, thus making the calf a partner, as it were, of the Lord. Hence the plural. In this, or a similar, manner, the Talmudic sages understood the text when they declared (B. Sanhedrin 63a): 'Were it not for the *Wāw* of הֶעֱלוּךְ *heʿĕlūkhā* [which makes the verb plural — (they) 'brought you up'], Israel's foes [a euphemism for the Israelites themselves] would have been liable to extinction'; and when they expounded (Exodus Rabba iii 3): 'I have seen this people' (Exod. xxxii 9). [This means, I foresee] that when I come to Sinai to give them the Torah, descending in My *τετράμουλος (the four creatures in the Divine Chariot, each of which has four faces, one being that of an ox [see Ezekiel i 5 ff.])*, they will scrutinize Me and extract one of the creatures and provoke Me therewith.' This, then, was their sin: they transgressed against the commandment, 'You shall have no other gods before Me' — in My presence, associated with Me. In the reference to the making of the calf found in Nehemiah ix 18, the text does actually read the singular: 'This is your God who brought [singular] you up out of Egypt'; but there the author wishes to give the utmost emphasis to Israel's transgression.

5 *And Aaron saw.* The sense is: And when Aaron saw (on this syntactical construction see above, on *v.* 1) the evil trend of the people, he endeavoured to curb them, *and he built an altar before it* — before the throne of the deity in the form of a calf — *and Aaron made proclamation and said, Tomorrow shall be a feast to the Lord* — to the Lord, not to the calf. But the people, who had 6 already broken down every barrier, were beyond control: *And*

---

* Compare M. Jastrow, *A. Dictionary of the Targumim, the Talmud Babli and Jerushalmi, and Midrashic Literature*, London–New York 1886-1903, p. 528. Tr.

they rose up early on the morrow, and offered burnt offerings and brought peace offerings in honour of the calf (v. 8: 'and have sacrificed to it'); *and the people sat down to eat and drink, and rose up to play*, in accordance with the custom obtaining at the feasts of the peoples addicted to the worship of the gods of fertility and the inchastity connected therewith.

SECOND PARAGRAPH

ON MOUNT SINAI

(XXXII 7–14)

The morning when the people abandoned themselves to idolatrous licentiousness was apparently the one on which Moses wished to descend the mountain (see above, my commentary to xxxi 18). He was getting ready to bring to his people the Tables of the Covenant, and his soul was tranquil and filled with religious joy, when suddenly the word of the Lord came to him and brought him news that dumbfounded him: *And the Lord said unto Moses, Go down* — make haste to descend at once — *for your people have corrupted themselves* — your people, for they are no longer worthy of being called My people — the people *whom you brought up out of the land of Egypt*, for they no longer deserve the honour that I should attribute their exodus to Myself, seeing that they have associated a partner with Me, to whom they give a share of the credit for it. *They have turned aside quickly out of the way which I commanded them*: only a few weeks have passed since they heard My voice proclaiming the Ten Words, but they have been quick to turn away from them. *They have made for themselves a molten calf*; now this in itself would not yet have constituted a grave iniquity, but in addition *they have prostrated themselves and sacrificed to it* after the manner of the heathen peoples, *and said, These are your gods, O Israel, who brought you up out of the land of Egypt*. They rebelled against Me, and also against you, since it was you who brought the exodus about.

Moses stands listening in amazement to what he is told, and apparently he is unable to utter a word to voice the feelings of his heart — feelings of deep sorrow at what has happened, but also of love for his people, which impel him to entreat for mercy on their behalf. But before he is able to open his mouth and pray for them, the Lord, who looks on the heart, turns to him again and bids him not to plead for them, for they are undeserving of compassion. *And the Lord said to Moses, I have seen this people* (in the expression *this people* one can sense an intended rebuke), *and behold it is a stiff-necked people*: I have seen that they are stiff-necked and it is impossible to instil new ideas into their obdurate mentality; they are accustomed to the cult prevailing round about them, namely, that of image worship, and it is not possible to make them understand that this mode of worship is unfitting and unacceptable. *And now*, this being the case (the expression indicates the conclusion reached by God), *let Me alone* — do not intercede for them — *that My wrath may burn hot against them and I may consume them*, and the promise that I gave to your ancestor Abraham to make of him a great nation (Gen. xii 2) I shall fulfil in you and in your descendants: *and I will make of you a great nation*. Moses, however (the greatness of the faithful shepherd is seen here in all its glory), does not retreat before the Lord's burning anger, but, as soon as he is able to utter a word, he endeavours to shield his people. In the words *Let Me alone* he discerns that also in the Lord's mind there is an element of doubt, as it were, and that even in the moment of His anger God feels love for His people, and hints, so to speak, that there is still a possibility *not to let* His anger continue to burn. Thereupon, Moses immediately begins to plead for mercy: *And Moses implored* [literally, 'besought the face of'] *the Lord his God*, etc.

The verb וַיְחַל *way^eḥal* [rendered above, 'besought'] is derived from the stem חָלָה *ḥālā*, the primary meaning of which is 'to be weak' (Jud. xvi 7 ff.), and in the *Pi^eēl* conjugation 'to make weak', 'to soften'. When connected with פָּנִים *pānīm* ['face'] as object, it signifies 'to endeavour to calm and soften the angry countenance.'

Moses does not attempt to justify the people. He realizes that they committed a great sin, and that strict justice requires them to be severely punished, but he appeals to the Divine attribute of mercy, and relies on the Lord's paternal love for his people. *And he said, O Lord, why does Thy wrath burn hot* (v. 10: 'that My wrath may burn hot') *against Thy people* — They are after all Thy people, whom Thou hast chosen and concerning whom Thou didst say to me, 'Israel is My son, My first-born' (iv 22) — the people *whom Thou Thyself hast brought forth out of the land of*

Egypt, for when I brought them out from there, I did so at Thy bidding and in fulfillment of Thy mission, and in the final analysis it was Thou who didst bring them forth *with great power and with a mighty hand,* for my humble powers were insufficient for so tremendous an undertaking. Let not Thy work, pray, which Thou hast wrought by Thy power and might be in vain!

After stating the first reason for his plea for mercy, namely, the Lord's love for His people, Moses supplements it with a second argument, to wit, that of the sanctification of the Divine Name, as though to say: Do it for Thine own sake if not for ours. It was Thy wish that the Egyptians should learn to acknowledge Thee (vii 5, *et passim*). *Why* then *should the Egyptians* have the
12 opportunity to *speak, saying, with evil did He bring them forth* (that is, *for evil,* see my commentary to x 10, and compare also Deut. ix 28), *to slay them in the mountains* — among the mountains of the Sinaitic desert — *and to consume them* (v. 10: 'and that I may consume them') *from the face of the earth?* Permit me to repeat Thy words and pray before Thee: *Turn from Thy fierce wrath* (v. 10: 'that My wrath may burn hot') *and repent* [וְהִנָּחֵם] *wᵉhinnāḥēm*] (it is true Thou didst say, הַנִּיחָה לִּי *hannīḥā lī* ['Let Me alone'], but I refuse to let Thee alone, and on the contrary, I beseech Thee, הִנָּחֵם *hinnāḥēm* ['repent'] — there is a word-play here: הַנִּיחָה־הִנָּחֵם *hannīḥā–hinnāḥēm*) *of this evil* (again the word, *evil*) *that Thou didst think to do against Thy people* — they are Thy people — so that the Egyptians shall not say that this evil was intended by Thee from the first.

He advances yet a third reason: the merit of the Patriarchs. Human beings are not isolated creatures; persons and generations are but links in a chain. When you judge this generation, this link in the chain of generations, pray remember the preceding links:
13 *Remember Abraham, Isaac, and Israel,* who were *Thy* faithful *servants, to whom Thou didst sware by Thine own self* — by Thy great name — *and didst say to them, I will multiply your offspring as the stars of heaven, and all this land that I have spoken of will I give to your offspring* — to all your descendants, and not merely to those of one man like myself (Moses does not wish to be built up at the cost of his people's destruction), *and* all your offspring *shall inherit* it *for ever.* Thy promise is everlasting.

Moses' entreaty to save his people from sentence of annihilation
14 was received with compassion and favour: *And the Lord repented of the evil* (the word *evil* occurs here for the third time) *which He*

said that He would do unto His people (compare the passages, Jer. xxvi 19 and Jonah iii 10, which are based on our verse). The decree of destruction contemplated by God initially was annulled. The text now speaks of *His people* — the Lord's people. This is the first stage in the process of forgiveness — the first mitigation of the sentence. Thereby the Torah comes to teach us that three things avert calamity: the Lord's love for His creatures; the glory of the Divine name; the merit of the Patriarchs.

However, to his plea that the Promised Land assured to the patriarchs should be given to the whole people Moses received no answer. He was given only a negative promise that the nation would not suffer annihilation, but his positive request was not yet acceded to in the first phase.

THIRD PARAGRAPH

MOSES' ACTION

(XXXII 15–29)

Now that Moses has been assured that the people will not be destroyed, he must take action as the national leader to bring them back to the path of rectitude. Forthwith he descends the mountain and devotes himself energetically to the accomplishment of this task.

15 *And Moses turned and went down* [וַיִּפֶן וַיֵּרֶד מֹשֶׁה *wayyiphen wayyēredh Mōše*] *from the mountain.* In Biblical diction the subject of two verbs sometimes comes after the second verb [here, in the Hebrew, 'Moses' follows the two verbs]. This obtains not only when both verbs denote a single action, as in this sentence, which means 'And he turned to go down', or as in the first verse of the Book of Leviticus: וַיִּקְרָא אֶל־מֹשֶׁה וַיְדַבֵּר ה' אֵלָיו *wayyiqrā' 'el Mōše wayᵉdhabbēr YHWH 'ēlāw* ['And the Lord called Moses, and spoke to him'; in the Hebrew 'the Lord' comes after the second verb 'spoke'], which can easily be explained, since 'calling' and 'speaking' are ultimately the same thing. But the usage is also found in cases where the two verbs signify two separate actions: see, for example, xxxiv 4. *And the two tables of the testimony in his hand* — the tables that had been given to him, as was stated in xxxi 18 — *tables that were written on both their sides; on the one side and on*

the other were they written. This detail is given here in order that the reader may visualize the approximate size of the tablets, which were neither large nor thick, but could be carried by Moses in his hand, and were easily broken (v. 19). They were not huge tables like the stone monuments set up for all to see — for example, the stele of Mesha, king of Moab — slabs that no human being could carry in his hand, but tablets like those on which were inscribed or engraved, in letters of moderate size, records and documents intended for preservation in archives or libraries. Since the text was divided into two, spread over both sides of the tables (according to the natural meaning of the words, half of the text was on one side and half on the other, as we often find in the Mesopotamian and Ugaritic tablets), there was no need for large-sized stones. We may assume that their length was approximately thirty centimetres, with corresponding width and thickness. On the way the tables were placed inside the ark, see above, my commentary to xxv 16.

16 Scripture adds further, in order to emphasize the sublime worth of the gift that Moses was bringing the children of Israel: *And the tables were the work of God* — a cautious expression like the one in xxxi 18 (see my note thereto), that is, generally speaking, a Divine creation. *And the writing was the writing of God* — here, too, the wording is circumspect, and connotes only Divine writing — *graven on the tables*, that is, incised on the stone with a sharp instrument.

17 *And Joshua*, who remained in the lower part of the mountain to await there the return of his master Moses (see my commentary on the end of chapter xxiv), *heard the noise of the people as they shouted* in orgiastic celebration in honour of the calf. The Masoretes retained the archaic spelling of the word בְּרֵעֹה *bᵉrēʿō* ['as they shouted'], with a *Hē'* at the end, thus making it identical with the consonants of the word בְּרָעָה *bᵉrāʿā* ['with evil'] in v. 12, in order to emphasize the word-play, which apparently was intended by the text. *And* Joshua *said to Moses*, when the latter reached him as he descended from the mountain: *There is a noise of war in the camp* — he was afraid that desert marauders might have

18 attacked the Israelite camp. *And* Moses *said* to Joshua: *It is not the sound of the answering* [עֲנוֹת *ʿănōth*] *of might* — it is not the sound of the shouting for victory — *neither is it the sound of the answering of weakness* — neither is it the sound of the cry of the defeated — *the sound of answering-in-song* [עֲנּוֹת *ʿannōth*] (a play on the twofold meaning of the stem עָנָה *ʿānā*) *do I hear*: what I hear is the sound

EXODUS XXXII 21

of singing and music (compare Isa. xxvii 2; Psa. lxxxviii 1).

19 *And it came to pass, as soon as* Moses, accompanied by Joshua, *came near the camp, and he saw the calf*, of which we were informed earlier and hence it occurs with the definite article, *and* the *dances* around it, then *Moses' anger burned hot.* Although he had asked at first (*v.* 11): 'O Lord, why does Thy wrath burn hot against Thy people?' now, when he sees with his own eyes what the Lord had observed from heaven, he, too, is wroth, *and he hurled the tables from his hands*, for, seeing that the people had broken the covenant, the testimony of the covenant had, perforce, to be annulled (compare Ibn Ezra *ad locum*), *and he shattered them at the foot of the mountain* — at the very place where the covenant had been made (xxiv 4: 'and built an altar at the foot of the mountain').

In accord with his strong character, he immediately took drastic action. The rioting people, on seeing Moses approaching with angry mien, instantly stopped their singing and dancing, and scattered in all directions. Moses now drew near to the calf to
20 destroy it completely: *And he took the calf which they had made*, as an idol (compare Hosea ii 8 [Hebrew, *v.* 10]: 'and who lavished upon her silver and gold which they used for Baal'), *and burnt* it *with fire*, for the greater part of the calf's body, beneath the gold plating, was made of wood, as we have noted, *and ground* the burnt wood *to powder*, thereby showing the people the impotence of the image that they had considered a god, *and strewed* the ash *upon the water* (Deut. ix 21: 'into the brook that descended out of the mountain'), *and made the children of Israel drink* that water, so as to test them like a wife suspected of unfaithfulness (Talmud and modern commentators). The reaction of the people who drank would indicate psychologically who were guilty and who were not.

This was the first step taken by Moses. Whilst his loyal followers were occupied, on his orders, with the destruction of the calf and the testing of the Israelites by making them drink of the water, he took the next step, and summoned Aaron to give him an account
21 of what had taken place. He asked him: *What did this people* (here it has a compassionate sense: this hapless people) *do to you that you have brought a great sin upon them?* The meaning is: Did this people, then, do you previously a great wrong, so that you did not refrain from acting towards them carelessly, and from doing a thing that was liable to lead them, and actually did lead them, to so great a sin? Compare with this question Genesis xx 9: 'What have you done to us? And how have I sinned against you,

that you have brought upon me and my kingdom (by your careless
22 words) a great sin?' *And Aaron said, Let not the anger of my lord burn hot*, etc. Moses is now enabled to perceive how the Lord's anger is to be understood; not only did he become wroth upon seeing what had happened, but he, too, is entreated that his anger should not burn hot, exactly as he had at first made supplication before the Lord. Aaron addresses his brother as 'my lord', since he is obliged to give him an account of his actions and to justify himself before him; he thus seeks to appease him. Similarly it is related of Jacob that he called his brother Esau 'my lord' (Gen. xxxii 5 ff.), when he endeavoured to mollify him in regard to the wrong he had done him.

In order to excuse himself, Aaron begins his statement with a preparatory observation: *you know the people that they are set on evil* [בְּרָע *bh^erā^ʻ*, literally, 'are in evil'] — you are acquainted with the nature of this people, that they are inclined to do evil; given the least opportunity, they immediately fall into great sin (the word בְּרָע *bh^erā^ʻ* contains a further allusion to the expression בְּרָעָה *b^erā^ʻā* ['with evil intent'] in *v.* 12 and to the verb בְּרֵעֹה *b^erē^ʻō* ['as
23 they shouted'] in *v.* 17). *For they said unto me, Make us gods, who shall go before us; for as for this Moses, the man who brought us up out of the land of Egypt, we do not know what has become of him.* They asked me to make for them an image to take your place — not, Heaven forfend!, the place of the Lord — and consequently I saw no necessity to refuse their request. At all events, my action was partly passive, and even in its active aspect lacked
24 any evil intent. *And I said to them, Let any who have gold*, hoping thereby to gain time, but they immediately *took it off and gave it to me, and I threw it into the fire, and there came out this calf*; in other words, I did not specifically intend to fashion this calf, but it emerged from my hands fortuitously, just as anything else might have resulted.

Moses understood the position, and realized Aaron's limited
25 responsibility and the greater culpability of the people. *And Moses saw that the people* (compare *v.* 9) *had broken loose* [פָּרֻעַ *phārūaʻ*] — were undisciplined, completely given over to their desire (compare Num. vi 5: 'he shall let the locks [פֶּרַע *peraʻ*] of hair of his head grow long', that is to say, the Nazirite shall allow the hair of his head to grow untended), *for Aaron had let them break loose* — he had not taken the helm in his hand and restrained the people — *for an object of derision among them that rose up against them* —

so that the Israelites became a proverb and byword among their enemies. In these poetic expressions there is possibly to be heard an echo of the ancient epic poem to which we have alluded earlier. Likewise the word-play, which may also have formed part of that poem, still continues. In order to focus attention on it, the Masoretes retained here, too, in the word פְרָעֹה *ph*ᵉ*rāʿō(h)* ['let break loose'], the archaic spelling with a *Hē*' at the end (v. 12, בְּרָעָה *b*ᵉ*rāʿā(h)* ['with evil']; ibid., הָרָעָה *hārāʿā(h)* ['the (rendered: 'this') evil']; v. 14, הָרָעָה *hārāʿā(h)* ['the evil']; v. 17, בְּרֵעֹה *b*ᵉ*rēʿō(h)* ['as they shouted']; v. 22, בְרָע *b*ᵉ*rāʿ* ['in evil']; v. 25, פָרֻעַ *phārūaʿ* ['broken loose']; ibid., פְרָעֹה *ph*ᵉ*rāʿō(h)* ['let break loose']; in all, seven words of similar sound).

Seeing that the people had broken loose, it was necessary to bring them under control and restore them to the right path. For this purpose, Moses adopted drastic measures, which constituted the third stage in his course of action. *Then Moses stood*, a dominant figure, *in the gate of the camp* — that is, in one of the gates of the camp (v. 27) — *and called*, in a loud voice, *and said, Who is for the Lord? To me. And all the sons of Levi gathered themselves together to him*; his fellow tribesmen are prepared to listen to his commands and execute them, come what may. The word *all* is employed, as usual, in a hyperbolical sense and connotes a large number (compare v. 27: 'every man his brother'). *And he said to them, Thus says the Lord God of Israel* (it was not previously stated that the Lord had said this to him, but Moses feels that such is God's will, and he speaks like a prophet, using prophetic phraseology): *Put every man his sword on his thigh, go back and forth* — come from all directions hither and thither, passing to and fro — *from gate to gate in the camp* — from one end of the camp to the other — *and slay every man his brother, and every man his companion, and every man his neighbour* — put to death all those who, you know of a certainty sinned, in connection with the calf, either because you were actually witnesses, or because they were found guilty by the ordeal of drinking; spare no one, even if he be your brother, or companion, or neighbour. It is better that a few Israelites lose their lives rather than that the entire people should perish.

28 *And the sons of Levi did according to the word of Moses.* It was a terrible thing, hence Scripture does not go into details, but is content to observe that the Levites did what Moses had told them, and to indicate the number that fell: *and there fell of the people that day about three thousand men* — a round figure based on the

²⁹ sexagesimal system, a half of 6,000. *And Moses said* to the Levites: *Your hand is filled* מִלְאוּ יֶדְכֶם *milᵉʾū yedhᵉkhem*, literally: 'They filled your hand'] *today to the Lord*, etc. The word *milᵉʾū* here is not the *Qal* imperative, as it is usually explained, for if it were the imperative its place would have been in the preceding verse; furthermore, the expression 'to fill the hands' (see xxviii 41) requires the *Piʿēl* conjugation. Hence this word is to be understood as the third person [plural] perfect of the *Piʿēl*, used in an indefinite or impersonal sense, to wit, 'they who filled filled', that is to say, your hand was filled — you have been inducted — to minister in the holy place, apparently instead of the first-born who were hitherto in charge of every sacred function, but were now deposed because they had sinned in connection with the golden calf. You have been appointed to minister in the holy place, *because* [כִּי *kī*] *every man was against his son and his brother* — precisely because you evinced, by your action, that your zeal for the Lord's honour superseded your natural human affection for your kith and kin. For the sense of the word כִּי *kī* ['because, precisely'] in this expression compare xviii 11: 'precisely in those things of which they boasted, He is (greater) than they.' Your installation serves to consecrate you for ministering *and to bestow upon you a blessing this day*. A poetic rhythm is noticeable in this verse, possibly an echo of the ancient epic poem that recounted the episode.

This completes Moses' action vis-à-vis the people; it brings forgiveness nearer, since suffering purges, and death even more so.

FOURTH PARAGRAPH

MOSES IS ASSURED THAT ISRAEL WILL POSSESS THE LAND

(XXXII 30–35)

But Moses was not content with severe punishment being meted out to the chief culprits; general responsibility rested on the people as whole, for even those who did not participate actively in the worship of the calf but did not oppose it or protest against it were not guiltless. Therefore Moses makes ready now to entreat again for mercy and pardon for the entire people. He is concerned about Israel's future, since he has not yet received a reply to his request regarding the possession of the Land.

EXODUS XXXII 33

30 *And it came to pass on the morrow, that Moses said to the people, You have* all — even you who were not the primary sinners and consequently were not put to death — *sinned a great sin, and now I will go up* again upon Mount Sinai *to the Lord* to intercede for
31 *you; perhaps I can make atonement for your sin. So Moses returned to the Lord*; he offered up his prayer in a clean place, not in the midst of the camp, which had been defiled by idolatrous worship. *And he said*, using the phraseology of confession, *Ah, now! this people have sinned a great sin* (this expression occurs here for the third time, after *v.* 21 and *v.* 30), *and have made for themselves gods of gold*, transgressing Thy commandments, which Thou didst enjoin on them through me (xx 23): 'You shall not make gods of silver to be with Me, nor shall you make for yourselves gods of gold.' After the confession, Moses entreats for forgiveness and identifies himself with his people's fate: *But now,* — in the present
32 situation — *if Thou wilt forgive their sin* — if Thou wilt be willing to pardon their sin, and not withhold from them the assurance that Thou didst give to their ancestors, well and good! The apodosis of the conditional sentence, *good*, is not expressly stated, because it is self-understood. (So, too, for example, we find in i Sam. xii 14–15: 'If you will fear the Lord and serve Him and hearken to His voice and not rebel against the commandment of the Lord, and if both you and the king who reigns over you will follow the Lord your God, [well and good!]; but if you will not hearken to the voice of the Lord, but rebel against the commandment of the Lord, then the hand of the Lord will be against you and your fathers'). *And if not,* — if Thou art unwilling to forgive the people for their general responsibility, punish me, too, with them: *Blot me, I pray Thee, out of Thy book which Thou hast written* — blot out, pray, my name from the book in which are inscribed by the Heavenly Court the names of Thy chosen ones (compare Isa. iv 3); I do not wish my fate to be better than that of the rest of my people. Some exegetes have regarded this request as a suggestion by Moses to receive the punishment instead of his people. Such a proposal would undoubtedly have been very noble on Moses' part, but this does not appear to be the actual meaning of the text.

Moses' prayer on behalf of his people was accepted, even though with certain reservations for the time being (see, further, the next paragraph). The Lord's reply begins with a prefatory observation:
33 *Whoever has sinned against Me, him will I blot out from My book*, that means to say, in regard to your last request, to blot out your

name from My book, I do not agree, for it is impossible to inflict punishment on one who has not sinned; of this there is no need
34 to speak at all. *But now* — in so far as your main plea for the entire people is concerned, I am inclined to accede to it. I have already granted your first petition, and have assured you that I shall not condemn your people to complete annihilation, and now I add, more positively, that I shall give the children of Israel all that I have promised their ancestors, and confirmed to you, in regard to the acquisition of the Land: *go, lead the people* (no longer is the term *your people* used, but neither is the expression *My people*) *to* the good land *of which I have spoken to you* (iii 8, etc.). *Behold My angel will go before you* as I promised you (xxiii 20), that is to say, I shall vouchsafe you My protection and help that your way may be prosperous and that you may conquer your country (see my comments on xxiii 20). The general punishment for their collective sin will be postponed to some future time, and will take whatever form it has to take: *nevertheless, in the day when I visit, I will visit their sin upon them* (compare xxxiv 7: 'but who will by no means clear the guilty', and my commentary thereon), but at all events I will not deprive them of their right to take possession of the Land.

35   The words of the last verse, *And the Lord smote the people*, etc., do not necessarily refer to that very day; the meaning is that the Lord smote the people with a plague, as a collective punishment, at some undefined time, visiting on the day that He visited. The Bible does not specify how and when the punishment was inflicted, but only alludes to the matter in order to conclude the subject of the preceding verse, and to inform us at this stage that as it had been announced previously, even so it came to pass. This chastisement was meted out to the people *for* the things *which they had done in connection with* [אֶת *'eth*] *the calf that Aaron had made*. After this verse, which speaks of the future and interrupts the narrative, the Torah reverts to its theme in the next paragraph. A similar procedure is adopted in Numbers xiv, where, immediately after the Divine rebuke on account of the episode of the spies (*vv.* 26–35), we are told (*vv.* 36–38) that the spies 'who brought up an evil report of the land died by plague before the Lord' (when this occurred is not stated), and only two of them, Joshua and Caleb, remained alive. Thereafter (*v.* 39), the Torah goes back and relates that Moses reported the Lord's reprimand to the people and they mourned greatly, just as it is stated here, next paragraph, *v.* 4.

EXODUS XXXIII 2

Thus the people attained the second stage of their forgiveness: all the promises given to the Patriarchs would receive fulfilment in them as a whole. But the pardon was not yet complete, for there still remained an element of reservation, which will be explained in the following verses.

FIFTH PARAGRAPH

THE DIRECTIVES FOR THE CONSTRUCTION OF THE TABERNACLE ARE ANNULLED

(XXXIII 1–4)

Chapter XXXIII
This paragraph parallels the one preceding, and deals with the same subject. For two consecutive passages to treat of the same theme, with a few variations, was a common feature of epic poetry. It will suffice, for instance, to point out that in the Ugaritic epic of Aqhat, Daniel's action in a year of dearth is recounted in two successive paragraphs, which are identical except for the change of a few synonyms, like the two words for 'ear of corn' (in one case *bṣql*, and in the other *šblt*); and similar examples. Here, in our section, the prose version of the story may have given us these two paragraphs in conformity with the two found in the ancient epic poem. Both were actually needed, because the narrative was interrupted in the foregoing paragraph by the reference to the plague in *v*. 35, and was not finished; thus the reservation that God made to Moses' appeal was omitted. In order to add this new point it was necessary to go over the ground again and to explain the position in greater detail.

1 *And the Lord spoke to Moses*, as was stated in the previous paragraph: *Depart, go up hence, you and the people whom you have brought up out of the land of Egypt.* You began this undertaking and you will complete it; you have already brought the people up, now go up once again — *to the land of which I swore to Abraham, Isaac and Jacob, saying, To your descendants I will give it*, and I shall fulfil this oath through the people as a whole, in accordance
2 with your request (xxxii 13). *And I will send an angel before you* (xxiii 20), *and I will drive out the Canaanites, the Amorites, the Hittites, the Perizzites, the Hivites, and the Jebusites* (xxiii, 23,

425

27-30). After *v.* 2, which forms, as it were, a parenthesis, *v.* 3 is again linked to the last clause of *v.* 1, in parallelism to it: Go up hence, you and the people, *to a land flowing with milk and honey* — to a land filled with all manner of good, as I promised you when you started out on your mission (iii 8, 17). But I wish to make this reservation: *but* (כִּי *kī* in the sense of אֶפֶס כִּי *'ephes kī* ['but', 'however'] as in Isa. xxviii 28; Psa. cxli 8) *I* — I Myself — *will not go up among you*. All that I have promised the Patriarchs I shall carry out, but on no account shall I cause My Presence to dwell in the midst of Israel's camp through the Tabernacle that they will build to My name, as I said I would, because the people are no longer worthy thereof. Although I gave you detailed directions with regard to the construction of the Tabernacle, and at the commencement of these instructions I said to you (xxv 8): 'And let them make Me a sanctuary that I may dwell in their midst', and at the end I said to you (xxix 46) that I brought the children of Israel forth out of the land of Egypt that 'I might dwell among them', yet now, seeing that they were unfaithful to Me, I do not permit them to build a Tabernacle for Me, and I shall not dwell in their midst. I shall give them My protection and help from afar, but they shall not be privileged to see the symbol of My presence in the midst of their camp.

In the light of our interpretation of this verse and of those passages that refer to the sending of the angel (xxiii 20 ff.; xxxiii 2, 12 ff.), all the problems that have exercised the exegetes fall away, and everything becomes clear. It also opens up for us the possibility of understanding the connection between the section dealing with the calf and that of the Tabernacle (see above, pp. 407 ff.), and also of comprehending the significance of the paragraph about the Tent of Meeting, which comprises *vv.* 7–11.

This reservation, to wit, that I shall not cause My Presence to dwell in your midst, is after all in your interest, *for you are a stiff-necked people* — you do not readily accept My new teachings but cling to the old idolatrous concepts, and consequently if you sin against Me again when My tabernacle is in your midst, as you have sinned now, and you defile the place sanctified to Me, there is the danger *that I may consume you* (אֲכֶלְךָ *'ăkhelᵉkhā*; cf. xxxii 10 וַאֲכַלֵּם *wa'ăkhallēm* ['and I may consume them']) *on the way*. It was My intention to honour you in My tabernacle, but every added honour imposes on the one honoured an added obligation and responsibility. If, now, I cause My Presence to dwell among you, your responsibility will be so much the greater and the punishment for your sins so much severer.

4 *And when the people heard* from Moses *these evil tidings, they mourned* like people under God's displeasure, *and no man put on his ornaments* as a sign of mourning. It is particularly this sign of grief, and not others, that is mentioned here, because it was precisely with their ornaments that they sinned, in as much as they gave their ear-rings for the making of the calf — measure for measure.

SIXTH PARAGRAPH

A PARALLEL PASSAGE TO THE PREVIOUS THEME

(XXXIII 5–6)

This paragraph parallels the second part of the preceding paragraph, which came to add a detail not included in the fourth paragraph. The repetition here of what has already been stated is to be explained, as we explained the last paragraph, in the light of the technique employed in epic poetry: it also helps to elucidate the subject further. Now the two paragraphs are necessary from the literary viewpoint, since each one uses one of the two expressions that are to serve as key-words in the continuation of the narrative: the term פָּנִים *pānīm* ['face', 'before'] in *v.* 2 ['before you'], and יָדַע *yādha'* ['know'] in *v.* 5 ['that I may know']. By understanding this paragraph as a parallel account to the preceding passage, we can explain a point that is otherwise extremely difficult to comprehend, namely, that the command, 'So now put off your ornaments from you' (*v.* 5), comes after it has already been related that the Israelites refrained from putting on ornaments (*v.* 4).

5 *And the Lord said to Moses: Say to the people of Israel*, in order to make it clear to them that what I tell you now is only for their good. It is a fact that *you are a stiff-necked people* and are inclined to sin, and there is the danger that *if for a single moment I should go up among you, I would consume you* (this is all in accord with the parallel verse, *v.* 3). *And now* — therefore — *put off your ornaments from you* — act unostentatiously, take off the finery from yourselves, for they do not befit those deserving of punishment for

the sin they have committed — *and I shall know what to do with you* — and I shall see in future, in accordance with your conduct, what treatment you merit (compare xxxii 34: 'nevertheless, in the day when I visit, I will visit their sin upon them'). *So the children of Israel stripped themselves of their ornaments from Mount Horeb* (paralleling *v.* 4: 'and no man put on his ornaments') — they took off the adornments with which they had decked themselves when they prepared for the Revelation at Mount Sinai, dressing themselves, for that occasion, in fine, washed garments (xix 10, 14). Although there is no reference to ornaments in the Biblical account of the Sinaitic Revelation, they constituted apparently one of the details featured in the ancient epic poem that the Torah passed over in silence, because they were irrelevant to its purpose; nevertheless, traces of them were preserved in Scripture and are still discernible. Possibly it was precisely the poetic phrase *their ornaments from Mount Horeb* that was taken verbatim from the epic poem. In the expression *stripped themselves* [וַיִּתְנַצְּלוּ *wayyithnaṣṣᵉlū*] there may be an allusion to the words, '*Thus they despoiled* [וַיְנַצְּלוּ *wayᵉnaṣṣᵉlū*] *the Egyptians*' (xii 36; compare iii 22). These adornments consisted, in part at least, of the jewellery of silver and of gold that the Israelites had received from the Egyptians; and since they had made improper use of some of the gold ornaments in donating them for the making of the calf, it was only right that they should themselves be deprived of what still remained in their possession of the spoil they had taken from others. Conceivably there is another significance to be discerned in the matter of the jewellery: these ornaments [עֲדָיִים *ʿădhāyīm*], with which the Israelites adorned themselves when they stood before Mount Sinai, may have appeared to them as witnesses [עֵדִים *ʿēdhīm*] — note the word-play — a testimony and memorial, as it were, to that sublime event and to the establishment of the covenant between them and the Lord. But now that they had broken the covenant, they were no longer worthy of wearing the symbol of the voided compact. The removal of the ornaments corresponds to the breaking of the tablets by Moses.

SEVENTH PARAGRAPH
THE TENT OF MEETING
(XXXIII 7–11)

This paragraph differs from its surrounding context in respect of its verb forms. They occur here in the 'imperfect' or in the 'perfect converted to the imperfect', instead of the forms customarily found in Biblical narrative style, namely, those of 'imperfect converted to perfect' or the simple 'perfect'. For this reason, and because of the disparity between the Tent of Meeting mentioned here and the Tabernacle or Tent of Meeting described in the preceding, and also in the following section, many have thought that we have here a difference of sources: the sections speaking of the Tabernacle (it is supposed) belong to source P, whereas our passage is an excerpt from another document that refers to a Sacred Tent of the wilderness period, which is to be distinguished from the Tabernacle (a fiction, according to this view) of source P, and the form of the verbs [to be construed as frequentative] denotes acts that used to be repeated from time to time, at every encampment of the Israelites in the desert.

However, those who take this view have failed to understand the text properly. Let us endeavour to find the correct interpretation. Since Moses saw that for the present the Lord would not permit the building of the Tabernacle in accordance with His original plan, because of the unworthiness of the children of Israel, he thought of the idea of establishing a temporary surrogate for the Tabernacle, 'until the wrath be past.' It was not possible for him to commune with the Divine Presence in the midst of Israel's camp, because it had become defiled by the iniquity of idolatry, and the Lord did not wish to let His Presence dwell there; hence Moses took his tent and pitched it without the camp so that it might serve as a place of meeting between himself and the Lord. This is the substance of the paragraph. As for the verbs and their form, it is impossible for all of them to signify action that is repeated at each place of encampment. At the beginning of *v.* 7 reference is made to the *taking* of the tent, to its erection outside the camp — that is to say to its removal from the camp where it had been hitherto — and to its naming. Without doubt, these acts were performed only once (even from the passage in Num. xi

24–30 it is not to be deduced that the Tent of Meeting was at that time outside the camp; it simply implies a distinction between the Israelite zone and that of the Divine Presence within it). The verbs that occur in the continuation of the paragraph — that is, after the first verbs — undoubtedly denote acts that continued till the establishment of the Tabernacle; but the first verbs — יִקַּח *yiqqaḥ* ['took'; imperfect], וְנָטָה *wᵉnāṭā* ['and pitched'; perfect with *Wāw* consecutive], וְקָרָא *wᵉqārā'* ['and called'; perfect with *Wāw* consecutive] — are only additional examples of the use of verbal forms in accordance with poetic diction, like the form of the verb תִּשָּׁחֵת *tiššāḥēth* ['was ruined'; imperfect], which we have already discussed in viii 20. The entire paragraph is written in poetic style and has a poetic rhythm, and traces of the ancient epic poem are discernible in it. The aforementioned verbs of *v.* 7 were left apparently, in the form they had in the poem for the very reason that in the rest of the passage there are so many similar forms that are permissible also in prose, since they signify frequentative actions.

7   The subject *Moses* precedes the verb יִקַּח *yiqqaḥ* ['took'] in accordance with the rule, explained earlier (see above, on ix 20–21), that when the subject is placed before the predicate it expresses antithesis or marks a parallelism with the action of another subject. In the preceding verse we were told what the people did on hearing the Lord's decree not to permit His Divine Presence to dwell in their midst, and now we are informed what Moses did on his part. The people did one thing, and Moses did another. He took his *tent* (compare xviii, 7) *and pitched* this tent *for himself outside the camp*, which was not yet worthy of God's manifestation; not just outside the camp, but even *far off from the camp* (this removal to a distance must be understood as due to the excommunication of the camp, which had been rendered unclean by the iniquity of the calf), *and he called it the Tent of Meeting*, He gave it this name because the real Tent of Meeting, to wit, the Tabernacle, which had already been called by this designation several times previously, was not yet in existence, and, for the time being, could not be constructed. Thus, it is customary for people to call a substitute by the name of the thing whose place it takes. Moses was hoping that the Lord would be willing to meet with him in this Tent of Meeting and his hope was not disappointed. It was right that all this should be recorded here, for otherwise we should not be able to understand where the words of the Lord reported in *vv.* 12 ff. were communicated to Moses, since it is not stated there that Moses had

gone up to Mount Sinai, nor are we given any indication that he had retired in solitude to hear the Lord's communication.

After informing us that Moses called his tent the Tent of Meeting, the text continues: *And it came to pass,* from that day onward until the Tabernacle was erected, *that every* one of the children of Israel who went *to seek the Lord* — that means to say, who wished to hear instruction from Moses in the Lord's name — *would go out to the tent of meeting* — would go out from the camp and make his way to that tent — *which was outside the camp* — repeated for emphasis, in order to stress still further the fact that the camp was unfit for this purpose. This applied, needless to say, even more so to Moses, who, whenever he sought the Lord, would go out there.

In vv. 8–10, we have a description of the behaviour of the Israelites, who treated Moses with great deference, and conducted themselves with reverence and humility towards God's manifestation — an indication of the spirit of repentance and of perfect faith in the Lord their God and in Moses His servant that inspired them then. This portrayal is rightly introduced at this stage, because it enables us to understand that on account of this penitent mood of theirs the children of Israel won complete forgiveness, as will be related subsequently.

8 *And it came to pass, whenever Moses went out to the tent* (a parallel to the preceding verse: 'And it came to pass... would go out to the tent of meeting') — every time Moses left the camp to go to the Tent of Meeting, as soon as he went forth — *all the people rose up and stood* — they remained standing — *every man at his tent door, and looked after Moses,* with respect and affection, *until*
9 *he had gone into the tent. And it came to pass* [וְהָיָה‎ w*e*hāyā] (the third occurrence of this expression at the beginning of a sentence serves to introduce a third description) *when Moses entered the tent, the pillar of cloud would descend and stand at the door of the tent and He would speak with Moses.* The subject of the verb דִּבֶּר‎ *dibber* ['would speak'] is the Lord; this is easily understood even
10 though not expressly stated. *And all the people saw* — that is: And when all the people would see — *the pillar of cloud standing at the door of the tent,* and understood by this sign that the Divine Glory had come to speak with Moses, then *all the people,* who had sat down again after Moses had entered the Tent, *would rise up and do obeisance* (this time they not only stood but also prostrated themselves) *every man at his tent door.* The phrase *the door of his tent* or *the door of the tent* also occurs three times in succession,

and, without doubt, this is not fortuitous but is intended for rhetorical emphasis, just as a rhetorical purpose is to be discerned in the word-play עַמּוּד *'ammūdh* ['pillar'], עָמַד *'āmadh* ['would stand'], עֹמֵד *'ōmēdh* ['standing'] in vv. 9–10.

After the digression in *v.* 10, the text reverts to the end of *v.* 9: 11 *And the Lord used to speak to Moses face to face, as a man speaks to his friend.* Moses was not like one who sees visions, or falls into a trance; he was in possession of his senses and heard the sound of words. When the Lord finished speaking to him, Moses *would return to the camp.* He did not dwell constantly in the Tent of Meeting, since he had public matters to attend to, but the Tent was never left without a guard of honour: *but* Moses' *attendant, Joshua the son of Nun,* was *a youth* — that is, a minister in the sanctuary — and *he did not depart from the tent.* There is a parallelism here with xiii 22: 'The pillar of cloud by day and the pillar of fire by night did not depart from before the people.' Just as the Lord watches over His people, even so His people watches over the shrine dedicated to Him — perpetually.

EIGHTH PARAGRAPH

A DIALOGUE BETWEEN MOSES AND THE LORD

(XXXIII 12–23)

In the Tent, which was outside the camp, Moses prayed to the Lord that he should forgive his people completely, and waive the last reservation that He had made, when He said (xxxiii 3), 'I will not go up among you', and permit the Tabernacle to be built and His Presence to dwell in Israel's camp. The people had already shown signs of penitence (see the preceding paragraph); hence the moment was opportune for this prayer.

In order to comprehend the dialogue in this paragraph properly, heed must be paid to the fact that this conversation is not conducted in accord with Greek or modern processes of logical thinking, but follows the pattern of eastern dialogues, which convey the intention of the speakers more by way of allusion than through explicit statements.

Moses begins his speech as would a man addressing his friend 12 (*v.* 11), and says: *See* — consider, I pray Thee, the situation. He

EXODUS XXXIII 13

draws attention particularly to three things, in three clauses commencing with *Thou* or *and Thou*: (1) On the one hand, *Thou sayest to Me* (xxxii 34; xxxiii 1), *Bring up this people*; (2) and on the other, Thou dost abide by Thy decision not to go up with us Thyself, but only to send an angel before us, that means to say, to help us from afar; but how this help is to be rendered Thou hast not told me: *but Thou hast not let me know whom Thou wilt send with me* — what or whom Thou wilt send to our aid — and this promise of general, indirect assistance gives no satisfaction to my spirit, which yearns for Thee to be near to us and for Thy Presence to dwell in our midst; (3) and I now make bold to entreat Thee once again to fulfil this my desire, since *Thou hast said*, in Thy grace, *I know you by name* — that is, I have chosen you specifically (compare Jer. i 5; Amos iii 2) — *and you have also found favour in My sight*. In the Book of Exodus we do not find that these words were said to Moses; but apparently this Divine communication was expressly recounted in one of the passages of the epic poem current among the people. Although the Torah did not cite the exact statement before, it did not refrain from alluding to it in this verse, since the matter was known to the people from another source, and, at all events, agreed in substance with what Scripture itself had recorded and, as it were, included between the lines in its account of the theophany at the thorn-bush.

13 After these three introductory sentences Moses states the conclusion, which begins as usual with the word וְעַתָּה *we'attā* ['Now therefore'], and continues with the customary deferential expression, *if, I pray Thee, I have found favour in Thy sight*, whose meaning is similar to that of the phrase in use in post-Biblical Hebrew, בְּבַקָּשָׁה מִמְּךָ *bebhaqqăšā mimmekhā* ['pray, please'] (the word *if* in phrases of this kind does not express doubt but has the significance of 'since', or some similar word). What Moses asks for first and foremost is: *pray, let me know Thy ways* (דְּרָכֶךָ *derākhekhā*: the word is spelt without a *Yōdh*, but is vocalized like the plural, דְּרָכֶיךָ *derākhe(y)khā*), that is to say, pray, let me know the principles by which Thy Court of Justice is guided, what criteria Thou dost employ in the bestowal of reward and punishment to people, and in what way man can obtain forgiveness from Thee for his sins, that I may be privileged *to know Thee*; and when I know Thy ways I shall know how to act and on what basis I may prevail on Thee to forgive my people and allow Thy Presence to dwell in their midst, *to the end that I may find* real *favour in Thy sight*, and behold practical benefit, in

this grace that I find, for the good of my people. At the end of his plea Moses reverts to his opening expression, *and see* — consider, pray, the fact — *that this nation*, for whom I entreat Thee, *is Thy people*. Forget not that Thou hast already chosen them and drawn them near unto Thee and called them 'My son, My first-born'; therefore, I pray Thee, continue to treat them as *Thy people*.

Moses phrases his prayer with finesse, employing, as we have stated, allusions, but his intent is clear to the Lord, who looks on
14 the heart, and He answers him accordingly: *My presence* [literally, 'My face'] *will go*, that means, I Myself (compare ii Sam. xvii 11: 'and that you go to battle in person' [literally, 'and that thy face go in battle']) shall go with the children of Israel, and I shall cause My Presence to dwell in their midst in all their wanderings, *and I will give you rest* — I shall give peace to your spirit and let your mind be at ease. To Moses' first request, 'pray, let me know Thy ways', no specific answer is given here; he is assured that he will achieve his goal, and there is no need for him to know the means by which it will be attained.

The merit of Moses' prayer and the Lord's compassion had already changed the outlook. At first God had said to Moses, *Let Me alone* [הַנִּיחָה לִי *hannīḥā lī*] (xxxii 10), whereas now He said to him, *and I will give you rest* [וַהֲנִחֹתִי לָךְ *wahănīḥōthī lākh*]. The parallelism underlines the radical change in the situation.

Thus the third stage of the Divine Forgiveness is concluded. The pardon is now complete: The Lord will cause His Presence to dwell in the midst of Israel's camp, and to this end He will permit the Tabernacle to be built.

Nevertheless, Moses remains dissatisfied, for he yearns to know the ways of the Lord. At this point the educational aim of the Torah becomes clear. It seeks to teach its readers the Lord's ways in conducting the affairs of the world, and in the bestowal of reward and punishment, as well as the means for winning forgiveness. Hence the dialogue continues.

15 *And* Moses *said to Him: If Thy presence will not go* [with us], *do not carry us up from here*, that is to say (here, too, we must understand the speaker's underlying intent rather than the superficial meaning of his words): This is actually what I wished to achieve, otherwise the survival of the people of Israel would be valueless; unless Thou didst consent to go with us Thyself, it were better for us not to leave this desert. And he proceeds to give
16 his reason: *For how shall it be known that I have found favour in*

Thy sight, I and Thy people? Is it not in Thy going with us? It were better for us not to go forth from here, for it is only by Thy going with us that the world will know that we have found grace in Thine eyes and that Thou hast chosen us, *so that we are distinct —* separated thereby to our advantage—*I and Thy people, from all the people that are upon the face of the earth*. The distinction that Thou hast already made between Israel and the Egyptians (viii 22 [Heb. v. 18]; ix 4; xi 7) will have no real value unless it persists also in the future. For the third time Moses emphasizes here the expression *Thy people*, and again he associates himself with his people.

In regard to the question of making a distinction, the Divine answer is also affirmative: *I will also do this thing that you have asked* (namely, 'so that we are distinct, I and Thy people'), *for you have found favour in My sight, and I know you by name* (compare v. 12). Here Scripture seeks to teach us how meritorious is the one who pleads for the good of others.

But Moses had not yet attained all that he wished; hence he reverts, in slightly different words, to his initial request when he had said: 'pray, let me know Thy ways.' He now formulates his request thus: *I pray Thee, let me behold Thy glory*, that means: grant me, pray, the privilege of Thy manifesting Thyself to me. The signification of the word *glory* in this verse, as above (xvi 7, 10; xxiv 16, and in several other pentateuchal passages), is 'theophany'.

From this point till the end of the paragraph it is clear from the wording that a number of things are expressed metaphorically. This is to be observed immediately in the answer given to Moses' last request. Although the reply is positive, yet it contains a certain reservation: as far as a human being can understand. It is possible for you to hear the voice of the Lord speaking to you as one hears that of his friend (v. 11), but as far as seeing is concerned, that is to say, in regard to the comprehension of the Divine attributes, there is a boundary that man cannot cross. It is impossible for you to contemplate My attributes as one contemplates the face of his fellow who stands before him. You will be able to achieve no more than this: *I will make all My goodness* — all My virtues (it is already implied here that fundamentally the Divine qualities are compassionate) — *pass before you*, that is, I shall not cause them to stand before you, so that you may contemplate them, but I shall make them pass before you in a momentary flash, whilst you stand at the side (regarding the expression *before you*, compare

Gen. xxxii 21 [Heb. *v.* 22]: 'So the present passed on before him'; and concerning the passing of God, note the story of Elijah, in i Kings xix 11: 'And behold, the Lord passed by'). *And I will proclaim the name of the Lord before you*: the proclamation will not be just generally speaking before you but literally so; it will announce the name of the Lord [*YHWH*] and the significance implicit therein, to wit, the attributes to which it alludes. *And I will be gracious to whom I will be gracious, and show compassion to whom I will show compassion*, the meaning being: but the exercise of these qualities depends entirely on My will; you may know that I am compassionate and gracious, and that I love to go beyond the strict letter of the law, but the decision to act according to these virtues is at all times in My discretion, and it is impossible for you to know when, or if, I shall act thus. If I were constantly to let the quality of mercy prevail over that of justice, and were to forgive every sinner, I should not be a righteous judge, and every man would permit himself all kinds of wickedness in the assurance that he would be forgiven. I shall be gracious and compassionate if it pleases Me, when it pleases Me, and for the reasons that please Me.

20 Verse 20, in accordance with the rule that we established in respect of the repetition of the words *And He said — And He said* (see above, at the end of my annotation to iii 14), does not introduce a new communication from the Lord, but elucidates the purport of the previous communication. The conclusion of *v.* 19, 'and I will be gracious to whom I will be gracious, and show compassion to whom I will show compassion', means, *you cannot see My face* as you see that of your fellow man, nor know the workings of My attributes in the same way as you are able to know the reactions of human qualities of character, *for man shall not see Me and live*, because to perceive the face of My glory is beyond the power of man's comprehension throughout the days of his life upon earth. The commentators who see in these words a reference to the belief that whoever sees God dies, or to the doctrine that after his death a man can see God, are merely reading into the Biblical text concepts that are not there.

21 Verse 21, which does not commence, like *v.* 20, just with the words *And He said*, but with the full sentence, *And the Lord said*, marks a new Divine communication, or the continuation of the utterance cited in *v.* 19, after the interruption by the explanatory verse [*v.* 20]. *Behold, there is a place by Me* — one known to Me

436

where it is suitable for you to hide, when *My glory passes by you* — *and you shall station yourself* at that place *on the rock*. When the time comes, Moses will be given fuller instructions (xxxiv 2): 'and you shall station yourself for Me there on the top of the mountain.' *And it shall come to pass, while My glory passes by before you, that I will put you in a cleft of the rock*, that is, in one of the caves there (compare the mention of the cave in the account of the Lord's manifestation to Elijah, i Kings xix, 9, 13), *and I will cover* [וְשַׂכֹּתִי *w^eśakkōthī*] *you with My hand* — I shall cover the entrance of the cave with My hand in order to shield you, so that you do not see what a human being may not see — *until I pass by* — until I shall have passed by before you (the verbs שָׂכַךְ *śākhakh* and סָכַךְ *sākhakh* are similar in form and identical in meaning ['cover'], like the verb חָשַׂף *ḥāśaph* ['draw (water)'] in Hebrew and the verb *ḥsp* in Ugaritic; for the construction of the sentence, compare xl 3: 'and you shall screen [וְסַכֹּתָ *w^esakkōthā*] the ark with the veil'). *After I have passed by, then I will take away My hand, and you shall see My back; but My face shall not be seen*. Here it is obvious that figurative expressions are being used: you will be able to perceive only My works and to discern from them some of My attributes, but you will be unable to comprehend My essential nature.

NINTH PARAGRAPH

PREPARATIONS FOR THE RENEWAL OF THE COVENANT AND THE REVELATION OF THE LORD TO MOSES

(XXXIV 1–10)

Chapter XXXIV

Since complete forgiveness had been attained, it is now possible to renew the Covenant that had been broken by the people's guilt; and together with the renewal of the Covenant there would take place the Revelation promised to Moses — the revelation of God's attributes in so far as a human being could comprehend them.

The tangible token of the renewal is the handing over of two tables of the testimony like the first, which had been shattered at the time when the original covenant had been annulled. The ceremony was to be similar to the first one, but not so festive, just as the second wedding of one who remarries his divorced wife is not quite the same as the first. The breach has been healed, but it is not possible to undo the fact that at some time the breach had existed.

1 *And the Lord said to Moses* — possibly not on the same day, but on the morrow or some time later: *Carve for yourself*, in order to bring them with you when you ascend to Me, *two tables of stone like the first*. As far as possible endeavour to make them similar to the first, but they will not be identical; of the first it was stated that they were 'the work of God' (xxxii 16), whereas the second tablets would be the work of Moses' hands. *And I will write upon the tables the words that were on the first tables, which you broke*. The first tablets were broken because they testified to the first covenant that had been annulled; the second writing would be a witness to the covenant that was to be renewed. *And be ready*
2 *by the morning* (this recalls the injunctions given in connection with the first ceremony (xix 11): 'And let them be ready for the third day', and thereafter (*ibid.*, v. 15): 'Be ready for the third day'). *And come up in the morning to Mount Sinai*, as you went up on the first occasion, *and station yourself for Me there on the top of the mountain*
3 (compare xxxiii 21). *And no one shall come up with you* — not even Aaron, who at the first ceremony ascended up to a certain point (xix 24); to the second 'wedding', after a divorce, a large assembly is not invited. *Neither let any one be seen anywhere on the mountain; neither let the flocks and the herds graze in front of that mountain* (compare xix 12–13).

Moses did as he was bidden, and the account of his acts is formulated, as usual, in language paralleling the instruction he
4 received. *And he carved two tables of stone like the first; and Moses rose early* [וַיַּשְׁכֵּם מֹשֶׁה *wayyaškēm Mōše*] (on the position, in the Hebrew, of the subject after the second verb, see above, xxxii 15), *and went up on Mount Sinai, as the Lord had commanded him*. Furthermore: *and he took in his hand two tables of stone*. He was not expressly told to do this, but it was self-understood. The reading in our verse is *two tables of stone* without the definite article, although the tablets had already been mentioned at the beginning of the verse. The reason, apparently, is the desire that the expression *two tables of stone*, which occurs three times, should be identical in each instance; this uniformity gives the phrase a specific connotation, as though the definite article were expressly written.

EXODUS XXXIV 6

5 *And the Lord descended in the cloud* from heaven on to Mount Sinai as at the first Revelation described in chapter xix. (There it is stated in *v.* 20: 'And the Lord came down upon Mount Sinai', and the cloud is mentioned earlier in the chapter, in *v.* 16). *And He took His stand with him* — with Moses — *there.* With regard to Moses it is said, וְנִצַּבְתָּ *w^eniṣṣabhtā* ['and you shall station yourself'] (xxxiii 21), or וְנִצַּבְתָּ לִי *w^eniṣṣabhtā lī* ['and station yourself for Me'] (xxxiv 2), whereas relative to the Lord the verb is used in the *Hithpāʿēl* conjugation, out of reverence, in the same way as the *Hithpāʿēl* of the verb דָּבַר *dābhar* ['speak'], which occurs according to the masoretic vocalization in Num. vii 89; Ezek. ii 2; xliii 6. *And called upon the name of the Lord* — proclaimed His name and His attributes, that is, the connotation of His name. How He did this is recorded in *v.* 6, in accordance with the literary method of first making a general statement and subsequently giving the

6 details. *And the Lord passed before him* — before Moses, as he was told previously (xxxiii 19 ff.) — *and proclaimed*: *The Lord, the Lord*, etc. Great importance is attached to this declaration of the Thirteen Attributes in Jewish tradition, and even according to the simple interpretation of the text it is imbued with great significance as one of the fundamental teachings inculcated by this section. The meaning of the two Names that occur at the beginning, *The Lord, the Lord*, is apparently: 'The Lord, He is the Lord', and it is impossible to define His nature in any other words (compare iii 14: 'I am who I am'). In the continuation of the Divine communication are mentioned the attributes that describe God's deeds, His 'back', but His 'face' it is not possible to portray: The Lord, He is the Lord — that must suffice. The proclamation of the attributes comes, as it were, to sum up in synthetic form what is to be deduced from the preceding narrative:

1) First and foremost *a God compassionate and gracious* — the moral qualities of grace and compassion, which had already conceded Moses' requests on behalf of the people (compare also xxxiii 19: 'And I will be gracious to whom I will be gracious, and show compassion to whom I will show compassion').

2) *Slow to* [literally, 'long of'] *anger*, that is, His anger prolongs itself and is not quick to inflict punishment on the sinner, in order that he may repent, as happened on this occasion.

3) *Abounding in lovingkindness and truth*: this is a single attribute, since lovingkindness and truth are dual elements of a unitary quality — lovingkindness of truth, true and faithful lovingkindness.

He keeps, with complete faithfulness, His promises to shew lovingkindness and bestow good, and so, in fact, he is fulfilling them in this instance.

7 4) *Keeping lovingkindness for the thousands*: He continues to shew His lovingkindness even for thousands of generations, to the distant descendants of those to whom the promises were made, and thus He will do on this occasion to the people of Israel.

5) *Forgiving iniquity, and transgression and sin*, even as God had answered Moses' entreaty when he prayed to Him to forgive Israel's sin (xxxii 32). It is actually difficult to determine the distinction between the three synonyms *iniquity* (עָוֹן ʿāwōn from the root עָוָה ʿāwā, which signifies to turn actions aside from the straight course), *transgression* (פֶּשַׁע pešaʿ: essentially an expression of 'rebellion'), and *sin* (חַטָּאָה ḥaṭṭāʾā: etymologically an act that misses the desired mark). Possibly, however, it was not intended here to differentiate between three varieties of sin, but to mention various synonyms in order to cover the entire range of wrongdoing (the same applies to the two synonyms *our iniquity and our sin* in v. 9).

6) *But who will by no means clear the guilty*, that is to say, that the first-named attributes of the Lord, the qualities of compassion and grace, are not signs of weakness and do not imply perversion of justice. Sin is not completely expunged by mercy; the punishment is suspended, and if a man sins again, the Lord exacts retribution from him for both the present and the former sin (compare above, xxxii 34: *nevertheless, in the day when I visit*, etc.).

7) *Visiting the iniquity of the fathers upon the children and the children's children*: even if it entails waiting several generations, and the children or children's children sin, God will visit upon them the iniquity of their fathers. Nevertheless, the influence of evil is limited, and affects only a few generations — *to the third and fourth generation* — whereas the influence of good extends to thousands of generations, as it is stated earlier: 'keeping lovingkindness for thousands' (on all this see above, my commentary on xx 5).

8 *And Moses made haste*, when he began to hear the words of the Lord, *and bowed his head toward the earth and prostrated himself.*

9 *And he said*, when the Lord's communication ended, *If, pray, I have found favour in Thy sight* — that is, I pray Thee (see above, on xxxiii 13) — *O Lord* (אֲדֹנָי ʾĂdhōnāy; this is the customary expression in addressing God), *let the Lord, I pray Thee, go* (a formula of reverence, in the third person) *in the midst of us* constantly — not only at present, as Thou hast already assured us, but also in

the future, irrespective of the people's conduct, *for* although *it is a stiff-necked people* and liable to sin also in the future, I nevertheless hope, and I make it the subject of my prayer to Thee, that Thy merciful qualities, which Thou hast made known to me, may prevail over the attribute of justice, *and that Thou wilt pardon our iniquity and our sin* — two synonyms to include all forms of transgression. The pronominal suffix is in the first person plural because Moses, out of love for his people, associates himself with the collective deeds of the children of Israel, and includes himself among the transgressors. *And take us for Thine inheritance* — and accept us, all of us, as the people of Thine inheritance.

The answer to this petition is given in *v.* 10 (it is not missing as many scholars have supposed); God not only agrees to the request 10 but even augments it. Firstly it is stated: *Behold, I make a covenant* — I am now about to establish for the second time My covenant with the children of Israel as the people of Mine inheritance, and, that apart, I assure you that *before all your people I will do marvels* (here it is clear from the context that the expression *your people* is not intended to deprive Israel of the designation of honour, *My people*, but serves to emphasize that they are Moses' people, the people that were privileged to have a leader and pleader like Moses). Before all of them, and not before Moses only (xxxii 10), will the Lord do marvels (נִפְלָאוֹת *niphlā'ōth*: the stem פלא *pl'* and the stem פלה *pl(h)*, which occurs in Moses' supplication, xxxiii 16, are related to each other, and the Hebrew-speaking ancients did not refrain from using them for word-plays and reciprocal allusions), namely, wonderful deeds in protecting them against the dangers of the journey, in providing water and food in the wilderness, in enabling them to vanquish their foes, and in the conquest of the land on both sides of the Jordan, which is more than was promised to the Patriarchs, who were given an assurance only with respect to the western side. All these will be marvellous and amazing acts, *such as have not been wrought* [literally, 'created'] hitherto, being, as it were, a new creation the like of which has not existed *in all the earth or in any nation* (in Moses' plea, xxxiii 16: 'from all the people that are upon the face of the earth'). *And all the people* (again the totality of the people is emphasized) *among whom you are* (once more Moses' personality is stressed) *shall see the work of the Lord* — the aforementioned marvels — *that it* — this work — *is an awesome thing that I* Myself, in going with you, *will do with you.* The threefold occurrence of the stem עָשָׂה *'āśā* ['do'] is for emphasis. For the syntactical construction וְרָאָה... כִּי נוֹרָא הוּא *wᵉrā'ā... kī nōrā' hū'* ['shall see... that it is an awesome thing'] comparison may be made with verses like וַתֵּרֶא אֹתוֹ כִּי טוֹב הוּא *wattēre' 'ōthō kī ṭōbh hū'* ['and when she saw that he was a goodly child'] (ii 2).

TENTH PARAGRAPH

INSTRUCTIONS FOR THE OBSERVANCE OF THE COVENANT

(XXXIV 11–26)

In the same way as when the first covenant was made detailed directions were given with a view to preventing the children of Israel from falling into idolatry (ch. xxiii), so also now, when the second covenant is established, detailed instructions are issued for the identical purpose. But they are sterner than the first, since the people had already committed a sin of this nature.

Hence it is not surprising that this paragraph forms a parallel, with some variations in the phrasing and in the sequence of the words and verses, to what has already been stated earlier in ch. xxiii. Such repetitions are customary in the literatures of the ancient East, and there is no room for all the complicated theories that have been advanced, to the effect that there were various redactions of these parallel paragraphs in different stages, times and circles. The renewal of the covenant requires here, according to the principles of literary composition obtaining in the ancient East, a restatement of the covenant's terms. If we dissect the Book limb by limb, and regard each paragraph as a separate and isolated entity, we are conscious of a difficulty in the existence of two similar passages; but if we treat the Book as a unitary literary work, although composed of different ancient elements, we encounter no problem in this regard.

Concerning the theory that we have here, in *vv.* 14–26, an early form of the Decalogue, see above, pp. 237 ff.

Since we have already annotated ch. xxiii, it will be unnecessary to comment on this paragraph in detail. We shall therefore explain only the new points and the variants; with regard to the verses that are identical, or nearly so, with the text in chapter xxiii, we

EXODUS XXXIV 14

shall content ourselves with giving the reference to the corresponding passage. From my observations on the earlier chapter it will be seen that the primary purpose of the two parallel paragraphs is to keep the children of Israel away from the influence of the Canaanite religion.

11 Just as in chapter xxiii the stem שָׁמַר *šāmar* ['keep', 'observe'] occurs several times in the *Qal* or *Niphʿal*, so our paragraph opens with this verb. *Observe well* [literally, 'to yourself'], Moses, *what I command you this day, so that you may teach the Israelites. Behold*
12 *I am about to drive out before you*, etc.: see xxiii 23, 28. *Take heed to yourself*, etc.: see xxiii 32. It is with Me that you are making a covenant; therefore, take heed to yourself *lest you make a covenant with the inhabitants of the land whither you go* — to conquer it and be masters of it; *lest* the inhabitants of the land become *a snare to you*, if they remain *in the midst of you* and are able to seduce you from Me and induce you to serve their gods. (See xxiii 32–33, and, *inter alia*, note my observations on the difference between making a covenant *with* [אֶת *'eth*] and *to* [לְ *le-*] someone).
13 *But, on the contrary, you shall tear down their altars, and break their pillars* (see xxiii 24), *and cut down their Asherim*. The Asherim were cultic objects made of wood, which were apparently named after the Canaanite goddess *Asherah*, and represented and symbolized her or her fertility. It is not possible to determine their form; by most scholars they are considered to have been tree stems or wooden posts that were set up next to the altars (compare Deut. xvi 21: 'You shall not plant [i.e. erect] any tree [or, wooden pole] as an Asherah beside the altar of the Lord your God which you shall make'). Appropriate to this interpretation is the use of the verb כָּרַת *kārath* ['cut', 'cut down'], found here, and also of the synonymous verbs גָּדַע *gādhaʿ* ['hew down', 'hew off'] and נָתַשׁ *nāthaš* ['pluck up'], which occur elsewhere. In view of this, and seeing that the entire passage here speaks in general terms and not with reference to the worship of specific deities, it appears that the word *Asherim* in this verse does not denote images of the goddess Asherah, as several exegetes have supposed.
14 The word כִּי *kī* ['for'] at the beginning of *v.* 14 gives the reason for the injunctions in *v.* 13: 'Tear down the altars' etc., *for* the worship of the gentiles is forbidden to you, and *you shall not prostrate yourself to any other god*, save to the Lord alone (the Masoretes have directed that the *Rēš* in the word אַחֵר *'aḥēR* ['other'] should be written large [*litera majuscula*] so as to prevent

443

it being misread as אֶחָד 'eḥādh), *because the Lord, His name is Impassioned,* and by this name He designated Himself in the Decalogue (xx 5; see my annotation *ad locum*), and as His name is, so is He: *He is an impassioned God.* This proves that this verse echoes the phrasing of the Ten Words in Chapter xx. The word
15 *lest* at the beginning of *v*. 15 does not come to admonish the Israelites not to commit the act mentioned immediately thereafter, [*lest*] *you make a covenant with the inhabitants of the land,* for in this respect a warning was already given in *v*. 12, but its purpose is to exhort them to eschew the things mentioned after this first act, as its consequences, to wit, *and when they play the harlot,* etc. A similar construction is found in Deuteronomy iv 19: 'And beware lest you lift up your eyes to heaven... you be drawn away and prostrate yourself to them and serve them'; and *ibid*. viii 12–14: 'lest when you have eaten and are full... then your heart be lifted up, and you forget the Lord your God', etc. The verb זָנָה *zānā* ['to commit fornication'] connotes here idol-worship due to the concept that the relationship between Israel and God is similar to that between a wife and her husband, and consequently the worship of idols is a form of harlotry (hence also the idea of קַנָּא *qannā'* [literally, 'Jealous', rendered: 'Impassioned'], the term applied above to the Lord). The verb also contains an allusion to sexual rites that characterized pagan worship. The evil results that the making of a covenant with the inhabitants of the land was liable to bring about are described here in consecutive stages, like links in a chain. The first phase is: *and when they* — the inhabitants of the land — *play the harlot after their gods, and slaughter* sacrifices *to their gods, and* some one from among them *calls you* — that is, invites you to partake of the flesh of his sacrifice at his sacred meal (the change from plural to singular is common in Biblical style, and is not to be regarded as an indication of different sources) — *you eat of his sacrifice.* Such eating may be the beginning of an extremely dangerous process, for as a result of the habit of eating with aliens you may become friendly with them, and the friendliness may
16 lead to the second stage, namely, intermarriage: *and you take of their daughters for your sons.* This stage, in turn, may engender the third: *and their daughters play the harlot after their gods and make your sons play the harlot after their gods.* The verbs used [in the Hebrew] in picturing this development are seven in number: *play the harlot — slaughter — calls — eat — take — play the harlot — make play the harlot.*

17 Yet another warning against dangerous action: *You shall make for yourself no molten gods* — no likeness whatsoever, even to symbolize the Lord God, for this may have evil consequences, as you have seen in the case of the golden calf. Needless to say, not only molden gods, in the precise sense of the term, are included in this prohibition, but all images, of every kind of material, are intended, only Scripture refers to the most common type.

18 *The feast of unleavened bread you shall keep.* On this subject and on the link with the heathen festivals, see xxiii 15. Mention of the feast of unleavened bread leads, by association of ideas, to the laws of the firstlings, which are cited in detail in order to make clear in what respects it is permissible to act in a manner resembling the Canaanite practices, and in which respects it is forbidden. Of particular importance is the new law concerning human first-born, whom the Canaanites, at least in certain instances, used to sacri-

19-20 fice to their gods. *All that opens the womb is Mine*, etc.; see xiii 2, 12–13. The verb תִּזָּכָר *tizzākhār* ['drop a male'] refers to cattle [בְּהֵמָה *bᵉhēmā*, which is feminine] giving birth, and hence takes the feminine form. All the laws of the firstlings, from *All that opens the womb* up to the second occurrence of *shall redeem*, are in parenthesis, and are omitted in chapter xxiii. *And none shall appear before Me* [literally, 'My face shall not be seen'] *empty-handed*, but you shall bring with you the firstlings of your sheep and herd; see xxiii 15, at the end. The expression 'to see the face' is used here in a different sense from that in xxxiii 23, and connotes: 'to enter the sanctuary'.

21 *Six days you shall work*, etc. Compare xxiii 12. In our paragraph the law of the Sabbath follows immediately after that of the feast of unleavened bread, because this festival marks the commencement of the harvest, and the Bible wished to rule that the work of harvesting, despite its importance, should not override the Sabbath: even *at plowing time and harvest time you shall cease from labour*.

22 *And you shall observe the feast of weeks*, etc., *and the feast of ingathering*, etc.; see xxiii 16. Here the term *feast of weeks* is used instead of *the feast of harvest*, which occurs in the parallel passage, in order to give added emphasis to the septimal system that prevails in the arrangement of the sacred seasons. In our verse the phrase תְּקוּפַת הַשָּׁנָה *tᵉqūphath haššānā* ['the turn of the year'] replaces בְּצֵאת הַשָּׁנָה *bᵉṣē'th haššānā* ['at the going out of the year'] in xxiii 16, but the meaning is the same. The stem קוּף *qūph*, which is akin to the stem נָקַף *nāqaph*, signifies 'to revolve', 'to go round

EXODUS XXXIV 22

in a cycle'; here the sense is: when the cycle of the agricultural year comes to an end. Compare i Sam. i 20; ii Chron. xxiv 23; in Ugaritic the stem *nqp* has a like connotation.

After the mention of these three festivals, several commandments relative to them are stated, beginning (*vv.* 23–24) with the precept to go on pilgrimage to the Sanctuary, which is common to all three. The injunction begins and ends with the identical words,
23 *three times a year*, which form, as it were, a framework round the subject. On *v.* 23, see xxiii 17. Emphasis is given in our verse not only to the designation *Lord* [אָדוֹן 'ādhōn], which occurs also there, in chapter xxiii, in contradistinction to the Canaanite title *Baal* [which likewise means 'lord'], but also to the most distinctive Divine appellation, *the God of Israel*. Verse 24 comes to relieve the anxiety of any one who may fear that his estate might be im-
24 perilled during his pilgrimage to the Sanctuary: *For I will cast out nations before you, and enlarge your borders*, and though your possessions be very far from the Sanctuary, yet even so you have no need to worry; I shall protect you, *and no man shall desire your land* — not only will he not take it, but it will not even enter his mind to desire or covet it (see above, my notes to xx 17), *when you go up to appear before the Lord your God three times in the year.*
25 Finally, we have laws relating to specific festivals. *You shall not offer My blood-sacrifice with leaven; neither shall the sacrifice of the feast of the passover remain all night until the morning*; see xxiii 18. There the reading is *My feast*, whereas here *the feast of the passover* is distinctly stated. The scholars who distinguish between the Feast of Passover celebrated by the nomads and the Feast of Unleavened Bread observed by the settled inhabitants, encounter a difficulty in the fact that in *v.* 18 the festival is designated *the feast of unleavened bread* and here it is called *the feast of the passover*; hence it has been suggested to read in our verse *My feast* as in chapter xxiii, or *My sacrifice*. But it is more satisfactory to conclude that at the time when this section was written the two
26 festivals had become fused into a single celebration. *The first* [i.e. choicest] *of the first fruits of your ground*... *You shall not boil a kid*, etc.; see xxiii 19.

ELEVENTH PARAGRAPH

THE WRITING OF THE COVENANT DOCUMENTS

(XXXIV 27–28)

27 The directions for the observance of the Covenant having been completed, another Divine communication commences at this point, and hence it is preceded by the formula, *And the Lord said to Moses*. The command now given to Moses is: *Write you* in a book, on a special scroll, as a memorial for generations, *these words* — that is, the instructions that I have given you for the observance of the covenant — *for in accordance with these words* — on the basis of these conditions (compare xxiv 8) — *I have made a covenant with you and with Israel*. The exegetes who take the view that at the end of the preceding paragraph we find the recension of the earliest Decalogue regard this verse and the latter part of *v*. 28 as referring to the writing down of this recension. But this interpretation is implausible, for here it is enjoined, *Write you* [literally, 'for you']; but it is not stated *upon the tables*, whereas in *v*. 28 occurs the phrase *upon the tables* but not the word *you;* it is thus clear that two different matters are referred to in these verses. Furthermore, there is a manifest difference between 'the words of the covenant' (*v*. 28) and the 'words' [i.e. conditions] in accordance with which the covenant was made, as is stated in *v*. 27.

28 *And he* — Moses — *was there*, on Mount Sinai (*v*. 4), *with the Lord forty days and forty nights*, the same period that he stayed there when he first received the Decalogue (xxiv 18). But this time it is stated *with the Lord*, possibly because on this occasion he was vouchsafed a unique revelation (*vv*. 5–6), and on account of his devotion to his people he attained to an exceedingly lofty spiritual height and drew very near to the Lord. Hence it is further recorded here: *he neither ate bread nor drank water*, indicating that he was uplifted above the everyday plane of life and tangibly approached the Divine sphere. In the light of this development, we can understand the statement in the next paragraph that the skin of Moses' face shone.

And He wrote upon the tables, which Moses had brought with him to the mountain top, *the words of the covenant*, the Decalogue. The subject of the verb *wrote* is apparently the Lord (*v*. 1: 'And

EXODUS XXXIV 28

I will write upon the tables'). But Scripture, following its principle of caution, was purposely vague and refrained from stating expressly that the Lord wrote, so as not to attribute an actual physical act to the Lord Himself; it thus left the matter shrouded, as it were, in mystery. Possibly the verb וַיִּכְתֹּב *wayyikhtōbh* ['and wrote', 3rd person sing. masc.] may also be understood as an indefinite, impersonal form, used in a similar sense to that of the passive: 'And the words of the covenant were written upon the tables.'

TWELFTH PARAGRAPH

THE SKIN OF MOSES' FACE BECOMES RADIANT

(XXXIV 29–35)

This paragraph is written in an elevated style that is almost poetic, with epic amplitude, and with a rhythm resembling that of poetry.

Verse 29 is divisible into three parts, each of which is ternary
29 [in the Hebrew]: *And it came to pass, | when Moses came down | from Mount Sinai, || with the two tables of the testimony | in Moses' hand | as he came down from the mountain, || that Moses did not know | that the skin of his face shone | because he had been talking with Him.* The verse speaks of two matters: (a) of the tables of the testimony that Moses brought with him when he came down from the mountain (parts 1–2 of the verse); (b) of the radiance of the skin of Moses' face (part 3). The twofold reference to Moses' descent, at the commencement and conclusion of the first theme, and likewise the threefold mention of Moses' name have the manifest purpose of lending beauty and grace to the verse and elevating its style.

The verb קָרַן *qāran* ['shine'] is derived from the noun קֶרֶן *qeren* in the sense of a 'ray of light', in accordance with Habakkuk iii 4: 'rays [קַרְנַיִם *qarnayim*] has He at His side.' According to the belief of the Mesopotamian peoples a radiant brightness (*melammu*) shone from the faces of the gods, which resembled in shape those of human beings and were differentiated from the latter by this very radiance. The Israelite prophet does not actually refer to the 'face' of the Lord, but only to His radiance. Since Moses was privileged to enjoy special intimacy with God and to speak with Him (Scripture says *with Him* and not *with the Lord* out of reverence;

448

compare the omission, for the same reason, of the subject of the verb וַיִּכְתֹּב *wayyikhtōbh* ['and wrote'] in *v.* 28), something of the Divine glory remained with him, and on an infinitesimal scale he also had rays at his side — enveloping his countenance. In the Greek translation of Aquila and in the Latin Vulgate the verse is rendered as though it referred to actual horns [which is the primary meaning of קֶרֶן *qeren*], like the horns of an ox; and so, in truth, is Moses portrayed in European art. Recently, A. Jirku defended this interpretation on the ground that in the ancient East horns were a symbol of the strength and prowess of the gods, and he supposed that Moses covered his face with a mask adorned with horns, when he approached the Deity (on the question of the mask see further below). This interpretation is implausible because the subject of the verb קָרַן *qāran* is 'the *skin* of his face'; and because it is stated *that Moses did not know*; but, above all, because an idolatrous emblem is out of place here, especially the horns of an ox, which would be particularly liable to recall the episode of the calf.

Verse 30 is divisible into two parts, which are also ternary:
30 *And when Aaron | and all the children of Israel | saw Moses || behold |, the skin of his face shone | and they were afraid to come near him* — that is to say, when Aaron and all the children of Israel saw the face of Moses, and perceived that the skin of his face shone, they were filled with awe, and were afraid to come near to him, and drew back (note the word-play: וַיַּרְא-וַיִּירְאוּ *wayyar'–wayyīr^eū* ['... saw' — '...feared']).

In *v.* 31, the first part is ternary, followed by a brief conclusion
31 consisting of three words: *But Moses called to them; | and Aaron and all the chieftains in the congregation | returned to him, || and Moses spoke to them*. Moses called to all of them, in love and humility, to draw near to him, and first Aaron his brother and the chieftains of the congregation went back to him, and Moses spoke to them as he did every day, for the man Moses was very humble and did not act proudly on account of the honour that he had been vouchsafed.

32 Verse 32 is divisible into two ternary parts: *And afterward | all the children of Israel | came near, || and he gave them in commandment | all that the Lord had spoken with him | in Mount Sinai*. After Aaron and the chieftains had come near, the common folk also drew near to Moses, and he reported to them what the Almighty had said to him. The meaning is not that he told them

everything at once, at this first meeting; the word *all* must not be taken literally (see above, on ix 6, etc.). Later, in chapter xxxv ff., we shall be told how Moses transmitted to the Israelites the Divine injunctions relating to the construction of the Tabernacle.

33 Also in verse 33, *And when Moses had finished speaking with them, He put a veil on his face,* poetic rhythm is discernible. The sense is: After Moses had completed his report to them of the Lord's communication (on the word וַיְכַל *way^{e}khal* ['when... had finished'] and its idiomatic usage, see my note on Gen. ii 2), he put over his face, out of a sense of humility and modesty, a kind of veil, like the veil or head-scarf that women in Israel usually wear over their faces during summer to protect themselves from the sun's glare. Such a veil permits one to see out, but is able to reduce the brightness of the light, be it the rays of the sun coming from without or radiance issuing from within, like the glow of the skin of Moses' face. Some exegetes have regarded Moses' 'veil' [מַסְוֶה *maswe*] as a kind of mask such as the priests of certain primitive peoples are accustomed to put on their faces during the performance of their ritual — not unlike the mask with horns envisaged by Jirku in his aforementioned conjecture. But this is also impossible, since it was the reverse position that obtained. It was precisely when Moses was speaking to the people as God's messenger and when he was alone with the Divine Presence (*v.* 34) that he did not put the veil over his face, whilst in his daily life he covered his face with it. For the selfsame reason it is difficult to agree with the theory of Wellhausen, who identifies Moses' veil with the shawl with which the Arab seers used to cover their faces during their visions. It is also implausible for the reason mentioned earlier [see the author's argument against Jirku's view in the commentary on *v.* 29].

Verses 34 and 35 describe the habitual practice of Moses from that day onward; hence the verbs occur in the imperfect or in the perfect with the *Wāw* consecutive. In these verses, too, a poetic
34-35 rhythm is noticeable, in part ternary: *But when Moses went in | before the Lord | to speak with Him, || he would take the veil off, | until he came out; || and he would come out, | and speak to the children of Israel | what he was commanded.* The meaning is: Whenever Moses would go into the Tent of Meeting to speak with the Lord (here, too, the text has only *with Him*, as in *v.* 29), he used to remove the veil from his face and remain with uncovered face till the Divine communication was ended, and he went out; and even after he

had gone out he would leave his face uncovered whilst he told the Israelites what he was enjoined to tell them. *And the children of Israel would see | the face of Moses, | that the skin of Moses' face shone; | and Moses would put the veil again | upon his face, | until he went in to speak with Him.* The sense is: And whilst Moses addressed the people, the Israelites saw the Divine radiance that shone from the skin of his face, and only after he had finished speaking to them did Moses (in this verse, too, as in *v.* 29, Moses' name occurs three times) put back the veil over his face, leaving it there until he again entered the Tent of Meeting to commune alone with God (also here the reading is, *with Him*).

The poetic character of the passage is evident not only from the rhythm and the repetitions to which we have already referred, but also from other schematic reiterations: the fact that the skin of Moses' face shone is stated three times (*vv.* 29, 30, 35); the veil is mentioned thrice (*vv.* 33, 34, 35); it is thrice recorded that Moses spoke *with Him*, that is, with the Lord (*vv.* 29, 34, 35); on three occasions, we are informed, Moses spoke with the children of Israel (*vv.* 31, 33, 34); and once, we are told, the Lord spoke to Moses (*v.* 32). Thus there are seven references, in all, to speaking.

SECTION THREE

THE EXECUTION OF THE WORK OF THE
TABERNACLE AND ITS ERECTION

CHAPTER XXXV, VERSE 1 — CHAPTER XL, VERSE 38

Now that complete forgiveness, and with it permission to build the Tabernacle, had been obtained, Moses and the Israelites must carry out the work of construction and establish the sanctuary. How the task was executed is narrated in detail in the present section, in language that is almost identical with that used earlier in ch. xxv 1– ch. xxx 10, in the injunctions given by the Lord to Moses in regard to the making of the Tabernacle. Each item is dealt with in the same or almost the same words. Needless to say, instead of verbs in the imperative or the imperfect, like תַּעֲשֶׂה *taʿăśe* ['you (masc. sing.) shall make'], וְעָשִׂיתָ *weʿāśîthā* ['and you (masc. sing.) shall make'], וְעָשׂוּ *weʿāśû* ['and they shall make'], and so on, there occur in our section verbs referring to the past, as, for example, וַיַּעַשׂ *wayyaʿaś* ['and he made'], וַיַּעֲשׂוּ *wayyaʿăśû* ['and they made'], עָשָׂה *ʿāśā* ['he màde'], and עָשׂוּ *ʿāśû* ['they made'], and so forth. Apart from this, and apart from several variations of form, such as a *Wāw* conjunctive more or less, the substitution of synonyms, changes in the order of the words and the paragraphs, and the like, there are a few divergences, and these are due to the difference of context. Thus, for instance, since chapters xxxv-xxxix speak only of the construction of the Tabernacle and its vessels and of nothing else, they do not repeat what was stated earlier concerning the arrangement of the parts of the shrine and its furniture, and their use. All this is described again in chapter xl, which speaks of the erection of the Tabernacle.

In view of the fact that the repetition is mainly literal, it has not met with the approval of the majority of exegetes. Without paying attention to the differences or to the reasons for them, they expressed surprise at the lengthy passages that are iterated word for word, and almost letter for letter. Since in their view it is inconceivable that the same author should repeat himself at length and verbatim, they came to the conclusion that we have here an addition posterior to the date of the sections containing the instructions.

THE ERECTION OF THE TABERNACLE

The first to express this view was Julius Popper (1862); and after the leading exegetes of the time, Kuenen and Wellhausen, had approved his main thesis, the theory gained wide acceptance among Biblical scholars. Even today this section is attributed to the secondary strata of P, whilst some distinguish as many as five different literary strands in it. However, this conjecture is based on ignorance of the methods employed in the composition of books in the ancient East. The theme of the founding and building of a shrine was a stereotyped literary category in the early writings of the Eastern countries; and it was usual for such passages to record first the divine utterance describing the plan of the sanctuary in minutest detail, and thereafter to give an account of the construction, which repeated in identical or similar phrasing the description given in the divine communication. This is, indeed, only a specific facet of the general technique of repetition, which was dearly beloved of the writers of the ancient East. The literary tradition of the land of Canaan, which is continued in Biblical writings, is also fond of this practice. It will suffice to cite here one example from the Canaanite works discovered at Ugarit. In the Ugaritic epic of King Keret it is narrated that this monarch saw El the father of the gods in a dream, and received from him instructions concerning the offering of sacrifices, the mustering of a great army, the organization of a military expedition to the land of King Pabel, the request that Pabel's daughter or granddaughter be given him for a wife, and so on and so forth; these directives contain more than ninety lines. At the conclusion of the instructions we are informed that King Keret did as El had directed him in his dream, and his actions are described by the literal repetition of the terms of the instructions, except for changes in the forms of the verbs to indicate the past tense and other variations of formulation, such as a *Wāw* conjunctive more or less, the substitution of synonyms, differences in the sequence of the words and the like, as well as other divergences arising from the altered character of the narrative — precisely what we find in the present section of the Book of Exodus. In the light of this style of composition, our section is not only not to be regarded as a later addition, but is required where it is, and, were it not here, we should have to assume that it was missing from the text.

In our exposition of this section we shall follow the same method that we adopted in annotating the parts of chapter xxxiv that correspond to parts of chapter xxiii: we shall comment on the new features and on the divergences, in so far as this is necessary, whereas when we come to passages that we have already explained earlier, we shall content ourselves with giving the references to the parallel verses, and this will suffice.

FIRST PARAGRAPH

CESSATION OF WORK ON THE SABBATH

(XXXV 1-3)

Chapter XXXV

1 Moses called together a solemn assembly of the people for the purpose of giving them the instructions for the work of the Tabernacle. *And Moses assembled all the congregation of the children of Israel*: not, of course, all six hundred thousand, nor yet a *congregation* in the sense of an assembly or council, as has been suggested, but the majority of the heads of the clans, who represented the people as a whole; the word *all* is used, as a rule, imprecisely. *And he said to them*: *These are the things that the Lord has commanded that you should do them*. The plural *things* and the expression *that you should do them* prove that this introductory note does not refer to the observance of the Sabbath but to the construction of the Tabernacle (*vv.* 4–19), and that the law of the Sabbath is mentioned only as a prefatory admonition. When Moses was given the instructions, it was sufficient to cite this prohibition at the end (xxxi 12 ff.), as the time had not yet come for the commands to be carried out, but now, at the moment of implementation, it was necessary to proclaim the prohibition at the very beginning,

2 and to tell the Israelites from the outset that only *six days shall work be done* — work of any kind — and, therefore, when, in the continuation of his address, he will speak to them of work, it must be clear to them from the first that even this work does not abrogate the Sabbath. *But on the seventh day* — even at the time when the Tabernacle is being built — *there shall be to you a holy (day), a sabbath of entire rest unto the Lord; whoever does any work on it* — even sacred work — *shall be put to death*.

3 *You shall kindle no fire in all your habitations on the sabbath day*. According to the simple meaning of the verse, the kindling of fire was treated as an exception and received special emphasis so that

no one should suppose that making a fire — a prerequisite for various kinds of work in the construction of the Tabernacle — was not real labour but only a preparation for it (so it was regarded by the Canaanites, who used to tell of a fire being kindled for six days in order to prepare the gold and silver plating, with which the walls of Baal's palace were covered, on the seventh day).

Incidentally the Torah says, *in all your habitations*, to inform us that the prohibition does not apply only to work done in the Tabernacle, but also to that performed in the private dwellings of the Israelites, in their tents in the desert, and, subsequently, in their houses in the Promised Land. The addition of this restriction was necessary, for without it one might have supposed that a fire had to be kindled in honour of the Sabbath day, as candles are lit, in Jewish tradition [on the eve of a holy day]. It is also possible that the expression implies opposition to the pagan custom of lighting a fire in the homes in honour of the festivals. In Mesopotamia a special festival was dedicated to fire, and in one of the texts referring to this festival it is stated: The people of the place shall make a fire in their dwelling-places.

SECOND PARAGRAPH

THE CONTRIBUTION TO THE TABERNACLE

(XXXV 4–20)

After the admonishment in regard to the Sabbath, Moses continues his address and explains the primary purpose of the assembly:
4 *This is the thing which the Lord has commanded*—this in particular is what I have wished to tell you in the name of the Lord. This repetition of what had already been stated in *v.* 1 ('These are the things that the Lord has commanded', etc.) was necessary in order to revert to the primary theme after the prefatory injunction concerning the cessation of work on the Sabbath. A similar sequence is found in the section of the Festivals in Leviticus xxiii. To begin with it is stated there (*v.* 2): 'The fixed times of the Lord, which you shall proclaim as holy convocations; these are My fixed times.' In *v.* 3 we have a note on the Sabbath to indicate that it is also holy, nay more, it is the chief of the sacred seasons; and in *v.* 4, in order to return to the subject after this preliminary note, it is

again stated: 'These are the fixed times of the Lord, the holy convocations, which you shall proclaim at the time appointed for them.'

5-10 Now this is what you are commanded: *Take from among you a contribution to the Lord*, etc.; see xxv 1–7. The differences are few: *Wāw* conjunctive has been added in a number of instances; the sentence, *And this is the contribution that you shall take from them*, is omitted, because it would have been out of place here; and there are also several other variations due to the changed circumstances (for example, *from among you*, in *v.* 5). On the words *and every wise hearted man* in *v.* 10, see xxxi 6.

11-19 In *vv.* 11–19 there is repeated the list of all the articles that are to be made; see xxxi 7–11. In the latter passage, in the summing up of the instructions that have already been stated, the list is formulated more briefly, whereas here, at the beginning of the announcement, it is fitting to mention each item separately. There is no need to point out all the divergences in detail. On the change of gender in the words אֶת־עַמֻּדָיו וְאֶת־אֲדָנֶיהָ *'eth ʿammūdhāw* [masc. pronominal suffix] *wᵉʾeth 'ădhānehā* [fem. pronominal suffix] — 'his pillars and her sockets' — in *v.* 17, compare i Kings xix 11, רוּחַ גְּדוֹלָה וְחָזָק *rūaḥ gᵉdhōlā* [fem. adjective] *wᵉḥāzāq* [masc. adjective] — 'a great and strong wind' — and the like.

20 *Then all the congregation of the children of Israel* — the men of the congregation mentioned in *v.* 1 — *departed from the presence of Moses* — after Moses had concluded his speech, and had told them what they had to bring as a contribution to the Tabernacle.

THIRD PARAGRAPH

THE BRINGING OF THE CONTRIBUTION

(XXXV 21–29)

Corresponding to the last verse of the preceding paragraph, which begins with the expression *And... departed*, we have here two verses commencing with the words *And they came* — a fine stylistic parallel, which, at the same time, contains an allusion to the swift response of the children of Israel to the request for contributions to the Sanctuary. As soon as Moses ended his address they left to fetch their gifts, and immediately returned with their offerings. The description of the donors is long and detailed, as though Scripture were depicting for us the long and crowded queue of people in their multitudes bringing their contributions. The fact that the word *brought* occurs seven times in this paragraph is not without significance.

21 *And they came, every one whose heart stirred him*, as Moses had said in v. 5: 'whoever is of a generous heart.' Then again, as a poetic parallelism, the thought is repeated in different words: *and every one whose spirit moved him*. The two terms used by Moses in his speech, נָדַב *nādhabh* ['to impel, be willing, be generous'] and לֵב *lēbh* ['heart'], are here divided between the two parts of the verse. *Brought the Lord's contribution* — precisely as Moses phrased it in v. 5; *for the work of the tent of meeting and for all its service and for the holy garments* — a concise summary of the inventory given above.

The general statement is followed by details. First it is stated:
22 *And they came, both men and women* [literally, 'the men upon the women'], so as to avoid the misapprehension that the expression *every one* [literally, 'every man'] in the preceding verse refers to men only. In the continuation of v. 22 and in vv. 23–24 the men are specifically mentioned, but the women are included by implication, whilst in vv. 25–26 the women are expressly referred to.

All who were of a willing heart, whether men or women, *brought various articles of gold*, for example (the nouns occur in the singular to indicate the type, but they have a plural signification): חָח *ḥāḥ*, that is, 'brooches'; *and* נֶזֶם *nezem*, ear or nose ornaments [rendered: 'earrings' or 'nose-rings']; *and* טַבַּעַת *ṭabbaʿath*, finger ornaments [rendered: 'rings'], derived from a stem meaning 'to imprint', since as a rule the ring contained a signet; *and* כּוּמָז *kūmāz*, apparently a globe-shaped ornament (Arabic كمزة *kumza*, 'a little ball'); and, in general, *all sorts of gold objects. And every man that waved a wave-offering of gold unto the Lord* — in whatever form, even if it were not an article but consisted, for example, of bars of gold or of broken jewellery and the like — he brought his contribution forthwith. The predicate of this subject, with which v. 22 concludes, occurs at the end of v. 23 (*brought* [*them*]), after the second subject ('And every man with whom was found', etc.). The verb הֵנִיף *hēnīph* ['to wave'] and the noun תְּנוּפָה *tᵉnūphā* ['wave-offering'] are synonymous with the verb הֵרִים *hērīm* ['lift'] and the noun תְּרוּמָה *tᵉrūmā* ['offering', 'contribution']: one who presents a gift in a celebrative manner

does so on his outstretched hands as though he were waving it
23 (see xxix 24–28). *And every man with whom was found deep violet or dark red wool*, etc. — all these *brought* their contribution at
24 once. Similarly, *every one who brought a contribution of silver or bronze* — the other metals that Moses required, beside the gold mentioned in *v.* 22. These donors also *brought the Lord's contribution*; and the same applied to those who offered acacia wood: *and every man with whom was found acacia wood for any work of the service brought* [*that*]. The word *brought* at the end [in the Hebrew] of *v.* 23 and *v.* 24 is emphasized, and we have already noted that it occurs seven times in this paragraph.

The expression *with whom was found* does not exclude other possibilities, for instance, that a man would go and cut down acacia trees in the vicinity of the camp and bring them to Moses, or that another would buy something for the purpose from the caravan merchants who passed through the nearby places; only Scripture cites the most common examples, and its primary purpose is really to stress the bringing of the gifts.

Now just as the men carried out their part, so the women did their duty, particularly the tasks that fall within their specific com-
25 petence. *And all the women that were wise hearted* [i.e. skilled] (compare Moses' words in *v.* 10: 'and every wise hearted man among you') *spun with her hands* (the transition from singular to plural, or vice versa, is not uncommon in Biblical diction), *and brought what they had spun* — in the form of spun thread — *in deep violet and dark red*, etc. The same, of course, was done by the women who were expert at spinning goats' hair, a coarser type of work but
26 just as necessary: *And all the women whose heart moved them in wisdom spun the goats' hair*.

After the ordinary folk, both men and women, we have the chieftains. They brought the costly gifts. There is a clear word-play here: אֲנָשִׁים *'ănāšīm* ['men'] — נָשִׁים *nāšīm* ['women'] — נְשִׂיאִים *neśī'īm* ['chieftains']; compare also the verb נָשָׂא *nāśā'* ['lift up';
27 rendered: 'moved'] in *v.* 26. *And the chieftains brought* — as gifts befitting their rank — *the šohām stones and stones to be set, for
28 the ephod and for the breastpiece*, as required by Moses (*v.* 9), *and the spice* (הַבֹּשֶׂם *habbośem* — a collective noun; in *v.* 8: בְּשָׂמִים *beśāmīm* [plural]), *and the oil, for the light, and for the anointing oil and for the fragrant incense* (*v.* 8, and *vv.* 14–15).

After the enumeration of the three categories of contributors, verse 29 provides a general summary with which to conclude the account. The syntax of the verse appears difficult, at first sight, since the verb *brought* has two subjects, one before the verb (*All the men and women*, etc.), and one after it (*the children of Israel*). But possibly we have here a construction with a twofold subject; compare, for example, קוֹלִי אֶל ה' אֶקְרָא *qōlī 'el YHWH 'eqrā'* [literally, 'My voice unto the Lord I cry'; usually rendered: 'I cry aloud unto the Lord'] (Psa. iii 5). The verse, then, has to be construed thus: In this way, by the voluntary contributions of *every man and woman whose heart moved them to bring anything for the work which the Lord had commanded by Moses to be done, the children of Israel brought a freewill offering to the Lord.*

FOURTH PARAGRAPH

THE APPOINTMENT OF THE CRAFTSMEN AND
THE COMMENCEMENT OF THE WORK

(XXXV 30—XXXVI 7)

30-34 At the very time that the children of Israel were bringing their contributions for the construction of the Tabernacle, Moses announced the selection of the craftsmen who would be in charge of the work.

There is repeated here, in chapter xxxv 30–34, *mutatis mutandis*, and with a few variations of form, what was stated above, in chapter xxxi 1 ff.; see *ibid*. on the particulars. The new features, apart from changes of *Wāw* conjunctive and the like, are:

(a) In *v.* 33 it is stated: בְּכָל־מְלֶאכֶת מַחֲשָׁבֶת *bekhol mele'kheth maḥăšābheth* [literally, 'in every work of thought'] — that is, in every work that represents the implementation of a thought or project planned previously; compare also above, xxxi 4: 'to think thoughts', etc.

(b) In *v.* 34 we find: *And He has put in his heart that he may teach* — He had also put in Bezalel's heart the capacity to instruct others and to guide them in their work. There would be two men to whom this gift would be granted: *He* — Bezalel — *and Oholiab the son of Ahisamach, of the tribe of Dan.* Since we have here already an allusion to assitants working with the two chief artificers, who would receive instruction from them, there was no need to cite here the continuation of the passage in xxxi 6: 'and in the hearts of all that are wise hearted', etc.

35 (c) Verse 35 is almost new. Its meaning is: *He has filled them* — Bezalel and Oholiab — *with wisdom of heart*, so that it may be possible *to do*, under their direction, *every sort of work done by a craftsman* — a worker in wood or metal — *or by a designer or by an embroiderer*, etc. — even to the simple work of weaving: *or by a weaver*; and in general the work done *by any sort of workman or skilled designer*.

Chapter XXXVI

1 The chapter division here is incorrect; it is based on a mistaken interpretation of the word וְעָשָׂה *we'āśā* in the sense of וַיַּעַשׂ *wayya-'aś* ['and he worked'], as though the account of the execution of the work by Bezalel and Oholiab and their helpers began at this point. But of this we shall be told only later. The correct meaning of the word וְעָשָׂה *we'āśā* is וְיַעֲשֶׂה *weya'ăśe* ['and he shall work'], and the whole verse is the continuation and conclusion of Moses' address. After Moses had spoken of the choice of Bezalel and Oholiab and the attributes with which the Lord had endowed them, he added: *And Bezalel and Oholiab shall work, and every wise hearted man, in whom the Lord has put wisdom and understanding* (compare xxxi 6) *to know to work*—so that they may know how to do their work — *all the work* (these words are the object of the verb *shall work*) *for the service of the sanctuary, in accordance with all* (לְכֹל *lekhōl* — the initial *Lāmedh* expresses inclusion; cf. above, on xxvii 3) *that the Lord has commanded*. Here ends Moses' oration.

2 *And Moses called Bezalel and Oholiab, and every wise hearted man, in whose heart the Lord had put wisdom, even every one whose heart stirred him up to draw near to the work to do it* — not only the bringing of a gift was an act of freewill offering, but the service of every skilled man was equally so.

Moses delivered to the craftsmen all the materials that the children of Israel were bringing as a contribution for the Taber-
3 nacle: *And they took from before Moses all the contribution, which the children of Israel had brought* (the repetition of the word *brought* recalls the uncoerced giving that was emphasized earlier by means of this word) *for the work of the service of the sanctuary, to do it* — to wit, the work of the service of the sanctuary. *Now they* — the children of Israel — *still brought* (the word is again reiterated) *to him* — to Moses — *freewill offerings every morning*. Even after the craftsmen had begun to receive the raw material from Moses,
4 freewill gifts continued to arrive early each morning. *And all the wise men* — 'the wise hearted' [skilled] — *who were doing all the*

EXODUS XXXVI 8

work of the sanctuary (the word *all* occurs here twice, in, as usual, a general sense, signifying various wise men skilled in various types of work), *came, every man from his work* — that is, every
5 one came from the place of the work *that he was doing, and spoke to Moses, saying*: *The people are bringing much more than enough for the service* required *for the work, which the Lord commanded to do*. All this is narrated at length in order to underline still further the spirit of voluntary giving, which did not abate until Moses announced that no more gifts were to be brought. But for this proclamation, they would have brought more offerings still.
6 *And Moses gave command, and they* — the people charged with the task, the verb being used impersonally — *caused it to be proclaimed throughout the camp, saying, Let neither man nor woman* (a further allusion to what was stated earlier, that both the men and the women contributed liberally) *do any more work for the contribution for the sanctuary* — let them not occupy themselves any more with the work of preparing and bringing the contributions. Only then, after Moses' proclamation, *were the people restrained from bringing* — they were stopped, as it were, against their will.
7 *For the stuff* [מְלָאכָה *mᵉlā'khā*, literally, 'the work'] — the quantity of material that they had already prepared and brought — *was sufficient* for the artisans *for all the work* (מְלָאכָה *mᵉlā'khā*: the word is used in two different senses here as a word-play) *to do it, and more* — the great liberality of the people is again underscored.

From the beginning of the section up to this point the word תְּרוּמָה *tᵉrūmā* ['contribution'] has occurred seven times. Likewise the verb בּוֹא *bō'* ['come'], in the *Qal* or *Hiph'îl*, is used seven times, quite apart from the seven occurrences of the word הֵבִיאוּ *hēbhī'ū* ['they brought'] in the preceding paragraph.

FIFTH PARAGRAPH

THE TABERNACLE AND THE TENT

(XXXVI 8–19)

8-19 Here begins the detailed description of the tasks that were performed for the work of the Tabernacle; but the order followed is

461

different from that of the section containing the injunctions. The first and principal divergence is that the construction of the Tabernacle precedes here the making of its vessels. It is not Scripture's intention to indicate that the Tabernacle was made first and thereafter the vessels, for generally speaking the different artisans carried out their various tasks simultaneously; at the same time that the weavers wove the curtains the carpenters made the wooden articles and the metal workers fashioned the metal objects. Nor is it to be assumed that the Bible wished to tell us, that the Tabernacle was constructed first in order to provide a place where to house the holy articles, for the Tabernacle was erected only at the end (chapter xl), when the entire work was complete in all ist details. The reason for the different sequence is only a literary one, namely, the tendency to use a chiastic order, which was so beloved of the Biblical writers: articles — Tabernacle; Tabernacle — articles.

In this paragraph, since it is the first to describe the work, the opening sentence is characterized by a longer and more detailed formulation: *And all the wise hearted men among the workmen*, etc.; whereas in the succeeding paragraphs the phrasing is simpler: *And he made* or *And they made*, and once (xxxvii 1), *And Bezalel made*.

The account of the making of the curtains of the Tabernacle and the Tent corresponds almost word for word to the injunction regarding them (xxvi 1–14); see, in detail, my annotations *ad locum*. On the verbal differences, such as אַחַת אֶל אֶחָת *'aḥath 'el 'eḥāth* [literally, 'one to one'; rendered: 'one to another'] instead of אִשָּׁה אֶל אֲחוֹתָהּ *'iššā 'el 'ăḥōthah* [literally, 'a woman to her sister'; rendered: 'one to another'], or בַּמַּחְבֶּרֶת *bammaḥbereth* ['in the set'] in place of בַּחֹבֶרֶת *baḥōbhereth* [also translated: 'in the set'], and the like, there is no need to enlarge. There are missing here the particulars that do not appertain to the making of the curtains but to the manner in which they were to be fitted over the boards when the Tabernacle would be erected (xxvi 9: 'and the sixth curtain you shall double over at the front of the tent'; *ibid. v.* 12: 'And the part that remains of the curtains of the tent', etc.; *ibid. v.* 13: 'And the cubit on the one side, and the cubit on the other side', etc.); this is entirely in accord with the context, since we deal here only with the making of the curtains as a separate entity.

SIXTH PARAGRAPH

THE BOARDS

(XXXVI 20-34)

20-34 This paragraph agrees with the instructions in xxvi 15 ff., almost verbatim; see my commentary *ad locum*. There are only a few changes of form here, such as עֶשְׂרִים קְרָשִׁים *'eśrīm qerāšīm* for עֶשְׂרִים קֶרֶשׁ *'eśrīm qāreš* ['twenty boards']; or בְּרִיחֵי עֲצֵי שִׁטִּים *berīḥē 'ăṣē šiṭṭīm* instead of בְרִיחִים עֲצֵי שִׁטִּים *bherīḥīm 'ăṣē šiṭṭīm* ['bars of acacia wood']; whilst אַחַת אֶל אֶחָת *'aḥath 'el 'eḥāth* ['one to another'] iterates the wording of the preceding paragraph, and so forth. The last verse *ibid*. (xxvi 30) is not repeated in our passage, because it relates to the erection of the Tabernacle and not to the making of the boards.

SEVENTH PARAGRAPH

THE VEIL AND THE SCREEN

(XXXVI 35-38)

35-38 This paragraph corresponds to xxvi 31 f.; see my annotations *ad locum*. Here, too, only the particulars appertaining to the making of the objects are given, but not those that belong to the erection and inner arrangement of the Tabernacle (xxvi 33-35), whose proper place is in chapter xl (*vv*. 20-24). In this passage, likewise, we find several variations of wording, particularly where a change is necessary in order to restrict the account to a description of the making of the things (xxvi 32: 'And you shall put it upon four pillars of acacia'; whereas here in *v*. 36 it is written: *And for it he made four pillars of acacia*).

EIGHTH PARAGRAPH
THE ARK AND THE KAPPŌRETH
(XXXVII 1-9)

Chapter XXXVII

1-9 A reproduction of xxv 10 ff.; see my commentary *ad locum*. In v. 1 Bezalel's name is specifically mentioned, possibly because the manufacture of the furniture begins at this point. Here, too, certain changes of phrasing occur (thus, for example, the word בָּהֶם *bāhem* ['by them'], which occurs above, in xxv 14, is omitted in v. 5). Likewise in this passage the details concerning the arrangement of the Tabernacle and its appurtenances and their use (xxv 15-16, 21-22) are omitted; the execution of these matters is dealt with later, in xl 20. There are also differences of spelling and grammatical form: above, xxv 19, we find קְצוֹתָיו *qᵉṣōthāw*, and here, in v. 8, it is written קצוותו *qṣwwthw* (the *Qᵉrē* [the Masoretic reading and vocalization] is: קְצוֹתָיו *qᵉṣōthāw* ['its ends']).

NINTH PARAGRAPH
THE TABLE
(XXXVII 10-16)

10-16 A duplication of xxv 23 ff.; see my commentary *ad locum*. Here again there are verbal variations (e.g., *ibid.*, v. 26, וְעָשִׂיתָ *wᵉʿāśithā* ['And you shall make'], and here, v. 13, וַיִּצֹק *wayyiṣōq* ['And he cast']; *ibid.* v. 27, לְבָתִּים לְבַדִּים *lᵉbhāttīm lᵉbhaddīm*, and in this paragraph, v. 14, בָּתִּים לְבַדִּים *bāttīm lᵉbhaddīm* ['(as) holders for the poles']; in our passage, v. 16, there is added, before the list of articles, the general expression, *the vessels which were upon the table*; and other divergences such as the addition of the particle אֶת *'eth* [sign of the accusative], the changed order in which the 'beakers' and 'chalices' are listed, and the omission of the final suffix in the word הַקְּשָׂוֹת *haqqᵉśāwōth* ['the beakers']). In this paragraph, too, what appertains to the ritual of the sanctuary (the bread of the Presence; see xxv 30) is omitted; this omission, however, is made good later in its due place (xl 23).

TENTH PARAGRAPH

THE LAMPSTAND

(XXXVII 17–24)

17-24 This paragraph iterates xxv 31 ff.; see my notes *ad locum*. There are a few verbal changes in our passage (*ibid.*, *v.* 33: 'of the lampstand'; here at the end of *v.* 21: *of it*). In keeping with the overall theme there are omitted here the references to the kindling [or, fixing on] of the lamps (xxv 37) and to the vision Moses saw on the mountain (xxv 40). The kindling [or affixing] of the lamps will be mentioned in its proper place later on (xl 25).

ELEVENTH PARAGRAPH

THE ALTAR OF INCENSE

(XXXVII 25–29)

25-28 We have a repetition here of xxx 1–5; see my annotations *ad locum*. The reasons for which the injunction to make the altar of incense was separated from the directives relative to the other sacred articles [of the Tabernacle proper], and placed as an appendix at the end, do not apply here, and therefore this paragraph follows immediately after those dealing with the rest of the internal furniture. Naturally, our passage is restricted to an account of the construction of the incense altar, whereas the data given in chapter xxx regarding the location of the altar, the burning thereon of incense, and the putting of blood upon its horns once a year, are not mentioned till later, in their proper context (xl 26–27; Lev. xvi 18–19).

Brief reference is also made incidentally here to the preparation of the anointing oil and the incense of spices, forming an addendum, as it were, to the description of the making of the altar of incense:
29 *And he made the holy anointing oil* (compare xxx 25), *and the pure incense of spices* (compare xxx 35), both being *the work of the perfumer* (compare xxx 25, 35).

TWELFTH PARAGRAPH

THE ALTAR OF BURNT OFFERING

(XXXVIII 1–7)

Chapter XXXVIII
1-7 This notice parallels chapter xxvii 1–8; see my commentary *ad locum*. Here, too, there are only a few variations of form. Thus, for example, we find אָרְכּוֹ *'orkō* ['its length'] and רָחְבּוֹ *roḥbō* ['its breadth'] in *v.* 1 instead of אֹרֶךְ *'ōrekh* ['length'] and רֹחַב *rōḥabh* ['breadth'], which occur in xxvii 1, without the pronominal suffix; the addition of the general expression *all the utensils of the altar* before the list of vessels in *v.* 3; the omission of the pronominal ending in the names of the vessels (compare the divergences that were pointed out above in connection with the table utensils), and the like. The phrase *to receive its ashes* that occurs in xxvii 3 is not used here because it relates to the sanctuary service and not to the making of the vessels. Similarly, the second half of the last verse of the earlier passage is not reproduced here since it refers only to Moses' vision. A few particulars are abbreviated in our paragraph.

THIRTEENTH PARAGRAPH

THE LAVER AND ITS BASE

(XXXVIII 8)

8 The position of this paragraph here is to be explained in the same way as that of the eleventh paragraph, which treats of the altar of incense (see on this above). The command relating to the making of the laver and its base, and the manner of using it, is cited above, in xxx 17–21; see my annotations *ad locum*. Here only the construction is mentioned, but whatever appertains to its use, even the words *for washing*, is omitted.

Our passage records a new fact, namely, the material of which the laver and the base were made: *from the mirrors of the women in array* [צֹבְאֹת *ṣōbhe'ōth*] *who stood in array at the door of the tent of meeting.* This is an obscure detail, concerning which the haggadists have developed various fanciful interpretations and modern exegetes have advanced a number of conjectures. According to the simple sense of the verse, its intention seems to be to indicate that the laver and its base were not made from the material of the Lord's contribution, which was designated for the service in the sanctuary, since these articles did not serve this purpose, but were used for the preparation of the priests for their ministrations (see above, p. 395). What is stated here explicitly accords with what Scripture implies later on (*vv.* 29–31), when it enumerates all the articles made from the bronze of the wave-offerings, and neither the laver nor its base is mentioned among them. The mirrors brought by the women constitute an exceptional gift, which was not included in the contribution to the sanctuary. Possibly the ancient poetic tradition related that the women, in their generosity of heart, came in their multitudes to offer to Moses their most precious treasures such as the mirrors, forming a long queue for the purpose, literally צֹבְאֹת *ṣōbhe'ōth* ['standing in array'] *at the door of the tent of meeting* — in front of Moses' tent, which served at the time as a Tent of Meeting and was so designated (see above, on xxxiii 7–11). Although the Torah did not incorporate this particular in its narrative, and only alluded to it incidentally, yet since the episode was known to the Congregation as part of its poetic tradition, the allusion was understood without difficulty.

The wording of the text in i Samuel ii 22 ('how they lay with the women who stood in array' [הַצֹּבְאֹת *haṣṣōbhe'ōth*, usually rendered: 'who served']) is derived from our verse or from the ancient source on which our own verse is dependent.

FOURTEENTH PARAGRAPH

THE COURT OF THE TABERNACLE

(XXXVIII 9–20)

9-20 A repetition of xxvii 9–19; see my commentary *ad locum*. In this paragraph there are more changes in connection with the words, their order, and the arrangement of the subject-matter than in the preceding paragraphs, but in the final analysis these, too, are to be classified as variations of form. The following are examples: in xxvii 9 we read, 'hangings for the court', and in *v.* 9 of our chapter, *hangings of the court*; at the end of the same verse in the earlier passage we find, 'a hundred cubits long for one side', and here only, *a hundred cubits*; in xxvii 10, 'and its pillars' [i.e., of the court], and in our paragraph, *their pillars* [i.e., of the hangings]; and other variant readings of the same kind. Verse 16 here states what is implied in the middle of xxvii 18. In *v.* 17 and in *v.* 19 of our chapter there are added the words, *and the overlay of their tops* (compare *v.* 28: 'and overlaid their tops'), but possibly 'the overlay of the tops' simply means the topmost band, and consequently is included in the expression 'their bands' in chapter xxvii. The height, which is noted with extreme brevity in xxvii 18 ('and the height five cubits') is indicated in *v.* 18 of our chapter with greater detail: *and the height* of the screen *in the breadth* — that means to say, measured in the breadth of the fabric when it was hung perpendicularly — *was five cubits*, this height *corresponding to* that of *the hangings of the court*, that is, their height equalled that of the screen, namely, five cubits.

FIFTEENTH PARAGRAPH

AN INVENTORY OF MATERIALS USED
FOR THE TABERNACLE

(XXXVIII 21–XXXIX 1)

After the account of the bringing of the Tabernacle contribution, and of the construction of the sanctuary and its appurtenances, we are given here a general review of the sum of the materials that were dedicated to this purpose.

21   *These* — the things mentioned below — *are the reckonings of the tabernacle* — that is, the details of the inventory of the materials that were donated and used for the work of the Tabernacle, namely, *the tabernacle of the testimony*, which incorporated the ark of the testimony, *which was* [sing. in the Hebrew] *reckoned* — whose inventory (i.e. of the tabernacle) was made — *according to the commandment* (literally, 'mouth') *of Moses*; and this reckoning was *the work of the Levites, under the hand of Ithamar the son of Aaron the priest* — that is, work performed by the Levites under the direction and supervision of Ithamar.

Scripture's purpose in this verse is to inform us that Moses

EXODUS XXXVIII 25

specifically appointed the Levites to keep the accounts of the construction of the Tabernacle — to record the gifts that were brought and the use to which they were put in the course of the work, to draw up a balance sheet, as it were, of the income and expenditure of the whole enterprise — and that he appointed Ithamar the son of Aaron as the head officer in charge of these accounts. Having referred to the Chief of Accounts, the chief officers in charge of the work, who were responsible to Ithamar and to Moses, are

22 also mentioned: *And Bezalel the son of Uri, the son of Hur, of the tribe of Judah, made all that the Lord had commanded Moses*;
23 *and with him*, working and supervising the workers, *was Oholiab, the son of Ahisamach, of the tribe of Dan, a craftsman and designer*, in general, of all types of work, and more particularly *an embroiderer in deep violet and dark red*, etc.

After these introductory remarks, the particulars are given — first and foremost the amount of gold.

24 *All the gold that was used for the work, in all the work of the sanctuary* (in the Hebrew these words form a *casus pendens*, followed by the apodosis beginning with *Wāw*), namely, *the gold of the wave-offering*, which the Israelites had waved [i.e. contributed] (xxxv 22), *was twenty-nine talents and seven hundred and thirty shekels*, the equivalent, since a talent comprised three throusand shekels, of 87,730 shekels. This figure is built up according to the usual method, which we discussed earlier (pp. 86 f., and in my commentary on Genesis, Pt. I, pp. 251–264), that is to say, a basic number related to the sexagesimal system serves as a foundation, to which are added multiples of seven, and sometimes also the half of a round number in accordance with the septimal, decimal or sexagesimal system. Here, too, the figure of the thousands of shekels is based on the sexagesimal system, to wit, six times twelve, plus another dozen, plus half of six ($6 \times 12 + 12 + \frac{6}{2} = 87$), the total being augmented by 700 — a hundred times seven — and another 30 shekels, that is, half the unit of sixty in the sexagesimal system. The number 730, which follows the thousands, occurs also in the census of the Israelites in Numbers xxvi 51. All these shekels refer to *the sacred shekel*, which is the heavy shekel; see on this above, p. 394.

After the gold comes the silver. The amount recorded here is
25 the sum of *the silver of them that were numbered of the congregation*, namely, the half shekels that were given at the time of the Israelites' census, as was stated in xxx 11–16. We are also informed in our

EXODUS XXXVIII 25

chapter, *vv.* 27–28, how this silver was used for the construction of the tabernacle. At this stage, however, two difficult problems arise:

(a) The date of the census of the children of Israel was, according to Numbers i 1, 18, the first day of the second month in the second year of the exodus of the Israelites from the land of Egypt, whereas the Tabernacle was erected, according to Exodus xl 2, 17, on the first day of the first month of that year, that is, a full month before the census. If so, how is it possible that for the work of the Tabernacle, which was already completed before the first month, there was used the silver of the population-count organized in the second month?

(b) Another difficulty is the fact that in *v.* 26 the total of those numbered, 603,550, is mentioned as something already known at the time of the construction of the Tabernacle; but according to Numbers i 46, this figure emerged from the census taken in the second month.

The harmonizing interpretations that have been advanced in order to explain these difficulties (two consecutive numberings, or that new pedestals were made a second time after the census recorded in the Book of Numbers) are improbable; and the division of the passages among different strata of P does not solve the problem, for there still remains the question: How did the final editor understand the matter. The solution must therefore be sought in another direction.

Apparently there was a tradition among the Israelites that the number of the Israelites who went forth from Egypt, which is given only approximately in Exodus xii 37 as *about six hundred thousand*, was more precisely 603,550. This figure is also composed in the manner described earlier: it consists, firstly, of a basic number related to the sexagesimal system (600,000), augmented by two additions, half of 7,000 and half of 100 ($600,000 + \frac{7,000}{2} + \frac{100}{2} = 603,550$); and this tradition, which was widely diffused among the Israelites, forms the basis of verse 26, which cites this figure as a previously known statistic. As for the problem of the dates, this may be solved in the light of the knowledge gained from the documents discovered at Mari (eighteenth century B.C.E.) with regard to the census taken there. These documents show that the organization of a census was not an easy matter accomplished in a single day, but one that required considerable time (see ii Sam. xxiv 8). The officers used to draw up lists of names on clay tablets, and at the end special officials classified and examined the tablets, and on the basis of this information made their calculations and computed the results of the census. The Israelites, in so far as it is possible to determine, did not make use of clay tablets as did the people of Mesopotamia, but employed potsherds (the Ophel ostracon and the list of names on ostracon no. 1 of the Lachish potsherds may be documents of this kind), nevertheless their methods were undoubtedly the same. In view of this, we may assume the purport of the verse to be as follows: In the first year of the exodus of the Israelites from the land of Egypt, at the same time as the artisans were occupied with the construction of the Tabernacle, the first steps were taken in connection with the census. The children of Israel presented themselves one by one before the officers in charge, who registered their names on ostraca and received from each one silver weighing half a shekel. This silver was used for the work of the Tabernacle, for the making of the pedestals. After all the measures requisite to the registration of the Israelites had been taken and after the month of Nisan — the month dedicated to the festival of the erection of the Tabernacle and the Feast of Passover — was ended, work began, on the first day of the second month of the second year, on the classification and examination of the ostraca and the calculation of the figures by the men in charge of these duties, namely, the chieftains of the congregation who are mentioned in Numbers i 4 ff. These tasks were carried out, as is expressly stated *ibid.* (*v.* 2, and elsewhere), *according to the number of names*, that is, by counting the names inscribed on the potsherds. Now although several months had passed since the commencement of the census, and some of those registered had already died, and, on the other hand, a number of young people had, in the meantime reached the age of twenty and had become eligible for inclusion in the population-count, nevertheless the total resulting from the census computations was exactly the same as the number of half shekels that had been contributed in the first year, because the figures were worked out on the basis of ostraca inscribed at the time when the half shekels were handed in.

In this way it is possible to understand the particulars of the verses before us: *And the silver of them that were numbered of the congregation was a hundred talents* — that is, three hundred thousand shekels — *and a thousand seven hundred and seventy-five shekels, according to the sacred shekel.* And this is how this weight of silver was accumulated: *A beka* — half a shekel — *a head*, that is, *half*

a shekel, according to the sacred shekel, was the amount devolving *on every one who passed over to those who were numbered* — that means, on every one who passed before the men who were taking the census, so as to be recorded in the number of the people counted — *from twenty years old and upward* (we have already noted that also in Mari there were recorded in the census only men who had reached military age), *totalling six hundred and three thousand, five hundred and fifty men,* — that is, the known number of 603,550 Israelites. Since each one of them had given half a shekel, the total amount of silver was $\frac{603{,}550}{2}$ shekels, that is to say 301,775 shekels — according to the sacred shekel, of course. Of this sum, 300,000 shekels come to one hundred talents, leaving
27 over 1,775 shekels. *And the hundred talents of silver were* used *for casting the pedestals of the sanctuary* — the ninety-six pedestals for the boards — *and the* four *pedestals of the veil, a hundred pedestals for a hundred talents, a talent for a pedestal* (see above,
28 p. 358). *And of the thousand seven hundred and seventy-five* shekels that were left over *he made hooks for the pillars and overlaid their tops* with the topmost band (*vv.* 17, 19) *and made bands for them* — other bands to go round them.

Here another difficulty may be indicated. In these two verses are enumerated all the silver articles in the Tabernacle, and it is stated that they were all made from the silver of those of the congregation who were numbered. If such be the case, for what purpose was the contribution of silver mentioned earlier, in the account of the bringing of the contributions (xxxv 24), used? However, this problem easily solves itself when we note the fact that there, too, in the narrative relating to the bringing of the contributions, the reference is to the silver of those who were numbered. It is stated *ibid.*: 'Every one who brought a contribution of silver or bronze brought *the Lord's contribution*', and in the paragraph dealing with the silver of the census (xxx 11–16) this silver is specifically called *a contribution to the Lord* or *the Lord's contribution.*

With the specific object of indicating the use to which the census silver was put, Scripture states here expressly what was made of the silver, although in *v.* 24 we are not told what was done with the gold. Having given these details here in connection with the silver, the Torah continues this practice subsequently, too.

29 *And the bronze of the wave-offering* (on this word see xxxv 22) *was seventy talents, and two thousand and four hundred shekels.*

EXODUS XXXIX 2

This figure is mainly based (seventy — ten time seven) on the septenary system, and the addition, 2,400 shekels, belongs to sexagesimal system (600 × 4). The sum-total of the bronze shekels is 212,400, and, if we add it to the 87,730 gold shekels and the 301,775 silver shekels, the aggregate is 601,905 shekels. This figure, too, is built up in the aforementioned manner: it comprises a big number based on the sexagesimal system (600,000), to which are added twice times six hundred, plus seven times one hundred, plus half

30 of ten (600,000 + 1,200 + 700 + $\frac{10}{2}$ = 601, 905). *And therewith* — with the bronze — *he made the pedestals for the door of the tent of*
31 *meeting, the bronze altar*, etc., *and the pedestals of the court round about*, etc. — all the bronze articles of the Tabernacle.

Chapter XXXIX

Just as we are told what was made out of the silver and bronze, so we are also informed of the use made of the materials intended for weaving (here, too, the chapters are wrongly divided; the correct division is that given by the Masorah, which indicates an open
1 section after *v*. 1): *And of the deep violet and dark red and scarlet wool they made the plaited garments for ministering in the holy place* (xxxi 10), *and they made* — of these materials and of flax, as was stated earlier and will again be mentioned later — *the holy garments for Aaron, as the Lord had commanded Moses.*

After referring to the holy garments generally, the Torah deals, in the next paragraph, with each item in detail. The general statement is thus followed by a detailed account.

SIXTEENTH PARAGRAPH

THE PRIESTLY GARMENTS

(XXXIX 2–31)

2-21 Verses 2–21 deal with the Ephod and the Pouch. Here, too, we have only a repetition of what was stated earlier (xxviii 6 ff.); see my commentary *ad locum*. In this passage, also, there are differences like those that occur in the account of the construction of the Tabernacle and its appurtenances:

(a) Changes of form: for example, in xxviii 7 we find 'two shoulder-pieces', but here only *shoulder-pieces*; in the earlier passage, *ibid*., קְצוֹתָיו וְחֻבָּר *qᵉṣōthāw wᵉḥubbār* ['its edges, that it may be

473

joined together'], but in our passage קצוותיו *qṣwwthyw* (the *Qᵉrē* [the Masoretic reading and vocalization] is קְצוֹתָיו *qᵉṣōthāw*; see p. 464) חֻבָּר *ḥubbār* ['(at) its (two) edges was it joined']; there (*loc. cit.*) *v.* 8, כְּמַעֲשֵׂהוּ מִמֶּנּוּ יִהְיֶה *kᵉmaʿăśēhū mimmennū yihᵉye* ['(shall be) like the work thereof, of it (i.e. of the same piece) shall it be'], but here, מִמֶּנּוּ הוּא כְּמַעֲשֵׂהוּ *mimmennū hū kᵉmaʿăśēhū* ['was of it (i.e. of the same piece) like the work thereof']; in *v.* 9 of our chapter are added the words *they made the pouch*, and also the word *double* at the end; and other variations of the same kind.

(b) Changes due to the fact that here only the execution of the work, and nothing more, is narrated. Before the words *the work of the designer*, which occur at the end of xxviii 6, there is added here, in *v.* 3, an explanation of the technique employed for the weaving of gold threads in with those of wool and flax. *And they hammered out sheets of gold* — that is to say, by beating with a hammer they flattened out the gold until they made thereof thin leaves (פַּחִים *paḥīm*) — *and one cut threads* — that is, they cut up the leaves, making of them fine wires like threads or narrow strips — *to make* — to work and weave them — *into the deep violet and dark red and scarlet wool, and fine linen*. The subject-matter of xxviii 9–11 appears in *v.* 6 of our chapter in an abridged form that suffices to explain what was done by the craftsmen. Similarly, the content of 12a in the earlier passage is given in a shorter version here in *v.* 7; whilst *vv.* 13–14 there are summarized here in a few words at the beginning of *v.* 16. Verses 12b and 29–30 in ch. xxviii, which refer not to the making of the articles but to the manner in which they were worn, are not repeated here. At the end of the description of the ephod (*v.* 7) and of the pouch (*v.* 21) there is added in this chapter, *as the Lord had commanded Moses*, in order to stress that everything was done in conformity with the Divine injunction, as had already been stated in general terms in *v.* 1. A similar ending occurs later on, when Scripture speaks of the other sacred vestments.

22-26 Verses 22–26, which deal with the Robe, reproduce xxviii 31–35; see my annotations *ad locum*. Likewise here we find variations of form; for example, *the work of the weaver* occurs there in the second verse [*v.* 32], and here in the first verse [*v.* 21]; there in *v.* 33 we read 'its skirts', here in *v.* 24 *the skirts of the robe*; and similar variants. In the present case, too, we have an example of an abridged description; compare *v.* 23 here with *v.* 32 there, which is more detailed. Also here the text does not iterate the concluding verse

EXODUS XXXIX 31

of the instruction (*ibid. v.* 35), which refers to the manner of using it, but cites only the general term *for ministering*. Again we have here the ending, *As the Lord had commanded Moses*, as in *v.* 7 and in *v.* 21.

27-29 The other woven garments of the priests are enumerated in *vv.* 27–29, before mention is made of the plate and contrary to the order followed in the section containing the instructions, because here, in the account of the making of the articles, there was no need to make any distinction between Aaron's vestments and those of his sons; thus all the woven garments are taken together, and described seriatim.

Here, also, the narrative is condensed, and only one particular, appertaining to the making of the sash, is added (*v.* 29): *of fine twined linen and deep violet and dark red and scarlet wool, the work of the embroiderer*. In this passage, too, the details of the order of service and the consecration of the priests (xxviii 41, 43) are omitted; *v.* 42 [*ibid.*] is one of those abridged here. The ending of *v.* 29 [of our chapter] is the same as that with which the description of each of the priestly vestments concludes.

30-31 Finally, after the account of the making of the woven garments has been completed, the text deals with the gold plate. Chapter xxviii 36–37 is repeated here *mutatis mutandis*; see my commentary *ad locum*. A new feature, however, is introduced here, namely, the designation of the plate as *the holy diadem*; see on this appellation my note on the parallel passage. Instead of the verb פִּתַּח *pittaḥ* ['engrave'] we have here the synonym כָּתַב *kāthabh* ['write']. In *v.* 31 there is repeated, in an abridged form, the more elaborate statement of xxviii 37. The difference between וַיִּתְּנוּ עָלָיו פְּתִיל תְּכֵלֶת *wayyittᵉnū ʿālāw pᵉthīl tᵉkhēleth* ['And they gave upon it [i.e. attached to it] a lace of deep violet'] (*v.* 31 of our chapter) and וְשַׂמְתָּ אֹתוֹ עַל פְּתִיל תְּכֵלֶת *wᵉśamtā ʾōthō ʿal pᵉthīl tᵉkhēleth* ['And you shall put it on a lace of deep violet'] (xxviii 37) is, according to the actual sense of the text, only a variation of form (the haggadic interpretation is well known), for the word עַל *ʿal* has not the literal signification of 'above', but simply connotes proximity. Since *v.* 38 in the earlier section deals with the ritual purpose of the plate, it is not repeated here. The ending of *v.* 31 is identical with the wording found at the conclusion of the preceding passages.

SEVENTEENTH PARAGRAPH

COMPLETION OF THE WORK

(XXXIX 32)

32 At this point the account of the construction of the Tabernacle is brought to a close with a formal ending: *Thus all the work of the tabernacle of the tent of meeting* (the two synonymous expressions standing in juxtaposition serve to stress the formal solemnity of the statement) *was finished*. Here, and still more later, the language of the text recalls the conclusion of the story of Creation. In the narrative portraying how God formed the universe, the Bible ends with the words (Gen. ii 1–2): 'Thus the heavens and the earth were finished and all the host of them. And since God was finished... with His work', etc.; and here, when the Torah recounts how the sanctuary of God was made by man, the text concludes: 'Thus all the work... was finished', etc. Other parallels to the work of Creation, which are clearer still, will be noted later on.

The wording of the conclusion of this final paragraph is fuller and more stately than the parallel formulations in the earlier paragraphs: *and the children of Israel did according to all that the Lord commanded Moses, so they did* (compare Gen. vi 22, etc.). The *children of Israel* as a whole are mentioned here, because the artisans did their work on behalf of the entire people, and with materials that had been given them from the offerings of all the people.

EIGHTEENTH PARAGRAPH

THE WORK IS BROUGHT TO MOSES

(XXXIX 33–43)

33-41 *And* the workmen *brought*, in the name of all the Israelites, *the tabernacle to Moses: the tent and all its furnishings*, etc. From this verse as far as *v.* 41, there is repeated the list of articles recorded earlier, in a shorter version, in xxxi 7–11, and again, in a more complete form, in xxxv 11–19. The duplication of lists of this kind is common in the epic poetry of the ancient East, and it represents one of the characteristic features of the literary tradition of the

Orient. The list here is almost identical with that of chapter xxxv; the differences are only few and slight, and also the order of the subject-matter varies but little, at the beginning. The covering of the tent, which was mentioned only briefly in chapter xxxv (v. 11: *and its covering*) is here depicted in great detail (v. 34: *and the covering of rams' skins dyed red and the covering of dugong skins*), and on account of the fullness of this description it was necessary to make prior mention of *its clasps, its boards* (קְרָסָיו קְרָשָׁיו $q^e r\bar{a}s\bar{a}w\ q^e\bar{a}rš\bar{a}w$; note the word-play!), etc. *The veil of the screen* (v. 34, end) precedes here the ark (v. 35). Thereafter the order is identical in all its details with that of chapter xxxv. Our passage contains the following additions — v. 33: *and all its furnishings* (i.e. of the tent); v. 40: *and all the furnishings for the service of the tabernacle*, which belonged *to the tent of meeting*. These are general expressions that serve to include everything, even small articles not warranting detailed enumeration. A new term appearing here is *lamps of the order* (v. 37), that is, the lamps set in proper order on the branches of the lampstand; compare above, xxvii 21: 'shall set it in order', (namely, the perpetual lamp, in a collective sense); similarly Leviticus xxiv 3: 'shall set it in order'; *ibid.*, v. 4: 'He shall set the lamps in order'; Psalms cxxxii 17: 'I have set in order a lamp for my anointed.' On the change in the gender of the pronominal suffixes in v. 40, אֶת־מֵיתָרָיו וִיתֵדוֹתֶיהָ *'eth mēthārāw wīthēdhōthehā* [literally, '*his* cords and *her* pegs'], see above, on xxxv 17.

At the end of the list, the Torah again indicates that everything included in it was made in conformity with the Divine instruction:

42 *According to all that the Lord commanded Moses, so the children of Israel had done all the work.*

The last verse forms another parallel with the narrative in the Book of Genesis relating to the completion of the creation of the
43 world: *And Moses saw all the work and behold they had done it as the Lord had commanded; so had they done it.* Compare Genesis i 31: 'And God saw everything that He had made, and behold, it was very good.'

And Moses blessed them: compare Genesis i 22, 28: 'And God blessed them'; *ibid.*, ii 3: 'So God blessed the seventh day.' We shall point to another parallelism later on, when we come to xl 33.

NINETEENTH PARAGRAPH

THE COMMAND TO ERECT THE TABERNACLE

(XL 1–16)

Chapter XL

1 All the components of the Tabernacle, its furniture and its utensils are ready for use, and each one of them has been duly delivered to Moses. The time has now arrived to put the parts together and to set up the Tabernacle properly. After reading so many unrelated paragraphs, which show us each item as a separate and independent entity, we now wait for the process of dissection to be followed by one of integration, and we hope to be given an overall picture that will unify all the various elements into one whole structure, in which each constituent will occupy the place due to it and befitting its function. This complete view is now vouchsafed us in the last chapter of the Book.

The chapter is composed in accordance with the technique frequently employed in various Biblical sections, and, in general, in the literary tradition of the ancient East: one paragraph tells of the Divine injunction and the next records its implementation.

2 God's command commences: *On the first day of the first month* — the beginning of the new year, when you enter upon a new period of your life, will also mark the inception for you of a new epoch in the Lord's service. On that day *you shall erect the tabernacle of the tent of meeting*, after which the Tabernacle will be ready for the celebration in it of the festival dedicated to the commemoration of the exodus from Egypt.

Verses 3–8 recapitulate, in broad outline, as befits a final summation, the instructions given to Moses at the beginning concerning each component and furnishing of the tabernacle. First of all, the

3 holiest article, is mentioned: *And you shall put there* — inside the Tabernacle — *the ark of the testimony* (xxvi 33), the ark in which the tables of the testimony are kept. In conformity with the brevity of style that characterizes our paragraph, even this slight allusion to the tablets is adequate, just as the term 'ark' suffices to include also the *kappōreth* (see the end of my commentary on xxv 20). *And you shall cover* [וְסַכֹּתָ֥ wᵉsakkōthā] *the ark with the veil* — you shall hang in front of the ark the veil that will screen it. In the Samaritan Pentateuch and in several Hebrew manuscripts, the

EXODUS XL 9

reading here is: 'and you shall cover the ark with the *kappōreth*' [substituting the latter word for פָּרֹכֶת *pārōkheth*, 'veil']. At first glance this reading would appear to be correct, but only at first glance, because subsequently, in the account of the execution of this command, it is stated: 'and set up the veil of the screen, and screened [וַיָּסֶךְ *wayyāsekh*] the ark of the testimony' [*v*. 21]. Furthermore, it was not possible for reference to the veil to have been omitted here, whilst the *kappōreth* was included, as we explained, in the term 'ark'. Corresponding to what was stated in detail earlier (xxvi 35), mention is made in *v*. 4, also with extreme brevity, of

4 the table and the lampstand: *And you shall bring* into the Tabernacle *the table, and set in order* — at the proper time, of course, after the Tabernacle has been completely erected — *its arrangement* — the bread of the Presence (xxv 30) — *and you shall bring in the lampstand, and light* [or *set up*] — when the Tabernacle is fully erected — *its lamps. And you shall put the golden altar for incense*

5 *before the ark of the testimony* — as stated in xxx 6 — *and set up the screen of the entrance of the tabernacle* — as indicated in xxvi 36.

6 *And you shall place the altar of burnt offering before the entrance of the tabernacle of the tent of meeting* — that is to say, in the court (the position of the altar was not defined earlier, in the relevant paragraph, xxvii 1–8, but it can be inferred there from the context,

7 as I noted at the end of my commentary on that passage). *And you shall place the laver between the tent of meeting and the altar* (here, too, the location is stated, as it was explicitly specified in xxx 18), *and put water in it*. Finally, there is a brief reference to the court

8 and screen at its gate: *And you shall set up the court round about, and hang up the screen of the gate of the court.*

Even when the tabernacle has been duly erected and put in order, it will still not be deemed the sanctuary of the Lord until a special ceremony of consecration has been performed by anointing it with the oil of anointment. On the significance of this ceremony and on the manner of carrying it out, see my observations

9 above, on xxx 22 ff. *And you shall take* — upon completing the erection of the Tabernacle — *the anointing oil, and anoint the tabernacle and all that is in it, and consecrate it and all its furniture* by this anointment, *and it* — the Tabernacle with all its furnishings — *shall become*, from that moment, a *holy* thing. The inner vessels were included in the expression *and all that is in it*, and there was no need, therefore, to enumerate them all individually; but the case of the outer vessels was different, for they were not *in it* — in

10 the Tabernacle — and hence they are mentioned in detail: *And you shall anoint the altar of the burnt offering and all its utensils, and consecrate the altar; and the altar shall be most holy.* It, too, shall be most holy like the inner vessels; the point is specifically stated so that none should think that since its place was outside the Tabernacle, its sanctity was of a lower order. Similarly, Moses
11 must anoint the laver and its base: *And you shall anoint the laver and its base, and consecrate it.*

The consecration of the tabernacle is to be followed by that of its ministers, Aaron and his sons. The ritual of this consecration will comprise three stages. The first is the same for all the priests:
12 *And you shall bring Aaron and his sons to the entrance of the tent of meeting, and wash them with water.* The second phase, the clothing with the priestly vestments, is different for Aaron, since
13 there are special garments that he alone must wear: *And you shall put upon Aaron the holy garments.* Similarly the third stage, that of the anointing, which is the central rite of the consecration, is not identical for all; Aaron alone is anointed for the high-priesthood (on this difference see above, on xxviii 41): *and you shall anoint him and consecrate him, that he may serve Me as a priest.* Thereafter the Torah enumerates the three phases of the consecration of Aaron's sons: first, brief mention is again made of bringing
14 them to the entrance of the tent of meeting, *And you shall bring his sons*; regarding the second stage it is stated, *and put tunics on them*, since these alone were their priestly vestments; at the end,
15 reference is made to the anointing of the ordinary priests, *And you shall anoint them, as you anointed their father, that they may serve Me as priests*. And concerning all of them, both Aaron and his sons, it is said: *and it* — this act — *shall be* conducive to the end *that their anointing shall be to them for an everlasting priesthood throughout their generations*, that means to say, that by virtue of this ceremony their anointing would be a token of everlasting priesthood to them and their children and their children's children after them.

The paragraph concludes with the customary formula employed
16 to indicate that the Divine commands were carried out: *Thus Moses did according to all that the Lord had commanded him; so he did.* After this general statement, the particulars of the fulfilment of the injunctions mentioned in vv. 2–8 will be recorded in the next paragraph. Regarding the execution of the instructions cited in vv. 9–15 nothing is said in the coming paragraph (which ends

with the completion of the work of setting up the tabernacle), since these were fulfilled subsequently, and the account of the ceremonies will be given elsewhere. The story of Moses' anointing the Tabernacle and all its vessels will be told in its proper context in Numbers vii 1, and the account of his anointing and consecrating Aaron and his sons will be given in its due place in the section of the Installation of the Priests in the Book of Leviticus viii 6 ff.

TWENTIETH PARAGRAPH

THE ERECTION OF THE TABERNACLE

(XL 17-33)

In this paragraph is recounted, as we stated above, how Moses carried out the commandments he was given regarding the erection of the Tabernacle. In accordance with the usual practice, the wording corresponds to that of the directions.

Verse 17 parallels *v.* 2; it begins with the expression, *And it came to pass*, which indicates that on the day specified by the Lord it happened as He had said (compare, for example, Gen. vii 10;
17 Exod. xix 16): *And it came to pass in the first month in the second year, on the first day of the month, that the tabernacle was erected*—entirely as was stated in *v.* 2, almost word for word. After this general parallelism the particulars are given in separate, successive passages, and their formulation corresponds not only to the abridged directions contained in *vv.* 3-8, but also to the detailed instructions set forth earlier, in chapter xxv ff. At the end of each passage is reiterated, like an echo reverberating seven times, *as the Lord commanded Moses*. Moses' name occurs expressly, as the subject of the verbs, once at the beginning (*v.* 18: *And Moses erected*) and once at the end (*v.* 33: *So Moses finished*). All the other verbs are impersonal in form ('and laid', 'and set up', 'and raised up', 'and spread', etc.), but the subject, even though not stated, is self-evident; it is always Moses. He directed the whole enterprise, and to him belongs the merit.

Following are the seven subsections that conclude with the stereotyped formula, *as the Lord commanded Moses*:
18 (1) *And Moses erected the tabernacle*; here the word *tabernacle* is used primarily in its restricted sense, namely, the curtains of deep

481

violet and dark red and scarlet wool and fine twined linen. In the first place *he laid its pedestals* upon the ground; then *he set up on the pedestals its boards, and put in its bars*, which held the boards fast, *and raised up its pillars*, but not yet in their exact position, so that the ark could be taken through between them (see above, p. 360); they would be put in their correct place when the veil of the screen would be hung upon them (v. 21). Over all this Moses

19 stretched out the curtains of the tabernacle. Thereafter *he spread the tent* — that is, the curtains of goats' hair — *over the curtains of the tabernacle, and put the covering of the tent* — the covering of rams' skins dyed red — *on top of it*, etc. (Regarding the dugong skins, see my annotations above, on xxvi 14). All this corresponds to v. 2 and to what was stated in detail in chapter xxvi.

20 (2) *And he took and put the testimony into the ark* — in conformity with xxv 16, 21 — *and set the poles on the ark* — in agreement with xxv 14 — *and put the kappōreth on top of the ark* — in accordance

21 with xxv 21 — *and he brought the ark into the tabernacle, and set up the veil of the screen, and screened the ark of the testimony*, etc.

22 (3) *And he put the table in the tent of meeting, on the north side of the tabernacle, outside the veil* — corresponding to v. 4 and xxvi

23 35 — *and set the bread in order on it before the Lord* — in agreement with v. 4 ('and set in order its arrangement') and with xxv 30.

24 (4) *And he put the lampstand in the tent of meeting, opposite the table on the south side of the tabernacle* — conforming to v. 4 and

25 xxvi 35. *And he lighted* [or, *set up*] *the lamps before the Lord* — as enjoined in xxv 37. Needless to say, this was not done as soon as the lampstand was put in its place, but after the completion of the erection and consecration of the Tabernacle. The verb is impersonal and it signifies, 'the kindler kindled' [or, 'the lamp-setter set the lamps up']. It thus includes both Moses, who ministered as a priest until the last day of the installation, and Aaron, who kindled the lights after his induction. Evidence that Moses also is implied can be found in v. 31; see my note *ad locum*.

26 (5) *And he put the golden altar in the tent of meeting before the*
27 *veil* — in accord with v. 5 and xxx 6; *and he burnt on it incense of spices*, etc. — paralleling xxx 7. What we stated with regard to the subject of *kindled* [or, *set up*] in v. 25 applies with equal force to the subject of the verb *burnt*.

28 (6) *And he put in place the screen of the entrance of the tabernacle* —
29 in accord with v. 5 — *And the altar of burnt offering he set at the entrance of the tabernacle of the tent of meeting* — in agreement

with *v.* 6; *and offered* — whoever offered; the construction is the same as in the case of *kindled* [or, *set up*] in *v.* 25 — *the burnt offering and the meal offering,* etc.

30 (7) *And he set the laver between the tent of meeting and the altar, and put water in it for washing* — corresponding to *v.* 7 and xxx 18.

31 *And Moses and Aaron and his sons shall wash* — so that they should wash — *their hands and their feet from it.* This verse repeats almost verbatim what was stated in xxx 19, adding however, the name of Moses to 'Aaron and his sons', who form the subject of the earlier verse, because during the period of installation, before Aaron and his sons entered upon their ministry in the holy place, Moses served as a priest, and he, too, had to wash his hands and feet before approaching the sanctuary to perform his ministrations.

32 *When they come into the tent of meeting, and when they draw near to the altar, they shall wash,* etc. — as stated in xxx 20.

The last verse, which lacks the usual concluding formula because
33 it has another ending, speaks of the court: *And he erected the court round the tabernacle and the altar* — in conformity with the beginning of *v.* 8 — *and set up the screen of the gate of the court* — in accordance with the end of *v.* 8.

Finally comes the closing sentence: *So Moses finished the work,* in which, too, is discernible a parallelism with the story of Creation (Gen. ii 2): 'And since God was finished on the seventh day with His work which He had done.'

CONCLUSION OF THE SECTION

AND THE BOOK

(XL 34–38)

The Tabernacle was erected. The children of Israel had constructed in the midst of their camp a sanctuary to the Lord their God, in accordance with the injunction that was delivered to Moses (xxv 8): 'And let them make Me a sanctuary.' Here, immediately after the description of the setting up of the Tabernacle, it is narrated that the promise given to Moses in the very next words following this command, to wit, 'that I may dwell in their midst', and which was confirmed at the end of the Divine communication (xxix 45), 'And I will dwell among the children of Israel', is now receiving

EXODUS XL 34

fulfilment: the Lord causes His Divine Presence to dwell among the children of Israel.

These verses, which are phrased in an elevated, poetic style, depict the manifestation of the Divine Glory in expressions that parallel those used at the end of chapter xxiv to portray God's presence on Mount Sinai. The Tabernacle is a kind of miniature Sinai, which can be transported from place to place, in order to accompany the children of Israel in their wanderings and to serve as a palpable token of the Divine Presence in their midst throughout their journeyings. Just as the Lord had revealed Himself to them on Mount Sinai in the awe-inspiring theophany of the third month, even so He manifests Himself to them now, and will reveal Himself in the future, in the sanctuary that they have made to Him.

Verse 34 is clearly poetic in structure (2:2 // 2:2), its two parts corresponding to each other in conformity with the laws of poetic

34 parallelism. *Then the cloud covered the tent of meeting, and the glory of the Lord filled the tabernacle* — entirely like the theophany on Mount Sinai: 'and the cloud covered the mountain; and the glory

35 of the Lord dwelt upon Mount Sinai' (xxiv 15–16). *And Moses was not able to enter the tent of meeting, | because the cloud abode upon it, | and the glory of the Lord filled the tabernacle.* Between the first two parts of this verse there is a parallelism similar to that in the preceding verse, while the last clause solemnly repeats the concluding words of the previous verse. With regard to the Revelation on Mount Sinai it is stated that only after the cloud had covered the mountain six days did the Lord call to Moses on the seventh day out of the midst of the cloud (xxiv 16), that means to say, that Moses was unable to ascend to the top of the mountain and to enter into the cloud until the Lord called to him. Similarly we are told here that Moses could not come into the tent of meeting on account of the Divine Presence that dwelt in it, until the Lord called him, as we are told at the beginning of the volume following the Book of Exodus (Leviticus i 1): 'The Lord called to Moses and spoke to him from the tent of meeting saying', etc.

These verses are the source of what is stated in i Kings viii 10–11, in the account of the dedication of the Temple at Jerusalem: 'And when the priests came out of the holy place, a cloud filled the house of the Lord, so that the priests could not stand to minister because of the cloud; for the glory of the Lord filled the house of the Lord.'

Since it is said here that the cloud abode upon the Tabernacle,

Scripture proceeds to recount how this cloud used to lead the people continually during their wanderings in the wilderness and direct them when to journey and when to encamp. This subject will be referred to again at length in Numbers ix, but it was necessary to allude to it also here, in order to link it with the first theophany in the Tabernacle, and to emphasize that this Divine revelation was not unique, but a recurring phenomenon. In parallelism with this allusion there occurs in Numbers ix, in the detailed description of the manifestation of the cloud during Israel's journey through the desert, a reference to its first appearance on the day when the Tabernacle was set up (*ibid.*, v. 15).

Also the verses dealing with this theme are written in an exalted,
36 poetic style: *And when the cloud lifted from the tabernacle, the children of Israel would set out* (the imperfect tense here has a frequentative meaning, signifying that the action was oft-times
37 repeated) *throughout all their journeys; but if the cloud did not lift, they would not set out till the day that it did lift.* Thus it happened
38 continually; *for*, as the pillar of cloud by day and the pillar of fire by night showed the Israelites the way during the exodus from Egypt, so *the cloud of the Lord was upon the tabernacle by day, and there was fire in it by night, in the sight of all the house of Israel, throughout all their journeys.* The last words of this verse parallel those of *v.* 36, and reverberate like a final echo of what was narrated previously in xiii 21–22. With this echo, and with this allusion oriented towards the future, the passage closes — a fitting and noble ending to the Book.

ABBREVIATIONS

AANAL	*Atti della Accademia Nazionale dei Lincei*
AASOR	*Annual of the American Schools of Oriental Research*
AJA	*American Journal of Archaeology*
AJSL	*American Journal of Semitic Languages and Literatures*
ANET	J. B. Pritchard (ed.) *Ancient Near Eastern Texts, relating to the Old Testament*, 2nd ed., Princeton 1955
ARI	W. F. Albright, *Archaeology and the Religion of Israel*, Baltimore 1942
BAr	*Biblical Archaeologist*
BASOR	*Bulletin of the American Schools of Oriental Research*
BDB	F. Brown, S. R. Driver and C. A. Briggs, *A Hebrew and English Lexicon of the Old Testament*... based on the Lexicon of W. Gesenius
BIES	*Bulletin of the Israel Exploration Society* (In Hebrew)
BRL	K. Galling, *Biblisches Reallexikon*, Tübingen 1957
E.V.	English Version(s) of the O.T.
FSAC	W.F. Albright. *From Stone Age to Christianity*, Baltimore 1940.
HUCA	*Hebrew Union College Annual*
JBL	*Journal of Biblical Literature*
P	*Priestly Code*
PEF QS	*Palestine Exploration Fund, Quarterly Statement*
PEQ	*Palestine Exploration Quarterly*
RB	*Revue Biblique*
ZAW	*Zeitschrift für die alttestamentliche Wissenchaft*
ZDPV	*Zeitschrift des deutschen Palästina–Vereins*

BIBLIOGRAPHICAL NOTES
AND ADDENDA*

It is not the purpose of these notes to mention all the books that I have laid under tribute, nor even a small fraction of them; a complete bibliography — indeed, even a selected book list — would have lengthened the volume unduly. It is only with regard to those parts of my commentary that contain brief allusions requiring explanation or justification or proof that I have given references here with a view to meeting these requirements.

I have also added here and there in the following pages a few supplementary observations to the annotations in my commentary.

p. 7 (i 1). On the associations of tribes or amphictyonies see especially, M. Noth, *Das System der zwölf Stämme Israels*, Stuttgart 1930.

p. 11 (i 11). The identification of Raamses with Zoan of Egypt won the consensus of scholarly opinion after the evidence advanced by P. Montet in his book *Les nouvelles fouilles de Tanis*, Paris 1933, and in his essay in the periodical *Syria* 17 (1936), pp. 200–202; see: W. F. Albright, *FSAC*, p. 194; *idem.*, *BASOR* 109 (1948), p. 15. On the identification of Pithom see Albright, *ibid.* Cf. further on the whole problem: B. Couroyer, *RB* 53 (1946), pp. 75–98.

p. 13 (i 15). On 'the Hebrew slaves' in the Nuzu documents: J. Lewy, *HUCA* 14 (1939), pp. 587–623.

p. 14 (i 16). On the Egyptian representations of the god Khnum, who formed human beings on the potter's wheel, see my article in the *Encyclopaedia Biblica* [Hebrew], I, pp. 58–59, and the illustration *ibid.*, p. 58.

p. 18 (ii 3). On the use of bitumen and pitch: R. J. Forbes, *Bitumen and Petroleum in Antiquity*, Leiden 1936, pp. 8–9, 85–87.

p. 44 (iii 22). On 'the jewels of silver, and jewels of gold, and raiment' see my book, *La Questione della Genesi*, pp. 240–241.

p. 68 (v 7). On the method of making bricks in Egypt: A. Lucas, *Ancient Egyptian Materials and Industries*[3], London 1948, p. 62.

p. 72 (v 19). On the allusion to the Egyptian god *Re'*: S. Rosenblatt, *JBL*, 60 (1941), pp. 183–185.

p. 93. The division of the sequence of the plagues according to the

---

* The bibliographical notes and addenda are reproduced here in the form in which they appeared in 1951, when the book was first published. No attempt has been made to bring them up to date, since it is felt that this is a task that only the author, had he lived, could properly have performed. *Tr.*

change of meeting-place (outside Pharaoh's palace; inside the palace; the place unstated) has now been suggested also in the book by F. V. Winnett, *The Mosaic Tradition*, Toronto 1949, pp. 3–15. In a review of this book (*Theol. Rundschau* 18 [1950], pp. 267–287) this suggestion was rejected by O. Eissfeldt, who still favours the prevailing method of source analysis.

p. 103 (viii 9 [Heb., v. 5]). See Tur-Sinai, *Lāšōn wāSēpher* [Hebrew], I, pp. 364–365.

p. 106 (viii 19 [Heb., v. 15]). On 'the finger of *Aširat*' see W. F. Albright, *BASOR* 94 (1944), p. 18.

p. 112 (ix 8). On the firing of bricks in Egypt: A. Lucas, *op. cit.*, pp. 63–64.

p. 133 (xi 7). On another interpretation of the verb יֶחֱרַץ *yeḥĕraṣ* [rendered in the Commentary, 'whet'] see Tur-Sinai, *Lāšōn wāSēpher*, [Hebrew], I, p. 347.

p. 156 (xiii 18). On the view that the route taken by the Israelites when they left Egypt is to be located in the north, along the Mediterranean seaboard, see in particular: O. Eissfeldt, *Baal Zaphon, Zeus Kasios, und der Durchzug der Israeliten durchs Meer*, Halle 1932.

pp. 159, 167 ff. On the identification of the Sea of Reeds and the meaning of its division, see the aforementioned book by Eissfeldt, and the articles that advance a different view, such as: C. Bourdon, *RB* 61 (1932), pp. 370–392; Th. Robinson, *ZAW* 51 (1933), pp. 171–173. Cf. also M. Noth, 'Der Schauplatz des Meereswunders', *Eissfeldt-Festschrift*, Halle 1947, pp. 181–190. The author agrees with Eissfeldt's conjecture, but considers that this was how the parting of the sea was described only in the late tradition, whereas the early tradition had in mind the Gulf of ʿAqaba.

p. 182 (xv 20). On the word מְחוֹלוֹת *mᵉḥōlōth* see Tur-Sinai, *Lāšōn wāSēpher* [Hebrew], I, pp. 342–343; II, p. 365, note 22.

p. 184 (xv 25). On the testimony of travellers, see Holzinger's commentary, p. 56.

p. 195 (xvi 14) see: F. S. Bodenheimer, *BAr* 10 (1947), pp. 2–6.

p. 203 (xvii 6). On the account of the occurrence at Jebel Musa, see Holzinger's commentary, p. 60; in regard to the second story, see C. S. Jarvis, *PEQ* 1938, pp. 35–36.

p. 206 (xvii 14). On the meaning of the word סֵפֶר *sēpher* here, see H. S. Gehman, *JBL* 63 (1949), pp. 303–307.

p. 225 (xix 2). On the various theories concerning the identification of Mount Sinai, see the commentary by Beer, pp. 25–26.

pp. 235 ff. Concerning the different views expressed on the question of the Decalogue, see my article דִּבְּרוֹת הַדִּבְּרוֹת, עֲשֶׂרֶת, *Dibberōth*, *'Ăsereth Haddibberoth* in *Encyclopaedia Biblica* [Hebrew], II, and the detailed bibliography *ibid*.

p. 244 (xx 8). On the Sabbath and its antecedents in the civilization of the ancient East, see my observations in my book *From Adam To Noah*, pp. 61–70, and the bibliography given there, pp. 18–19; cf. now the essay of Tur-Sinai in *Bibliotheca Orientalis* 8 (1951), pp. 14–24.

p. 255 (xx 24). On the altar of Megiddo see G. Loud, *Megiddo* II, Text, Chicago 1948, figs. 164–165.

p. 257 ff. When I wrote my commentary it was my intention to provide a detailed bibliography for each collection of laws of the ancient East, but this is superfluous now, for in the meantime there was published the anthology, *Ancient Near Eastern Texts relating to the Old Testament*, edited by James B. Pritchard, Princeton 1950, where the reader can find a complete translation of all the legal texts and bibliographical information bearing on them, which should, however, be supplemented by the following:

(a) Another fragment from the laws of Lipit-Ishtar: F. R. Steele, 'An Additional Fragment of the Lipit-Ishtar Code Tablet from Nippur', *Archiv Orientální* 18, No. 1–2 (1950), pp. 489–493.

(b) A new edition of the code of Ḥammurabi: *Codex Hammurabi, Transcriptio et versio latina* (A. Deimel), editio tertia denuo retractata, auctoribus A. Pohl S. J., R. Follet S. J., Romae 1950.

(c) A few other publications that will be of interest to the reader: M. David, 'The Codex Hammurabi and its Relations to the Provisions of Law in Exodus', *Oudtestamentische Studiën* 7 (1950), pp. 149–178; E. Neufeld, *The Hittite Laws*, translated into English and Hebrew with Commentary, London 1951; P. Artzi, 'Two Pre-Hammurabi Codes Newly Discovered', *BIES XVI*, 1–2 (1951), pp. 30–37. [Hebrew; also English summary].

pp. 259 ff. Views approximating in part to my own in regard to the Pentateuchal statutes were expressed in a book by M. Noth, *Die Gesetze im Pentateuch, ihre Voraussetzungen und ihr Sinn*, Halle 1940. He is of the opinion that the Torah laws were not laws of the monarchy but of the sacred amphictyony of the Israelite tribes. It is impossible, however, to concur in his view that the kings of Israel and Judah promulgated no laws. The religious character of the Pentateuchal precepts is also emphasized by J. van der Ploeg, *The Catholic Biblical Quarterly* 13 (1951), pp. 164–169. But he considers that they also include non-religious statutes.

BIBLIOGRAPHICAL NOTES

pp. 270 f. (xxi 16). My friend Dr. J. J. Rabinowitz (in private conversation) suggested that the words 'or is found in his possession' be interpreted as a reference tho the manner of attesting the theft by means of witnesses who saw the perpetration of the crime, as the Talmudic sages declared: 'Wherever the term "finding" is used it refers to attestation by witnesses.' He finds support for this view in the parallel passage (Deut. xxiv 7): 'If a man is found stealing one of his brethren, the children of Israel, and if he treats him as a slave or sells him, then that thief shall die.' It may be added that the term 'finding' occurs also in the Hittite laws with reference to kidnapping (clause 19). Possibly we have here a stylistic tradition in legal language.

p. 273 (xxi 20–21). The words נָקֹם יִנָּקֵם *nāqōm yinnāqēm* [literally, 'he shall surely suffer vengeance'; rendered: 'he shall surely be punished'] (v. 20) and [לֹא] יֻקַּם [*lō'*] *yuqqam* [literally, 'he is not to suffer vengeance'; rendered: 'he is not to be punished'] (v. 21) are apparently relics of the ancient language that survived as verbal 'fossils' from the era in which blood-vengeance was customary, and are comparable to the linguistic survivals that I have indicated on p. 268 f. (שְׁאֵרָהּ *šeʾērāh* ['her food'; literally, 'her flesh']) and on p. 272 (אֶבֶן *ʾebhen* [literally, 'stone', i.e. weapon]). Here, undoubtedly, the reference is to sentence of death passed by the court, for blood-vengeance, which a man takes in hot anger (Deut. xix 6), is not a matter that is subject to legal provisions.

p. 305 (xxiii 19). See my article '*Gedhī baḥălēbh ʾimmō*', *Encyclopaedia Biblica* [Hebrew], II, and the comprehensive bibliography there.

p. 309 (xxiii 31). See Tur-Sinai, *Lešōnēnū* [Hebrew], X, (1939), pp. 30–39.

pp. 319 f. On new views with regard to the Tabernacle, see: W. F. Albright, *FSAC*, p. 203; F. M. Cross, *BAr* 10 (1947), pp. 45–68.

p. 329 (xxv 11). On the techniques of overlaying wooden articles with gold, see A. Lucas, *op. cit.*, pp. 492–493.

p. 331 (xxv 16). On the letter of Ramses II see H. Torczyner [Tur-Sinai], *Die Bundeslade*[1], pp. 37–38; and his article '*Ārōn, Encyclopaedia Biblica* [Hebrew], I, p. 542.

pp. 332 f. (xxv 19). On the cherubim see the bibliography cited in my book, *From Adam To Noah*, p. 174–176.

p. 338 (xxv 24). For examples of Egyptian tables, adorned by a hieroglyphic inscription on the frame surrounding their surface, see: Schäfer-Andrae, *Die Kunst des alten Orients*, 6–10. Tausend, Berlin s.a., p. 269 (top, left side); p. 311 (below, right side); p. 416 (top). For a new discovery of this kind cf. *Orientalia* 19 (1950), Tab. 39.

p. 341, lines 6–15. On candelabra with seven spouts, see, for instance:

BIBLIOGRAPHICAL NOTES

E. Sellin, *Eine Nachlese aus dem Tell Ta'annek in Palästina*, Wien 1905, Abb. 19; W.F. Albright, *AASOR* 12, New Haven 1932, p. 71, pl. 23, 3; Grant-Wright, *Ain Shems V*, Haverford 1939, p. 142; Lamon-Shipton, *Megiddo I*, Chicago 1939, p. 171, pl. 37, 16; J. Carson Wampler, *Tell en-Nasbe II*, Berkeley–New Haven 1947, p. 45, pl. 71, 1625; C. F. A. Schäffer, *Ugaritica II*, Paris 1949, fig. 52, 29; fig. 71, 15; fig. 114, 1, 7; N. Glueck, *The Excavations of Solomon's Seaport: Ezion-Geber*, Washington 1942, pl. 8:2.

Ibid., lines 15–21. On the metal pedestals found at Megiddo and Bethshean, see C. Watzinger, *Tell el Mutesellim II*, Leipzig 1929, pp. 26 ff.; G. M. Fitzgerald, *PEF QS*, 1934, pp. 133–134, pl. 7, 2. Compare also H. G. May, *Material Remains of the Megiddo Cult*, Chicago 1935, p. 19, pl. 17. He is inclined to the view that these pedestals were not used as supports for lamps but were *offering-stands*.

Ibid., lines 25–28: J. Lewy, *Tablettes Cappadociennes*, Paris 1935, pl. 235, 74.

Ibid., lines 29–31. For the view in favour of a late date, see for example, K. Galling, *BRL*, p. 349.

p. 363 (xxvii 5). On the ledge, see a number of examples in the book by K. Galling, *Der Altar in den Kulturen des alten Orients*, Berlin 1925; also May, *op. cit.*, pl. 12; and many others.

p. 381, line 24. On *dyn* in Akkadian in this sense: G. Furlani, 'La sentenza di dio nella religione babilonese e assira', *AANAL*, Memorie, Cl. di sc. mor. stor. e filol., serie 8, vol. 2 (1950), pp. 219–279.

p. 383 (xxviii 33). On the round pedestal of Ugarit: C. F. Schaeffer, *The Cuneiform Texts of Ras Shamra-Ugarit*, London 1939, pl. 23, 2, and thence in the *Encyclopaedia Biblica* [Hebrew], I, plate ג, 1. On the mould for making ornaments: Schaeffer, *op. cit.*, pl. 19, 2.

p. 389. On the incense altars with four horns, see: May, *op. cit.*, pp. 12–13, pl. 12; Loud, *op. cit.*, fig. 102, pl. 254; Albright, *AASOR* 21–22, New Haven 1943, pp. 29–30.

p. 392. For the use of a special dish for the burning of incense, see, for instance, May, *ibid.*

p. 393 (xxx 12). On the taking of the census in Mesopotamia, see: J. R. Kupper, 'Le recensement dans les textes de Mari', *Studia Mariana*, Leiden 1950, pp. 99–110.

p. 399 (xxx 34). On the burning of resins that are considered malodorous today, see Lucas, *op. cit.*, p. 119. For another interpretation of חֶלְבְּנָה *ḥelbᵉnā*, or *galbanum*, as a fragrant resin that is exuded by plants of the genus *Peucedanum*, which grow in Persia, see Lucas, *op. cit.*, p. 115.

p. 407. On the interpretation of the golden calves as the abode of the invisible deity, see K. Th. Obbink, *ZAW* 47 (1929), pp. 264–274; W. F. Albright, *FSAC*, pp. 229, 332; *idem*, *ARI*, pp. 156, 219.

pp. 408 f.. On the conjecture that the story of Nadab and Abihu, the sons of Aaron, was based on the acts of Jeroboam the father of Nadab and Abijah, see T. J. Meek, *AJSL* 45 (1928–29), pp. 157 ff.; F. Dornseiff, *ZAW* 53 (1935), p. 164.

p. 412 (xxxii 4). On the method of making silver and gold images in the ancient world, see H. Maryon, *AJA* 53 (1949), pp. 99–100, 102, 122.

p. 419 (xxxii 19). On the word מְחֹלֹת *mᵉḥōlōth* [rendered here: 'dances'], see Tur-Sinai, cited above in the note on p. 182. [he regards מָחוֹל *māḥōl* as a kind of flute].

p. 449 (xxxiv 29). On the theory of the mask with horns, see A. Jirku, *ZDPV* 67 (1943), pp. 43–45.

p. 450 (xxxiv 33). For the view held by several scholars, who regard Moses' veil as a kind of mask, similar to those worn by the priests of primitive peoples, see the commentaries, for example, that of Beer, pp. 164–165.

p. 453, line 1. J. Popper, *Der biblische Bericht über die Stiftshütte*, Leipzig 1862.

p. 470. On the census at Mari, see above, the note on p. 393.

INDEXES*

I. Biblical References

GENESIS			
I: 20	101	13	13
21	180	20	216
22	477	23	387
24	371	XV: 6	71
28	9 477	9–10	216
29	196	9	324 412
31	477	13	44 85 86 214
II: 1–2	476	14	41 44 (twice)
2	450 483	16	86 f.
3	244 245 404 477	XVI: 11	29
11–12	376	16	91
15	335	XVII: 1–2	78
III: 24	335	2–6	9
VI: 1–4	61	24–25	91
11	296	XVIII: 16	221
18	79 (twice)	XIX: 29	29
22	476	XX: 13	256
VII: 2	137	XXI: 17	29
10	481	XXII: 4	183
VIII: 1	29	XXIII: 1	86
20	216	10	363
IX: 1	9	XXIV: 7	305
5	279 (twice) 280	27	306
6	279	30	97
X	7 8	37 ff.	250
21	87 182	40	306
XI: 1	205 227	48	306
7	34	56	306
28	241	XXV: 26	91
31	53	XXVIII: 3	78
XII: 1–4	20	10 ff.	54
2	415	10	224
3	146	XXIX	26
12	14 16	10	25
XIII: 12	117	31	29
XIV: 7	159 204	33	29
		XXX: 6	29

* References are to pages.

17	29	7	15
22	29	9	13
XXXI: 12	29	10	146
42	29	11	22 80 147 486
XXXII: 5 ff.	420	12	15
10 [Heb. 11]	266	14	113 139
16 [Heb. 17]	202	15	22 265 486
21 [Heb. 22]	202 436	16	25 101 486
XXXIII: 3	202	17	15 25 (twice)
XXXIV: 5	71	18	23 25
29	125	22	170
XXXV: 11	78	II–IV	213
XXXVI	176	II: 2	196 442
XXXVII: 3	385	3	20 97 486
13	35	4	97
15	97	5	20 312
23	385	10	21
XXXVIII: 24	97	11 ff.	91
XXXIX: 11	21	11	28 53 80
14	13	14	22
17	13	15	53
XL: 13	105	16	28
19	105	17	26
XLI: 1	97	22	54 214
12	13	23	80 91
33	220	24	33 79 80
41	401	25	33 63
46	91	III: 1	26 62 214
XLIII: 8	125	2	41
14	78 f.	4	33
XLIV: 2 ff.	343	6 ff.	174
XLV: 3	53	6	214 335
19	125	7	30 32 41 63 73 292
XLVI: 5	125	8 ff.	424
XLVII: 4	214	8–9	63
7	146	8	41 73 80 152 306 426
10	146	9	30 291
XLVIII: 2	215	10–20	63
3–4	78	10	36 80
XLIX: 18	16	11	80
25	78	12	38 49 80 156 176 226
L: 8	125	14–15	77 174
15	18	14	33 67 192 439
24	41	15	33
25	41 157	16–17	63
		16	62 63
EXODUS		17	152 426
I: 1	15 486	18	45 65 66
5	310	19	55 f. 74

I. BIBLICAL REFERENCES

20	132	13	88
21–22	132 147	14	88
22	132 428 486	16–26	148
IV: 1–9	63	23	310 371
1	47	26	90 142
2–9	55	VII: 1	401
2–4	51 97	3	55
4–23	63	4	96
10–17	52 63	5	416
12	50	8–XI 10	486 f.
14	62	8–12	55
15–16	62	11	99
16	89	13	56 97 (twice)
17	54 94	18	104
19	29 59	21	98 104
20	51	24	98 184
21–23	59 132	25	98
21	90	VIII: 1 [Heb. VII 26]	111
22	59 295 415	2 [Heb. VII 27]	111
23	59 100	3–4 [Heb. VII 28–29]	102
24–26	138	3 [Heb. VII 29]	99
25	54 59 139 325	5 [Heb. 1]	123
27	59 72	8 [Heb. 4]	102
28	63 64	9–13 [Heb. 5–9]	193
30	64	9 [Heb. 5]	487
31	30 83	13–14 [Heb. 9–10]	102
V: 1	69 74	13 [Heb. 9]	110
2	42 74 81 90 103 115 160	14 [Heb. 10]	101
3	69 73 75	19 [Heb. 15]	405 487
4	70 74 80 103	21 [Heb. 17]	108
5	80	22 [Heb. 18]	111 435
7–19	113	24 [Heb. 20]	123 430
7	486	29–30 [Heb. 25–26]	193
9	74 80	IX: 3	116 117
11	80	4	435
13	74	5	140
14	68	6	119
19	126 486	8	487
21	104 164	9–10	117
23	80	10	116
VI: 1	43	11	116
2–8	88	12	56
2	241 256	14	120 121
5	30	16	120
6	77 90	18	115 124
7	77	20–21	121 147 252
8	77	21	119
10–11	88	22	129
12	88	23	231

INDEXES

24	115 117 124	29–31	167
25	121	32	130
27	122 128	33	74
28	122	34	148
30	118 124 160	35–36	132
32	119 124	36	428
X: 2	196	37	126 157 162 470
4–5	126	38	327
5	119	39	146 (twice)
8–10	130	40–41	44
9	147	40	85 86 162
10	129	41	151
11	123 147	43	153
12	119 127	48	138
13	167	XIII: 2	153 445
14	115	3–10	144
15	119 128	3	154
16	123	5	153
21	262	8	154
24	145	9	154 158
28	145 216	12–14	151
29	132	12–13	445
XI: 1	134	13	295
2	248	16	152
4–8	131	17–22	172
4–5	140	18	159 163 171 487
4	134	19	41
5	145	20	165
6	115 145	21–22	485
7	435 487	21	185
8	145	22	432
9–10	55	XIV–XV	129
XII: 1–42	149	XIV	487
2–13	136	2	163 170
2	140	3–4	162
3	138	5	164
4–5	196	7	175
6	142 198 200	10	165 184 202
7	140 143	13	172 253
8	11	14	170 174 180
11	143 144	15	103 201
13	138 f.	16	167 170 180 (twice)
14–20	136	17	169
14	142 151	18	170
15	303	19	158 306
17	148	21	180
21	197	22	171 180
24–25	151	23	171
27	138	25	180

I. BIBLICAL REFERENCES

26	171	16	212
27	174	XVIII: 1	218 222 226
28	129 175	2	222 (twice)
29	180	4	216
30–31	164	5	211 212 225
31	228	7	212 222 430
XV: 1–18	173 177 ff.	8–10	214
1	163 181	12	222 324
3	38 164	13	212 (twice)
4	163	14	212 (twice) 219
9	163	15–16	211
11	115	18	212 221
16	308	19	221
19	163	23	212 222
20	487	24	222
22–27	185	25	212 220
22	184 229	XIX: 1–2	211
24	187 201	2	224 487
25	187 190 201 202 487	3	235 252 254
26	307	4 ff.	255
XVI: 1	194 200	4	228
2	187	5–6	81 211 238 312 313
3	192 194 202	5	235 241 312
4	187 197 201	6	241 295 385
5	244	9	234
7	187 435	10	428
8	187	11	438
9	187	12–13	233 438
10	314 435	12	234
11–12	193	13	231
12	187	14	428
13	195	15	438
14	487	16	232 252 253 439 481
15	199 (twice)	17	233 235 253 311
16	199	18	252
20	198 (twice)	19	235
22	198	20	439
23	199 200	23	233
XVII: 1	225	24	438
2	187 203 205	XX: 1–17	487 f.
3	188	2	256
4	103	5	444
6	487	8	488
7	187 201 (twice)	9–10	198
8	212	19	252 255
9	51 212 (three times)	21	311 (twice)
10	401	22–XXIII	238
12	212 (four times) 401	22–XXIII 33	311 313
14	487	22 ff.	39 305

INDEXES

22	262	28	443
23	309 423	31	489
24–25	362	32–33	443
24	311 312 488	32	443
26	387	XXIV: 1	254 314
XXI–XXIII	312 488	2	315
XXI:2–6	301	4	419
10	276	7	264
12	273	8	447
13	56	10	376
14	261	12	310 316 330 405
16	489	14	401 411
17	293	15 ff.	194 484
18	276	16	435
20–21	489	17	314
22	281	18	324 406 447
26	292	XXV ff.	452 481 489
27	292	XXV	390
32	292	1–7	456
34	292	2–3	369
XXII: 4[Heb. 3]	286	2	369
7 [Heb. 6]	283 292	5	353
9 [Heb. 8]	292	6	369
9 (Heb.)	284	7	374
12 (Heb.)	284	8	328 426 483
17 [Heb. 16]	261	9	322 347
18–20 [Heb. 17–19]	298	10 ff.	464
20 [Heb. 19]	312	10	372
21 [Heb. 20]	299	11	338 489
24 (Heb.)	284	13	339
30 [Heb. 29]	301	14	482
XXIII	442	16	336 482 489
2	284	18 ff.	407
5	284	19	489
9	291 300	21	482
10 ff.	239	22	370 388
12	198 445	23 ff.	464
13–15	306	24	489
16	445	28	319
17	302 446	29	337 (twice)
18	446	30	337 479 482
19	446 489	31 ff.	369 465 489 f.
20 ff.	426	37	370 482
20	308 424 425	XXVI	482
21	313	1–14	462
22	313	1	375
23	308 425 443	2	397
24	302 443	3	373
27–30	426	9	352

I. BIBLICAL REFERENCES

15 ff.	463	9	339
17	329	11–16	469 472
18	365	12	490
30	322 351	13	397
31 f.	463	17–21	466
33–35	463	18	364 479 483
33	478	19	483
35	370 479 482	20	483
36	385 479	23	400
XXVII: 1–8	466 479	24	400
1	373	25	400 465
5	490	28–29	395
7	279	30	386
8	322	34–35	392
9–19	467	34	490
10	367	35	465
19	351 365	XXXI: 1 ff.	459
20	327	6	371 460
21	477	7–11	456 476
XXVIII: 4	373 383	10	473
6 ff.	473 f.	12 ff.	454
7 ff.	329	18	330 411 417 418
8	372	XXXII ff.	491
9–10	376	XXXII: 4	408 491
11	376	9	413 420
12	377	10	416 426 434
14	377	11	409 419
29	376	12 ff.	430
30	375 490	12	126 418 420 421
31–35	474 f.	13	425
33	490	14	421
36–37	475	16	315 438
41	422 475	17	420 421
42	257	19	418 491
43	403 475	20	412
XXIX: 5	385	22	421
6	384	25	421
7	397	26	409
24–28	458	29	216
37	398	32	440
38–42	371	34	428 433
42–43	370	XXXIII: 1	433
43	336	2	426
46	426	3	432
XXX: 1–5	465 490	4	424
3	362	7–11	426 467
6	336 388 479 482	11	435
7–8	370 399 400 490	12 ff.	410 426
7	482	12	435

499

16	441	XXXIX: 1	403
19 ff.	439	27	386
19	439	28	387
21	438 439	29	385 386
23	445	31	384
XXXIV: 1	447 f.	41	403
2	437 439	XL	462
4	417 447	2	470 481 482
5–6	447	3–8	481
7	424	3	437
9	410	4	482
14–26	237 239	5	482
18–20	303	6	364 482 f.
18	446	7	483
21	198	8	483
22	303	10	392
24	248	15	386
25	305	17	470
28	251 315 (twice) 330 337	19	354
29	450 491	20–24	463
33	491	20–21	360
XXXV ff.	450	20	464
XXXV: 1	456	21	479
4–19	454	23	464
5	457	25	465
8–9	327	26–27	465
8	458	29	364
9	458	33	481
10	458		
11–19	476 f.	LEVITICUS	
11	354		
12	359	I: 1	484
14–15	458	II: 11	304
18	365	VI: 11	398
19	403	VII: 13	304
22	469	VIII: 6 ff.	481
24	472	7	385 (twice)
33	348	8	378
XXXVII	390	11	398
1	462	X: 1–2	409
16	339	XIII: 19	114
XXXVIII: 17	472	XVI: 2	332
19	472	8	380
24 ff.	345	12–13	400
24	472	12	113
25 ff.	393 395	13–15	332
27–28	470	18–19	465
27	357 358	18	392
29–31	467	XVIII: 23	290

I. BIBLICAL REFERENCES

XIX: 1 ff.	77	2	411
15	297	16	306
18	247	XXII: 3	11
34	247 291	5	124
XX: 9	271	6	10
16	290	28	302
XXIII: 2–4	455 f.	32	302
3	139	33	302
17	304	XXIV: 5	346
XXIV: 2–3	369	XXVI: 51	469
3	370 477	XXVII: 21	378 380
4	477	XXXIII: 3	161 162
5–9	337 340	8	183
20	275	12–14	201
XXV: 20–21	199	XXXV: 20–25	270
		21–22	270
NUMBERS		23	270
I: 1	470	31	277
4 ff.	471		
18	470	DEUTERONOMY	
19	328	1: 9 ff.	217
46	470	II: 30	57
IV: 6	330	IV: 13	251
7	339	19	444
VI: 5	420	V: 6–21 [Heb. 6–18]	249
VII: 1	481	21 [Heb. 18]	249
89	439	VII: 9	243
VIII: 4	322	14	307
IX	485	15	307
15	485	16	307 309
X: 11	195	20	308
33	183	VIII: 12–14	444
XI	194 200	IX: 9	315 337
4	148	11	406
24-30	429 f.	18	315 337
XIII: 27	35	21	419
29	204	28	416
XIV: 4	156	X: 4	251
25	204	19	291
26–35	424	XI: 26	401
35	77	XV: 11	298
36–38	424	13–14	44
39	424	XVI: 19	299
43	204	21	443
XV: 38	385	XVIII: 9 ff.	95
XVI: 3	411	10	290
XVIII: 2	50	XIX: 6	489
27	294	15	273
XX: 1–11	204	21	277

501

XXII: 1–3	297	23	379
3	301	27–28	379
4	297		
9	294	I SAMUEL	
23–29	288 f.	I: 5	56
XXIV: 1	268	20	446
7	489	II: 18	373
XXV: 17–19	206	22	467
18	204 206	30	271
XXVII: 6	257	III: 2	21
21	290	3	370
XXVIII: 27	113	IV: 4	333
35	113	XII: 14–15	423
XXXII: 11	226	XIV: 19	382
XXXIII: 8	378	36	382
20	345	37	378
27	81	38 ff.	379
		XV: 9	197
JOSHUA		XVIII: 6	182
I: 8–9	158	XXI: 10	373
III: 3–4	330	XXII: 18	373
V: 2–7	59 (twice)	XXIII: 2 ff.	379
11	200	2	382
VI: 4 ff.	330	10–12	380
5	230	11	382
VII: 21	248	XXIV: 11	270
IX: 17	183	XXX: 7–8	379
X: 12	173		
XXIII: 13	309	II SAMUEL	
XXIV: 12	308	I: 2	183
		II: 1	379
JUDGES		V: 19	379
I: 1–2	379	VI: 2	333
II: 3	309	14	373
VII: 2	103	22	271
VIII: 11	345 f.	XIII: 18	385
27	309	XVII: 11	434
IX: 7	226	XXII: 11	333
27	303	14	118
XIV: 18	412	15	169
XV: 16	104	XXIV: 8	470
XVII: 5	373	XXX: 24–25	260
10–11	26		
XVIII: 7	71	I KINGS	
14	373	VII: 49	344
17	373	VIII: 7	334
18	373	10–11	484
20	373	XII	408
XX: 18	379	28	408

I. BIBLICAL REFERENCES

31	409	LXVI: 1	331
XIII: 6	409		
XIV–XV	409	**JEREMIAH**	
XIX: 9	437	I: 5	433
11–13	231	10	401
11	436 456	VIII: 5	71
13	437	X: 13	194
XXI: 10	293	XVIII: 3	14
		XXVI: 19	417
II KINGS		XXX: 18	346
I: 3	163	XXXI: 4 [Heb. 3]	182 374
6	163	XXXIV: 8	261
16	163	9	265
II: 17	183	L: 11	412
19–22	185		
IX: 22	95 290	**EZEKIEL**	
XX: 7	114	I: 4	119
		5 ff.	413
ISAIAH		22	314
I: 16	304	II: 2	439
II: 20	148	X	333
III: 14	284	XVII: 24	77
VI: 1	314	XX: 9–10	78
2	335	XXI: 21 [Heb. 26]	381
VII: 21–22	412	XXII: 14	77
VIII: 21	293 (twice)	XXVII: 22	396
IX: 5	374	XXVIII: 2	172
X: 1	260	13	375
15	103	14–16	334
XII: 2	174	XXXVI: 36	77
XXVI: 8	39	XL: 39	338
XXVII: 2	419	XLI: 22	338
XXVIII: 17	363	XLIII: 6	439
28	426	XLIV: 16	338
XXX: 22	412	XLV: 12	394
XXXVII: 24	304		
XXXVIII: 21	114	**HOSEA**	
XLII: 14	14	II: 8 [Heb. 10]	419
XLVII: 9	290	V: 6	125
12–13	290	X: 11	412
LI: 9–10	178 180	XII: 1 [Heb. 2]	127
9	80 f.	5 [Heb. 6]	39
10	172		
LII: 12	158	**JOEL**	
LIV: 2	346	II: 2	127
LXI: 1	148		
LXIII: 5	22	**AMOS**	
11	21 30	III: 2	433
LXV: 11	337	12	287
		VIII: 12	309

503

INDEXES

JONAH

I: 9	13
III: 10	417

MICAH

II: 2	248
13	158
IV: 10	345
VII: 6	116
12	309

NAHUM

III: 4	290

HABAKKUK

III: 8	180

MALACHI

I: 7	338
12	338

PSALMS

III: 5	459
XV: 1	346
XVIII: 10 [Heb. 11]	333
13 [Heb. 14]	118 (twice)
14 [Heb. 15]	169
XXIII: 1–2	185
XXVI: 8	346
XXIX: 3	118
7	31
XXXII: 1	332
XLVI: 6 [Heb. 7]	118
LVIII: 5 [Heb. 6]	95
LXVIII: 4 [Heb. 5]	78 333
25 [Heb. 26]	182
33 [Heb. 34]	118
LXXII: 8	309
LXXIII: 9	118 f.
LXXVIII: 24	196
45	107
53–54	177
LXXXVIII: 1	419
LXXXIX: 10 [Heb. 11]	81
13 [Heb. 14]	81
XCIX: 5	330
CII: 12 [Heb. 6]	39
CV: 40	196
CVI: 19–20	412
36	309
CXVIII: 14	174
CXXXII: 7–8	330
17	477
18	384
CXXXV: 7	194
13	39
CXXXIX: 9	345
CXLI: 8	426

PROVERBS

VII: 26	299
VIII: 5	270
12	270
16	23
X: 7	39
XX: 20	271
XXX: 11	271
XXXI: 10	220

JOB

II: 7	113
9	293
VI: 15–20	201
XV: 2	127
XVIII: 17	39
XXI: 28	346
XXXI: 22	344
XXXVIII: 13	171
22	119
XXXIX: 8	31

CANTICLES

I: 8	346
IV: 14	396
VII: 9	101

RUTH

I: 20–21	79
IV: 7	261

LAMENTATIONS

II: 1	331
IV: 7	314

ECCLESIASTES

III: 11	163

ESTHER

I: 1	86

I. BIBLICAL REFERENCES

VIII: 9	86	XIII: 6	333
IX: 30	86	XV: 27	373
		XXVIII: 2	330 f.
EZRA		11	335
II: 63	382	18	333 334
		19	322
NEHEMIAH			
III: 8	297		
V: 13	171	**II CHRONICLES**	
VII: 65	382	II: 6	325
IX: 18	413	13	325
X: 32 [Heb. 33]	394	III: 14	325
		XXIV: 23	446
I CHRONICLES		XXXII: 28	11
IV: 4	401		

II. OTHER LITERARY REFRENCES

(Ancient and Modern)

Abravanel, Isaac 92
Albright, W.F. 486 487 489 490 (twice) 491
Alt, A. 263
Andrae, W. 489
Antonine, Itinerary of 159
Apocrypha and Pseudepigrapha 178; Ecclesiasticus 299
Aquila see Bible translations, ancient
Artzi, P. 488

Baraitha On The Erection Of The Tabernacle 321 352
Beer, G. 487 491
Ben Asher, school of 272
Bible, Masoretic text 3 78 192 250 252 255 342 360 418 421 443 473
Bible, Samaritan Pentateuch 3 f. 31 68 70 86 105 117 126 128 199 201 215 230 234 284 328 478
Bible translations, ancient 3 f. 68 70 78
  Aquila 449
  Peshiṭta 201 256
  Septuagint 23 54 86 105 118 201 215 (twice) 216 250 327 328 382
  Targum Onkelos 31 400
  Vulgata 449
Bodenheimer, F.S. 195 487
Bourdon, C. 159 f. 487

Carson Wampler, J. 490
Cassuto, U.
  The Documentary Hypothesis and the Composition of the Pentateuch 188
  Encyclopaedia Bilbica [Hebrew]
    article אֲבָנִים 486
    article גְּדִי בַּחֲלֵב אִמּוֹ 489
    article דִּבְּרוֹת, עֲשֶׂרֶת הַדִּבְּרוֹת 488
  "From Adam to Noah" A Commentary on the Book of Genesis Pt. I 86 180 188 488 489
  "From Noah to Abraham" A Commentary on the Book of Genesis Pt. II 53 79 87 188
  Keneseth [Hebrew] VIII *pp. 121–142.* 178
  La Questione della Genesi 486
  Tarbiz [Hebrew] XX (= Jubilee Volume presented to J.N. Epstein) *pp. 1–7.* 54
  World Congress of Jewish Studies, Summer 1947 [Hebrew] I *pp. 165–169.* 187
Christian scholars 251
Clay, A.T. 258 273
Cross, F.M. 489
Couroyer, B. 486

David, M. 488

INDEXES

Deimel, A. 488
Dillmann, A. 173
Dornseiff, F. 491

Eissfeldt, O. 487 (four times)

Fergusson, J. 350
Fitzgerald, G.M. 490
Follet, R. 488
Forbes, R.J. 486
Furlani, G. 490

Galling, K. 490 (twice)
Gehman, H.S. 487
Glueck, N. 490
Goethe, J.W. von 237
Goetze, A. 258
Grant, E. N. 490

Haggada 91 126
Heinemann, J. 188
Herodotus 11
Holzinger, H. 487 (twice)
Hrozný, F. 259

Ibn Ezra 211 419

Jarvis, C.S. 487
Jewish exegesis *see* Rabbinic literature
Jirku, A. 449 450 491
Josephus Flavius 341

Kuenen, A. 453
Kupper, J.R. 490

Lamon, R.S. 490
Lewy, J. 486 490
Loud, G. 488 490
Lucas, A. 486 487 489 490
Lutz, H.J. 258

Maimonides 305
Maryon, H. 491
Masoretes *see* Bible, Masoretic text
May, G.M. 490 (four times)
Medieval philosophers 55
Meek, T.J. 491
Midrashim
  Exodus Rabba 52 413

Mekhilta 233 241 294
Mekhilta of Rabbi Ishmael 251
Mekhilta of Rabbi Simeon ben Yoḥai 38 251
Sifre Num. 217 251
  see also Baraitha; Rabbinic literature
Mishna 199 284 345
  Shabbath 154
  Yoma 113
  Baba Qamma 279
  Kelim 343
  Oholoth 343
  see also Rabbinic literature
Montet, P. 486
Müller 173

Naḥmanides 10 43
Neufeld, E. 488
New Testament 250
Noth, M. 486 487 488

Obbink, K. Th. 491
Onkelos *see* Bible translations, ancient

Peiser, F.E. 258
Peshiṭta *see* Bible translations, ancient
Philo of Alexandria 250 251
Pohl, A. 488
Popper, J. 453 491
Pritchard, J.B. 488

Rabbinic literature 169 178 187 217 256 264 275 284 353 397 399 400
  see also Midrashim, Mishna, Talmud
Rabinowitz, J.J. 489
Rashbam 38 87 92 107
Rashi 85 124 159 363 400
Robinson, Th. 487
Rosenblatt, S. 486

Samaritan Pentateuch *see* Bible, Samaritan Pentateuch
Schäfer, H. 489
Schäffer, C.F.A. 490 (twice)
Scheil, V. 258
Schick, H.C. 350
Schroeder, O. 259
Sellin, E. 490
Septuagint *see* Bible translations, ancient

II. OTHER LITERARY REFERENCES

Shipton, G.M. 490
Sforno, R. Obadiah 400
Steele, F.R. 258 488

Talmud 3 152 f. 321 322 326 341 398 399 419 489
  B. Berakhoth 37 38
    Shabbath 325 353
    Ḥagiga 334
    Qiddushin 246
    Sanhedrin 216 413
    Horayot 397
    Kerithoth 397
  see also Rabbinic literature

Torczyner, N.H. see Tur-Sinai, N.H.
Traditional interpretation see Rabbinic literature
Tur-Sinai (Torczyner), N.H. 103 309 487 (three times) 488 489 (twice) 491

van der Ploeg, J. 488
Vulgate see Bible translations, ancient

Watzinger, C. 490
Wellhausen, J. 237 450 453
Winnett, F.V. 487
Wright, G.E. 490

III. NOTABILIA

Akhenaten 236
Akkadian 11 13 42 95 106 118 176 258 265 325 326 339 359 372 376 380 381 386 393 397 399 490
  see also Amarna letters
'Al'iyn Ba'al 160
altars 364 389 490
Amarna letters 118 196
Amenemhet 356
Amon 242
Amphictyonies 7 486
Anath 42 230
ancient East 57 76 77 f. 84 86 137 178 187 229 235 f. 239 241 250 257 258 259 262 265 270 289 f. 300 320 321 331 333 334 336 f. 338 381 393 407 449 453 476 488 see also Israel's neighbours; legal tradition of the ancient East; literary methods and traditions of the ancient East
Apis 133
Aqhat, son of Daniel 42 230 323 425
Arabic 10 29 105 174 193 196 199 269 270 297 298 302 208 325 (twice) 326 332 375 457
Arabs (modern) 215
Aramaic 24 29 95 403
archaeological research and finds 329 341 364 383 389 486 ff.
archaic expressions and linguistic survivals 272 276 286 294 323 489

Asherah 106 443 487
Ashur 259
Aširat see Asherah
Assyrian Laws 258 274 289 290
Assyrian seals 341
Aten 236
Azitawadda 19 76 248

Baal 118 178 290 303 307 323 333 340 455
Babylonian Laws 258 280
Babylonian story 178
Babylonians 322
Bedouins 199 305 326 346 353 354
Beth-Shean 341 342 490
Boğazköy 259

Canaan 34 118 183 226 (twice) 231 334 402 453 see also Ugaritica
Canaanites 408 455
candelabra with seven spouts 341 489 f.
Cappadocia 259 341
Carthage inscription 304
conservatism in religious matters 60 139 325 346

Daniel (Ugar.) 42 230 425
Dead Sea scrolls 3 268
decimal system see numbers, decimal system
Delphi, Amphictyonic Council 7

507

INDEXES

desert nomads 346 *see also* Bedouins
divination, magic and incantation 46 95 f. 381 382
Divine names 16 32 37 f. 41 77 ff. 106 111 120 121 157 174 213 215 216 ff. 235 253 254 314 315 401 405 f. 440 446

Egyptian belief 304
Egyptian cult 336 384
Egyptian language 13 21 105 265 325
Egyptian paintings and reliefs 334 346 f.
Egyptian priests, kings 257
Egyptian texts 13 117 133 235 240 265
El (Canaanite) 322 453
Elisha b. Abuyah 242
Esagila 322
Ešnunna 258 276 278 279 280 281
European art 449

fire festival 455
foreknowledge of God 43 55 ff.
fratriarchy 181 f.

Gilgameš 183 229 290
Greek 325 399
Gudea 322

Ḫabiru or Ḫapiru 13 265
Ḥammurabi 258 259 260 266 267 268 270 (three times) 272 274 275 f. 278 (twice) 279 280 281 282 284 286 (passim) 288 (twice) 290 305 488
Hathor 133
Hebrew [עברי '*bry*] 13 42
Hebrew language, later 284 397 403
Hebrew slave 44 265 f. 301 486
Ḥeḳet 101
Hittite Laws 259 272 274 276 277 278 280 284 (twice) 290 489
Hittite texts 260 294
Hittites 331

incantation *see* divination, magic and incantation
Israel, Land of 341 364
Israel s neighbours 364 390 396 *see also* ancient East
Ištar 230 290

Jewish Law, later 285
Jewish slave 265

Keret 183 322 453
Khnum 14 101 486
Kilamuwa 76
Kition (Cyprus) 359

Lachish ostraca 36 48 471
Latin 325 399
legal tradition of the ancient East 267 273 277 280 281 284
linguistic survivals *see* archaic expressions
Lipit Ištar 258 305 488
literary methods and traditions of the ancient East 3 34 53 54 118 141 151 183 191 231 232 442 453 476 f. 478 489

magic *see* divination, magic and incantation
Marduk 178 322
Mari 259 393 394 470 472 490
mask 449 450 491
Megiddo 255 257 334 341 342 389 488 490
Mesha, stele of 76
Mesopotamia 259 333 336 381 393
Mesopotamian calendar 244
Mesopotamian census 490
Mesopotamian cult 384
Mesopotamian fire festival 455
Mesopotamian kings 87 260
Mesopotamian mythology 229
Mesopotamian peoples 448
Mesopotamian pictures and reliefs 346f.
Mesopotamian texts 236
Min 242
Mira 331
moon-god 244
Mōse (Egyptian word) 21
Mot 178 290

Napoleon I 167
Nash papyrus 3 250
Ningirsu 322
Nippur 258 488
number seven 9 12 15 21 27 32 52 63 f.

508

III. NOTABILIA

75 81 91 100 110 120 122 135 140 141 148 149 150 185 207 222 245 249 266 300 303 316 320 338 341 344 358 372 392 405 411 421 444 445 451 457 458 461 469 470 473 481
number seventy 8
number six 35
number ten 222 269 278 288
number three 21 22 24 25 27 32 62 64 71 75 82 104 119 145 167 172 183 188 200 216 229 230 233 325 338 371 384 389 395 396 399 405 416 423 431 435 438 441 f. 446 451
numbers 86; decimal system 320 354 358 368 469 470; sexagesimal system 35 86 135 147 148 162 185 320 368 422 469 470 473
numbers, symbolism of 3
numerical symmetry and schematism 3 63 320 354 358 368
Nuzu 13 259 265 266 486

observance, post-exodus 138 146
Ophel ostracon 471

Pabel 453
penitential texts, Egyptian 235 240; Mesopotamian 236
Petra 257
Phoenician art 334
Pheonician inscriptions 248 359
Phoenician language 19
phylacteries 152
poem, ancient epic, on exodus 2 10 51 54 61 91 92 108 118 119 121 122 125 158 172 f. 205 206 213 f. 421 422 425 428 430 433 *see also* sources of the book of Exodus
Ptah-Hotep 133

Rā'a (star) 126
Rahab 178
Ramseses II 11 112 331 489
Re' 72 126 129 331 486
Roman Law 275

Šabattu or *Šapattu* 244

Samaria 334
Samaria ostraca 326
satire 96 99
sexagesimal system *see* numbers, sexagesimal system
sources of the Book of Exodus 2 320 386 429 442 444 770 487
see also poem, ancient epic
stereotyped common formula 276 281 301
see also traditionary expression
Sumerian King list 87
Sumerian Laws 258 273
Sumerians 257
Susa 258
Syria 334 341
Syriac 153 339

Taanach 106 341
techniques, ancient 329 412 489 491
Tell Harmal 258
Tešub 331
Thothmes III 117
Tiamat 178
Titus, Arch of 341
tradition of ancient East *see* ancient East; legal tradition of the ancient East; literary methods and traditions of the ancient East
tradition, ancient Israelite 51 f. 59 61 86 f. 91 187 190 f. 194 205 211 f. 213 294 322 334 467
see also poem, ancient epic
tradition, later 224 225 229 269
tradition of the 'Sages' 299
traditionary expression 309 *see also* stereotyped common formula

Ugaritica 8 10 13 23 34 39 42 45 53 54 65 82 95 104 118 122 153 160 162 163 174 176 178 183 195 196 221 230 232 265 267 271 290 297 304 305 314 322f. 332 339 340 341 346 359 372 374 375 383 399 412 418 425 437 446 453 490

Yehawmilk 76

509